THE
POETRY OF
RIMBAUD

THE

POETRY OF

Rimbaud

ROBERT GREER

COHN

PRINCETON

UNIVERSITY PRESS

Library of Congress Catalog card number: 72-5377
ISBN: 0-691-06244-7

Library of Congress Cataloging in Publication Data
will be found on the last printed
page of this book.

Publication of this book
has been assisted by grants from
STANFORD UNIVERSITY and the
JOHN SIMON GUGGENHEIM
MEMORIAL FOUNDATION

The Author and Publishers
gratefully acknowledge permission from
Harcourt Brace Jovanovich, Inc., to reproduce
material from T. S. Eliot's "Sweeney Among the Nightingales,"
from *Collected Poems, 1909-1962*, and from Richard Wilbur's "The Terrace,"
from *Ceremony and Other Poems*, and "Song,"
from *The Beautiful Changes*.

Composed in Linotype Granjon and
Printed in the United States of America
by Princeton University Press,
Princeton, New Jersey

FOR VALENTINA

CONTENTS

Contents

Contents

Contents

PREFACE

AFTER AN INTRODUCTION, presenting an overview of Rimbaud, the following pages offer a set of readings of his important poems in what is normally assumed to be their chronological order. Each chapter is designed to make independent sense for those seeking guidance to the meaning of individual poems. Accordingly, some allowance must be granted for the inevitable repetition of certain key ideas or references, when the book is read as a whole.

Among previous Rimbaud commentators, I admire particularly C. A. Hackett, Wallace Fowlie, J.-P. Richard, Claude-Edmonde Magny, Yves Bonnefoy, Marcel Ruff, John Houston Porter, Pierre Arnoult, Émilie Noulet, Wilbur Frohock. I owe much to them and to many others (as will be acknowledged *passim*), above all to Suzanne Bernard who brought together so much varied and pertinent material along with insights of her own. I doubt that I would have dared to undertake this lengthy task without her superb backing. Because the scholarly references—attribution of sources, problems of dating, and the like—can be found in her readily-available book I have by and large refrained from going over that ground again and have usually limited myself to commentary on the poetry as such.

Albert Py's study of the *Illuminations* has recently confirmed some of my notions and taught me some new ones. Mr. Stéphane Taute, the Librarian of Charleville, was most courteous and helpful. And it seems that almost no book of mine can come into being without the midwifery, as well as the inspiration, of my great *maître*, Henri Peyre.

I owe a great deal to the fresh minds of my graduate students, particularly Leda Lebidois, who gave invaluable editorial assistance as well, Thomas Hanson, and Hélène Davis.

Financial aid was generously provided by the American Council of Learned Societies, the National Endowment for the Humanities, the Center for Research in International Studies of Stanford University, the John Simon Guggenheim Memorial Foundation, and Stanford University. Mr. Ronald Herring gave wise and friendly counsel. Dean Peter Foulkes was especially understanding and encouraging. I am deeply grateful for all this confidence and support.

My wife, Valentina, helped in all sorts of ways; to her the book is appropriately and dotingly dedicated.

*   *   *

Page references without other indication are to the Garnier edition of Rimbaud's *Œuvres*, edited by Suzanne Bernard. I have relied consistently on this edition for correct versions of the texts.

Robert Greer Cohn

THE
POETRY OF
RIMBAUD

INTRODUCTION

To BEGIN WITH, there was the soul of the poet, awakening, a babe in the woods, assaulted by the morning splendor and the deep shadows of "Aube." Very likely it was born more susceptible to pain or delight than others but in any event it is certain that a crucially individual path was determined here by the extraordinary intellect which came into being simultaneously and, equally, by the circumstances the soul and mind encountered not long after appearing in the world.

Chief among these circumstances was the fact of Rimbaud's peculiar upbringing in what must have been one of the unhappiest family ambiences ever inflicted on a very sensitive child. Surrounding this familiar core in a vaster circle was the France into which, fortunately for us, he came forth at a time when his native culture was reaching its prime. Rimbaud received the particularly literary education of a nineteenth-century *collège* and, having been nourished on the Greek and Roman and early French classics (presented though they were in however deadly a style, he was at least exposed to them), he was prepared to move on by himself, with the encouragement of his young mentor Izambard, to a discovery of the later classics, Lamartine, Hugo,[1] Baudelaire—"un vrai Dieu"—and thus, at a relatively tender age, to reach the point where he could appreciate coeval masters like Verlaine and, perhaps, Mallarmé.[2]

All these happenings together account for the precocious and meteoric shape of Rimbaud's career: within the span of three or four adolescent years he produced a major body of poetry and then lapsed, for practical purposes, into total artistic silence. However, when we remind ourselves

[1] It is generally recognized that the political poems of Rimbaud owe a good deal to the *Châtiments*.

[2] The influence of Baudelaire is the most prominent: the cloacal, the satanic, the "artificial Paradise" elements, scattered images of childhood, of mingled light and ocean, the "cher corps," the mud and gold of city streets, the "alchimie du verbe." What Rimbaud learned from Verlaine is evident in the impressionistic early poems ("Tête de Faune," etc.). Mondor has demonstrated that he must have been considerably more aware of Mallarmé than he let on: for example his pastiche of Mallarmé's "Fleurs" (as of the equally admired Banville) indicates, in the same way as Proust's imitations of Flaubert and Balzac do, the very power of the challenge.

of the special rhythm of serious creativity, as described for example by Eugene Kretschmer, we are somewhat less surprised at the pattern, for we are aware that the alternation of time-oases of fertility and long-lasting interregnums of spiritual aridity is almost the hallmark of Rimbaud's kind of genius. In his case the rhythm is radically reduced to one intense wave or phase. If his comparatively early death, at thirty-seven, had not intervened, there might have been a repetition of the cycle; moreover, there is evidence to indicate that he was preparing a "rentrée dans la littérature" (reported by Bardey, his associate in Harrar) not long before his disappearance. It is also conceivable, though less likely, that he condensed into this one exultation of expression enough to expiate over a normal lifetime: "shot his wad," burned himself out creatively once and for all. This is mere speculation, but in one way or another the phenomenon of Rimbaud is quite understandable in sympathetic literary terms which can do very well without the reasons assigned by the religious philistinism of Claudel, Daniel-Rops, Mauriac and company or the scientific philistinism of a professional analyst like Fretet. However frightening the implications—and the biographers' account of his years of restless wandering, self-inflicted pain, final agony and death is nothing if not frightening—the strictly artistic achievement is there, deserving of our appreciation and respect.

In order to begin to understand how all this came about we must consider the known or guessed factors of his childhood existence together, with perhaps a particular insistence on those vicissitudes of family life which—"encore une tuile"—aggravated a, no doubt, already precarious emotionality and pushed Rimbaud over into his extraordinary poetic adventure. Simply because it is available to rational analysis we will single out momentarily the lasting effect of his boyhood plight as a modern Perceval, deprived, by separation, of a father and further exposed to the neglect or the stings of an unfeminine, harshly dutiful mother.

We plan to return to these tangled matters in greater detail later, but for the moment it will be useful to point out one result these events helped bring about within the intimate shaping of his career. In sum, it meant that Rimbaud, far more than most men, and even most poets, was thrown back upon himself and nature for comfort and love; that he confronted each of the emotional crises of growing up with additional handicaps; that his lag in overcoming these was correspondingly great. This lag and its accompanying introversion, together with the fact that he produced all of his poetry before emerging from physical boyhood, caused him to become the classic poet of earliest infancy, childhood, and fumbling, staggering adolescence, increasingly escaping into a fantasy-world of powerful *voyance*.

What Rimbaud sought in his past was not so much the childhood experiences in themselves but rather how the child *felt* in his most aware moments, all the way back to the Source, the original Glory which, as Wordsworth tells us, we can only recollect, and that very rarely, in this life. This is an "addiction" that makes for what appears to normal beings as arrested development. As much as Baudelaire or Mallarmé or Proust or Faulkner, we may say, Rimbaud looked backwards obsessively *through* childhood, or the past, for authentic Being.

*   *   *

By far the most important source of our knowledge of Rimbaud, the *inner* biography, is the recorded poetry. But a summary sketch of the more traditional sort at this point will help us to keep our bearings later.

Rimbaud was born in 1854 in Charleville, in the Ardennes near the Belgian border. His mother Vitalie (née Cuif) came from a family of small landowning farmers of the nearby village of Roche. His father Frédéric was an infantry captain, of some literary propensity, a restless man who evidently could not bear the pinched and narrowly bourgeois temperament of his wife. He stayed away with his regiment for long periods, appearing at intervals to get Vitalie with a succession of children: Frédéric (1853), Arthur a year later, then the girls Vitalie (1858) and Isabelle (1860). After that he simply dropped out of view, which devastating act was of determining importance to his genius son. Rimbaud later remembered little of him besides a violent quarrel between the two parents during which a metal household object was dashed to the floor in turn by both.

The house where Rimbaud was born still stands, but it is difficult to locate the series of other dwellings to which his mother moved the little family in search of decent surroundings for her brood; the street numbers have changed so many times. Still, one can see approximately where he must have lived in the rue Bourbon during those crucial years around his seventh to which "Les Poètes de sept ans" looks back, and one gets the feel of that *peuple* atmosphere in which his mother was forced to settle for awhile—I am told by local people that it has not changed much in a century. Rimbaud trumpeted often enough his hatred of Charleville, but his poetry attests at times to a contrary mood; given his temperament and need he would have found natural objects for his wayward affection regardless, but actually there is much to please the eye along the banks of the Meuse, where he played with his brother in a little moored boat (near the old Mill which is still there and has become in part a Rimbaud museum), or in the surrounding countryside where he rambled with his friend Delahaye in adolescent years. The landscape around Roche, where his mother maintained her father's old property and where Rimbaud spent some miserable summers is lushly green, poplar-lined, charming in the French manner.

At eleven Arthur became a day-student at the Collège de Charleville and promptly amazed everyone with his brilliance, winning all the honors. He was a model child as well as student and, for a brief while, a devout Catholic, the latter to the extent of irritating his peers; he received his First Communion in 1866. All this was *too* good, suspiciously so: soon he would be scrawling "Merde à Dieu" on local walls. He wrote some remarkable Latin verse as school exercises. The first French poem we have was published in 1870: "Les Étrennes des orphelins." That same year Rimbaud wrote to Théodore de Banville offering him "Sensation," "Ophélie," and "Credo in unam" ("Soleil et chair") for the *Parnasse contemporain*—without success.

In this year, the advent of Izambard, a young professor of literature, to the school was of determining importance to Rimbaud: the fatherless boy gave his all to win this kindly and intelligent mentor's approval. His letters prove that he saw in him "presque un père"; he wrote poetry feverishly to show to him, and he worked even harder at his studies. But eventually, inevitably, Izambard fell short of the implacably ideal model Rimbaud demanded. Stirred by his old wounds, new disappointments and the infectiously restless climate of war in his region—the Franco-Prussian conflict began that same fateful year—Rimbaud took off on the first of his famous flights from home. Not being able to pay the full train fare, when he got off at Paris he was imprisoned. Izambard managed to have him released and, on the way back, he stayed for two weeks at Douai, in Belgium, with the former's maiden aunts who were very sweet to him; and this moved him to a pathetic poem of childhood emotional deprivation. He returned home—he always did in the end. Within this most stubborn of rebels—politically as well as artistically: the Commune filled him with enthusiastic hope—was a yearning for the quiet source, of course.

Two months later, the *bougeotte* welled up irresistibly, and he fled to Belgium. Once again he stayed with the aunts, the demoiselles Gindre, and met a young poet, Demeny, to whom he offered copies of all the poems (twenty-two of them) he had written and kept so far. His mother had him sent back by the police and punished him with her usual severity by depriving him of pocket money. In 1871 came another escapade, to Paris for a month, where he almost starved. Perhaps a fourth flight occurred that year, during which Rimbaud may have endured sexual humiliation at the hands of soldiers, recorded obliquely in "Le Cœur volé"—this has never been solidly established. At any rate, in May of 1871 he wrote his two "Lettres du voyant," addressed to Izambard and Demeny, in which he outlined his revolutionary poetic program, dismissing most of the art of the past, excepting Baudelaire and a few other writers, proposing a wide-open and visionary art of his own to be bought at the cost of terrible sufferings and a methodical "dérèglement de tous les sens."

Full of his new perspective and boundlessly confident, Rimbaud wrote to Verlaine, whom he admired, and sent him some sample verse. Verlaine was enormously impressed and invited Rimbaud to come join him in Paris. Rimbaud, with the newly composed "Bateau ivre" in his pocket, joyously took off for the big city and the future. He promptly made himself *non grata* with Verlaine's inlaws, at whose home the older poet was staying, and with a number of literati. Together the remarkable pair— "ivres de réciprocité" as Mallarmé put it—began a wildly bohemian existence with some homosexual undertones which scandalized almost everybody.

In the spring of 1872, Rimbaud left for home to allow Verlaine to patch things up with his wife; then he wrote his late poems, sometimes called the "Illuminations in verse." But he was soon back in Paris with Verlaine, and together they set off for freedom, first in Belgium then in England, where they studied English, bummed around, lived in some misery and quarreled and drank and made up endlessly. Most of the prose *Illuminations* were probably composed in this setting.

Rimbaud returned to Charleville for a few weeks at the end of the year, leaving Verlaine in London where he became quite ill. Accompanied, surprisingly, by his mother, Rimbaud went to his aid in early 1873. Shortly thereafter he was back in Roche, at work on the *Saison en enfer*. In May he set off again with Verlaine for London where they quarrelled fiercely. Verlaine ran off to Belgium; Verlaine's own mother and Rimbaud together followed him there; Verlaine talked wildly of suicide; Rimbaud threatened to leave; Verlaine shot him in the wrist and was condemned to two years in prison (where he would be converted, to Rimbaud's disgust). After a few weeks in a Brussels hospital and, apparently, a near-conversion on his own part, Rimbaud went back to Roche where he finished, in a terrible agitation of spirit, his great work of poetic confession, the *Saison en enfer*.

In 1874 Rimbaud revisited England, this time with a new poet-friend, Germain Nouveau. There he wrote some of the *Illuminations*, according to various scholars; although the matter is still controversial, it seems that the *Saison en enfer* was after all not Rimbaud's last word, artistically speaking. Be that as it may, for practical purposes this is where the meteoric phenomenon of Rimbaud as poet ends.

The rest of his brief life makes fantastic reading: his conversion into a money-grubbing son of his mother, his only intellectual interests now being technical manuals, the learning of countless languages for commercial reasons; the story of his wanderings over the face of Europe, the Far East; the explorations, trading, and gun-running in Ethiopia, the sufferings and the amputation of his leg in Marseilles, the final agony and death, the possible conversion on his deathbed, according to the more-than-suspicious testimony of his sister Isabelle (who in cahoots with her husband Paterne Berrichon perpetrated a notorious pious forgery to establish her brother's faith)—but all this is really beside our present purpose. It is time to return to more pertinent and intimate matters, starting with our point of origin.

* * *

"First the infant," the babe in his private and mysterious woods, with his extreme emotional rhythm—the characteristic steep rises and falls followed by prolonged exhaustion, emptiness of spirit which is observable universally in the newborn but which we may suspect were even more extreme in little Rimbaud. The daemonic quality of the juvenile psyche with its infinite dream of omnipotence is supposed, in healthy development, to give way, through the normal devices of mitigation—forgetting, "bad faith," activity, interest in other things and people—to more mature patterns of behavior and temperament. But in some—the budding artists—the original sense of glory and its concomitant complementary pain are apparently too powerful for easy taming. Or they may become too powerful through the aggravating circumstances of neglect or shock (in notable cases like Rimbaud's both levels are likely). Much as in the classic treatment of shellshock, as described by Freud—the recurrent homeopathic *reliving* of traumatic experience—the youthful psyche may choose to *deal with* its horror by facing it inwardly, repeatedly, in the same way as Baudelaire chose to remain an *enfant boudeur*, in Sartre's well-known existential analysis. Whence the evident phenomena, in Rimbaud, of ambivalence, introversion, visions of catastrophe (as well as glory), fixation on the inner life. The day-dreaming lag, when exasperated by outer goading (from his mother, from the achievement-oriented French bourgeois society) of equally unusual insistence, led to the aggravated élan of ultimate expression. We may easily reconstruct this pattern from all we know of Rimbaud: in "Les Poètes de sept ans" we see him sulking in the outhouse, "vaincu, stupide. . . . Il pensait là, tranquille et livrant les narines," or again, hanging from a banister, or hiding in a secret corner of the attic. Here the rhythm was contained within an outer obedience to his mother's rule, "il suait d'obéissance" and won all the honors at school; he had not yet the strength to break from this hated régime—which was not only accepted but even at times undoubtedly loved: "the poet performs well only under torture," as René Char puts it—but, underneath, "quelques traits semblaient prouver en lui d'âcres hypocrisies. . . . En passant il tirait la langue." Later, when he had broken physically with his home, his rhythm was released to its full spontaneous expression. Then the sulking lag became incredible taciturnity and "paresse" ("plus oisif que le crapaud"— "Mauvais sang") followed by the "travail humain . . . l'explosion qui éclaire mon abîme de temps en temps" ("L'Éclair"), with its marvelous flow of expression. After such an outburst he was so empty that if he went among people he felt "[ils] *ne m'ont peut-être pas vu*" ("Mauvais sang"); if he wandered in the country, the inevitable dogs—to which he fearfully alludes in "Nocturne vulgaire" and "Les Douaniers"—probably then barked at him in the especially penetrating way registered by the humbled souls of tramps.

In all these moments, of extreme rise and fall and of nothingness, he was so out of phase, so different, that he considered "nous sommes hors du monde" ("Nuit de l'enfer"), out of the ordinary reality whose terms and judgment, however, he could no more escape, eventually—despite the characteristic delay—than the hurtful fact of the dogs. But he was condemned to this fearful freedom. Once the original tragedy of his vulnerability and parental neglect had established the depth of his emotional rhythm, it spontaneously repeated itself: compulsively, by his provocative actions, he had to recreate the neglect in others (in addition to his own self-torture) in order to purge the original pain and, conversely, to refresh the resultant acute sense of glory, in order to feel alive. Only a major crisis, a dead end, could change or mitigate the rhythm, and this did occur later.

The well-known summation "Je est un autre"—which refers to the impersonal, original, objective, cosmically-rooted self, the "other" behind the social "I"—simultaneously asserted both his being at odds with society, his uniqueness, and, in another direction, his being at odds with himself, constituting what would be, if pathological, schizophrenia. But fortunately for art his power of integration was as strong as the menacing split, and, in direct opposition to what Fretet claims, he *did* face himself with a courage seldom equaled on a spiritual terrain, the irrefutable proof being the granitic presence of his work.

By further backward extrapolations from the writings of Rimbaud we may follow this exemplary temperament along its way as it encounters successive emotional crises, each characterized by the renunciation of a particular form of love, which are the milestones of the writer's fate. The method and the subject will often coalesce, since Rimbaud's writings for the most part incarnate his own search for things past as keys to the future, and the persistent central image of his poetry is that of a child or youth wandering curiously along a forest path, a country road, a city street. Not that he is really going anywhere; at his best and most characteristic, he is merely varying the modalities of his Being and Knowing, as he moves: ". . . je vis que tous les êtres ont une fatalité de bonheur: l'action n'est pas la vie, mais une façon de gâcher quelque force, un énervement" ("Délires II").

His point of departure was birth from an unfathomable beyond, to which, like all men, he occasionally yearned consciously to return: "O Mort mystérieuse, o sœur de charité." Language itself, as in this lifeline of verse, happily stands between him and the total abdication: we are reminded of its origin as a talismanic babbling in such exultant utterances as the "ô ia, io, ia, io" of "Bruxelles" or the free associations of "Voyelles." In moments of lowest despair Rimbaud spoke of his "gourmandise de Dieu," a primitively sensual form of nostalgia which is far removed from organized religious belief. The constant images[3] of flight and departure: "des plages sans fin. . . . Un grand vaisseau d'or," of abandonment and laziness: "le vin de la Paresse"; "Ce charme! il prit âme et corps, / Et dispersa tous efforts," and the thresholds of flight, such as windows—"par la fenêtre, on voit là-bas un beau ciel bleu"—or garden walls—"Autour du parc, . . . Les palissades sont si hautes qu'on ne voit que les cimes bruissantes"—all these are early exfoliations of the original desire. The invisible garden—an inaccessible earthly version of the beyond, like the first lost Eden—has a remote, exotic equivalent in Rimbaud's persistent dream of an ancient magical Orient.

Perhaps the most poetic of all such expressions is the "O saisons! ô châteaux!" of "Le Bonheur." For Rimbaud, the château ("O! joli château! Que ta vie est claire!" "Age d'or"), as for Mallarmé (the *manoir* of "Hérodiade," "Un Coup de Dés") or Shakespeare ("this vision, The cloud-capped towers, the gorgeous palaces" of *The Tempest*) or Poe (*The House of Usher*), is the experience of sheer innocence and beauty wrung from the guilty, suffering life—"Quelle âme est sans défauts?"—and so comes to stand for the soul's ideal image of itself. It has the architectural quality of pure artistic form surrounded and suffused by the relatively "feminine" (but the opposites merge in a mystery) holy ghostly *saisons*, not one particular season but all of them in one heavenly, vibrant climate.

An eventual form of narcissism is masturbation, and when this is renounced the phallic symbol emerges as its vicarious equivalent, somewhat present in the image of the tower[4]—a detail of the deeper inward and more integral vision of the *château*. Although a scarcely veiled description of

---

[3] Successively from "Matin," "Les Chercheuses de poux," "Le Bateau ivre," "Les Étrennes des orphelins," "Enfance."

[4] As in the "Chanson de la plus haute tour."

the act is the substance of the prose poem entitled "H,"[5] generally the deed is as thoroughly condemned in the mind of Rimbaud[6] as in that of most individuals (even today, despite the indulgent modern analytic view)[7] because this kind of direct short-circuiting is simply, like the repeated notion of death, too close to flat nothingness to be of any prolonged interest to literature or culture.

The sweeping return of the death urge and of physical narcissism is, for the obvious reasons mentioned, usually subsumed into subsequent forms of desire, mingled with the elements of nature and with other levels of reality. Earth and stones are, after the cadaver, the most concrete representations of death, objects of a heavily sensual form of nostalgia for nature and the beyond, which desire in the child is expressed through the central appetitive conatus,[8] communion by eating: "Si j'ai du *goût*, ce n'est guères / Que pour la terre et les pierres" ("Fêtes de la Faim"). At another point there is the womb-attraction of "ce tombeau, blanchi à la chaux" ("Enfance"). Closely corollary is the anal eroticism, the scatology of poems including "Les Premières Communions," "Bateau ivre," with varying nuances of bitterly "expulsive" aggressiveness ("Les Assis") or self-consolation ("Les Poètes de sept ans").

Under the element earth (and stones) we may subsume metals as well as more complex forms such as crystals, jewels. Crystals represent for certain modern thinkers (e.g., Hans Kayser) an important, perhaps crucial, link between inanimate and animate. Thus the solidity of crystals tends to rise up in the imagery of Rimbaud to give male artistic hardness to threateningly soft organic substances, such as flowers, most notably in "Fleurs." But combinations of the various elements among each other (giving mud from water and earth, vapor from water and fire, etc.) and with subsequent levels of reality (vegetation, animals . . .) are too complex for more than this preliminary mention here.

Water, which we have called (in *The Writer's Way in France*) a "feminine, undulating, caressing presence of the all" is, beyond its own irreducible value, associated with the woman and mother;[9] "je me suis

---

[5] Arnoult and Etiemble concur in this view.

[6] See the self-critical tone of "gland tenace trop consulté" in "Remembrances du vieillard idiot." Passages in Rousseau, Gide, Proust reveal the subject as a painful problem.

[7] This is no puritan bias, and, as Rimbaud recalls, masturbation has always been the "ardente hygiène des races"; at an early stage it is a step toward genitality and might even, as in ancient India, be subtly encouraged on these grounds. Thus the modern view, like Freudian ones generally, may have been a useful corrective. But the problem remains.

[8] Of which genitality is a byway, a derivative channel.

[9] In addition to, but overlapping with, the pervasive sense of "the sea of life"

baigné dans le Poème / De la Mer" ("Bateau ivre," recalling the medieval association of *mer-mère-Marie*, e.g. in Robert de Boron; Marie, linked with *la mer*, occurs later in the poem). But Rimbaud's mother was a failure as a woman, had failed to hold on to the affections or the presence of the longed-for father who would have given direction and meaning to the family and the son; on the other hand, she was almost all Rimbaud had as a small child to cling to, and so she is intensely loved and hated (indeed, in the poetry, her constantly hovering presence approaches the mythic proportions of Jung's "Terrible Mother" as Rimbaud emerges in his own imaginative mind as the "divine child"). Water is both a fearful menace in which "un noyé pensif parfois descend" and a source of bottomless comfort. A contrast is then set up with the element fire, the sun, which is quite consistently associated with the father (or Father). Rimbaud dubbed himself "fils du Soleil," and we shall find the father-sun coupling prominent in "Soleil et Chair," "Mémoire," *Une Saison en enfer*, "Génie." Yellow or gold is the sun's color, and his mother's eyes were blue, "Elle avait le bleu regard,—qui ment!" ("Les Poètes de sept ans"). This blackly hateful element, "qui ment," is refound in the remarkable outburst "j'écartai du ciel l'azur, qui est du noir, et je vécus, étincelle d'or de la lumière *nature*" ("Alchimie du verbe").[10] We will establish these connections more firmly later on, but it is already fairly clear that Rimbaud's purest desire was, at some points, as we have seen so often, for the ideal distant father as well as the light with which he is mingled. At other times, he was in equal need of a woman's tender affection. The two yearnings—for he was deprived of the sympathetic attention of both parents—are commingled in this phrase which is one of his most poignant expressions of a total Return through love of nature: "Elle est retrouvée. / Quoi? L'éternité / C'est la mer allée / Avec le soleil."[11]

(the *Ewig-Weibliche*), especially in the "Bateau ivre"; cf. Bernard Weinberg, "*Le Bateau ivre*; or the limits of symbolism," *PMLA*, vol. 72 (March, 1957), pp. 165-93. In the realm of undifferentiated psychic energy (as occasionally in the sun image), the male-female distinction tends to fade. At a certain point, however, this Jungian atmosphere begins to pall: life itself, in creating sexuality, demands a sense of direction. The critic, while justly suspicious of pseudo-Freudian simplifications, occasionally has the same obligation to follow these life-given lines of orientation as the poet—with varying consciousness—does. Thus the general elemental image of water overlaps with the more particularized version, amniotic fluid in the mother. An image like "source de soie" implies the original well-spring, the womb-source and an even later entity: the silky skin of the mother or her garments, cf. "soie des mers" in "Barbare."

[10] This pairing of yellow (gold) and blue shows up in various contexts, e.g., the "phosphores chanteurs" of "Bateau ivre."

[11] A variant has "mêlée" for "allée." Frequent expressions such as "flots bleus,"

The elemental water, to repeat, emanates through subsequent over-lapping levels of reality, spirally, through its more particularized, human-ized, and *sexualized* (here Jungian becomes Freudian) form as amniotic fluid within the mother-womb or a general climate of *mer-mère*, etc. Water wells up again and again in the imagery of Rimbaud as a basic life sub-stance, (involved in sap or milk or blood or tears), for example in "Après le déluge." One of his central themes is thirst ("Comédie de la soif").

The last, and most volatile, element, air, like the sunlight which it is near to in fact and spirit, is also associated with the father (Hölderlin's "Father Aether") or divinity: "le ciel angélique." Rimbaud's "gourman-dise de Dieu" is represented by his "goût . . . pour la terre et les pierres" but also by the childishly direct, superbly poetic "mangeons l'air." Here, as almost always with Rimbaud, we must speak of pre-lyric nature mingled with lyric (relatively sentimentalized, humanized) nature, just as both levels of nature fuse with the human into the object of an aboriginally possessive and immediate form of desire: "les tendresses profondes [de l'enfant] se jetaient sur cet étonnement [de sa mère]."

Following upon, but intermingled with, the level of inanimate elements are what we have called elsewhere (in *The Writer's Way in France*) "ani-mate essences, sensual surrogates of pure and undefined love," typically the sap, blood, milk, which permeate and nourish life, physical and spiritual. Thus the thirst for light and air, the "vin de vigueur" which Rimbaud, "sobre surnaturellement," drinks in along the open road often becomes, more sensually, its fluid corporeal form, the blood of the grape, the essential virtue of "Quelque liqueur d'or . . . qui fait suer" ("Larme"),[12] perhaps made present to him through a sunlit glass of white wine; and Rimbaud dreamed of "une fête où tous les vins coulèrent." If we divorce this from righteous glosses, we might think of the eternal *sitio*.[13] Tears, transparent, brimming with light, suspending a sort of "salt" of distilled love, are close in spirit to this "liqueur," especially remembering the childlike sulking habit of drinking one's own tears (as Larbaud's Rose Lourdin did): "L'eau claire; comme le sel des larmes d'enfance, / L'assaut au soleil des blancheurs des corps de femmes . . . " ("Mémoire"); "la mer faite d'une éternité de chaudes larmes" again brings together the tears and the woman-water motif. Tears are the vehicle of communion in forbidden or frustrated relationships such as between father and son or, here, the cold mother and her son; just as profoundly, they are the substance of communion with self

---

"fleuve bleu" support the association of his mother's eyes with water; cf. "cet œil d'eau" ("Mémoire").

[12] Note the title, "Larme"; see, below, our remarks on tears.

[13] Thirst, like hunger, is one of Rimbaud's very essential themes; see particularly "Comédie de la soif": "Que faut-il à l'homme? boire."

in that dangerously infinite sentiment which is self-pity: "vrai j'ai pleuré plus que tous les enfants du monde."

Adding a nuance of density, there is milk, white like the salt of the sea or of tears,[14] "Le pur ruissellement de la vie infinie. L'homme suçait . . . " ("Soleil et chair"), "ému jusqu'à la mort par le murmure du lait du matin" (*Les Déserts de l'amour*); in a fantasy of universal doom, apocalypse— with the significantly fluid form of a flood—which is one way of hitting bottom for the vertical rebound which alone can fully satisfy him, he imagines that "Le sang et le lait coulèrent" ("Après le déluge"), bringing in the even more incarnate blood. The blood communion easily coalesces with the later homoerotic phase ("Le Dormeur du val"), and the notion of apocalyptic war[15] and carnage: "Petite veille d'ivresse . . . Voici le temps des ASSASSINS" ("Matinée d'ivresse") or "Je songe à une Guerre, . . ." ("Guerre"), all of which is mainly based on a renunciation of homosexuality, far more important to an understanding of Rimbaud than his actual fitful practices with Verlaine and Nouveau.

Blood communion also interfuses with another, closer, level, that of animals, whence the "abattoirs" of "Après le déluge." But the level of imagery which hypothetically follows directly upon the life essences is that of vegetative nature: the flowers, trees, fields of grain which inspire one of Rimbaud's richest veins of expression. In "Soleil et chair," "Aube" ("J'ai embrassé l'aube d'été.") and "Sensation" ("j'irai . . . / Par la Nature,— heureux comme avec une femme."), there are the shifts to anthropomorphized nature—"les pierreries regardèrent," "une fleur . . . me dit son nom" ("Aube")—and an atmosphere of promiscuous magic which had almost disappeared from French literature between the end of the Middle Ages and the coming of the Romantics. All growing things, as Jean-Pierre Richard has observed, represent Rimbaud's fundamental dynamism of elevation, life vigorously rising and sometimes bursting into a new form, a metamorphosis, like a calyx from a stem—or even breaking free into

[14] Also, in "Mémoire," there is a complex linkage of these essences not only with the white bodies of women but, in an aesthetic orgy, with the lilies of France and eventually the angelic whiteness of the sun's core, for white is the source of all color; it is easily the "principal personnage" of this poem as it is of similarly inspired Impressionist paintings (e.g., Pissarro's white-drenched flowering orchard at Pontoise). Thus, at one level, although actual outgoing relationships with all kinds of people and things are vicariously expressed in the imagery of such art works at a more hidden level, the harmonizing "hero," light, stands in part for the drama of vicarious self-possession, in part for the equally strong gift of self, "vocational" love, through effective expression.

[15] His father was a professional soldier. Rimbaud gave his birthplace as being his father's (Dôle, in the Jura) to Bardey, a hardy type himself. Clearly Rimbaud desired at such points to be hard, to become like his father.

flight, like the birds from the trees of "Mémoire." The grove of trees is a shadowy womb-source of new life ("Après le déluge").

The free spirit of communion informs as well the overlapping animal kingdom of Rimbaud: "des bêtes d'une élégance fabuleuse circulaient";[16] "Cette famille est une nichée de chiens"; "million d'oiseaux d'or, ô future Vigueur." In "Soleil et chair" the dryads, nymphs, and beast-shaped gods descend to earth again with some of that original power which is felt to be generally resurgent in nineteenth-century poetry. One whole obscure prose poem, "Antique," is given to the fascinated description of what is probably a centaur in the Louvre,[17] or in any case a part-human creature with four legs. In "Bottom" Rimbaud identifies with a bear and a bird, and in the "Lettres du voyant" he announces that the poet's mission includes a responsibility for animals.

In the Oedipal phase, the next halting place in our journey, typically there is the partial ousting from the home into an elementary sense of reality, generating historically, and ever anew individually, the quests of fairydom. At one time Rimbaud pictures himself as the prince, complete with damsel, together triumphant in their rediscovered majesty ("Royauté"). At another time there is the familiar combining figure of the beast and the prince which is incorporated in the prose poem entitled "Bottom." But the most compelling fantasy from this early period which Rimbaud took up in his later poetry is that of the sadly retarded "Petit Poucet," a sort of baby Perceval, a handicapped miniature soul but who may yet "faire le bonheur de sa famille" (Perrault). In "Ma Bohème" he calls himself "Petit-Poucet rêveur," and the image of the tiny fellow advancing through the mysterious woods with infinite gingerliness, pathetic tentativeness,[18] but advancing all the same, fearfully, curiously, is found very prominently in the important prose poem called "Enfance":

> Je suis le piéton de la grand'route par les bois nains; la rumeur des écluses couvre mes pas.[19] Je vois longtemps la mélancolique lessive d'or du couchant.

> Je serais bien l'enfant abandonné sur la jetée partie à la haute mer, le petit valet[20] suivant l'allée dont le front touche le ciel.

[16] One thinks of the blue-eyed creature in Larbaud's "Hour with the Face."

[17] Arnoult's good guess.

[18] Ravel has captured this mood in the exquisite "Petit Poucet" passages of the *Ma Mère l'Oye* suite.

[19] Cf. the sound of mysterious waters accompanying the approach of le Grand Meaulnes toward his unknown desire.

[20] Perceval was identified as a "valet," a farm-boy.

> Les sentiers sont âpres. Les monticules se couvrent de genêts.
> L'air est immobile. Que les oiseaux et les sources sont loin! Ce
> ne peut être que la fin du monde, en avançant.

In the late versions of the fairy tales, the fantasy is mingled with realism, and this is very much truer of our strong-minded nineteenth-century poet.

When Rimbaud's affections, drawing force like the embottled genie from its prolonged compression—"j'ai ravalé mes rêves" ("Oraison du soir")—finally went out to fully human beings, it was with the familiar explosion, in whatever direction. During the Oedipal phase (around the fifth year), there is normally, and in Rimbaud's case with an enhanced drive, a new canalization and intensification of the emotions. Love is centered on individuals, at first the parents, and with differing rhythms: the mother is loved more directly by the boy child, tenderly or passionately, opening the path of the affections to future heterosexuality, through the nuanced interdiction of relations with her followed by transfer to another woman, the mate. The relation with the father is more complex: the analysts, starting with Freud, make a rather hard distinction between the desire to "imitate" the father (creating the superego) and the desire to "possess" the mother. This is roughly acceptable if we realize that imitation is really a subtle (sublimated) form of possession, rivaling the latter in power. It brings about the infinite, ideal love of the Father which is the seminal dimension of Western culture. In Rimbaud's case, the localization of his desire upon his parents met with a harsh rebuff: the total absence of his father brought about that intense yearning for ideal direction which we may identify with the title of his lost masterpiece, "La Chasse spirituelle." This search, or "hunt," for the Father, is perhaps the most important thread running throughout his work.

Simultaneously, given the untender nature of his mother, Rimbaud felt himself at times to be totally abandoned, alone. The ousting from the home is a part of normal life (often with the arrival of a new baby) and is a kind of spiritual weaning which is necessary to the child's emotional growth. Obviously it ought to be tempered with affection and understanding, particularly in the case of a sensitive child with added family-imposed difficulties, but for Rimbaud understanding was conspicuously absent. From this sad situation there emerged the self-pity of the orphan and "une éternité de chaudes larmes," often transferred to other homeless children in early poems like "Les Étrennes des orphelins," "Les Effarés," and even "Ophélie" (with its possible echo of Ophélie-*orphelin*), floating whitely, abandoned in death, on the dark tide ("they'll be sorry then"). In "Les Poètes de sept ans," we learn that "Ces enfants seuls étaient ses familiers / Qui, chétifs, fronts nus, œil déteignant sur la joue, / Cachant de maigres doigts jaunes et noirs de boue / Sous des habits puant la foire et tout vieillots, / Conversaient avec la douceur des idiots!" In their *peuple* way they shared some of Rimbaud's spiritual misery, and their physical wretchedness gave a further hold to his imaginative sympathy. His relations with the little proletarian neighbor girl are more direct: "La petite brutale, et qu'elle avait sauté, / Dans un coin, sur son dos, en secouant ses tresses, / Et qu'il était sous elle, il lui mordait les fesses," adding the charming detail "Car elle ne portait jamais de pantalons"; he then, triumphantly, "Remportait les saveurs de sa peau dans sa chambre."

In all of this, Rimbaud as the adolescent writing the poems reveals in more honest, sensual fashion the intense love for children which one finds in writers generally: Shakespeare, Montaigne, Pushkin and, more particularly, some contemporaneous figures such as Andersen (Little Match Girl), Dostoevsky (Kolia Krassotkin), Lewis Carroll or Charles Kingsley and their naked babes, or, a bit later, Gide and his Georges, and Mann's "Kirghiz-eyed boy," with varying nuances of puritan or premodern sentimentality. Even in Rimbaud's case the relationship had to be eventually denied in part, and the love of children he carried into the future betrayed some of this "pastoral spirit" ("the child as swain"), which is Empson's term for the sentimental variation. But the sheer poetry of Rimbaud has never been equaled by any of these milder figures: we need cite only this little quatrain which is perhaps without peer in any literature:

> Si je désire une eau d'Europe, c'est la flache
> Noire et froide où vers le crépuscule embaumé
> Un enfant accroupi plein de tristesses, lâche
> Un bateau frêle comme un papillon de mai.
>
> ("Bateau ivre"[21])

In his relation with his sisters as children there is an added flavor of renounced incest:

> Quelqu'une des voix
> Toujours angélique
> —Il s'agit de moi,—
> Vertement s'explique
> . . .
>
> Reconnais ce tour
> Si gai, si facile:
> Ce n'est qu'onde, flore,
> Et c'est ta famille!
> . . .

[21] This *accroupi* position is the essence of introverted lonely childhood; cf. "un pied contre mon cœur" ("Ma Bohème").

> Je chante aussi, moi :
> Multiples sœurs ! voix
> Pas du tout publiques !
> Environnez-moi
> De gloire pudique ... etc.

("Age d'or")

The intimations of guilt are included, and partially accepted, in the quatrain:

> Le monde est vicieux;
> Si cela t'étonne !
> Vis et laisse au feu
> L'obscure infortune.

In "Mémoire," "l'assaut au soleil des blancheurs des corps de femmes . . . les robes vertes et déteintes des fillettes" are his sisters, as if caught by the brush of Renoir, embraced in the trembling light of his summer love.

The word *sœur*[22] is used frequently by French writers, particularly Symbolist poets (Baudelaire: "mon enfant, ma sœur"; Mallarmé: "ô calme sœur"), to express a somewhat idealized, somewhat perversely sensuous desire. With Rimbaud, it tends to become the Queen who is mingled with various forms of Eros as Muse of Beauty, Justice, and Death: "les sœurs de charité." But the Queen is Woman: mother, divinity, as well as *jeune fille*.

When one has waited so long as Rimbaud, steeped in oneself, the love and the guilt interpenetrate ambivalently in what is to other men perversity, so that no moment of joy is ever entirely divorced from some hint of defeat or death, either contrasting, as the immediate counterpart or consequence of such sheer purity, innocence, and beauty: "O saisons, O châteaux / Quelle âme est sans défauts?" ("Le Bonheur"); "Elle est retrouvée. Quoi?—L'Éternité . . . Science avec patience, / Le supplice est sûr" ("L'Éternité"), or mingled in like the "bonne voix d'anges . . . Chers corbeaux délicieux!" ("La Rivière de Cassis"), their blackness and reedy caws spicing the keenest delight in nature through which he wanders, a latter-day Perceval, recalling "Les passions mortes des chevaliers errants: / Mais que salubre est le vent!" (ibid).

At times his love for his mother partially tunneled through the barriers of rejection—she was not altogether inhuman or unfeminine and sporadically made comforting gestures toward her son—and we have the

---

[22] Partly because it is so much lovelier than the English "sister" (it rimes with *douceur*); we are apt to use the word "daughter."

nocturnal scene of "Les Déserts de l'amour."[23] The mother image appears white, the very color of desire, often localized in the pale nightgown of any visitant mother pitted against the darkness (recalling Ophelia on her black tide), for some of his orphaned feeling, as we shall see in "Mémoire," is transferred to the deserted mother.[24] Despite the intensity of the long desire and sulking which brought about this juxtaposition of white and black, the love is not consummated in the fantasy, and the boy and the woman fall hopelessly from the bed in a well-known sequence of dream events.[25] There can be no full breakthrough of the emotions in this direction as yet; the resentment and the normal incest-guilt together set up a thick barrier zone, and without a father to guide him through it by steadying discipline he had not yet the strength, the manhood, to go it alone; he will, however, gradually attain it via accepted or inherited father substitutes: socially determined work, spiritual fathers, a certain spontaneous inner toughening which comes with years. For a long time, the only satisfying and uncensored outlet for Rimbaud will be through his poetry.

During his protracted striving to be a man, Rimbaud's misogyny is mainly apparent, a protective device not radically dissimilar to that of all young men who lack the honesty to admit their dependency upon womanly affection: "ô Femme, monceau d'entrailles, pitié douce, . . . C'est toi qui pends à nous, porteuse de mamelles" ("Les Sœurs de charité"). But at other moments he calls out desperately for a "sœur de charité." It is therefore a mistake to emphasize Rimbaud's homosexuality: with him as with all true poets there is rather an enhanced case of the doubleness (at least) of the civilized temperament, revealing the need both to love

---

[23] In Ethiopia, he seems to have made the beginnings of a breakthrough, expressing the desire to marry.

[24] Or, inversely, the mother's Madame Butterfly sorrow often molds the child's emotions.

[25] The sequence is somewhat duplicated in "Après le déluge," where the Queen, "la Reine, la Sorcière qui allume sa braise dans le pot de terre, ne voudra jamais nous raconter ce qu'elle sait, et que nous ignorons." In the preface to the *Saison en enfer*, he refers to a pair of Muses in the following terms: "La Beauté . . . la justice . . . O sorcières . . . c'est à vous que mon trésor a été confié." Further on in the work ("Mauvais sang"), we find "la boue m'apparaissait soudainement rouge et noire, comme une glace quand la lampe circule dans la chambre voisine, comme un trésor dans la forêt!" Thus we come full cycle, back to the "mother" in "Les Déserts de l'amour" with: "La lampe de la famille rougissait l'une après l'autre les chambres voisines. Alors la femme disparut." In sum, the treasure, like embers in an earthen pot (gold in mud, a lamp in the night), is the love of the "mother," or Beauty, half-buried in guilt and forbidden passage, a consummation hidden in ignorance. Commentators have given the "Reine" all sorts of dry, scholarly sources. Why not?

actively, aggressively, as well as tenderly, and to be loved, passively in a similarly ambiguous way (in men, including Rimbaud, there is some tilt toward the active mode). Recalling our notion that "the creator has, in his narrow way, something more of both modes than his counterpart: he is at once more penetrating, virile, form-creating, and more gently available and open to the world's various impressions," there is still a resolving tone of proud, free-swimming initiative (crowned by the total visionary stasis), hence the frequency of phrases like "Je courus! et les Péninsules dé-marrées / N'ont pas subi tohu-bohus plus triomphants." (Note the impact of *Péninsules*.) "Je sais les cieux crevant en éclairs" . . . "Et j'ai vu quelque-fois ce que l'homme a cru voir" ("Bateau ivre"). One may think first of the obvious narcissism, but that is a powerful element of all vocational striving. With the "Bateau ivre" Rimbaud has precisely "found his voice" in an exultantly confident way. And although there is a note of failure at the end of the poem,[26] there is clear promise in this boy, even in the world's most ordinary terms. There are, of course, alternations of passive phases: "L'eau verte pénétra ma coque" (the boat is an excellent symbol of this doubleness, being an outer penetrating shape and an inner con-tainer). But, to repeat, his larger openness is more than balanced by his stronger creative virility, and the final shape of the career is a monument, perdurable through the wearing years and before which the swaggering male must eventually bend the knee. The poet who courageously saw himself to be "ainsi qu'une femme à genoux" ("Bateau ivre") then rises up "Majestueusement debout" ("Soleil et chair").

And now we come to a crucial juncture of Petit Poucet's journey, when amidst the scintillating light playing upon the flowers, the pebbles, and the myriad things of this world, he is pierced through to his soul by a distant mysterious call;[27] at first he is haunted by an unknown presence, a voice of undifferentiated nature, but slowly he becomes aware of a distinct source of this yearning, the absence of a father, as crucial to his dangerous

---

[26] The true artist, poet or musician, often eschews the pompous fanfare of a positive close, which is too obvious a way of *affirming*; the quieter conclusion, often leaving the issue unsolved or returning to the beginning spirally, rounds out the work more nearly in the tentative spirit of life itself, allows it to stand up as a whole and assert its presence tactfully. But Molly Bloom's gentle final "Yes," the "vers le bonheur d'autres m'entraîneront" of Mallarmé's "Faune," or the quiet re-minder that the "play's the thing" concluding Shakespeare's best tragedies are all solutions superior to Rimbaud's abrupt drop here.

[27] Madeleine Smith has mentioned the affinity with St. Paul on the road to Da-mascus in an interesting attempt to reconstruct the "chasse spirituelle" from the known writings, "The Theme of the Hunt in Rimbaud: *La Chasse spirituelle*," *PMLA*, LXIV, no. 3 (June, 1949), pp. 325-39.

genius as it was to Hölderlin's (according to Jean Laplanche) or Nietzsche's (according to Walter Kaufmann).

We have tried in *The Writer's Way in France* to follow the arabesque of this golden thread of inspiration running throughout French (and world) literature, from *Tristan* to the present. In Rimbaud we may trace it from the very first poem, "Les Etrennes des orphelins," where it is, however, as yet relegated to a secondary role: "Plus de mère au logis!—et le père est bien loin!" In the same juvenile piece, there is a promise of its subsequent development: "Ils écoutent, pensifs, comme un lointain murmure . . . / Ils tressaillent souvent à la claire voix d'or / Du timbre matinal, qui frappe et frappe encor / Son refrain métallique en son globe de verre." We observed, in our study, that the distant horn of *Tristan*, which seemed an echo bridging the original sundering, had later equivalents in the far-off sound of bells[28] or hailing voices.

In a subsequent poem, the fantasy metamorphoses into the image of a *Forgeron*, a quasi-mythical Worker, with a mingling-in of the hunt theme: "Ouvriers! Nous sommes / Pour les grands temps nouveaux où l'on voudra savoir, / Où l'Homme forgera du matin jusqu'au soir, / Chasseur des grands effets, chasseur des grandes causes, / Où, lentement vainqueur, il domptera les choses / Et montera sur Tout, comme sur un cheval! / O! splendides lueurs des forges![29] Plus de mal, / Plus! . . . "

The theme of the father is here attached, as in "Génie," to the idealized notion of political justice which arises typically in adolescence, but it picks up the earlier nostalgia from childhood, when the worker, though apotheosized, is not at all abstract: we have only to recall the immensely real and sensuous prestige the locomotive driver or the carpenter had for any of us as children,[30]

> Il n'aimait pas Dieu; mais les hommes, qu'au soir fauve,
> Noirs, en blouse, il voyait rentrer dans le faubourg . . .
> ("Les Poètes de sept ans")

and the prose poem "Ouvriers" recounts a fumbling attempt to live their lives. "Bonne pensée du matin" is based entirely on the theme of workmen as the favorites of Venus:

[28] Whether through the golden sun which measures time, the village bell, or the "golden voice" of the living-room—possibly "grandfather"—clock, there is some link between "Father Time" and the poetic expression of nostalgia for the father.

[29] Cf. the Greek blacksmith, fireworker, and Father God, Zeus, or Norse Thor.

[30] He alludes briefly ("Oraison du soir") to an angel in a barber's chair: this is a poignant situation for the fatherless child, to be held in tender subjection (by a man with a razor), as in "Les Chercheuses de poux"; here the "motherless" child received similar attention from a pair of maiden ladies, and it moved him to tears.

> Mais là-bas dans l'immense chantier
> Vers le soleil des Hespérides,
> En bras de chemise, les charpentiers
> Déjà s'agitent.
>
> . . .
>
> O Reine des Bergers!
> Porte aux travailleurs l'eau-de-vie,
> Pour que leurs forces soient en paix
> En attendant le bain dans la mer à midi.[31]

The sunlit *chantier* is found again in "Mémoire," "chantiers riverains,"[32] and leads us to a brief consideration of this major work. A complete analysis will be found in a separate chapter.

The hero of the poem is white or golden-yellow light itself, the pure love of the poet aspiring to come into his own through the absent father. The universal drama of the struggle for identity is cast at different levels of reality, the most important *dramatis personae* being the actual parents. But first the light itself appears as an angelic Presence; its feminine half is the wide background of earthly nature over which it hovers (the classic man-sun and woman-earth paradigm is the core of "Soleil et chair," based on Greek myth and Lucretius). The earth-woman is partially associated with darkness, but in various myths she takes on her own whiteness and brightness ("Aphrodité marine," daughter of foam, "Soleil et chair"), as the opposites interpenetrate with some of the complexity of life itself. Here the sisters incarnate this womanly fairness: "blancheur des corps de femmes," but the mother is soon singled out as "Elle, toute / froide, et noire," for, by her failure as a woman, her usurpation of masculinity, she has upset the balance of nature; with the departure of the man her feminine light has gone out of her: "Madame se tient trop debout" [the male stance]; she disdainfully treads upon field flowers which are "trop fière[s] pour elle." "Hélas, Lui, comme / mille anges blancs qui se séparent sur la route, / s'éloigne par delà la montagne! Elle, toute / froide, et noire, court! après le départ de l'homme!" The "Lui" is primarily the father but conceivably a prevision of the son who aspires to be one with him, to become a father.[33] *Lui* happens also to be the past participle of *luire*, to shine, and Rimbaud returns to this poetic harmony in "le soleil, de la montagne fière, / Luit" ("Le Dormeur du val," note the reappearance

---

[31] Cf. the communion of the men in the sea in Camus's *Noces* and *La Peste*, Giraudoux's *Bella*.

[32] This points to a possible suggestion of workers in the "fils du travail" of strophe III.

[33] For the moment, in the irresponsible adventurous image of his parent; later, in a more universally acceptable way.

22

of the mountain). By coincidence, Mallarmé used one of his well-known echo ambiguities to describe Rimbaud himself: "météore, lui" ("Arthur Rimbaud"). In "Le Bonheur" Rimbaud similarly writes: "vive lui, [or, as a variant, "salut à lui"] chaque fois / Que chante son coq gaulois," which is another instance of the spatial nostalgia (cock-cry, horn, one's own name called at a distance).

The dramatic man-woman opposition is found also at the level of two flowers: the yellow-gold marigold is like the father: "Plus pure qu'un louis, jaune et chaude paupière / le souci d'eau—ta foi conjugale, ô l'Épouse!— / au midi prompt . . ." (recall Father Time as sun). In the final strophe it is juxtaposed to the blue flower, and both are seen as being beyond Rimbaud's reach for the reasons we have understood: "Oh! bras trop courts! ni l'une / ni l'autre fleur: ni la jaune qui m'importune, / là; ni la bleue, amie à l'eau couleur de cendre." Now we clearly see the woman-water image, but through a body of water with the light gone out of it: "la nappe, sans reflets, sans source, grise." And we may understand better why his resentment of his mother, with her "bleu regard—qui ment," is exhaled in the later phrase "j'écartai du ciel l'azur qui est du noir." At other moments, however, we remember that he will dream about the nuptials of ideal parents, hidden like faces in a picture puzzle amid "la mer mêlée au soleil" ("L'Éternité"), "L'azur et l'onde communient" ("Bannières de mai").

These grasses, flowers, rivers, mountains, seas, and suns are—regardless of whether we call Rimbaud a "symbolist" or not (the point seems idle)— symbols in the proper literary sense: the objects all have their own absolute value as well as their place in that fluid hierarchy of phenomena which characterizes universal analogy, the "jeu suprême" of any worthwhile (symbolist, in the broad sense which would include Shakespeare, Dante) poet;[34] a "jeu," incidentally, of which Rimbaud was, varyingly and increasingly, quite conscious.

From the poetic theme of the sun derives directly that of the hunt, as in "Bannières de mai": "Aux branches claires des tilleuls / Meurt un maladif hallali."[35] The beauty of the light—"Le ciel est joli comme un ange"—is doomed to a sacrificial end in the eternal drama of nature, to which sacrificial communion the son aspires, at first through the stabbing intervention of the father himself; he desires to be hunted down, as if by the Greek archer and sun-god, Apollo, wounded into manhood and more: "Je sors! Si un rayon me blesse / Je succomberai sur la mousse." "Je

---

[34] The same is to be said of the "armoire" or "buffet" ("Les Étrennes des orphelins," "Le Buffet"), mother symbols, yes, but also wonderful things-in-themselves (cf. Mallarmé's *console*, which plays on ambiguity).

[35] "On entend dans les bois lointains des hallalis" ("Ophélie").

veux que l'été dramatique [the drama just mentioned] / Me lie à son char de fortune." (This is the myth of Apollo as huntsman and charioteer.) "A toi, Nature, je me rends; / Et ma faim et toute ma soif. . . . C'est rire aux parents,[36] qu'au soleil." Elsewhere, in "O saisons, ô châteaux," the poetry of the distant sun is refound in its herald, the time-telling morning cock crow:

> J'ai fait la magique étude
> Du bonheur, que nul n'élude.
>
> . . .
>
> O vive lui, chaque fois
> Que chante son coq gaulois

The fiercely fatherly quality of this *bonheur* is clear for it pierces him to the quick with "sa dent douce à la mort." The distance the cock call[37] traverses to end in "me," arising from slumber to refind the world, seems to encompass all of sweet France, given back to the waking poet. He is as passively receptive here—in one aspect—as in the preceding "Bannières de mai": "Il [le bonheur] s'est chargé de ma vie / Ce charme, il prit âme et corps, / Et dispersa tous efforts." ("O saisons, ô châteaux.") We may further recall the aspect of passivity in "Le Bateau ivre," this time associated with the mother-sea: "L'eau . . . me lava, dispersant gouvernail et grappin" (standing for self-guidance, of which he was understandably weary, as well as meaningless family duties). In the same way, there is little that is more penetrating than the sound of one's own name[38] spoken from a distance, like the mysterious sundown call to sainthood in Debussy's *Martyre de Saint Sébastien*:

[36] Inanimate nature and the sun are still conceived as sexless here, which of course they are, and some of their poetic value depends precisely upon their innocence, their being apart from the human struggle. But the advanced critic is no more afraid of the underlying, and eventually overlying, drift in this imagery, than the mature creative artist comes to be (*vide* Joyce's pages on the father-son relationship in *Ulysses*), as we grow toward a serener awareness. Incidentally, the obvious resistance in the young Rimbaud to this acceptance is somewhat paralleled by the young Mallarmé, who substituted a *Mère* for *Père* divinity in "Les Fleurs"; but his later work resolves all this ("Un Coup de dés": "le Maître," Man as a universal Father, takes a prominent role. Cf. "Confrontation"). With Rimbaud, even in his final poems, because he is so much younger, the victory is less clear-cut; he is still somewhat dominated by his theme: but its rising to consciousness as clearly as it does is a tribute to the power of his precocious intellect. His pitiless self-analysis is well illustrated by the "Remembrances du vieillard idiot."

[37] In a secondary way, there is an obvious association between male and "coq."

[38] Cf. Richard Wilbur's "June Light."

Quelqu'une des voix
Toujours angélique
—Il s'agit de moi—

("Age d'or")

If we speak of religion here, of course, it can only be the undefined, perhaps pantheistic, faith of the artist.

From all of this we may understand the impact of a prose poem entitled "A une raison" (*raison*, here, is a fatherly, almost military, "musical" logic or ordering of reality; *new* reason, to be sure, and yet not without reminiscences; we recall that Rimbaud's father was a professional soldier; cf. "L'idéal, la pensée invincible, éternelle," "Soleil et chair"):

> Un coup de ton doigt sur le tambour décharge tous les sons et commence la nouvelle harmonie.
> Un pas de toi c'est la levée des nouveaux hommes et leur en marche.
> Ta tête se détourne: le nouvel amour! Ta tête se retourne:— le nouvel amour!
> "Change nos lots, crible les fléaux, à commencer par le temps", te chantent ces enfants. "Élève n'importe où la substance de nos fortunes et de nos vœux", on t'en prie.
> Arrivée de toujours, qui t'en iras partout.[39]

Here, according to an obviously military theme, the father image is of a general (with some dictatorlike[40] qualities); we find the same linkage, and further with light, in "Alchimie du Verbe": ". . . je m'offrais su soleil, dieu de feu. / 'Général . . . bombarde-nous.' . . . Oh! le moucheron . . . que dissout un rayon!"

The "tête [qui] se détourne . . . [et] se retourne" is not only a probable allusion to the "right face" (passing in review) sort of military movement—a wooden, masculine gesture of love par excellence—but may contain some hidden reminiscence of the abrupt absence-presence of his military parent, the excruciating "concession" of "Génie."

Rimbaud's social rebellion—which, politically, has the radical left quality of permanent revolt (as opposed to an eventually consolidated revolution) and is of relatively little interest despite some silly recent attempts to make Rimbaud "relevant"—may be thus understood as a bid

---

[39] The attractiveness of this figure, like his gone father, is his utterly above-it-all dynamism; he comes only to go: what a flash!

[40] The political right and left extremism of Rimbaud, like that of poets generally, is a corollary of the daemonic rhythm.

for castigation,[41] for the sharp disciplined attention of the father-society: this, whether we mean his revolutionary fling during the Commune, his personal misdemeanors (which were mild), his theoretical fierce admiration for the *forçat*, the hardened criminal who is released only to be locked up again, or his blasphemy, which is a bid for attention from the Highest Authority: "Général . . . bombarde-nous. . . ."

The culmination of this mood appears in the last, and most glorious, of the *Illuminations*, "Génie": it is too long to quote in its entirety here but the complete text will be found in the special chapter devoted to it. Along with the more general or diffusive sense of a pure spirit of genius[42]—whatever inspires us to keenest feelings of aliveness, embracing the whole world as it is or could be—the poem is permeated with something more specifically male (which is unsurprising in our Judaeo-Christian tradition) and even more specifically fatherly. It can be summed up as a sophisticated and subtle hymn to the ideal father (or Father).

The repeated (five times) "lui," is clearly enough, and brightly (the overtone of "shone"), male. The "lui et nous" formula is distinctly fatherly as is the extensive series of protective, providing, or indulgent acts emerging from the spirit: "il a fait . . . ," "lui qui a purifié les boissons et les aliments"; "sa concession"; "Il nous a connus tous et nous a tous aimés"; "l'abolition de toutes souffrances. . . ." The "raison merveilleuse" has been previously associated with the orderly father-principle ("À une raison"). In a more direct personal way, the "lui qui nous aime . . . Et nous nous le rappelons et il voyage" certainly bears on Rimbaud's intimate family drama. And the whole feeling of meteoric passage—"la force et l'amour que nous, debout dans les rages et les ennuis, nous voyons passer dans le ciel de tempête et les drapeaux d'extase"[43]—is in harmony with the awesome independence of his sire who swept into and out of his life like an above-it-all God, whom Rimbaud would strive to emulate in his own "meteoric" career.

In another prose poem, "Conte," the *Génie* is again the spirit of the male parent with a presence of the father principle within the son, the Prince; the tone of it is on the whole more narcissistically[44] self-involved:

[41] Sartre, and others, have shown the same to be true for Baudelaire's relations with his stepfather, le Général Aupick.

[42] Cf. "Le jeune homme [qu'eût] Adoré, dans la Perse, un Génie inconnu" ("Les Sœurs de charité").

[43] The "rage et les ennuis" are clearly in the mood of the abandoned child left to the stagnant life and neglect of the woman-dominated family as we see in "Mémoire" (where the sun-father was *lui*) or "Jeunesse."

[44] It is a spirit of Rimbaud *beyond* Rimbaud so to speak; his higher self he wishes to join. J.-P. Richard confirms this point.

"Un soir il [the Prince] galopait fièrement. Un Génie apparut, d'une beauté ineffable, inavouable même. . . . Le Prince et le Génie s'anéantirent probablement dans la santé[45] essentielle. . . . Le Prince était le Génie. Le Génie était le Prince. . . ."

Izambard was enormously important to Rimbaud as a (young) father-figure of the sort the male school-teacher is to the needy boy: "Je vous aimerai comme un père . . . j'espère en vous comme en ma mère," Arthur wrote him. The arduous school labors, the first poems, were all meant to get his attention, earn his affection. His leaving and his bourgeois "feet of clay" were an enormous letdown, as always happens sooner or later in cases like this. It is no use blaming anyone; but for Rimbaud, here again, fate was extraordinarily harsh, and a deep pathos is to be read between the lines of his letters to his mentor.

In a different, yet corollary, way—he too played a somewhat fatherly role for a while—Verlaine was the target of comparable hopes and comparable disappointment.

At its most extreme, as in the case of Hölderlin or Vigny, the absence of the father becomes in Rimbaud a shocking total void. These traumas are reflected in the rare moments of the poetry where we glimpse his sense of utter abandonment by, and hence his utter rejection of, deity, as in "L'Homme juste." This void is the male-womb of Promethean creativity, the riskiest of prides. It is among the deepest and most frightening of human phenomena: spiritual death, to even think of it is painful.

For most children, following the exhausting struggle of the Oedipal crisis, there is a relatively calm transitional ("latency") period. Then come the crises of puberty, with the flowering of romantic love and, with its disappointments, the further growth of potentially adult realism and striving, together with the idealization of certain principles embodied in the young vocation. We have noted that the Oedipal struggle was uncommonly protracted for Rimbaud; still, there are grounds for believing that he was making good headway toward the end of his life and, in any case, there were partial victories on this front all along. The struggle is never decisively won by any sensitive person, least of all artists, but rather recurrently subdued, allowing subsequent emotional growth. In this relativistic light, even Rimbaud can be said to have matured: the partial ascent into the phase of romantic love is evidenced by a series of poems like "À la musique," "L'Étoile a pleuré rose . . . ," "Première soirée," later the prose "Ouvriers" and "Bottom" (despite the *arrière-goût*, which is scarcely unique to our poet).

---

[45] The suggestion of masturbation jibes with "L'ardente hygiène" of "H."

> Je ne dis pas un mot: je regarde toujours
> La chair de leurs cous blancs brodés de mèches folles:
> Je suis, sous le corsage et les frêles atours,
> Le dos divin après la courbe des épaules.
>
> J'ai bientôt déniché la bottine, le bas . . .
> —Je reconstruis le corps, brûlé de belles fièvres.
> Elles me trouvent drôle et se parlent tout bas . . .
> —Et je sens les baisers qui me viennent aux lèvres . . .
> ("À la Musique")

From all this it seems likely that Rimbaud's homosexual experience was of less than determining importance, merely an episode. Even the "Je n'aime pas les femmes" of "Délires I" is immediately followed by Rimbaud's recognition of "femmes, avec les signes du bonheur, dont, moi, j'aurais pu faire de bonnes camarades" (even though, alas, they have been spoiled by brutal men . . .). In Rimbaud, as Painter said of Proust, there was a heterosexual "screaming to be let out." Perhaps his sexual abuse by the *communards,* described pathetically in "Le cœur volé," and his awareness that he *enjoyed* his humiliation, made the struggle even harder, though from such tussles there emerge correspondingly firm victories. Eventually he rejected this heresy along with all the other forms of personal love in his "Adieu" to Verlaine and the West. Later, in his letters from Harrar, he expresses the desire to marry and have a son. This probably represents a significant step in his inner progress, and his wish to marry sounds sincere: he seems to have lived with a native woman during his stay in Abyssinia. When he returned to France he could not bear to see his mother, and let her know it. We are aware, from analysis, that this exhalation of his resentment against her is a useful part of the "spiritual weaning" from her. His ambition to have a son represents his need to continue the struggle for self-mastery by becoming a father, his need to accept demands from and exert discipline upon something other than his own ego, to get outside of himself, to be effective and grow in the time-proven way. But before all this there was the precocious burst of vocational activity culminating in *Une Saison en enfer,* his most concerted attempt to publish and make a name as an author, to find and nail down his adult male identity.

Few identities have ever been more firmly fixed.

I

THE EARLY

POEMS

Les Étrennes des Orphelins

THIS IS the earliest of Rimbaud's published poems and the first poem in verse we have of his aside from the Latin exercises. It appeared in the *Revue pour tous* in January 1870, having been written in Rimbaud's fourteenth or fifteenth year. Various influences have been discovered: Reboul's "L'Ange et l'enfant" (which was the subject given in his school for a Latin verse-composition: Rimbaud's "Ver erat"); Coppée's "Enfants trouvés," Hugo's "Pauvres gens." The following lines from Hugo's "La Prière pour tous" (*Les Feuilles d'automne*) seem to me to have impressed young Rimbaud even more:

> C'est l'heure où les enfants parlent avec les anges
>   .   .   .
> Et puis ils dormiront.—Alors, épars dans l'ombre,
> Les rêves d'or, essaim tumultueux, sans nombre,
> Qui naît aux derniers bruits du jour à son déclin
>   .   .   .
> Viendront s'abattre en foule à leurs rideaux de lin.
>   .   .   .
> Ainsi que l'oiseau met sa tête sous son aile,
> L'enfant dans la prière endort son jeune esprit.

The poem has been described as a pastiche (of Coppée, among others), but the self-pitying sincerity of it strikes one even more than whatever ironic intention. This is the earliest of the many references Rimbaud makes to his abandoned state. It is a typical fantasy of nostalgia for nest- or womb-warmth and the lost "happy family"—one is aware of many such sentimental evocations in literature, for example, Dickens' *David Copperfield*, Charles Kingsley's *Water Babies*. Whether we regard it as shallow, sentimental pathos or the expression of tragically profound deprivation may depend on how defensive we ourselves are: knowing what was behind it, in Rimbaud's case, I find it suggestive of genuine pain in certain passages.

The poem is useful to us because it presents numerous important themes in simple forms which can help us to see through some very complex imageries.

2. De deux enfants le triste et doux chuchotement.

The presence of two conspiratorial children lightens the orphan burden somewhat, puts the poem in the realm of gentle pathos, the mood of "triste et doux." Richard would call this *fadeur*—I find that to be a too systematic and condescending approach to such Verlainian moods.

> 4. Sous le long rideau blanc qui tremble et se soulève . . .

The "rideau" is the bed-curtain, by context; like the lovely presence of air lifting and billowing out window-curtains, the "tremble et se soulève" delicately hints at the ghostly hovering of absent and dreamed-of ("rêve" in line 3) parents or of some such consoling notion: "il y avait des visions derrière la gaze des rideaux" (second "Lettre du voyant").

> 5. —Au dehors les oiseaux se rapprochent frileux;
>   Leur aile s'engourdit sous le ton gris des cieux;

As in "Les Effarés," there is an ambivalent tone of warmth and cold which dominates the poem; it exists mainly in a mid-realm—something like a delightful shiver—between the pleasure of nostalgia and indoor snugness versus deprivation and external cold. The birds, victims of the outer chill, are associated with the deprivation as are the poor worker's children in "Les Poètes de sept ans," "Les Effarés." The double mood is carried on in:

> 9. Sourit avec les pleurs, et chante en grelottant . . .

> 12. Ils écoutent, pensifs, comme un lointain murmure . . .
>   Ils tressaillent souvent à la claire voix d'or
>   Du timbre matinal, qui frappe et frappe encor
>   Son refrain métallique en son globe de verre . . .

There is, to repeat, the hint of a major theme here: the distant "golden" bell (or hailing voice, or cock-crow . . .), which mysteriously evokes a possible salvation (as in Goethe's *Faust I*), often at the dramatic moment of daybreak (or sunset): "Le Bonheur! Sa dent, douce à la mort, m'avertissait au chant du coq,—*ad matutinum*, au *Christus venit*,—dans les plus sombres villes." (*Une Saison en enfer*: "Alchimie du Verbe"). Baudelaire's "Crépuscule du matin" evokes this shiveringly alive moment with the same cock-crow.

The clock ("grandfather clock"; "Father Time") is vaguely associated with the original Father who divided the light from the dark (the etymon of time is "to cut," according to Cassirer) and ordered Creation (as in "À une raison" or the "ordre, éternel veilleur" of "L'Homme juste"); the "golden voice" reminds us that Rimbaud will later identify himself as "fils du Soleil." In "La Maline" we get a faint echo of this nostalgia: "En mangeant, j'écoutais l'horloge,—heureux et coi." And in "Enfance," there is a numb suspension of life when the clock stops, as if the sun had gone behind a cloud.

> 21. —Il n'est donc point de mère à ces petits enfants,
>   De mère au frais sourire, aux regards triomphants?

Rimbaud, of course, had a mother; but she was scarcely inclined to "cool smiles" according to descriptions we have of her. Even a more usual mother is often rejected by the sensitive child in moments of inevitable bitterness occasioned simply by the imposition of harsh reality onto the original king-like infinite of his lost paradise of "juvenile omnipotence"; then, as in the well-known spiritual, sometimes we feel like a "motherless child."

> 23. Elle a donc oublié, le soir, seule et penchée,
>   D'exciter une flamme à la cendre arrachée,

Here too we witness the germination of a major theme: the ambivalent black and red pairing—ashes and fire, death and life-blood—which runs through the poetry.

> 29. —Le rêve maternel, c'est le tiède tapis,

We will re-encounter this maternal carpet in "Veillées," III: "Les lampes et les tapis de la veillée."

> 30. C'est le nid cotonneux où les enfants tapis,
>   Comme de beaux oiseaux que balancent les branches,
>   Dorment leur doux sommeil plein de visions blanches! ...

The white visions involve a complex maternal fantasy of milk, mother's skin or night-dress, the white bed-curtains (mentioned earlier) around the secure "nest." Mallarmé's early poems—and sometimes later ones ("Brise marine," "Une Dentelle s'abolit")—are steeped in these reminiscences.

> 36. Votre cœur l'a compris:—ces enfants sont sans mère.
>   Plus de mère au logis!—et le père est bien loin! ...

Despite the possible ironic echo of Coppée in the "Votre cœur l'a compris," the theme of the absent father is solidly sounded. It overlaps with and aggravates the general human condition of the Adamic fall, exile from the All-Father, the lost paradise which is echoed in earthy images of the invisible garden ("Enfance"), the closed inns ("Comédie de la soif"), and the ancient Orient (*Une Saison en enfer*).

In an essay, "Plumes and Prisons,"[1] we took note of the extraordinary number of French writers who were fatherless, in various ways. The male parent teaches one the prevailing games, the male role, which helps one to tame one's emotions and fit in with a group and live somewhat automatically. Failing this, one is inclined to change the rules of the game through new visions, creativity. In any event, one doesn't fit in—one is an "ugly duckling"—and must find unusual compensatory self-justifications. The writer finds father-figures in previous creators who justify his peculiar type (the budding swan). In Rimbaud the father-image will vary considerably, including writers like Baudelaire ("un vrai Dieu"), adventurers, and even criminal types. All represent his need to "smash reality like a moneybox" (Sartre), his revolutionary—both politically and artistically—temperament.

> 45. Dans quelque songe étrange où l'on voyait joujoux,
> Bonbons habillés d'or, étincelants bijoux,
> Tourbillonner, danser une danse sonore,
> Puis fuir sous les rideaux, puis reparaître encore!

The movement from reality through a process of sublimation or etherealization often, in art or fantasy, takes the form of a whirlwind, which not only lifts but accelerates reality and, despite the exciting experience of escape, involves it in a narcissistically contained *round* like the traditional magic circle which expresses a centripetal impulse toward a center of intimate meaning, the focus of depth, the beyond. Hence Mallarmé used it as a symbol of art on page 6 of the "Coup de Dés" (as well as in an early story, "Ce que disaient les trois cigognes" which is rather close in mood to this poem). Essentially, this is Rimbaud's notion of his art: the contained *delirium* of "Délires II: Alchimie du Verbe" in which he boasts "Je fixais des vertiges." In more sophisticated guise, this pattern will repeat itself in various *Illuminations* such as "Being beauteous": "Les couleurs propres de la vie se foncent, dansent, et se dégagent autour de la Vision." Compare also "Cimmérie, patrie de l'ombre et des tourbillons" ("Délires II"), and "Ce qu'on dit au poète à propos de fleurs," part II, where there is a whirlwind of roses à la Banville.

[1] Robert G. Cohn, "From Chrétien to Camus: Plumes and Prisons," *MLN*, Vol. 80, No. 5, pp. 601-609.

59. Un grand feu pétillait, clair, dans la cheminée,
    Toute la vieille chambre était illuminée;
    Et les reflets vermeils, sortis du grand foyer,
    Sur les meubles vernis aimaient à tournoyer . . .
    —L'armoire était sans clefs! . . . sans clefs, la grande armoire!
    On regardait souvent sa porte brune et noire . . .
    Sans clefs! . . . c'était étrange! . . . on rêvait bien des fois
    Aux mystères dormant entre ses flancs de bois,
    Et l'on croyait ouïr, au fond de la serrure
    Béante, un bruit lointain, vague et joyeux murmure . . .

The warmth of the quondam "happy family" was embodied in the fire on the hearth[2] (later, the *foyer* will become sadly rejected, a mere point of departure for wild fantasy, in the prose poem "Nocturne vulgaire": "Un souffle disperse les limites du foyer").

The "tournoyer" again speaks of a welling- or spiraling-up of joy. But the ambivalent mood again is in the red firelight versus the dark ("noire") mood of the *armoire* which is clearly associated, as in the later poem "Le Buffet," with the deepest maternal mystery—the same that gave rise to those childhood dreams of a fairy godmother who lives up high in a secret room (as in *The Princess and the Goblins*) when one's own mother had too seriously let one down.

The opposition of the fire and the dark (ashes) will be found again associated with a mysterious and sad mother-figure (the sorrow of loss often seeps into the substitute figure, as in the *Sad King* of Rouault, the wounded Fisher King, or the wistful King of playing cards). Thus: "la Reine, la Sorcière qui allume sa braise dans le pot de terre, ne voudra jamais nous raconter ce qu'elle sait, et que nous ignorons" ("Après le Déluge").

Mothers are in a major sense a source,[3] and we depend on them utterly at first—until they let us down thoroughly and we are spiritually weaned. We believe for a while that they are rooted in deep wisdom, are omniscient, like Norns, or Sibyls. Ousted, this belief remains at our core, but often the bitter disappointments and the emotional blockage ("noire . . . sans clefs!") causes the image to be transferred to other figures, perhaps a

---

[2] Which is a fantasy of a consoling mother-like presence "devant une neige" stirring up beauty, the warmth of life: "un Être de Beauté de haute taille . . . des blessures écarlates et noires" ("Being beauteous"), compare Hopkins' "gash gold" ("The Windhover").

[3] The writings of Jung ("the terrible mother"), Neumann (*ouroboros*), Robert Graves ("White Goddess") have reminded us of her power recently in discursive terms.

kindly aunt, or the Virgin, or, in this case, the generous cornucopia-like maternal totem of the buffet, with its frequent breast-like *bombé* shape (as in Baudelaire's "Le Beau Navire": "Ta gorge triomphante est une belle armoire / Dont les panneaux bombés. . . ."). In the present instance it is womb-like, with its "flancs de bois."

Finally the quoted "bruit lointain, vague et joyeux murmure" is a quasi-divine calling to us to join the source of joy (perhaps the stir of a distant fête or fair), like the golden voice of the clock mentioned earlier.

> 74. leurs grands yeux bleus.

Rimbaud's eyes were blue, like his mother's. It is a symbol of this childish sublime innocence (as in line 90: "Par la fenêtre on voit là-bas un beau ciel bleu") and a desired communion with the mother's intimacy—but *that* blue lies, as we learn in "Les Poètes de sept ans."

> 88. paradis rose.

The pink (and blue) is a baby-joy color par excellence, originally symbolic no doubt of the warmly suffused cheeks of maternal love. It is again in "une fée a passée . . . près du lit maternel, sous un beau rayon rose" in line 99. Compare Mallarmé's "Apparition."

> 91. La nature s'éveille et de rayons s'enivre . . .
>   La terre, demi-nue, heureuse de revivre,
>   A des frissons de joie aux baisers du soleil . . .

The simple paradigm of sun-father and earth-mother goes back to the Greeks (passing perhaps by way of Banville's "La Voie lactée"), and Lucretius; it will remain persistent in Rimbaud's most advanced art, such as "Mémoire." It is part of the "Happy family" fantasy, here dispersed amid consoling nature.

> 100. Là, sur le grand tapis, resplendit quelque chose . . .
>   Ce sont des médaillons argentés, noirs et blancs,
>
>   •   •   •
>
>   Ayant trois mots gravés en or: "À NOTRE MÈRE!"

Rimbaud clearly had trouble finishing this poem; the emotion is exhausted and the infinite mystery is not. How familiar this is: all our adolescent poems came a cropper in this way! The medallions engraved with *À notre mère* offer an air of monumental (or tomb-like) finality, but, even leaving room for the possible irony, how pathetically clumsy and juvenile![4]

Sensation

Par les soirs bleus d'été, j'irai dans les sentiers,
Picoté par les blés, fouler l'herbe menue:
Rêveur, j'en sentirai la fraîcheur à mes pieds.
Je laisserai le vent baigner ma tête nue.

Je ne parlerai pas, je ne penserai rien:
Mais l'amour infini me montera dans l'âme,
Et j'irai loin, bien loin, comme un bohémien,
Par la Nature,—heureux comme avec une femme.

In this poem one feels some roundly Rimbaldian qualities; "roundly" in the sense that in his world the beyond and the here and now are fully integrated; the poetic and the real are blissfully married. An earthily concrete yet transcendent world, like a fresh evening stroll on a *sentier*, which is a "male" Way embedded in mother earth.[1]

The title embodies the Romantic acceptance of the "lower" self, the child's immediate apprehension of the world through his senses. And like the later title, "Mémoire," it indicates Rimbaud's awareness of the modern psychological phenomenon. "Sensation" is in a Romantic, or late-Romantic, vein on its way to Symbolism—very close in tone to Paul Bourget's "Beau soir" from about the same period. The incipient Symbolism, or Impressionism, is evident in the delicacy of "l'herbe menue" and "picoté."

The expression of the boy's wedding with an eternal-womanly nature is put in immediate, familiar, personal terms—as in "Aube" he will "embrass[er] l'aube d'été." He is "heureux comme avec une femme." Nature responds: like a woman, she hits back, penetrates physically into his intimacy: he is "picoté par les blés" (these drypoint touches dialectically raise the Romantic emotion to something finer). The wind is like a caress, a generous maternal attention he lacked: "Je laisserai le vent baigner ma tête nue." And altogether he *bathes*—as in the mother-sea of the "Bateau

---

[4] A parallel to this naive final fantasy is found in *Lancelot del lac*: Queen Evaine awakens from a dream of children to find the names "Bohort" and "Lionel" inscribed in her hand.

---

[1] This theme of roundness as expressed in characteristic words like "bon" is discussed under "Les Reparties de Nina."

ivre"[2]—in the surpassing calm and splendor of a summer evening, "blue" as the waters of the later poem which cradle and hold him up in life and through their transparency offer communion with the allsoul. But, too, he has his moments of male initiative: the wandering along paths far, far away—"loin, bien loin"—in the wake of his errant and ecstatically free father. At first, Rimbaud as a young schoolboy lacked the courage to break with the stifling home; here his escape is as wildly imaginary as his physical life was restricted. The dream of a bohemian freedom was later fulfilled and then described in passages of "Ma Bohème," in certain *Illuminations* and in the *Saison en Enfer*.

The underlying tone is a Romantic *legato*, almost Lamartinian. In "l'amour infini me montera dans l'âme" the a's do much to sustain the broad, calm, sweepingly melodious effects. "Loin, bien loin," by its neutral sound and repetition, prolongs this mood.

Soleil et chair
(Credo in unam)

Romanticism, in France as in Germany, was accompanied by a wave of neo-classicism in the specific sense of a utopian or Arcadian cult of the ancient Greeks. The Germans, with Herder, Schiller, Hölderlin, and Novalis, spoke of a "third realm" of history which, after a prolonged, dark *second* era—the Western tradition between the Greeks and the modern age—would rejoin the *first* original ("naive" in Schiller's term) and "Golden" Age. Hegel's dialectic easily fit here, and indeed the idea is a natural one for all men of late (or "sentimental"—Schiller) culture and applies to all spiral returns to the source, all moods of neo-primitive sophistication, the artistic moods which Empson identifies as "pastoral." Lamartine, Hugo, Musset (in "Novissima verba," "Le Satyre," and "Rolla," respectively) and the Parnassians: Banville, Leconte de Lisle, Heredia, Louis Ménard—even Baudelaire ("J'aime le souvenir de ces époques nues") and actually the whole era—carried the cult well into the second half of the century where the neophyte Rimbaud imitatively yet gracefully picked it up, beginning with this long Lucretian poem.

It is interesting to us largely because, along with the automatic neo-classical emulation, the glibly melodious and somewhat rhetorical and precious tone, there is much that is sincerely felt and, more important, there are scattered examples of the personal symbols that will evolve into the fully original work, miraculously soon.[1]

---

[2] The theme of the maternal sea was discussed in our Introduction and will be further treated in our remarks on the "Bateau ivre."

---

[1] Rhetoric, schematically speaking, occurs along a horizontal axis of expression

The first of these is the pairing of sun-father and earth-mother which in increasingly complex form will remain constant through Rimbaud's work. "The prototype of all such [sacred] unions of male and female is the *hieros gamos* of Earth and Sky inducing the fertilization of the ground . . . Sky God marrying . . . Earth Goddess" (John W. Perry, *Lord of the Four Quarters*).

> Le Soleil, le foyer de tendresse et de vie,
> Verse l'amour brûlant à la terre ravie,
> Et, quand on est couché sur la vallée, on sent
> Que la terre est nubile et déborde de sang;
> Que son immense sein, soulevé par une âme,
> Est d'amour comme Dieu, de chair comme la femme,

From the last two lines cited, it is clear that the pair is already complex: the earth is a fleshly woman but has a soul of its own, and the soul, or its "love," is paradoxically a God-principle within the flesh. Likewise, the Sun is a male being, aggressively "pouring" its love into the earth in a clearly sexual act which fecundates it; but this being is, passively, a "foyer de tendresse et de vie."

After Freud and Jung, we now tend to think of each of the two sexes as containing its opposite (Freud's famous "when I think of a couple, I imagine four people"; Jung's *animus* and *anima* personae in each individual). Rimbaud spontaneously felt the same way, and recognition of this conception will help to explain some difficult passages in the later poems.

> 14. Je regrette les temps où la sève du monde,
> L'eau du fleuve, le sang rose des arbres verts
> Dans les veines de Pan mettaient un univers!

This rising "sap of the world," welling up and at times spinning like *tourbillons*,[2] is the stuff of joy, recalling a lost paradise which can come back in privileged moments, such as the evolved paean of "Génie" or of "Being beauteous" or the "delirium" of "Alchimie du verbe."

> 23. La terre berçant l'homme, et tout l'Océan bleu

---

as opposed to the vertical axis of the plunge into one's own depths (and return to the surface of life) which is "originality." If the original expression is *added* to rhetorical expression (i.e., not organically evolved from it but superimposed, so that a feeling of gap remains between the two forms of expression), the result is preciosity, or mere pretty *décor*, *plaqué*.

[2] God's voice came at times from a whirlwind (for example to Abraham).

In the "Dormeur du Val" Rimbaud will ask mother-Nature to cradle the dead soldier: "berce-le chaudement."

> 28. Son double sein versait dans les immensités
> Le pur ruissellement de la vie infinie.
> L'Homme suçait, heureux, sa mamelle bénie,
> Comme un petit enfant, jouant sur ses genoux.

As in Baudelaire's "La Géante" (or Shakespeare's *Venus and Adonis*) the awesome mother-spirit is seen as gigantic. The pure milk—akin to the "sève" above—will return in fantasies of communion with the long-lost source, for example, in "Après le déluge": "Le sang et le lait coulèrent."

> 39.   . . . l'immortelle Astarté
> Qui jadis, émergeant dans l'immense clarté
> Des flots bleus, fleur de chair que la vague parfume,
> Montra son nombril rose où vint neiger l'écume,

Here Rimbaud begins, in the spirit of the medieval *blason*, the detailed homage to the female body which we will find scattered throughout the work; see, for example, in "L'Étoile a pleuré rose. . . . "

> 43. "Déesse aux grands yeux noirs."

His, probably feminine, idol in "Enfance" will have black eyes too; the generic woman of "Les Sœurs de charité" has a "regard noir."

II

> 46. . . . —Oh! la route est amère
> Depuis que l'autre Dieu nous attelle à sa croix;

The myth of the return of the Golden Age naturally implies that Christianity was a sad error. With its advent, whole men then turned one part of themselves (puritanical conscience) against the rest. Christ is thus a "voleur d'énergie" ("Les Premières Communions") in the sense that energy is wasted in this struggle with self instead of flowing wholeheartedly outward. This is, of course, a naive view of reality: the kind of spontaneous energy that flows on and out is like an undammed river: it never "gets off the ground," as we say.

But, as usual, there is a germ of truth in this nineteenth-century idea. The trick is to rediscover wholeheartedness, or authenticity, despite, or through, the sophistications which we cannot shuck—"After such knowledge what forgiveness?" (T. S. Eliot). Or to create higher syntheses of civilized-yet-authentic art, as Rimbaud will eventually do.[3] But because the cost of this feat runs so high, poets will frequently sigh to be simpler, and they then are apt to fantasy an easier, child-like or Arcadian mood of running naked and gleefully in nature: "Il a des vêtements, parce qu'il n'est plus chaste" (l. 50).

At times there is a more reflective attitude which turns back not to Arcadia but to the tragic (or "existential") mood of the Greeks who accepted life whole or compacted in the sense that they accepted no false solace (no "leap," as Camus would say), no belief in an afterlife. Mallarmé's "Toast funèbre" is a hymn to this rediscovered pagan, stoic, and lucid spirit in Gautier.[4] Here is Rimbaud's equivalent expression:

> 54. Oui, même après la mort, dans les squelettes pâles
> Il veut vivre, insultant la première beauté!

This same modern corruption, Rimbaud will exclaim after Michelet, has contaminated woman:

> 60. La Femme ne sait plus même être courtisane!

This was a handy alibi for a basic maladjustment which owed much to his mother's insufficiencies: it is all woman's (or society's) fault if I can't love; she stinks. Thus all the notes of disgust ("monceau d'entrailles," "Les Sœurs de charité," "Vénus Anadyomène") along with fellow-pity for her fallen state. The second "Lettre du voyant" calls for her renaissance to equality in the revolutionary spirit of Michelet. He can only accept woman in the awe-inspiring guise of Venus (Cybèle-Astarté-Aphrodité), to whom this whole section is addressed: far above him or, conversely, far below him (or, as a putative equal, only in the remote ideal future). Never head on. This is the typical stance of the artist vis-à-vis woman; but all this is characteristically aggravated.

III

> 65. —Car l'Homme a fini! l'Homme a joué tous les rôles!

Rimbaud will remain true to this disabused view of Western striving in the *Saison en enfer*: "Prêtres, professeurs, maîtres . . . Les saints! des forts!

---

[3] This cake-and-eat-it is bought at frightful cost, as Camus suggested in *La Chute*: the route to innocence by way of true baptism (rebirth; Mallarmé's *renaître*; Gide's *palingenesis*; Malraux's metamorphosis) is very painful (that water is cold: "brrr").

[4] Compare Valéry's epigraph to the "Cimetière Marin" taken from Pindar.

les anachorètes, des artistes . . . Farce continuelle!" ("Mauvais Sang"). But when the Western idols—religious and other false values ("fatigué de briser des idoles / Il [l'Homme] ressuscitera, libre de tous ses Dieux," l. 66)—are broken in a Nietzschean pattern of "breaking the tables" and "transvaluation," there will be a new, free, lucid, male Ideal: "l'Idéal, la pensée invincible, éternelle" (l. 67), along with the feminine force of love symbolized—not by the Christian Virgin—by the ancient Venus who will, in a sense, return: "Tu [Vénus] viendras lui donner la Rédemption sainte!" (l. 72). These are obvious extensions of the ideal male and female pair of the title, "Soleil" and "Chair," and they will continue to function throughout Rimbaud's work.[5] The male (*animus*) "Idéal, pensée" will become, for example the *raison* of "À une raison" and the *Génie*. The female (*anima*) force of love will become the *nouvel amour* which accompanies the changes of the *raison* in "À une raison" and is particularly evident in expressions such as "nos os sont revêtus d'un nouveau corps amoureux" ("Being beauteous") which clearly prolongs the feminine "Chair": love as the force of embodiment, female equivalent of the male *pensée* (cf. light versus heat; Mallarmé's St. Jean versus Hérodiade; Apollo or Hephaestus versus Venus).

The total female figure satisfies an immense thirst for love in the deprived boy; she is everything his mother was not:

> 76. Tu surgiras, jetant sur le vaste Univers
> L'Amour infini dans un infini sourire!
> Le Monde vibrera comme une immense lyre
> Dans le frémissement d'un immense baiser!
>
> —Le Monde a soif d'amour: tu viendras l'apaiser.

The total male figure slakes an equally immense thirst to emulate an ideal father (or Father) in creativity and omniscient thought; to be a demigod. The stirring of beauty, impelled by the female force of love, arouses the young divinity in his body, which is like a setting, an altar, for the new light.

> 82. O! L'Homme a relevé sa tête libre et fière!
> Et le rayon soudain de la beauté première
> Fait palpiter le dieu dans l'autel de la chair!
> Heureux du bien présent, pâle du mal souffert,

[5] One parent is too monolithic; this situation forces the child to put all his emotional eggs in one basket, so to speak. Two parents help him to learn emotional balancing, to play off one against the other; he begins to learn thus a very human trick of duplicity, mobility, healthy "bad faith" which helps him to forget and survive.

This was literally true. The poor schoolboy had swotted too much, crushed and stifled by maternal and societal constraints. So the inner source of freedom rising in adolescence exasperated beyond bearing sprang one April day into this quelling self-assertion.

> 86. L'Homme veut tout sonder,—et savoir! La Pensée,
>   La cavale longtemps, si longtemps oppressée
>   S'élance de son front!

The image of the mare is the spontaneous opposite of the image of restraint. The fiery power of the horse—as in Plato's myth of the aspiring soul (*Phaedrus*)—is expressed in headlong flight as opposed to stagnant arrest. In "Le Forgeron" horseback will express the *elevation* of the human male, dominating the world of natural animal forces, and retains echoes of virile equestrian powers, accompanying traditional themes of the hunt, the quest, the conquest.

Then follows the eternal questions about our origins, the stars in space, in the Baroque-Romantic-Modern vein of Montaigne, Pascal, Hugo. Is there a Godhead, after all? ("Un Pasteur mène-t-il cet immense troupeau?" l. 98); is there "une éternelle voix," a *logos*? (l. 101). Is there any meaning or, as Shakespeare queried and the Baroque era worried, is thought just a dream: "La voix de la pensée est-elle plus qu'un rêve?" (l. 103). As do his contemporaries, Leconte de Lisle, Nietzsche, and Mallarmé, Rimbaud raises the question of eternal return: ". . . Sombre-t-il dans l'Océan profond / Des Germes, des Fœtus, des Embryons, au fond / De l'immense Creuset d'où la Mère-Nature / Le ressuscitera . . . ?" (l. 105). But the questions are not answered, and like Socrates or Montaigne and our modern absurdists, he confesses his ultimate and fatal limitation: "Nous ne pouvons savoir! . . . Notre pâle raison nous cache l'infini!" (l. 107). Mallarmé will speak similarly of our "petite raison virile [en opposition au ciel]"; Montaigne, after Plutarch, ended his "Apologie de Raymond Sebond" with a similar sigh.

There is, alas, a negative force which prevents us from rising, a sort of spiritual gravity incarnated and represented by the old serpent; the insinuating Doubt stimulates thought but also infects the apple of knowledge: "le Doute nous punit!" (l. 108). Birds are evolved from snakes; doubt becomes a black bird (shades of Poe's raven or Nerval's) which swoops down from above like a lightning-stroke revenge for our hubris, the obverse of the angelic dove of belief: "Le doute, morne oiseau, nous frappe de son aile" (l. 109). The spirit falls after a sustained soaring of aspiration, as at the close of the "Bateau ivre." But here the mood lifts again, and the paean persists, neatly lined up in pairs in the following two lines:

I V

117. O splendeur de la chair! ô splendeur idéale!
     O renouveau d'amour, aurore triomphale

Two lines containing:

129. . . . les tigres lascifs et les panthères rousses,
             . . . les sombres mousses

indicate a possible reason (the rime of "rousse/mousse") for the association of russet with love in the "Bateau ivre" and the quatrain "L'Étoile a pleuré rose." Compare the later lines referring to Venus (l. 145): "Et son ventre neigeux brodé de mousse noire."

160.   —Une brise d'amour dans la nuit a passé

This is pure Musset. But Suzanne Bernard and others have found here numerous echoes of Musset (especially "Rolla")—Rimbaud later will detest him—as well as Chénier, Banville, Hugo.[6]

Ophélie

Despite its echoes of Banville and the clumsy collage of two radically different tones—the lyrically personal in part I and the rhetorically ideological in part II—this is a poem which can proudly represent its sixteen-year-old maker in anthologies.

Shakespeare's wistful heroine was a natural magnet for Rimbaud's sympathy: she too was a waif left behind by the male. Rimbaud, like many children of abandoned mothers,[1] partially identifies with the woman's sorrow in a sort of Madame Butterfly complex,[2] of which we

[6] In lines 119-20 the rime "Héros/Eros" followed by the rime in "roses/écloses" reminds us of one of Mallarmé's favorite image-clusters (see "Hérodiade" in *Toward the Poems of Mallarmé*) with a similar white and red coloring ("la neige des roses").
"La Source pleure" (l. 157) is a fine liquid (and spilling-over) effect. The trill of "sombres Marbres" (l. 162) is one of Verlaine's and Valéry's favorite vibrant effects. Compare "l'ombre des arbres dans la rivière embrumée" of Verlaine, and Valéry's "tant de marbre tremblant sur tant d'ombre."

[1] Sartre, in *Les Mots*, describes such a moment of identification with his widowed mother when a strange man accosts her on the *quais* of Paris.
[2] The identification is mainly between his own *anima* and the woman, in a complex superimposition of the one upon the other.

44

have particular echoes in "Mémoire" and "Enfance." The name Ophélie[3] bears a probable echo of *orphelin*, one of Rimbaud's key words. Her pale visage cast against the black waters ("fleuve noir") is an ideal image of narcissistic love, self-pity, as in the classic fantasy of the neglected child running away from home and dreaming of his death: "They'll be sorry then." She, the too-sensitive-to-live darling ("ton sein d'enfant, trop humain et trop doux"), is at romantic peace now, in a familiar, pathetically fallacious, communion with Nature, the immemorial consoler of the deprived: "Le vent baise ses seins."

I

    4. —On entend dans les bois lointains des hallalis.

The distant sound of the hunt no doubt evokes an ancient sacrificial theme as in "Bannières de mai." There Rimbaud dreams of being martyred into something like godhead amidst nature by hunter-Apollo's arrows:

> Aux branches claires des tilleuls
> Meurt un maladif hallali
>   .   .   .
> Je sors. Si un rayon me blesse
> Je succomberai sur la mousse.

The distance is a reflection of the spirituality of the theme, like a far-off voice calling to sainthood the similarly wounded St. Sebastian in Debussy's score. One also senses a reminiscence of "La Belle au bois dormant," the creature born of adolescent yearning who is distilled from the woods themselves, sums them up, and makes them available for human caress, like the "Baiser d'or du Bois" of "Tête de faune." Such was the origin of Greek nymphs as it will be of those peasant-girls conjured up by little Marcel's need from the trees of Roussainville in *Du Côté de chez Swann*; thus the "hallali" distantly echoes the huntsman prince who came to awaken her. Rimbaud's identification here—like Valéry's with the Young Fate awaiting her swan-god—is partly (through his *anima*) with the passive beauty waiting to be released by the divinely virile intervention of a male spirit, as in "Les Sœurs de charité" or "Génie"; partly (through his *animus*) he aspires to fulfill that role of Awakener.

    5. Voici plus de mille ans que la triste Ophélie
        Passe, fantôme blanc, sur le long fleuve noir.

---

[3] See also the waifs in the snow of "Les Effarés" (she [Ophélie] too is *effarée*), confronted by the male figure. Also "Les Étrennes des orphelins."

Why this length of time? A mythic depth is achieved, as in temporal dream-distortions similar to "l'autre hiver" of "Le Bateau ivre," or the "nuits d'hiver" of "Les Déserts de l'amour." Ophélie becomes, like the Wandering Jew of the "Comédie de la soif," an eternal type: a victimized *anima* vaguely recalling Eurydice or Syrinx, transfigured into music.

The tone is softly melodious in the Romantic and Parnassian manner (e.g., "Phydilé," "La Vérandah" of Leconte de Lisle) with hints of delicate impressionism in the Baudelairian ("Harmonie du soir") or Verlainian vein: the "saules frissonants," the "nénuphars froissés," the "frisson d'aile."

> 14. Elle éveille parfois, dans un aune qui dort,
>   Quelque nid, d'où s'échappe un petit frisson d'aile

Rimbaud identified very readily with birds, as we saw (above, p. 32) in "Les Étrennes des orphelins." For complex reasons: one is the common fantasy of lost womb-snugness, the baby bird in his nest. The sympathy Rimbaud felt with nature is furthered by this image and in a related way by the feeling of a responsive shivering in the trees as she passes: "Les saules frissonnants pleurent sur son épaule." Thus, in "Mémoire," "Ah! la poudre des saules qu'une aile sécoue!" is like a personal sigh.

> 16. —Un chant mystérieux tombe des astres d'or.

This recalls Verlaine's "Un vaste et tendre / Apaisement / Semble descendre / du firmament" ("La lune blanche" from the collection *La Bonne chanson*, 1870). The Pythagorean idea of star-music is found again in "Ma Bohème." Suzanne Bernard finds a possible immediate source for this in Victor Hugo.

II

> 19. Norwège

Although the setting of Hamlet, as Rimbaud undoubtedly knew, is Denmark, the idea of a wind from the neighboring Scandinavian country of Norway was probably influenced by the appropriate sound of "Nord/ Norwège." He uses it again in "Comédie de la soif" and "Villes, II" for similar reasons of resonance, I suspect.

> 20. Liberté

This is somewhat abstract and contrasts jarringly with the preceding lyricism. It may have some overtones of political liberty, but mainly it refers to the individual surge of adolescent revolt welling in Rimbaud's breast. The urge which sent this dreaming girl-child down a dark river was the same one which released the drunken boat down a nocturnal river to the open sea in "Le Bateau ivre." Compare: "[hommes] pâles du baiser fort de la liberté" ("Morts de Quatre-vingt-douze").

The voices in the wind speak of "âpre liberté." This modulates to "le chant de la Nature / Dans les plaintes de l'arbre et les soupirs des nuits." Fundamentally, it is the siren call that Nature, the world, addresses to the poet, saying: "give yourself to me, even at the cost of your life." We hear it again in "Age d'or."

> 27. C'est qu'un matin d'avril, un beau cavalier pâle,
>   Un pauvre fou, s'assit muet à tes genoux!

The mad young girl ("ô pauvre Folle!") became, as it were, contaminated by the madness of Hamlet, sitting at her feet. This drama of *animus/ anima* is made explicit in the lines below:

> 29. Ciel! Amour! Liberté! Quel rêve, ô pauvre Folle!
>   Tu te fondais à lui comme une neige au feu;
>   Tes grandes visions étranglaient ta parole
>   —Et l'Infini terrible effara ton œil bleu!

There is a male, godlike principle, here in the form of intransigent vision and duty, which intervenes violently in the gentle *anima*, the instinctive life, and upsets it, makes it difficult for the emotions to be controlled for articulation. But the principle is irresistible and brings a grateful flush of the whole passive soul which *believes*, so strongly that it flings itself head-long to possible perdition. Keats heard a similar voice in nature, a similar wild injunction, in "Sleep and Poetry," which likewise drove him to near-madness.

That "blue eye" echoes the color of Rimbaud's eyes. The innocent victim of this descending fateful thrust of spiritual fire (like Leonardo's vulture or St. Paul's rays of light), he is as submissive as his mother will be toward the departing male, in "Mémoire," or as he himself will be toward the "Génie" in the poem of that name. Compare "un rayon me blesse" ("Bannières de mai"), or "je m'offrais au soleil, dieu de feu" ("Alchimie du verbe"). His mother's eyes, too, were blue.

Bal des Pendus

This poem mainly illustrates Rimbaud's virtuosity and his savoring of medieval crispness and frankness and the fat grief of Villon (whom he had already parodied lustily in his juvenile piece "Charles d'Orléans à Louis XI"). Thus, as in Villon's "Ballade des pendus," the joy here is largely necrophilic and adolescent-spooky or Hallowe'eny, in a mode which might be called the "medieval agony." It is akin to the well-known Romantic agony. Both modes embody a jagged union of opposites, as in grotesque face-making which is both funny and pathetic. The gawky sensitive adolescent in France often expresses his strong need for both pleasure and pain in this intensely ambivalent way. Among the better known literary practitioners of this vein are Lautréamont, Corbière, Laforgue, and Jarry. The total effect of the formula is clearly evident in abrupt couplings such as "hideux amour" (l. 12).

Medieval art—particularly Romanesque—was haunted by this effect in façade statuary, gargoyles, and grotesque literary imagery. Rabelais's Panurge is a later verbal version of troubled adolescent *canular*: we think particularly of the sexual prank he plays against some haughty ladies. The underlying emotion is explosive, but tamed—horizontalized—by geometry, tinkering science (including the elaborate techniques of the prank) and humor. The explosions are rhythmically released as in an internal combustion engine. The effects are precisely a series of staccato noises, crisp sounds in c, q, t, d.

Adolescents or children see more spooks than anyone because they need to: horror movies are mostly made for teenagers. So much instinctive life is buried or stifled by the bourgeois regime of a Rimbaud that it pops way up into the air, doing usually-forbidden things. If sex is condemned as horrible, it will spring up mixed with horror ("J'ai horreur de ça!" says the classic modern virgin in France, e.g., Sartre's Ivich). In place of the alternations of exertion and joy in a sex act, one has the intermittances of *disembodied* pleasure and pain, free-floating joy and horror, mingled in the sensational thrill of fascination. This disembodied aspect combined with the simple, childish effects of color and shape (bright reds and oranges versus blacks, neat patterns of this versus that) creates a Hallowe'eny impression. The crisp imagery is like that of a decorative cut-out: starkly contrasted pantomimic or Chinese-shadow effects of geometric gibbet and dangling creatures against the sky: "grimaçant sur le ciel."

Among the characteristic linguistic effects: the hard d's in the first quatrain alone: "dansent . . . dansent . . . paladins . . . diable . . . saladins." Likewise the hard crisp c or q of "squelettes . . . cravate . . . claquant . . . choqués . . . racle . . . macabre . . . crispe . . . craque . . . cris . . . ricanements . . . baraque."

The only image which is germane to Rimbaud's important future development is this:

27. Les loups vont répondant des forêts violettes

The wolves and forests are out of Villon's "Testament": "Et faim [fait] saillir le loup du bois," but the "forêt violette" is an association of vaguer ancestry. Rimbaud favors the pairing: the plunge into the woods is refreshing; moist violets there are like a blue air-and-water bath. Compare Mallarmé's: "abreuve-toi d'azur" (letter to Cazalis). Here the color alone gives merely a hint of that later-developed flavor, which we will discuss in "Comédie de la soif." The lustfully low wolves and the lyrically sublime violets are a startling and artistic union of extreme opposites. The wolves and violets reappear, separated, in "Le Loup criait." There too the wolf is a fleshly, lustful (Villonesque) representative of man's *animal* (and paradoxically sublime: the "violet" aspect) appetites (as in Hesse's *Steppenwolf*). In "Mauvais sang," the wolf is a cowardly rapacious beast associated with Rimbaud's Gallic ancestors.

Le Châtiment de Tartufe

This is a poem of childish revolt against constraint; specifically, religious constraint. Rimbaud debunks the zealot in the wake of Molière, stripping his metaphysicality to reveal the ugly underside: "—Peuh! Tartufe était nu." The same technique is employed in "Les Premières Communions" where the priest's shoes stink of sweat. It is a juvenile device, because it is, characteristically, perfectionistic and puritanical children who regard the revelation of a human underside as a demonstration of defeat. But the revolt in the name of purity is not always meaningless. There can be a lingering "sickness unto death" (Kierkegaard) in hypocrisy, bourgeois or religious, carried beyond a certain point, and the symptoms are appropriately namby-pambiness, sallow sickliness, expressed here by the color yellow, by Tartuffe's mealy-mouthed sweetness, his pallor, the clammy moistness of his skin, the covertness of his gloves, the stirring embers of unavowed love concealed under a black robe.

Le Forgeron

This poem of political (and total) revolt, it has been noted, owes much to the Hugo of "La Légende des Siècles" and *Les Châtiments*. Under the guise of an account of a historical event—when Louis XVI, confronted by a butcher in a revolutionary crowd, donned a *bonnet rouge* (Rimbaud converts the butcher to a blacksmith)—Rimbaud is striking obliquely at Hugo's favorite butt, Napoleon III. The poem suffers from its public nature; it is Rimbaud's most rhetorical and self-indulgently righteous work.

The blacksmith is, however, a compelling personage. Rimbaud's need to worship a father-figure inflates him to gigantic, legendary size—a Paul Bunyan, a Gargantua—and he joins with some other *ouvriers*, as in "Les Poètes de sept ans," in this bath of adoration:

> Il n'aimait pas Dieu; mais les hommes, qu'au soir fauve,
> Noirs, en blouse, il voyait rentrer dans le faubourg

(See also "Bonne pensée du matin.") Blacksmiths, since at least Hephaestus, have always had this power over youthful imagination. They are as strong as bulls, work with awe-inspiring fire, make an impressive clatter; "God is a noise in the street," says Joyce. Longfellow's smith was as solid and "rooted" as the chestnut tree he forged under. Alain-Fournier's village youth stood entranced at the door of the local smithy, gingerly edging up to the powers of virility and adult vocation.

2. . . . riant / Comme un clairon d'airain

The "clair-" of "clairon" is the brightness of male authenticity as in the dazzling blast of a Last Judgment (compare Hugo's "Dieu"), the "suprême Clairon plein des strideurs étranges / Silences traversés des mondes et des Anges" of "Voyelles," or "le chant clair" of "Génie"; "trompettes … irradiant un sacre" (Mallarmé's "Hommage à Wagner"). Compare the later "Écoutant le devoir comme un clairon qui sonne" of line 151.

25. On nous faisait flamber nos taudis dans la nuit;
    Nos petits y faisaient un gâteau fort bien cuit.

The vehement Protestant revolt of d'Aubigné's "Tragiques" led to comparably extreme or baroque imagery; fire in night, stinging accusations of child-murder couched in rhymed verse.

29. Or, n'est-ce pas joyeux de voir, au mois de juin,
    Dans les granges entrer des voitures de foin
    Énormes? . . .

Siding with spontaneous nature, as against stale forms of Church and bourgeois society, the peasant that was in Rimbaud's immediate ancestry here revels in the simple, healthy, Keatsean sensuality of consumption of scene by ogling eyes, hay by barn. More, there is a "happy family" joint joy of consuming and being consumed, male and female as in "L'Eternité."

It goes on in this vein:

> 31. ... De sentir l'odeur de ce qui pousse,
>   Des vergers quand il pleut un peu, de l'herbe rousse?
>   De voir des blés, des blés, des épis pleins de grain,
>   De penser que cela prépare bien du pain? ...

This welling sap of healthy, fertile nature rises in the boy at rare moments. The wheat is like palpable stored sunshine (compare the sun trapped in the straw of "Les Assis"), the amassed force of which, like "gold"-charged blood in the body, will plump up the blond loaf even more palpably, so that, like a bodily host, it can be consumed. The participation is, in fact, double: identification with the consumed bread, and consumption of it. Thus the "lourd pain blond" goes into the oven, in "Les Effarés," like a male and/or, as Hackett suggests, a child's body back into a life-giving womb. Not that all of this is explicit in the lines quoted. But it usefully illustrates some of the valences of these images which will be exploited later.

> 51. Ils ont rempli ton nid de l'odeur de nos filles

The extremely low and natural animal realism here is spontaneously sought in a downward movement that digs beneath the stale bourgeois social forms to undermine them. This is "grassroots" radicalism (*radix*: root), in the pattern of humanistic naturalism. Perhaps we ought not to emphasize the peasant in Rimbaud. His home atmosphere was petit-bourgeois, and he had deliberately to rediscover the rustic in him, as Rousseau, Tolstoy, and most of us do.

> 72. Enfin! Nous nous sentions Hommes!

The fatherless boy has difficulty in making it to male maturity (whence the bitter irony, "Quels hommes mûrs!" in "Parade"). When belatedly or in flashes he *does* make it, the triumph is quelling. Thus he sides with the long-downtrodden, in class terms, and revels in their moment of domination. Similarly, in the *Saison en Enfer*, he will side with the "enfants de Cham."

The mature *Homme* is an amalgam of *animus* and *anima*; both kinds of forces rise together in his celibate striving:

> 77. Nous nous sentions si forts, nous voulions être doux!

This was true as well of the lonely "androgynous angel" that was the adolescent Rimbaud.

108. Tas sombre de haillons saignant de bonnets rouges

This is the black-red pairing we first witnessed in "Les Étrennes des orphelins."

135.   . . . Oh! ceux-là, sont les Hommes!
Nous sommes Ouvriers, Sire! Ouvriers! Nous sommes
Pour les grands temps nouveaux où l'on voudra savoir,
Où l'Homme forgera du matin jusqu'au soir,
Chasseur des grands effets, chasseur des grandes causes,
Où, lentement vainqueur, il domptera les choses
Et montera sur Tout, comme sur un cheval!
Oh! splendides lueurs des forges! Plus de mal . . .

Here the theme of the quasi-deified, Promethean, fire-stealing workman (as in "Les Poètes de sept ans" or "Bonne pensée du matin") joins with the hunt-theme, equally associated with mature virility.[1] The sound of the horn is a key part of the powerful male-sacrificial theme, for example in *La Chanson de Roland* and Vigny's "Le Cor." Thus, a few lines below, we find:

Écoutant le devoir comme un clairon qui sonne (l. 151)

and:

On aurait un fusil au-dessus du foyer (l. 154)

and:

—Oh! quand nous serons morts, nous les [les pavés avec notre sang] aurons lavés (l. 166)

In "Génie," the powerful spiritual figure will likewise effect "l'abolition de toutes souffrances" in a mood approaching the miraculous, the mood of "Plus de mal" here. Thus, in spite of the modernity and socialistic secularism of Rimbaud's political program, a magic note is introduced, as in the *Saison en Enfer* ("Je ferai de l'or, des remèdes") as the troubled boy's emotional life wells up too overwhelmingly—for a moment—for ordinary reason to control. But this easily happened to other Utopians,

[1] In *Le Grand Meaulnes*, the worshiped older boy—Meaulnes—is a hunter; the men in the blacksmith shop are another expression of this prestigious male quality. Faulkner's "The Bear" is a well-known comparable case: the boy, Ike MacCaslin, finds a legendary father-figure in the Indian guide Sam Fathers as he is initiated into manhood through the hunt.

most notably Fourier (even Marx had his wildly messianic moments, as Camus noted in *L'Homme révolté*). Nietzsche convincingly proclaimed in the *Genealogy of Morals* that the socialist tradition concealed a religious zeal, was the Hebrew-Christian transcendental tradition in new guise. And his own stubborn, rational lucidity ended in fiery gushes of poetry and madness. Jung is right: the fountain of life at our core is religious and we cannot quell it for long.

Morts de Quatre-vingt-douze

An unimportant poem, it heavily satirizes a journalist who had the gall to evoke the memory of the revolutionary soldiers of 1792 and 1793 (Valmy, etc.) to propagandize the nationalistic cause of Napoleon III's war against Prussia.

There is only one memorable image:

> O Soldats que la Mort a semés, noble Amante,
> Pour les régénérer, dans tous les vieux sillons;

The conception of death or war as a whore is ancient: she takes you back into her sterile womb. But here she has the fertile, regenerating qualities of a Lover. Baudelaire occasionally thought of Death that way, most notably in "Les Deux Bonnes Sœurs." Rimbaud will likewise turn to her in utter distress as an ultimate "Sœur de charité."

The image also takes up the old Deucalion myth: its hero sowed dragon's bones that became men. Also remembered are the *sillons* of "La Marseillaise."

The "million de Christs" (l. 16) is in the sacrificial lineage of the deprived soldier-workers in "Le Forgeron," of which the starving children of "Les Effarés" ("les pauvres Jésus") are embryonic versions.

À la musique

Verlaine's *Poèmes saturniens* had aroused Rimbaud's enthusiasm, according to Izambard.[1] Certainly there is an echo here of the "Nuit du Walpurgis classique" from that collection. For Verlaine the French neo-classic garden à la Watteau was "correct, ridicule et charmant"; here is a "Square où tout est correct, les arbres et les fleurs." That crisp c and ct of "correct" are just right for this effect of geometric neo-classic order, whether monarchic or bourgeois. The humor of both poets adds to the

---

[1] "M. Prudhomme" is another satiric poem in that collection; Rimbaud alludes to him in "L'Impossible."

flattening (or "deadening," as Spitzer would say) effect; the dry anti-romantic tone which ironically defeats the announced ardor of the title: "À la musique" (to paraphrase Nabokov, the poem is about ardor or order). The initial discouragement caused by the provincial setting—the oompahs of the military band, the strutting of the petty local *notables*—only superficially represses the true ardor here, the inner fire of the strolling adolescent Rimbaud. The bitter-sweetness wells up so, it spirals retroactively even to the banal scene which may end by charming some of us, like Vuillard or even Pop Art. The banality is expiated, as in Joyce's Gerty MacDowell episode or Brecht-Weill's *Threepenny Opera*, by the spoof, and the sentimentality thus gets by our defenses. It is like much of Laforgue in this respect, for example the crisply ironic (c-sound) plus sentimental: "Quand l'orchestre attaqua sa dernière polka" or "Bref, j'allais me donner d'un 'Je vous aime'" ("Dimanches"). At least the poem is mostly in this covert vein. In the end there is the pathetically honest:

> Et je sens les baisers qui me viennent aux lèvres

And altogether I find here a sincere though unfulfilled longing.

    11. Des rentiers à lorgnons soulignent tous les couacs

What a wicked eye Rimbaud has, like Proust in a similar scene at the musicale of Madame de Saint-Euverte! The devastating item, that of provincial would-be-snobs showing they are "with" pompously vulgar military music! The "couacs" break "henormously" through this subtlety, like low-down "lazzi"—its sound and mimetic substantial quality are suitably impertinent, refreshing. The parading fat wives, with their flounces as big as ad-posters, as "cornacs" (elephant drivers) is another low blow.

    16. Puis prisent en argent, et prennent: "En somme! . . ."

    20. Déborde—vous savez, c'est de la contrabande;

The pithy quotes "En somme" and "vous savez c'est de la contrebande" are also *substantial*, take us to the naked texture of reality under this art, like a bared canvas amidst paint, with refreshingly real effect.

    22. Le long des gazons verts ricanent les voyous;
        Et, rendus amoureux par le chant des trombones,
        Très naïfs, et fumant des roses, les pioupious
        Caressent les bébés pour enjôler les bonnes . . .

The scene of the soldiers and the "bonnes" will be re-enacted in Verlaine's "Chevaux de bois" (*Romances sans paroles*, 1874).

> 25. —Moi, je suis, débraillé comme un étudiant,
>   Sous les marronniers verts les alertes fillettes:
>   Elles le savent bien; et tournent en riant,
>   Vers moi, leurs yeux tout pleins de choses indiscrètes.

Rimbaud plays with the "suis" (it means "follow" but momentarily looks like its French homonym for "am"):[2] in a sense he *is* the girls, identifies with them, as well as follows them, just as, below, he *is* their divine backs, as well as follows them.

Rimbaud's lucidity is astonishing, as usual. The girls use the same device ("riant") to deal with dangerously deep emotions as Rimbaud does in the poem as a whole. But on this terrain they are far more courageous, as women almost always are, than the young male, and he fearfully glimpses the depth of their intent. They are tough, *alertes*, and mean business or "choses indiscrètes," and he quails. Thus the adolescent band in *Le Grand Meaulnes* trailed Gilberte Poquelin with bravado cock-calls, but they dared not approach too closely, and ended in a strangely embarrassed silence, when they gazed suddenly into the depth of nature's intent in her hip-motion.

Rimbaud's courage will take him only as far as an imagined undressing, an inner possession, of their lissom bodies. With sharp female realism and some cruelty, they are quick to sense their advantage on this terrain (and get even with would-be-domineering males). They are aware of the shyness or cowardice and find him "drôle" and, nudging each other, "se parlent tout bas."

Undoubtedly such girls, if given a chance, would see the unusual depth behind that shyness and meet him halfway—but Rimbaud couldn't go that far, as yet. He had too much to contend with in the bottom of his psyche.

The *belles fièvres* were there and were genuine, I believe. But the in-security was too great to overcome. In the form of his family, people had betrayed him too much for him to have any confidence in this realm. Nature seemed more reliable, it had not dealt him any major blows as yet. . . . And he had not yet seen the cancerous cruelties the narcissistic spirit of art could dish out—not before the *Saison en Enfer* when he discovered the "bitter" qualities of the Muse.

---

[2] Compare Mallarmé's "Va-t-il nous déchirer . . . Le transparent glacier" ("Le Vierge, le vivace et le bel aujourd'hui"): the "nous" momentarily wavers between a direct object and a dative of interest.

Vénus Anadyomène

All sensitive male adolescents, we now know, have difficulty accepting the opposite sex. First, because love (Eros) is dialectically entangled with its opposite, death (Thanatos), or general psychic negation including all the sub-forms: fear, hate, pain, disgust. But, normally, the negation is overcome in a stubbornly persistent commitment to the opposite sex—at least for a while, through an affair and various "acts" of love—either by dialectically turning it into its opposite or by dissociating the positive phase from the dialectic cycle and investing it alone in the relationship (the negative phase going into work, private suffering, or strife with others, etc.).[1]

But in order for the dialectic to run its course, for a young man to win the inner struggle against all the demons of doubt, fear, and inhibitory guilt which a bourgeois puritanical order has used to keep him from sex, he must *believe* in the relationship, have a basic confidence in its purpose and future. In Rimbaud's case he had too much hatred for his mother to allow for this, or at least it made the situation highly problematical. His mother had, he felt, failed as a woman, failed to hold on to the affections of the father, and so the family was ruined and the boy's inner life was unbalanced. Besides, his mother was harshly dutiful and cold, making it difficult to love her. But the boy needed a woman's tender love all the more; under the rough exterior, the *Forgeron* said: "Nous voulions être doux!" In another poem Rimbaud cries out for "une sœur de charité." And so we realize that the poems, like "Vénus Anadyomène" (or "Mes petites amoureuses," or "Adieu"), in which he scorns female beauty, are redolent of sour grapes, or bitter ones. It is all very familiar: the juvenile psyche flinging excrement is trying homeopathically to blot out its own terror of "love's bitter mystery," playing on the fact that "love has pitched its mansion in the place of excrement," in a way that is absolutely unconvincing to it and to us who know that it is precisely because of the dirty dangerous aspect of love that the baptismal plunge into its dark waters leads to a birth of holy joy (in Apuleius' *The Golden Ass*, Eros came to Psyche as a monster; Beauty learned to overcome her disgust, whereupon the Beast became a Prince). But only the initiated know this and learn to have faith in the process, learn to "swim"; Rimbaud—from all we know of him—had yet to plunge in.

1. Comme d'un cercueil vert en fer blanc, . . .

There is an obvious association between the *cercueil* and the idea of

---

[1] These two rhythms of love-hate (pleasure-pain) are usually combined in varying doses.

decay—love as a disgusting pit, like the whore-death who symbolized war in "Morts de Quatre-vingt-douze"—which is borne out in the "vieille baignoire" and the ugly aspects of the female flesh, including the ulcer. The verdigris quality of the tin is associated with this decay, rather than with nature, *pace* Hackett.

12. Les reins portent deux mots gravés: *Clara Venus*

Gengoux has demonstrated that Rimbaud here was probably copying a poem by Glatigny depicting a prostitute with a pair of names tattooed on her arm. But the idea of "Clara Venus" ("bright, or renowned, Venus") inscribed on or above the behind is absurd and pathetically juvenile, like scrawling a moustache on a poster picture of a woman. The Venus Kallipygia seems to be confusedly involved in the image of Venus Anadyomene.

14. Belle hideusement d'un ulcère à l'anus.

A *fleur du mal?* Suzanne Bernard rightly distinguishes between the spirituality of such couplings in Baudelaire versus the snickering realism here. But the bitterness of misogyny is at least sincere in Rimbaud and leads to further developments in the *Saison en Enfer.*

Première Soirée

Inspired by music hall librettists like the eighteenth-century Favart, whom he is known to have admired, Rimbaud wrote here in a light *chanson* vein, with a Boucher prettiness, frivolity, and mild indecency. There are delicate pointillist touches which bring the picture closer to the Impressionists than to Boucher, and some realistic details which add a note of drily mocking modernity.

1. —Elle était fort déshabillée
   Et de grands arbres indiscrets
   Aux vitres jetaient leur feuillée
   Malinement, tout près, tout près.

The girl, despite her half-naked charms, is almost drowned by the surrounding nature, revealing Rimbaud's truer tastes; we think of Proust's preference for Albertine asleep as an objective, "vegetable" part of the world.[1]

[1] Or La Fontaine's preference in "Le Songe de Vaux." Compare also Théophile's ode: "Le Matin."

These trees will poke their heads in again in "Jeune ménage" and "Mémoire" or "Enfance": "Les branches et la pluie se jettent à la croisée de la bibliothèque" (257).

> 7. Sur le plancher frissonnaient d'aise
>   Ses petits pieds si fins, si fins.

They seem to have an independent, impersonal existence. Compare Baudelaire's rhapsody over the self-sufficient parts of Jeanne ("ces grappes de ma vigne," etc.).

> 9. —Je regardai, couleur de cire,
>   Un petit rayon buissonnier
>   Papillonner dans son sourire
>   Et sur son sein,—mouche au rosier.

As much as Vermeer or the Impressionists, Rimbaud was enamored of light, which is the rock-bottom substance to get at for authenticity (akin to Eros itself). A description of its varied tones and nuances in his work would make a little study in itself.

> 13. —Je baisai ses fines chevilles.
>   Elle eut un doux rire brutal
>   Qui s'égrenait en claires trilles,
>   Un joli rire de cristal.

As with the "alertes fillettes" of "À la musique," Rimbaud learned young that women are the true realists, sometimes brutally so. As Camus says in *The Rebel*, the nineteenth-century notion that women are sentimental, idealistic, is mystification. The realism passes into laughter as light crystalline ("clair," "cristal") hardness, a quality Rimbaud obviously appreciates.

> 18. . . . "Veux-tu finir!"

The reality of the directly present woman (speaking) adds a refreshingly modern note. Rimbaud obviously enjoys the irony of this new anti-romanticism, but there is a hint of Laforguian bitterness too that women should be so *plates*. Compare the end of "Les Reparties de Nina," where all the girl is thinking of is getting back to her desk job.

> 19. —La première audace permise,
>   Le rire feignait de punir!

There is more than a hint of Verlaine's *Fêtes galantes* (much admired by Rimbaud) in this entire half-serious sequence.

A complex dialectic is at work here: the girl leads the boy on by coquettish alternation of restraints (the punishing laugh) and permissiveness (the first gesture is allowed, moreover the laugh only feigns to punish). Rimbaud senses she means business. He is no doubt uneasy underneath the pretense of man-of-the-world insouciance and the false implication of an intent to go through with it. Thus upon reflection one is unconvinced by the follow-up, the kiss on the eyes and the kiss on the breast and the satisfaction that her resultant laugh augured well for a consummation: "un bon rire qui voulait bien . . ." (l. 28). One doubts he ever did consummate in this usual way, though it is interesting enough that he dreamed of it, indicating that the heterosexual only needed to be brought out.

Les Reparties de Nina
(*variant title*: Ce qui retient Nina)

This remarkable early poem is in the lineage of poetic realism starting approximately from Sainte-Beuve's *Rayons jaunes* or the *Sylvie* of Nerval, with echoes of French genre painting à la Chardin or Greuze.[1]

It is appropriate to speak here of the "phenomenological" quality of Rimbaud's art, its frequently immediate or transparent nature. That is to say, he seeks the direct substance of life functions by using simple, direct, almost invisible words like *bon* (Hemingway's "good"). Thus "nous irions" (l. 2), "bon matin bleu" (l. 5), "Ton grand œil noir" (l. 16). Or apposite images are evoked to create a general tone of transparency, especially *air*, as in "Ayant de l'air plein la narine" (l. 3). Or qualities which seem to speak directly to our senses are invoked: "vin de jour" (l. 6).

A corollary quality is the wholeness of this art: the phenomenological world is rendered entire, not separated into abstract mind and concrete nature (or fragmented through conventional social formulas of human attitudinizing, oughts instead of is-es). The effect is of Nietzschean or Camusian lucidity, freshness, and very often of *roundedness*. Thus the interpenetration or one-ness of man and nature is rendered when the nostril is full of air, "Ayant de l'air plein la narine," or when the couple are *bathed* in the air, "Du bon matin bleu, qui vous baigne / Du vin de jour." The wood is rendered as a whole, "*tout* le bois," and it is silent, giving forth unbroken the world-love, out of the world's body which *bleeds* it: "tout le bois frissonnant saigne / Muet d'amour" (l. 8).

---

[1] See our article "From Poetic Realism to Pop Art," *MLN*, vol. 84, no. 4 (May, 1969), pp. 668-74.

The roundedness is sometimes rendered by appropriate image-objects (or more subtly by the hieroglyphic effect of o's: as in the "O monde" of "Génie" which has both: the globular real entity and the pair of o's). The "bon matin" has this double roundedness: the vault of the spacious day, the o (and b) in *bon*, as in "Les bons vergers à l'herbe bleue, / Aux pommiers tors" (l. 65-66); "ce bleu qui cerne / ton grand œil noir" (l. 15-16), where three o's are a circular microcosm of the day, or of the world. Heavier examples are "le pot de bière / Cerclé de plomb" (l. 83-84), or "la face ronde / Du cher petit" (l. 99-100) which is a fine illustration of the Flemish quality of accepted wholeness of flesh and spirit together, as in Breughel, Rubens, or Verhaeren's *Flamandes*; and this worldly quality extends somewhat to Chardin and Greuze and Nerval. Various of the poems inspired by the trip to Belgian Flanders bring this happy globularity: the "chope immense" of "Au Cabaret-Vert" and the "tétons énormes" of the hefty girl who serves it.

The letter b offers a similar bubbly or buoyant quality, as Mallarmé had observed in *Les Mots anglais* (compare Keats' "Beaded bubbles winking at the brim" where the b's are singularly graphic). This is evident in "Du bon matin bleu, qui vous baigne" (l. 5) or "Des bourgeons clairs" (l. 10).[2]

Rimbaud uses his "rondeur," in both senses (candor and general roundedness) to cut beneath and rise above the stale, flaccid, median bourgeois setting. A simple example is the scene of the stable (l. 72-80), with its quasi-divine light from above, "Blanchissant sous quelque lumière" but "pleine / De fumiers chauds." A variant for "Alchimie du verbe" reads, "Le soleil souverain [descendait] donnait vers . . . une merde." For the banal realism of the bourgeois, he substitutes a new robust reality on sane middle ground, so to speak, well-centered at human eye-level but vibrant there (*au point*) with the new vital *up-and-down* (or "far-out" all-around) which he has explored. It is as if an optician suddenly put into his refractor a lens so much more encompassing and still so limpid (as well as precisely focussed) it made us gasp.

"Les Reparties de Nina" is initially a poem of simple communion with nature through its representative—its queen—woman; in "Sensation" he had merely dreamed of a possible woman. Thus the first strophe features the contact of the lover with his lass; he drinks in with her presence the morning air in which she bathes, the "vin de jour." It is the same "vin de vigueur" he feels on his body along the roads of "Ma Bohème." And the taste of that wine of life is still present in the reminisced "sobre surnaturellement" of "L'Impossible."

---

[2] A prime example is in the buoyancy of "Aube," especially the last line which overcomes all hints of defeat in the meaning: "L'aube et l'enfant tombèrent au bas du bois."

From all of nature, this female force of universal love rises up like the *sève* of "Soleil et chair":

> 9. De chaque branche, gouttes vertes,
>   Des bourgeons clairs,
>   On sent dans les choses ouvertes
>   Frémir des chairs:

The liquidity of love-communion makes the buds seem fluid, "gouttes vertes," part of the universal flowingness of spring. Later, "nos grands bois sentiraient la sève" (l. 57).

Through universal analogy, the hierarchy of being, the world's body and the human (woman's) body overlap: in the intoxicated eyes of poetry, vegetation and flesh are one. This communion was prominent in "Soleil et chair" ("fleur de chair") and is repeated in "O chair de fleur!" (l. 26); later there will again be "fleurs de chair" ("Les Poètes de sept ans").

> 13. Tu plongerais dans la luzerne
>   Ton blanc peignoir,

The woman is commingled with her sister-nature, the grass, as in "Mémoire." She is "Amoureuse de la campagne" (l. 17) which is ambiguously "in love with the countryside" or "the lover [springing out] of the countryside." Later, the countryside itself easily becomes the mistress, as in "Sensation," or the "pubescences d'or" of wheatfields in "Les Poètes de sept ans": "la prairie amoureuse."

> 18.   Semant partout,
>   Comme une mousse de champagne,
>   Ton rire fou:

Mallarmé also thought of laughter as champagne (Pléiade, p. 181).

> 21. Riant à moi, brutal d'ivresse,
>   Qui te prendrais

This, though probably a fantasy like the other poems about Rimbaud's love-affairs—was he really a "brutal" conqueror of women?—is again indication of at least a desire.

> 27. Riant au vent vif qui te baise
>   Comme un voleur,

In "Jeune ménage," only the wind betrays the young husband. In certain primitive cultures, the wind is believed to fecundate women.[3]

> 39. Lents, nous gagnerions la ravine,
>   Puis les grands bois! . . .

To sink into the ravine, or the deep woods, is to commune intimately with Magna Mater.

> 41. Puis, comme une petite morte,

Echo of "la petite mort," sexual consummation.

> 52.   Ivre du sang
>
>   Qui coule, bleu, sous ta peau blanche

The almost cannibalistic desire to commune with the woman through oral consumption is universal. Babies like to bite their nursing mothers.[4] Milk and blood thus overlap. And they are often associated, as in Chrétien's "Perceval" or Mallarmé's "Hérodiade," with the white and red cheeks of a woman. In the promiscuous infantile urges of "Après le déluge," "Le sang et le lait coulèrent."

> 61. Le soir? . . .

The evening descending adds a graver note, elegiac, to the preceding sweetness, speaks gently of death, *Homecoming* in the total sense which always lies behind the impulse of love. (Robert Frost spoke of the twin motives of his poetry as love-sickness and home-sickness.) The theme of *le sentier* leading to the peaceful village, redolent of Home in everyone's dreams—and the corollary family interior—now dominates the poem. Of course, given Rimbaud's family background, the Home here is a wishful fantasy, like Rousseau's utopian village, which joins, in an ideal union, human organization (houses) and countryside: man and his source.[5] The green inn of "Comédie de la soif" is another such substitute, similarly plunged into the setting-source.

[3] John Steinbeck, in *The Grapes of Wrath*, refers to man as "a seed blowing by."

[4] In the fancied nuptials of St. John and Hérodiade, Mallarmé speaks of "le mets délicieux qu'on goûte l'un à l'autre" and, in a note for *le Livre*: "Mangez la dame."

[5] The city too (more rarely) can join with its natural setting in various ways, either by plunging views to water or sky, or by invading nature (parks); compare the intrusive forest in "Métropolitain."

69. Nous regagnons le village

This section of "Les Reparties de Nina," like Nerval's *Sylvie*, is full of family-warmth, humble, almost popular poetic realism in the Chardin manner. The family, too, is a substitute. Not actual parents, or even middle-aged people who could be, but "grand-parents" who are thus removed from the generation struggle. Similarly in *Le Grand Meaulnes*, at the Strange Festival there were only elderly people (or children) "qui seraient capables de vous pardonner."[6]

71. Et ça sentira le laitage
     Dans l'air du soir;

The liquidity of the milk passes insensibly into the flow of *air* and *soir* (with their liquid r).

73. Ça sentira l'étable, pleine
     De fumiers chauds,
     Pleine d'un lent rhythme d'haleine,
     Et de grands dos

The communion with Home, the union with the cosmos, occurs through all the levels of nature overlapping, as we have seen in our Introduction. It includes not only the air and light and all the other elements, the trees and grasses, but also the sap and the "animate essences" which are the human sap, milk and blood; even excrement can participate in the warmth of communion (as Freud has told us it can for infants) as a humble "animate essence." Then there are the animals at the next level of hierarchy, and finally the people who overlap with all the foregoing in this mobile mood. Thus the baby has a "museau" and is promiscuously caressed by the dog's fraternal "mufle"; the grandfather's "effroyables lippes" are similarly animal in an affectionate sense.

77. Blanchissant sous quelque lumière;
     Et, tout là-bas,
     Une vache fientera, fière,
     A chaque pas . . .

[6] And children (the equivalent here are the orphans of "Les Effarés" or the *peuple* children next door in "Les Poètes de sept ans"). The workman is another such "removed" idealized fantasy, not a typical *bourgeois* adult (removed sideways, so to speak, instead of up like the old people or down like the children).

The "vache fientera" continues the warm excremental communion as in "Oraison du soir":

> Tels que les excréments chauds d'un vieux colombier,
> Mille Rêves en moi font de douces brûlures:

(At other times the scatological expresses a bitter expulsive aggression, like excrement flung at an adversary.) The light from above in "Blanchissant sous quelque lumière," recalling the light that is suspended from the roof in "Les Poètes de sept ans," is like an intervention of the divine amid the everyday.[7] But the other extreme, the humbleness of the "vache fientera" or the "fumiers chauds," rises from the bottom up to the human level. Rimbaud's world vibrates at its core from the tensions set up between these vitally opposed (yet conjoined) reals—like Baudelaire's "ciel ou enfer, qu'importe" ("Hymne à la Beauté").

The following strophes are in fine *genre* style and very visual (particularly the profile of the old lady against the fire). We think naturally of the Flemish and French genre painters. And Rimbaud himself says "Que de choses *verrons*-nous ... !"

> 81. —Les lunettes de la grand'mère
>   Et son nez long
> Dans son missel; le pot de bière
>   Cerclé de plomb,
>
> Moussant entre les larges pipes
>   Qui, crânement,
> Fument: les effroyables lippes
>   Qui, tout fumant,
>
> Happent le jambon aux fourchettes
>   Tant, tant et plus:
> Le feu qui claire les couchettes
>   Et les bahuts.
>
> Les fesses luisantes et grasses
>   D'un gros enfant
> Qui fourre, à genoux, dans les tasses,
>   Son museau blanc
>
> Frôlé par un mufle qui gronde
>   D'un ton gentil,
> Et pourlèche la face ronde
>   Du cher petit ...

---

[7] Jacques Rivière has commented at length on this aspect of Rimbaud's vision in his well-known study.

Noire, rogue au bord de sa chaise,
  Affreux profil,
Une vieille devant la braise
  Qui fait du fil;

Que de choses verrons-nous, chère,
  Dans ces taudis,
Quand la flamme illumine, claire,
  Les carreaux gris! . . .

—Puis, petite et toute nichée
  Dans les lilas
Noirs et frais: la vitre cachée,
  Qui rit là-bas . . .

Tu viendras, tu viendras, je t'aime!
  Ce sera beau.
Tu viendras, n'est-ce pas, et même . . .

ELLE.—*Et mon bureau?*

I think of the Green Inn which symbolizes for Rimbaud (as for Baudelaire) the pathetic longing for the happy home he never had, a resting place, "l'auberge verte" of "Comédie de la soif." The inn, half-glimpsed behind foliage like so many mysterious figures in Rimbaud (and in art generally), beckons as we pass eternally by. I remember particularly Richard Wilbur's:

> I thought if I should begin
>
> To enter entirely that door,
> Saying, "I am a son of this house,
> My birth and my love are here,"
> I might never come forth any more:

112. Qui rit là-bas . . .

The end is tricky, a bitterly wry let-down; it happens often that closes are defeated in Rimbaud (notably in "Le Bateau ivre"); he tried too hard to soar and, Icarus, fell again and again.

Les Effarés

This is one of Rimbaud's finest early efforts,[1] powerfully sincere and pathetic. It barely skirts sentimentality, escaping it through remarkably

---

[1] He himself thought so; he exempted it (along with "Sensation") from a proposed destruction of his first twenty-two poems, the "recueil Demeny."

self-possessed art and whimsical irony. It owes something to Villon (whom Rimbaud pastiched so well in "Charles d'Orléans à Louis XI"):

> Les autres mendient tous nus
> Et pain ne voient qu'aux fenêtres;
>
> ("Le Testament," l. 233)

The "effarés" are no doubt worker-children of the sort that offered Rimbaud's spiritual misery such a natural hold of sympathy in "Les Poètes de sept ans." The word *effarés*, "frightened ones," brings out the pristine quality of children, who are essentially timid, not ready to participate: "effaré comme trente-six millions de caniches nouveau-nés."[2] These children moreover have a *peuple* timidity: power is not theirs.

The deprived child finds delight in a complex fantasy. This is centered around the adult, courageous and powerful, almost godlike, worker, the *Boulanger*, who is in touch—by his earthy laboring role and his graceful skill and spontaneity—with the source of life; he is a creator, not only of bread but the life it nourishes, and of joy. One watches him *make*: "faire / Le lourd pain blond." He is a father-provider of the sort Rimbaud thought would have brought light and strength into his sombre household. As a creator-provider he is gentle as well as strong, a mixture of maternal and paternal qualities which will be most explicitly drawn in the ideal father-figure of "Génie":[3] "la force et l'amour." The bread emerges from the Baker almost like a baby.[4] The capital B[5] underlines this aspect of him. But the capable arms which authoritatively and gently fashion the loaf, rather like a mother swaddling a child, also thrust it into a recipient oven, in a male act, "le fort bras blanc ... Dans un trou clair." Further, through a sort of symbolized sexual union of the male Baker's thrusting gesture, and the recipient womb-like oven, there is a resultant birth from that oven of the "bon pain," like a warmly fulfilled child, made whole, heavy or solid, round (the o of "bon") like a mandala (Jung). The Baker is an ideal comforter, combined with something of a ritualist, an earthy priest, celebrating the fundamental processes of life.

The joy of communion is primarily with the bread, like a host. The child dreams of consubstantiality, an identity which would raise him to an ideal or even divine child-status; this is echoed in the "pauvres Jésus" below. This shadowy and primitively sublime notion is merely sug-

---

[2] In Jean-Marie Carré, *Les deux Rimbaud, l'Ardennais, l'Éthiopien*, p. 23.

[3] Compare Mallarmé's comments on the letter M, "le pouvoir de faire mâle et maternel" ("Les Mots anglais").

[4] Hackett describes the baby fantasy in an acute original analysis, which we have tried to extend somewhat.

[5] James Joyce plays with the buttock shape of the B in *Finnegans Wake*.

gested—it is certainly less explicit than the imagery of physical hunger. And it is only one level (a pure happy Being) of the poem's total Eros. The warmth of the contact occurs not only with the bread but also between the emotionally hungry and cold children and the good man[6] and his generous stove (the maternal "trou clair"; compare "Le Buffet"). Another obvious level of union is of food and physically hungry stomachs, overlapping with the earlier-suggested "sexual" union of bread and oven (we are using "sexual" to stand for the more total psychological phenomenon such as Sartre speaks of in his passage on "the hole" in *L'Être et le Néant*). Then there is the corollary dynamic of their cold bodies outside yearning for contact with the warmth inside—the "trou clair" of the stove is extended to the "trou chaud [qui] souffle la vie" of the room—and so on.

The pathos, or initial alienation, underlying the ideal of union runs fluidly from level to level. Thus the "misère" (l. 4) which is their physical hunger is also clearly related to their spiritual hunger. The physical darkness ("noirs") of the children and the cold of the snow certainly underline their emotional deprivation, like the fireless hearth of "Les Étrennes des orphelins."

1. Noirs dans la neige et dans la brume,

It is midnight according to a variant from line 16: "Et quand pendant que minuit sonne," hence dark. Their ragged garments also probably make a dingy splash against the snow, since, being poor, they and their clothes are no doubt dirty. But the chief effect is the spiritual one: sombre misery, outside in the cold and fog.

2. Au grand soupirail qui s'allume

The air-vent leads to an underground room, all the mysteriously snugger and more womb-like for that, akin to Hobbit-dwellings or similar habitations in animal-stories for children.

3. Leurs culs en rond,

The whimsical cuteness à la Disney helps to offset the pathos, especially when their breeches burst later. Note the pleasant roundness (and the o).

4. A genoux, cinq petits,—misère!—

[6] The desire for contact with the Baker is, of course, complex: to be *with* him, as a child is with his father (and to be handled and *molded* by him like the bread), and eventually to *be* him (as the Logos was *with* God and *was* God).

67

The "five children" were found in Hugo's "Pauvres Gens" according to Emilie Noulet. The "misère!" is a general cry of spiritual distress, as well as a description of their condition of poverty. Compare the repeated "pitié!" of "Les Poètes de sept ans."

> 5. Regardent le Boulanger faire
>   Le lourd pain blond.

There is a resonance between the overtone of *boule* and the heavy (*lourd*), round solidity of the bread. The round o's and the pendulous u's of "Boulanger" and "lourd" are instrumental in this effect, to which the b's and p also contribute; compare Keats' "swell the gourd, and plump the hazel shells" ("To Autumn").

> 9. Dans un trou clair.

We recall the *armoire* of "Les Étrennes des orphelins"; here is a similar womb-like or cornucopia source of nourishment and spiritual strength which we will find again in the later poem, "Le Buffet." (Also in Baudelaire's "Le Beau Navire" and "Le Flacon.")

> 14. Au souffle du soupirail rouge
>   Chaud comme un sein.

The whole warm room ("ce trou chaud," l. 22)—extension of the stove ("trou clair")—is here explicitly maternal. Suzanne Bernard is, we think, wrong to slight Hackett's penetrating and thoroughly convincing analysis.

> 16. Quand pour quelque médianoche,

Since Rimbaud conceived the scene as occurring at midnight, he thinks of the bread as being prepared for a "midnight snack" of the privileged, nocturnal cousins to the decadent rich who are contrasted with the idealized morning workers of "Bonne pensée du matin."

> 17. Façonné comme une brioche

The variant "Faconné, pétillant et jaune" indicates how much Rimbaud enjoyed the idea of this wholesome loaf, healthy and solid as he would be by consuming it: well-*molded* by its maker.

22. Que ce trou chaud souffle la vie,
    Ils ont leur âme si ravie
        Sous leurs haillons,

    Ils se ressentent si bien vivre,
    Les pauvres Jésus pleins de givre,

The warm air enters them like the breath of life from the parents (*âme* <
anima, breath). "Jésus" is a conventional term for "babies," but it may
refer here also to their misery—the martyred soldiers were called "Christs"
in "Morts de Quatre-vingt-douze"—so deep that they are as if sacrificed
for a spiritual rebirth. We think of Andersen's "Little Matchgirl" and
other such tragic children in Shakespeare, Pushkin, Dickens.

28. Collant leurs petits museaux roses
    Au treillage, grognant des choses
        Entre les trous,

    Tout bêtes, . . .

The "museaux," "grognant," "bêtes" all exhale an animal tone: Rimbaud
looks upon the worker-children in the somewhat condescending, pitying
way one looks upon humble and victimized animals. The tone is also
affectionately whimsical. The animal-worker (or peasant) sympathy is
part of a Romantic—Rousseau, Barbizon school, Hugo, Sand, Pissarro—
heritage.

31. . . . faisant leurs prières
    Et repliés vers ces lumières
        Du ciel rouvert,

The religious note of "Jésus" leads to this image of a heaven opened to
them: "Blessed are the meek." Or the deprived, Rimbaud himself. This is
one of many steeply vertical moments in Rimbaud, like the light of the
stable of "Les Reparties de Nina." The light from the cellar room—below
human level—is felt to be descended from the heavenly source, above. So
that a new and fuller reality all *around* the observer has been opened up
in the poem as a whole.

34. Si fort, qu'ils crèvent leur culotte

They are bent so eagerly they burst their breeches. A whimsical, cute
close, not quite worthy of the poem. Rimbaud had difficulty ending his
poems generally, and occasionally relied on gimmicks like this.

Roman

Close in mood to "À la musique," this poem is somewhat less ironic and more romantically sincere, with some particularly promising touches.

> 1. On n'est pas sérieux, quand on a dix-sept ans.

Rimbaud means that in the eyes of his mother, or society, he is part of the *jeunesse étourdie*; in a sense, he accepts this judgment, as a defense against his tumultuous emotions which lead him out in quest of girls—or at least he ironizes about himself, for the same timid reason.

The delightful rhyme "limonade / promenade" probably engendered this first strophe and the echoing last one.

If Rimbaud foregoes *bocks* and *limonade*, that is a real sacrifice since thirst is so important to him and his poetry.[1] (Another illustration of the point is Proust's Marcel who admitted preferring, on occasion, orangeade to Albertine's kisses.)

> 5. Les tilleuls sentent bon dans les bons soirs de juin!

Transparency and roundness, again, are in these two "bons" (see our earlier remarks on this effect in "Les Reparties de Nina").

> 7. Le vent chargé de bruits,—la ville n'est pas loin,—
>   A des parfums de vigne et des parfums de bière . . .

This exquisitely delicate, vibrant presence-absence of "bruits" is the most promising note so far in Rimbaud. Similarly, in "Départ," the trembling between staying and departure, the tension between distance from and nearness to the city (cf. Verlaine's "Le ciel est, par-dessus le toit") engenders the vibrancy of "rumeurs." Here he dares, in almost Zen spirit, to include in this all-encompassing beauty the vulgar "bière."

II

> 9. —Voilà qu'on aperçoit un tout petit chiffon
>   D'azur sombre, encadré d'une petite branche,

This is "phenomenological" or immediate imagery (*données im-médiates*), which gives a feeling of startling presence because it calls attention to the stuff, the texture, of reality. The phenomenon seems to be

---

[1] Jean Fretet in *L'Aliénation poétique* builds a whole pathological case on this constant theme in Rimbaud's poems and letters.

at one with the eye of the beholder or even lodged in it; so that the effect is of union between viewer and viewed. Here the fragment of sky stands out surprisingly because one expects to see it in normal perspective *behind* the framing branches, but because the sky-color is of higher saturation it leaps forward into the vision (like those incandescent bright letters on bumper stickers). A quite comparable effect is the "rivière / Accrochant follement aux herbes des haillons / D'argent" ("Le Dormeur du val": note "haillon" and "chiffon"). Or the "mouches volantes" or dark specks the child sees after pressing his eyes in "Les Poètes de sept ans": "pour des visions écrasant son œil." A corollary effect, occurring in the matrix of vision, is the "J'ai vu quelquefois ce que l'homme a cru voir" of "Le Bateau ivre."

> 11. Piqué d'une mauvaise étoile, qui se fond
>   Avec de doux frissons, petite et toute blanche . . .

The star is, no doubt, "mauvaise" because it sharply pushes through the softness of amorous June air and linden trees—almost like a prick of conscience or a hard judging male eye (as in "Les Assis"). But when it melts with "sweet shivers" and appears milkily "white," all is well. The "doux frou-frou" in "Ma Bohème" evokes a comparably amiable aspect of the stars.

> 13. Nuit de juin! Dix-sept ans!—On se laisse griser.
>   La sève est du champagne et vous monte à la tête . . .
>   On divague; on se sent aux lèvres un baiser
>   Qui palpite là, comme une petite bête . . .

Rimbaud convincingly describes the amorous drunkenness of adolescence, the desire for kisses, with scarcely a trace of irony.

III

> 17. Le cœur fou Robinsonne à travers les romans,

His timidity leads to the substitute expression of dreaming, fictitious adventure in the mode of *Swiss Family Robinson*, or other *romans* (hence the title).

> 20. Sous l'ombre du faux-col effrayant de son père . . .

Rimbaud, like all adolescent males, is frightened at the prospect of a confrontation with the experienced older male, the father, in a pattern which echoes an Oedipal archetype: this would-be Don Juan is tempered at the mere suggestion of an avenging Don Luis. The stiff collar stands for the toughness of the proven (if only by experience and work) adult male, as in "Les Assis," or for the hard laws of initiation wherein youth defeats the adversaries of fear and guilt-feeling and earns the right to take a lady love.

> 21. Et, comme elle vous trouve immensément naïf
> Tout en faisant trotter ses petites bottines,
> Elle se tourne, alerte et d'un mouvement vif . . .
> —Sur vos lèvres alors meurent les cavatines . . .

Some of the toughness of the father, and of the *reality* he is associated with, is in the naturally realistic woman, *alerte* like the "alertes fillettes" of "À la musique." It is even somewhat in the neat, precise, hard movement ("trotter") of her "bottines," or the "mouvement vif" she executes to get a glimpse at her potential suitor, who already, he suggests in the first line, she had suspected was not yet up to serious encounters ("naïf"). All this is disenchanting and brings shocking recognition in the boy of a lack of strength or readiness: the song dies as did the whistle in the mouths of the callow youths following Gilberte Poquelin in *Le Grand Meaulnes*. But the object is not forsaken—the girl is felt to be more *real* than one's own self and hence infinitely desirable. Rimbaud is stung to the quick in this challenge to his courage to live, desire, possess. As the next section opens, he falls all the way in love: "Vous êtes amoureux. Loué jusqu'au mois d'août."

I V

26. Vous êtes amoureux.—Vos sonnets La font rire.

There is probably an actual incident behind all this, recounted by Jean-Marie Carré. Rimbaud apparently wrote to Delahaye in 1871 to tell him of a rendezvous with a girl whose father frightened him, "effaré comme trente-six millions de caniches nouveau-nés." Rimbaud, then, probably did write the girl and send her sonnets—which naturally were less than to the point.

The tone, here, is amusedly and bitterly Laforguian.

The capital initial of "La" anticipates the awe-inspiring *Elle* of some important later poems. Compare "À * * * Elle," the dedication of "Rêvé pour l'hiver." When She writes to him the result is ambiguous. Does he return to the café in a burst of new manly confidence? Or is he frightened off in earnest?

29. —Ce soir-là, . . . —vous rentrez aux cafés éclatants,
     Vous demandez des bocks ou de la limonade . . .

It is like the close of "Alchimie du verbe": "Cela s'est passé," vibrant and
unsure.

Le Mal

This is a poem of reconciliation, of salvation through sacrifice. First, the
soldiers: they are like the "million de Christs" in "Morts de Quatre-vingt-
douze. . . ." As in the "Dormeur du val," their death amidst the joys of
summer in the grass is a scandal (hence the title). But at this stage of his
career Rimbaud can imagine a God who is sensitive to the depth of this
sacrifice and gives it meaning. In His sight sacrificial woman is saved too.
A poor and bereft mother is redeemed where the rich woman—as in "Les
Pauvres à l'église"—is not. Behind all this I suspect Rimbaud's need for
reconciliation with his mother. If she is totally abandoned by the male—as
by Hamlet, "Ophélie"; as here she is by her potentially dead son; as she
will be by father and son symbolically in "Mémoire"—she can finally
attract Rimbaud's sympathy. Rimbaud was planning further such sacri-
fices for her and instinctively knew it.

Rages de Césars

There is little or no poetic interest to this primarily vindictive piece,
which pitilessly jumps on Napoleon III, prisoner of the Prussians, and
asserts that the liberty he had tried to stamp out as dictator now relives
in the Commune. Napoleon is pictured as having no regrets for his mis-
deeds and his failure. The "œil mort" Rimbaud ascribes to him seems to
have been a well-known aspect of the Emperor. Perhaps in the final image
of smoking a cigar in solitude, as the Emperor did in the evenings at his
palace of St. Cloud, there is a note of a poet's sympathy for an exile.
Though perhaps unintentional, there is a curious echo between the
Cloud and the *nuage* ("cloud").

Rêvé pour l'hiver

The dedication "À * * * Elle" (the "She" is unknown) echoes a number
of such *Elles* in the poems and the *Illuminations* ("Roman," "Being
beauteous"). This capitalized awe-inspiring entity may well owe some-
thing to Baudelaire's "C'est Elle! noire et pourtant lumineuse" ("Un
Fantôme"). Later, Proust and Gide will use *Elle* in precisely the same
spirit (the incest-barrier of the dream in *Les Cahiers d'André Walter* is

exactly parallel to the foiled encounter of *Les Déserts de l'amour*; Proust and Gide, like Rimbaud, loved woman *too* much to love her normally).

The poem, modest and brief, is another sincere adolescent tribute to female being. Under the heterosexual object, as usual, lies the maternal: the fantasy of the cozy love-nest in a train coach is a familiar one. By contrast, outside the window are fugitive demons, the obverse of the love-object, as in all fairy stories or medieval *romans*. The imagery recurs in "Jeune ménage," amusedly, and, more seriously, in the dream-fantasy of "Nocturne vulgaire":

> . . . le véhicule vire sur le gazon de la grande route effacée: et dans un défaut en haut de la glace de droite tournoient les blêmes figures lunaires, feuilles, seins.

Verlaine, in his "Charleroi" (*Romances sans paroles*) will see similar "Kobolds" outside the train window. These two examples, the Rimbaud and the Verlaine, are among the earliest images of train-traveling recorded in poetry.

> 1. L'hiver, nous irons dans un petit wagon rose
>   Avec des coussins bleus.
>   Nous serons bien. Un nid de baisers fous repose
>   Dans chaque coin moelleux.

The winter of the title and of the first line, the demons later, provide a pleasurable contrast: *suave mari magno*. This ambivalent theme will figure again in the *Saison en enfer*: "je redoute l'hiver parce que c'est la saison du comfort!" Also in the "Bateau ivre," the winter is the outside setting for the snugly dreaming child indoors; here the "rose" and the "bleu" are infantile colors, and the "nid" recalls the one in "Les Étrennes des orphelins."

Le Dormeur du val

The sacrificial soldiers of "Morts de Quatre-vingt-douze" and "Le Mal" are here summed up in a single representative, a young one, almost a child, with whom Rimbaud can easily identify his own intimate life-sorrow. As in the famous cinematic documentary *Le Sang des bêtes* we are set up for the shocking or scandalous let-down by an initial pastoral scene. There is a deep bitterness here, and some of it may be obliquely directed toward his mother: nature is clearly a womb-shaped *magna mater*: "un trou de verdure . . . un petit val." This reminds us of Mallar-

74

mé's "Mère qui créas les fleurs avec la balsamique mort" ("Les Fleurs"), or Du Bellay's "marâtre" ("Défense et Illustration"): "Nature, berce-le chaudement" (l. 11), is thus a cutting irony. Everything is arranged to make us feel sympathy for the cruelly rejected innocent boy-child here. In this sense "Le Dormeur du val" is the male version of "Ophélie."

> 1. C'est un trou de verdure où chante une rivière
>   Accrochant follement aux herbes des haillons
>   D'argent; où le soleil, de la montagne fière,
>   Luit: c'est un petit val qui mousse de rayons.

The setting is very like the later and fuller one in "Mémoire": both have a male sun (with "lui/luit" echo) at the mountain top sending down angel-sons of light in impressionistic splendor amidst the grass. Here too, as in "Mémoire," the feminine river is a passive reflector of the light. And like that of "Ophélie," there is a potentially fickle, *mobile* feminine folly—and melody—in the river's frolic.

We noted earlier, in our comments on "Roman," the effects of "phenomenological imagery" in the silver fragments ("haillons") which stand out, as something solid and assertive between the grass blades.

> 5. Un soldat jeune, bouche ouverte, tête nue,

He is vulnerable, innocent, with open mouth and naked head. We are not yet told of his true condition....

> 6. Et la nuque baignant dans le frais cresson bleu

This "fresh" grass will recur in "Mémoire."

The "baignant" is like that infantile "baigné dans le Poème / De la Mer" [echoing *mère*] of "Le Bateau ivre." Surely Rimbaud felt like all children that he was safe, cradled, bathing in that fresh, gentle summer morning grass. "Danger [of war] is sunk in the pastures . . . Sunshiny field grass, the woods floor, are so mixed up with earliest trusts [of] the dumb child" (Richard Wilbur, *Mined Country*).

> 8. Pâle dans son lit vert où la lumière pleut.

The "lit" of "Mémoire" is the same natural maternal site. But the "pâle" begins to give away the horrible secret. The impressionistic light is generous ("pleut"): it feeds life. Is there a favoring of the male principle here?

9. Les pieds dans les glaïeuls, il dort. Souriant comme
   Sourirait un enfant malade, il fait un somme:

He is mingled with nature. But the "smiling sick child" readily evokes sympathy; it also further arouses our suspicion that all is not well here. And we know it in the next line:

11. Nature, berce-le chaudement: il a froid.

Cold (like thirst and hunger) was Rimbaud's characteristic fear, the fear of the early-ousted from the breast and nest.

12. Les parfums ne font pas frissonner sa narine;

As in Sartre's analysis of Baudelaire (for example his allusion to "Le Flacon") the smell of perfume, a pure volatile spirit, is most *penetrating*; it goes to the sensuous, intimate core of life. For the poet, to breathe no longer deeply of nature's sweet smells is total deprivation—death.

18. . . . Il a deux trous rouges au côté droit.

The hard dry "cold" fact of death—in contrast to the vibrant animation of warm, light, foamy, odorous nature—is partly in the symmetrical, unmagical number two. The short, crisp, almost clinical, final sentence adds to this deadly effect.

Au Cabaret-Vert

This is the Rimbaud of the *fugues*, the man with the wind-soles, hungry for life, on the road leading wildly away to anywhere. . . . After his season in hell he would seek a "réalité rugueuse à étreindre," but his earlier resilient and buoyant youth had already found it in the rugged joy of tearing his boots on the pebbles of the road. The inn, as it had been for Stendhal (*Lucien Leuwen*: "le Vert Chasseur") and Baudelaire ("l'espérance qui brille aux carreaux de l'Auberge," "L'Irréparable") is the ideal fantasy of a substitute "nest," replacing and somehow restoring the impossible original one. Thus in "Comédie de la soif" he dreams:

Peut-être un Soir m'attend
Où je boirai tranquille
En quelque vieille Ville

The *evening* (capitalized here) is a grave time of reconciliation, of homecoming, and we note the hour of the present poem: "cinq heures du soir."

The "Comédie" goes on bitterly:

> Jamais l'auberge verte
> Ne peut bien m'être ouverte.

This echoes the "green" of the title here and perhaps of Stendhal's "Vert Chasseur." The disappointment recalls Baudelaire's inn whose windows were extinguished: "Le Diable a tout éteint aux carreaux de l'Auberge!" And this note will recur elsewhere in Rimbaud, for example, "Enfance."

But in this earlier poem, the tone is all up-beat. He is warm, he is fed, he feasts his eyes on a very present and sumptuous Flemish woman, he drinks.[1] And his thirst is doubly quenched since the "male" light streaming into his beer-mug joins in a supremely satisfying union with the "feminine" fluid. Or the sky comes down and fuses happily with earth as in the "mer allée / Avec le soleil" or (variant) "mer mêlée au soleil" of "L'Éternité" or the "L'azur et l'onde communient" of "Bannières de mai."

> 5. Bienheureux, j'allongeai les jambes sous la table
> Verte: je contemplai les sujets très naïfs
> De la tapisserie.

This propensity to take joy in the naive expands into a well-known and influential passage of "Alchimie du verbe." The "table verte" emphasizes the at-home-in-maternal-nature feeling, in the Green Inn.

> 8. Quand la fille aux tétons énormes, aux yeux vifs,

The roundness, again, is emphasized by the two o's. And as previously seen in "Roman" and "À la musique," woman is alert, realistic, for Rimbaud; but this healthy peasant girl is less threatening than the earlier figures.

> 13. ... et m'emplit la chope immense, avec sa mousse
> Que dorait un rayon de soleil arriéré.

[1] As Marie Bonaparte noted of Poe's drinking, there was a reminiscence of the long-lost breast of the mother who died young. Compare Mallarmé's similar breast-haunting in "Mes bouquins refermés."

The mood is still Flemish or Dutch *rondeur*, and we easily conjure up a scene of De Hooch or Vermeer (or Hals, Teniers or Terborch). But there are complex levels here: the simple full joy of the round "chope" (with its o) is joined to the more sophisticated ambivalent pleasure of the half-light of the evening, in which the homecoming motif mingles as always its "underside" of return to sleep—and death. We recall the last—as is fitting—line of Baudelaire's "Chant d'Automne"; or of Mallarmé's autumnal "Soupir."

"Mousse" is a half-way substance in which air (or light) and water conjoin. It is suspended, fleeting as this artistic notation of a privileged moment.

La Maline

This is, practically speaking, another version of the "Cabaret-Vert." Rimbaud's ripe adolescent sensuality evokes in fantasy, and probably in reality, a mood of plenitude and availability about him. The buxom servant woman is so responsive she employs a ruse to attract his kiss, hence the title: "the clever one" (*maline*: *maligne*); the word can also mean "spring tide," referring possibly to his emotion; there may be a further reference to the Belgian town Malines, though this poem was written in Charleroi.

> 1. Dans la salle à manger brune, que parfumait
>   Une odeur de vernis et de fruits, à mon aise

The solidly provincial and reassuring atmosphere recalls the one in Proust's Combray.

> 5. En mangeant, j'écoutais l'horloge,—heureux et coi.
>   La cuisine s'ouvrit avec une bouffée,

This is a sort of symbolic pair: the "male" clock ticking or chiming away its classic orderliness—like the distant clock the fatherless children listened for in "Les Étrennes des orphelins"—and the generously warm "female" kitchen, like the "trou chaud [qui] souffle la vie" of "Les Effarés." There is in the combination something of the lowland "ordre et beauté, / Luxe, calme et volupté" of Baudelaire's "Invitation au Voyage."

L'Éclatante Victoire de Sarrebruck

Another satiric piece leveled against Napoleon III and of little interest to poetry.

1.   . . . dans une apothéose
     Bleue et jaune,

The colors here have nothing to do with the curious pair at the end of
"Mémoire"; they are rather the actual naive colors of a "gravure belge"
Rimbaud is describing. The "poem" draws its main effects from a number
of such amusing color touches.

12. Un schako surgit, comme un soleil noir . . .

A possible reminiscence of Nerval ("El Desdichado") or Hugo ("Magni-
tudo Parvi"), as Suzanne Bernard notes; it is another apt color-splash in
the series.

Le Buffet

Baudelaire had used the image of the *armoire* for a sumptuous woman
in "Le Beau Navire":[1]

> Ta gorge triomphante est une belle armoire
>   Dont les panneaux bombés et clairs
> Comme les boucliers accrochent des éclairs;
>
> Boucliers provoquants, armés de pointes roses!
> Armoire à doux secrets, pleine de bonnes choses,
>   De vins, de parfums, de liqueurs
> Qui feraient délirer les cerveaux et les cœurs!

Rimbaud's buffet is closely related to this *armoire*: it too is a repository
of time: "O buffet du vieux temps" and further recalls the drawers rum-
maged through for nostalgic items in a *Spleen* poem (LXXVI):

> Un gros meuble à tiroirs encombré de bilans,
> De vers, de billets doux, de procès, de romances,
> Avec de lourds cheveux roulés dans des quittances,

In Rimbaud's poem, the memories and associations are mainly those
of a *mundus muliebris*, which befits the obvious maternal symbolism of
the buffet: a womb-source, like a cornucopia, of comfort, nourishment
and life. But the wine and fruits, emblems of this generosity, are mingled
with more ambivalent memories.

---

[1] The same *armoire*, only musty, is found in "Le Flacon": "quelque armoire /
Pleine de l'âcre odeur des temps."

Suzanne Bernard has provided a note to another poem ("Jeune mé-
nage") which is helpful here: "Ce sont . . . des fées (souvent *marraines*
d'un enfant dans les contes) qui entrent dans les buffets" (p. 440). We
spoke earlier of this fantasy, referring to the buffet in "Les Étrennes des
orphelins": for the absent or unloving mother the child often substitutes
an ideal fairy-godmother, mysteriously hiding in the buffet, or the gen-
erous buffet itself comes to stand for her. Such fairy *marraines* are often
old ladies since old people are usually indulgent to children; hence "cet
air si bon des vieilles gens" ("qui vous pardonneraient," Alain-Fournier
would say). By extension these figures can also become maternal deities,
like the *Sorcière* who could tell us the universal secrets of childhood
unhappiness: what went wrong?—where does happiness lie? (see for
example the end of "Après le déluge"). Here too the buffet seems to
reveal such secrets: "O buffet du vieux temps, tu sais bien des histoires, /
Et tu voudrais conter tes contes. . . ." In the *Saison en Enfer* ("Mauvais
sang") Rimbaud will go back to the beginning and interrogate his an-
cestors in much the same troubled and questioning spirit (compare
Mallarmé's "Igitur").

But, as Baudelaire knew and said in "Le Flacon," at the bottom of that
well—or at the top of those fairy-godmother's spiral stairs—is not only
pure joy, but Death. And indeed the oldness of these "vieilles vieilleries"
is part of a death-urge, a desire to sink back into the womb, perhaps for a
better rebirth, or perhaps just to disappear from a sorrowful world. In
any case Paradise—whose price is death—needs no justification, and all
poetry, like this, is a more-or-less gingerly approach to it: "all poems are
epitaphs" (T. S. Eliot).

> 4. Le buffet est ouvert, et verse dans son ombre
>   Comme un flot de vin vieux, des parfums engageants;

As in Baudelaire's "Le Flacon," this is a tomb-overtone of the womb
(Baudelaire speaks of Lazarus rising from his grave). Old wine is easily
part of this flavor, and the perfume in both poets is *engageant*, like a
siren-call back to the lost and dangerous source.

> 5. Tout plein, c'est un fouillis de vieilles vieilleries,
>   De linges odorants et jaunes, de chiffons
>   De femmes ou d'enfants, de dentelles flétries,
>   De fichus de grand'mère où sont peints des griffons;

Here the tone is fascinatingly faded and old, redolent of mild death-as-
time. The series of double l's and diphthongs in "fouillis de vieilles

vieilleries" renders somewhat this complexity: the convoluted twistings of jumbled old clothes is like the messy spirals of the self-involved *fascinated* psyche, sucked down into this deep whirlpool of death-past-darkness, recalling the *Vertige*, with its cone-shaped V, of Baudelaire's "Flacon." Here too the two v's have a pleasantly down-sucking maelstrom—"rummaging"—effect.

> 12. —O buffet du vieux temps, tu sais bien des histoires,
> Et tu voudrais conter tes contes, et tu bruis
> Quand s'ouvrent lentement tes grandes portes noires.

We have commented on this above; the darkness (of past, death) is in the "noires." The "bruis" recalls the "grince et rechigne en criant" of Baudelaire's *armoire* in "Le Flacon"; the creaky sound is expressive of age, and seems like a voice of the past and, more mysteriously, of things, a cry rooted all the way down in nature, wood, like the cricket sound admired by Mallarmé as a voice of the earth (letter to Lefébure). Compare the forest and earth-rooted *Sorcière* of "Après le déluge":

> . . . la Reine, la Sorcière qui allume sa braise
> dans le pot de terre, ne voudra jamais nous
> raconter ce qu'elle sait, et que nous ignorons.

Ma Bohème
(Fantaisie)

A winning and much-anthologized piece, this poem has done much to fix the image of Rimbaud as the boy wanderer of the country roads. Under the wayward independence of the earth-and-air-flavored flights there is a vestigial childish powerlessness and wounded pathos, fully present in the poem. But there is inner courage too, born of these tragic escapes and defeats, more important than the outer courage of the adventure. Rimbaud speaks of himself as a "Petit-Poucet rêveur," and there is no more accurate and compelling identification in all his poetry. A psychically handicapped miniature soul—like the tentative toddler in dwarf woods of "Enfance"—a sort of infant Perceval,[1] is at the core of this inner struggle for strength to survive, which went far back into his past.

---

[1] See my analysis of Perceval in *The Writer's Way in France* (chapter entitled: "Tristan; Perceval"). Although we do not know whether Rimbaud was significantly aware of the Perceval story (beyond a reference to the "Saint-Graal" in "Les Lèvres closes," *Album Zutique*), folklore versions of it were current in the Ardennes. A modern edition of *Perceval* came out in 1866, in Belgium, edited by Alfred Pettiot.

Petit-Poucet was small but, like the biblical David, he developed a giant spiritual strength from his very shortcomings. The corollary dialectic in time (characteristic of the creative temperament) is retardation followed by enhanced duration: "Tel qu'en lui-même enfin l'éternité le change." As Perrault tells us at the end of his *Contes de ma mère l'oie* version of "Hop o' my Thumb," ultimately "Il fera le bonheur de sa famille"—he who laughs last laughs best (or longest). Perceval's delayed entrance into manhood turned into a similar lasting triumph. Surely there is an echo of this inner drama in the juvenile prose sketch written at age nine: "Mes frères étaient moins vaillants que moi et cependant plus grands" (Pléiade, p. 6). It will be the old fairy story of the disinherited younger brother coming at long last into his own.

At the end of the poem, it is true—as at the end of the "Bateau ivre"—there is a note of provisional defeat, of curling on the crushed self for comfort. But we now have the promise in the central image. Rimbaud's whole career ended on a down-curve. But after all, whose does not? The poetry goes on victoriously.

1. Je m'en allais, les poings dans mes poches crevées;

The imperfect tense running through the poem implies a summed-up-in-memory series of experiences, which was the case: four or five such *fugues* are recorded before Rimbaud finally left home for good. The "poings" thrust down (a characteristic gesture recorded in a well-known pencil sketch) so hard as to burst the pockets indicate aggressiveness, a child's pent-up anger at what he has left behind and perhaps at being psychically ousted from that home prematurely. The "crevées" also indicates a Bohemian raggedness, as does the next line:

2. Mon paletot aussi devenait idéal;

It was becoming an airy nothing, being full of holes, echoing the ideality of his poetic dreams.

3. . . . et j'étais ton féal.

"Féal": Mallarmé's "Sonneur," which Suzanne Bernard thinks Rimbaud imitated for other reasons (p. 442), contains this unusual word; its medieval flavor (liege) may have to do with the hint of Perceval (see footnote 1).

4. Oh! là là! que d'amours splendides j'ai rêvées!

A somewhat bitter, self-mocking adolescent tone favored also by Lautréa-mont, Laforgue, Jarry is part of the *déculture* (as is the folksy "Oh! là là!") Rimbaud was to do so much to further, particularly with the "Alchimie du verbe."

> 7. —Petit-Poucet rêveur, j'égrenais dans ma course
>   Des rimes. Mon auberge était à la Grande-Ourse.
>   —Mes étoiles au ciel avaient un doux frou-frou.

The scattering of rimes instead of the bread-crumbs or pebbles of the fairy story is a fine stretch of extended metaphor. For indeed his poems were a lifeline going back to his home and core, a kind of extended umbilical cord, or Ariadne's thread, the rosary of words which accompanies all of us "whistling in the dark" through dreadful experiences.

The "auberge à la Grande-Ourse" is another fine invention echoing both real inn names and the saying "coucher à la belle étoile." The stars are close to this child-in-nature. He speaks of them with the *déculture* familiarity of "frou-frou." They are *"mes* étoiles." They seem to come down to touch him with that sweet intimate rustling reminiscent of "Mystique":

> La douceur fleurie des étoiles et du ciel et du reste descend en
> face du talus, comme un panier,[2]—contre notre face, et fait
> l'abîme fleurant et bleu là-dessous.

Or again, Yeats: "And hid his face amid a crowd of stars."

> 9. Et je les écoutais, assis au bord des routes,

The "frou-frou" is a sassy version of the Pythagorean "music of the spheres." A more solemn version occurred in "Soleil et chair": "tous ces mondes-là, que l'éther vaste embrasse, / Vibrent-ils aux accents d'une eternelle voix?" (above, p. 43). See also "Phrases."

> 10. Ces bons soirs de septembre où je sentais des gouttes
>   De rosée à mon front, comme un vin de vigueur;

We commented on the round freshness of "bons soirs" under "Roman." The dewdrops are another form of nature's coming down solicitously to him, caressing him and refreshing him, like the sea of the "Bateau ivre."

---

[2] They are white like manna, a spiritual nourishment (*panier*).

"Vin de vigueur" suggests rubbing alcohol but, even more, a restoration of *strength*.

    12. ... des ombres fantastiques,

We have seen these hobgoblins menacing an intimate scene of joy in "Rêvé pour l'hiver"; we will see more in "Jeune ménage" and "Nocturne vulgaire."

    13. Comme des lyres, je tirais les élastiques
        De mes souliers blessés, un pied près de mon cœur!

This humble earthy touch—poetry of shoes, with holes into which earth seeps—is, despite the bantering tone, a true contribution to modernity. The final image is doleful. The child curled on himself, like an embryo, or a sorrowing, womb-nostalgic being in bed. We recall the sadly crouching child at the close of the "Bateau ivre."

(The subtitle *Fantaisie* may exist just because Rimbaud enjoys the word. But perhaps at this stage of his development he thought the imagery was disjointed and wanted to justify it.)

Les Corbeaux

This is full and fine Rimbaud.

Nature is numb in winter. Light is suspended. There is a mysterious pall of powerlessness, like a magic enchantment, over the dead-seeming hamlets of the countryside. It is the affective paralysis—love neglected and overcast by duty—of Rimbaud's own childhood, waiting for some event to release it. Like the bee which Valéry calls upon—"j'ai besoin d'une prompte douleur"—the crows are allies of this potential liberation. They are ambivalent, black angels of delight, with the quality of pepper—"les plaines poivrées" ("Vies")—strong seasoning that will turn this dull interim into savoriness. Later, Rimbaud will call upon the blacks of Africa to deliver Europe from its civilized pall, in just this spirit: "Noirs inconnus, si nous allions!" ("Qu'est-ce pour nous, mon cœur . . . ?").

Here the birds are summoned like avenging angels to remind the appalling powers-that-be (Napoleon III, the hated bourgeois order generally) of all the death and destruction they have wrought in their dirty wars. Again, as in so many of the poems ("Morts de Quatre-vingt-douze," "Le Mal," "Le Dormeur du val") Rimbaud identifies his own murdered childhood with the sacrificed soldiers.

But Rimbaud's daemonic spirit, as always, was only part of him. That need for violence, retribution, had been forced on him by sad circumstances. Underneath lay a harried creature who wanted to be left alone, to be allowed to love more quietly, tenderly. And so when the violent flurry of revengeful screaming is over, mingled with the reward of pleasure-in-reprisal is an outwardly calmer spirit. Not action, but passion. The sacrifice of the soldiers, or Rimbaud's own suffering, is seen in a contemplative Christian light as part of a universal tragedy. The last stanza is this quiet beauty—the flutings of a May warbler—born of grief.

>   1. Seigneur, quand froide est la prairie,
>   Quand dans les hameaux abattus,
>   Les longs angelus se sont tus . . .

Although there is a suggestion of villages ravaged by war (with the Franco-Prussian conflict particularly in mind), the likelier interpretation is an assault by "General Winter." This mood of suspended potential light is exactly the one of the Grand Meaulnes's journey in mid-winter, past dead-seeming hamlets and villages or nature. In "Enfance" there is this same still scene: "Les prés remontent aux hameaux sans coqs, sans enclumes." For Rimbaud—as in "Le Forgeron"—the fiery forge was a source of male life, light and stir, like the sun. The *coq* was an equally powerful symbol of *awakening* life; in "O Saisons, ô chateaux" he cries, "vive lui [echo of *luire*] chaque fois / Que chante son coq gaulois." The morning sun greeted the workers of "Bonne pensée du matin" and stirred the *chantiers* into joyous activity—but this cold day is dead. Here, the bells, another "male" source of sound and aural light which ordinarily pours forth into the passive villages or countryside, are silent. The angelic angelus no longer sounds; there is no fatherly voice to quicken life. Hence, as in "Mémoire," once the light has departed, nature is an abandoned woman: "la nature défleurie" of the following line.

>   6. Les chers corbeaux délicieux.

In "La Rivière de Cassis," another poem of a tentative boy-child's wandering through mysterious landscapes (or "inscapes"), seeking answers to deeply puzzling questions, the crows are identified in exactly the same terms. And Rimbaud addresses them as: "Soldats des forêts que le Seigneur envoie" which (echoing the "Seigneur" of "Les Corbeaux") makes them into the same militant angels. (In "La Rivière de Cassis," however, the enemy is the wily peasant rather than the bourgeois.)

>   7. Armée étrange aux cris sévères,
>   Les vents froids attaquent vos nids!

Rimbaud's own sensitivity was insulted by the coldness of life—winter, rigid mother, no father—and we have seen his earlier references to the nest ("Les Étrennes des orphelins"). Like the avenging birds, at this point of the poem he comes out fighting.

> 9. Vous, le long des fleuves jaunis,

The river which is an image of (feminine) life reflecting (masculine) light, in "Le Dormeur du val" and "Mémoire," is here yellowed with the general pall. To go along a river, as in "La Rivière de Cassis," is the essence of a life-journey, towards a mysterious source (as in "Enfance"; we remember also the hidden river Meaulnes followed along).

> 10. Sur les routes aux vieux calvaires,

The road is like the river, an obvious image of the moving quest. It is punctuated by arresting events, like the Pilgrim's Progress. These crosses lead to the sacrificial final theme. But they are also themselves: old, half-rooted in nature, parts of the ambivalent scene.

> 11. Sur les fossés et sur les trous
> Dispersez-vous, ralliez-vous!

Rimbaud's imagery is humbly and wonderfully concrete. His consolation was nature in its kinder moments; he went to her for refuge, and the familiar ditches and holes and banks (the *talus* is a frequent image) and ruts and groves were like the parts of a loved-one's body he intimately knew. The wheeling dispersion and condensation of the bird-flights is rightly observed and caught in this and the subsequent lines.

> 13. Par milliers, sur les champs de France,
> Où dorment des morts d'avant-hier,
> Tournoyez, n'est-ce pas, l'hiver,
> Pour que chaque passant repense!
> Sois donc le crieur du devoir,
> O notre funèbre oiseau noir!

The bird is to be an angel of retribution, a solemn black *justicier*; he recalls somewhat Poe's raven (who was an emissary of the total justice of Fate).

"Les morts d'avant-hier" are possibly the fallen soldiers of the Franco-Prussian war (preceding more recent battles of the Commune, as Suzanne

Bernard suggests), but the feeling is of something older, though not necessarily the dead of 1793 (suggested by Gengoux).

> 19. Mais, saints du ciel, en haut du chêne,
>   Mât perdu dans le soir charmé,
>   Laissez les fauvettes de mai
>   Pour ceux qu'au fond du bois enchaîne,
>   Dans l'herbe d'où l'on ne peut fuir,
>   La défaite sans avenir.

The "saints du ciel" are the crows whom he asks to leave the May warblers alone to sing the grief of the dead; their activity is to give way to passion and quiet beauty.

The "chêne, / Mât perdu dans le soir charmé," is one of those land-sea vibrancies Rimbaud favored, as in "Marine" or the dreams of sails in the attic of "Les Poètes de sept ans." The "charmé" indicates a gentle turn to appeasing light and warming color.

That grass is the site of many such limit-situations of total beauty-in-death in Rimbaud: "Le Dormeur du val," "Mémoire." He was fascinated by the burial places of the soldiers around Mézières, according to Delahaye. The "futureless defeat" is the full swallowing of the bitter existential draught that alone makes possible such beauty.

Les Assis

Rimbaud was the classic outsider, at times above, at times below his conventional contemporaries, seldom on a level with them. Because he lacked a father-model, he despaired of attaining normal maturity and alternately envied and hated and showed contempt for those who could. "Quels hommes mûrs!" is the characteristically ambivalent outburst ("Parade"). And, like that of our young militants of today, lacking the truly virile ingredients in his upbringing, his need for authority was so great that it often took the form of a scandalous provocation. "Général . . . bombarde-nous," he cries to the pitiless sun, in the *Saison en enfer* ("Alchimie du verbe"). He empathized with the hardened criminal who provoked the father-society over and over again to close the doors of the jail on him, thus giving him at least the firm identity he, like Sartre's Genet, lacked. "Je veux bien que les saisons m'usent" ("Bannières de mai") is another such bid for attention from the Highest Authority.

The old librarians of "Les Assis" have a deep French concierge-like nastiness of petty power—i.e., legitimate sadism, which few bureaucrats of any sort can resist—which makes them good targets for Rimbaud's fear, hatred, and fascinated interest; perhaps even secret veneration. Like the old Wandering Jew antique-dealer of Balzac's *Peau de chagrin* or Baudelaire's kindred *vieillards* ("Les Sept Vieillards"), they are immemorial father-time figures, venerable crocodiles or amphibia from the primeval slime, "Tremblant du tremblement douloureux du crapaud" (l. 12); certainly, close to death and illness, they are sacrificial and have earned a kind of pitying awe; and there is also fear of that death-depth in their eyes:

> 30. . . . leur regard filtre ce venin noir
>   Qui charge l'œil souffrant de la chienne battue,
>   Et vous suez, pris dans un atroce entonnoir.

(Baudelaire's *vieillards* had a similar vertigo in their eyes.) Even their buttons are authority-eyes:

> 27. Et leurs boutons d'habit sont des prunelles fauves
>   Qui vous accrochent l'œil du fond des corridors!

Though they seem weak, "ils ont une main invisible qui tue" (l. 19), a surreptitious lethal power from the dark backward and abysm of time.

> 1. Noirs de loupes, grêlés, les yeux cerclés de bagues
>   Vertes, leurs doigts boulus crispés à leurs fémurs,
>   Le sinciput plaqué de hargnosités vagues
>   Comme les floraisons lépreuses des vieux murs;

This describes wizened and funky creatures, half-rooted or embedded in primeval vegetal and elemental nature, like the "crapaud" of line 12. "Boulus," according to Emilie Noulet, is a neologism based on *boulures*, excrescences arising at the base of plants (in Suzanne Bernard, p. 386). The old men's rashy skulls are like "leprous walls," covered with dark mossy growths.

> 5. Ils ont greffé dans des amours épileptiques
>   Leur fantasque ossature aux grands squelettes noirs
>   De leurs chaises; leurs pieds aux barreaux rachitiques
>   S'entrelacent pour les matins et pour les soirs!

Here they are seen entwined in their inert chairs, almost organically; they are "grafted" onto them. The mating of the human "skeletons" and the "skeletons" of the rickety (*rachitiques*) wooden chairs is a grotesque encounter of angularities, recalling the dancing bones of "Bal des Pendus," hence "épileptiques." "Pour les matins et pour les soirs!" is an indication of their fixed inertia ("les assis").

> 9. Ces vieillards ont toujours fait tresse avec leurs sièges,
>   Sentant les soleils vifs percaliser leur peau,
>   Ou, les yeux à la vitre où se fanent les neiges,
>   Tremblant du tremblement douloureux du crapaud.

Here there is a gentler note of contact with nature—"fait tresse" gives the old men a plant quality—the sun and the seasons. This is carried out in the next strophe.

> 13. Et les Sièges leur ont des bontés: culottée
>   De brun, la paille cède aux angles de leurs reins;
>   L'âme des vieux soleils s'allume, emmaillotée
>   Dans ces tresses d'épis où fermentaient les grains.

The chairs' straw is kind to them, and it is authentic straw, savored by the poet in depth for its fascinating ambivalent qualities of nature captured (vibrant between living and dead, motion and rest). The formerly fecund sun trapped in this pale straw similarly vibrates between light and dark.

> 17. Et les Assis, genoux aux dents, verts pianistes,
>   Les dix doigts sous leur siège aux rumeurs de tambour,
>   S'écoutent clapoter des barcarolles tristes,
>   Et leurs caboches vont dans des roulis d'amour.

I detect some sympathy here. Old men drumming on chairs are humbly homey; "roulis d'amour" indicates warmth.

> 24. Tout leur pantalon bouffe à leurs reins boursouflés.

All the o's (for roundness) and f's (for puffing out) are effective.

> 37. Quand l'austère sommeil a baissé leurs visières,
>   Ils rêvent sur leur bras de sièges fécondés,
>   De vrais petits amours de chaises en lisière
>   Par lesquelles de fiers bureaux seront bordés;
>
>   Des fleurs d'encre crachant des pollens en virgule
>   Les bercent, le long des calices accroupis
>   Tels qu'au fil des glaïeuls le vol des libellules
>   —Et leur membre s'agace à des barbes d'épis.

They fall asleep on their arms. They dream that the "epileptic loves" described above could result in darling baby chairs lining offices (*en lisière* can also mean babies "on leashes"). Hence the final line about their male organ being in (irritating) contact with the straw of the chairs.

Meanwhile, dream-flowers made of ink, like Rorschach blots, apparently send out fantastic comma-shaped pollen—a reference to the librarians' clerical ink-scratchings—and, dreaming, the old men pass along the rows of "squatting" calyxes—"cradled" by them, i.e., between the rows—like dragonflies down a line of gladioli. These weird flowers will grow more profusely in "Ce qu'on dit au poète."

Tête de faune

This is an impressionist poem, in the Verlaine manner, filled out by Rimbaldian earthiness and concreteness. The faun is distilled organically from nature by need, as his Greek original was. More poignantly, like the *Belle au bois dormant*, or William Hudson's Rima, the "Baiser d'or du Bois, qui se recueille" is the summing-up of the wood's beauty, their "puckering," so to speak, into an available or "instrumental" *graspable* human form, as the pucker is a résumé of the mouth in *kissable* form. Proust's Marcel similarly dreamt of peasant girls emerging from the tree trunks of the woods of Roussainville, as their "organ" ("dont la structure permet d'approcher") as it were, to appease his own summed-up desire: "de ces bois le trésor caché, la beauté profonde." In "La Belle au bois dormant" (whom Ophélie also recalled) the climactic image is the kiss that would awaken her, a kiss during which the Prince would undoubtedly "know" the whole woods in which she steeped (like the impressionistic little orange-lipped girl of "Enfance" at the forest's edge). With the "dormant" she provides a key word, "dort" (cf. line 3), from which two full echoes grow: "d'or" of line 1 and its repetition in line 12.[1] The gold is the sweetness and warmth of the kiss itself and is very close to the elixir of love that the sad child-prince tried to draw or distill from a light-brimming forest pond in "Larme," "tel qu'un pêcheur d'or."

> 1. Dans la feuillée, écrin vert taché d'or,
> Dans la feuillée incertaine et fleurie
> De fleurs splendides où le baiser dort,
> Vif et crevant l'exquise broderie,

The greenness is frank and fresh in the Verlaine tone ("Green"). The

---

[1] Compare Mallarmé's similarly gold- and sleep-haunted "se dore / Tristement dort une mandore" ("Une dentelle s'abolit").

"feuillée incertaine et fleurie" is the kind of impressionistic *impair* effect of magic wildness Verlaine favored ("Art Poétique"), like the "fouillis de fleurs" of "Les Chercheuses de poux."

"Vif et crevant": the two v's are incisive like the teeth of the faun, seen in line 6. The bright i sounds of "splendides," "vif," "exquise broderie" are the sparks of light in the leaves.

> 7. Brunie et sanglante ainsi qu'un vin vieux,

In "Antique" Rimbaud will describe a faun-like creature (centaur): "Tâchées de lies brunes, tes joues se creusent." The "lie [de vin]" obviously echoes the "vin vieux" and both probably come from "vieux faune de terre cuite" of Verlaine's *Fêtes galantes* (Rimbaud had enthused over them to Izambard).

> 10. Son rire tremble encore à chaque feuille,

All that is left is his breezy spirit, a sparkling ghost, a laugh in the leaves like the Cheshire cat's smile of *Alice in Wonderland*. A sigh in the poplars of "Mémoire" is a similarly apt "pathetic fallacy." These delicate and delicious shivers in nature—"un petit frisson d'aile" ("Ophélie")— were a source of consoling communion: a current of erotic electricity, of shared pleasure, passes between the faun and the trees. These shivers titillate and exasperate to a desire for climax, full possession, the summing-up "golden kiss" of the last line.

Les Douaniers

An unimportant satire, in the vein of "Les Assis," directed against authority: the customs agents who patrolled the Franco-Belgian frontier and arrested runners of contraband tobacco, etc.

The only memorable line is: "Quand l'ombre bave aux bois comme un mufle de vache." This will be echoed in the "océans poussifs" of the "Bateau ivre." *Baver* is a favorite adolescent word—American youngsters enjoy and over-use "drool" as much as Rimbaud—no doubt because it has the violent opposites which are characteristic of that age; a person who "drools" after something is full of desire and frustration. Its repeated use in Rimbaud is partly unconscious homeopathic release. The "baiser qui palpite aux lèvres" of "Roman" and the "salives / Reprises sur la lèvre ou désirs de baisers" of "Les Chercheuses de poux" are part of the same troubled mood. So is Rimbaud's notorious thirst.

Oraison du soir

Rimbaud saw himself with amazing honesty. Few men have dared to speak directly for the child buried in us all, no one with such moving sincerity. Apparently his need to express his emotional tragedy was so great that he did not care what people thought. Today we accept this directness and pathos easily from the Salingers and Goyens. But in 1870!

The central image is simply a melancholy boy sitting alone over a drink, puzzling hopelessly over his muddled beginnings and subsequent experiences, seething in revolt against his stifled life, going out and relieving himself in more than the usual sense. For here, the humble act is felt to be an emotional outlet, like an infant's, making up for all the personal feelings which are blocked in him. With Hamlet he would bitterly agree, "man delights not me; no, nor woman either."

> 1. Je vis assis, tel qu'un ange aux mains d'un barbier,

"Je vis assis": Rimbaud here classes himself with the inert librarians ("Les Assis"); it is an image of his passivity and numbness as he gathers strength for a flight. The scene seems to be outside, in his own yard or a beer garden.

The rest of the line is an epiphany of the fatherless child for whom to be in the care of a barber for a few moments means receiving at least some mature virile attention. Similarly, in "Les Chercheuses de poux," the unaccustomed care lavished on him by the Gindre sisters moved him to tears.

There is a secret father-son confrontation in the situation: the man with the razor standing over the youth, like Abraham over Isaac (or the equivalent in the ritual of circumcision).[1] But we will return to this father-son theme at length in our comments on "Bannières de mai."

The image of an innocent, nay, angelic victim is easily associated with the usual picture we have of Rimbaud (with hair needing cutting, perhaps), as in the painting of Fantin-Latour. The narcissism and child-martyr complex in all of us goes out to this surefire image.

> 2. Empoignant une chope à fortes cannelures,
>   L'hypogastre et le col cambrés, une Gambier
>   Aux dents, sous l'air gonflé d'impalpables voilures.

There is a fumbling and amusing and touching youthful attempt to

---

[1] Joyce plays with the name Swiney Tod (German: "death") the Demon Barber, which echoes "Sweeny Todd the Demon Barber of Fleet Street," a well-known ballad about a murderous hairdresser.

appear manly in these accoutrements and this aggressive "Empoignant."
He was only sixteen.

The "impalpables voilures" are clouds in the swollen air, as the
atmosphere, like his fuller mood, seems to be gathering toward a storm.
(But it will only be a flash in the pan.)

> 5. Tels que les excréments chauds d'un vieux colombier,
> Mille Rêves en moi font de douces brûlures:
> Puis par instants mon cœur triste est comme un aubier
> Qu'ensanglante l'or jeune et sombre des coulures.

The emotional outlet in evasive dreams is associated with the excremental
outlet, here of a passive sort, a warm consolation—"douces brûlures"—from
the self's own humbly expressed bodily substances. Bird's droppings with
similar cathexis will reappear in the "Bateau ivre." These oozings modu-
late to an image (closer to the more conventional seepage of blood and
tears) which expresses the welling-over sorrow of his "sad" heart and, by
the yellowness of the fluid, further modulates toward the release through
urination: "a willow / Bloodied by the young dark gold of washed-down
pollen." Pollen as sexual exudation helps orient the ensuing passage.

The "sad heart" (and the "ravalé") will appear again in "Le Cœur
volé."

> 9. Puis, quand j'ai ravalé mes rêves avec soin,
> Je me tourne, ayant bu trente ou quarante chopes,
> Et me recueille, pour lâcher l'âcre besoin:

"Ravalé": Rimbaud had to painfully pull in (swallow) his dream-horns
to face reality, over and over again; *ravale* can also mean "abase" as in
"Il ravalait ma poésie" ("Un Cœur sous une soutane"). As to the "trente
ou quarante chopes": he had a stupendous thirst, as we know, but this
seems to be mere adolescent bragging. The gathering toward an expression
in "me recueille" is obviously analogous to the "puckering" of "se re-
cueille" in "Tête de faune." Rimbaud was a keen observer of these
universal organic processes.

> 12. Doux comme le Seigneur du cèdre et des hysopes,
> Je pisse vers les cieux bruns, très haut et très loin,
> Avec l'assentiment des grands héliotropes.

Suzanne Bernard informs us that the "Lord of cedars and hyssops" is a
familiar biblical expression; it adds an amusing pompous touch to the
blasphemous image of "pissing towards the heavens" as a prayer (hence

the title). Perhaps too the image of salvation of the lowly ("hysopes") as well as the great ("cèdres") can apply to this benediction of our humblest parts. Moreover, hyssop served in a ritual of purgation, which may have some bearing here. Rimbaud's revolt against his mother's religion makes this gesture a sort of minor Black Mass. The "héliotropes," his idly assenting brothers, are like the chorus in a church; they too turn toward the sun-source in the sky.

The blasphemous irony changes into something natural and innocent. For in the light of nature, or modern all-acceptance, what difference does it make? The act is as much a part of creation as any other human gesture. This seems to have been felt by Rimbaud under the blasphemy itself—certainly the situation has evolved very quickly into one of sympathy on our part.

Chant de guerre parisien

The clever and often obscure images of this historical satire have been thoroughly explained by the brilliant research of Gengoux, and others. See Suzanne Bernard, p. 390. Rimbaud, entirely sympathetic to the Commune, ridicules the "Versaillais" with fantastic virtuosity. But the poetic *apport* is slight; no light is shed hence on the lyric works.

Mes petites amoureuses

Here again excessive spleen, in a mocking tirade against women, vitiates poetry. The result is—usually grating—cleverness, though Rimbaud's verbal resources are remarkable. Some of the images are effective and memorable. Most of the difficulties have been explained (see Bernard, p. 391).

> 1. Un hydrolat lacrymal lave
>   Les cieux vert-chou:
>   Sous l'arbre tendronnier qui bave,
>   Vos caoutchoucs

The chemical or technical terms bring a sassy modern note in the Corbière manner: a biting, acidly mocking, hard quality which can refresh art after too much softness and beauty. But that happens effectively only when part of a sustained effort; here Rimbaud is too nervous and merely illustrates the possibilities *en passant* (further illustrated in a corollary way through neo-primitivism or *déculture* in the famous passage of "Alchimie du verbe"). "Un hydrolat lacrymal" is a "tearlike chemical water" which makes a "cabbage-green sky" and reminds one of T. S. Eliot's (Corbière-influenced) evening "spread out against the sky / Like a patient etherised upon a table." The image is of rain. A mocking effect in the "la . . . la . . . la" is noted by Baudry.

The view of the girls appearing in their raincoats under the springtime tree is poignant, adolescently lyrical à la Laforgue and is similarly touched with bitterness, here excessive. It is like an inversion of the spring promenade scene in "Roman."

"Tendronnier" refers to the young trees in spring, as well as to the young girls. They are similarly paired in "Mémoire" (the willows and the faded green dresses of his sisters).

"Qui bave" is reminiscent of the tree's heart-oozings of "Oraison du soir" and the kindred adolescent "bave" of "Les Douaniers."

> 5. Blancs de lunes particulières
>   Aux pialats ronds,
> Entrechoquez vos genouillères,
>   Mes laiderons!

Lunes is argot for "behinds" (compare Cocteau's comment on the *coucher de lune romantique* as a "derrière qui disparaît"). The "ronds" remind Suzanne Bernard, therefore, of "culs en rond" ("Les Effarés"); compare the "sein rond" of the sixth strophe. This leads to the slapped-together thighs: "Clash your garters, my ugly-ones!"[1]

Baudelaire's similar image was more enticing:

> Tes nobles jambes, sous les volants qu'elles chassent,
> Tourmentent les désirs obscurs et les agacent,
>   Comme deux sorcières qui font
> Tourner un philtre noir dans un vase profond.

> 31. —Hop donc! soyez-moi ballerines
>   Pour un moment! . . .

He sends them in imagination into a grotesque dance—vaguely recalling the "Bal des Pendus"—that mocks their femininity: their "sheep-shoulders" become unhinged. "Une étoile" (later "Fade amas d'étoiles ratées") refers satirically to a ballet dancer, almost in a Degas spirit.

"Je voudrais vous casser les hanches / D'avoir aimé!" is more than bitter misogyny. It is frightening and sick.

---

[1] "Genouillères" is used in a comparably mocking context in "L'Homme juste."

41. Fade amas d'étoiles ratées,
    Comblez les coins!
    —Vous crèverez en Dieu, bâtées
    D'ignobles soins!

This is exactly the tone of the "Premières Communions." The women have been spoiled by Christianity and their ignoble acquiescence to the conventional Western life. So Rimbaud sends them into a metaphorical corner, as at a dance: "Aujourd'hui qu'elles sont si peu d'accord avec nous" ("L'Impossible").

Accroupissements

Here Rimbaud combines a scatological bent with satire. Whereas the librarians of "Les Assis" were merely seated, this butt, a banal bourgeois, is squatting (hence the title; note the *pisse* in it) over a pot for the usual purpose. The implication is similar: human inertia in a provincal town where no one is going anywhere by Rimbaud's standards. But the satire is not entirely aggressive; the excremental aspect is almost sympathetic, like the warm consolation of the bird-droppings to which he compared his dreams in "Oraison du soir."

Only a minimum of imagery merits detailed attention:

12. . . . grelottant au clair soleil qui plaque
    Des jaunes de brioche aux vitres de papier;

The time is morning (the poem ends at evening). Rimbaud describes sunlight in various remarkable ways: this one is typically concrete, the way a child perceives, orally: "Si j'ai du *goût*, ce n'est guères / Que pour la terre et les pierres" ("Fêtes de la faim").

23. Des escabeaux, crapauds étranges, . . .

Rimbaud refers to the old men as toads in "Les Assis" and refers to his toad-like laziness in the *Saison en Enfer*. This image is equally apt and contributes to the atmosphere of bourgeois stagnation.

24. . . . des buffets ont des gueules de chantres
    Qu'entr'ouvre un sommeil plein d'horribles appétits.

The generously maternal "buffet" ("Le Buffet") turns here from a cornucopia-womb to a frightening devouring mouth, like the death-depths Rimbaud feared in the maw of the established provincial religion which could swallow him as it did "Un Cœur sous une soutane." His mother, "la Bouche d'ombre," was part of this frightening pit in which he could sink and disappear.

32. . . . des bavures de lumière

One of the many uses of the "adolescent" *baver* discussed in "Les Douaniers."

The close of the satire is mock-poetic: squatting on his pot, again, the bourgeois seeks the evening star. He is like a hollyhock against a pink snowy background of crepuscular wall, combining floral lyricism with the excremental act in a way similar to the close of "Oraison du soir." The floral (vegetal) and the earthy (fertile or fecal) are often combined in Rimbaud in this way. The end of "Les Assis" is an example; the "campagne en rut" of "Les Premières Communions" is another.

Les Poètes de Sept Ans

This is one of the pivotal poems of the *œuvre* and of our tradition. Rimbaud, aged sixteen, turns back to his seventh year. Why? This, it is clear from the poem, was a crucial year in his early development. A new awareness came alive in him. Through a painful crisis, a revolt, a spiritual weaning, his ego precociously found its separate identity, or a major stage of its evolution. Obviously he did not yet have the courage to break totally with the home. This is that time when sad little boys run away and get as far as the corner, where they stand lingering for a terrible wistful moment; then, fear of the vast unknown sends them skulking back to a hateful, but fundamentally safe, hearth.

No doubt sent back to his origins by some current crisis, Rimbaud reconstructs in a crystallized, almost cubistic, simultaneity, the basic childhood drama, much as he does more subtly and complexly in "Mémoire," in an effort to puzzle through his problems and grow on. Both comforting and enlightening, the communion with the lost little boy that was is a wedding of present and past selves, in Proust-like memory.

We see the harshly dutiful Mother, smug and "proud" (as in "Mémoire") of her role, unaware of the revolt breeding in her sensitive and intelligent son. We see too his hopeless love for her—primarily in the sense that all children's loves for their parents are hopeless (Bergman portrays this superbly in the frustrated yet glorious final scene of *Wild Strawberries*). Hopeless too in the sense that his mother, stiffer and perhaps more obtuse than most, would never understand him; and the *mésentente* was compounded by the terrible loss that was the family breakdown, the deep special need for affection of this extraordinary soul (true, perhaps she could not afford to give him such love, but that is *hors jeu*).

So we see a very lonely child, seeking consolation in odd places as children do, hanging partly upside down from a banister—that odd posture seems to take one out of an impossible reality for a breather—lying in an out-of-the-way spot of the garden, etc.[1] These evasions bring him to "friendly" or at least inoffensive objects in nature which he is learning to observe and appreciate as reflectors of his own affections. He seeks to escape through inner visions by pressing his eyes, as we all did—anything for diversion! Then there are all sorts of daydreams, romantic adventures read in books, and finally the marvelous game which rehearses future total flight by boat (or dream-boat) and seems to anticipate the "Bateau ivre."

> 1. Et la Mère, fermant le livre du devoir,
>   S'en allait satisfaite et très fière, sans voir,
>   Dans les yeux bleus et sous le front plein d'éminences,
>   L'âme de son enfant livrée aux répugnances.

The poem begins with a biblical "Et"; this is a solemn epiphany of the past. The Mother is capitalized to bring out what Jung would call a Terrible Parent figure. Elsewhere, in the correspondence, he called her "la Bouche d'ombre," which renders well the mythical quality of black womb into which one could sink and lose one's identity. In "Accroupissements" we saw the association of the maternal buffet with the "gueules de chantres / Qu'entr'ouvre un sommeil plein d'horribles appétits." This dark sleep of church and mother was the provincial pit he, like James Joyce (who imitated Rimbaud's dress in Paris), had to run for his life from. Her characteristic act here is the religious one, closing the "book of duty," the Bible.[2]

The Mother is terrible in more than one way. She is a pit *and* she is a rod, or stiff as one, trying to make up, as women in this situation often do, for the absent father, and thus depriving her son of full female affection. (Since Arthur also lacked a father, he was doubly deprived.) But even when fathers are present, some bourgeois mothers, particularly late nineteenth-century French mothers, are overly rigid and arouse unneces-

---

[1] The paintings of Balthus perfectly catch this adolescent phenomenon.

[2] Suzanne Bernard has demonstrated that, since Arthur first went to school only at the age of eight, the book is not a school book, contrary to the supposition of certain commentators. Actually, in a Catholic family, it was apt to be a *Histoire sainte*, stories from the Bible with illustrations.

sary revolt in their children; Claude Debussy's mother, for example, was quite comparable in this respect.

The mother did not see the repugnance in the child's eyes; she was too proud and satisfied with herself, too smug, obtuse. The imperfect tense of the whole poem, like the shift in seasons below, indicates an experience lasting over a stretch of time. Rimbaud's eyes *were* blue, it is known (hers were too; see below). The "forehead full of protuberances" is curious, since Rimbaud's pictures don't reveal it. But Lacoste's conjecture, that Rimbaud implies a phrenological sign of future genius, is convincing.

> 5. Tout le jour il suait d'obéissance; très
> Intelligent; pourtant des tics noirs, quelques traits,
> Semblaient prouver en lui d'âcres hypocrisies.
> Dans l'ombre des couloirs aux tentures moisies,
> En passant il tirait la langue, les deux poings
> A l'aine, et dans ses yeux fermés voyait des points.

Rimbaud did "sweat with obedience" and later won all the prizes at school; "very intelligent" echoes, no doubt, a pat adult verdict. Until he had the strength, years, and courage for a full break, what could he do but obey? Children in such circumstances have the choice of constant punishment and disarray, or of knuckling down. This regime is internalized to some extent, accepted, even cherished at times. Rimbaud knew how to work and live with discipline, like many French children. And at times they all do what he did: hypocritically stick their tongues out behind adult backs. But perhaps Rimbaud more so, with a greater vengeance. This gesture, or gestures of evasion such as closing his eyes to see light-points, or vaguely sexual gestures of putting his fists in his groin, he considers to be "black tics" leading to his future outbursts of nastiness and revolt, pathological urges bordering on the criminal. He judges his hypocrisies to be "harsh."

> 11. Une porte s'ouvrait sur le soir: à la lampe
> On le voyait, là-haut, qui râlait sur la rampe,
> Sous un golfe de jour pendant du toit. L'été
> Surtout, vaincu, stupide, il était entêté
> A se renfermer dans la fraîcheur des latrines:
> Il pensait là, tranquille et livrant ses narines.

Any distracting event is welcome in this dark childhood atmosphere which Rimbaud is passing through as though through the "shadow of corridors with moldy wallpaper"; a door opening is a happy possibility of escape, lets air into a stifling domestic setting. But its opening onto evening indicates an ambivalence, an enveloping fear of oncoming night which keeps him back.

He hangs on the banisters in the awkward way children do. (Anything out of the way.) An upside-down world is thus created, different from the hated real one. One even *feels* different, as the blood rushes to the head.

Then the "gulf of light" intervenes from above; this vertical escape, unlike the horizontal one through a door, is more acceptable since it is merely symbolic, a "golden stairs" like the one De Quincey described in his *Confessions* (and Baudelaire after him), the essential sublimated dream-escape of fantasy in art. Such descents of the supernatural into the ordinary will be a hallmark of Rimbaud, as Rivière noted.

In summer, the heat closes him further in on himself and he stifles even more. He seeks the coolness, and the narcissistic comfort of bodily excretion, odors, in the WC. Richard Wilbur, in his "Potato," comparably speaks of "breaching strangely refreshing tombs" (Thanatos and feces or corruption are involved together, as usual).

> 17. Quand, lavé des odeurs du jour, le jardinet
> Derrière la maison, en hiver, s'illunait,
> Gisant au pied d'un mur, enterré dans la marne
> Et pour des visions écrasant son œil darne,
> Il écoutait grouiller les galeux espaliers.

The moonlit yard has a new light-harmony and a new smell: the day odors are "washed" by the evening (Proust's Marcel was moved by a similar phenomenon in his aunt's garden in Combray). The specification "en hiver" contrasts with the immediately preceding "L'été" indicating that this portrait encompasses several seasons in his seventh year. The winter, a strange sad time, as in the beginning lines describing the dreaming child in the "Bateau ivre" ("l'autre hiver") and at the end of "Les Déserts de l'amour," opens new poignant modes of escape through dream even as it blocks physical possibilities, like the drunken beat of wings of the swan trapped in ice. Thus the little Rimbaud lies ("enterré") in the soil, at the base of a wall, as if at a limit-situation, dreaming his way through the barrier which curiously abets the flight like the palisades around the vacant house in "Enfance." (Mallarmé liked to sit just outside the wall of a garden.) This out-of-the-way place is all his own. He can go no farther from the house and still belong to its security (the wall reappears in the "Bateau ivre"). Here, visions take over and carry him beyond the limiting horizon: he helps them along by pressing on his eyes, as children do. It is a very tentative process, not yet the triumphant severing of an umbilical tow-rope ("haleurs") as in the "Bateau ivre," though there are premonitions of this at the end of the poem. He is, still or again, held by the wall and reads and listens to its crawling leprous life for signs, meanings.

The flight is not only beyond the wall, upward and outward in fancy, but momentarily downward in a telluric communion with damp earth, the maternal element, as if the child was seeking to be buried ("enterré") in order to be reborn into a more meaningful existence. The damp soil by the wall is strangely fertile and potential in winter, preparing a renewal of the seasons and perhaps, subliminally, of the child himself. This dark chthonian tone is further developed in the final section: "Et comme il savourait surtout les sombres choses . . . humidité." Later he will speak of this "goût . . . pour la terre" ("Fêtes de la faim"). Rimbaud, as in "Mémoire," seeks in all directions for a way out. Do we not all? Try this way and then that: "A quelle force me dévouer?" (*Saison en Enfer*).

> 22. Pitié! Ces enfants seuls étaient ses familiers
> Qui, chétifs, fronts nus, œil déteignant sur la joue,
> Cachant de maigres doigts jaunes et noirs de boue
> Sous des habits puant la foire et tout vieillots,
> Conversaient avec la douceur des idiots!
> Et si, l'ayant surpris à des pitiés immondes,
> Sa mère s'effrayait; les tendresses, profondes,
> De l'enfant se jetaient sur cet étonnement.
> C'était bon. Elle avait le bleu regard,—qui ment!

"Pitié!" This refers ambiguously to the lamentable picture of the poor neighbor children, to Rimbaud's sympathy for them, to his mother's horrified misunderstanding of her child's contact with them, their "filthy pities." But mostly it is a total cry of distress as in the repeated use at the end—"déroutes et pitié!"—and numerous such cries in Rimbaud ("Vrai . . . j'ai pleuré plus que tous les enfants du monde," "Les Déserts de l'amour.")

The poor children of the *quartier* provided objective correlatives for his inner misery, as in "Les Pauvres à l'église." They are, beyond populism, perfectly caught, as they are. How childhood returns through that "conversed with the sweetness of idiots"! (One thinks in passing of Faulkner's Benjy.)

"Pitiés immondes" is vague but expresses, no doubt, the mother's horror at some contact, probably bodily, of Rimbaud with the unwashed poor. Such a contact, with the specific flavor of childhood sexuality ("playing doctor"), is described in detail a few lines on. The mother was shocked, and the child's profound need threw itself on that astonished look as if a sincere passage were suddenly opened to her heart. Then comes an expression of momentary contentment—"C'était bon"—followed by the bitter disappointment of seeing something black and hateful in the eyes of his mother: her "blue look" lied. Another interpretation is possible here; my reasons for preferring the foregoing one are too complex to discuss in the main body of commentary. Hence I have relegated them, somewhat reluctantly, to a very long footnote since the evidence is largely new and, I think, compelling.[3]

[3] The "c'était bon" has been construed by some as meaning "OK" (as in the familiar expression: "c'est bon")—but this is most unusual and quite unlikely in the imperfect, the tense of description. In "Les Pauvres à l'église" Rimbaud uses "c'est bien bon" and "c'est bon" to mean simply "it is good." In "Les Premières Communions" "c'est bon pour vous, / Hommes" means "it's all right for you, men." But the form is very different from that of our text (present tense and the *pour*).

Similarly, "She would get the blue look—which lies" would mean she got only Rimbaud's lying *appearances* of love. But that is at variance with the sudden outburst of affection and with the imperfect of description, *avait*. "[On] a eu" (*passé composé*) is the formula for "got," and this expression is never used in the imperfect.

The likelier interpretation, as Suzanne Bernard and most commentators agree, is "It was good"—that moment of love. We have seen how often Rimbaud, like Hemingway, uses this round term; and the mother's eyes were in fact blue, and had their familiar "blue look—which lies!" For that was the profound disappointment, the barrier of bourgeois hypocrisy, which separated him from true communion with her. In "Les Sœurs de charité" the wounded boy looks into a woman's eyes for deep answers and comfort, but "Tout notre embrassement n'est qu'une question." Indeed "la femme . . . l'épouvante" (this is partly incest fear as in "Les Déserts de l'amour"). Thus it is probable that when Rimbaud cries out "j'écartai du ciel l'azur, qui est du noir, et je vécus, étincelle d'or de la lumière *nature*" (*Saison en Enfer*, Bernard, p. 232), he is exorcising this blackly hateful element in his mother's eyes. Again in "Fêtes de la faim" his deep spiritual hunger is described: "Mes faims, c'est les bouts d'air noir; / L'azur sonneur." The blue azure, which as in Mallarmé was a milky source of filial joy (compare "Don du poème") —and Suzanne Bernard has surmised that Rimbaud owed to Mallarmé this *azur sonneur* (from "Le Sonneur")—was thus again contaminated by the black hunger of separation, alienation. Hence the turning to the male light (as *fils du Soleil*), the "golden spark" of the "Alchimie du verbe," like the filial angels of light in "Mémoire."

The "azur noir" of "Ce qu'on dit au poète à propos de fleurs" confirms all this fully. It is the sky of the Parnassian poets contaminated by sentimentality (and Rimbaud's scorn). It is also the sky of sentimental religion blackened by Rimbaud's disgust: "le bleu dégoût . . . des Proses religieuses." Suzanne Bernard writes: "L'adjectif *bleu* donne . . . une nuance chrétienne" (p. 417).

Rimbaud liked ambiguities (compare the many levels of "Mémoire")—the lying blue look belonged to both his mother and himself—and it may be that both interpretations are true: but one is primary, I believe, and more deeply poetic.

31. A sept ans, il faisait des romans, sur la vie
    Du grand désert, où luit la Liberté ravie,
    Forêts, soleils, rives, savanes!—Il s'aidait
    De journaux illustrés où, rouge, il regardait
    Des Espagnoles rire et des Italiennes.
    Quand venait, l'œil brun, folle, en robes d'indiennes,
    —Huit ans,—la fille des ouvriers d'à côté,
    La petite brutale, et qu'elle avait sauté,
    Dans un coin, sur son dos, en secouant ses tresses,
    Et qu'il était sous elle, il lui mordait les fesses,
    Car elle ne portait jamais de pantalons;
    —Et, par elle meurtri des poings et des talons,
    Remportait les saveurs de sa peau dans sa chambre.

Like little J.-P. Sartre (*Les Mots*), Rimbaud made novels of adventures, avenues of escape and self-aggrandizement, small-fry dreams of glory. In the vast open spaces (of America, à la Chateaubriand?) he would find lost Liberty. There would be forests, suns (a symbol of male independence for Rimbaud, compare "Mémoire"), the "banks" of rivers which also represent in their dynamic aspect a male going-somewhere, or maybe seashores which represent an exotic getting-somewhere. Savannahs are as distant, open, free as the desert.

There is a modulation of images from the warm southern women (totally unlike his mother)—"Espagnoles, Italiennes"—gleaned from books to the direct sexual experimentation with the little neighbor girl. Probably no more charming or accurate taking-us-back exists in literature. We are there. The taste of salty childhood flesh is there, the lively little girl springing from earth despite all that maternal and churchly horror can do; the stimulating tussles (as in Proust's *Champs Elysées*), the savory guerdon. In the precociously available naked "fesses," Rimbaud tastes a joy with more than a touch of infantile cannibalism, and communes through oral possession. His deprivation knew the consolation of eating dirt, communing with the source in the most direct way, as he proclaims his "goût . . . pour la terre" in "Fêtes de la faim."

44. Il craignait les blafards dimanches de décembre,
    Où, pommadé, sur un guéridon d'acajou,
    Il lisait une Bible à la tranche vert-chou;
    Des rêves l'oppressaient chaque nuit dans l'alcôve.
    Il n'aimait pas Dieu; mais les hommes, qu'au soir fauve,
    Noirs, en blouse, il voyait rentrer dans le faubourg
    Où les crieurs, en trois roulements de tambour,

Font autour des édits rire et gronder les foules.
—Il rêvait la prairie amoureuse, où des houles
Lumineuses, parfums sains, pubescences d'or,
Font leur remuement calme et prennent leur essor!

All children hate "dreary" Sundays (as Charles Trenet sentimentally reminds us): the day of official piety, the stiff routine promenade, musty old people, dullness. In December the death of nature makes it all drearier, and he recalls with horror the sitting like a fixture in his Sunday-best, miserably slicked up (like Huck Finn) on a bourgeois mahogany "guéri-don," reading the Bible. The "cabbage-green" is scarcely a compliment, even though the skies of "Mes petites amoureuses" are that color. Cabbages are eaten by the silly hero of "Un Cœur sous une soutane."

The dreams that oppress him are born no doubt of bad conscience because of his inner revolt, developed in the next lines. He found he really did not love God, that abstract image contaminated by association with the bourgeois and societal prison. The workers are real and part of the stir and bustle of the weekdays which led away from the home; they are awe-inspiring to boy-children, as we have seen in "Le Forgeron," and certainly to boy-children who lack fathers. "Bonne pensée du matin" and "Ouvriers" will bring out this truth even further, as well as certain passages of the *Saison en Enfer*.

The workers are "noirs," partly because of shadowy evening, partly perhaps because they return dirty from work. The father in the juvenile prose-sketch entitled "Prologue" has "chevelure noire, barbe, yeux, peau de même couleur." Blackness can be an uncompromising "color," an aspect of a tough male ideal.

The town crier offers more stir, crowds, promise of escape.

The "prairie" is like the other open spaces but with an added nuance, as in "Sensation," of sexualized nature: "pubescences." It is the feminine undulation of fields of wheat that mingle, as in other fantasies (compare "L'Eternité"), with a male element, the light. The doubleness is made evident in the pairing of their calm motion and their flight, as in "Génie": the "stations" and the "lieux fuyants" come together in a higher meta-psychological synthesis.

55. Et comme il savourait surtout les sombres choses,
    Quand, dans la chambre nue aux persiennes closes,
    Haute et bleue, âcrement prise d'humidité,
    Il lisait son roman sans cesse médité,
    Plein de lourds ciels ocreux et de forêts noyées,
    De fleurs de chair aux bois sidérals déployées,

Vertige, écroulements, déroutes et pitié!
—Tandis que se faisait la rumeur du quartier,
En bas,—seul, et couché sur des pièces de toile
Écrue, et pressentant violemment la voile!

We have commented upon the maternal dark and damp of the room (like strangely fertile winter—damp soil preparing the rebirth of the year [perhaps a child?]—outside near the fence).

In this room, rather like little Marcel's private place of "sin" and evasion at the top of the house in Combray,[4] Rimbaud mulls over "his" novel, either read or personally invented. Here are ochre-colored skies, heavy with apocalyptic portent like Hérodiade's. Drowned forests represent a pleasing communion or wedding of the different parts of nature, as in "Après le déluge." The flesh-flowers—like the "fleur de chair" of "Soleil et chair"—are a similar coming together of man and nature, repeated in the watchful flowers of "Aube." Sidereal woods further this promiscuity (compare the mingling of sea and sky in the "Bateau ivre"), bringing the sky intimately close, as in "Ma Bohème" and "Mystique."

"Vertige, écroulements, déroutes et pitié!" is a kind of orgiastic climax of the various couplings all balled together in an apocalyptic moment like "Après le déluge" (or Mallarmé's sundown: "Sang par écume, tison, gloire," or Victor Hugo's "avalanches d'or"). But Rimbaud's climax is more fearful; as at the close of the "Bateau ivre" or of his young career's curve, the very excess of his revolt has led to a hint of repentance, retreat, passivity, self-pity. The "déroutes" are partly his disaster, the "pitié" is like that which we feel for the sad and lonely little boy squatting by the crepuscular pond in the "Bateau ivre." But Rimbaud's most exquisite poetry comes from just such defeats, as all true lyric poetry does (see Sartre's parallel view in *Qu'est-ce que la littérature?*). He is going nowhere.

So to him now in his upstairs prison comes "Such a vision of the street as the street hardly knows" (T. S. Eliot): "Tandis que se faisait la rumeur du quartier, / En bas." The "rumeur" is absolutely Rimbaldian in this respect: motion arrested, multiplicity harmonized in an impressionistic vibrancy of the pure epiphany, the far-away filtered into its spiritual essence of presence. Such are the "rumeurs" of the distant city in "Départ," or the "bruissements" of inaccessible trees beyond the fence in "Enfance."

J.-P. Richard, who sees these moments as *merely* paralysis, is missing the main point of Rimbaud (his Rimbaud is far too dynamic for good poetry). The final image is comparably vibrant—presence-absence of a sailboat,

---

[4] Proust, too, was fascinated by damp smells, for example that of his uncle Adolphe's room or that of the public WC in the Champs Elysées.

summed up in a piece of unbleached linen cloth lying on the attic floor with the lad on top of it dreaming furiously of escape.

"Violemment la voile" is a pleasing harmony of letter-sequences, and brings out the erotic undertone woven into "voile" (*viole*), in a way comparable to the outburst "que j'aille à la mer" of the "Bateau ivre."

In "Les Déserts de l'amour" an association between the "toiles de navire" and the maternal "Elle"—"Je la renversai dans une corbeille de coussins et de toiles de navire, en un coin noir"—indicates that he carried a memory of his mother into the attic and his imaginary quest. The "Poème / De la Mer" of the "Bateau ivre" bears this out.

Les Pauvres à l'Église

Almost in the populist manner which would be developed by twentieth-century writers like Eugène Dabit and Francis Carco, this poem is really closer to the people than that. Although Rimbaud was not *peuple* himself (rather *petite bourgeoisie*), his spiritual misery and French-youthful humility together put him well in range of their feelings.[1] But in a complex way: the direct earthy sensuality—good sordidness—combines with intellect to produce a refined imaginative synthesis. The ambivalent sensuality of "good sordidness" reminds me of Baudelaire's *Spleen* (LXXV): "un jeu plein de sales parfums" or the "Paris . . . vieillard laborieux" of "Le Crépuscule du Matin," or "Le Vin des chiffonniers." Baudelaire, the "vrai Dieu," was certainly the masterly predecessor of Rimbaud here. The solid ground-bass of feeling is made up of simple chunks of heavy reality, for example, the "soupe" of "ces mangeuses de soupe" (l. 13).

Rimbaud's usual communion through eating combines here with something almost fleshly, cannibalistic. "Leurs seins crasseux dehors," he savors the women almost like meat in soup. We remember that Rimbaud tasted the little working-class girl who lived next door in a very direct way: "Il lui mordait les fesses, / Car elle ne portait jamais de pantalons; . . . Remportait les saveurs de sa peau dans sa chambre." This is healthy, however dirt-flavored, sensuality. By contrast, the "Dames des quartiers / Distingués" seem decadent, liver-sick, pale, yellow. In this poem, then, Rimbaud is looking frankly in the downward direction for Antaean strength, a *vis a fundo*. At the same time he is showing us how to dredge extreme ambivalent delight from the dark sunless interior of a provincial church in bitter winter, in "nefs où périt le soleil."

---

[1] For slightly different reasons, the Camus of *L'Envers et l'endroit* and *Noces* briefly enjoyed a similar position (he almost got it back in "Les Muets"; *L'Exil et le royaume*).

1. Parqués entre des bancs de chêne, aux coins d'église
   Qu'attiédit puamment leur souffle, tous leurs yeux
   Vers le chœur ruisselant d'orrie et la maîtrise
   Aux vingt gueules gueulant les cantiques pieux;

In "Parqués" there is the hint of an animal *parc*; the women are like "chiens battus" (see below).

The choir-loft dripping with tasteless gilt is their idea of class, like the awful doves and angels sculpted on tombstones described by Camus in *Noces*; both writers see, and accept, the people as they are.

5. Comme un parfum de pain humant l'odeur de cire,
   Heureux, humiliés comme des chiens battus,
   Les Pauvres au bon Dieu, le patron et le sire,
   Tendent leurs oremus risibles et têtus.

They are happy with the smell of wax from votive candles mingled with the manna of hymns, as if with the perfume of bread (there is an overtone of the host-wafers, bread and wine, perhaps also incense), reminding us of the similarly humble orphans of "Les Effarés" inhaling the bread odors emanating from the oven of the almost priest-like Baker.

"Les Pauvres au bon Dieu" seems to be a mixture of sincere respect for the blessed meek (as in "Le Mal")—since "Dieu les fait souffrir" (l. 10)—and irony. These attitudes can cohabit in a sophisticated mind or merely in a humanly inconsistent one. It is hard to know which or how much of each of these two Rimbaud represents at this stage. But surely new evidence of adolescent anti-religious revolt is implicit in the "souffrir."

13. Leurs seins crasseux dehors, ces mangeuses de soupe,
    Une prière aux yeux et ne priant jamais,
    Regardent parader mauvaisement un groupe
    De gamines avec leurs chapeaux déformés.

"Une prière aux yeux et ne priant jamais" bears out the *authenticity* of these poor women who need no official cult to be holy. By contrast, the children and frivolous *gamines* are spiritually sterile like the "Dames des quartiers / Distingués."

17. Dehors, le froid, la faim, l'homme en ribote:
    C'est bon. Encore une heure; après, les maux sans noms!

The stark contrast of cold, hunger, irresponsible husband gives a cozy savor to the simple well-being of warmth and music and human and spiritual presence inside. "C'est bon" is that pleasure and perhaps also, ambiguously, an "all right" referring resignedly to the sordid facts of life outside.

> 21. Ces effarés y sont et ces épileptiques

The grotesque parishioners—the frightened, the epileptic, the blind, the old—drool out their stupid faith. Rimbaud is on the side of the little people but obviously not of their religion.

> 27. Qui rêve en haut, jauni par le vitrail livide,

Jesus is "yellowed by the livid stained glass window"; that is to say, it is winter outside and no light vivifies the *vitrail*.

> 29. Loin des senteurs de viande et d'étoffes moisies,
> Farce prostrée et sombre aux gestes repoussants;
> —Et l'oraison fleurit d'expressions choisies,
> Et les mysticités prennent des tons pressants,

Rimbaud is fascinated by the contrast between the sublimity of the Jesus figure up there "far from the smells of wet and mildewed clothes" and the abjectness of the congregation which in its silly religiosity is a "prostrate and somber farce with repulsive gestures." The remoteness of Jesus is paralleled by the highflown ceremony with "select expressions" and *mysticités*, adding to the "farce"; the peak of derision is reached in the next strophe.

> 33. Quand, des nefs où périt le soleil, plis de soie
> Banals, sourires verts, les Dames des quartiers
> Distingués,—ô Jésus!—les malades du foie
> Font baiser leurs longs doigts jaunes aux bénitiers.

The height of absurdity is a Christian church, preaching the blessedness of humility, where the rich swagger, backed by the religious establishment itself. The jaundiced pallor of the ladies symbolizes decadence, contrasted with the *natural* strength of the poor.

The "nefs où périt le soleil" give, again, an effect of winter, of light extinguished in a ruined establishment; compare the last strophe of "Mémoire."

Le Cœur volé

An obscure poem, the best guess is that it refers to a moment of profound sexual humiliation at the hands of soldiers ("pioupious" = infantrymen). The whole shadowy event is akin to T. E. Lawrence's similar homosexual ordeal in Turkey with quite comparable results: his life was radically changed. The "stolen heart" refers no doubt to the brutal removal of his childhood belief in simple human goodness.[1] But the Rimbaud of the poems after "Le Cœur volé" is not really a cynic, as we shall soon see.

Whether Rimbaud's humiliation occurred, as some think, while on a flight to Paris during the Commune, or not, is of secondary importance. There were soldiers all around Charleville and Mézières, as well as in Paris; the incident may have occurred near to home. The poem is interesting fundamentally because it is curious and Rimbaud's and, secondarily, for the possible anecdote behind it. Basically it is a deliberate adolescent mystification, using "big" words, melodramatic play-acting, and secret formulas (almost like the pig Latin used by James Joyce and his friends in *Stephen Hero*) to hide as well as confess. He needs to make a clean breast of something, but he is afraid too of what people (or himself) might think. The familiar *baver* is very much in this adolescent vein (Steinbeck refers to the "drool and acne" of that age): the exudation compounded of desire and frustration, of outpouring and sexual shame together.

Sensitive youths (Gide's Armand is a good example) try to hide their feelings behind the mask of the ridiculous.[2] The protective self-mockery is clear in the alternate title: "Le Cœur du pitre."[3] The other side, the tragic, is in the first version of the title, "Le Cœur supplicié," as well as the final one.

The reason for the sea-setting is as obscure as the rest. Rimbaud dreamed of a sea voyage on the famous little boat attached to the bank of the Meuse. Perhaps it was there that he went to "drool" or vomit out his rage and sorrow. At any rate sea-sickness and soul-sickness combined are the key theme. The boat-on-the-dream-sea as the voyage of psychic life (including

---

[1] The "sans cœur" of a letter to Izambard was in quotes, i.e., people thought of him that way but he was not, in his own mind.

[2] Compare the "convulsion vulgaire" of Valéry's *Mon Faust*. The self-chosen negative image of derisiveness thus homeopathically deals with the pain of one's own negative judgment of self (or that of others), anticipates it or confronts it and so controls it or cancels it out. At times, too, a more violent outburst of humor expresses the convulsive solution of colliding crude psychic forces at this celibate age. Such is the *fou rire* (often brought on by the corollary *canular*, of which Rabelais's Panurge was an archetypal practitioner).

[3] This reminds us of Mallarmé's similarly self-deprecatory "Le Pitre châtié."

sick moments) is the core of the "Bateau ivre," just over the horizon, and it was previously prepared by the end of the "Poètes de sept ans," so that there is a thread binding these three poems. Thus it is possible that the shocking events dimly described here were the turning point in Rimbaud's career, after which he developed—as some have surmised—a more hermetic and anarchic manner, to hide his feelings and change a hateful world. We may further suppose that the development of the triumphant voyage in the "Bateau ivre" (which includes an episode of nausea, and a "gouvernail" vaguely echoing the rudder here) represents at least a momentary victory of independence wrung from the deep spiritual distress recounted here.

First strophe:
> Mon triste cœur bave à la poupe,
> Mon cœur couvert de caporal :
> Ils y lancent des jets de soupe,
> Mon triste cœur bave à la poupe :
> Sous les quolibets de la troupe
> Qui pousse un rire général,
> Mon triste cœur bave à la poupe,
> Mon cœur couvert de caporal !

The "poupe," the stern, is a place of dejection (compare Mallarmé's "moi déjà à la poupe," i.e., old age, "Salut"). The poet's heart is covered with "caporal," a cheap tobacco used by soldiers. The "jets de soupe" is uncertain, possibly sexual because of the "Ithyphalliques et pioupiesques" below. The "troop" gibes at him and gives off a "general laugh," which sounds pretty much like a scene of victimization by a group of men, a male horde like the rough bunch of "Parade."

Second strophe:
> Ithyphalliques et pioupiesques
> Leurs quolibets l'ont dépravé !
> Au gouvernail on voit des fresques
> Ithyphalliques et pioupiesques.
> O flots abracadabrantesques,
> Prenez mon cœur, qu'il soit lavé !
> Ithyphalliques et pioupiesques
> Leurs quolibets l'ont dépravé !

"Au gouvernail on voit des fresques / Ithyphalliques et pioupiesques" has a variant "A la vesprée, ils font des fresques, etc." One sees sexually prepared males silhouetted. But, again, why "at the rudder"? No good answer has been found. The "flots abracadabrantesques" are equally puzzling:

we are told that Rimbaud had a paper marker with the magic triangle "abracadabra" printed on it, and he wrote on the paper "pour préserver de la fièvre" (Bernard, p. 399). Thus there may be a connection with the idea of purification, but obviously not important or clear. Maybe the triangular form has to do with the shape of waves, but again that is unsure. More certainly, it is a "big" adolescent secret-formula term, in line with the other pretentiously feeling-concealing words in the poem. "Prenez mon cœur, qu'il soit lavé!" referring to the waves, is comparable to a passage in the "Bateau ivre": "L'eau verte . . . me lava"; and to "la mer, que j'aimais comme si elle eût dû me laver d'une souillure" ("Alchimie du verbe").

Third strophe:
> Quand ils auront tari leurs chiques,
> Comment agir, ô cœur volé?
> Ce seront des hoquets bachiques
> Quand ils auront tari leurs chiques:
> J'aurai des sursauts stomachiques,
> Moi, si mon cœur est ravalé:
> Quand ils auront tari leurs chiques
> Comment agir, ô cœur volé?

The chewing tobacco, the Bacchic hiccoughs, the stomach revulsions as after a debauch, all point to the same probable experience of a military drinking-and-sex orgy of the sort Sartre describes in *La Mort dans l'âme*.

Rimbaud felt degraded ("cœur . . . ravalé") to his core: he had accused the monarchist aristocracy of doing just that to the people in "Le Forgeron": "Vous leur avez sali leur âme" (variant to line 130: "Vous [leur] avez craché sur l'âme").

L'Orgie parisienne ou Paris se repeuple

In this vehement satire, Rimbaud decries the *putain* Paris for accepting the Versaillais swarming back after the Commune.[1] The city is a woman, like nature or life itself, an all-too-accommodating one, or so it seemed to Rimbaud in his frustration after the bitter political debacle, which no doubt echoed in him all his own defeats. But he admires this creature for her awesome power and indifference. He still wants to be on her side, appeal to her. He calls on the city to throw off these false sons and lovers, and at one point confidently proclaims: "Elle se secouera de vous, hargneux

---

[1] Marcel Ruff insists that the poem refers to the return of the bourgeois who had fled the city after the Prussian attack on it and before the Commune. But it is hard to believe that Rimbaud could work up this much spleen over such a minor event.

pourris!" At the end the "Poet" castigates her, vengefully, yet hoping she will heed him. Unlike certain lines of *Une Saison en Enfer*, this is not yet an outcry of pure misogyny.

> 4. Voilà la Cité sainte, assise à l'occident!

This is in opposition to the *oriental* Jerusalem; he will invoke a vision suggesting the latter at the end of *Une Saison en Enfer*.

> 9. Cachez les palais morts dans des niches de planches!

They were emptied by the exodus during the Commune. Rimbaud is haunted by empty houses, like the general's in "Enfance," the silent palaces in "Aube."

> 10. L'ancien jour effaré rafraîchit vos regards.

The Versaillais enjoyed seeing daylight "frightened" by bombs' glare, killing workers.

> 11. Voici le troupeau roux des tordeuses de hanches:

Red-haired prostitutes represent, no doubt, the unfaithful city, "la putain Paris" (l. 38), like the scarlet woman of Babylon. Later Rimbaud will associate this reddish color with woman's sexuality in the "Bateau ivre." "La Reine aux fesses cascadantes" (l. 21) is another image of the harlot-city.

These prostitutes are called to the gambling houses.

> 14. Le cri des maisons d'or vous réclame. Volez!
> Mangez! Voici la nuit de joie aux profonds spasmes
> Qui descend dans la rue. O buveurs désolés,
>
> Buvez! Quand la lumière arrive intense et folle,

The image of decadent revellers followed by innocent light ("Quand la lumière arrive intense et folle / Fouillant à vos côtés les luxes ruisselants"—i.e., streaming in their wine glasses) is like that of "Bonne pensée du matin":

> A quatre heures du matin, l'été
> . . .
> Sous les bosquets l'aube évapore
> L'odeur du soir fêté.

In a famous letter to Izambard, Rimbaud described this favorite time of day for him (see under "Aube"). The morning innocence is like that of the workers (the carpenters in "Bonne pensée du matin," or the "Forgeron"). Morning represents a "revolution," in a sense, of radical new light from past darkness.

This section describing Parisian debauchery is reminiscent of Baudelaire's *Crépuscule* poems. Rimbaud sees the drunks at daybreak, drooling in their glasses with haggard eyes lost in the distances (l. 19-20). The "hoquets" of drinking (l. 22) recall the "Cœur volé" and Rimbaud's revolt against such degradation.

Ninth and tenth strophes:
>   Parce que vous fouillez le ventre de la Femme,
>   Vous craignez d'elle encore une convulsion
>   Qui crie, asphyxiant votre nichée infâme
>   Sur sa poitrine, en une horrible pression.
>
>   Syphilitiques, fous, rois, pantins, ventriloques,
>   Qu'est-ce que ça peut faire à la putain Paris,
>   Vos âmes et vos corps, vos poisons et vos loques?
>   Elle se secouera de vous, hargneux pourris!

The image is of a rape followed by a convulsive revolt on the part of the violated City. In the tenth strophe the poet says that the "putain Paris" will throw off the "rotten" ones.

In the following three strophes the City, "red courtesan, heavy-breasted with battles" is seen as aroused to a new era ("retenant dans tes prunelles claires / Un peu de la bonté du fauve renouveau"—a wild spring renaissance) as in Delacroix's familiar painting of the giantess Liberty leading the people: "La tête et les deux seins jetés vers l'Avenir." This image of rebirth is borne out in the reference to her "Corps remagnétisé" (l. 53) and "ton souffle de Progrès" (l. 58).

>   57.   . . . Les vers, les vers livides
>   Ne gêneront pas plus ton souffle de Progrès
>   Que les Stryx n'éteignaient l'œil des Cariatides
>   Où des pleurs d'or astral tombaient des bleus degrés.

"The [bourgeois] worms will no more stop the breath of your [Paris'] Progress than the Stryx [nocturnal vampires] could put out the eyes of Caryatides where golden astral tears fell from the blue steps [of heaven]." This is the failure of night and death to extinguish classic beauty in Greece, where innocent light fell from heaven, as described above ("la lumière intense et folle"). "Or astral" is simply sunlight, contrary to

Gengoux's occultist explanation ("le silence astral" of "Fairy" refers to other stars).

Sixteenth and seventeenth strophes:
> Quoique ce soit affreux de te revoir couverte
> Ainsi; quoiqu'on n'ait fait jamais d'une cité
> Ulcère plus puant à la Nature verte,
> Le Poète te dit: "Splendide est ta Beauté!"

> L'orage t'a sacrée suprême poésie;
> L'immense remuement des forces te secourt;
> Ton œuvre bout, la mort gronde, Cité choisie!
> Amasse les strideurs au cœur du clairon sourd.

Paris can be rehabilitated; indeed, she is tragically beautiful, emerging from the "storm" of conflict as "supreme poetry" (compare the refreshing floods of "Après le déluge" or the "paradis des orages" of "Villes," I, and the "clair déluge" of "Michel et Christine").

The poet tells the "chosen City": "Amasse les strideurs au cœur du clairon sourd." That is to say, "Summon up the call to a revolutionary Last Judgment." This image is echoed in "Voyelles": "suprême Clairon plein des strideurs étranges."

The poet takes up the cause of the little people, the oppressed: the *Infâmes* (as in "Les Pauvres à l'église"), the *Forçats* (as in the *Saison en Enfer*), the *Maudits* (as in "L'Homme juste"). He also undoubtedly wants to espouse the cause of woman, as in the "Lettre du Voyant" (and after Michelet). But here she has been called unfaithful, running to the rich, so the Poet's "rayons d'amour flagelleront les Femmes" (l. 71). These love-rays are similar to the violent and awakening flashes the sun will be called upon to emit in "Alchimie du verbe."

Hackett has finely observed the "muscular" quality of Rimbaud's ex-postulations: "Ses strophes bondiront: Voilà! voilà! bandits!" This has something to do with the dramatic rise from dark nasal *on* to bright *i* (and *an* to *i*), as well as the petulant b's.

Les Mains de Jeanne-Marie

A hymn to the worker women—"Jeanne-Marie" is a fittingly solid *prénom populaire*—who participated in the Commune uprising. It has been convincingly demonstrated that here Rimbaud is parodying poems addressed to female hands by Gautier and Mérat, in much the same spirit as is evidenced in his pastiche of sentimental flower-poems ("Ce qu'on dit au poète à propos de fleurs").

Baudelaire's "L'Idéal" is just as likely a source:

> Ce ne seront jamais ces beautés de vignettes,
> Produits avariés, nés d'un siècle vaurien,
> Ces pieds à brodequins, ces doigts à castagnettes,
> Qui sauront satisfaire un cœur comme le mien.

> 1. Jeanne-Marie a des mains fortes,
>   Mains sombres que l'été tanna,
>   Mains pâles comme des mains mortes.
>   —Sont-ce des mains de Juana?

Exposed to work and nature, she has strong hands, darkened by the sun—like Rimbaud's idealized father in his first prose ("chevelure noire . . . peau de même couleur"), or the returning hero in the *Saison en Enfer*, or the young man with "la peau brune" in "Les Sœurs de charité." But she also has "hands pale as death," alluding to her deadly revolutionary task:

> Elles ont pâli, merveilleuses,
> Au grand soleil d'amour chargé,
> Sur le bronze des mitrailleuses
> A travers Paris insurgé!

They are pale with the tension of grimly holding machine-guns or other weapons. Like the fingers of the "chercheuses de poux" they are "terribles et charmeurs."

"Sont-ce des mains de Juana?" is probably an allusion to the pretty hands of a girl by that name from a poem of Musset (whom Rimbaud detested; see Bernard, p. 402).

> 5. Ont-elles pris les crèmes brunes
>   Sur les mares des voluptés?

The "crèmes brunes sur les mares des voluptés" recalls the lines from "Comédie de la soif" where Rimbaud evokes the hours of drunkenness from absinthe:

> Qu'est l'ivresse, Amis?

> J'aime autant, mieux, même,
> Pourrir dans l'étang,
> Sous l'affreuse crème,
> Près des bois flottants.

Hangover is associated with scum on a pond, and there may be some vaguely sexual overtones (see under "Comédie de la soif"). Rimbaud's image here of cream taken from a pond (*mare*) of voluptuous delight has a general aura of decadence related to drinking or sex, but it can also refer to creamy desserts: *gourmandise*. In sum, decadent luxury of the sort described in "Paris se repeuple."

> 7. Ont-elles trempé dans des lunes
> Aux étangs de sérénité?

This might be a reference to Verlaine's sentimental marriage mood in *La Bonne chanson*, specifically "La Lune blanche": "La *lune* blanche . . . L'*étang* reflète, / Profond miroir, / La silhouette / Du saule noir . . . Un vaste et tendre / *Apaisement* [cf. sérénité]." Jeanne-Marie is the opposite kind of woman. Verlaine specifically refers to his wife's hands in "Sagesse," no. XX of *La Bonne chanson*: "vos chères mains furent mes guides."

> 9. Ont-elles bu des cieux barbares,
> Calmes sur les genoux charmants?
> Ont-elles roulé des cigares
> Ou trafiqué des diamants?

"Roulé des cigares"—Madame Bovary did that for Rodolphe. Maybe Carmen is in the picture, as Suzanne Bernard says.

> 13. Sur les pieds ardents des Madones
> Ont-elles fané des fleurs d'or?
> C'est le sang noir des belladones
> Qui dans leur paume éclate et dort.

An atheist, she has not placed religious flowers at a Madonna's feet. Her flowers are fiercely poisonous ones, "belladones" (compare "Fêtes de la faim": "le gai venin / Des liserons"). Black blood is a union of opposites, life and death, in an essence of vehemence, life at a deadly pitch of tension. This vital and urgent imagery re-emerges in "Being beauteous" together with the "éclate" and the flesh: "des blessures écarlates et noires éclatent dans les chairs superbes."

> 21. Oh! quel Rêve les a saisies
> Dans les pandiculations?
> Un rêve inouï des Asies,
> Des Khenghavars ou des Sions?

The Dream of these hands is not for Oriental or Jewish ("Sions") gestures ("pandiculations"); it is for a Dream unheard of in the "Asias." In the next strophe this idea is repeated: "These hands have not darkened on the feet of gods"; compare the "Sur les pieds ardents des Madones" above.

> 25. —Ces mains n'ont pas vendu d'oranges,
>   Ni bruni sur les pieds des dieux:
>   Ces mains n'ont pas lavé les langes
>   Des lourds petits enfants sans yeux.

This strophe is preceded by a dash which seems to connect it with the preceding one; unlike Oriental women's hands, Jeanne-Marie's have not sold oranges, darkened over gods' feet, washed swaddling clothes of sightless infants (affected with trachoma—Bernard, p. 402).

> 29. Ce ne sont pas mains de cousine
>   Ni d'ouvrières aux gros fronts
>   Que brûle, aux bois puant l'usine,
>   Un soleil ivre de goudrons.

They are not the hands of a docile "cousin," nor of a stupid worker (member of the *Lumpenproletariat*) with vast forehead (like the medieval boor), burned by the sun in woods contaminated by a factory—a sun which beats on industrial tar.

> 33. Ce sont des ployeuses d'échines,
>   Des mains qui ne font jamais mal,
>   Plus fatales que des machines,
>   Plus fortes que tout un cheval!

They are strong hands, capable as a peasant girl's, which bend backbones (see below: "Tourne le crâne des brebis"). They are irresistible as fate, as machines, compare "Génie": "machine aimée des qualités fatales." So efficient are they, no pain is felt: "Des mains qui ne font jamais mal."

> 41. Ça serrerait vos cous, ô femmes
>   Mauvaises, ça broierait vos mains,
>   Femmes nobles, vos mains infâmes
>   Pleines de blancs et de carmins.

The noble ladies' hands are decadent, full of "whites" and "carmines" (diamonds, rubies?). In "Les Pauvres à l'église" the "Dames des quartiers / Distingués" had "yellow" hands, but the idea is the same.[1]

---

[1] See Verlaine's "Une Sainte en son auréole" (*La Bonne Chanson*):

45. L'éclat de ces mains amoureuses
    Tourne le crâne des brebis!
    Dans leurs phalanges savoureuses
    Le grand soleil met un rubis!

The hands are implacable, turn the heads of sheep and perhaps sheep-like people. Similarly the good efficient hands of the ladies in "Les Chercheuses de poux" killed the little pests. The sun putting a ruby in their fingers is like the "General sun" which bombards with ruby-dust in "Alchimie du verbe": "soleil . . . Général . . . emplis les boudoirs de poudre de rubis brûlante."

49. Une tache de populace
    Les brunit comme un sein d'hier;
    Le dos de ces Mains est la place
    Qu'en baisa tout Révolté fier!

A *peuple* freckle browns them, as it did bosoms in open-necked dresses of yesteryear (eighteenth century). See the final strophe. The backs of the hands are kissed by every proud *Révolté*. This is extended in lines 60-64: "A vos poings, Mains où tremblent nos / Lèvres jamais désenivrées."

57. Ah! quelquefois, ô Mains sacrées,
    A vos poings, Mains où tremblent nos
    Lèvres jamais désenivrées,
    Crie une chaîne aux clairs anneaux!

The chains on the hands are prison chains; in the next strophe they are "bled"; the worker-women pay with their lives and freedom.

61. Et c'est un soubresaut étrange
    Dans nos êtres, quand, quelquefois,
    On veut vous déhâler, Mains d'ange,
    En vous faisant saigner les doigts!

The "déhâler" refers back to the "tache" in lines 49-52.

Des nobles Dames d'autrefois;

. . .

Des aspects nacrés, blancs et roses,
Un doux accord patricien.

Les Sœurs de charité[1]

This is not a great poem, but it is an important one, with many of Rimbaud's central images. The idea seems to come from Baudelaire's "Les Deux Bonnes Sœurs" ("La Débauche et la Mort ... ") which ends as this poem does: "O Mort, quand viendras-tu ... ?"

Rimbaud takes stock of himself as an adolescent, in one of his deeper crises, and then, having found himself full of potentiality, looks around for help, or a cause. He finds none in woman—she is not a true "sister of charity" in the religious sense of comforter—or womanly muses of various sorts, and at the end he turns desperately to the final "Sister of Charity": Death.

There is a real possibility that the mood reflects a bitter experience with the girl who—according to his friends Delahaye, Pierquin, Millot—was his mistress and accompanied him to Paris in the spring of 1871, where she apparently deserted him. A letter of April 17 to Delahaye, who had just gotten married, seems to confirm this, according to Ruff: "Oui vous êtes heureux, vous ... il est des misérables qui, femme ou idée, ne trouveront pas leur Sœur de charité."

> 1. Le jeune homme dont l'œil est brillant, la peau brune,
> Le beau corps de vingt ans qui devrait aller nu,
> Et qu'eût, le front cerclé de cuivre, sous la lune
> Adoré, dans la Perse, un Génie inconnu,

Rimbaud sees himself as the young man, with brilliant eye (full of life, light, and sap), and brown skin (healthy, tanned like the hands of Jeanne-Marie), with a handsome body "twenty years old" which "ought to go naked"—that is, he wants to accept himself whole, the way young people tend to do today, as the admired, "integrated," unashamed and pagan Greeks did in Rimbaud's view ("Soleil et chair"; compare the second "Lettre du Voyant"). Note that Rimbaud exaggerates by four years to make a fuller figure of an ephebe, or aggrandize himself: he more than once added years to his age, as in his letter to Banville.

In Persia, an unknown *Génie* (with its head circled by copper, as in hieratic Syrian statues, and under an exotic moon, worshiped in the East), would have adored that body. That is to say, the father (or Father) figure which will be more fully developed in "Génie" is naturally enough the first person to whom the disoriented boy looks for a model, to emulate

---

[1] Baudelaire speaks of a painting entitled *Sœurs de charité* (by Armand Gautier) in his *Salon de 1859.*

and to grow towards. But he is way off in Persia, which is tantamount to rejection. Surely the essence of his own father, perhaps gone off to exotic lands like Algeria (where we know he was stationed for a long while) and leaving Rimbaud derelict, is mirrored here, as in "Mémoire." Rimbaud's early Latin poem "Jugurtha" ends with the evocation of an Algerian Genius: "the Genius of Arab shores."

> 5. Impétueux avec des douceurs virginales
> Et noires, fier de ses premiers entêtements,
> Pareil aux jeunes mers, pleurs de nuits estivales,
> Qui se retournent sur des lits de diamants;

He is full of potentiality, hard and soft (*animus* and *anima*), in sum an "androgynous angel"—as Joyce called his adolescent self and Hamlet. The typically adolescent narcissistic self-sufficiency vaguely recalls Balzac's Séraphitus-Séraphita and a whole poetic tradition. Thus he is both (male) impetuous and (female) given to virginal "douceurs." These "douceurs" are ambivalently also "noires," recalling the "tics noirs" of "Les Poètes de sept ans." The girl of "Les Premières Communions" will be similarly torn between pleasure and pain.[2] He is buffeted, like Mallarmé's Hérodiade[3] (representing an aspect of his adolescent self), between all sorts of opposite urges, for example yearning and repulsion, and the struggle makes him toss on his bed like waves in a storm-tormented sea: "Pareil aux jeunes mers . . . / Qui se retournent sur des lits de diamants." This is the inner stretch of dream-sea which will be explored in "Le Bateau ivre."

The "pleurs de nuits estivales" is a poetically ambiguous combination of his actual tears on restless summer nights[4] and also of the sea; they are similarly combined in "mer faite d'une éternité de chaudes larmes" ("Enfance"). The whole is recalled in "la rumeur tournante et bondissante des conques des mers et des nuits humaines" ("Mystique").

The "lits de diamants" are his own bed plus the ocean bed (this pun is used again in "Mémoire"); compare the "nuits sanglantes" of "L'Homme juste." The "diamonds" are the buried potential delight, precisely as in "Hérodiade."[5]

---

[2] She is complexly related to Rimbaud as Hérodiade is to Mallarmé and the Jeune Parque to Valéry.

[3] Compare "la mer contrairement poussée" of Philippe Desportes, which describes a love-tossed swain. This is a generally Baroque theme.

[4] "Serene" winter is easier on the troubled emotions, as Mallarmé observed: "L'hiver, saison de l'art serein" ("Renouveau").

[5] See *Toward the Poems of Mallarmé*, p. 81.

> 9. Le jeune homme, devant les laideurs de ce monde
> Tressaille dans son cœur largement irrité,
> Et plein de la blessure éternelle et profonde,
> Se prend à désirer sa sœur de charité.

The original wound—the initial problem of evil, aggravated by an inborn hypersensitivity plus family-imposed difficulties—is described as the "blessure éternelle et profonde," which makes the world, the Others, seem very ugly at times: "les laideurs de ce monde." Having been rejected by man, he seeks aid and comfort from a second source, "Woman." She is called a *sœur de charité*, the first in a series of female figures, personal or abstract.

> 13. Mais, ô Femme, monceau d'entrailles, pitié douce,
> Tu n'es jamais la Sœur de charité, jamais,
> Ni regard noir, ni ventre où dort une ombre rousse,
> Ni doigts légers, ni seins splendidement formés.

But "Woman" is too soft, doesn't satisfy his deep need for virile attention, a model to emulate, to help him find a way of purging his pain, through work ("souffrir en mesure"—Sartre), competition with males, sacrifice, creativity, and the like. The pain, thus unexpressed, piles up and finds an outlet in resentment of his mother for letting him down (by losing the father, destroying the family; compare "Mémoire"). Her softness (Sartre's "viscosity," fear of octopuses; as Hugo said in *Les Travailleurs de la mer*: "chose affreuse, c'est mou") becomes a source of horror. It is the subversive attraction of matter, gravity, which, unleavened by male rigor, threatens to drag him down like alluring quicksand, a fly in honey. God's word, the law, is cutting. It intervenes. It is hard and above-it-all like the copper in the *Génie*'s headband. The threatening softness is referred to as "monceau d'entrailles, pitié douce."

So personal woman is rejected; she is never a rock of solid comfort, strength, no true "sister of charity." Then follows a miniature *blason* (the medieval verse which ticked off a model woman's beauty) like the little quatrain "L'étoile a pleuré rose." Her look is black, which probably refers to the general theme of woman as the dark chthonian force—she is called "Nuit" in line 23—as in "Soleil et chair" (see also under "Les Poètes de sept ans"). The "reddish" shadow which is her sex, pubic hair, reminds us of other such allusions in Rimbaud, and one speculates that the first glimpse of a woman's *bas-ventre* gave him that abiding impression. Similarly, the prostitutes are described as a "troupeau roux des tordeuses de hanches" in "Paris se repeuple," and "Le Bateau ivre" speaks of the "rousseurs amerès de l'amour." The quatrain "L'étoile a pleuré rose" has "La mer a perlé rousse à tes mammes vermeilles" which indicates probably a russet-colored aureola; also, from the same quotation, "L'Homme a saigné noir" (in the pubic region) may imply, in the "saigné," a red tinge.

The light fingers are admired (but they were also condemned in "Les Mains de Jeanne-Marie"); the breasts are "splendidly formed," as in "Soleil et chair": he admires, but finds nothing to support him here (unlike the Baudelaire of "La Géante").

> 17. Aveugle irréveillée aux immenses prunelles,
> Tout notre embrassement n'est qu'une question:
> C'est toi qui pends à nous, porteuse de mamelles,
> Nous te berçons, charmante et grave Passion.

"Unawakened blindwoman with immense pupils,"[6] she has no answers, no more than does the *Sorcière* of "Après le Déluge." She is like an unconscious force of nature. We put questions to her in vain as we embrace her. It is very reminiscent of the moment in "Les Poètes de sept ans" when the boy-child hurled himself at his mother and was thrown back in bitter disappointment (as was Golaud in *Pelléas et Mélisande* desperately trying to get "truth" out of Mélisande).

Suzanne Bernard quotes Baudelaire's "Semper eadem":

> Laissez, laissez mon cœur s'enivrer d'un *mensonge*,
> Plonger dans vos beaux yeux comme dans un beau songe ...

Whether Rimbaud remembered this or not, the root-experience here (and in "Les Poètes de sept ans") is the same.

Ironically he observes that although the woman is "porteuse de mamelles," it is she who depends on *us*, males. Tender, yet scornful of her dependency, he announces: "Nous te berçons, charmante et grave Passion"; compare Vigny's "Colère de Samson": "la Femme, . . . enfant malade et douze fois impur."

> 21. Tes haines, tes torpeurs fixes, tes défaillances,
> Et les brutalités souffertes autrefois,
> Tu nous rends tout, ô Nuit pourtant sans malveillances,
> Comme un excès de sang épanché tous les mois.

All that woman has suffered from her fate which she hates ("tes haines"), such as her periodic "curse" ("tes torpeurs fixes" and "excès de sang

---

[6] This may remind us of Baudelaire's "La Beauté: "Mes larges yeux aux clartés éternelles," and Vigny's Eva in "La Maison du Berger."

épanché tous les mois"), and mistreatment at the hands of men ("brutalités souffertes autrefois"; cf. "Les Pauvres à l'église"), for all this she gets even with man: "Tu nous rends tout, ô Nuit pourtant sans malveillances"; she is so punished by fate and really innocent. It all comes out of her periodically like her menstrual flow, moved by universal laws. This is Olympian or Nietzschean realism, surprising in a sixteen-year-old (but what isn't in Rimbaud?).

The combination of "Nuit" and "sang" is another of the many examples of Rimbaldian vehemence—life or love at a hate-driven peak, like a purple rage ("tes haines"). Here the vehemence is mainly natural: blood and hate together in Woman. But the "Nuit" ambiguously refers also to the general "darkness" of Woman.

> 25. —Quand la femme, portée un instant, l'épouvante,
> Amour, appel de vie et chanson d'action,
> Viennent la Muse verte et la Justice ardente
> Le déchirer de leur auguste obsession.

"When woman, borne an instant"—i.e., perhaps turned to in a momentary love affair—"frightens him," he gives up *this* sister of charity. Why does she frighten him? As we noted earlier, Rimbaud's misogyny came from an excess, not a lack of interest (see under "À la musique"). He was clearly overawed by the "white Goddess" as Robert Graves calls the universal mother-figure present at times in all women. Whereas a normal child has two parents and learns to play off one against the other, internally as well as externally, i.e., learns the act of emotional equilibrium and "keeping it moving," Rimbaud was too monistic in his emotional life. He loved and hated his mother too much—and his father too and perhaps everyone else.

When Rimbaud looks into a woman's eyes he sees Her (cf. our later discussion under "Bruxelles") and is too honest to deny it—unlike those who learn to play the ordinary bourgeois game of duplicity and *mauvaise foi*. He sees the spontaneous depths ("Aveugle irréveillée . . . Passion") of Woman and is terrified, as all men are at times (sometimes in incest nightmares as in the passage of the *Cahiers d'André Walter* where a monkey lifts André's mother's skirts—and underneath is ghastly Nothing; cf. *Les Déserts de l'amour*).

The rest of the strophe tells of the third and fourth ways sought (after Man and Woman), those of poetry and social action, respectively: "la Muse verte et la Justice ardente." Thus in a letter to Banville (Pléiade, p. 257) we read: "Je jure, cher maître, d'adorer toujours les deux déesses, Muse et Liberté." These are confused, referred to together as "Love, call of life and song of action" in the 26th line (in apposition to the following line). In "Génie" this dynamism (action) and stasis (lyric passion) are together the essence of spiritual life, genius.

> 29. Ah! sans cesse altéré des splendeurs et des calmes,
> Délaissé des deux Sœurs implacables, geignant
> Avec tendresse après la science aux bras almes,
> Il porte à la nature en fleur son front saignant.

The two "sisters" (sisters of charity), the Muse and Liberty, desert him after a while. The endless quest or "thirst" for the "splendors" and "calms" of poetry and justice is exhausting, and Rimbaud seems to foresee the spiritual exhaustion portrayed in the *Saison en Enfer*, which opens with exactly this image:

> Un soir, j'ai assis la Beauté sur mes genoux.
> —Et je l'ai trouvée amère. . . .
> Je me suis armé contre la justice.
> Je me suis enfui. O sorcières, ô misère, ô haine,
> c'est à vous que mon trésor a été confié!

So he briefly tries a fifth and sixth way, the first of which vaguely predicts future events, for in fact, after giving up poetry and social revolution, Rimbaud went back to nature and the simple life. Here he moans tenderly after "science" (knowledge) with "nourishing arms," and also takes his "bleeding forehead"—his psychic wounds—to "flowering nature" for healing as he did in "Soleil et chair," "Sensation," and "Ma Bohème," etc.

> 33. Mais la noire alchimie et les saintes études
> Répugnent au blessé, sombre savant d'orgueil;
> Il sent marcher sur lui d'atroces solitudes.
> Alors, et toujours beau, sans dégoût du cercueil,

Knowledge (or "science") is identified as "holy studies" of the mystic, occult sort Rimbaud is known to have pursued for a while in Charleville under the tutelage of Charles Bretagne. Enid Starkie and Gengoux, of course, exaggerate the extent of his readings. Inwardly, all authentic poets work out the basic ideas for themselves; they get the visions of deep reality direct, with, at most, a side glance at the musty tomes whose authors are almost always "cultish," impatient, eager to make outward capital of their evanescent truths. But these are unexploitable, except by genius, by artistic originality working it all up anew from scratch. The expression "saintes études" undoubtedly refers to these purer insights, the "noire alchimie" to the spiritually immature magic aspect of them. Rimbaud, "sombre savant d'orgueil," is too independent, and these studies "repel" him, are no balm for his psychic "wounds" ("blessé"). It is vaguely suggested that the immature magic is responsible for his repulsion (as in "ce sont des erreurs . . . les magies, les alchimies"—sketch for "Nuit de l'enfer")—this is enough to refute Starkie and Gengoux—but the magic is confusedly lumped with the "saintes études" here, and one gets the definite impression that mainly he is just too tired and sick for study of any kind, or too weary to discriminate between the kinds. He has simply given up: "Il sent marcher sur lui d'atroces solitudes." It is like the "dernier couac" of the *Saison en Enfer*.

But the last line of the strophe protests that it is not his fault: he is still "beautiful." It is like Camus's remark, at the end of the *Myth of Sisyphus*, that any defeat can be overcome by scorn. It is a sort of *amor fati*: from the unfair contest he has emerged a spiritual victor. The expression "sans dégoût du cercueil" links with the next strophe. Rimbaud has been defeated in this life—in all ways but the spiritual spark—and yearns for death.

> 37. Qu'il croie aux vastes fins, Rêves ou Promenades
> Immenses, à travers les nuits de Vérité,
> Et t'appelle en son âme et ses membres malades,
> O Mort mystérieuse, ô sœur de charité.

"Let him [the wounded one] believe in vast ends, Dreams or immense Promenades, through nights of Truth." This vision of consoling death is like the end of Baudelaire's "Le Voyage," "Au fond de l'Inconnu pour trouver du nouveau," and anticipates at another level the inner night-voyaging of the "Bateau ivre."

The final "sister" is the classic image of smothering maternal death, the receptive grave which is a microcosm of the receiving All—the womb-tomb: "la charité serait-elle sœur de la mort, pour moi?" ("Adieu"). Rimbaud's yearning for death had been there all along since his first traumatic experience, falling in a cosmic disaster (cf. "Après le déluge") from the All-womb. But only in a total crisis, total defeat, do we come down to that: Bach's "komm süsser Tod," Keats' "I am half in love with easeful death," Baudelaire's "Appareillons!" ("Le Voyage"), Mallarmé's "frisson à l'unisson" ("Cantique de Saint-Jean"). And usually it is put in more positive terms: the nostalgia for Paradise. That is the way Rimbaud will usually see it.

Voyelles

Much fuss has been made about this little poem, far too much of it sensational, whooping it up for a misunderstood Rimbaud or demeaning of Symbolism generally. I regard it as one of Rimbaud's minor efforts, mainly a curiosity. True, Rimbaud bragged about it in the *Saison en enfer*: "J'inventai la couleur des voyelles!", but critical perspective is very often lacking in that work, which is scarcely the last word in mature balance. So, pleading guilty of exegetic frustration and hesitation, I will nonetheless risk a judgment that it is an arbitrary and inchoate poem.

There seems to be no fixed physiological nor psychological basis for synesthesia in the sense of a particular color associated with a specific sound (René Ghil likewise went astray here). Though a given person may always see red when a bugle blows, this is an individual experience, of little or no interest to literature or criticism. But I think Rimbaud's impressions were based usually on more general qualities, associations which can be universally understood or felt, although not properly synesthetic in the above-mentioned sense. They overlap with Mallarmé's insights as described in "Les Mots anglais" (or applied in his texts),[1] at least enough to make some comparison useful. Mallarmé commented in various places on the brightness of the letter i and the darkness of ou.[2] This corresponds to an objective fact, the frequency of sound waves. There is a whole scale of these frequencies from highest i to lowest on (with ou being quite low). So there would be an objective basis for associating brightness with i, blackness or darkness with ou or on. Theoretically (aside from bright light), the color with the highest frequency, violet, ought to be associated with i. But Rimbaud sees red here. He sees violet when confronted with an o which is fairly neutral in level of frequency. Red, very low in frequency, would be associated with on or ou. (This is leaving out the relative saturation and brilliancy factors; Rimbaud also neglects these and speaks only of hues). But, again, Rimbaud sees red in conjunction with the letter i! His association of blackness with a, which is smack in the middle of the frequency-scale (and which Mallarmé accordingly associates with banality, flatness, mat-ness, etc.), is then equally arbitrary on these grounds of sound (and shape offers no direct clues as to color). We must grant then that Rimbaud's associations are much less controlled, less maturely worked out, than Mallarmé's, which is likely enough, given his youth and haste versus Mallarmé's lifetime evolution of a poetics.

[1] See *Toward the Poems of Mallarmé*, Appendix c.

[2] See "Crise de vers," Pléiade, p. 364. Claude Lévi-Strauss took note of this passage in his *Anthropologie structurale*. He approved. Roman Jakobson has also shown interest in this passage.

Verlaine, when queried about Rimbaud's color-vowel correspondences, answered: "Il les voyait comme ça," and that is the likeliest explanation. It is possible that Rimbaud retained from an old primer, where the letters were associated with several of the creatures and things he mentions, some abiding impressions, but this does not conform to general experience. The usually-cited primers are not consistent.

Gengoux's occult scheme is even less convincing; he has to push and prod to get the colors to fit the scheme. Rimbaud was a poet, no doubt of that; however, there is much doubt (see under "Les Sœurs de charité") that he ever took occultism seriously in detail, i.e., other than for its essential visionary stance. As for the *blason* presented by Faurisson, it is merely wacky (*I* as the shape of a woman's smile—*voyons!*).

In the instances of at least two of the letters, the associations are very clearly based on evident properties of the letters, for example, the o is easily seen as round, like the mouth of the *clairon* (and the o in it), or the "Oméga," and the eyes, including the four o's again in "O l'Oméga, rayon violet de Ses Yeux" (Mallarmé favored this obvious effect, for example the "ô miroir" in *Hérodiade* or the famous "aboli bibelot"). The other instance is the u, which is equivalent to the upsilon in the etymon of *cycle* (and generally almost all the images under u can be shown to have a rather direct connection of this sort). Logically, then, we are induced to pursue this sort of associationism in a relaxed spirit of probability, being assured of no fixed final result. The present effort is not the first of its kind; nor will it be, I am confident, the last. Any number can play. My only claim on the reader's attention herein is that I have had some experience in this sort of thing and that I believe in rigorous honesty—never claim a hit until *ça saute aux yeux*—having learned from my classes how enthusiastically wrong people can go here.

> 1. A noir, E blanc, I rouge, U vert, O bleu: voyelles,
> Je dirai quelque jour vos naissances latentes:
> A, noir corset velu des mouches éclatantes
> Qui bombinent autour des puanteurs cruelles,
>
> Golfes d'ombre; ...

One has the grouped impressions of blackness or darkness, hole, death, perhaps excrement, black hair, buzzing flies. In "Chanson de la plus haute tour" we have an image of dirty buzzing flies in a corrupt weed-grown summer meadow, together with Rimbaud's own passivity, laziness. In "Dévotion" we have "l'herbe d'été bourdonnante et puante.—Pour la fièvre des mères et des enfants." In the fourth strophe of "Mémoire" there is this same mixture of mother and decaying yet darkly fecund summer: "en proie / aux soirs d'août qui faisaient germer ces pourritures!"[3]

In provisional sum, the feeling is of the dark pit of maternity which threatened to engulf him—his mother, his mother's "dark" church, the obscurantist provinces, etc. He called his mother "la Bouche d'ombre"; in "Mémoire" she is "Elle sombre" (versus the male light). In "Les Sœurs de charité" the essence of woman is her "regard noir" and "Nuit." In "Les Premières Communions" there is "la nuit, Vierge-Mère impalpable."

The flies are associated with the feminine "stinking pit" (*King Lear*) and the nearby excrement, death, etc., rather naturally. Thus Sartre's *Les Mouches*, which is essentially a drama of his triumph over the mother-spirit (Clytemnestra, his own fear of feminine viscosity, cf. *Les Mots*), associated the flies with the corruption of reactionary guilt and obscurantist religion.[4] And we have seen that Rimbaud in "Dévotion" and "La Chanson de la plus haute tour" linked flies with passive corruption.

This corruption is fascinatingly double, ambivalent, latent with life, like Baudelaire's "charogne" which gave off a "strange music" akin to the "bombinent" here. Hence, as J.-P. Richard observes, the "éclatantes" (like the "éclate" of "Being beauteous" or "Enfance") represents a sort of bursting forth of vigor. But here, obviously, the negative note is strong and the vigor is rather special.

But why the letter A? Here we are on even less sure ground, but let us plunge in anyway. A is a, and perhaps *the*, characteristically feminine letter, in the Latin tradition, including French (feminine articles and endings, feminine names like Marie, etc.). Jacques Duchesne-Guillemin has observed that the phonetic vowel sound of *noir* (*nwar*) is ā. A is alpha, the original *abîme*, as "oméga" closes the little poem cycle; a is in *cadavre, cave, caca*: "Un noir angelot . . . fait caca . . . son caca maudit" ("L'Angelot maudit"). A is a curiously apt sound for death, as Mallarmé knew (the flat middling is connected with nothingness). Thus in "Quand l'ombre menaça de la fatale loi" the flat line of death-horizon is emphasized

---

[3] In "Les Premières Communions" we have:

> La pierre sent toujours la terre maternelle.
> Vous verrez des monceaux de ces cailloux terreux
> Dans la campagne en rut qui frémit solennelle,
> Portant près des blés lourds, dans les sentiers ocreux,
> Ces arbrisseaux brûlés . . .

The dark fertility of earth-mother is associated with the dark pit of provincial religion: the *curé* is a *"noir* grotesque" (l. 4).

[4] Sartre is a devoted Rimbaldian. He quotes "O Saisons, ô châteaux" more than once; he refers to Rimbaud in *L'Enfance d'un chef* and he admires him totally along with Van Gogh in *Qu'est-ce que la littérature?* and *Genet*.

by nine a sounds; compare "la massive nuit," ending of "Toast funèbre," or "le hasard" at the mid-line of the "Coup de Dés." A is a back sound, and when we say "Ah-h" for the doctor, we open a "golfe d'ombre." Finally, the capital A (see the manuscript in Faurisson) looks a bit like a fly seen from the back. As an inverted V shape (cf. "velu"), it may have to do with the *vagin*, as Faurisson surmised.[5] He also indicates that this may be related to the "corset." The black hairy sex is implied in the little *blason* printed next in the collection: "L'Homme a saigné noir à ton flanc souverain."[6] But all this, I must allow, is merely approximate.

> 5. . . . E, candeurs des vapeurs et des tentes,
>   Lances des glaciers fiers, rois blancs, frissons d'ombelles;

As mute *e*, this letter is often not pronounced. The feeling here is of coldness, bland or blank neutrality. E is pronounced *eu* in the alphabet, which is a neutral sound *par excellence*, middling in the sound-scale, unobtrusive, discreet (contrast é). It is present in *neutre* and is brought out by the immediate grouping after E of "candeurs" and "vapeurs." The blankly cold effects of both images are clear as in "rois blancs" ("blanc" and "lances" are echoes) and "frissons."[7] Perhaps the "ombelles" here are related to the "ombelles" in "Mémoire," chilly and "proud" ("trop fières," compare "glaciers fiers" like her, Rimbaud's mother). The "pride" in the lances (or "icicles" of the variant: note the element *acier* in "glacier"), in purely erect kings and cool spikey flowers has probably to do with the three projections of the E shape.

In *Qu'est-ce que la littérature?* Sartre says that the word *Florence* "s'abandonne avec décence et prolonge indéfiniment par l'affaiblissement continu de l'*e* muet son épanouissement plein de réserves." The discreetness of "réserves" and "décence" and "affaiblissement" is partly due to the neutrality described as the main quality of the letter e in my study of Mallarmé's use of letter-symbolism (see *Toward the Poems of Mallarmé*, p. 267).

> 7. I, pourpres, sang craché, rire des lèvres belles
>   Dans la colère ou les ivresses pénitentes;

---

[5] Charles Baudoin says that v is another spontaneous symbol for woman; see *Toward the Poems of Mallarmé*, Appendix c.

[6] Compare "blessures écarlates et noires éclatent dans les chairs superbes" ("Being beauteous").

[7] "Toujours frissonnent ces fleurs blanches!" ("Ce qu'on dit au poète à propos de fleurs," 4th strophe).

I should be bright (on the sound-scale), but Rimbaud seems to have a dark shade of red in mind. Still, red can be acute, fierce in psychological effect, by association with blood, etc. Thus Proust associated the fiery title of Nerval's *Filles de feu* with "Ce nom pourpré de ces deux I . . . Sylvie" (*Contre Sainte-Beuve*, p. 168).

"Rire" and "ivresse," featuring the letter, are sharp, dynamic. In "rire" we have the notion of a jet of expression, which has to do with acute sound and the straight shape. "Sang craché" is a similar spurt of brightness. We commented on the frequent vehement association of *sang* and *noir* ("Les Mains de Jeanne-Marie"), and that is the case here where the "sang craché" and the "rire des lèvres belles / Dans la colère ou les ivresses pénitentes" both involve blackness ("colère," "pénitent"). The "pourpres"—as in a "purple rage"—has this same feeling, like Mallarmé's tumescent pomegranates:

> Tu sais ma passion que pourpre et déjà mûre,
> Chaque grenade éclate et d'abeilles murmure;
> Et notre sang, épris de qui le va saisir,
> Coule pour tout l'essaim éternel du désir.
> ("L'Après-midi d'un faune")

"Pourpre . . . sang . . . désir . . . coule [jet, cf. 'craché'] . . . ivresse," ferocity, are all linked here with i ("épris . . . désir . . . saisir") as in the Rimbaud poem.

"Pénitentes" has an undertone of "pénis" which is in line with all this (the shape and the acuteness of I, cf. the Hebrew *jod*: I, male principle, as Rimbaud could easily have learned from occult lore, or guessed himself).

> 9. U, cycles, vibrements divins des mers virides,
> Paix des pâtis semés d'animaux, paix des rides
> Que l'alchimie imprime aux grands fronts studieux;

We mentioned previously the Greek upsilon behind the y of "cycles," akin to the essential Greek word *rhythmos*. The u sound is basically a cyclic, rhythmic *vibrancy*, combining a bright, acute, "male" i with a relaxed, open, "female" mouth (and a receptacle shape). Hence all the images are developments of an initial tension between male and female poles (or negative and positive), resulting in vibrancy and hence the phenomenon of cyclic rhythm. First comes the rhythm of waves, "vibrements divins des mers virides," then of rolling meadows:[8] "Paix des

---

[8] Rimbaud often enjoyed this earth-sea confusion; see "Marine," in particular. Leconte de Lisle in his "Epiphanie" has played on the same ambiguity.

pâtis semés d'animaux," then of wrinkles on a human forehead "paix des rides . . . aux grands fronts studieux" (this evolution from universal rhythm through land and sea undulations to human rhythms is found in the little quatrain "L'Etoile a pleuré rose").

The tension-become-rhythm (alternation of troughs and crests) is also in the female-male combination of vi thrice repeated in "vibrements," "divins," "virides."[9]

The u is reminiscent of a whole Rimbaldian cluster: "la Muse verte," "Nature verte," *pâture* ("pâtis"), *études*, or *studieux*, *sucer*. This last is connected with Cybèle, the rhythmic earth-mother and ocean:

> La terre berçant l'homme, et tout l'Océan bleu
>
>   .   .   .
>
> Son double sein [cf. rhythm of hills] versait dans les immensités
> Le pur ruissellement de la vie infinie.
> L'Homme suçait, heureux, sa mamelle bénie,
> Comme un petit enfant, jouant sur ses genoux.
>
> ("Soleil et chair")

Compare the breast undulation of "Veillées," III: "La mer de la veillée, telle que les seins . . . " and "au sein des sillons" ("Fêtes de la faim").

The image of "la noire alchimie et les saintes études" was linked with "la nature" as a consoling *Magna Mater* ("bras almes") in the preceding poem, "Les Sœurs de charité." The ideas of *saint* and *études* and *mer* are linked with meadows in:

> Je suis le saint, en prière sur la terrasse,—comme les bêtes pacifiques paissent jusqu'à la mer de Palestine.
> Je suis le savant . . .
>
> ("Enfance")

All this will be further discussed in connection with the second and third lines of the *blason*: "L'Etoile a pleuré rose."

12. O, suprême Clairon plein des strideurs étranges,
    Silences traversés des Mondes et des Anges:
    —O l'Oméga, rayon violet de Ses Yeux!

The tone here is of pure ethereality: one thinks of Baudelaire's "L'Imprévu"

> Le son de la trompette est si délicieux,
> Dans ces soirs solennels de célestes vendanges,

[9] Compare the wing-beat vibrancy of "vierge, vivace" in Mallarmé's swan poem.

(Note the obvious undertone of *anges* in "vendanges"). One thinks even more of the "strideurs" accompanying the "clairon" and Rimbaud's injunction to Paris to build up to a Last Judgement:

> Amasse les strideurs au cœur du clairon sourd.

These "strideurs" are a harsh virile strain of rigorous, inflexible judgement, akin to the "fanfare atroce" of "Matinée d'ivresse." In male-invented myth generally—because of the severe (Logos: the cutting interdiction) separation of male Eros from male in our Judeo-Christian tradition and the resulting radical sublimation or spirituality—the upper and ethereal is assigned to man.[10] (Compare "Soleil et chair" and our Introduction generally). I feel that this "violet ray" and "Ses Yeux" refer to a male essence like "Génie," where the possessive adjective "Son corps! . . . Sa vue, sa vue!" echoes this one persuasively. Seeing that (ultra)violet is a blue sublimated toward pure light, we may bring in the mystic "ton Bleu" of "Bruxelles." True, his mother's eyes were blue, like Rimbaud's own, so we have a theoretical choice here. But the (ultra)violet seems purified in the same way as in "j'écartai du ciel l'azur, qui est du noir, et je vécus, étincelle d'or de la lumière *nature*." ("Alchimie du verbe"). Thus in "Fleurs" we have "un dieu aux énormes yeux bleus." That the eyes of the father-god ("Génie") should resemble the narcissistic son-god's ("fils du Soleil") own blue eyes—"couleur de myosotis ou de pervenche" according to Delahaye—is an obvious probability. "Conte," indeed, merges the two (the "Génie" and the "Prince") mystically. Rimbaud had pined for a girl with violet eyes according to Delahaye: those exquisite depths where opposites merge summed up, as the Mona Lisa does, all the major forms of Eros. As Valéry put it, the love a woman arouses in us can only be satisfied by God. Violet is linked with Rimbaud's spiritual ascent in the "Bateau ivre": "Libre, fumant, monté de brumes violettes" and with a sundown's "horreurs mystiques," not unlike the *strideurs* in the final awe-inspiring aspect of the Apocalypse:

> J'ai vu le soleil bas, taché d'horreurs mystiques,
> Illuminant de longs figements violets,

("figement" is very close to *strideurs* in effect). The "violettes" of "Comédie de la soif" also represent an ethereal ultimate of thirst. As Léon Cellier reminded me, violet is also the color of grief or of death itself—which is near in spirit, or coalesces with the ultimate thirst: "De la couleur violette (amour contenu, mystérieux, voilé, couleur de chanoinesse)" (Baudelaire

---

[10] See the chapter on "The Hunt" in our *The Writer's Way in France*.

Fusées, II) and "violet . . . braise qui s'éteint derrière un rideau d'azur ("Le Peintre de la vie moderne").

So the effect of o is the roundness of totality (of love, death), as in "Oméga," the final letter (Last Judgment). The fact that through violet the apex of the spectrum circularly links with its nadir, red—"the extremes meet"—hinting, further, at a fusion of light and dark, life and death, male and female, all this may have some bearing on this o. There are echoing o's in "Clairon . . . Mondes . . . O . . . Oméga . . . rayon . . . violet." The shape of the circle is often symbolic of woman, but it can be equally that of wholeness as in the sun-disc (the sun is at times sexually ambiguous for Rimbaud).[11] "O Monde," which echoes the wholeness rediscovered of the "Mondes" here is an exultant cry of praise to the *Génie* in the prose poem of that name. The roundness of the eyes here is echoed, similarly, in the "dieu aux énormes yeux bleus . . . la mer et le ciel" ("Fleurs")—two immense horizon circles.

"L'Étoile a pleuré rose . . . "

This is a minor little *blason*.

1. L'Étoile a pleuré rose au cœur de tes oreilles,

In "Accroupissements," moonlight created an effect of "neige rose" on the backdrop. Here starlight does something similar in the feminine ear (the "blanc" is nearby; see the next line). In "Ce qu'on dit au poète à propos de fleurs" there is a similar (though amusing) image concerning sad flowers "qu'allaitèrent de couleurs / De méchants astres." The etymology of the word "influence," which literally is the "pouring" down of effects from stars—combined with the milky way ("astres lactés" in "L'Homme juste")—seems to be behind this strange image. The derivation of parts of the female body from nature began in "Soleil et chair": "Astarté . . . Montra son nombril rose où vint neiger l'écume." (Note the similarity between the cup of the "nombril rose" and that of the ear.) The effect of "pleuré" is in its direct image, in its liquid sound (r) and in the graphic spilling-over effect from the container of the u to the over-brimming r.[1] There are four r's in the line. In "cœur" the effect of the u is again related

[11] The sun is male-female in "Bannières de mai": "C'est rire aux parents, qu'au soleil"; Rimbaud thus calls himself ambiguously "fils du Soleil" ("Vagabonds"). Even the male sun of "Soleil et chair" has a generous female component, as ideal fathers do. But at times, as in the "Général, . . . bombarde-nous" of "Alchimie du verbe" the maleness is emphasized.

[1] See *Toward the Poems of Mallarmé*, p. 17.

to a cup shape, like an ear, and the diphthong gives an effect of the inner convolutions.

    2. L'infini roulé blanc de ta nuque à tes reins;

This is a universal rhythm, which began in the stars, the cycles of the cosmos, and extended through sea or land undulations into human shapes, an evolution much like the one described under u, "cycles" in "Voyelles"; the "nuque" may echo that u. The feeling is in the lineage of Shakespeare's *Venus and Adonis* or Baudelaire's "La Géante":

> . . . quand les soleils malsains,
> Lasse, la font s'étendre à travers la campagne,
> Dormir nonchalamment à l'ombre de ses seins,

(Note the rhythmic ripple as of flesh in "nonchalamment").
Compare Rimbaud's "Soleil et chair":

> La terre berçant l'homme, et tout l'Océan bleu
>   .   .   .
> Je regrette les temps de la grande Cybèle
>   .   .   .
> Son double sein versait dans les immensités
> Le pur ruissellement de la vie infinie.
> L'Homme suçait, heureux, sa mamelle bénie,
> Comme un petit enfant, jouant sur ses genoux.

This rolling sweep of land and ocean behind "la grande Cybèle . . . au sein des grandes mers" (with her "double sein," cf. "au sein du sillon" in "Fêtes de la faim") is close to the infinite evolving into the spontaneously feminine rhythms of the *blason*, the convolutions of the ear or the hollow of the back.[2]

    3. La mer a perlé rousse à tes mammes vermeilles

The foregoing evolution of universal rhythms from the sky-source through land and water rhythms to human shapes obviously applies here. In the "Soleil et chair" excerpt we saw the "double sein" as an example of

---

[2] Compare the similar evolution in Mallarmé's "Un Coup de Dés"; also the arabesque of the nymph's back in the "Après-midi d'un faune": "songe ordinaire de dos . . . une sonore, vaine et monotone ligne." See *L'Oeuvre de Mallarmé*, "Un Coup de Dés," p. 150.

this.[3] Here the *mammes* (*mer-mère*), with their rippling effect of three m's (like Baudelaire's "nonchalamment"), combined with two other m's in the line, give a wave effect: "la mer, telle que les seins d'Amélie" ("Veillées," III). In "Le Bateau ivre" the sea's "rhythmes [sic] lents" were directly linked with "les rousseurs amères de l'amour."[4] The "rousse" in the quatrain refers no doubt to the aureola surrounding the vermilion nipples.

> 4. Et l'Homme saigné noir à ton flanc souverain.

In the three preceding lines the colors were true colors, or hues. Now the quatrain ends with a leap to a masculine image, rather like the final effect of the "Oméga" in "Voyelles." A *final* or limiting "color," black, puts a period here. The effect of fluid Becoming, universal rhythms pouring into human shapes, is maintained; but here the source itself is a human one: Man. And the world, by passing through the human, has become contaminated with sin, corruption: "caca maudit . . . sang noir" ("L'Angelot maudit"); "bad blood" (Mauvais sang"). Rimbaud on occasion sees woman as put-upon by man—for example "les brutalités souffertes autrefois" of "Les Sœurs de charité." In "Les Premières Communions," Man's Church, the Christian one, has "soiled" her, with the "baiser putride de Jésus."

In "La Lettre du voyant," he speaks (after Michelet) of emancipating her from Western thralldom. But how much of this is present in the quatrain is hard to ascertain. At any rate, as so often in Rimbaud, the life-red and the death-black combine in an acute ambivalence, a human vehemence pitted against a calm natural background, "flanc souverain."

L'Homme juste

This is the most bitterly anti-Christian of Rimbaud's poems, in the vein of Leconte de Lisle's "Quaïn," Baudelaire's "Reniement de Saint-Pierre," and Lautréamont's *Chants de Maldoror*. Rimbaud outdoes all these other figures in bitterness. But it is not a very rewarding effort; the result is scarcely more than a messy and scattered fragment.

Rimbaud identifies with the "Maudit suprême," the *révolté par excel-*

---

[3] This is much developed in Mallarmé's vision; see *Toward the Poems of Mallarmé*, p. 208.

[4] "Amère" goes with *mer* and *mère* and *amer* (old French for *aimer*) in an important harmony. Thus Robert de Boron speaks of "Marie . . . son nom veut dire mer amère . . . elle est Sa mère." And Verlaine: "Je ne veux aimer que ma mère Marie." Baudelaire rhymes *mer*, *mère*, and *amère* in "Chant d'automne," II.

lence, Satan. It is the age-old cry of Cain—or Ivan Karamazov—against
the ironies of a divine "Justice" which can favor an Abel or kill innocent
children (l. 53: "un tas d'enfants près / De mourir"). It is the *cri de cœur*
of a youth who is full of sap and wants to *do* something and feels helpless
before an implacable order, the status quo of the Establishment (and its
Church) reflecting a similarly static universe of natural law:

> 44. L'ordre, éternel veilleur, rame aux cieux lumineux
> Et de sa drague en feu laisse filer les astres!

This cry wants action (as Baudelaire's Saint-Pierre did), hates the "torpor"
of Christianity, and sides with man in the manner of Nietzsche, only less
confidently.

The allusions have been well explained, the major influences detected:
I have little to add to that beyond a few reflections here and there.

> 1st and 2nd strophes:
> > Le Juste restait droit sur ses hanches solides:
> > Un rayon lui dorait l'épaule; des sueurs
> > Me prirent: "Tu veux voir rutiler les bolides?
> > Et, debout, écouter bourdonner les flueurs
> > D'astres lactés, et les essaims d'astéroïdes?
> >
> > "Par des farces de nuit ton front est épié,
> > O Juste! Il faut gagner un toit. Dis ta prière,
> > La bouche dans ton drap doucement expié;
> > Et si quelque égaré choque ton ostiaire,
> > Dis: Frère, va plus loin, je suis estropié!"

Here, Rimbaud describes Jesus, the "juste" (as he is called in the Gospels),
and sweats with metaphysical anguish. He ironically alludes to celestial
phenomena as "farces de nuit," i.e., the naïve belief of the masses in these
outward displays.[1] (See "Les Pauvres à l'église"). He mocks the man who
bows down to these superstitions, says his prayer, then buries his mouth
contentedly under his bed-sheet. If somebody bumps into his bones
(*ostiaire* = *ossuaire*?), Jesus should say, "Move on, brother, I am lame,"
meaning impotent (so Rimbaud tells him).

> 3rd strophe:
> > Et le Juste restait debout, dans l'épouvante
> > Bleuâtre des gazons après le soleil mort:
> > "Alors, mettrais-tu tes genouillères en vente,
> > O Vieillard? Pèlerin sacré! barde d'Armor!
> > Pleureur des Oliviers! main que la pitié gante!

[1] Compare Mallarmé's "Quand l'ombre menaça": "luxe . . . astres vils."

He imagines Jesus as shocked by this blasphemy; there is a feeling that Rimbaud himself is deeply shocked by this death of God in him: "l'épouvante / Bleuâtre des gazons après le soleil mort." This recalls the "Pauvres à l'église" with the yellow Jesus hovering in a nave "where the sun perishes"; also "Mémoire," where the absent father leaves the grass empty of light.

Then Rimbaud mocks the idea of relics: "genouillères" are ridiculous relics of a lame man, "O vieillard" an old impotent God, like Lautréamont's. He is curiously mixed with dead Norse gods in an allusion to Ossian ("barde d'Armor"; cf. "thrènes" in strophe 6), who pops up again in "Métropolitain": "mers d'Ossian."

In the fourth strophe Rimbaud calls him "disgusting" and sees himself as the true sufferer: "Je suis celui qui souffre et qui s'est révolté." And in the fifth strophe he laughs at the idea of the divine pardon, calls himself "maudit," describes his fury and mad despair.

6th strophe:
> "C'est toi le Juste, enfin, le Juste! C'est assez!
> C'est vrai que ta tendresse et ta raison sereines
> Reniflent dans la nuit comme des cétacés,
> Que tu te fais proscrire et dégoises des thrènes
> Sur d'effroyables becs-de-canne fracassés!

He compares Jesus' "tendresse et ta raison sereines" to whales (images no doubt of torpor, emptiness, stupidity) sniffling in the night—surprisingly close to Lautréamont in mood here. The "becs-de-canne" are probably a misspelling for "becs-de-cane," aloes, referring possibly to the palms over which Jesus rode triumphantly into Jerusalem.

7th strophe:
> "Et c'est toi l'œil de Dieu! le lâche! Quand les plantes
> Froides des pieds divins passeraient sur mon cou,
> Tu es lâche! O ton front qui fourmille de lentes!
> Socrates et Jésus, Saints et Justes, dégoût!
> Respectez le Maudit suprême aux nuits sanglantes!"

Rimbaud says that even if cold soles of the divine feet passed over his neck (an allusion perhaps to the kneeling onlooker of the divine procession into Jerusalem) he would still think Jesus (and God) a coward—which is curiously reminiscent of Pascal's cry that if a rock crushed him he would still be superior to the rock (for radically different reasons than Rimbaud's!).

8th strophe:

> J'avais crié cela sur la terre, et la nuit
> Calme et blanche occupait les cieux pendant ma fièvre.
> Je relevai mon front: le fantôme avait fui,
> Emportant l'ironie atroce de ma lèvre . . .
> —Vents nocturnes, venez au Maudit! Parlez-lui,

His insults are in vain; Jesus has disappeared, carrying off "the atrocious irony of my lips." Rimbaud addresses the nocturnal winds, tells them to come talk to him—he obviously feels "atroces solitudes" ("Les Sœurs de charité"), metaphysical emptiness after the hollow Nietzschean triumph.

9th strophe:

> Cependant que silencieux sous les pilastres
> D'azur, allongeant les comètes et les nœuds
> D'univers, remuement énorme sans désastres,
> L'ordre, éternel veilleur, rame aux cieux lumineux
> Et de sa drague en feu laisse filer les astres!

The heavens go on in their meaningless rounds: nothing is changed by the revolt. The rage is vain, a storm and fury signifying nothing—*une passion inutile*.

10th strophe:

> Ah! qu'il s'en aille, lui, la gorge cravatée
> De honte, ruminant toujours mon ennui, doux
> Comme le sucre sur la denture gâtée.
> —Tel que la chienne après l'assaut des fiers toutous,
> Léchant son flanc d'où pend une entraille emportée.

Another (useless) insult to Jesus, comparing him again to a bitch (compare the hound-bitches, "lices," of line 19), passively female (as Nietzsche would agree)—licking her wounds after Rimbaud's assault (which is compared to proud male puppies' attacks).

11th strophe:

> Qu'il dise charités crasseuses et progrès . . .
> —J'exècre tous ces yeux de Chinois à [be]daines,
> Puis qui chante: nana, comme un tas d'enfants près
> De mourir, idiots doux aux chansons soudaines:
> O Justes, nous chierons dans vos ventres de grès!

The invective continues against "dirty charity" and "progress" (this will be repeated often in the *Saison en Enfer*, etc.). There is a mockery of prayers (here the text is particularly fragmentary, unclear): singing *"nana* like a bunch of children near death, sweet idiots with sudden songs." Compare the "divins babillages" of "Les Premières Communions" (Suzanne Bernard) or the "oremus risibles et têtus" of the flock in "Les Pauvres à l'église." The *nana* (*nanan*: "yum yum") refers to paradise, promised sweets which Rimbaud thinks a farce. Even as he mocks feeble mankind in them, one senses Rimbaud's bitterness at the idea of children dying. We recall his sympathy for the poor children who "conversed with the sweetness of idiots" in "Les Poètes de sept ans."

The *Chinois* is a typical French usage for something foreign-incomprehensible-silly. In "Parade" Rimbaud uses it in just that way at the head of a list of mocking names for ridiculous role-players: "Chinois, Hottentots, bohémiens," etc. I do not know what the "ventres de grès" are. Leda Lebidois suggests holy-water fonts, which is the most convincing possibility I have encountered.

A Monsieur Théodore de Banville
Ce qu'on dit au poète à propos de fleurs

This pastiche of the Romantic and Late-Romantic (Parnassian) cult of flowers in verse is remarkable for its virtuosity, its modern images, its biting satire; but I do not like it. Virtuosity leaves me cold; satire—"la pointe assassine" (Verlaine)—is not a good ground for genuine poetry. Besides, a lot of this is just frivolous word-play, thrown together as it came to Rimbaud. The scholarly spadework has been done by a succession of Rimbaud critics, and I have little to add on that score.

1st and 2nd strophes:
> Ainsi, toujours, vers l'azur noir
> Où tremble la mer des topazes,
> Fonctionneront dans ton soir
> Les Lys, ces clystères d'extases!
>
> A notre époque de sagous,
> Quand les Plantes sont travailleuses,
> Le Lys boira les bleus dégoûts
> Dans tes Proses religieuses!

Lilies shall always "function" (the mechanical term is satiric, like the medicinal "clystères") in the evenings as symbols of prayer. The "azur" is a Late-Romantic cliché and seems to stand for the outworn religion (as well as art); hence *black*, "noir," (compare "Le ciel est mort" in Mallarmé's "L'Azur," published in *Le Parnasse contemporain*, where Rimbaud could have seen it along with "Les Fleurs," which is parodied here). Rimbaud will later say that he has removed from heaven "l'azur qui est du noir" ("Alchimie du verbe"). We commented on this at length in our Introduction. This hateful religious blue (which he also saw in his mother's eyes: "Les Poètes de sept ans") is called "les bleus dégoûts" and will be drunk by the lily (i.e., its calyx resembles a mouth receiving it like a host). This insipid process occurs in simple religious verse, "Proses religieuses." These lilies are "Plantes . . . travailleuses," unlike the biblical ones which "toil not, neither do they spin."

"La mer des topazes" no doubt is used partly for its liaison: *mer de* (cf. "Açoka cadre" in part II, strophe 6). It describes a sentimentally jeweled sky.

3rd strophe:

> —Le lys de monsieur de Kedrel,
> Le Sonnet de mil huit cent trente,
> Le Lys qu'on donne au Ménestrel
> Avec l'œillet et l'amarante!

This mocks the lily as royalist emblem (Kedrel, we are told, is a well-known royalist).

4th strophe:

> Des lys! Des lys! On n'en voit pas!
> Et dans ton Vers, tel que les manches
> Des Pécheresses aux doux pas,
> Toujours frissonnent ces fleurs blanches!

An allusion to the *Dame aux camélias*? Something like. The shivering white flowers are also found in "Voyelles."

"On n'en voit pas!" They are not real, just in poetry.

5th strophe:

> Toujours, Cher, quand tu prends un bain,
> Ta chemise aux aisselles blondes
> Se gonfle aux brises du matin
> Sur les myosotis immondes!

Rimbaud addresses Banville (to whom this letter-poem was sent) as "Cher." Gengoux explains the rest: Gautier had written of Banville that "il voltige au-dessus des fleurs de la prairie, enlevé par des souffles qui gonflent sa draperie aux couleurs changeantes." The Botticelli *Birth of Venus* is clearly involved here.

6th strophe:

> L'amour ne passe à tes octrois
> Que les Lilas,—ô balançoires!
> Et les Violettes du Bois,
> Crachats sucrés des Nymphes noires! . . .

"Love only allows lilies to pass through your [Banville's] customs." And Rimbaud calls the "wood-violets" (equally stereotyped in Parnassian poetry) prettily-mockingly: "sugary spittle gobs from black Nymphs." There is a violet-colored sugar-coated confection (called "Violets") made in Toulouse and which looks for all the world like *crachats*; they may well have existed in Rimbaud's era.

The "balançoires" could be a pastiche of Mallarmé's "Fleurs," "balançant la fiole future." Rimbaud applies the term to lilies in "Lys" (*Album Zutique*).

II

We pass from lilies to roses, equally hackneyed.

1st and 2nd strophes:

> O Poètes, quand vous auriez
> Les Roses, les Roses soufflées,
> Rouges sur tiges de lauriers,
> Et de mille octaves enflées!
>
> Quand BANVILLE en ferait neiger,
> Sanguinolentes, tournoyantes,
> Pochant l'œil fou de l'étranger
> Aux lectures mal bienveillantes!

Rimbaud imagines a whirlwind[1] storm of roses, as in some poem of Banville (or Botticelli's *Birth of Venus*), hitting some poor reader in the eyes and puffing them up ("Pochant l'œil fou de l'étranger"). The "readings" hence are "not friendly."[2] The main idea is that even if ("Quand . . . ") Banville storms the landscape with roses, we in France (strophe 4) still have only ridiculous flowers ("Toujours . . . ," strophes 4 and 5).

3rd and 4th strophes:

> De vos forêts et de vos prés,
> O très paisibles photographes!
> La Flore est diverse à peu près
> Comme des bouchons de carafes!

---

[1] Compare the *tourbillon* of toys in "Les Étrennes des orphelins."
[2] "Mille octaves" refers to octosyllabic verse, according to Suzanne Bernard.

> Toujours les végétaux Français,
> Hargneux, phtisiques, ridicules,
> Où le ventre des chiens bassets
> Navigue en paix, aux crépuscules;

Rimbaud complains that ordinary forests and meadows (photographic) have dull flora, no variety. The same old French vegetation, ridiculous, lowly (traversed by a low-slung dog, the basset hound).

5th strophe:

> Toujours, après d'affreux dessins
> De Lotos bleus ou d'Hélianthes,
> Estampes roses, sujets saints
> Pour de jeunes communiantes!

More complaints: horrid drawings of blue lotuses, pink "estampes" for "jeunes communiantes." It is implied that the poetic flowers of Banville replace them in vain.

6th strophe:

> L'Ode Açoka cadre avec la
> Strophe en fenêtre de lorette;
> Et de lourds papillons d'éclat
> Fientent sur la Pâquerette.

Rimbaud mocks at exotic poetic flowers, like *açokas* (favored by Leconte de Lisle), as well as humble *pâquerettes* (complete with butterflies). An ode containing the *açokas* is compared to a courtesan's window. The *pâquerettes* are soiled by butterflies—an excremental technique of satire much used in this poem.

8th strophe:

> Ces poupards végétaux en pleurs
> Que Grandville eût mis aux lisières,
> Et qu'allaitèrent de couleurs
> De méchants astres à visières!

"Ces poupards végétaux en pleurs . . . qu'allaitèrent de couleurs / De méchants astres à visières" seems to come from the word "influence" (literally a "pouring"-down of effects from stars) and from the milky way, cf. "astres lactés" in "L'Homme juste" and "lactescents" in the "Bateau ivre." There is a similar image in "L'Etoile a pleuré rose."

The stars, as painters, wear *visières*. Grandville, an illustrator, would have put these weeping vegetal babes only on margins.

10th strophe:

> Oui, vos bavures de pipeaux
> Font de précieuses glucoses!
> —Tas d'œufs frits dans de vieux chapeaux,
> Lys, Açokas, Lilas et Roses! . . .

sums up this section in which Rimbaud has made fun of vulgar illustrations, as well as the Parnassian flora.

III

> O blanc Chasseur, qui cours sans bas
> A travers le Pâtis panique,
> Ne peux-tu pas, ne dois-tu pas
> Connaître un peu ta botanique?

In the first strophe Banville is addressed as a "white Hunter" (the Parnassians describe many animals) and is told he should learn botany.

2nd strophe:

> Tu ferais succéder, je crains,
> Aux Grillons roux les Cantharides,
> L'or des Rios au bleu des Rhins,—
> Bref, aux Norwèges les Florides:

Otherwise he will mix up all sorts of things: crickets and Spanish flies, Norway and Florida, etc.

3rd strophe:

> Mais, Cher, l'Art n'est plus, maintenant,
> —C'est la verité,—de permettre
> A l'Eucalyptus étonnant
> Des constrictors d'un hexamètre;

Modern Art no longer permits mixing (for example, eucalyptus trees with hexameter-constrictors). He amusingly criticizes Parnassian verse forms, inappropriate to their objects.

5th strophe:

> —En somme, une Fleur, Romarin
> Ou Lys, vive ou morte, vaut-elle
> Un excrément d'oiseau marin?
> Vaut-elle un seul pleur de chandelle?

A famous statement announcing desentimentalized modern art: a flower isn't worth an "excrément d'oiseau marin" or a "pleur de chandelle." Corbière would agree. The bird-droppings are found in "Oraison du soir" and the "Bateau ivre"; in "Alchimie du verbe" we have the well-known passage about *déculture*.

I V

1st strophe:

> Dis, non les pampas printaniers
> Noirs d'épouvantables révoltes,
> Mais les tabacs, les cotonniers!
> Dis les exotiques récoltes!

Rimbaud tells Banville what to replace his vapid flowers with: fresh, surprising plants like "tabacs, . . . cotonniers."

2nd strophe:

> Dis, front blanc que Phébus tanna,
> De combien de dollars se rente
> Pedro Velasquez, Habana;
> Incague la mer de Sorrente

Or brute facts like the income of so-and-so. Crap on the sentimental sea of Sorrento, where thousands of Swans go (next strophe).

3rd strophe:

> Où vont les Cygnes par milliers;
> Que tes strophes soient des réclames
> Pour l'abatis des mangliers
> Fouillés des hydres et des lames!

Let your strophes be (rather) advertising posters for weird animals. The 4th, 5th, and 6th strophes offer more such suggestions.

7th strophe:

> Trouve, aux abords du Bois qui dort,
> Les fleurs, pareilles à des mufles,
> D'où bavent des pommades d'or
> Sur les cheveux sombres des Buffles!

The "Bois qui dort" rhymed with "or" is reminiscent of "Tête de faune"; the "mufles . . . bavent" announces an image of the "Bateau ivre."

8th strophe:

> Trouve, aux prés fous, où sur le Bleu
> Tremble l'argent des pubescences,
> Des calices pleins d'Œufs de feu
> Qui cuisent parmi les essences!

The "pubescences" are like those of the fields in "Les Poètes de sept ans."

9th strophe:

> Trouve des Chardons cotonneux
> Dont dix ânes aux yeux de braises
> Travaillent à filer les nœuds!
> Trouve des Fleurs qui soient des chaises!

Flower-chairs anticipate surrealism; this image may have arisen from the dreams of the chair-ridden "Assis." This in-between reality—human artifact-natural object—is characteristic (see next strophe).

10th strophe:

> Oui, trouve au cœur des noirs filons
> Des fleurs presque pierres,—fameuses!—
> Qui vers leurs durs ovaires blonds
> Aient des amygdales gemmeuses!

"Des fleurs presque pierres." Rimbaud's poetic reality is often a higher synthesis of this sort, between motion and rest, soft and hard, etc.; see under "Génie." The softness of ordinary pretty-pretty flowers is rejected likewise in "Métropolitain": "atroces fleurs qu'on appellerait cœurs et sœurs."

V

More advice to the poet:

1st strophe:

> Quelqu'un dira le grand Amour,
> Voleur des sombres Indulgences:
> Mais ni Renan, ni le chat Murr
> N'ont vu les Bleus Thyrses immenses!

Rimbaud suggests a daring image to replace the flowers of traditional mysticism: "Bleus Thyrses immenses!" which is a combination of pagan emblem and blue for Christianity (Bernard). Blue is a Christian symbol in "Les Premières Communions": "chastes bleuités" (IV). The "thyrse" may have come from Baudelaire's prose poem of the same name.

2nd strophe:
> Toi, fais jouer dans nos torpeurs,
> Par les parfums les hystéries;
> Exalte-nous vers des candeurs
> Plus candides que les Maries . . .

Here are more mocking suggestions of super-religious imagery; compare "Les Premières Communions" for these "hystéries" and the plural use of "Maries."

In the third to fifth strophes Rimbaud proposes a democratic and ridiculous variety of modern or bourgeois types as the new poets, and he sees their industrial products as the fresh new images, often recalling Laforgue's. Some, like the "poteaux télégraphiques . . . lyre aux chants de fer" are almost seriously surreal. But I doubt, unlike Suzanne Bernard, that he really means this seriously. It is just youthful impetuosity thumbing its nose and throwing anything it can get its hands on.

In strophes six and seven, tongue in cheek, Rimbaud recommends for the composition of mysterious poems a standard reference work (published by Hachette!) with namby-pamby illustrations.

The signature *Bava* is a perfect example of the tone of the whole; see our remarks on adolescent "drool" under "Le Cœur volé."

Les Premières Communions

Rimbaud's revolt against Christianity, in this lengthy and interesting poem, is put in terms of a very concrete and often rather affectionate regionalism, at times reminiscent of Alain-Fournier. One is made to feel how good pagan Nature is as against the contaminating cult (in "Soleil et chair" this was specifically Greek Nature, rather than French). There are also streaks of genuine bitterness. One wonders why he became thus exercised over the specific instance of a girl's—perhaps a sister's—First Communion. Perhaps, like so many French men, he was jealous of the priest's interference in the emotional life of his women.

I

3. "les divins babillages"

No doubt about his opinion of liturgy here; compare the end of "L'Homme juste."

4. Un noir grotesque dont fermentent les souliers:

A humble detail reminiscent of Joyce's cops "sweating Irish stew"; the young priest in "Un Cœur sous une soutane" had similar problems with his sweaty shoes. This is an effective subversion, reminding us of his all-too-human feet, at the pole opposite to spirituality, so to speak. Rimbaud must realize that it creates a human sympathy—those feet itch with a desire to dance, later.

5. Mais le soleil éveille, à travers les feuillages,
   Les vieilles couleurs des vitraux irréguliers.

We think of the uneven stained glass at Combray. Note the bright sounds in "Mais le soleil éveille."

7. La pierre sent toujours la terre maternelle.
   Vous verrez des monceaux de ces cailloux terreux
   Dans la campagne en rut qui frémit solennelle,
   Portant près des blés lourds, dans les sentiers ocreux,
   Ces arbrisseaux brûlés ou bleuit la prunelle,
   Des nœuds de mûriers noirs et de rosiers fuireux.

The stones of the church are still earthy, rooted in the maternal ground and half *of* it, like Sartre's shingle, dirty on one side. The Sartre of *Nausea* was trying to break free from the viscous, maternal, provincial dampness ("il pleuvra sur Bouville") and fly free with the clean, hard, metallic quality of jazz.[1] Rimbaud is equally eager to fly here, but like the early Sartre, he is ambivalent, still half held by the province, the home, and certainly the nature underlying them. So the feeling is mixed. The "rosiers fuireux" indicate a nausea, like the "campagne en rut," a slight male disgust at the too-natural. This countryside has some of the overripe, already slightly decaying quality ("arbrisseaux brûlés") of the last part of "Mémoire."

13. Tous les cent ans on rend ces granges respectables
    Par un badigeon d'eau bleue et de lait caillé:
    Si des mysticités grotesques sont notables
    Près de la Notre-Dame ou du Saint empaillé,
    Des mouches sentant bon l'auberge et les étables
    Se gorgent de cire au plancher ensoleillé.

[1] The porosity of human dwellings in the countryside reminds me of the interior-exterior, art-nature vibrancy in Meaulnes's and François's attic which was difficult to shut against the outdoors.

Here, there is a direct contrast between the "mysticités grotesques" and the goodness of natural life. The "mouches" are like living emanations of the light itself (Proust's "chamber music of Summer," referring to the buzzing); instead of praying before the candles, they *eat* their drippings in a true communion according to Rimbaud (as in "Fêtes de la faim"). The round wholesome "bon" is active again, and the stables imply the same acceptance of the whole man as does the similar image in "Les Reparties de Nina." The sun on the floor, like Mallarmé's sun on the stones (or wanting to freckle the panes in "Les Fenêtres"), is this full union of the above and the below.

> 19. L'enfant se doit surtout à la maison, famille
> Des soins naïfs, des bons travaux abrutissants;
> Ils sortent, oubliant que la peau leur fourmille
> Où le Prêtre du Christ plaqua ses doigts puissants.
> On paie au Prêtre un toit ombré d'une charmille
> Pour qu'il laisse au soleil tous ces fronts brunissants.

The simple life of the village children—good honest work—is contrasted with the contamination of Christianity: their skin has contracted a sort of itch from the contact with the priest. But they soon forget it. The priest is given a cottage (by the community), in the shade of a grove—perhaps a symbol of his dark work—in exchange for letting them go their pagan ways in the sun.

> 25. Le premier habit noir, le plus beau jour de tartes,
> Sous le Napoléon ou le Petit Tambour
> Quelque enluminure où les Josephs et les Marthes
> Tirent la langue avec un excessif amour
> Et que joindront, au jour de science, deux cartes,
> Ces seuls doux souvenirs lui restent du grand Jour.

A clear description of the souvenirs of the great day (the First Communion) which remain with the village lad.

> 31. Les filles vont toujours à l'église, contentes
> De s'entendre appeler garces par les garçons
> Qui font du genre après Messe ou vêpres chantantes.
> Eux qui sont destinés au chic des garnisons,
> Ils narguent au café les maisons importantes,
> Blousés neuf, et gueulant d'effroyables chansons.

An unproblematic description of the Sunday scene—boys teasing girls, swaggering around after the Mass.

37. Cependant le Curé choisit pour les enfances
    Des dessins; dans son clos, les vêpres dites, quand
    L'air s'emplit du lointain nasillement des danses,
    Il se sent, en dépit des célestes défenses,
    Les doigts de pied ravis et le mollet marquant;

—La Nuit vient, noir pirate aux cieux d'or débarquant.

The Curé putters around after vespers and, hearing distant music, feels an urge to dance, despite hierarchical interdictions. No bitterness here. The coming on of night is decoratively dramatic rather than portentous.

I I

A girl is singled out by the Priest for special distinction on the Great Day—our sad heroine.

I I I

The night before, the girl is deeply disturbed, feels sick. She has visions of angels, Jesus, the Virgin, taken from naïve religious pictures: "vermilion Foreheads bathed in watery green skies." (This image, for all its naïveté, is repeated in "Michel et Christine" and "Enfance.") She tastes of the "coolness" of innocence as a reward for her virginity, but Rimbaud sees the price as being too high. "Tes pardons sont glacés," he says to the Virgin.

I V

1. Puis la Vierge n'est plus que la vierge du livre.
   Les mystiques élans se cassent quelquefois . . .
   Et vient la pauvreté des images, que cuivre
   L'ennui, l'enluminure atroce et les vieux bois;

Sometimes mystic *élans* break, and one sees the underlying poverty of the religious imagery. Those "enluminures" are as awful as the one in "L'Éclatante victoire de Sarrebrück." Rimbaud will be kinder to popular art in "Alchimie du verbe."

5. Des curiosités vaguement impudiques
   Épouvantent le rêve aux chastes bleuités
   Qui s'est surpris autour des célestes tuniques,
   Du linge dont Jésus voile ses nudités.

Into the girl's imaginings creep oddly shameful thoughts about Jesus' body under his clothes. (We note "bleuités," blue as a religious color, as in "Ce qu'on dit au poète," "Fêtes de la faim," etc.)

9. Elle veut, elle veut, pourtant, l'âme en détresse,
   Le front dans l'oreiller creusé par les cris sourds,
   Prolonger les éclairs suprêmes de tendresse,
   Et bave . . . —L'ombre emplit les maisons et les cours.

But the girl tries to prolong her sublimity, struggles, and "drools."

13. Et l'enfant ne peut plus. Elle s'agite, cambre
    Les reins et d'une main ouvre le rideau bleu
    Pour amener un peu la fraîcheur de la chambre
    Sous le drap, vers son ventre et sa poitrine en feu . . .

She gets up to cool her fevered body.

V

1. A son réveil,—minuit,—la fenêtre était blanche.
   Devant le sommeil bleu des rideaux illunés,
   La vision la prit des candeurs du dimanche;
   Elle avait rêvé rouge. Elle saigna du nez,

Seeing the moonlit curtain, she thinks of the Sunday "candor." Her nose bleeds. The play between realistic details and vision is psychologically canny (one thinks of the woman who grew from Marcel's thigh when he slept; or her cheek from his pillow).

5. Et se sentant bien chaste et pleine de faiblesse
   Pour savourer en Dieu son amour revenant,
   Elle eut soif de la nuit où s'exalte et s'abaisse
   Le cœur, sous l'œil des cieux doux, en les devinant;

   De la nuit, Vierge-Mère impalpable, qui baigne
   Tous les jeunes émois de ses silences gris;
   Elle eut soif de la nuit forte où le cœur qui saigne
   Écoule sans témoin sa révolte sans cris.

She has regained her feeling of chastity but it is weak. She "thirsts for the night," silence, in a sort of death-wish. The silent night is compared to the Virgin-mother. Goethe's Mephistopheles too spoke of *Mutter Nacht*.

13. Et faisant la Victime et la petite épouse,
    Son étoile la vit, une chandelle aux doigts,
    Descendre dans la cour où séchait une blouse,
    Spectre blanc, et lever les spectres noirs des toits.

Like a Victim and little bride of Christ, she goes down to the courtyard, candle in hand; her blouse, ready for the morrow, is drying there, dangling like a white ghost. Dark ghosts rise from the roofs—shadows cast by her candle (cf. "Entends comme brame").

V I

1. Elle passa sa nuit sainte dans des latrines.
   Vers la chandelle, aux trous du toit coulait l'air blanc,
   Et quelque vigne folle aux noirceurs purpurines,
   En deçà d'une cour voisine s'écroulant.

   La lucarne faisait un cœur de lueur vive
   Dans la cour où les cieux bas plaquaient d'ors vermeils
   Les vitres; les pavés puant l'eau de lessive
   Souffraient l'ombre des murs bondés de noirs sommeils

She passes the holy night in the outhouse. We remember the "seven-year-old poet" seeking solace in the same place. Like the stable, the outhouse for Rimbaud is a site of humble poetry, recalling Richard Wilbur's "strangely refreshing tomb" (inside a potato). Nature is impartial, and its shy moonlit loveliness is glimpsed through openings, just as the little Marcel discovered a friendly vine entering his place of boyish sin. The white air circulates in the roof holes illumined by the candle: immediate, transparent life is affectionately observed. The gable window is a heart of brightness in the courtyard when low skies lay vermeil-gold effects on the panes: dawn is near. The paving stones, smelling of laundry water, color sulphur the shadow of walls filled with "dark slumbers" (shadows; compare Mallarmé's woods filled with "sommeils touffus," "L'Après-Midi d'un faune").

V I I

1. Qui dira ces langueurs et ces pitiés immondes,
   Et ce qu'il lui viendra de haine, ô sales fous
   Dont le travail divin déforme encor les mondes,
   Quand la lèpre à la fin mangera ce corps doux?

Rimbaud exclaims bitterly against these "languors and filthy pities." As in "Les Poètes de sept ans" the word *pitiés* means something like "the pity of it all" (*Othello*); the filth is the "souillure" (below) brought by the religious institution, as Rimbaud sees it, "whose divine work still deforms the world." The "sales fous" are the religionists (priests, etc.). And "when leprosy finally eats away this gentle body" implies that somehow the Church will be responsible for the rot. Then who will say what "hatred will come to her?"

VIII

> 1. Et quand, ayant rentré tous ses nœuds d'hystéries,
> Elle verra, sous les tristesses du bonheur,
> L'amant rêver au blanc million des Maries,
> Au matin de la nuit d'amour, avec douleur:

Having swallowed all her hysteria—her sick reaction to genuine love later, on her marriage bed—she will see, under the sorrows of happiness (her corrupted love-experience), the husband-lover "sorrowfully" dreaming of the myriad white-clad young *communiantes* (Maries), and he will regret "on the morning after the night of love" what has been done to them all to spoil his happiness.

> 5. "Sais-tu que je t'ai fait mourir? J'ai pris ta bouche,
> Ton cœur, tout ce qu'on a, tout ce que vous avez;
> Et moi, je suis malade: Oh! je veux qu'on me couche
> Parmi les Morts des eaux nocturnes abreuvés!

She addresses the husband with regret and guilt: "I made you die. I took your mouth and heart, all you have; and I am sick. Oh! I want to be lain among the Dead steeped in nocturnal waters." Here, the death-wish expressed earlier (V), and in "Les Sœurs de charité," becomes a compelling theme, comparable to the death-drinking of "Comédie de la soif": the "cimetière / Ah! tarir toutes les urnes."

> 9. "J'étais bien jeune, et Christ a souillé mes haleines.
> Il me bonda jusqu'à la gorge de dégoûts!
> Tu baisais mes cheveux profonds comme les laines,
> Et je me laissais faire ... ah! va, c'est bon pour vous,
>
> "Hommes! qui songez peu que la plus amoureuse
> Est, sous sa conscience aux ignobles terreurs,
> La plus prostituée et la plus douloureuse,
> Et que tous nos élans vers vous sont des erreurs!
>
> "Car ma Communion première est bien passée.
> Tes baisers, je ne puis jamais les avoir sus:
> Et mon cœur et ma chair par ta chair embrassée
> Fourmillent du baiser putride de Jésus!"

"Christ soiled my breaths, filled me with disgusts," cries the future bride, revolting against the puritanism that made her body seem dirty and befouled her mind (so Rimbaud's rather naïve analysis goes—as if the Church monopolized the negations of the body's impulses, by which civilization rises).

Addressing her husband she says: "You kissed me and I allowed it—it is all right for you men [i.e., they enjoy making love], unaware that the most amorous of women is also the most prostituted [i.e., her guilt, and espousal of Christ, at her core makes it a false love, really ungiving of the self, like an act of prostitution] and the most sorrowful, and that all our élans toward you are errors [i.e., in the eyes of the inner self, committed to Christ]."

She goes on: "My First Communion is now over, I can't even know your kisses [that is, really feel them inside]. And my heart and flesh embraced by your flesh swarm with the putrid kiss of Jesus." (That "swarming" also was felt on the boys' skin after the priest touched them, in part I.)

I X

1. Alors l'âme pourrie et l'âme désolée
   Sentiront ruisseler tes malédictions.
   —Ils auront couché sur ta Haine inviolée,
   Échappés, pour la mort, des justes passions,

   Christ! ô Christ, éternel voleur des énergies,
   Dieu qui pour deux mille ans vouas à ta pâleur,
   Cloués au sol, de honte et de céphalalgies,
   Ou renversés, les fronts des femmes de douleur.

"The rotten soul [the woman's] and the desolate soul [the man's] will feel your [religion's] curses pour down. They will have slept on your [God's] inviolable Hatred, escaped [i.e., deprived] until death, from just passions, Christ, O Christ, eternal stealer of energies [he absorbs all the woman's deep love], God who for two thousand years destined to Your pallor [—whether] nailed to the ground [i.e., prostrate, "crucified"] with shame and headaches or thrown back [in agony—] the foreheads of women in sorrow."

This was the theme, less bitterly put then, of "Soleil et chair." It will remain active throughout the *Saison en Enfer*, though in more complex form.

Les Chercheuses de poux

Rimbaud is going nowhere here; only glowing. Like the "angel in the hands of a barber" ("Oraison du soir"), he was touchingly pleased to be granted the sort of affectionate parental attention he had lacked on both sides. He got it a-plenty from the demoiselles Gindre, aunts of Izambard, who took him in during one of his flights and returns and were good to him (even to delousing his head) as only such childless spinsters can be.

Marcel Ruff thinks the "enfant" was a baby and the two sisters were young girls, all this merely witnessed by Rimbaud. That may be so (though the "lourds cheveux" seem to preclude it) but it hardly makes any difference to our understanding of the poem: with that *enfant* Rimbaud is totally identified.

The "voyou" is a sad little boy underneath the rough mask, a heart deprived rather than depraved. Despite the obvious sincerity and depth of the emotions, Rimbaud avoids excessive sentimentality by modern touches, realism, fresh imagery, general inventiveness. The title, for example, is gently plain-speaking, calling lice "lice." It has a faintly Barbizon ring, like *Les Glaneuses*, or a quality of mild, veristic genre painting.

> 1. Quand le front de l'enfant, plein de rouges tourmentes,
>   Implore l'essaim blanc des rêves indistincts,
>   Il vient près de son lit deux grandes sœurs charmantes
>   Avec de frêles doigts aux ongles argentins.

The child's head is infested with "red torments" and, to forget his pain, he seeks sleep: "the white swarm of indistinct dreams." Then the two charming sisters (probably Gindre) come to his bedside—almost like magic creatures from the dream-swarm—with their frail fingers and silvery nails. In "Les Sœurs de charité" he had already, more generally, admired the fragility of feminine fingers. The hands of these ladies, however, are also *competent*, even deadly so, like those of Jeanne-Marie.

> 5. Elles assoient l'enfant devant une croisée
>   Grande ouverte où l'air bleu baigne un fouillis de fleurs,
>   Et dans ses lourds cheveux où tombe la rosée
>   Promènent leurs doigts fins, terribles et charmeurs.

Here the color blue is *not* associated with religion—showing again how delicate and contextual a matter association ("symbolism") is—but is part of a fully accepted beauty of open air coming through a window, with an impressionistic jumble of flowers recalling "Tête de faune."

The "terrible" fingers, fatal to the lice, are also "charmeurs," cf. "machine aimée des qualités fatales" in "Génie," as well as the already-mentioned hands of Jeanne-Marie.

9. Il écoute chanter leurs haleines craintives
   Qui fleurent de longs miels végétaux et rosés,
   Et qu'interrompt parfois un sifflement, salives
   Reprises sur la lèvre ou désirs de baisers.

The realism of the saliva of the good single ladies, set flowing by the contact with a person (the boy), is remarkable for that era. The "sifflement," Rimbaud says, can be the breath holding back that flow, or a sigh, "désirs de baisers."

As Suzanne Bernard notes, there are many sibilant sounds in the strophe, which is alive with the described emotion. The breath is as intimately analyzed as Proust would have done, or Natalie Sarraute, for its delicate components and overtones: "slow vegetal and roseate honeys." This will be echoed by the "sèves inouïes" and the "confiture exquise aux bons poètes, / Des lichens de soleil . . . " of "the Bateau ivre."

13. Il entend leurs cils noirs battant sous les silences
    Parfumés; et leurs doigts électriques et doux
    Font crépiter parmi ses grises indolences
    Sous leurs ongles royaux la mort des petits poux.

Rimbaud mines the atmosphere for its full poetic worth. As so often he goes down to the sheer phenomena, the *données immédiates*, such as the air in a previous strophe and here the electric and perfumed silences (between the breaths, the inspiration of saliva, the crackling sounds of the lice being killed). This silence is as obsessively alive as a Chardin genre scene. The tension between the nothingness of silence and the little drama of death is the essence of "électrique": a stillness paradoxically alive. The sweet and deadly precision of those feminine fingers is wonderfully caught: the nails are stained royal red by the blood of the lice. What a span of being is integrated in this vibrantly real middle-ground of life!

17. Voilà que monte en lui le vin de la Paresse,
    Soupir d'harmonica qui pourrait délirer;
    L'enfant se sent, selon la lenteur des caresses,
    Sourdre et mourir sans cesse un désir de pleurer.

The electric tension reaches a peak by sobbing stages, and spills over into a kinetic phrase; *le courant passe*, it flows. The "wine of Laziness"—which La Rochefoucauld called "the greatest of all beatitudes"—is sheer passive delight, disinterested bliss, almost religious in nature, certainly innocently infantile. Rimbaud calls himself with total honesty "l'enfant." The feeling is so steep it is mingled, as authentic love of self, of life, always is, with *lacrimae rerum*, somewhat aggravated by the special self-pity Rimbaud was entitled to. The emotion is infinite and borders on hysteria like a harmonica's "sigh." This is unsurpassably modern, unsentimental and totally sentimental at once, like good contemporary music, Sartre's idolized saxophone air, Steppenwolf's jazz. And as with such music, the "blues" or whatever, a desire to weep is mingled in, in suspension, and wells up again and again.

Le Bateau ivre

Rimbaud's most famous poem had so long been overpraised (particularly in relation to some of his other works, like "Mémoire" or "Génie") that more recently there has been a tendency to underestimate it. I still regard it as a fantastic achievement by a boy of sixteen, or of any other age. It is less original than used to be thought—this is always the fate of originality, given time and historical critics—but powerfully inventive for all that, and absolutely characteristic of Rimbaud, linking up with the rest of his writings in countless ways.

The form is traditional Late Romantic, Parnassian, but the imagery and general tone are Impressionist-Symbolist. There is no use quibbling about its being a true Symbolist poem or not. Certainly it belongs to its cultural era, which is being increasingly defined as the Symbolist one (for example by René Wellek, after Edmund Wilson), by virtue of its impressionist-pointillist delicacy and refinement; and by its fluidity (as opposed to neo-classic discursive rigidity), including connotations, suggestive qualities of imagery, touches of synesthesia, the vibrant relation between sign and designatum, and the like.

Since the true meaning of Symbolism depends mainly on the foregoing qualities, it is idle to hunt for individual "symbols." Symbolism implies, to me, that the key images are in a fluid continuum, a chain (or net) of Being. Each symbol is a monad or microcosm, standing for the subjective-objective whole. It relates theoretically to all, and in practice to many of the verbal phenomena, through overtones, associations, echoes, rhymes.

There are myriad symbols in the poem. Some are more obvious than others, like the boat of the title itself, which crystallizes varied aspects of reality floating about in the world or the work. It stands (or, rather, lies) for the boy-poet himself, on the threshold of a special manhood—prefiguring the departing vessel of "Adieu"—timorously launching into the sea of independence, adult human life or, more deeply, the unknown force of the whole cosmos (including prominently the feminine waters of birth and mother-nature or life *qua* experience). As such, it vibrates with reminiscences of all sorts of literary boats, from the *Odyssey* through Poe's *Arthur Gordon Pym* to Baudelaire's "Le Voyage" and "le vaisseau fantôme" of Wagner (and, later, the "Coup de Dés").

But this vessel is far more "Symbolist" than any of its predecessors in the sense that the relation between the concrete form (the boat as symbol) and the substantive reality is constantly alive, fluid, vibrant. Many aspects of the boat reflect aspects of the boy *sensually*: his body *feels* like a boat, lying down in a dark room awash with memories and potentialities; its rocking and *élans*—later, its rotting timbers—are perceived as direct parts of the self. And the sea is apprehended with equal *intimacy* as expression of a life's vicissitudes.

The poem tells of the moment when, after a long "winter" of childhood numbness ("l'autre hiver," strophe 3) and of powerlessness under the resented regime of a harshly dutiful mother, the gathering life-forces, the "sèves inouïes" (strophe 16) of the adolescent rise to spiritual revolt. The spirituality is emphasized by the fact that there is no outer action: it all occurs in a dream, or in a state of intoxication, *n'importe*; in any case, it is an inner crisis and evolution.

The disaffection and dissidence here are extraordinarily pronounced, primarily because the child was so full of life, so exceptional (to start with, undoubtedly, but also aggravatedly, because of his circumstances), and secondly because both the later-19th-century provincial France generally and the mother were so repressive. Strong as she obviously was, she had failed as a female parent, had not succeeded in keeping the family together, had lost her husband by divorce or separation, so, partly for this reason too, the revolt came sooner than most.

Such revolts are seldom complete—what in life is?—and we need not exaggerate: at the end of the poem it is clear that Rimbaud is not yet ready to let go of the ropes of the "haulers" (strophe 1)—umbilical cords or their later extension, apron strings—and that he still fears the adult world with its prisons ("pontons," last strophe). And, as it has been observed, his later wanderings, like his earlier ones, always returned to his only Penelope, his mother. So let us not talk too soon about "smashing reality like a money box," as the schematic and often heavy-handed Sartre does. Although Rimbaud makes genuine advances in syntactical fluidity and openness both here in "Le Bateau ivre" and more remarkably in the works that follow, his reality is nonetheless recognizably inscribed in a specific time, place and tradition which also must be taken into account. Rimbaud is also us, an almost predictable, immensely appealing (French) boy—not unlike Meaulnes—who makes sense if we read him and his times right. This is not finally to "tame" him—on the contrary. As Norge says, there is nothing more *intimate* than a symmetric French garden. Or, as Richard Wilbur puts it, when decorum prevails, "there are most tigers in the woods."

1st strophe:
> Comme je descendais des Fleuves impassibles,
> Je ne me sentis plus guidé par les haleurs:
> Des Peaux-Rouges criards les avaient pris pour cibles,
> Les ayant cloués nus aux poteaux de couleurs.

The "impassive Rivers" are the numbly suspended, dull course of his life to this point, seen as a river itinerary in a dream, heading for the open ocean of freedom, widening. It is like the underground rushing waters that sound the approach to a mystic experience in *Le Grand Meaulnes*,[1] or a release, a thaw to maturity, emotional openness, like the close of "Hérodiade." The suspension is humming with new possibilities, we sense, when we are aware that the guidelines, the "tow-ropes," the spiritual umbilical cords of childhood dependency, have been dropped.

Right away there is the fear of "anguished freedom." The "haulers," resented but mild symbols of everyday familial or societal authority (mothers, teachers, priests, etc.) are done in by savage creatures, "shrieking Redskins." They avenge Rimbaud momentarily, and he identifies with them, sadistically—with sexual undertones to this sadism in the "nus" (as the fake zealot was said to be naked under his hypocritical clothes in "Le Châtiment de Tartufe"). But these figures are also frightening, with something of the bogeyman mothers use to keep their young in line (more deeply rooted than the societal ones). Antoine Adam found a likely source a line in Verlaine's *La Bonne Chanson*, XVII: "Il [le monde] peut . . . nous prendre pour cibles." The Indians may come from Chateaubriand's *Les Natchez*.

---

[1] This mysterious combination of homecoming (to freedom) and Outward-Bound is like the opening scene of Broch's *Death of Virgil*, Tennyson's "Crossing the Bar," or the long rivery closes of Brahms' symphonies (particularly No. 2). It involves a mysterious close-of-cycle fusion of death and life, of old man and infant (as in the symbolism of the New Year). See our later comment on the "noyé pensif," the Old Man of the Sea (Shakespeare's "father" who lies "full fathom five" in *The Tempest*, Keats' Glaucon in "Endymion," who is the spectral father of the poet; Mallarmé's *vieillard* in the "Coup de Dés," who carries the *ombre juvénile* in him). Wordsworth's "child is the father of the man" expresses the awesome paradox, as does the enigmatic stained-glass King of Proust's Combray, who partly represents the child's kingdom of innocence and magic omnipotence. Compare the old space traveler with the embryo in him at the close of *2001, a Space Odyssey*. Or the endlessly fascinating and puzzling king of playing cards and Tarot.

2nd strophe:

> J'étais insoucieux de tous les équipages,
> Porteur de blés flamands ou de cotons anglais.
> Quand avec mes haleurs ont fini ces tapages,
> Les Fleuves m'ont laissé descendre où je voulais.

The child-man, advancing tentatively, fearfully but advancing all the same like Petit-Poucet ("Ma Bohème"), comes into intimate view. There is youthful braggadoccio—as well as some genuine new confidence, a daring *élan*—in the "heedless of all crews." For, at the end, those adult "crews" will cow him anew. They are associated with boats of commerce, a busy adult northern (Flemish, English) world which is coldly efficient like his mother and the bourgeois generally—there is probably some connection here with the "hiver" of the next strophe.

The final fearful stirrings, trepidations, qualms die away. He "lets go."[2] It is like being taken over by a roller coaster, or childbirth, birth of the new self: exhilarating. One accepts being a part of the subjective-objective order, the cosmos, as Nietzsche did in his privileged moments.

3rd strophe:

> Dans les clapotements furieux des marées,
> Moi, l'autre hiver, plus sourd que les cerveaux d'enfants,
> Je courus! Et les Péninsules démarrées
> N'ont pas subi tohu-bohus plus triomphants.

Like a contemporary surfer, he rides the excitingly challenging waves of freedom, independence. The "other winter" is a mixture of the long numb winter of discontent in childhood thralldom, now thawing, a northern, coldly efficient atmosphere of duty in a society against which he is now rebelling (cf. the northern commercial boats above), plus a more general feeling of cold openness—sweeping as blank snow—which is part of the daring, new free scene. Winter is a time of fresh resolve: New Year's resolutions, birth from year-end. Having ventured forth into the freezing outdoors and "made it," the child draws confidence, like the Mallarmé of "Le vierge, le vivace et le bel aujourd'hui." The "autre" gives a timeless, eternal quality which corresponds to the spatial openness. Both are typical of crucial dreams (cf. "la neige éternelle," "Villes," II; and "hiver éternel," Baudelaire, "Le Poème du haschisch"). Thus in "Les Déserts de l'amour" he is moved "to death" in his sleep by the murmur of "the night of the last century." This is linked to "hiver" and "sourd" in

---

[2] This is the hardest thing for a sensitive being, like Rimbaud, to do. For example, James Joyce was deadly afraid of one thing above all: losing consciousness, control, his identity (see Richard Ellman's biography).

> Je sortis dans la ville sans fin. O fatigue! [numbness]. Noyé
> dans la nuit *sourde* et dans la fuite du bonheur. C'était comme
> une nuit d'*hiver*, avec une neige pour étouffer le monde dé-
> cidément [the smothering of independent life].

In "Génie," the "nuit d'hiver" is a dream of strength and summer amid
winter rigors: "au haut des déserts de neige." The "deafer than children's
brains" is related ambiguously to this wintery pall and the stubborn isola-
tion in new night- or day-dreaming individuality (cf. the "unheeding"
above), like a sulking, in-turned child, which he had been in "Les Poètes
de sept ans" (rehearsing in the last lines this flight by imaginary boat).
This rapt inwardness is closely akin to the later image of the drowning
men (seeing their whole lives roll by), or an embryo in its amniotic fluid
(or a foetus in a bottle).[3] That "sourd" has a dull reverberating quality
like a dream echo-chamber.[4]

"I ran!" he brags, beginning a series of self-assertive *Je*'s. The image of
a detached peninsula (no doubt from some legendary or exotic source,
such as the floating islands of Mexico) is apt for this new freedom: the
child-peninsula, or part, breaking away from the mainland-mother, a
whole, and becoming a new full entity, as in mitosis. The peninsula is a
good shape and sound for male pride. The swelling-at-the-top P in
"Péninsule" and "triomphants" (plus all the o's) adds to the pride, or
mushroom-cloud, hubris feeling. This goes with the numerous b's in
"subi . . . bohu . . . béni . . . bouchons," which are rounded, buoyant,
bubbly, etc.[5] This rocky and rackety trial is being triumphantly sur-
mounted.

    4th strophe:
            La tempête a béni mes éveils maritimes.
            Plus léger qu'un bouchon j'ai dansé sur les flots
            Qu'on appelle rouleurs éternels de victimes,
            Dix nuits, sans regretter l'œil niais des falots!

The "maritime awakenings" are the new fuller awareness of self, as when
we say a woman is "awakened" to love. Note the bright é and i for this

---

[3] Recall the embryonic coil of "Ma Bohème." The "hippocampes" of strophe 20 is
a faintly related image.

[4] Curiously appropriate to the sonorous quality of distant sounds in winter, com-
pare Baudelaire's "Chant d'automne": "Tout l'hiver va rentrer dans mon être . . .
écho . . . sourd." Gide's André Walter, in a crisis of inward listening spoke of his
"tête sonore." Verlaine in his "Green" has a "tête toute sonore" rolling on his mis-
tress' lap.

[5] See *Toward the Poems of Mallarmé*, Appendix c, under *p* and *b*. Compare Keats'
"beaded bubbles winking at the brim" ("Ode to a Nightingale").

effect in "béni ... éveil ... maritimes ... léger." Lightness, buoyancy, is the essence of freedom, the defeat of enslaving gravity. Rimbaud mocks the vaguely Hugolian ("Oceano nox") fears of the ocean as "eternal roller of victims." He regrets not the silly shore beacons. The essence of mother as secure "mainland" for the perhaps sick or frightened child is the light down the hall at night, "La lampe de la famille rougissait l'une après l'autre les chambres voisines." ("Les Déserts de l'amour," Bernard, p. 189). Compare the "braise" in the dark forest of the "Sorcière" in "Après le déluge." In "Veillées" III, "Les lampes et les tapis de la veillée font le bruit des vagues, la nuit" which links the maternal lamp with the nocturnal sea voyage here. Rejection of this security as "silly" is absolutely appropriate to the mood of new confidence (and yet?).

5th strophe:
> Plus douce qu'aux enfants la chair des pommes sures,
> L'eau verte pénétra ma coque de sapin
> Et des taches de vins bleus et des vomissures
> Me lava, dispersant gouvernail et grappin.

The "sour apples" have the tartness of challenging, fresh life. The green water (associated with green apples as well as, no doubt, absinthe) envelops and invades him; as a boat he is a passive-female inner shape as well as an active-male outer one, and these two modes alternate frequently. Part of the passivity here is the admitted child-status ("enfants") and the being "bathed"; his "letting go" is to abandon himself to a greater force—the ocean (like the "Génie" of "Les Sœurs de charité" and of "Génie" and "Conte")—to be taken over, *possessed*, by something like a father-God (cf. "O saisons, ô châteaux": "dispersa tous efforts," and the "ange aux mains d'un barbier" of "Oraison du soir"; "Général . . . bombarde-nous" of the *Saison en Enfer*, the "je succomberai" of "Bannières de mai").[6]

The ocean here is at times neutral, and at times either "male" or "female" (even as the boat varies its mode between active and passive); in the next

---

[6] In this last poem, as often, both parents are merged in the sun ("c'est rire aux parents qu'au soleil"), the world-forces (as in "Génie," though the accent there is on the virile). The ocean of myth is a father (Oceanus) as well as a mother ("mère-mer"); for James Joyce it is both his "great gray mother" (the beginning of *Ulysses*) and his "cold feary father" (end of *Finnegans Wake*). Here too it is both, as nature is mainly neutral sexually, but there are different specific modes involving one or the other sex as an accented rhythm, or aspect, of nature, playing on universal analogy (or the fact that the sexes emerge from aspects of nature, metaphysical and physical laws). When a mother invades her child's mouth with a spoon, or its rectum with an enema, she is metaphysically male. When she washes and caresses him she is more "female" (see Sartre's analysis of the "hole" in *L'Être et le néant*, i.e., its reversible meaning).

strophe the "take charge" aspect of the ocean becomes pronouncedly feminine.

The "vins bleus" and the "vomissures" echo the *ivre* of the title, another obvious form of "letting go" but clearly rejected for something more total here. This dream-sea maternally washes away the spots of wine: the vomit of a night of debauchery as in "Bonne pensée du matin": "l'aube évapore / L'odeur du soir fêté . . . "; *vins bleus* is wine which makes spots—*taches*—that are hard to remove: "la mer, que j'aimais comme si elle eût dû me laver d'une souillure" ("Alchimie du verbe").

6th strophe:

> Et dès lors, je me suis baigné dans le Poème
> De la Mer, infusé d'astres, et lactescent,
> Dévorant les azurs verts; où, flottaison blême
> Et ravie, un noyé pensif parfois descend;

Here the child abandons himself to envelopment by the ocean of beauty ("Poème"), of life, as in "Génie": "Il nous a connus tous et nous a tous aimés"; but here there is a decided overtone of *mère*, in "mer," reinforced by the milk in "lactescent" and the "lava" in the last line of the preceding strophe.

The fantasy feeling of childhood communion with mother-essence is very much like Wynken, Blynken, and Nod on their sky-sailing dream-boat. Rimbaud was completely honest about this shamelessly plunging mood: in "Les Déserts de l'amour" he speaks of his being "ému jusqu'à la mort par le murmure du lait du matin et de la nuit du siècle dernier." He combines milk with the milky sky of dawn (precisely as Mallarmé does in "Don du poème") emerging from the depth of night-death, and all this is related to a clear dream-mother-figure; compare the Cybèle of "Soleil et chair" and "l'astre lacté" of "L'Homme juste." The "Mer . . . Dévorant les azurs verts" refers to the sea's absorption by reflection, fusion, with the sky; recall the trees mingling with the *azur* and its (milky) white star in "Roman."

The "flottaison blême / Et ravie, un noyé pensif" is discussed under strophe 3. The image recurs in strophe 17. The "ravie" is the rapt fascination of the "diving" child at the sea-change into rich and strange phenomena.[7]

---

[7] One easily thinks of Shakespeare's "Full fathom five": the conversion through death-in-life, to a new "undersea" world of art; the association with the dead father-figure who preceded the son into mystery. The "livres . . . qui avaient trempé dans l'océan" of "Les Déserts de l'amour" are similar to the end of *The Tempest*.

7th strophe:

> Où, teignant tout à coup les bleuités, délires
> Et rhythmes lents sous les rutilements du jour,
> Plus fortes que l'alcool, plus vastes que nos lyres,
> Fermentent les rousseurs amères de l'amour!

This strophe is full of mysterious undersea music and light flashes—bright gong-like effects of i and u in "délires . . . rhythmes . . . rutilements . . . lyres" versus dark effects of ou in "tout à coup . . . rousseurs . . . amour"—like a "happening," with synesthesia[8] matching the sea-sky fusion in the generalized promiscuity of a wonderful integrated magic world. The "bitter ruddinesses" spread happily, marrying the ocean "bluenesses."[9]

No doubt *amère* is called up by the harmony of *mer-mère-amère*, etc., which we discussed previously, and there may be a connection with his own mother, as in the similar instance of the "mer a perlé rousse" of "L'Étoile a pleuré rose." It may be too that the "bleu regard . . . qui ment" of his mother's eyes in "Les Poètes de sept ans" is vaguely recalled here, in the contamination of *amère*.

8th strophe:

> Je sais les cieux crevant en éclairs, et les trombes
> Et les ressacs et les courants: je sais le soir,
> L'Aube exaltée ainsi qu'un peuple de colombes,
> Et j'ai vu quelquefois ce que l'homme a cru voir!

Events—vertical, dramatic—happen: lightning going down, waterspouts shooting up. The repeated "Je sais" is pathetically boastful, like one child to another as in the later desire to show children the goldfish (strophe 15).

The "Aube exaltée ainsi qu'un peuple de colombes" is an exquisite epiphany of dawn spraying up (like Mallarmé's "Palmes!"). Dawn was Rimbaud's favorite experience; we will return to it under "Aube." The religious overtone is duplicated in the "croix consolatrice" over the ocean of "Délires," II. The fourth line is like Marianne Moore's famous "live toads in imaginary gardens" or Mallarmé's "De vue et non de visions" (the "vue" referring to true vision) in "Prose," i.e., a leap joining two radically distinct categories of Being:[10] fiction ("cru voir") and reality

---

[8] Sounds ("lyres"), tactile effects ("alcool," in part), visual effects (the colors), echo each other here. "Lyres" are "vastes," etc. In Yeats' "Byzantium" the gongs are similarly siren-seductive.

[9] "Bleuité" is invented by Rimbaud, cf. "bleuisons" of "Les Mains de Jeanne-Marie."

[10] Kant says we cannot *think* the color blue. True. But also, ultimately, not true.

("vu"); "Je n'exagère rien. J'ai vu. A la fin tous ces nuages aux formes fantastiques et lumineuses, ces ténèbres chaotiques, ces immensités vertes et roses. . . . Je reconnais ce que je n'ai jamais vu" (Baudelaire, *Salon de 1859*).

Rimbaud will use a flock of birds for the swarming life of vision once again in this poem and, later, in "Vies."

9th strophe:
> J'ai vu le soleil bas, taché d'horreurs mystiques.
> Illuminant de longs figements violets,
> Pareils à des acteurs de drames très antiques
> Les flots roulant au loin leurs frissons de volets!

This apocalyptic sun with its "figements violets" recalls the Last Judgement *strideurs* of "rayon violet" in "Voyelles." The "figements" are inspired, no doubt, by Baudelaire's sundown "sang qui se fige" ("Harmonie du soir"). The waves succeeding each other across the horizon are like mysterious actors moving hieratically, processionally, across a stage (perhaps a Greek chorus; cf. "Scènes"). "Frissons de volets" is marvelous for this rippling alternation of striated light-and-shadow on sea-surface.

10th strophe:
> J'ai rêvé la nuit verte aux neiges éblouies,
> Baiser montant aux yeux des mers avec lenteurs,
> La circulation des sèves inouïes,
> Et l'éveil jaune et bleu des phosphores chanteurs!

The winter night in his dream is like the one in "Les Déserts de l'amour" (already discussed under strophe 3); this one is oceanic green. It is probably associated with the mother, as in "Les Déserts": "Baiser montant aux yeux des mers" may recall the embrace he sought in his mother's blue look in "Les Poètes de sept ans." The effect recalls the "Baiser d'or du Bois qui se recueille" of "Tête de faune": love's beauty-light rising in the sea-eye (in "Fleurs" the sea is an eye, as is the river water in "Mémoire"). The blue in the last line is mingled with the "male" yellow as at the close of "Mémoire." Here in a promising moment the sap of life is rising full in his adolescent veins—"plein de sang!" ("Les Déserts")—and he seems to mate with a male-female life force (cf. "Génie"), which somehow includes the essence of his mother, one feels. But, of course, one cannot prove anything this complex. Still the theme of marriage, the restored happy family, is one of Rimbaud's clear and recurrent themes, which we discuss in our Introduction. Synesthesia ("phosphores chanteurs") helps to bring together magically (as does the coupling of the two colors, cf.

the frequent red and black pairing) the tragically split world—the crack of the "absurd"—represented in Rimbaud's broken home. In this sense I believe the ubiquitous coupling of red and black represents an attempt to overcome the most primordial split in the cosmos: between light and darkness, life and death. The marriage of yellow (gold) and blue is discussed under "Mémoire."

11th strophe:

> J'ai suivi, des mois pleins, pareille aux vacheries
> Hystériques, la houle à l'assaut des récifs,
> Sans songer que les pieds lumineux des Maries
> Pussent forcer le mufle aux Océans poussifs!

The hysterical herds, foaming at the mouth ("poussifs"), are a fairly apt metaphor for surf. In Greek myth the surf was imagined as the manes of horses of Poseidon, and the wild horses of Camargue are thought by some to be remembered here.

The feet of the Virgin Mary traditionally calm the sea. "Marie de la mer" is an important figure in Bretagne, hymned by Corbière. Verlaine has "La mer sur qui prie / La Vierge Marie," imitated by Rimbaud in "Chanson de la plus haute tour." Mallarmé too has "tes pieds qui calme-raient la mer" (Pléiade, p. 15). But Rimbaud is "unheeding" of her, doesn't even think of her power, but accepts the tumult, life as it is, in a Nietzschean-Camusian sense. The plural of Maries indicates a number of such statues (or places named after the Virgin) along the coast of France.

12th strophe:

> J'ai heurté, savez-vous, d'incroyables Florides
> Mêlant aux fleurs des yeux de panthères à peaux
> D'hommes! Des arcs-en-ciel tendus comme des brides
> Sous l'horizon des mers, à de glauques troupeaux!

Exotic notes from his youthful readings crop up: goodness knows where he got the "panthers with men's skins" but it is a pleasing idea, reversing the usual formula, like "man bites dog." The jungle picture here is in the manner of "le douanier" Rousseau. Rainbows are apparently like giant loops of bridles—perhaps an echo of the Ocean herd—attached undersea to watery herds; not so felicitous an image, rather forced in fact.

13th strophe:

> J'ai vu fermenter les marais énormes, nasses
> Où pourrit dans les joncs tout un Léviathan!
> Des écroulements d'eaux au milieu des bonaces,
> Et les lointains vers les gouffres cataractant!

The drunkenness moves into a hangover phase, *gueule de bois*, with some dramatic movements of water, full of potential menace ("gouffres").

14th strophe:

> Glaciers, soleils d'argent, flots nacreux, cieux de braises!
> Échouages hideux au fond des golfes bruns
> Où les serpents géants dévorés des punaises
> Choient, des arbres tordus, avec de noirs parfums!

More exotic spectacles parade by in the first line, none particularly poetic. The "Échouages hideux," etc., deepen the hangover effect, a heavy coming-aground after the free buoyancy, back to a viscous darkness rather like the "boue" at the end of "Mémoire." The snakes, like the rotting Leviathan, represent well the inner disgust (the throat lining, the dirty human plumbing generally). They also, with their "noirs parfums" (see our Introduction to the Derniers vers, below) represent a fear of homosexuality. The "cieux de braise" will have a rough later equivalent in the "brasiers, pleuvant" of "Barbare."

15th strophe:

> J'aurais voulu montrer aux enfants ces dorades
> Du flot bleu, ces poissons d'or, ces poissons chantants.
> —Des écumes de fleurs ont bercé mes dérades
> Et d'ineffables vents m'ont ailé par instants.

He bounces back with a new note of wistfulness—it's not all that easy, this freedom. The desire to show other children the goldfish and the other phenomena is typically infantile bragging; here it is brought in by the sophisticated Rimbaud as a note of honest humility and pathos so characteristic of him (as of Salinger: Holden Caulfield would have felt the same way). Besides, only they who spoke with the "sweetness of idiots" ("Les Poètes de sept ans")—like Faulkner's Benjy—would truly understand.

The second part of the strophe is as gently lyrical as the first. The last line is an exquisitely childish yielding to the breezes, the world. The ff of "ineffables" and the v of "vents" are windy (as Plato said in the *Cratylus*).[11]

16th strophe:

> Parfois, martyr lassé des pôles et des zones,
> La mer dont le sanglot faisait mon roulis doux
> Montait vers moi ses fleurs d'ombre aux ventouses jaunes
> Et je restais, ainsi qu'une femme à genoux . . .

---

[11] See *Toward the Poems of Mallarmé*, Appendix c. Compare Hugo ("Booz endormi"): "Un frais parfum sortait des touffes d'asphodèle; / Les souffles de la nuit flottaient sur Galgala." Leconte de Lisle speaks somewhere of "l'aile du vent."

The humility and passivity extend here into lassitude and drifting. He has traveled far in this inner world of vast space and time. The emotional charge (*cathexis*) of the crisis was clearly great. Now he floats rather like Ophélie on her river, gently, passively, and compares himself to a woman, a humbly kneeling one, foreshadowing the squatting child of the next-to-last strophe.

The verb tense, which has alternated between *passé défini* and *passé composé* heretofore, now becomes the imperfect for the next six strophes. The tone has changed from dramatic staccato events to a more fluid continuous effect of backdrop or reminiscence of a whole era: the bold striking-out is over.

The maternal aspect of *la mer* is strong again now in the flowery sucking-cups, emerging from the dark depths as a feverish child in the night might see them coming in his mother's hands.

17th strophe:

> Presque île, ballottant sur mes bords les querelles
> Et les fientes d'oiseaux clabaudeurs aux yeux blonds.
> Et je voguais, lorsqu'à travers mes liens frêles
> Des noyés descendaient dormir, à reculons!

The passivity is emphasized by the boat as container, carrying clamorous birds—lighter ("blond eyed") variants of the *gueule de bois* serpents, with similar fecal muddy quality in their "fientes." The drowning men are vaguely a threat now, though again they represent mainly, as in strophe 6, a rapt inner meditation.[12] The menace and the insecurity are implied too in the frailty of the "liens": Rimbaud seems almost to miss *les haleurs*. The curious expression "Presque île" emphasizes that he is not entirely independent (Eng.: "almost an island"). The "regret" of "old parapets" is not far off.

18th strophe:

> Or moi, bateau perdu sous les cheveux des anses,
> Jeté par l'ouragan dans l'éther sans oiseau,
> Moi dont les Monitors et les voiliers des Hanses
> N'auraient pas repêché la carcasse ivre d'eau;

The "cheveux des anses"[13] are a further example of the *échouages*, the running aground (strophe 14), the developing failure. The "éther" lacks

---

[12] And the strange combination of man-child (embryo) in the moment of death and rebirth to spiritual life (see footnote 1).

[13] Compare the "bras . . . d'herbe" of "Mémoire," and similar vegetation along the river banks in Flaubert's *Un Cœur Simple*.

the familiar orientation of birds, a part of the well-known European scene he is beginning to regret (strophe 21). Fearful gunboats, *Monitors*, somewhat nightmarish visions like the prison-boats (*pontons*) at the dark close of the poem, loom up from his past readings. The Hanseatic "voiliers" recall the commercial boats mentioned in strophe 2—the adult boats he ignored then, and now fears, or needs the help of, to fish his water-logged body out of the sea. He anxiously surmises they would not even bother: after all, he didn't give a hang for them.

19th strophe:
> Libre, fumant, monté de brumes violettes,
> Moi qui trouais le ciel rougeoyant comme un mur
> Qui porte, confiture exquise aux bons poètes,
> Des lichens de soleil et des morves d'azur;

Although the strophe begins with an assertion of freedom, the tone (furthered by the passive, fluid imperfect) is increasingly resigned. The imagery is more and more lyric, static, less dynamic or dramatic: more intimately Rimbaldian, in sum. Hence it returns to the numb scenes of childhood, "not going anywhere." We see the wall from his backyard, as in "Les Poètes de sept ans," closely observed by the little boy who was desperately in need of *something* to latch onto: insects, moss, anything gentle and apart from the forbidding world of people, adults and most of his peers too (who called him "sale cagot," etc.).

So the strophe, which begins with the forced confidence of "libre" and the "Moi qui" plus the image of voyaging to the exotic and new, soon turns insensibly (partly through the limp imperfect) to the humbly familiar. The wall, which began as a metaphor of the sky, takes over, in a remarkable modulation, the main interest. And although the ensuing images are extensions of the metaphor, we are aware that the "bons poètes" are linked with the imagery of a defeated childhood: the "reddening" of the sunset, "lichens of the sun," "exquisite jam"—the very essence of a child's solace—even the "morves," which are also comforting to deprived children, like other excrement or exudations, such as the "eye discoloring on the cheek" of the pauper children down the street in "Les Poètes de sept ans."

The "violet mists" too are associated with perfectly resigned beauty: the apocalypse of the sun described in one of the quieter moments earlier (strophe 9) was colored with "figements violets." In "Comédie de la soif" the violets represent the ultimate resignation, a beauty-in-death for which the poet finally thirsts (*sitio*) like the melting clouds ("fondre où fond ce nuage") which are akin to the violet mists (and curdlings) here. In

"Voyelles," too, the "rayon violet" is an ultimate refinement of light in divine Eyes.

20th strophe:

> Qui courais, taché de lunules électriques,
> Planche folle, escorté des hippocampes noirs,
> Quand les juillets faisaient crouler à coups de triques
> Les cieux ultramarins aux ardents entonnoirs;

Now he is a sadly diminished "boat," a mere "planche" and a "planche folle" at that. The "entonnoirs" are another example of growing threat. July makes the ultramarine sky crumble with cudgel-blows—excessive heat bringing on a storm, the hoped-for final release (as in many other poems: "Larme," "Michel et Christine," "Après le déluge"): "O que ma quille éclate!" (23rd strophe).

The imagery here is increasingly automatic, forced ("lunules électriques," etc.), marred by the brittle modernist virtuosity of "Ce qu'on dit au poète." It goes on for a while thus unconvincingly, but halfway through the next strophe he collapses; and the voyage is over.

21st strophe:

> Moi qui tremblais, sentant geindre à cinquante lieues
> Le rut des Béhémots et les Maelstroms épais,
> Fileur éternel des immobilités bleues,
> Je regrette l'Europe aux anciens parapets!

The imagery is repetitively and compulsively dramatic, exotic, visionary—large distances, Behemoths, Maelstroms, eternal skies—with a certain new note of aridity and defeat. All this infinity and wide-open liberty which can be anguish comes to a merciful halt, abruptly: he breaks down and confesses his regret for reality and the familiar life of Europe, with its limiting but old-friendly reassuring walls.

22nd strophe:

> J'ai vu des archipels sidéraux! et des îles
> Dont les cieux délirants sont ouverts au voyageur:
> —Est-ce en ces nuits sans fonds que tu dors et t'exiles,
> Million d'oiseaux d'or, ô future Vigueur?

A last look back over the adventure and a feeble attempt to crank up the dream, evoking the starry spaces he voyaged over. He scrapes at the bottom of the barrel, so to speak, digging desperately into his psyche for untapped resources. The hidden layers are like the depths of those dream-spaces, the "bottomless nights," the death Baudelaire sought at last in "Le Voyage," plunging into the *inconnu* to find *du nouveau*. The untapped strength itself—"future Vigor"—like dredged-up gold or stars in the night, is described as "a million golden birds." Birds, eternal symbols of man's Eros sublimated into spiritual aspiration, add dynamism to the gold.[14]

23rd strophe:

> Mais, vrai, j'ai trop pleuré! Les Aubes sont navrantes.
> Toute lune est atroce et tout soleil amer:
> L'âcre amour m'a gonflé de torpeurs enivrantes.
> O que ma quille éclate! O que j'aille à la mer!

The honest childish theme of weeping colors this return to earth, defeat, as it did tne close of "Les Déserts de l'amour" ("j'ai pleuré plus que tous les enfants du monde") and "Les Poètes de sept ans" ("pitié!").

Dawn, buoyant in an earlier strophe (as usual in Rimbaud), is "heartbreaking"—a broken promise! Moons, redolent of happy marriage, are likewise bitter disappointments: "atrocious," exactly as the "Or des lunes d'avril au cœur du saint lit" become a somber "regret" toward the sad close of "Mémoire." Suns (multiple in time or space), too, the very sources of light, are bitter in this psychic rout. Love itself, even deeper-rooted than light, which once soared up through the "sèves inouïes," has gone bad, has swollen him into drunken torpors.

Overinflated with hubris, excessive vision,[15] he yearns to burst, to sink back into easeful death, as at the end of "Les Sœurs de charité." Death is sought not for adventure's sake, not for *du nouveau*, but rather out of sheer fatigue. "O que j'aille à la mer!" is somewhat ambiguous: "to go into the sea," drown, as we said, is the main sense, but, like the close of *Une Saison en Enfer*: "Cela s'est passé," the formula leaves open a possibility of further voyaging, perhaps in a *real* sea (as he would do). Like the Lady of Shalott, Rimbaud must have been "sick of shadows" by now. And, as at the end of the "Scène" of "Hérodiade," a plunge into real life, a love, seemed a distinct possibility. The "j'aille" has an overtone of *jaillir*, spring forth, into new life, or physical love and a "future" of the body (compare "La vague . . . ose jaillir des rocs," the fresh élan at the end of Valéry's "Cimetière marin").

---

[14] They make us think a bit of those birds with blond eyes and of the goldfish of an earlier strophe (or perhaps Yeats' golden nightingale in "Sailing to Byzantium"). Rimbaud is similarly hyperbolic with his evocation: "O million de Christs aux yeux sombres et doux" in "Morts de Quatre-vingt-douze."

[15] This recalls Mallarmé's "Prose" with its "Hyperbole!" and repeated "trop." See *Toward the Poems of Mallarmé*, p. 240.

24th strophe:

> Si je désire une eau d'Europe, c'est la flache
> Noire et froide où vers le crépuscule embaumé
> Un enfant accroupi plein de tristesses, lâche
> Un bateau frêle comme un papillon de mai.

The real scene of his childhood—an Ardennes puddle, part of the regretted old Europe—turns out to be the hidden source of strength. Having resigned himself, in a sort of death of the outer-questing spirit (even though in fantasy), he is reborn to true inmost beauty, an epiphany worthy of the finest in art. The puddle[16] is a microcosm of the Ocean, an infinitely more intimate site for lyric poetry.

That child, bent over itself and nature for support—like the lonely wayside figure of "Ma Bohème," curled up almost embryo-fashion—is all of us, as we once were, martyrs of infinite grief, mirrored in the cold blackness of the soul-reflecting waters. But the dusk is perfumed, there is Balm in Gilead. And the spirit is lifted in a new tiny launching of a delicate hope, in the toy boat,[17] frail and ephemeral as a May butterfly. The most tactful comment here is silence.

25th strophe:

> Je ne puis plus, baigné de vos langueurs, ô lames,
> Enlever leur sillage aux porteurs de cotons,
> Ni traverser l'orgueil des drapeaux et des flammes,
> Ni nager sous les yeux horribles des pontons.

Rimbaud admits his defeat, his exhaustion of rebellious spirit. The waves—of varied inner life, experience—have been too numerous, wearing, "languorous." He has been drawn down by "Elle," the "Vampire," as in "Angoisse," undone by the feminine principle of on-going life which gets us all in the end, strive as we Icaruses may: "Mère qui créas . . . De grandes fleurs avec la balsamique Mort" (Mallarmé's "Les Fleurs").

He can no longer defy the grown-up boats, the cotton-bearing commercial ships he sailed blithely by in strophe 2. "Enlever leur sillage" means to follow in the adult-boat wake, with a suggestion of challenge or

---

[16] The little puddle is a reflection of the humility of the soul at this moment, "little me." We find a similar image in "Ouvriers": "une flache laissée par l'inondation du mois précédent à un sentier assez haut . . . [avec] de très petits poissons." This is the moment of defeat turning the gaze inward to intimate depth: to the "little fish in the little pond." In "Little Gidding" T. S. Eliot similarly pokes with a stick at a crab (like the ragged one he says he should have been in "Prufrock") in a pool on a mountain path. No doubt he had read his Rimbaud.

[17] The sail is gently indicated in the circumflex over "frêle" (or "lâche").

defiance in "enlever." "To cross the pride of flags and streamers" is definitely to challenge, referring no doubt to war-boats but, more generally, adult male pride and derring-do. He can no longer manage this, nor "swim" (as boat, as boy) under the horrible eyes (portholes) of prison ships—he cannot defy the law-giving male society that closes the doors on the hardened criminal he will dare, another sulking day, to admire in the *Saison en enfer*.

As he will later observe: "On ne part pas."[18]

---

[18] Rimbaud's voyage is faintly reminiscent of one in Balzac's *Les Proscrits* (which also has a New Jerusalem in the sunset skies, see the end of the *Saison en enfer*): "[L'Archange] franchit les sphères comme un vaisseau fend les ondes."

II

DERNIERS VERS

Introductory Note

"LE BATEAU IVRE" represents the new *voyant* manner of Rimbaud, after the shocking crisis of "Le Cœur volé." The *Derniers Vers* and the *Illuminations* which follow are without exception more or less in this daring later style. To me, however, it is all essentially Rimbaud, the early and the late. The temperament has not changed, the *petite sensation*, his flavor if you will. But the syntax loosens (and tightens in a new way), the references here and there become more obscure, the whole texture more complex.

The *Derniers Vers* are Rimbaud's last experiments in verse form, with a new suppleness, influenced by Verlaine no doubt (though the reverse is also possible). Verlaine wrote later in *Les Poètes maudits*:

> Après quelque séjour à Paris, puis diverses pérégrinations plus ou moins effrayantes [no doubt "Le Cœur volé" is important here], Rimbaud vira de bord et travailla (lui!) dans le naïf, le très et l'exprès trop simple, n'usant plus que d'assonances, de mots vagues, de phrases enfantines ou populaires. Il accomplit ainsi des prodiges de ténuité, de flou vrai, de charmant presque inappréciable à force d'être grêle et fluet.

Verlaine then quotes the first quatrain of "L'Eternité."

Later, Rimbaud seems to have regretted these experiments which were closer to Verlaine's personality. Suzanne Bernard believes the *Saison en enfer* shows a certain resentment of Verlaine in this respect and she quotes a sketch-fragment for the "Nuit de l'enfer": "ce sont des erreurs qu'on me souffle à l'oreille, les magies, les alchimies, les mysticismes, les parfums faux, les musiques naïves" (p. 147).

I believe Suzanne Bernard's intuition to be correct. No doubt Rimbaud feared the more feminine temperament of Verlaine would pull his stubborn virility, his *logos*, down. Sartre, whose work is haunted by the fear of homosexuality, speaks of "something too perfumed" in Baudelaire's poetry, exactly as Rimbaud does here.[1] Valéry's "Jeune Parque" is recurrently revolted by the "perfume" of sexuality symbolized by the "serpent." The no-doubt phallic (in part) serpents of "Le Bateau ivre" are accompanied by "noirs parfums."

The *Illuminations* often—like the later stubborn wanderings—represent the virile revolt. They are frequently dynamic, metallic. Sartre's develop-

---

[1] See *Les Mots* where he, the fatherless boy, identifies with his mother when she is approached by a man; his intimate understanding of Daniel in the novel trilogy; Lucien in *L'Enfance d'un chef*; his vulnerably heavy-handed attack on Proust. See our article "Sartre versus Proust," in *Partisan Review*, No. 2 (June-July 1951), pp. 633-45.

ment is curiously parallel here. After the dangers of sinking into maternal viscosity are barely averted in the youthful *Nausée* (which is alive with "charms" rivaling Proust's or Rimbaud's), Sartre, whose hero symbolically boards a train for Paris, *goes someplace* wilfully, and never really stops. His new aesthetic ideal, like Rimbaud's, is expressed by the unsentimental steely hardness of jazz (see under "Enfance": "des boules de saphir, de métal"). But Rimbaud, far more than Sartre, relapses. The *Illuminations* are, happily, just as often the defeated child in moments of glowing epiphany.

In the *Derniers Vers*, Rimbaud seems to be resigned to going nowhere; reassured by the presence of Verlaine, he provisionally accepts his role as a poet, sounding his still-deep moods for new effects in verbal music.

There are moments of solitary "blues" ("Larme," "Chanson de la plus haute tour"), of likewise exultation ("Bruxelles," "Michel et Christine"), of high-charged remembrance of some crucial scenes from a bewildered childhood ("Mémoire"), of amused self-observation: the odd couple he formed together with his mentor ("Jeune ménage"). The unprecedented insouciance of his wide-open manner, the incidence of perfect hits on sensibility, the intensity of—remarkably numerous—privileged moments, all this is hard to beat poetically.

Larme

This is one of Rimbaud's quietest poems. The tone is *estompé*, outwardly mild and inwardly intense, quite close to that of Baudelaire's Marie Daubrun mood. For example, "L'Invitation au voyage": "Les soleils mouillés / De ces ciels brouillés . . . tes traîtres yeux / Brillant à travers leurs *larmes*." Or "Ciel Brouillé": "ton regard d'une vapeur couvert . . . vert . . . tendre . . . tièdes et voilés . . . pleurs." Or "Chant d'automne": "J'aime de vos longs yeux la lumière verdâtre . . . tendre cœur . . . soyez mère . . . Amante ou sœur." In "Larme," the woods are *tendre*, the light is filtered by a tear-like (the title) "brouillard d'après-midi tiède et vert."

The "tear" of the overcast atmosphere reflects Rimbaud's frequent mood of sorrow combined with the comforting presence of nature in utter isolation. We remember that the woods yielded up a golden kiss in "Tête de faune." Here too he is a "fisher" of that "gold," but with less success. This wood is infinitely more troubled and wistful.

As the poem opens the climate is of early spring: the elm trees are yet birdless (or are the birds merely far?), the turf without flowers, the hazelnut groves "tender," the sky overcast. A storm comes and chills the landscape, and "we are back several months," as Robert Frost would say. Rimbaud imagines icicles falling into the pond. The mood saddens into a deep sigh.

The -ar- of the "larme" is in a cluster—of tear-like transparency—with "Par" and "brouillard" (see under "Départ").

1st strophe:

> Loin des oiseaux, des troupeaux, des villageoises,
> Je buvais, accroupi dans quelque bruyère
> Entourée de tendres bois de noisetiers,
> Par un brouillard d'après-midi tiède et vert.

"Far from the birds, flocks, and village girls" indicates an especially intimate solitude, beyond even the humble creatures of village, meadows, and woods. Coleridge expressed a remarkably similar sentiment in a letter: "The further I ascend from animated Nature (i.e., in the embracements of rocks and hills), from men and cattle, and the common birds of the woods and fields, the greater becomes in me the intensity of the feeling of life."

As Meaulnes approached the moment of despair, and death-like sleep in the sheepfold, he lost one by one his ties with normal life, and among the last creatures he saw were village-women and a shepherdess with her flock visually sinking into the earth as he rode on. For Rimbaud now even the birds are far off, as in "Enfance" where he is "l'enfant abandonné," so alone that he exclaims "Que les oiseaux et les sources sont loin!"

He drinks, seeking the childishly direct communion with the "milk" of natural life, as in "Comédie de la soif." (One remembers boys in primary school lapping water from muddy pools, pushed by some such impulse.) He is squatting, as he often was, like the child by the dark pond at the close of "Le Bateau ivre."

The "loin . . . oiseaux . . . villageoises . . . bois . . . noisetiers . . . boire . . . Oise . . . voix" form a haunting sound-group, an incantation like the "roses des roseaux dès longtemps dévorées" of "Mémoire," a childish babbling, a rosary of words to defend against a menacing sorrow. I suspect the last word of the poem, "boire"—repeated in the second strophe and in the form "buvais" in the first strophe—is the nucleus of the cluster. The oi sound is a release of tension, as in thirst satisfied. Thus in "Comédie de la soif" we have the appeasement and calm of "Peut-être un *Soir* m'attend / Où je *boirai* tranquille."

2nd strophe:

> Que pouvais-je boire dans cette jeune Oise,
> Ormeaux sans voix, gazon sans fleurs, ciel couvert.
> Que tirais-je à la gourde de colocase?
> Quelque liqueur d'or, fade et qui fait suer.

We need not know exactly what river is indicated by the "jeune Oise" to understand and enjoy the poem. It probably indicates a slender rivulet near the source—hence "young"—of a river; it also reflects the general early-spring mood. The nature of the "gourde" is puzzling—a variant simply calls them "gourdes vertes"—but of no great importance to us (maybe he needed a rhyme). The colocasia is found in a famous text which Rimbaud undoubtedly knew and which may indeed have helped arouse in him the sense of his "divine child" mission, the Fourth Eclogue of Virgil:

> . . . at that boy's birth, in whom the iron race shall begin to cease, and the *golden* to arise over all the world . . . on thee, o boy, untilled shall Earth first pour childish gifts, wandering ivy-tendrils and foxglove, and *colocasia* . . . (my italics).

The golden "liqueur" is no doubt the water reflecting light. The *or* sound runs as a secondary tone throughout the poem in "Ormeaux . . . d'or . . . orage . . . Or!" and "d'or," much as it did in "Tête de faune" and for similar reasons. It is the conjunction of the *light* and the water together that he would drink:

> Elle est retrouvée!
> Quoi? l'éternité.
> C'est la mer mêlée
> Au soleil.

They constitute a wedding of "male" and "female" elements in nature, a happy family reunion (see above, p. 36).[1] In just the same way Baudelaire exulted ("La Chevelure") in the boats' "glissant dans l'or [light] et dans la moire [water]"; here the wedding occurs in the words themselves ("or" in "moire").

3rd strophe:
> Tel, j'eusse été mauvaise enseigne d'auberge.
> Puis l'orage changea le ciel, jusqu'au soir.
> Ce furent des pays noirs, des lacs, des perches,
> Des colonnades sous la nuit bleue, des gares.

A drinking boy would have looked like a (poor) tavern sign. The storm, which refreshes and renews life totally, as in "Après le déluge," is one of

---

[1] In Chrétien de Troyes's *Perceval* there is such a "happy family" ending, with everyone related to everyone else; this is a further, if indirect, link of Rimbaud to Perceval.

Rimbaud's happiest moments, like dawn. Thus in "Bruxelles" there is the "paradis d'orage," echoed by "Le paradis des orages s'effondre" ("Villes, I").[2] In "Michel et Christine" he speaks of "Cette religieuse après-midi d'orage" (in "Larme," too, it occurs in the afternoon).

There is a vibrancy between "orage" and "changea."

Then all is transformed, and the spectacle goes on till evening: it is a phantasmagoria of wonderful things, like a continuing procession of fascinating phenomena going past a train window, "Le paysage dans le cadre des portières" (Verlaine, *La Bonne Chanson*). Some are spectral or frightening (as in "Rêvé pour l'hiver"): "des pays noirs." The "lacs" recall the "salon au fond d'un lac" or the "lacs sur les pierres" of the *Saison en enfer* and may have something to do with the shells below. The "colonnades under the blue night" could be like telegraph poles going by. The stations, "des gares," have a double delight as in "Génie": "le charme des lieux fuyants et le délice surhumain des stations." Thus in "Bruxelles" the

> Charmante station du chemin de fer,
> Au cœur d'un mont, comme au fond d'un verger

is an ideal place, like the "auberge," combining the excitement of travelling and the snugness of a resting-place.

4th strophe:

> L'eau des bois se perdait sur des sables vierges,
> Le vent, du ciel, jetait des glaçons aux mares . . .
> Or! tel qu'un pêcheur d'or ou de coquillages,
> Dire que je n'ai pas eu souci de boire!

The scene is chillier now: water—the "young" Oise?—trickles into the sandy ground, and "se perdait" inevitably sounds a desolate note. The wind is cold and knocks "icicles" into the ponds—imaginary icicles are the only possible ones in this setting, based on his feeling of being put back into winter plus possibly some flying twigs, etc. In a variant for "Voyelles," Rimbaud speaks of "Lances de glaçons fiers," and the feeling is similar, i.e., of being stung amidst the tender scene by some sharp "male" occurrences, a world of duty and pain, which tracks him here in his retreat. Deeper down is the bite of the hound of heaven, bitter and beautiful as in the "dent douce à la mort" of "le bonheur" ("Délires, II"). Thus a variant reads: "Le vent de Dieu jetait des glaçons." But Rimbaud is not ready for that supreme moment here. The cold thought merely makes him shiver and hunch further over himself, in self-pity.

[2] I think of Richard Wilbur's "The orchard spray gales in the eden trees."

The end of the poem is a deep sigh, the eternal unsatisfied *sitio* which will soon develop into a poem of thirst: the "Comédie de la soif." His thirst is for "gold" or "shells"; the gold reminds one of the untapped strength—"Million d'oiseaux d'or"—he sought at the end of "Le Bateau ivre." Or the goldfish, a pure visual delight he wanted to show other children, in that poem. Or the "golden kiss" of the woods, as from some Sleeping Beauty, the love bestowed by nature he seemed to have received in "Tête de faune." In "Comédie de la soif" he sighs: "Si j'ai jamais quelque or."[3] The shells are an obvious "thing" he might be seeking as he bends over in his puzzling thirst and sees objects in the water. But, for him as for Gide, it is the pure thirst itself that counts. "Don't tell me I wasn't concerned about drinking!" He is bent over in just this deeply questing spirit at the end of "Mémoire." There, in the water he sees a yellow and a blue flower. The yellow one is a *souci d'eau* (marsh-marigold). Maybe he had that somewhere in mind in the "souci" and "or" here.

La Rivière de Cassis

Here is another itinerant poem, like "Ma Bohème" and, even more, like "Les Corbeaux" where the crows are equally prominent and carry much the same poetic weight. Their reedy caws, like the brusque wind, spice a keen delight wrung with difficulty from a strange and challenging—at times cold and frightening—nature. Forbidding as the depths of landscape are the dark shadows of a medieval past which haunt the vague ruins he passes. A crafty peasant seems like a vestige of one of Chrétien de Troyes's boors, a sort of human equivalent of a dragon to challenge a *chevalier*. The crows, familiar sassy angels from Rimbaud's past, are like soldiers sent by the *Seigneur* to accompany him, he hopes, as well as to frighten away the peasant and, no doubt, all the other spectres. His courage, that of Petit-Poucet (as in "Ma Bohème"), is really special, after all, and he needs help, perhaps magic.

Rimbaud is a *spiritual* knight, with something of a Perceval about him. He was raised, like Perceval, exclusively by a woman and like him set out, despite her, to explore the virile world. There is a reference to the "Saint-Graal" in "Les Lèvres closes" (*Album Zutique*), and in "Enfance" he calls himself, as Perceval was called, a *valet*. The Perceval story was current in a popular version in the Ardennes region in Rimbaud's time. So, whether the *chevaliers errants* include this particular knight or not,

---

[3] Compare "Cherchant la fortune chimique personnelle" ("Mouvement"). Curiously, there is now a beer called Fischer Gold sold in France. But I doubt that it existed then.

something like that image may well have been in Rimbaud's mind when he conceived this compelling and sincere poem, which counts, in my opinion, among his better ones.

The poem is in alternate eleven- and six-syllable lines which give it a gravely rocking rhythm, as well as a mysterious freedom. The second strophe is a *laisse assonancée* (and there is other assonance) which befits the medieval memories.

1st strophe:
>La Rivière de Cassis roule ignorée
>>En des vaux étranges:
>La voix de cent corbeaux l'accompagne, vraie
>>Et bonne voix d'anges:
>Avec les grands mouvements des sapinaies
>>Quand plusieurs vents plongent.

The original of the river is uncertain, but the name Rimbaud gives it, Black Currant River—*Cassis* can refer to either the berries or the liqueur made from them—is appropriate to the dark, coldly liquid mood of the landscape. As happens to every boy—I think of Meaulnes lost in Sologne and his adolescence—the wanderer at some point goes "through a looking glass," and we are aware that "only the dead are safe" (Richard Wilbur). The river is "unknown," and valleys "strange." The crows, old friends, are reassuring companions. In "Les Corbeaux," Rimbaud had called them "saints"; like the "Noirs inconnus" of "Qu'est-ce pour nous, mon cœur?" they represent the particular—peppery—flavor of the freedom and poetic aspiration (sublimated Eros) birds have always stood, or flown, for. They echo the "tics noirs" of the "Poètes de sept ans"; their caw is impertinent, rebellious, almost razzing.

Winds, as they blow parallel, move the fir trees with a varying force (or resistance of branches).

2nd strophe:
>Tout roule avec des mystères révoltants
>>De campagnes d'anciens temps;
>De donjons visités, de parcs importants:
>>C'est en ces bords qu'on entend
>Les passions mortes des chevaliers errants:
>>Mais que salubre est le vent!

The "roule" here echoes the "roule" of the river in line 1: events roll past as a river flows. The flow is dark as if with the shadowy memories of ancient wars (or, ambiguously, "countrysides"), welling from the hostile scene all about.[1]

Probably he glimpses, as he wanders, something like, or suggestive of, the "important parks," the "dungeons" he "visited" or had once seen. Hereabouts, he says, one catches echoes of the dead passions of wandering knights; even as he rejects them for a refreshing present he is haunted by them, as Hamlet was by his soldier-father. Everything prepared Rimbaud for such a comparison with himself, as we have seen at various junctures (for example above, p. 81).

The keen delight fully emerges at last from the challenge of the dark and cold, his spiritual knight errantry. "Mais que salubre est le vent!" is his guerdon, Rimbaud's highest pleasure. One thinks of Wallace Stevens standing on the windswept hills: "This health is holy!" As the "rayon" of "Bannières de mai" will be, it is like an attention from the father he lacked. In "Génie" he exclaims "O ses souffles" and again "au haut des déserts de neige, suivre ses vues, ses souffles, son corps, son jour."[2] All of us know that wind, like a penetrating benediction making us weep with sudden joy, as François Seurel did when a gust flapped his scarf in his face.

> 3rd strophe:
> Que le piéton regarde à ces claires-voies:
>   Il ira plus courageux.
> Soldats des forêts que le Seigneur envoie,
>   Chers corbeaux délicieux!
> Faites fuir d'ici le paysan matois
>   Qui trinque d'un moignon vieux.

Let the "pedestrian"—Rimbaud's feet are in touch with "la réalité rigoureuse" and moving gingerly, not too fast, forward—look through the lattices and he will go more courageously, he tells himself. Agreed. What is lovelier and more inspiring than a lattice? It is human control and light from the source, together, an essence of French art,[3] particularly Symbolist (Classic and Romantic). Those lattices seem to be vaguely associated with the *châteaux* he passes.

The crows he calls on to chase away the crafty peasant remind us again of the ones in "Les Corbeaux"—he uses the exact same words: "Chers

---

[1] Just as in "Les Corbeaux," a war, probably recent, made him think of the cruel fate of buried soldiers. (Some echo of these is present in the second strophe.)

[2] Rimbaud also sees him "dans le ciel de tempête et les drapeaux d'extase" ("Génie").

[3] Compare Keats' "wreathed trellis of a working brain" ("Ode to Psyche").

corbeaux délicieux"—and his calling them soldiers of the forest—they are militant "angels" à la St. George—echoes the situation of "Les Corbeaux." There he called them "Armée étrange" and they flew over the "champs de France / Où dorment des morts d'avant-hier," referring to some recent war.

The "Seigneur" may refer to a feudal Lord who might send this help to his knight-errant envoy (this coincides with the rest of the medieval atmosphere), but more certainly *the* Lord. Thus "Les Corbeaux" began with "Seigneur, . . . Faites s'abattre . . . Les chers corbeaux délicieux."

Rimbaud didn't like the peasants of his farm neighborhood, that is, Roche. An echo of this distaste, as well as the medieval boor image, is probably present here.

Comédie de la soif

The theme of thirst is as important to Rimbaud's poetry as is the closely corollary theme of hunger ("Fêtes de la faim"). According to "Oraison du soir" he has drunk "thirty or forty" mugs of beer. In his early correspondence he speaks of his terrible thirst in Paris, and Fretet has speculated that there is some physical (glandular) disorder at its base. That may be so, but until this is proven one is inclined to remember, rather, that as emotionally frustrated adolescents many of us took to inordinate drinking of soft drinks, milk, whatever was around. Marie Bonaparte traces Poe's alcoholism to his motherless infancy. Alcohol as a partial replacement for such emotional deprivation—mixed mysteriously (psychosomatically, as we say) with concrete thirst—strikes us as convincing. The very expression and posture of the swigging bum are infantile.

Beyond the "objective correlative" of mother-milk and/or mother-love there lies a deeper hidden source which we may identify with Christ's *sitio*. One thinks here of Valéry's remark: "The desire that women arouse in us can only be satisfied by God." Or Poe: "I have drunk of a water / That quenches all thirst . . . From a spring but a very few / Feet under ground" ("For Annie"). Or Mallarmé's "boire . . . [dans] un peu profond ruisseau . . . la mort." In the *Saison en enfer* Rimbaud says: "J'attends Dieu avec gourmandise" and shortly thereafter "boire des liqueurs fortes comme du métal bouillant."

This thirst, in sum, can only be quenched through a fiery *possession* by the total force of the cosmos, as in "Génie," a force which would invade his lungs (*Une Saison en enfer*: "L'air marin brûlera mes poumons"), his inmost being, drive out homeopathically all pain (hence all fleshly life:

"The cost is not less than everything"), leaving only the innocence and beauty of "the milk of paradise": "fondre où fond ce nuage." There is nothing radically new here; but the childlike depth and sincerity with which the thirst is felt is exemplary. And certainly there is a newness in the remarkable span of Being, from the simple roots of that feeling in infancy (or before) to its sublimated flowering in the complex imagery of the brilliantly cultured adolescent.

The poem begins in a sort of delaying action, with the ordinary brews used to quench thirst. For, as in "Les Sœurs de charité," it takes time to recognize that the thirst is total, death the only answer. As if in a series of temptations of St. Anthony—to whom "Jeunesse" alludes—various substitutes are proposed by spectral figures. First the ancestors propose traditional palliatives. Not only the actual drinks they imbibed, but the whole ancestral scene is a "temptation": to sink into the past, give in, on *their* terms.

1. *Les Parents*

> 1. Nous sommes tes Grands-Parents,
>   Les Grands!
> Couverts des froides sueurs
> De la lune et des verdures.
> Nos vins secs avaient du cœur!
> Au soleil sans imposture
> Que faut-il à l'homme? boire.
>
> MOI.—Mourir aux fleuves barbares.

The grandparents are in the ground. They offer their drinks, "vins secs," and their way of life. Their graves are described poetically, and this is like a foretaste of what will be Rimbaud's deepest thirst. Death as an elixir, mixed with the rugged poetry of the Ground, has an immense ambivalent appeal (despite the apparent rejection of this by the grandparents: "Au soleil sans imposture"). The "cold sweats of the moon and verdures" recall Baudelaire's "cimetière abhorré de la lune" ("Spleen").[1] "Cold sweats of the moon" are apt for the eerie moonlight splashed around a burial ground and hinting at the *suintements* underground. It recalls also "Les Morts des eaux nocturnes abreuvés" ("Les Premières Communions") and Baudelaire's "La Servante au grand cœur":

[1] Compare also "Entends comme brame": "en avril la rame / *viride* du pois! / Dans sa vapeur nette / vers *Phoebé*! tu vois / s'agiter la tête / de saints d'autre-fois . . ." (my italics).

Et qui dort son sommeil sous une humble pelouse,

. . .

Ils sentent s'égoutter les neiges de l'hiver.

Or Milosz's savored and drenched "Morts de Lofoten."

But the grandparents immediately reject this death-urge and prefer the frank sun: "Au soleil sans imposture / Que faut-il à l'homme? boire." Does Rimbaud accept this ancestral, traditional, Tolstoyan, healthy-peasant solution? Obviously not. He answers them with a rich, exotic, ambivalent wish to die and, as in the *Saison en enfer*, in a distant place, a scene of revolt: "Mourir aux fleuves barbares."

> 9. Nous sommes tes Grands-Parents
> Des champs.
> L'eau est au fond des osiers:
> Vois le courant du fossé
> Autour du château mouillé.
> Descendons en nos celliers;
> Après, le cidre et le lait.

MOI.—Aller où boivent les vaches.

The castle with its deep moat is an image of Communion with ancestral splendors presented by the grandparents. Like Igitur, Rimbaud is invited by his ancestors to go down into that past. Here it is put as refreshment: "Après, le cidre et le lait."[2]

The "Vois le courant" is superbly poetic. This current in a moat is fascinating, like a writing on water, a wake, either an intimate and grave *impression* on the watery soul, or, reciprocally, the love-death furrow made by the self in nature as in a woman, a sort of momentary grave.[3] In "Mémoire" the river as a whole "toute froide, et noire, court!" but that is a less happy (because dark and cold), less intimate (because total) effect than a *courant*.

MOI answers disaffectedly with a resigned sigh; to go where the cows drink is to go apart, humbly, to nature, toward oblivion: "Loin des oiseaux, des troupeaux, des villageoises" ("Larme").

---

[2] The text is unsure here: is it "afterwards, cider and milk" or "[Go down] after cider and milk"? The second reading is parallel to "Après, le clair de lune" of "Michel et Christine." But the meanings are really very different.

[3] Compare, in Mallarmé's "Soupir": "creuse un froid sillon" and, more especially, "Le Pitre châtié": "dans l'onde . . . Mille sépulcres."

17. Nous sommes tes Grands-Parents;
    Tiens, prends
  Les liqueurs dans nos armoires;
  Le Thé, le Café, si rares,
  Frémissent dans les bouilloires.
  —Vois les images, les fleurs.
  Nous rentrons du cimetière.

MOI.—Ah! tarir toutes les urnes!

The grandparents come back at him and offer more refined, choice drinks: liqueurs from their "armoires" (realizing, apparently, what a hold of the past for Rimbaud was in these mysterious depths, see under "Le Buffet" and "Les Étrennes des orphelins"); also tea and coffee, "so rare."

Then the parents (the children of the grandparents) speak and point to religious pictures and flowers, saying "We are returning from the cemetery." But the MOI refuses these emblems of family tradition (more viciously maligned in "Ce qu'on dit au poète") and cries "dry up all urns" meaning, ambiguously, get rid of such traditions and quench your thirst in a total way that goes beyond such sentimentalities. Baudelaire in "Spleen" (LXXV) says "Pluviôse . . . De son urne à grands flots verse un froid ténébreux / Aux pâles habitants du voisin cimetière." Rimbaud's "urne" may retain some of this grave-seepage effect from the earlier part of the poem.

2. L'Esprit

1. Éternelles Ondines,
  Divisez l'eau fine.
  Vénus, sœur de l'azur,
  Émeus le flot pur.

  Juifs errants de Norwège,
  Dites-moi la neige.
  Anciens exilés chers,
  Dites-moi la mer.

MOI.—Non, plus ces boissons pures,
  Ces fleurs d'eau pour verres;
  Légendes ni figures
  Ne me désaltèrent;

  Chansonnier, ta filleule
  C'est ma soif si folle
  Hydre intime sans gueules
  Qui mine et désole.

A spirit comes and evokes legendary watery creatures; it is, as we saw earlier, a kind of temptation of the creative imagination, recalling the phantasmagorias of *Faust II* as well as St. Anthony.[4] The first creatures evoked are "Ondines," then Venus emerging from her sea. The muse-like spirit says: "Eternal Ondines, divide the fine water," i.e., swim or surface. To Venus he says: "Sister of the azure sky / Stir the pure wave," by rising. If less adoring of her than he was in "Soleil et chair," Rimbaud is also less bitter than in "Vénus Anadyomène."

Then:

> Wandering Jews of Norway,
> Tell me of the snow.

This may be a reminder of Quinet's version of the legend which became a paean to liberty. We recall that Rimbaud associated the winds of Norway with liberty in "Ophélie." So it is likely that the snows of Norway—quenchers of the thirst for freedom—are a parallel conception. Then:

> Dear ancient exiles
> Tell me of the sea.

An obvious total gratifier, especially in the symbolic sense of man's infinite restlessness which ever seeks and roams the ocean; this is closely tied to the preceding "Wandering Jews" theme and the "voyageur ancien" of part 4.

MOI answers: No more of these "pure drinks," which are empty abstractions. He calls them "water flowers for glasses," that is, pretty and vacuous designs on glassware. And adds: "Legends and [drawn] figures don't quench my thirst."

Then he addresses the "song-maker"—the creative spirit, seen as a muse, arid as the one Rimbaud forsakes at the beginning of the *Saison en enfer* or at the end of "Les Sœurs de charité." The spirit of singing leaves behind as "God-daughter" (from the same throat as song?) Rimbaud's mad thirst, an intimate hydra without mouths (i.e., it is merely his own unquenchable longing), which "undermines and desolates."

3. *Les Amis*

> 1. Viens, les Vins vont aux plages,
>   Et les flots par millions!
>   Vois le Bitter sauvage
>   Rouler du haut des monts!

---

[4] Not Flaubert's, yet unpublished at that date.

> Gagnons, pèlerins sages,
> L'Absinthe aux verts piliers . . .
>
> MOI.—Plus ces paysages.
> Qu'est l'ivresse, Amis?
>
> J'aime autant, mieux, même,
> Pourrir dans l'étang,
> Sous l'affreuse crème,
> Près des bois flottants.

"Les Amis" speak. They are drinking-companions of the sort Rimbaud met in Paris (Frenchmen readily refer to the people they habitually meet in cafés as "les amis"). They beckon to Rimbaud, invoking a plethora of wines; "vont aux plages" means *à go go* and arouses the obvious idea of nature's ocean waves. Like a flood, Bitter rolls down from the hills. As if they were pilgrims across the natural landscape thus allegorically evoked, the friends suggest they push on to absinthe, as if it were a temple (of drink) "aux verts piliers" in the Baudelaire manner of "Correspondances"; compare the early poem "Au Cabaret-Vert" and the "auberge verte" in part 4.

But Rimbaud answers: no more of these hallucinating landscapes, and he queries: "What is drunkenness?" in the tone of the first lines of the *Saison en enfer* where he regrets his past illusions. Rather than these artificial paradises, he prefers, he says, to rot in a *real* pond, amidst consoling nature. Instead of the disgust of hangover (recalling the "pourrit" of "Le Bateau ivre"), he prefers the "affreuse crème" of scum on the pond,[5] amid floating woods (reflected? or sticks? at any rate, natural). This same disgust was described in "les crèmes brunes / Sur les mares des voluptés" in "Les Mains de Jeanne-Marie."

The pond, *mutatis mutandis*, is the one he returned to in defeat at the end of "Le Bateau ivre" or "Larme." It is a microcosm of nature and of the whole world of his pre-sophisticated childhood self, as he seeks to start over from pure nothing.

4. *Le Pauvre songe*

> 1. Peut-être un Soir m'attend
> Où je boirai tranquille
> En quelque vieille Ville,
> Et mourrai plus content:
> Puisque je suis patient!

---

[5] Melville saw at times purest evil in white (*Moby Dick*). There are no doubt sexual undertones in both writers here.

Si mon mal se résigne,
Si j'ai jamais quelque or,
Choisirai-je le Nord
Ou le Pays des Vignes? . . .
—Ah! songer est indigne

Puisque c'est pure perte!
Et si je redeviens
Le voyageur ancien,
Jamais l'auberge verte
Ne peut bien m'être ouverte.

The final quenching of his thirst is described in exquisitely resigned terms reminiscent of Verlaine's "Le Ciel est, par-dessus le toit" ("Mon Dieu, mon Dieu, la vie est là / Simple et tranquille") or Baudelaire's "Moesta et errabunda."[6]

The old City is a part of the ancient and real Europe he sought in defeat at the close of "Le Bateau ivre." It is immemorial and, like his own ancestry that he will seek in the *Saison en enfer*, is connected all the way back with the roots of Being, hence Death: "mourrai plus content"; this is hardly promising but at least it is not fake or sentimental. This at last—Death accepted—is authentic, and it is appeasing or reassuring, Olympian calm. This is the core meaning of the word "patient" which will from now on become important in Rimbaud's poetry. The tone here is fully that of "Chanson de la plus haute tour."

In the second strophe, the "mal" is the same old metaphysical dissatis-faction of *soif* (*sitio*): "la soif malsaine" of the "Chanson de la plus haute tour." It is futile to try to specify it as Suzanne Bernard does. But the "gold" he needs to give him freedom of movement *is* specific; though its overtones are generic (as in "Larme," with Grail-like echoes). Yet he knows this "freedom" would lead nowhere: "On ne part pas" (*Saison en enfer*). So after idly vacillating between North and South (as if one could be cured by moving, like the sick Nietzsche), he quickly concludes it is futile: "Ah! songer est indigne / Puisque c'est pure perte!" That is what he means by "patience," and will mean by it. This is the central Rimbaud. Mondor calls him "le génie impatient," and there is truth to it in reference to his whole career (unlike the *patience* Mallarmé learned and described in "Prose"). But not in reference to his purest epiphanies! He knows that if he moves on, becomes the old traveler again (like the Wandering Jews of part 2), there is no ideal inn elsewhere. The "auberge verte" will remain closed to him: "Il y a des auberges qui pour toujours

---

[6] We have commented, under "Larme," on the relaxing effect of the oi in "Soir" and "boirai."

n'ouvrent déjà plus" ("Métropolitain"); "On suit la route rouge pour
arriver à l'auberge vide" ("Enfance"). We have discussed this poignant
image under "Au Cabaret-Vert," citing Baudelaire's "L'Irréparable":

> L'Espérance qui brille aux carreaux de l'Auberge
> Est soufflée, est morte à jamais!

5. *Conclusion*

> Les pigeons qui tremblent dans la prairie,
> Le gibier, qui court et qui voit la nuit,
> Les bêtes des eaux, la bête asservie,
> Les derniers papillons! . . . ont soif aussi.
>
> Mais fondre où fond ce nuage sans guide,
> —Oh! favorisé de ce qui est frais!
> Expirer en ces violettes humides
> Dont les aurores chargent ces forêts?

In the "Lettre du voyant" to Demeny Rimbaud writes: "le poète . . . est
chargé de l'humanité, des *animaux* même." In "Matin" of the *Saison en
enfer*, he glancingly demonstrated this sympathy: "des bêtes poussent des
sanglots de chagrin." Animals are numerous in his work, as intimately a
part of his world, of himself, as the flowers which eye him or dance.

There is "a flight of scarlet pigeons" in "Vies." The dynamism of
spiritual release is in them there, as traditionally, but here they are held in
the more typically Rimbaldian suspension between motion and rest:
"trembling." The rhythm of this vibrancy is in a whole series of similar
rhythms—he has wavered toward and away from this, then that, all the
"temptations" are trials—as in the last strophes of "Voyelles" and, as in that
poem, the frequency of the wave-movement increases toward the ultimate
vibrancy of exquisiteness in love-death: the ultra-violet of "ces violettes
humides" (in "Voyelles" it was "rayon violet").

Rimbaud has, like Igitur, reached the top of a spiral "staircase" of
Becoming, caught between the *be* and *not-to-be* of life with its constant
absurd oscillations, yearnings-and-frustrations, its ever-renewed thirst.
Here, so to speak, he leaps into the thin air of total resignation,[7] the final
repose of pure nothingness, as at the end of "Les Sœurs de charité" or "Le
Bateau ivre": "fondre où fond ce nuage sans guide."[8] Baudelaire's
"Étranger" (followed by the Debussy of *Nuages*) would sympathize.

---

[7] Compare the "sylphe" who breaks free from the top of the civilized structure in
Mallarmé's essay on Banville. Or Banville's own *pitre* who jumps into the stars ("Le
Tremplin").

[8] The fan in the charming hands of Mallarmé's daughter ("Autre éventail") seeks

The trembling of the pigeons is followed by the rhythm of ambivalence of "game which runs and sees the night" and, finally, the impressionist ephemeral flutterings of the "last butterflies," hovering on the edge of nothingness, sheer air, melting cloud, or the violet color which is close to that love-death in mood.[9]

The ephemerality of the mood will be caught again in the shadow of those thresholds of the infinite, the "talus" (so characteristic of the later Rimbaud poems): "Les talus de gauche tiennent dans leur ombre violette les mille rapides ornières de la route humide" ("Ornières"). Again, in a privileged moment of life emerging from the death of a flood—or those fantastic liquid tints which emerge, when it is moistened, from color-impregnated cardboard—there is "la futaie violette, bourgeonnante" ("Après le déluge"). The texture of the flowers themselves is a delightful shiver (compare the "frissons d'ombelles" in "Voyelles") of cool comfort mingled with the warmth of summer beauty. They appear at a vibrant moment of transition: dawn.

Bonne pensée du matin

Here is a dawn poem, in which this tingling privileged time of renewal and joy is mixed with affection for "Workers." This is partly, no doubt, on political-revolutionary grounds, but mainly, I feel, because of Rimbaud's childlike need for strong and prestigious father-figures, who would order life and make him happier, such as the *forgeron*, or the men in "blouses" whom he preferred to God in "Les Poètes de sept ans." The personal way, deeper than the political, underlies the latter and overlaps with it.

When he speaks of "Ces Ouvriers charmants / Sujets d'un roi de Babylone," we recall that in "Les Sœurs de charité" he would have been adored by a *Génie* in Persia. Rimbaud's Orient was a place of rebirth in better circumstances, "Orient . . . sagesse première et éternelle" ("L'Impossible"). The spoiled and decadent Western lovers are contrasted with these appealing men who are worthier of Venus. Sartre in his novels offers biased portraits of lovable workers (in *Le Sursis*) and disgusting lovers

---

the delight of pure space ("l'espace, comme un grand baiser"), and it is "sans chemin" as Rimbaud's clouds are "sans guide." "O to be nothing!" cries the Camus of *La Halte à Oran* in his turn. And Rimbaud had already expressed this yearning in "Le Bateau ivre": "O que ma quille éclate!"

[9] Léon Cellier reminded me that violet is the color of mourning, *demi deuil*. Degas noted that "le violet ombre" (quoted by Valéry in "Degas Danse Dessin"). Baudelaire, again, seems echoed in these final lines: "nous voltigerons vers l'infini, comme les oiseaux, les papillons, les fils de la Vierge, les parfums et toutes les choses ailés" ("Du Vin et du haschisch," II).

(in *La Nausée* and *L'Age de Raison*) in much the same spirit: he too had lacked a father.

The "bonne pensée" of the title is his wish for their happiness, in sum the *blessing* of the last strophe.

1st strophe:

> A quatre heures du matin, l'été,
> Le sommeil d'amour dure encore.
> Sous les bosquets l'aube évapore
> L'odeur du soir fêté.

The decadent lovers are still asleep in this fresh moment. Nature cleans away the odors of the debauchery as in "Le Bateau ivre": "L'eau . . . des taches de vin bleus et de vomissures / Me lava." In "L'Orgie parisienne" the description of "buveurs désolés" is followed by "la lumière arrive intense et folle, / Fouillant à vos côtés les luxes ruisselants." The "aube d'été" of "Aube" in the *Illuminations* is here observed evaporating under the woods—the veils lifting one by one.

2nd strophe:

> Mais là-bas dans l'immense chantier
> Vers le soleil des Hespérides,
> En bras de chemise, les charpentiers
> Déjà s'agitent.

Contrasted with the spoiled sleepers, the workers are already up and stirring, in their shirt-sleeves. The work yard[1] is intimately associated with the fresh light of the sun, together with a historically-young pagan authenticity (of the sort Rimbaud enthused about in his second "Lettre du voyant," and "Soleil et chair") in the allusion to the "Hespérides."[2] In "Mémoire" he sings of the "Joie / des chantiers riverains." In "Matin," the dawn moment of the *Saison en enfer*, he hails the "travail nouveau, la sagesse nouvelle." In "L'Éclair" he had already saluted "Le travail humain! . . . l'explosion qui éclaire mon abîme de temps en temps."

The descent of the sun's blessing upon the workers of the earth—specifically a young carpenter—is depicted in the early Latin poem "Jésus à Nazareth":

---

[1] A passing overtone of "chantier": *chanter* reinforces the feeling of joyful hum. *Chantier* is used in a similar way in "Being beauteous."

[2] There is an obvious problem about the "Hespérides," which were in the West originally.

> Au loin apparaissait le soleil brillant,
>> sur les hautes montagnes,
> et son rayon d'argent entrait par les humbles fenêtres . . .
>> le jeune ouvrier
> et les bruits du travail matinal.

3rd strophe:
> Dans leur désert de mousse, tranquilles,
> Ils préparent les lambris précieux
> Où la richesse de la ville
>> Rira sous de faux cieux.

They are "tranquil," at peace with themselves because of their authenticity, their work-sacrifice, their humility. They are preparing "precious wain-scotings" and the "fake skies" of décor—as opposed to their wide-open Nature setting—for the *fêtes* of rich people.

4th strophe:
> Ah! pour ces Ouvriers charmants
> Sujets d'un roi de Babylone,
> Vénus! laisse un peu les Amants,
>> Dont l'âme est en couronne.

Rimbaud implores Venus to leave for a bit the decadent lovers in favor of these charming Workers; in "Villes," I, she goes into the "cavernes des forgerons," ideal workers as was Hephaestus, favored by Venus. The ascription to the lovers of "souls in a wreath" seems to refer to their being entwined in love with a further allusion to the rococo preciosity of their décor, in line with the "Bergers" of the last strophe and the "lambris précieux" of the third strophe.

The workers are "sujets d'un roi de Babylone." As we said, this gives them marvelous Oriental auspices, like the Persian *Génie* of "Les Sœurs de charité." Babylone is perhaps one of the "splendides villes" in which he would enter "à l'aurore armés d'une ardente patience" at the end of the *Saison en enfer* ("Adieu").

5th strophe:
> O Reine des Bergers!
> Porte aux travailleurs l'eau-de-vie,
> Pour que leurs forces soient en paix
> En attendant le bain dans la mer, à midi.

He addresses Venus as "Queen of the Shepherds" in the rococo sense of the eighteenth century, when all lovers were shepherds (the heroine of "Un Cœur sous une soutane" is called "jeune bergère" by the sentimental priestling). He implores her to bring brandy to the workers, with the special overtone in "vie." At the end of the "Comédie de la soif," Rimbaud dreams of drinking "tranquille," and drink is also an obvious medium of male communion, just as the sea-bathing is. In *La Peste* that is the silent gesture of supreme fraternity between Rieux and Tarrou.[3]

The brandy will end their morning work session. The bathing will occur during this lunch-break at noon. That was the time when Rimbaud awoke after the magic of dawn in "Aube." It is the point, together with the *pointe de l'aube,* that defines the morning-curve. The moment is wide-awake, real, like the workers of this world.

Fêtes de la Patience

In "Comédie de la soif" the final note was a beautiful resignation, and a key word entered the late poetry: patience. The cycle of four poems beginning with "Bannières de mai" all feature this theme, and usually the word. Aside from this, and the out-of-doors setting with seasonal touches, the poems are linked by nothing but the (apparently) light and open quality of the later manner of Rimbaud's verse.

Bannières de mai

The title alludes to a folk festival of spring: the Maypole with its streamers.[1] The hint of Perceval we mentioned in "La Rivière de Cassis" is developed, whether intentionally or not, in this poem. Here is a tentative and thwarted young figure (raised by his mother alone) going forth in springtime to risk a sacrifice which will wound him—like the forefather and the Christ-like Fisher King—into manhood and more. It is close to being a Good Friday spell. The sacrifice, in the spirit of St. Paul's on the road to Damascus, is through a ray of light: "Si un rayon me blesse / Je succomberai sur la mousse."

The theme of the hunt, which runs throughout Rimbaud, is clearly sounded: "Aux branches claires des tilleuls / Meurt un maladif hallali." "April is the cruelest month" (T. S. Eliot): spring—"Le printemps maladif" ("Renouveau," Mallarmé)—is the time of suicidal urges, of bitter renewal.

The time in the first strophe is clearly spring, according to the title.

---

[3] In Giraudoux's *Bella* likewise.

---

[1] Compare the *oriflammes* of "Mémoire."

But the sacrifice implies a spiritual maturation into manhood, which is reflected in the seasonal progression to the summer of the second strophe. The third strophe comments on this process of participation in the drama of the cosmos: "Je veux bien que les saisons m'usent." This is, in a way, to acquire a family, a rootedness, a meaning. He would belong to parent-nature. Here the sun is not identified—unlike his occasional practice—as univalently male.[2] The parents are lumped together in the sun: "C'est rire aux parents, qu'au soleil." But he is obviously happy with "them" for an instant of imagined accommodation with the world. Alas, as often in Rimbaud, the mood darkens and the poem ends on a note of solitary woe.

1st strophe:
>Aux branches claires des tilleuls
>Meurt un maladif hallali.
>Mais des chansons spirituelles
>Voltigent parmi les groseilles.
>Que notre sang rie en nos veines,
>Voici s'enchevêtrer les vignes.
>Le ciel est joli comme un ange.
>L'azur et l'onde communient.
>Je sors. Si un rayon me blesse
>Je succomberai sur la mousse.

The May time implied by the title and borne out by the mood of the first strophe was the time of another sacrificial scene:

>Laissez les fauvettes de mai
>Pour ceux qu'au fond du bois enchaîne,
>Dans l'herbe d'où l'on ne peut fuir,
>La défaite sans avenir.
>
>("Les Corbeaux")

But like Perceval (whose mother had kept him away from the affairs of men because her husband and elder sons had all been killed in combat), Rimbaud goes forth not to a soldier's sacrifice but to a spiritual one. The reminiscence of the earlier struggle is strong in the hunt theme of the first two lines. In the third line there is a hint of those May "warblers" flitting about the currant bushes. Or is it the voices of children about the May-pole?[3] No matter: the tone is clear, regardless of the specifics of who or what is singing.

[2] In "Soleil et chair" it was rather ambiguous, but mainly a father, as it usually is in Rimbaud: see above, p. 39.
[3] Verlaine's Parsifal, in his sonnet of the same name, heard something holy or

There is a transparent effect in the a and r of "branches" and "claires."
The "maladif hallali" imitates somewhat the tootle of hunting horns.

In lines 5 and 6 the assonance of "vignes" and "veines" points to a
poetic analogy of vegetable vines and human veins. The tangle suggested
by "enchevêtrer" refers obliquely to this promiscuous communion of dif-
ferent analogous levels of nature or life in the orgy of light and vernal
Eros. "L'azur et l'onde communient" is one such espousal in a tentative
"happy family" coupling which Rimbaud depicts also in "la mer allée /
Avec le soleil," of "L'Éternité." In "Soleil et chair" this coupling was
between sun and earth. Here the sky is "pretty as an angel," which is
rather androgynous. But the light is piercing and male, like an arrow of
Apollo, whose chariot is invoked in the next strophe. In "Soleil et chair"
the analogy between sap and blood, vines and veins was similarly
described:

> Je regrette les temps où la sève du monde,
> L'eau du fleuve, le sang rose des arbres verts
> Dans les veines de Pan mettaient un univers!

"Je sors": in "Après le déluge" the child too "goes out" and it is He
who possesses all, who is a little Son of Man. The wounding by a Father's
light is repeated in "Alchimie du Verbe": "je m'offrais au soleil, dieu de
feu. / Général . . . bombarde-nous . . . ," etc. In the variant (Bernard, p.
334), it is quoted "je m'offrais au soleil, Dieu de feu, qu'il me ren-
versât. . . ."

2nd strophe:
> Qu'on patiente et qu'on s'ennuie
> C'est trop simple. Fi de mes peines.
> Je veux que l'été dramatique
> Me lie à son char de fortune.
> Que par toi beaucoup, ô Nature,
> —Ah moins seul et moins nul!—je meure.
> Au lieu que les Bergers, c'est drôle,
> Meurent à peu près par le monde.

He rejects suffering and, impulsively, the patience which he recom-
mended in "Comédie de la soif"; it is a genuine cry of distress. But deep
down Rimbaud, we are aware, knows there is no better remedy for life's

---

"spirituel" like that: "Et, ô ces voix d'enfants chantant dans la coupole!" Chrétien's
Perceval hearkened to "the sweet chanting of the birds / Who filled the forest with
their notes."

suffering. His wisdom will soon return in the 3rd strophe ("nothing fools me"), and the whole cycle, we remember, is named after the illuminations of patience.

The "trop simple" is like the impatient outburst of the *Saison en enfer*: "Je suis trop dissipé, trop faible. La vie fleurit par le travail, vieille vérité: moi, ma vie n'est pas assez pesante . . ." ("Mauvais sang") and "Le travail paraît trop léger à mon orgueil . . ." ("L'Éclair"). So he tries to shake off his suffering: "Fi de mes peines." He wants to be taken in charge, as when the sea "dispersed the rudder and anchor" of the boat in "Le Bateau ivre," or the Gindre sisters took him in hand in "Les Chercheuses de poux," or the barber in "Oraison du soir."

As a way out, then, he wants nature to take him brusquely, *dramatically* (like a piercing ray, or wind-thrust as in the "souffle" of "Génie"), in tow: "Je veux que l'été . . . me lie à son char de fortune" which is suggestive of the chariot of Apollo, the sun-archer. Like the Valéry of "Abeille," Rimbaud needs a "prompt tourment." He wants "to die" through nature as a man is reborn by sacrifice or humble submission to a Master, a cause: "j'offre à n'importe quelle divine image des élans vers la perfection" ("Mauvais sang"). Then he will be less "nothing," less "alone." As in the Gospel, or Kirilov's dramatic challenge of lose all to gain all, he would Be, or be Somebody: plunge to soar. By contrast the Bergers—spoiled creatures as in the "Bonne pensée du matin"—die through the mediocre "world" (*monde*: *mondain*), that is, the submission to a banal and futile cause of frivolous activity. He expresses an analogous futility in "Adieu's" "loin des gens qui meurent sur les saisons."[4]

3rd strophe:
> Je veux bien que les saisons m'usent.
> A toi, Nature, je me rends;
> Et ma faim et toute ma soif.
> Et, s'il te plaît, nourris, abreuve.
> Rien de rien ne m'illusionne;
> C'est rire aux parents, qu'au soleil,
> Mais moi je ne veux rire à rien;
> Et libre soit cette infortune.

The happy abandonment of self to the seasons is like the famous cry of *bonheur* of "O saisons!" The seasons of this poem are spring and summer, but the whole yearly round is implied, as in "Le Bonheur." The "thirst" ("Comédie de la soif") and "hunger" ("Fêtes de la faim") which are

---

[4] Here "saisons" signifies dreary routine, but in "Bannières de mai" (strophe 3) it has the positive sense of the deep life of nature.

major aspects of Rimbaud's total yearning, all this is given helplessly back to the source: Nature. Rimbaud is resigned again. If Nature *so pleases*, let her feed his hunger, water his thirst. He knows there is no way out: no illusions. He'd love to laugh up to the sun as a child does to its parents (cf. "rire aux anges"). Recalling the sun as ideal father (with some of the generosity and warmth of a mother) in "Soleil et chair," the lumping of the two parents in the sun image is not so surprising, especially since the "male" and "female" elements will be commingled in "Délires, II": "la mer mêlé / Au soleil," etc. In "Aube," Rimbaud's delight is expressed in this happy laugh: "Je ris au wasserfall."[5]

But the poem closes on something more somber than patience and resignation. The final note, as in "Le Bateau ivre," is pathetic defeat. He cries that he wants no one's love, to laugh at no one (Auden says he knows that he loves someone when they make him want to laugh; Mallarmé's *rire* is usually a happy Eros). He gives free rein to his grief, the "Déchirante infortune" of a moment of despair in the *Saison en enfer* ("L'Impossible").

Chanson de la plus haute tour

More than any of the preceding poems, this one comes close to being a pure incantation, a sort of delicate French "blues." The feminine rhymes: "vienne / s'éprennent," etc., are resonant with a solemn vibrancy of "good grief," the active passivity and joyful sorrow of *patience*. The poem is based on the sense of powerlessness of an adolescent with golden sap in his veins, much to offer. He is at the height of his inward rise to strength, as he is physically at the peak of his growth, but held there in a psychic cramp.[1] Accordingly he is like a prisoner at the top of a tower,[2] whence the title.[3]

Thus Rimbaud offers to descend the tower, "sans la promesse / De plus hautes joies." He has reached the end of his endurance and "wants down," desires reunion with humble nature—"une réalité rugueuse à étreindre" ("Adieu"). He has had enough of alienation from the body, brought on by Christianity: hence the "veuvages" of the "pauvre âme" from its source are linked with the officially pious image of the Virgin.

---

[5] It too was a mingling of opposites, light and water: "à la cime argentée."

[1] Mallarmé's late adolescent hero Igitur was in much the same situation: he had "spiraled up" to a position where he could not move, and could scarcely breathe.

[2] The slender shape of the poem on the page seems to reflect the tower-image.

[3] "Tower-songs" are a lovely topos, from Sophocles' *Agamemnon* through Provençal lyrics to Goethe's *Faust* (Rimbaud ordered a copy of Faust from Delahaye in June, 1872).

A line from "Ouvriers" comments on the mood: "les misérables incidents de mon enfance, mes désespoirs d'été, l'horrible quantité de force et de science que le sort a toujours éloignée de moi." The "Chanson," in its incantation of rhyme and rhythm, lacks some of the bitterness of the foregoing prose. Still it is bitter enough, and familiar to our memories of stagnant frustrated adolescent summers. And beautiful.

I see no need to attach the poem to the specifics of his defeated affair with Verlaine. It is more general than that. The personal event may, of course, have *catalyzed* the universal events of the poetry.

1st strophe:
> Oisive jeunesse
> A tout asservie,
> Par délicatesse
> J'ai perdu ma vie.
> Ah! Que le temps vienne
> Où les cœurs s'éprennent.

Rimbaud's laziness is at times the special inwardly active or daydreaming laziness of the creator[4] but often just stagnation. He called this negative aspect his "toad's laziness" in the *Saison en enfer* ("Mauvais Sang").

The essence of childhood, particularly in France, is to be subjugated, a kind of slave: "enslaved to all." According to "Les Poètes de sept ans" and other information "il suait d'obéissance"—this is the "délicatesse" which caused him to "lose his life," deprived him of his own affections which were now aching to go out, to love. The poetic act prolongs this abeyance and may be involved in the "délicatesse"; it is the whole culture he had absorbed as a dutiful child that he would now throw off (like the Gide of *The Immoralist*) anticipating the fuller revolt of *déculture* in the *Saison en enfer*. So let the time come when "hearts" (and the body) are moved to love.

2nd strophe:
> Je me suis dit: laisse,
> Et qu'on ne te voie:
> Et sans la promesse
> De plus hautes joies.
> Que rien ne t'arrête,
> Auguste retraite.

He told himself therefore to "let go" ("laisse") and to "drop out" ("qu'on ne te voie"), disappear from the burdensome bourgeois scene. In "Mauvais

---

[4] A positive moment of it is the "vin de la Paresse" in "Les Chercheuses de poux."

Sang" he says "ceux que j'ai rencontrés *ne m'ont peut-être pas vu.*" No
more striving upward, in career or even in art: "sans la promesse / De
plus hautes joies." He wants to retire from the struggle, hence let nothing
stop the move of "retreat."

   3rd strophe:
> J'ai tant fait patience
> Qu'à jamais j'oublie;
> Craintes et souffrances
> Aux cieux sont parties.
> Et la soif malsaine
> Obscurcit mes veines.

He has been so *flatly* dutiful, patient in the bourgeois sense, that all deep
or *vertical* meaning has gone, all authenticity: he "forgets," seemingly
"for good." This is the point of childhood and adolescent revolt when one
suddenly feels "I am nobody at all"—the black pit (*le vide*) before the
soaring discovery of one's true individual identity. But he doesn't know it
yet. This is still the time of stagnancy, utter dreariness. Even pain—"fear
and suffering"—seems to have fled from this deadly ennui (like Baude-
laire's *spleen*). All that he feels is a thirst for the deep waters, the well-
springs of true life. But in his limbo mood[5] the thirst itself is mixed and
muddy, *malsain*.

   4th strophe:
> Ainsi la Prairie
> A l'oubli livrée,
> Grandie, et fleurie
> D'encens et d'ivraies
> Au bourdon farouche
> De cent sales mouches.

His soul is like the spoiling countryside of late summer. "Things rank
and gross in nature / Possess it merely" as Shakespeare put it (*Hamlet*).
In "Mémoire" we will see the decaying scene of his deserted mother like
the abandoned river-fields, with the "roses des roseaux dès longtemps
dévorées." In "Dévotion" also, including the flies: "L'herbe d'été bour-
donnante et puante.—Pour la fièvre des mères et des enfants." In "Voy-
elles" we briefly heard their buzzing and smelled the stench of rot.

---

[5] He is like Mathieu in Sartre's *L'Age de Raison* who "never suffers enough," and
plunges a knife into his hand in exasperation; compare the same need in Rimbaud's
"Honte."

5th strophe:

> Ah! Mille veuvages
> De la si pauvre âme
> Qui n'a que l'image
> De la Notre-Dame!
> Est-ce que l'on prie
> La Vierge Marie?

We commented on this above. Rimbaud seems to be imitating Verlaine's "La mer sur qui prie / La Vierge Marie," but this does not prove Verlaine and his religion are foremost in his mind. Rimbaud is. Hence I do not interpret the *veuvage* as their particular separation. There are *"mille veuvages"*—it is the story of his young life. See the "cinq ou six veuvages" of "Vies," II, referring clearly to a number of such losses.

6th strophe:

> Oisive jeunesse
> A tout asservie,
> Par délicatesse
> J'ai perdu ma vie.
> Ah! Que le temps vienne
> Où les cœurs s'éprennent!

The repetition closes the circle. He is turning like an animal in a cage, or in a round tower.

L'Éternité

In "L'Éternité" there is an ideal union of sexual (and other) opposites,[1] with something like an equal balance of elements, "male" and "female," a "happy family" of nature, which represents an attempt to compensate for the disastrously unbalanced and futile family inflicted on the boy by circumstance. It is forcefully reminiscent of Baudelaire's dream of pure delight expressed in the mingling of light and water in "La Chevelure": "l'or et . . . la moire" (the poetic coalescence also occurs in the letters: *or* in *moire*).[2] Or, again, his "Chant d'automne": "rien . . . Ne me vaut le soleil rayonnant sur la mer." Both poets, rejecting concrete male and female, seek only a wedding of light and water. "Ce n'est qu'onde, flore / Et c'est ta famille" ("Age d'or").

[1] Rimbaud's "Génie" will represent a comparable union, but whereas "L'Éternité" is somewhat inclined to the feminine ("Elle"), "Génie" places the emphasis on the male Maker and Provider.

[2] Compare Mallarmé's "lampe" and "Palmes" in "Don du Poëme," with its fusion of the natural light of dawn and artificial light.

1st strophe:

> Elle est retrouvée.
> Quoi?—L'Éternité.
> C'est la mer allée
> Avec le soleil.

The "Elle," being posed as an unidentified entity, in momentary suspense, has for that moment an aura of the unknown and obliquely recalls—though we are on particularly unsure ground here—the many other mysterious *Elles* of Rimbaud's poetry. In "Les Déserts de l'amour" it is clearly a maternal figure: "J'ai compris qu'Elle était à sa vie de tous les jours. . . . Elle n'est pas revenue, et ne reviendra jamais, l'Adorable. . . ."[3] "Elle" is, as usually in Rimbaud and generally, a woman or girl, over-lapping with an infantile memory of his mother (as is always the case somewhat in a boy's love) or, farther back, Mother Nature. In "Mémoire," "She" is the mother and/or the landscape (river or grass). We might say that "Elle," and in any case the "Éternité" which she is, represents a feminine equivalent to the *Génie*—who, among other things, is "l'éternité" —like "notre mère de beauté" in "Being beauteous"; that is to say, a union of opposites in an Ideal, with a feminine emphasis. Thus the "tu te dégages" of strophe 3 corresponds to "Le dégagement rêvé" of "Génie."

Still, despite the momentary emphasis, which is borne out by the obvious overtone of "la mer" (*mère*, compare "Le Bateau ivre"), as soon as the maternal sea's partner is mentioned, the usually male (for Rimbaud) *soleil*, we have the union and balance, or synthesis, as in "L'azur et l'onde communient" of "Bannières de mai" or the wedding of sun and landscape in "Mémoire."

The variant "mêlée" (for "allée") in "Alchimie du verbe" seems prefer-able to me. Richard notes the added dynamism, leading to *another* reality, in "allée." Personally, like Joyce, I prefer stasis in epiphanies such as this one.

2nd strophe:

> Ame sentinelle,
> Murmurons l'aveu
> De la nuit si nulle
> Et du jour en feu.

The "sentinel soul" is the alert one, tall-standing; its inward brightness nullifies the dark, as does the outer day.[4] The simple proud assertion of

---

[3] The *elle* sound associated with the "Elle . . . Adorable" occurs four times in rapid succession in the 3rd paragraph plus the next line: "belle, maternelle, Elle, rappelle."

[4] A possible title for Rimbaud's lost masterpiece was "Veilleurs"; cf. the prose

light is like those Aristotelian (according to Sartre) essences in Giraudoux: "J'aime la lumière, je déteste les ténèbres."

Psalm 130 may be remembered here:

> My soul waiteth for the Lord
> More than they that watch for the morning.

In Hugo's "Stella," cited by Rimbaud in the second "Lettre du voyant," we find:

> Penseurs, esprits, montez sur la tour, sentinelles;

3rd strophe:
> Des humains suffrages,
> Des communs élans
> Là tu te dégages
> Et voles selon.

Here is another simple contrast, between the proud individual soul and the flat mass (its group votes or opinions, its ordinary impulses). The soul breaks free, as in the throwing-off of the *haleurs* in "Le Bateau ivre." It flies "selon," meaning probably "selon l'Éternité" but perhaps "appropriately" as in the expression "c'est selon" (or, again, "selon son idée").

Compare "voici que mon esprit vole" ("Michel et Christine").

4th strophe:
> Puisque de vous seules,
> Braises de satin,
> Le Devoir s'exhale
> Sans qu'on dise: enfin.

The "Braises de satin" are apt for light-in-water. Indeed, Baudelaire used a similar image in "La Chevelure," "l'or et . . . la moire," the *moire* being watered silk. "Braises" has an interesting overtone of *baiser* (compare the "Baiser montant aux yeux des mers" in "Le Bateau ivre" or Mallarmé's "clair baiser de feu" in "Tout l'âme résumée").

"Le Devoir" is the authentic (Nietzschean) duty toward the real cosmos, not his mother's variety of it; contrast "la Mère, fermant le livre du devoir" ("Les Poètes de sept ans"). She seems remembered and rejected in the line "Sans qu'on dise: enfin." Which is what such mothers are always saying: "Enfin, veux-tu!" and the like.[5] The last words of

---

poem "Veillées." Compare Mallarmé's "astre en fête . . . génie" versus "ténèbres" of "Quand l'ombre menaça."

[5] The smug rentiers of "A la musique" say "En somme! . . ."

"Dévotion" (which includes a memory of stagnant summer and "la fièvre des mères et des enfants") are similar: "Mais plus *alors*." In Rimbaud's particular situation "enfin" has the *limiting* quality of a nagging (maternal or societal) voice; more generally it ("enfin") is the clear and literal opposite of "Éternité."

The revolution of duty is commented on in "Vies" ("Mon devoir m'est remis"), and at the close of the *Saison en enfer* ("Adieu") he speaks of "un devoir à chercher."

5th strophe:
> Là pas d'espérance,
> Nul orietur.
> Science avec patience,
> Le supplice est sûr.

The Nietzschean reality (Duty) is, like Camus's, totally unsentimental with no false, Christian hope (Camus's "leap"): "pas d'espérance." No religion: "Nul orietur" ("Nor will any arise," a biblical term). Only lucidity ("science") and "patience" which accepts what is, including the inevitability of suffering (*amor fati*). "Patience" (from *patior*) implies that.

Age d'or

The light touch of the *Derniers Vers* leads, in "Age d'or," to something so evanescent that little that is solid or convincing has been said about it by the commentators.

To me, despite the fragility of manner, it is a poem based on a compelling theme: the calling (in the deep sense of vocation) of the world, or Nature, to the poet, the "chant de la Nature," or "la voix des mers folles," that siren-voice of poetry and freedom that Ophelia heard to her peril. Perhaps the calling is to be more *natural*, as is the inspiration generally of these later poems, with a childish, open-hearted quality of freshness or originality. In previous poems—"Bannières de mai," "L'Éternité"—we have seen the elements of nature wed in a "happy family" festival of patience. Here the water and flowers participate in a moment of joy, "Et c'est ta famille!" as Rimbaud is welcomed by the world and made a member of the wedding, one of its *belonging* creatures.

The voice specifically calls *him*: "Il s'agit de moi," just as the saints of legend are hailed by a mysterious distant appeal (like the faraway summons to Sebastian in Debussy's *Martyre de Saint Sebastien*). A humbler yet comparable moment is in Richard Wilbur's "June Light": "Your voice, with clear location of June days, / Called me—outside the window." That marvelous "location" is the essence of the experience for Rimbaud as well: one belongs, is in a clear focus, is identified: "Il s'agit de moi." Hence the "voix" is angelic for Rimbaud (as for Wilbur).

The voice may be a breeze, as in "Ophélie" (and "Mémoire"), or it could be some sweet unknown passing song like the one Wordsworth heard in "The Solitary Reaper"—which comes to much the same thing as a breeze. Conceivably it might even be one of Rimbaud's sisters, as in "Mémoire"—so close to nature they are like Ovidian laurel trees (metamorphosed, as Daphne was) in their faded green dresses—speaking indifferently, but gaily, like Nature, of himself. Similarly, the voice here is a "sœur des haleines" (7th strophe), and the "haleine des peupliers . . . la seule brise" of "Mémoire" locates this breath as wind in trees. All the singing voices are "Multiples sœurs" (10th strophe) as well as his "family" (3rd strophe); *Ophélie* too was a sister to nature and her breath was like its stirring.

It hardly matters what or who the voice is. The essence of the experience is familiar enough.

The title reminds one of Rimbaud's allusion to the Golden Age of poetry when man and (his) nature were one: "Vie harmonieuse" he wrote of this era in his famous letter to Demeny. When Rimbaud greets the castle (9th strophe)—as he will in "Le Bonheur"—as a bright pure "princely" essence of his soul, he asks what (Golden) Age it comes from; and we suspect the original Golden Age of Hesiod, or ancient Greece generally as Rimbaud looked back on it (see our comments under "Soleil et chair").

1st strophe:
>Quelqu'une des voix
>Toujours angélique
>—Il s'agit de moi,—
>Vertement s'explique:

The "Quelqu'une" indicates an initial jumble—of sounds in nature, of human voices—from which a single decisive and angelic note emerges. It seems to be telling him a deep truth in a sort of reprimand ("vertement"), telling Rimbaud to *be himself*: "Vis et laisse au feu / L'obscure infortune" (8th strophe). Apparently Rimbaud, like the rest of us at times, was all knotted up in a crisis with endless implications; in the second strophe the voice will tell him to abandon this confusion and return to the holy simplicity of nature ("facile," l. 10). "Vertement" may have an overtone of "green" nature.

2nd strophe:

> Ces mille questions
> Qui se ramifient
> N'amènent, au fond,
> Qu'ivresse et folie;

The futile human complexities lead only to "madness"; in the *Saison en enfer* he will denounce his whole vocation as "folie," but here he seems rather to be rejecting some nagging and tangled moral questions which merely exasperate him and lead to an unhealthy drunkenness: either a sort of helpless dizziness born of confusion or else the result of actual drinking bouts meant to kill the doubts and loosen the knots.

3rd strophe:

> Reconnais ce tour
> Si gai, si facile:
> Ce n'est qu'onde, flore,
> Et c'est ta famille!

The imperative "Reconnais" implies a homecoming. It is really all very simple and natural, "gai" and "facile." The water and flowers are certainly part of the same mood, for example in "Fleurs": "la mer et le ciel attirent . . . la foule des jeunes et fortes roses." This mood was evoked in Mallarmé's "enfance / Adorable des bois de roses sous l'azur / Naturel" ("Las de l'amer repos"), which he likewise penned in protest against Western complexities.

4th strophe:

> Puis elle chante. O
> Si gai, si facile,
> Et visible à l'œil nu . . .
> —Je chante avec elle,—

There is no problem here, except the "visible à l'œil nu," a banal expression for "evident." It is clumsy but I doubt if it is satiric, as some think; nothing else in the poem is. Perhaps it is just a relaxed insouciant expression for *immediate* or simple nature, "facile," etc.

The fifth and sixth strophes are quite straightforward.

7th strophe:

> Et chante à l'instant
> En sœur des haleines:
> D'un ton Allemand,
> Mais ardente et pleine:

The "sœur des haleines" is like the sisterly relation between the human voice or breath and the (other) natural voices ("haleines") in "Ophélie": "Les nénuphars froissés soupirent autour d'elle"; ". . . sa douce folie / Murmure sa romance à la brise du soir." And we have already observed that *haleine* means breeze in "Mémoire": "l'haleine / des peupliers . . . est pour la seule brise." Thus in "Mémoire," the blue flower is "amie à l'eau" and the "Elle," woman, is also the grass or river. Or: "Les robes vertes et déteintes des fillettes [his sisters] font les saules."

The "German tone" of the voice is no doubt like the "vertement," snappy and reprimanding, although it is also "ardent and full."[1] It dialectically reminds him of the harsh truth of reality which he must abandon—"Le monde est vicieux," etc.—even as the voice earlier explained "vertement" that the ugly complexities had to be left behind. Nonetheless, "German" can still be a natural voice, as in "Aube," where a waterfall takes on a Teutonic tone (*wasserfall*), and in "Entends comme brame" Germany is part of a moonlight effect as it is in "Soir historique": "l'Allemagne s'échafaude vers des lunes."

8th strophe:
> Le monde est vicieux;
> Si cela t'étonne!
> Vis et laisse au feu
> L'obscure infortune.

The voice reminds him of the ugliness of the "world" (that is, the ordinary or social world).[2] It ironically exclaims: What is surprising in that! and tells him to "live," preaches Life, like the château's "bright life" (l. 34). Throw away (leave to the fire—or the defunct?) "dark misfortune." A similar *darkness* in "Chanson de la plus haute tour" described the unhealthy thirst he wanted to abandon like the "questions" here. It contrasts with the brightness of the château, as the day does with the "nulle" night in "L'Éternité." At the end of "Bannières de mai" he was less buoyant: "Et libre soit cette infortune." Here he revolts against *infortune* in the name of joy.

9th strophe:
> O! joli château!
> Que ta vie est claire!
> De quel Age es-tu,
> Nature princière
> De notre grand frère! etc. . .

---

[1] It might be *nordic* German as the wind of liberty is Norwegian in "Ophélie."

[2] Compare "les Bergers . . . Meurent . . . par le monde" in "Bannières de mai."

The castle is awe-inspiring, as it is in "Le Bonheur." We have described it above (p. 10) as an ideal architecture of the soul. (Everybody's "dream-house" is a banal version of the same.) Here it is the "princely nature" of Rimbaud, who refers to himself as "notre grand frère." Just as the voice was a "sister" to other natural voices, he is the "brother" to the castle, etc.

> 10th strophe:
>> Je chante aussi, moi:
>> Multiples sœurs! voix
>> Pas du tout publiques!
>> Environnez-moi
>> De gloire pudique . . . etc. . . .

The "multiple sisters" are the nature he is called back to. The "modest glory" is exactly like the one Mallarmé returned to (in "La Gloire") amidst the Forest of Fontainebleau, away from the corrupt city and its meretricious success. The "voix / Pas du tout publiques" may indicate the specific bitter rejection of the artists of Paris, now left behind. Or of their art, as he listens to nature's voices, like Wordsworth exclaiming "The world is too much with us" and harking like Ophelia to "la voix des mers folles," to the fresh original "sea which bares its bosom to the moon."

Jeune ménage

This poem is unusually Verlainian—though more complex than Verlaine—in its fundamental tone: the evasiveness of adolescence, suspended in its dreams, play-acting, not ready for "It." The musical "key" is that of the enchanted *Fêtes galantes*, the mode, their mode mineur. Everything is *quasi* as in the "quasi-tristes" of "Clair de lune," in chromatic or *half* tones like moonlight itself. Humor, gallant badinage, the swirling movement of a youthful festival, all these are age-old means of avoidance. Another ploy is faëry, in the gossamer Shakespearean manner of *A Midsummer Night's Dream*,[1] where the couples endlessly grope toward each other, or in Watteau's frantically spinning *Commedia dell'arte* revels transcribed by Verlaine and Debussy (for example, "Mandoline").

In this poem, the couple of the title may refer to Verlaine and Rimbaud (cf. "drôle de ménage," "Délires I"), but, once again, that is of relatively little importance to the normal reader or to the universal and poetic experience of the piece. It makes lyric sense regardless of the

---

[1] Rimbaud's prose poem "Bottom" is earnest that he knew this play well.

specifics; almost any young couple will do for this frivolous, touching, and self-mocking scene.

1st strophe:

> La chambre est ouverte au ciel bleu-turquin;
> Pas de place: des coffrets et des huches!
> Dehors le mur est plein d'aristoloches
> Où vibrent les gencives des lutins.

The marriage room is a symptom of the numb ineptness of youth, disorderly, helpless (*jeunesse étourdie* in the stock phrase). Only the sky is serious: blue ("bleu-turquin: bleu tirant sur l'ardoise") is, in this poem, a color of affection—forgotten is the "lying blue" of "Les Poètes de sept ans." The sky-color begins and ends the poem (see the last line).

"Pas de place" sounds like an echo from *Alice in Wonderland*, but may not be (the first part of *Alice* was published in 1865). The chests and sideboards are domestic, somewhat excessively and unmanageably so, like the furniture in Colette-Ravel's *L'Enfant et les sortilèges*. Hence, no doubt, the exclamation mark.

These wayward householders are unusually aware of—indeed invaded by!—what goes on outside: for example, the birthwort on the wall (Rimbaud knew well what went on on walls, as we learned from "Les Poètes de sept ans" and "Le Bateau ivre"); also "vibrating gums" of elves. This grin in mid-air again suggests *Alice*, this time with shades of the Cheshire Cat (as well as the trembling "rire" of the comparable "Tête de faune"); it is the essence of the suspended mood of adolescence.

The vi ("vibrent") and reverse iv ("gencive") are quivering in sound as are the three vi's of "Voyelles": "vibrements divins des mers virides." The v is cutting here as in the similar effect of "Tête de faune": "Vif et crevant . . . Sa lèvre."

2nd strophe:

> Que ce sont bien intrigues de génies
> Cette dépense et ces désordres vains!
> C'est la fée africaine qui fournit
> La mûre, et les résilles dans les coins.

These comings and goings, "intrigues," are, as in the *Fêtes galantes*, busy frivolity to "keep moving," avoid *It*. T. S. Eliot caught the *Commedia dell'arte* mood nicely in his "Sweeney Among the Nightingales" (including the mid-air grin):

> She and the lady in the cape
> Are suspect, thought to be in league;
>
> . . .
>
> Leaves the room and reappears
> Outside the window, leaning in,
> Branches of wisteria
> Circumscribe a golden grin;

As we noted in our remarks on "Bal des Pendus," adolescents see more ghosts than anyone, for obvious reasons. Hence the *fées, génies, lutins,* and the like. A *génie* here is simply a spirit, a spectre; playful, willful, and naughty, he embodies all we buried then. The African fairy brings on a note of *black* magic, appropriate to slight guilt and fear, and may be associated with the "mûre," the somber color of the mulberry (compare "La Rivière de Cassis" for a mysterious dark berry counterpart). The hairnets are cobwebs, an intimate part of faëry for Shakespeare too, in *A Midsummer Night's Dream* (or for Mallarmé in "Frisson d'hiver").

3rd strophe:

> Plusieurs entrent, marraines mécontentes,
> En pans de lumière dans les buffets,
> Puis y restent! le ménage s'absente
> Peu sérieusement, et rien ne se fait.

The "plusieurs" refers to "génies."

The "marraines mécontentes" resemble the ill-tempered Duchess of *Alice in Wonderland*: again, the prudery of Victorian peevishness is related to the suspended mood. Suzanne Bernard explains these "marraines": they are said to enter buffets, in popular legend, as fairy godmothers (perhaps like the one in *The Princess and the Goblin*, by George MacDonald). See our earlier comments on "Le Buffet."

The "pans de lumière" are wonderfully evocative; the light-plots (flat a) inside the buffet are like a peepshow, a small private delight for a child.

The scene is so disembodied, even the couple is "absent"; frivolously so ("Peu sérieusement"). That is to say, they do not stay and do their household chores. So "nothing gets done," which is the whole story: ineffectuality.

4th strophe:

> Le marié a le vent qui le floue
> Pendant son absence, ici, tout le temps.
> Même des esprits des eaux, malfaisants
> Entrent vaguer aux sphères de l'alcôve.

The husband is "betrayed" by the wind during his absence. No real danger there (though the wind is thought to fertilize women by some primitive peoples).

The water-spirits[2] are the liquid light shadows on the walls. Rimbaud was also fascinated by this light-and-shadow play in "Les Poètes de sept ans" ("le soir . . . un golfe de jour pendant du toit"). These upper reaches or "sphères" of "alcôves," or the light-shafts in the barn in "Les Reparties de Nina," are part of the spiritual intervention from above which Jacques Rivière observed in Rimbaud. They are "malfaisants" only in the mild adolescent spirit of guilt (cf. "mécontentes," etc.), that is to say the tone of half-serious naughtiness and "disorder."

5th strophe:
>La nuit, l'amie oh! la lune de miel
>Cueillera leur sourire et remplira
>De mille bandeaux de cuivre le ciel.
>Puis ils auront affaire au malin rat.

The "honeymoon" is in the subtle *lunaire* mood of the rest, à la Verlaine. Not much is happening in the bed if they are looking at those coppery moonrays. The "sly rat" is another welcome diversion. Animals are substitutes for forbidden objects of desire in the hearts of children; like the Chagallesque ass and bird of "Bottom," they represent a defeat and metamorphosis, not adult direct doing.

6th strophe:
>—S'il n'arrive pas un feu follet blême,
>Comme un coup de fusil, après des vêpres.
>—O spectres saints et blancs de Bethléem,
>Charmez plutôt le bleu de leur fenêtre!

It is late evening or night. Now the possibility of a Hallowe'eny spirit is added, "pale will-o'-the-wisp." The syntax is as follows: in the preceding strophe, he has told what will happen on the "honeymoon" night; now he adds: "unless this happens . . . , etc."; i.e., it is an alternate possibility, which would occur with the violence of a gunshot. That is rather frightening. So he prays to the ghosts of the night—with a satirical reference to *religious* ghosts ("Bethléem")—for a return of the blue day which began the charming scene, the "premières heures bleues" ("Est-elle almée?") of morning.

---

[2] Compare the "Ondines" of "Comédie de la soif."

Bruxelles

A glorious paean to life, summer light, being on a boulevard in Brussels on a July day of the world.

1st strophe:
> Plates-bandes d'amarantes jusqu'à
> L'agréable palais de Jupiter.
> —Je sais que c'est Toi qui, dans ces lieux,
> Mêles ton Bleu presque de Sahara!

The "palais de Jupiter" is no cause for exegetic concern. Like the Hesperides of "Bonne pensée du matin" it merely gives a classic, antique depth or transcendence to something (a public building on the horizon?) which is more than itself on such a day.

But who is the "Toi"? The best bet is the spirit of poetry, the *génie* (of "Génie") who is "Lui," and whose eyes ("ses yeux") are present and if not quite blue, close to it: violet, in "Les Voyelles." In "Fleurs," there is "un dieu aux énormes yeux bleus . . . la mer et le ciel." If blue has at other times the blackness of deceit in it (see "Les Poètes de sept ans"), that is forgotten here.[1] This tint is pure as the "bleu de leur fenêtre" of "Jeune ménage" or his own eyes at their most innocent, mingled with the summer light as in Richard Wilbur's "Summer, luxuriant Sahara" ("My Father Paints the Summer").

Those three calm a's (Sahara) have to do with its luxuriant stretch (Baudelaire's "La langoureuse Asie et la brûlante Afrique" is a comparable effect in "La Chevelure").

2nd strophe:
> Puis, comme rose et sapin du soleil
> Et liane ont ici leurs jeux enclos,
> Cage de la petite veuve! . . .
> > > > Quelles
> Troupes d'oiseaux, ô ia io, ia io! . . .

The neatly enclosed gardens along the boulevard, with roses, firs (in the sun), lianas, perhaps a birdcage (the "cage" is seen again in the fifth strophe) glimpsed in the cottage of a "little widow." This is a fetching image in itself—no need to attach it to Verlaine. This image, linked with the "Kiosque de la Folle par affection" (l. 10), evokes that solitary, eccentric, lovelorn lady in her little house near the Vivonne along the way to

---

[1] "L'Épouse aux yeux bleus" ("Michel et Christine") is a sentimental and false evocation. I do not see this one as feminine, nor male either, but angelic.

Guermantes (or even Odette's *Charmettes*). A single and abandoned lady is a welcoming creature to a lonely wayfaring male, with echoes of long-past fairy godmothers (and buried mothers). Anyway, birds are in the air and a nameless enthusiasm like little Marcel's "zut zut zut." Rimbaud lets go his sheer self in that approximate twittering, more his own.[2]

3rd strophe:
> —Calmes maisons, anciennes passions!
> Kiosque de la Folle par affection.
> Après les fesses des rosiers, balcon
> Ombreux et très bas de la Juliette.

Calm houses, reminiscent of Vermeer or Pissarro (*Dimanche à Pontoise*). The "former passions" are the romantic depth that crosses the classic summer serenity in a plunging new dimension. There is more here than meets the eye. The image of the lovelorn *Folle*, discussed above, arises, suggestive—perhaps because of the low shadowy balcony—of Shakespeare's enamored and bereft Juliet. *En passant* there were the "fesses des rosiers," preferably the round "cheeks" of roses associated with behinds (like the "culs en rond" of "Les Effarés"), or maybe the Ardennes patois for flexible branches of rosebushes (the latter according to Suzanne Bernard).

4th strophe:
> —La Juliette, ça rappelle l'Henriette,
> Charmante station du chemin de fer,
> Au cœur d'un mont, comme au fond d'un verger
> Où mille diables bleus dansent dans l'air!

By echo, Juliet—romantic English heroine—recalls Henriette, lovely French heroine from Molière's *Les Femmes savantes*; according to Gengoux, Rimbaud found that pairing in Banville's "Voie lactée." Be that as it may, the playing-around with memory-echoes, like the bird-imitation outburst, is part of the spacious carefree day. Somehow the "Henriette," in a stream of consciousness, evokes a charming train station (perhaps by that name, so far unidentified). Rimbaud cherished train stations. We explained earlier how they are an ideal synthesis of free traveling and safe harbor, still repose. In "Génie" it is the "charme des lieux fuyants et le délice surhumain des stations." In "Départ" the "arrêts de la vie" are as compelling as the going. In "Larme," "des gares" were part of the fascinating sky-spectacle along with the flight of landscape in storm clouds.

---

[2] Compare Mallarmé's "Petit air II": "L'oiseau . . . [je ne sais] Si de mon sein pas du sien / A jailli le sanglot pire."

This station is really idyllic, snug as a womb, ensconced "in the heart of a mountain," no doubt surrounded by domestic and fruitful orchards, the sky vibrant with blue "spirits" like little devils.[3]

5th strophe:
> Banc vert où chante au paradis d'orage,
> Sur la guitare, la blanche Irlandaise.
> Puis, de la salle à manger guyanaise,
> Bavardage des enfants et des cages.

The storm, occasionally associated with the station, is a favorite moment for Rimbaud, a paradise of refreshing change. In "Villes, I": "Le paradis des orages s'effondre." In "Michel et Christine" it is equally heavenly: "Cette religieuse après-midi d'orage." In "Génie," there is the ecstatic *tempête.*

Then, surrealistically, a compelling figure appears from amidst the happy stir, as in "Being beauteous" or like the girl with the orange lips from the "bright deluge" of the woods in "Enfance." This "girl" is an Irishwoman (we recall the Spanish beauties of "Les Poètes de sept ans," the other foreign ladies—Mexican, Flemish—of "Enfance").

Some other house affords a glimpse of an exotic dining room, "Guyanan," with chattering of children and birdcages.

6th strophe:
> Fenêtre du duc qui fais que je pense
> Au poison des escargots et du buis
> Qui dort ici-bas au soleil.
> > Et puis
> C'est trop beau! trop! Gardons notre silence.

Another passing window, ducal in splendor, makes him think of Italian Renaissance poison (à la Lucrezia Borgia). Here the joy "turns" a bit (as "le rêve fraîchit" in "Veillées" or "la fanfare tournant" quoted below) into an underside dark dankness of snails, shadow of boxwood which "sleeps" in the sun. The gaiety is ambivalent, like the "gai venin" of "Fêtes de la faim," or the "soif malsaine" of his "veins" in "Chanson de la plus haute tour." Compare "Matinée d'ivresse": "Ce poison [drunken thirst for joy] va rester dans toutes nos veines même quand, la fanfare tournant, nous serons rendus à l'ancienne inharmonie."

But the mood lifts to pure delight again. It is too beautiful to express. He will say that anew in the next little poem, "Est-elle almée?"

---

[3] See Richard Wilbur: "The sky a deep and woven blue" ("Merlin"), and "While evening, with a million simple fissions" ("Place Pigalle").

7th strophe:

> —Boulevard sans mouvement ni commerce,
> Muet, tout drame et toute comédie,
> Réunion des scènes infinie,
> Je te connais et t'admire en silence.

Finally this is an Olympian epiphany; the perfection of the quiet (Sunday?) boulevard, usually astir with "movement and commerce," the business of the world, is now seen as alive with a private inner world, a unity-multiplicity, a kinetic-static "Réunion des scènes infinie." This reminds us of the "Rumeurs" of "Départ," the vibrant here-there of the *bruissement* of trees beyond the fence in "Enfance" or again of Valéry's "tumulte au silence pareil" ("Le Cimetière marin"). All scenes of life, the "human comedy"[4]—the scenes and characters he glimpsed and imagined, "l'Ancienne Comédie" of "Scènes"—are summed up in this silent microcosmic moment and site at this summit of the cultured West. He will soon abandon it all, having risen like Corneille's Augustus to a point from which he could only descend.

Est-elle almée?

"Elle" appears mysteriously, fleetingly, in this small poem. Who is She? Something like the feminine version of the *Génie*, as we said of "Her" in "L'Éternité"—a sort of distillation of all-woman rising up giddily in superior joy: life-breath itself, soul, *anima*, deliriously apprehended. A modest forerunner of *La Jeune Parque*. In the morning this spirit will disappear like Gautier's "specter of a rose."

1st strophe:

> Est-elle almée? . . . aux premières heures bleues
> Se détruira-t-elle comme les fleurs feues . . .
> Devant la splendide étendue où l'on sente
> Souffler la ville énormément florissante!

"Est-elle almée?" means: Is she an Oriental dancing-girl?—who will, no doubt, pirouette and disappear.

At the "first blue hours," she will be destroyed like defunct ("feues") flowers. This privileged moment seems to occur at dusk. Rimbaud is standing before the "enormously flourishing city," feeling its potential like Wordsworth on Westminster Bridge saying:

---

[4] Compare "Parade," in which there may be an echo of the Juliette, Henriette.

> This City now doth, like a garment, wear
> The beauty of the morning . . .
> And all that mighty heart is lying still!

2nd strophe:

> C'est trop beau! c'est trop beau! mais c'est nécessaire
> —Pour la Pêcheuse et la chanson du Corsaire,
> Et aussi puisque les derniers masques crurent
> Encore aux fêtes de nuit sur la mer pure!

Again, it is too much to express (as in "Bruxelles"). "Mais c'est nécessaire" is the usual Rimbaldian *amor fati*, as in "L'Éternité" where the vision of beauty is resignedly (*patience*) taken with its "supplice . . . sûr."

It is necessary for the "Pêcheuse" and the song of the "Corsaire," he says as an afterthought. Akin to the "human comedy" he thought of in sum at the end of "Bruxelles," these are role-playing worldly figures (with mysterious hints of musical theatre) which he imagines swirling gaily in the night that will come to an end, like a masked ball *sub specie aeternitatis*: "A quelque fête de nuit dans une cité du Nord; j'ai rencontré toutes les femmes des anciens peintres" ("Vies").[1] They are like those *Bergers* who disappear in the morning in "Bonne pensée du matin," only less wretched perhaps. These maskers naively *believed*, to the end, in their festival; that generous yielding of the self to too-great beauty is appropriate ("necessary") for the fulfillment of the drama of *éclat* and disappearance: "Nous savons donner notre vie tout entière" ("Matinée d'ivresse"). One thinks of the evanescent and persistent (through the dark hours) butterfly-figures of the "fête étrange" in *Le Grand Meaulnes*.

Does "sur la mer pure" recall Musset's "Nuit vénitienne" with its lantern-lit carnival on the sea-canals? In "Villes," "Des fêtes amoureuses sonnent sur les canaux," but it is hard to pin down just where. At any rate, the sea gives the proper backdrop of infinity, as it did for the phosphorescent events of "Le Bateau ivre." See our further discussion of this under "Being beauteous."

Fêtes de la faim

As in "Voyelles," Rimbaud lets himself go here in free childish association. The effect is fresh, innovative, and naturally uneven.

We have already seen hunger, like thirst ("Comédie de la soif"), to be among the handful of central Rimbaldian themes. It is full of his

---

[1] Similarly, in "Fête d'hiver" we see:

Nymphes d'Horace coiffées au Premier Empire—Rondes
Sibériennes, Chinoises de Boucher.

primitive directness, appropriation by eating, immediate communion through the most basic animal appetite. Yet the sensuality is dialectically accompanied and complicated by sophisticated form, studied word-effects, subtle art, and cultural references.

1-2.   Ma faim, Anne, Anne,
      Fuis sur ton âne.

The poem begins insouciantly with "Ma faim" which to the childlike ear sounds for all the world like the familiar breezy formula for "Mais enfin" (cf. the parallel sassiness of "Baou" in "Dévotion").

The immediate overtone of *faim* is *femme*, as in the rhyme "femme / affame" ("Don du Poëme"). The essence of mother is, at first, sustenance through nursing. The capitalized maternal m and the echo of *ma* (*maman*) support this feeling (m is the initial letter of the word mother in most European languages. Sir Richard Paget, in *Human Speech*, attributes this to the position of the lips in suckling). Hence the immediate association of a feminine name: "Anne."

The repetition no doubt is inspired by Perrault's "Anne, ma sœur Anne" from "Barbe-Bleu": the latter is significantly linked with milk in "Après le déluge." The obvious echo of donkey may be reinforced by a memory of a song in La Fontaine's "Le Meunier, son fils et l'âne": "[quand] Nicolas va voir Jeanne . . . [il] monte sur son âne" (Bernard, p. 442). I faintly suspect also an echo of *nanan*: "yumyum" (compare "nana" at the close of "L'Homme juste"), derived in turn from *maman*; *banane* and *ananas* have a particularly "yummy" quality. Nanette is a diminutive for Anne (or Annette). In any case, Rimbaud obviously enjoys mouthing the "Anne." The repetition "Anne . . . Anne . . . âne" is the essence of incantatory babbling, childish and narcissistic self-consolation through a rosary of reassuringly similar sound, a verbal substitute for suckling.[1]

3. Si j'ai du *goût*, ce n'est guères
   Que pour la terre et les pierres.
   Dinn! dinn! dinn! dinn! Mangeons l'air,
   Le roc, les charbons, le fer.

The earthy (and airy) communion is superbly poetic and not so unusual in practice. Not only children eat mud-pies; whole regions of grown people,

---

[1] See "ému jusqu'à la mort par le murmure du lait du matin" followed closely by "sa bouche, que la mienne saisit comme une petite vague désespérée minant sans fin quelque chose" ("Les Déserts de l'amour"). Also the "Le sang et le lait coulèrent" of "Après le déluge" and "L'Homme suçait, heureux, sa mamelle bénie" of "Soleil et chair."

not always primitive, have taken to eating earth in faddish waves. This is a form of death-urge, communion with the Ground, also a corollary to a burial-urge (as in India). Rimbaud's spiritual hunger is a sensual and *elemental* death-urge like Milosz's "Morts de Lofoten," Thomas Gray's "Elegy Written in a Country Churchyard," Dylan Thomas' "In Country Sleep," or Valéry's "Cimetière marin" ("Les morts cachés sont bien dans cette terre"; "L'argile rouge a bu la blanche espèce").

The emphasized "*goût*" indicates a sort of weak pun on physical taste and aesthetic taste. The two are thus explicitly combined in this image, as they usually are implicitly in Rimbaud.

The "Dinn! dinn! dinn! dinn!" is an overtone of *dîner* plus the sound of a distant bell (hint of dinner bell?)[2] thinned through the air—"L'azur sonneur" below—like the cock-crow of "O Saisons, ô châteaux" which comes to him from far off and seems to offer him the space, the air, the world for his complex hunger. Thus the "pré des sons" where his hunger "pastures" (in the next strophe) is partly this crop of "sounds." The air itself is eaten, like the earth, and what is more appetizing?

> Tasting the frothy mist, and freshest
> Fathoms of air
>
> .   .   .
>
> Imminent towns whose weatherbeaten walls
> Looked like the finest cheese.
> > (Richard Wilbur, "The Terrace")

Iron (flints?), coals, rocks, children stuff anything in their mouths and adults would too if we dared—we want all the world *in us* on certain privileged days of hunger.

> 7. Mes faims, tournez. Paissez, faims,
> > Le pré des sons!
> > Attirez le gai venin
> > Des liserons;

The hunger roves over the meadow with its sounds (or bran-like freckles, splotches), recalling the "Prairie . . . fleurie / D'encens et d'ivraies" and its "mouches" in "Chanson de la plus haute tour."[3]

---

[2] The sound *dinn*! *dinn*! is close to that made by bells at railway crossings, according to my French informants. Perhaps the coals and iron fragments are attached to this railroad image, frequent in Rimbaud (see "Michel et Christine," "Larme," "Bruxelles," etc.).

[3] Here is Richard Wilbur's equivalent for the same phenomenon in the just-quoted "Terrace":

Thus the "gay poison" of the convolvulus is like the *ivraies* (tares) of the spoiling *Prairie*, or the ambivalent emotional "poison" that invades the boxwood gardens of "Bruxelles."

11. Mangez
> Les cailloux qu'un pauvre brise,
> Les vieilles pierres d'église,
> Les galets, fils des déluges,
> Pains couchés aux vallées grises!

The pebbles a poor man breaks is a hint of communion with the *peuple* as in "Les Pauvres à l'église" ("mangeuses de soupe" brought in the oral communion there); compare also the poor toiling *dragueur* who echoes Rimbaud's misery and hunger at the end of "Mémoire."

The "old church stones" are like those "heaps" of stones in church walls he described in "Les Premières Communions." There the stones were earthy, redolent of "la terre maternelle," hence the same note of a Magna Mater's nursing, a Return.

The "galets" make one think of that original earth from which the child ("fils") emerged,[4] and echo the Deucalian (or Cadmus) myth. Compare "Après le déluge," where the child comes out renewed, reborn, as after an amniotic flood. The communion with the "galet" through eating (cf. *galette*) is the acquisition of this identity: a son-rock (the sulking child is a rock of self-sufficiency). "Les Effarés" told of a similar communion. But those stones on the gray valley floor *look* like bread; that is the main poetic point behind all these images.

16. Mes faims, c'est les bouts d'air noir;
> L'azur sonneur;
> —C'est l'estomac qui me tire.
> C'est le malheur.

Here, the hunger turns back to air but it is compromised now, like the meadow earlier. The "azur" is black (as "malheur"), as it is said to be in "Alchimie du verbe": "J'écartai du ciel l'azur, qui est du noir." Blue sky does, again, *look* like millions of black dots are mingled in, when you stare at it. This hints at the negative side of hunger: pain, the stomach which "pulls," and the overall *malheur* of his fate.

Mixt into all the day we heard the spice
Of many tangy bees
Eddying through the miles-deep
Salad of flowers.

[4] Hackett observed this meaning before us, in *Rimbaud l'enfant*.

The "azur sonneur"—recalling the "dinn! dinn!"—is based on the fact that French air in general is mingled with bells. Suzanne Bernard is probably right: Rimbaud did get the idea in part from Mallarmé's "Sonneur." And I think of Proust's Marcel reading in the garden where bell sounds emerged from the air as if they were squeezed like golden drops from its full-to-brim liquidity at noon. But church bells may well evoke Rimbaud's hatred of religion here. So in the next strophe he returns to pure pagan nature.

> 21. Sur terre ont paru les feuilles!
>   Je vais aux chairs de fruit blettes.
>   Au sein du sillon je cueille
>   La doucette et la violette.
>   Ma faim, Anne, Anne!
>   Fuis sur ton âne.

He turns to nature as nourisher, to its leaves; its overripe fruit offers a special *generosity*, something he notably had not received from his mother (and her Church). The *breast* is not hers, nor Mother Church's, but the plough-furrow's (we've seen those earth-woman shapes before, in "Soleil et chair," "L'Étoile a pleuré rose," etc.); see the later *talus (mamelon)*, a favorite image of the *Illuminations*. "Lamb's lettuce" and "violets" remind us of Shakespeare's love of nature and its humble flowerings. The *violets* have been scattered throughout the poems—an ultimate of thirst and hunger: in "Le loup criait sous les feuilles," the spider eats them joyously, at home in the world.

Qu'est-ce pour nous, mon cœur . . .

This apocalyptic piece is in the vein of various *Illuminations*, for example "Solde." It is not very good as poetry or anything else, but it is mildly interesting anyway.

Rimbaud calls frenziedly not so much for a *political* revolt as for a *cosmic* vengeance against the social order and its Powerful through the agency of (or with the aid of) the underdogs: "Noirs inconnus." This is the "déplacements de races et de continents" he will recall in "Délires II." Rimbaud wanted to pay back the forces of Order for all he had suffered at their hands. It is an orgy of vindictive youthful feeling or imagination ("mon cœur"), almost pathological. But the end, barely, saves sanity through a hint of humor.

Rimbaud had been preceded in this wild panorama not only by Sade but, closer in time and tone, by the anarchist Cœurderoy in his book

Hourrah ou la révolution par les cosaques, which called on exotic hordes to lay sack to everything. His only hope was in total disaster.

> 1. Qu'est-ce pour nous, mon cœur, que les nappes de sang
>   Et de braise, et mille meurtres, et les longs cris
>   De rage, sanglots de tout enfer renversant
>   Tout ordre; et l'Aquilon encor sur les débris;

Like a Caligula (or the Prince of his "Conte," or of Baudelaire in "Une Mort héroïque"), his hatred of pain in the world is so great that he homeopathically tries to blot out the cosmic cruelty by human cruelty. Or by a Nietzschean indifference to it.[1] Sade had called the heart "that weak spot of the intellect," and in a letter to Delahaye Rimbaud bragged of his heartlessness. Need we add that this is only fitful rage? (Rivière exaggerates this aspect of him. . . .)

> 5. Et toute vengeance? Rien! . . . —Mais si, toute encor,
>   Nous la voulons! Industriels, princes, sénats:
>   Périssez! puissance, justice, histoire: à bas!
>   Ça nous est dû. Le sang! le sang! la flamme d'or!
>
>   Tout à la guerre, à la vengeance, à la terreur,
>   Mon esprit! Tournons dans la morsure: Ah! passez,
>   Républiques de ce monde! Des empereurs,
>   Des régiments, des colons, des peuples, assez!
>
>   Qui remuerait les tourbillons de feu furieux,
>   Que nous et ceux que nous nous imaginons frères?
>   A nous, romanesques amis: ça va nous plaire.
>   Jamais nous ne travaillerons, ô flots de feux!

He sums up the list of horrors which will knock down the prevailing order with the expression: "all vengeance." He then states that all that mayhem is "nothing," which is temporarily puzzling: does he mean to say he is Olympian, indifferent to everything, including the worst pain, or is it "nothing" in relation to the vast sufferings inflicted by the Powerful? He goes on to clarify that he doesn't mean indifference: "yes," revenge *is* something ("si"), and "we want it." A lot goes under with the princes and senates, even "justice and history" and, in the next strophe, "peoples." This is a Sade-like rage against everything. A romantic frenzy of destruction, with only the romantic "romanesques amis" (l. 15) joining him in it:

[1] Camus describes the syndrome in *L'Homme revolté* and takes Rimbaud to task for his excesses.

Manichean men whose thirst for purity is so great they cannot accept the mediocre world and who might say like Villiers "our servants will live for us." Hence "Jamais nous ne travaillerons" (l. 16). In the *Saison en enfer* he will repeat more than once that work is not for him.

> 17. Europe, Asie, Amérique, disparaissez.
>   Notre marche vengeresse a tout occupé,
>   Cité et campagnes!—Nous serons écrasés!
>   Les volcans sauteront! Et l'Océan frappé . . .

He realizes he himself and his allies will perish too: "Nous serons écrasés!" And he goes on as if the Old Testament God were among his allies, to imagine that volcanoes will explode, the ocean will be hit. . . .

> 21. Oh! mes amis!—Mon cœur, c'est sûr, ils sont des frères:
>   Noirs inconnus, si nous allions! Allons! allons!
>   O malheur! je me sens frémir, la vieille terre,
>   Sur moi de plus en plus à vous! la terre fond,
>
>   Ce n'est rien! j'y suis! j'y suis toujours.

His imagination, or feeling, tells him the "unknown blacks" are indeed true friends, reassuring him despite the momentary fear and doubt. So he whips up his courage and says "Let's go." But the fear of this total destruction is too great for his heart. He imagines the called-for eruption as dumping on him: "O misfortune . . . the old earth [melts] on me, more and more yours [earth's, or misfortune's], the earth melts."

To quell this fear he calls up again the earlier "nothing" of indifference; ambiguously, this time it can also refer to the nothingness of the reality; it's all just his imagination, this catastrophe, like the dream-holocaust of "Conte": "I am here [on the earth] still." This is very like the close of Camus's *Caligula*: "Je suis encore vivant!" Or Rimbaud's surprise at still existing in "Mauvais sang": "te voilà, c'est ta force." The madman who wants to ruin all and calls down death at the end, when he is about to go under, screams the opposite urge: life. Moreover, this is a comment on all such *tricherie*, as Claude-Edmonde Magny would call it. In spite of their pretensions, the nay-sayers are always ultimately affirming, if only their "nay." Life is bigger than death as long as we are alive. Cretans call all Cretans liars; Brice Parrain loudly and incessantly proclaims the necessity of silence,[2] as do the Zen Buddhists. As Camus in the *Myth of Sisyphus* pokes fun at Schopenhauer for preaching suicide while staying around

---

[2] This is similar to Bertrand Russell's claim that Mr. Wittgenstein manages to say a great deal about the unsayable.

and enjoying good meals, Rimbaud here makes fun of himself for clinging to life. As he said in "Roman": "On n'est pas sérieux."

Entends comme brame

Perhaps the most puzzling of the verse poems, this one is a play of loose harmonies around a moonlit landscape, conjuring up specters and distant magic places. A possible source of inspiration is Verlaine's "L'Heure du berger"[1] from *Poèmes Saturniens*, well-known to Rimbaud. It has the key effects of *brume* and *prairie* ("la rame viride du pois") and *lune* ("Phœbé"), *spectres* ("ces chers Anciens"), trees ("peupliers" instead of "acacias"), *verts* ("viride"); and the *rament* ("row" with wings) echoes Rimbaud's "rame" ("row" of peas).

> La lune est rouge au brumeux horizon;
> Dans un brouillard qui danse la prairie
> S'endort fumeuse, et la grenouille crie
> Par les joncs verts où circule un frisson;
>
> Les fleurs des eaux referment leurs corolles;
> Des peupliers profilent aux lointains,
> Droits et serrés, leurs spectres incertains;
> Vers les buissons errent les lucioles;
>
> Les chat-huants s'éveillent, et sans bruit
> Rament l'air noir avec leurs ailes lourdes,
> Et le zénith s'emplit de lueurs sourdes.
> Blanche, Vénus émerge, et c'est la Nuit.
>   (Verlaine, "L'Heure du berger")

And Gautier's "Vieux de la vieille" is perhaps even closer:

> Passer des spectres en plein jour
>   .   .   .
> Pourtant c'est la nuit que les arbres,
> Par un clair de lune allemand,
> Dans les vieilles tours en décombres,
> Reviennent ordinairement;
>   .   .   .
> C'est la nuit que les Elfes sortent . . .

In Gautier's "Le Dernière Feuille" there is "le vent d'automne qui brame."

[1] Rimbaud played with the *berger*, as lover, in "Bannières de mai" and in "Bonne pensée du matin."

1. Entends comme brame
   près des acacias
   en avril la rame
   viride du pois!

   Dans sa vapeur nette,
   vers Phœbé! tu vois
   s'agiter la tête
   de saints d'autrefois . . .

The "brame" may be in part a play on "brume" (l. 15) which is the key note of the poem. In "Ophélie" the forest contained a mysterious sacrificial echo of stag-hunt ("hallali"). So did the springtime woods of "Bannières de mai" ("maladif hallali") and we note the comparable "April" here. In "Villes," I, stags are directly and curiously linked with the moon: "les cerfs tettent Diane" (see "Phœbé" below).

In "Métropolitain" the same scene of peas in a foggy vegetable garden is combined with moonlit specters: " . . . les nappes de brume . . . les derniers potagers . . . ces masques enluminés sous la lanterne fouettée par la nuit froide . . . ces crânes lumineux dans les plans de pois—et les autres fantasmagories—la campagne." Later in the same piece there is a suggestion of a mysterious Germany: "de féeriques aristocraties ultra-Rhénanes" together with "anciens" (cf. "Ma Saxe," an ideal vision, in "Nuit de l'enfer").

In "Comédie de la soif" we have similar "froides sueurs / De la lune et des verdures" associated with ancestors, the "Grands-Parents" (the "chers Anciens" below or the "saints d'autrefois," spiritual ancestors).

As we demonstrated at length in *The Writer's Way in France* (pp. 252-55), the stag is usually symbolic of the sacrificial father (for example Jouve writes that he represents "le plaisir de tuer le père") or deity (as in the St. Hubert legend), and ancestral figures generally.

"Phœbé" (a name for Artemis) is the moon.

9. Loin des claires meules
   des caps, des beaux toits,
   ces chers Anciens veulent
   ce philtre sournois . . .

The profiled poplars in the Verlaine poem have equivalents here in the hard, real objects—haystacks, hills ("caps"), roofs—projected starkly against the vapor ("philtre sournois"). The "philtre" recalls the ambiguous drink (light, like moon-sweat or rain seeping in the grassy graves) offered by the ancestors in "Comédie de la soif." In "Nuit de l'enfer" we catch a glimpse of "âmes honnêtes, qui me *veulent* du bien . . . fantômes":

they are vaguely ancestral. The "Anciens" here are "far off" beyond the foregoing scene, adding a mystic depth of immemoriality by their distance. As in "Comédie de la soif," they appeal to Rimbaud's death-instinct, hence they offer, or call for ("veulent") the subversive ("sournois") potion.

> 13. Or ni fériale
> ni astrale! n'est
> la brume qu'exhale
> ce nocturne effet.

The "Or" is "well, but," with an overtone of "gold" (moonlight). It is neither ordinary ("fériale") nor extraordinary ("astrale"[2]), this moonlit fog. A vibrant, hovering effect is implied, neither here nor there, as in the never-never yet real lands of Sicily and Germany in the last strophe. Rimbaud's poetry (like Kafka's prose) is often this way: both fully real and ethereal.

> 17. Néanmoins ils restent,
> —Sicile, Allemagne,
> dans ce brouillard triste
> et blêmi, justement!

The same vision of a magic, moonlit Germany is found in "Soir historique": " . . . l'Allemagne s'échafaude vers des lunes." We quoted earlier the "féeriques aristocraties ultra-Rhénanes" (from "Métropolitain") and Gautier's "clair de lune allemand." This connection of mystic and romantic Germany with the moon seems appropriate. Sicily is equally exotic, remote. Compare the childishly pure, fantastic, and real places of "Enfance": "[aux] noms . . . grecs, slaves, celtiques."

The end is defeated as usual in Rimbaud. The vision flags as the fog seems to become thicker, "sad and sallow"; "nevertheless," the fantasy of the exotic places stubbornly remains. But Rimbaud is losing heart for the game: the last word, "justement," is off-hand. It incidentally echoes the *désinvolture* of many of Verlaine's closing lines.

Michel et Christine

Only the title (or the two names of the idyllic couple) seems to have come from a vaudeville by Scribe, nothing else. The rest is a gorgeous storm, promising a rebirth, as refreshing as the flood of "Après le déluge."

---

[2] Cf. "le silence astral" of "Fairy," equally magic. In "L'Impossible," Rimbaud sees the "brume . . . légumes aqueux" as part of a benighted French heritage.

1st strophe:

> Zut alors, si le soleil quitte ces bords!
> Fuis, clair déluge! Voici l'ombre des routes.
> Dans les saules, dans la vieille cour d'honneur,
> L'orage d'abord jette ses larges gouttes.

At first Rimbaud is disappointed to see the sun go.[1] But he really feels ambivalent about the whole thing and tells the "bright flood" of light to "flee." Like all of us, he yearned to be overwhelmed by a larger force, submerged by God, or the *Génie* of poetry, which surely dictated this strophe.

2nd strophe:

> O cent agneaux, de l'idylle soldats blonds,
> Des aqueducs, des bruyères amaigries,
> Fuyez! plaine, déserts, prairie, horizons
> Sont à la toilette rouge de l'orage!

The lambs of the meadow resemble a horde of blond soldiers he will further imagine as dashing over the landscape (strophes 5 and 6), or an apocalypse reminiscent of "Qu'est-ce pour nous, mon cœur?" and the future *Saison en enfer*. But this is lyric, a "whee" of innocent change, a sweeping-out by wind, cleansing of the spirit by rainstorm. He tells the lambs and the whole landscape (aqueducts à la Cézanne, heath, etc.) to "flee" in this spirit. "Rouge" and "orage" (*orange*) are a colorful echo.

3rd strophe:

> Chien noir, brun pasteur dont le manteau s'engouffre,
> Fuyez l'heure des éclairs supérieurs;
> Blond troupeau, quand voici nager ombre et soufre,
> Tâchez de descendre à des retraits meilleurs.

The dog and the shepherd, he fantastically alive, his cloak engulfed by the vital spirit—wind—are told the same "flee," but it is modulated to a cautionary "flee the lightning." The lambs likewise are warned to go down to a snug retreat safe from this heaven-vengeance ("soufre"). He, Rimbaud, is made of bolder stuff, he will go on to say.[2]

---

[1] Proust's Marcel, when the sun reappeared from behind a cloud, cried "Zut zut zut," in a burst of enthusiasm.

[2] Richard Wilbur will similarly contrast the huddled ordinary folk below while superior Phipps and Starbuck stay on deck against the bracing storm ("Superiorities").

4th strophe:
> Mais moi, Seigneur! voici que mon esprit vole,
> Après les cieux glacés de rouge, sous les
> Nuages célestes qui courent et volent
> Sur cent Solognes longues comme un railway.

The "Seigneur" was similarly involved in the healthy landscape of "Les Corbeaux" and "La Rivière de Cassis" (the afternoon is a "religieuse après-midi d'orage," l. 49). The spirit recalls the "flying" of "L'Éternité." The red skies are aflame with delight, scarlet as the freewheeling pigeons of "Vies." The infinity in this poem is partly a vast participation, of change, new forces, migrations, horizontal as an anabasis in St.-John Perse or as the "déplacements de races et de continents" of "Délires II." Hence the emphasis on "long" in "Solognes," "longues," and the railway image, which is also dynamic, a way for new breath to come in (e.g., Izambard) and one of escape, which Rimbaud often took.

5th strophe:
> Voilà mille loups, mille graines sauvages
> Qu'emporte, non sans aimer les liserons,
> Cette religieuse après-midi d'orage
> Sur l'Europe ancienne où cent hordes iront!

The wolves (*herbe à loup*, wolfbane, may have aroused the image) are a fantasy of a savage horde bringing change, wild like the windblown grain (and weeds) close to the child-heart of Rimbaud, as transparent to vegetable nature as Shakespeare's was. In "Le loup criait," the lustful creature is mingled with the "leaves." In "Nuit de l'enfer," "Satan, Ferdinand [a local devil] court avec les graines sauvages." "Old Europe" is the vast perspective (not closed as in "Le Bateau ivre"), open to the winds of history with its barbaric invasions.

6th strophe:
> Après, le clair de lune! partout la lande,
> Rougis et leurs fronts aux cieux noirs, les guerriers
> Chevauchent lentement leurs pâles coursiers!
> Les cailloux sonnent sous cette fière bande!

With moonlight comes more fantasy, as in "Entends comme brame": specters of warriors, their foreheads reddened by the wind-storm. The "red forehead" is repeated in the last strophe. These heads in the dark sky are awesome. In "Enfance," "le front touche le ciel" refers to the brow of an uphill path but, by extension, the adventurous boy's drama.

227

7th strophe:

> —Et verrai-je le bois jaune et le val clair,
> L'Épouse aux yeux bleus, l'homme au front rouge, ô Gaule,
> Et le blanc Agneau Pascal, à leurs pieds chers,
> —Michel et Christine,—et Christ!—fin de l'Idylle.

It all ends in a defeat, again. Rimbaud hopes to see the ideal "blue eyes" of the woman joined in a true union with the wind-chafed male (from old pagan Gaul), in a bright valley of happiness . . . but there is only the same old religious sentimentality of the all-too-familiar Europe he lived in, with the *Agneau Pascal*, namby-pamby Christianity, as Nietzsche too would see it.

Honte

In "Au Lecteur" and "Examen de minuit" (and its prose version: "A une heure du matin"), Baudelaire confesses his shame for various sins and peccadillos. In "Honte," Rimbaud outdoes him in vehemence. The desire to cut his own nose (which recalls the double role of the "bourreau-victime" in "L'Héautontimorouménos") is a vicious Van Gogh-like aggression against the self, obverse of an equally deep narcissism. All men hate themselves on occasion, and poets, naturally, more so. Léon Cellier has recently compared Hugo to Claudel in respect to their thorough self-disgust. Rimbaud perhaps most of all! His lover's quarrel with himself is of an exemplary bitterness. The *Saison en enfer* will explore this vein at some length.

The poem is one long sentence, so breathlessly eager is Rimbaud to get at his *mal*, cut it out. He sees it as hopeless, incorrigible, never-ending. Still, in a sort of palinode, he calls for forgiveness, a prayer on his behalf. It is all very terrible, sincere and familiar. Alas!

1st strophe:

> Tant que la lame n'aura
> Pas coupé cette cervelle,
> Ce paquet blanc, vert et gras,
> A vapeur jamais nouvelle,

He says, in sum: as long as the blade has not cut his brain (source of devilish negation, the "spirit that always denies," according to Goethe), that "white, green, fat packet, with never-new vapor" (1st strophe), he, the "annoying child, the stupid beast," will never stop being "guileful and traiterous" (4th strophe). The "vapor" is no doubt an unflattering reference to the exudation of his brain: ideas or, rather, vague reveries or moods. The French used to refer to headaches as being caused by *vapeurs*. Rimbaud's "vapor" is obviously a kind of pall, mental stagnation, like Baudelaire's "Spleen LXXV" ("faubourgs brumeux," etc.).

2nd strophe:
> (Ah! Lui, devrait couper son
> Nez, sa lèvre, ses oreilles,
> Son ventre! et faire abandon
> De ses jambes! ô merveille!)

The "Lui" refers, I think, to the *enfant*, i.e., Rimbaud himself (and not to Verlaine, as some believe; this is too vehement to be directed toward another).

3rd strophe:
> Mais, non; vrai, je crois que tant
> Que pour sa tête la lame,
> Que les cailloux pour son flanc,
> Que pour ses boyaux la flamme,

More tortures proposed for his unworthy self.

4th strophe:
> N'auront pas agi, l'enfant
> Gêneur, la si sotte bête,
> Ne doit cesser un instant
> De ruser et d'être traître,

As long as these violent things remain undone, the child won't stop, etc., etc.

5th strophe:
> Comme un chat des Monts-Rocheux,
> D'empuantir toutes sphères!
> Qu'à sa mort pourtant, ô mon Dieu!
> S'élève quelque prière!

[He won't stop] stinking up the world ("all spheres"), like a Rocky Mountain cat (?? skunk?). This is the climacteric "moi aussi j'étais de trop" of Sartre's *La Nausée*. Still, at the end, like Baudelaire, he asks for clemency and a prayer. (Baudelaire had asked God to give him the strength to look at his body without disgust; Rimbaud merely asks for a vague general prayer.)

229

Mémoire

This important, though uneven, poem enacts the many-leveled drama of the poet's relation to the world and his divided family. The hero of the poem is light, standing for Rimbaud's love, seeking tentatively in various directions—nature, his sisters, his mother, particularly the absent father whom he would emulate to come into his own—and ultimately permeating the whole as the suffusion of his inspired artistic vocation.

The title is bemusing: does it mean "*un* mémoire" (a memorial, a report) or "*la* mémoire," the faculty of memory? Both, no doubt. And, gingerly, I feel that the soft maternal m's have to do with the spirit of his mother who pervades this remembered vision, while the liquid r echoes her and her sister-river.

That spirit is gone with the "jeune maman trépassée" ("Enfance," II), a sad memory of lost love which brings tears. . . .

I

L'eau claire; comme le sel des larmes d'enfance,
L'assaut au soleil des blancheurs des corps de femmes;
la soie, en foule et de lys pur, des oriflammes
sous les murs dont quelque pucelle eut la défense;

First the light of love appears as an all-embracing presence, scattered everywhere, as if by a Seurat, through nature and through the reflections upon the human figures which melt into it. Then it is in the water, like that pure distillation which is the salt in childhood tears or the sun-rivaling whiteness of the women's (perhaps bathers') bodies which are like lilies or the snowy banners of an army besieging the ramparts[1] he sees in the distance behind the fields.

The "tears" echo the title of "Larme" and will return in "Après le déluge" and "Barbare."

l'ébat des anges;—Non . . . le courant d'or en marche,
meut ses bras, noirs, et lourds, et frais surtout, d'herbe. Elle
sombre, ayant le Ciel bleu pour ciel-de-lit, appelle
pour rideaux l'ombre de la colline et de l'arche.

The light, as in "Soleil et chair," is now modulated to the male "lead" in a drama of nature. The sun woos the earth, who bears his "sons"—angels of light, "l'ébat des anges"—before he departs (cf. "ce reflet, pareil à un

---

[1] These ramparts, mentioned again in strophe IV, were probably those of a château.

ange blanc," "Beth-Saïda"). This theme will later modulate into a sug-
gestion of his actual father together with a specific image of his mother,
but at this level the anticipated nuptials will never take place.

Through the fluid imagery of the poem we see the impressionistic
outdoor scene as an expectant marriage chamber "ayant le Ciel bleu
pour ciel-de-lit . . . pour rideaux l'ombre de la colline et de l'arche"
("rideaux": bed curtains).[2] The river—"l'humide carreau tend ses bouil-
lons limpides"—forms a background, a floor, to the bed of earth, the
"couches prêtes." The grass, like the arms of the earth-mother embracing
the light—"la prairie amoureuse" ("Les Poètes de sept ans")—splits it into
separate little angels: "l'ébat des anges,—Non . . . le courant d'or en
marche, / meut ses bras, noirs, et lourds, et frais surtout, d'herbe." The
"courant d'or," the dazzled river seen through the grass of the bank, is a
fluid part of the earth-woman, her soul, as it were, wearing reflected light
of the sun, and the bank grass is seen as members of her body, her arms
(cf. "lilas / Noirs et frais," "Les Reparties de Nina").[3] (The *bras* also
refer ambiguously to the arms of the river, i.e., branches of it; cf. "bras de
mer" in "Les Ponts.") This same cluster of images is found in "Le
Dormeur du val":

> rivière
> Accrochant follement aux herbes des haillons
> D'argent, où le soleil, de la montagne fière,
> Luit . . .

The filial angels are attached to the cluster in "Sur la pente du talus les
anges tournent leurs robes de laine, dans les herbages . . . " ("Mystique").

"Elle/sombre" is this grass, standing for the earth-woman, now a prin-
cipal personage of the drama, later a mere setting for her human "sister,"
and, like her, appropriately dark (the true woman, or her water-sister,
will be described as "froide, et noire"). In Rimbaud the opposites inter-
penetrate with some of the complexity of life itself: woman has her own
fairness and brightness—"Aphrodité marine," born of foam ("Soleil et
chair")—and thus, in the first part of the strophe, there were the "blan-
cheurs des corps de femmes." But here her beauty is seen as sensually
dark; her arms are "noirs, et lourds, et frais surtout." (The real woman,
Madame Rimbaud, is excessively dark, "froide, et noire," because the
light of love is altogether gone from her.)

---

[2] The arch is probably that of a neighboring bridge.

[3] In "Le Bateau ivre," it was hair: "cheveux des anses," cf. "le vent agitait la
rivière; au fond, de grandes herbes s'y penchaient, comme des chevelures de ca-
davres flottant dans l'eau" (Flaubert, *Un Cœur simple*).

II

Eh! l'humide carreau tend ses bouillons limpides!
L'eau meuble d'or pâle et sans fond les couches prêtes.
Les robes vertes et déteintes des fillettes
font les saules, d'où sautent les oiseaux sans brides.

The first line is the river, perhaps like a floor of a marriage chamber in preparation, being washed, with bubbles here and there.[4] A complex association of roily water and "white" tears (strophe I) is indicated by "larmes blanches, bouillantes" ("Barbare") in conjunction with the "bouillons" here and in "Le loup criait." The reflected river-light puts pale gold, like the gilt of an ornate bed, on the "couches prêtes." The faded green dresses of his sisters by the river are like willow trees,[5] earth-daughters, probably implied to be outside the window—as in the "Première soirée": "de grands arbres indiscrets / Aux vitres jetaient leur feuillée"—from which the lovers would watch unfettered birds ecstatically darting up. In Verlaine's epithalamium "La Bonne Chanson," "L'alouette monte au ciel avec le jour" (no. V).

Plus pure qu'un louis, jaune et chaude paupière
le souci d'eau—ta foi conjugale, ô l'Épouse!—
au midi prompt, de son terne miroir, jalouse
au ciel gris de chaleur la Sphère rose et chère.

The marsh-marigold is a sort of emblem of the lover—"ta foi conjugale, ô l'Épouse"—worn by the earth-woman. Its golden glow, as if on time for a rendezvous at midday, rivals that of the sun, which is flushed, like a rapturous bridegroom, in the sky, gray, or drunk, with heat at noon: "gris comme l'atmosphère de l'été" (Baudelaire, *Salon de 1845*). The "terne miroir" is the reflection of this dull sky in the water seen from directly above as the poet bends over the flower.[6]

---

[4] Here, as in several other instances, Rimbaud's ambitious, inspired, but slightly impatient attempt to achieve interlocking complexity results in strained imagery. Wallace Fowlie's notion (in *Rimbaud*) of a window with rain-bubbles is possible, especially since "bouillons" can refer to imperfections in glass (cf. "Nocturne vulgaire"); in "Après le déluge" there are "vitres encore ruisselante[s]" and a similar image in "Vies"; having stared long at the Meuse in Charleville, I can see how the child assimilated it to glass distorted by rain (or imperfections); and yet the scene is really too sunny to allow for the suggestion of rain. Will we ever know what he meant? In *Eugénie Grandet* we read "le carreau est humide" referring to a floor.

[5] Trees as sisters go back to the *Aeneid*: "the shady sisterhood of poplar boughs" (Book X). Or Ovid's *Metamorphoses* ("The Story of Phaëthon"): "the new young trees, the sisters."

[6] Delahaye mentions that the yellow is the color of conjugal love. The flowers may also ambiguously be an image for the woman's warmth, even sexual.

III

Madame se tient trop debout dans la prairie
prochaine où neigent les fils du travail; l'ombrelle
aux doigts; foulant l'ombelle; trop fière pour elle;
des enfants lisant dans la verdure fleurie

leur livre de maroquin rouge! Hélas, Lui, comme
mille anges blancs qui se séparent sur la route,
s'éloigne par delà la montagne! Elle, toute
froide, et noire, court! après le départ de l'homme!   .

The modulation to the human: Rimbaud's mother standing upright in the field,[7] too proud and rigid to hold the affections of a man. The "ombrelle" goes with her darkness, refusing the sunlight; her haughty step crushes the "ombelle," nature, in a parallel symbolism; it is "trop fière pour elle," she cannot abide its rivalry. There is a hint that it is She who is too proud, given the loose syntax; likewise, knowing her character, we feel that her pride relates to the children. They seem ignored, isolated, mere filial objects, part of the tableau as they read their book in the grass. The "man" arrives only to depart: "Lui, comme / mille anges blancs qui se séparent sur la route, / s'éloigne par delà la montagne." Here is the familiar image of light split into angels but now in a solitary moment, on the male mountain top beyond womanly reach. The scene evokes the splendid "death" of a God, a self-sufficient "suicide beau" (Mallarmé), to which Rimbaud aspires in emulation of his lone-wandering heroic father; but humanly he still lacks the courage to follow. He remains earthbound, and homebound, in reluctant sympathy with his mother who is left alone and somber. Sympathetically, the splendor has gone out of the grass, her humble but happier sister: "Regret des bras épais et jeunes d'herbe pure!"

The water (woman) seems to "run" in its flow toward the departing sun, like the "courant du fossé" Rimbaud watches with fascination in "Comédie de la soif." Possibly the woman herself seems to be running in the shifting light and shadow.

The "Elle" is in the lineage of all the other awe-inspiring *Elles*, from "Rêvé pour l'hiver" to "Métropolitain."

---

[7] The phrase "neigent les fils du travail" refers probably to wispy white field flowers, strewn like bits of thread about a woman at her needlework; or it can be the threads (or "sons," products) of agricultural labor, cf. "le travail fleuri de la campagne" ("Mauvais sang"). In "Remembrances du vieillard idiot," the formula refers to a noise emerging from his hard-working mother.

IV

Regret des bras épais et jeunes d'herbe pure!
Or des lunes d'avril au cœur du saint lit! Joie
des chantier riverains à l'abandon, en proie
aux soirs d'août qui faisaient germer ces pourritures!

The sun which seasonally rises with hope, like young love, "lunes d'avril" (cf. the "lune de miel" of "Jeune ménage"),[8] is now nearing an autumn, "soirs d'août." The bank grass is now mere weeds, and the beauty of nubile woman is now seen in an unkind light as earthy femininity, as in "Les Premières Communions":

La pierre sent toujours la terre maternelle.
. . . Dans la campagne en rut qui frémit, solennelle,
Portant . . .
Ces arbrisseaux brûlés . . .[9]

The "chantiers riverains" which were once lit in joy are now extinguished; a similar cluster of workyard and sunlight (both being a part of the father theme) is found in "Bonne pensée du matin": "l'immense chantier / Vers le soleil. . . ."

Qu'elle pleure à présent sous les remparts! l'haleine
des peupliers d'en haut est pour la seule brise.
Puis, c'est la nappe, sans reflets, sans source, grise:
un vieux, dragueur, dans sa barque immobile, peine.

The mother, abandoned, weeping; or the river, her sister, in its liquid sounds, "weeps" under high banks. She is a "misérable femme de drame [qui] quelque part dans le monde, soupire après des abandons improbables" as "De petits enfants étouffent des malédictions le long des rivières"

---

[8] This poem has much of the feeling of "Mémoire": the longed-for vision of a happy marriage in which the poet, like a guardian elf hovering over the scene, would share; thus elves—"lutins"—and other spirits (some "malfaisants") invade the marriage room together with the beauty of nature, which was always the harmonizing innocence for Rimbaud:

La chambre est ouverte au ciel bleu-turquin;
. . .
—O spectres saints . . .
Charmez plutôt le bleu de leur fenêtre!

[9] Cf. "la terre est nubile et déborde de sang" ("Soleil et chair"). Suzanne Briet (*Madame Rimbaud*) sees an allusion to the lost male in the "bras épais." This is possible although it involves various difficulties.

("Jeunesse"). The breeze in the poplars,[10] like a sigh (see "Ophélie"), is the only life left in this landscape; the water without light is depthless, gray; an old fisherman laboring in his boat seems to echo the general defeat.

V

> Jouet de cet œil d'eau morne, je n'y puis prendre,
> ô canot immobile! oh! bras trop courts! ni l'une
> ni l'autre fleur: ni la jaune qui m'importune,
> là; ni la bleue, amie à l'eau couleur de cendre.

The drama now shifts to the child Rimbaud in a microcosmic close not unlike the little scene of the sad puddle at the end of "Le Bateau ivre." He is alone in a small boat, anchored at the bank, in which he is known to have played. The tethering chain (cf. the "haleurs" of "Le Bateau ivre") is the all-around defeat in his home, the failure of his mother's love which is reflected in the child's emotional frustration: he cannot "reach" either the yellow flower associated with the father-sun, nor the blue which is "amie à l'eau couleur de cendre," a sister of the water which is associated with the deserted soul of the woman, his mother. The cluster is very clear here: his mother had "le bleu regard—qui ment" ("Les Poètes de sept ans"); the eyes are the image of the water soul, hence "cet œil d'eau" (l. 40) or "énormes yeux bleus . . . le mer et le ciel" ("Fleurs"). The flower-eye association is clear from "paupière / de souci d'eau" of strophe III.

> Ah! la poudre des saules qu'une aile secoue!
> Les roses des roseaux dès longtemps dévorées!
> Mon canot, toujour fixe; et sa chaîne tirée
> Au fond de cet œil d'eau sans bords,—à quelle boue?

As in "Ophélie," a wing-stirring in the trees is a minor consolation. But the weeds are decaying, and there is scant comfort in the incantatory echoes accompanying the loss. The boat, unlike the drunken one of a happier moment, cannot set sail for flight. It is held fast by a chain which disappears into the mud of his troubled psyche, too deep as yet for the child Rimbaud to fathom.

[10] Stéphane Taute, the librarian of Charleville, showed me a photo of 1866 with a line of poplars on the Mt. Olympe directly across from where Rimbaud played in his boat. This scene probably became amalgamated with the old *prairie* between Charleville and Mézières where Rimbaud is known to have walked with his family (under a viaduct).

O Saisons, ô châteaux
(*Le Bonheur*)

In our Introduction (p. 10), we spoke of the climactic quality of this poem, conceived upon that height of awareness and being where the most minutely intimate is also the most expansive. Rimbaud wants to have it all, eternity, beauty, but, like Macbeth, here "upon this bank and shoal of time." Not one season alone but all, vibrant together in one heavenly presence of the round-of-the-year.[1] The seasons are like the holy ghostly "feminine" totality of his soul; the *châteaux* are the more "male"—specific and individual—architecture of his inner being, a metaphor for his vision: "Entre au divin séjour; habite le palais que tu as vu dans ton sommeil" ("L'Ange et l'enfant"). They are close kin to Shakespeare's "cloud-capp'd towers, the gorgeous palaces" (*The Tempest*)[2] in their evocation of all evanescent reality.

We have commented on a comparable pair, the tower by the sea, in *The Writer's Way in France* (p. 265). The marriage of the two—castles and seasons—is the source of the poem's birth in joy. The union of the *animus* and *anima* of the poet[3] makes him momentarily the seat of an androgynous, self-sufficient, angelic perfection. Like the sylph of Mallarmé's "Surgi de la croupe et du bond," his "Bonheur" (or his sylph-like happy poem) is the child of his own male and female principles, blissfully conjoined in a privileged moment. Every time the "male" principle—a cock-call as piercing as the tooth of the "hound of heaven"—stabs the "feminine" soul, there is conceived the new life:[4] "vive lui [Le Bonheur], chaque fois / Que chante son coq gaulois."

Of course, at this limit-point of experience, the male and the female are paradoxically related, integrated out of sight, with one emerging for a momentary flash from out the other: the "stab" may come from the image of the "feminine" source itself, the sky or seasons. Thus Baudelaire finely remarks that "il n'est pas de pointe plus acérée que celle de l'Infini [l'azur]" ("Le Confiteor de l'artiste").

---

[1] Compare the four seasons superimposed simultaneously up the mountainside in Rousseau's *Confessions*. The o's, including the one in "saisons" and the o-sound in "châteaux," seem to contribute to the round simultaneous feeling, recalling the cozily circular forms in *Les Très Riches Heures du duc de Berry*.

[2] Compare in Shakespeare's *Macbeth*: "this castle hath a pleasant seat. The air. . . ."

[3] An exact parallel in private drama occurs in Mallarmé's "Hérodiade," see *Toward the Poems of Mallarmé*, p. 82. See also *The Writer's Way in France*, p. 85. The castle was the symbol of inmost vision for Meister Eckhart.

[4] Compare "le nouvel amour" of "A une raison" (and equivalents throughout most of the poems of ecstasy).

Happiness of this sort is painful as true birth, hence frightening, and we attempt to "elude" it—in vain. Once this total life-event has taken possession of us (in spite of our fear—or the final doubt of the "Quelle âme est sans défauts?"), we are as aware of the insignificance of our usual days as is a mother fresh from childbirth.[5] It is a surpassing splendor far bigger than we are. It takes us over "soul and body" and "disperses all efforts," like the cosmic-ocean in "Le Bateau ivre": "dispersant gouvernail et grappin." Then the words of the hymn of joy—the poem—"fly" on their own as they did in "L'Éternité." At the end, as so often in Rimbaud, the total glory results in a sort of reprisal, a fear of let-down, or guilt: "Le supplice est sûr" ("L'Éternité"). But in "Délires II" ("Alchimie du verbe") where he quotes this poem with variants, Rimbaud speaks of "Le Bonheur" as a "fatality." Despite the ambiguity of his remarks here (does he mean lived happiness or creative happiness?—in a certain sense it does not matter, for all great art like this is a vibrant paradox of spontaneous life and deliberate expression), the main point is clear: *amor fati*, it is all, the pain and the joy, accepted. "C'est trop beau! mais c'est nécessaire" ("Est-elle almée?").

> 1. O saisons, ô châteaux,
>   Quelle âme est sans défauts?

A similar summing-up mood—an open, natural scene in time apprehended vibrantly, movingly-in-stasis, with an ecstatic total embrace—characterizes the beginning of "Barbare": "Bien après les jours et les saisons et les êtres et les pays." Only, in that text the mood is less elevated, more resigned, like "I've seen it all." Later in that prose poem the pair, "ô monde, ô musique," is closer to our present season-castle coupling.

In "Bannières de mai," "Je veux bien que les saisons m'usent" approximates this same giving over of self to a convergent moment of All in space and time (the *totum simul* of mystic experience).

Such perfection, to repeat, is hard to accept. We falter in lingering doubt on the edge of total joy: this is the scruple of "Quelle âme est sans défauts?" Anyone going forth to confront innocent nature is apt to quail, aware how demanding it is, how unworthy we come to the baptism which "cost[s] not less than everything" ("Little Gidding," T. S. Eliot). But at his best Rimbaud is supremely confident: "Nous savons donner notre vie tout entière" ("Matinée d'ivresse").

---

[5] Or as Proust's little Marcel who wanted to crow like a hen who had laid an egg when he had given birth to his "three steeples" passage.

3. O saisons, ô châteaux,

J'ai fait la magique étude
Du Bonheur, que nul n'élude.

Like the several o's, and o-sounds in the line, the repetition brings out the cyclical quality of seasons, the circular shapes of castles.

In the sketches of the *Saison en enfer*, Rimbaud writes: "vie éternelle, non écrite, non chantée . . . Je . . . vis une fatalité de bonheur dans tous les êtres." The "Bonheur" is pure experience.

It is as frightening as the experience Baudelaire describes in his "Confiteor de l'artiste": "L'étude du beau est un duel où l'artiste crie de frayeur avant d'être vaincu." But, as we said, somehow (like Wittgenstein's "form") he records it, "sings" it.

The "magic" study is no doubt the well-known method of *dérèglement*, as described in "Alchimie du verbe" where the passage on *Bonheur* also occurs. Now, curiously, although he describes the *Bonheur* as pure experience, in that passage (and in the "magic" of this poem) he goes on to *sophisticate* it by his "method."

So Rimbaud was guilty here, I feel, of a certain gimmickry.[6] He tries to exploit, control, or manipulate something too vast; and later on he confesses it, at the end of the "Alchimie du verbe" passage where he speaks of his hallucinations and suffering and gives up: "l'art est une sottise."[7] He was, as Mondor put it, a "génie impatient." Hence I regard that "magique" as the sign of his error, his spiritual greed that put too prompt an end to his poetic vocation. I wish it were not present in this otherwise splendid poem. "Magic" could mean merely "in depth," or "visionary," but I am afraid that the context of Rimbaud's life and of the cited passage from "Alchimie du verbe" incline us to take the messier meaning.

But the *Bonheur* itself, fortunately, is pure, innocent; it stabs us like the ray of light in "Bannières de mai" or the tooth of the "hound of heaven" (with its shadow obverse or overtone of remorse—like the "défauts"—from *morsus*, bite): "Sa dent, douce à la mort, m'avertissait au chant du coq—*ad matutinum*, au *Christus venit*,—" ("Alchimie du verbe"). That piercing cock-crow, giving back all of sweet France to the boy waking to delight, also reminds us of the dawn of Christ's agony and the cock-crow which revealed Peter's frailty, original human fallibility and guilt;[8] "la lumière / Suppose d'ombre une morne moitié" (Valéry, "Le Cimetière marin").

---

[6] Arthur Koestler accuses certain oriental mystics of similar tactics in *The Lotus*.
[7] Camus was right to berate him for this in *L'Homme révolté*.
[8] There are memorable equivalents of this in Bach's *St. Matthew Passion* and in Stendhal's *Lucien Leuwen*.

6. O vive lui, chaque fois
   Que chante son coq gaulois.

Note the piercing incisive (tooth) quality of the v, the sharp i and u of "vive" and "lui."

8. Mais! je n'aurai plus d'envie,
   Il s'est chargé de ma vie.

"No more desire" means *ordinary* desire. He wants it all. For which the price is to be nothing, to be taken over. "And His will is our peace" (Dante, *The Divine Comedy*).

10. Ce Charme! il prit âme et corps,
    Et dispersa tous efforts.

The charm is that totality that possesses us. It recalls the "vin de la Paresse" of "Les Chercheuses de poux," a letting-go as in "Le Bateau ivre," baptismal immersion in the cosmic ocean of disinterested beatitude, like Rousseau drifting in his boat in *Les Rêveries d'un promeneur solitaire.* "Veillées" catches this charm: "C'est le repos éclairé, ni fièvre, ni langueur, sur le lit ou sur le pré . . . L'air et le monde point cherchés. La vie."

12. Que comprendre à ma parole?
    Il fait qu'elle fuie et vole!

The "Il" is the "Charme." The flight is quite like that of "L'Éternité," a spontaneous outpouring, gratuitous, disinterested, a voice of the earth or of nature itself.[9]

14. O saisons, ô châteaux!

    Et, si le malheur m'entraîne,
    Sa disgrâce m'est certaine.

Now enters a shadow of reprisal for the pure Icarian flight, as at the close of "Le Bateau ivre," or the "supplice est sûr" ending the transport of "L'Éternité." The "malheur" is the obvious opposite of the "bonheur." And a fall from such grace is simply "disgrâce."

[9] Compare Mallarmé's cricket in a famous letter to Lefébure or the bird in "Petit air II."

17. Il faut que son dédain, las!
    Me livre au plus prompt trépas!

    —O Saisons, ô Châteaux!

By extension, the taking-away of grace is a sign of "disdain" on the part of the powers-that-be. And if that is so, Rimbaud asks for a quick merciful end: a "prompt trépas."

In the variant in "Alchimie du verbe" the flight and fall are put together more succinctly:

L'heure de sa fuite, hélas!
Sera l'heure du trépas.

Le loup criait . . .

Le loup criait sous les feuilles
En crachant les belles plumes
De son repas de volailles:
Comme lui je me consume.

Les salades, les fruits
N'attendent que la cueillette;
Mais l'araignée de la haie
Ne mange que des violettes.

Que je dorme! que je bouille
Aux autels de Salomon.
Le bouillon court sur la rouille,
Et se mêle au Cédron.

A cry of adolescent despair—I am ripe, Someone or Something take me—is at the core of these modest few lines. "Les Sœurs de charité" and various passages of the *Saison en enfer* are written out of this same crucial need. In "Jeunesse (Sonnet)" he takes stock of himself: "*Homme* de constitution ordinaire, la chair n'était-elle pas un fruit pendu dans le verger, ô journées enfantes! [recall the sexual scenes of "Les Poètes de sept ans"] le corps un trésor à prodiguer; ô aimer, le péril ou la force de Psyché?"

It is Rimbaud's strict religious upbringing that makes him, more than most people today or ever, so afraid of and awed by his body. *There* it is—not quite accepted as part of the self—big and heavy with its demands (as Sartre knew: *La Nausée*). It is *over*-present, it swells into horrifying assertion, flows like the burst-open overripe pomegranate of Mallarmé's timid faun.

In this poem he is at such a tumescent, crucial moment: he has the anguishing option to try to sublimate these forces into spiritual endeavor (but this time it is so difficult) or give in to the pagan force. He is revolted by his own sensuality—the note of distaste is obvious from the choice of image ("wolf")—which he regards here, as sensitive men often have, as a loss of spirit, Shakespeare's "waste of shame" (Sonnet 129). Perhaps, like Mallarmé in an early letter (Dec. 1864, to Cazalis), he is speaking of some youthful priapism or autoerotic act; or perhaps just of erotic daydreaming, the languid torpors typical of adolescence which Rimbaud describes in "Les Sœurs de charité." At any rate he feels he is "consuming" himself through loathsome appetites; the wolf too was just using up his life in his gluttony. A self-protest is in the "cry": even as he indulges, something sticks in his throat, hurts him, makes him cry out. The "beautiful feathers" might refer to the delight which, he cannot deny, is part of the process; but they are, after all, spat out, and hence we may assume they are the beauty lost through this waste.[1]

The wolf, like Hesse's, is one pole of his psychic dilemma (in "Mauvais sang" wolves are inferior rapacious beasts associated with his Gallic ancestors). The ravenous creature eats heavily sensual flesh. At the other extreme, the spider—with some of the abstract qualities Swift assigned to it (*The Battle of the Books*)—eats only ethereal violets. Their hue is at the extreme upper end of the color-spectrum (as we saw in "Voyelles") as opposed to the dark red of the body's blood. The salads and fruits seem to be midway between these two poles, as Rimbaud casts about for a compromise solution. If he sees his body—or a partner's—as a fruit, as he did in "Jeunesse," that takes some of the sting out of the idea of "plucking" it, consuming it as opposed to the heavy experience of the ravenous wolf. It is an attempted solution like Rousseau's idyllic village, halfway between savage nature and corrupt city.

In "Fêtes de la faim," Rimbaud's hunger migrates from the "chairs de fruit blettes" and "la doucette" (the equivalent of salad) to "la violette,"

---

[1] If we accept the "belles plumes" as being something produced by the experience (in spite of the disgust, the "crachant"), this could also be, rather than bodily delights, the bright images cast up from an *artistic* debauchery. At times Rimbaud thought of art that way; in "Les Sœurs de charité" as well as the *Saison en enfer*, he berates the Muse as a witch who led him astray.

If we pursued the hypothesis of art, the wolf would be a loner (like the spider) indulging and "consuming" itself as the poet narcissistically does. The salads and fruits would be the ordinary foods of society compared to these solitary repasts.

The final strophe could be then a release from art as in the *Saison en enfer*. But there is nothing in the immediate text to substantiate this more specific interpretation, so I prefer to fall back, undogmatically, on the broader and more general level of Eros.

but without the "mais" which here indicates a struggle, an opposition (though we may, by the nature of the images, read that mildly into them).

The "salads and fruits," he says, are there for the picking, but the spider (his mind) scants them, feasts only on airier matters; the body, in short (as in "Jeunesse") is left waiting—oh, so long!

Thus the final strophe is a climax of despair brought on by the continuing struggle and lack of release. He wants to sleep and let the natural forces take over, solve his problem for him, by, no doubt, a nocturnal emission. The image of Solomon is, I think, a good one for hopeless conflict (the Solomonic dilemma and decision). The bubbling brew rises from this seething—an obviously apt image (cf. Joyce's "fraudstuff" in *Finnegans Wake*)—and spills over, running down over the rusted pots ("rust" is probably an image for the stagnancy of long-waiting) and simply disperses amid nature, as, in fantasy, Baudelaire's nocturnal blood did (in "Rêve d'un curieux" and "Rêve parisien").

The "Cédron" is a torrent (between Jerusalem and the Mount of Olives), and I suppose the image implies, like the river of "Le Bateau ivre," a letting-go, a release into a natural relaxed world bigger than the self, and the dynamic rush of the whole self that accompanies that release. But its biblical quality (like the "Seigneur du cèdre et des hysopes" that accompanied a similar release in "Oraison du soir") is a way of solemnizing the experience, perhaps out of partial mockery, but also out of a desire to generalize, to universalize the experience and hence mitigate its specificity, its concentrated guilt and pain.

III

ILLUMINATIONS

Introductory Note

The deft touch of the finer, more evanescent *Derniers Vers*—such as "Age d'or," "Bruxelles"—volatilizes further in the best of the prose poems, the *Illuminations*, which are often thought to include the high points of Rimbaud's art. Well, it is not worth quibbling about: the high points are scattered widely amidst the different stages or manners, and the fact of being in verse or prose scarcely matters at all.

There is a higher concentration of *poésie pure* in the *Illuminations* as a whole; there is also much that is too private, autobiographical, confessional, scarcely-distilled. But, as usual, we will gratefully take the poetry where we find it, trying to admit honestly what escapes us or what is unworthy in Rimbaud.

How revolutionary are the *Illuminations*?

Aloysius Bertrand, Baudelaire, the young Mallarmé, had all preceded Rimbaud with masterpieces in this genre. But all had maintained a relatively "classical" clarity, despite the lyricism. At times, in Baudelaire and Mallarmé, the very tension between these two directions of the spirit—the discursive or communicative classical and the intensely personal, romantic, or daemonic—brought about that "curdled" complexity, that density and richness characteristic of the greatest art, "loading every rift with ore."

Rimbaud goes perhaps no further than these absolute masters, at their best, but his brew has a childishly fresh, open, free, "irresponsible" tonality all its own.

For Paul Valéry, the *Illuminations* are a borderline case, a *ne plus ultra* of expression of the chaotic and the spontaneous, the fundamentally unorganizable in reality.[1] This, I submit, is an exaggeration, although it points vaguely in the right direction. Valéry, under the cover of glamorous generalization, obviously prefers to abdicate here just as he did in the case of the "Coup de Dés" or *A la Recherche du temps perdu*. Rimbaud offers much more meaning, even of the ordinary sort, than Valéry allows; where he does not seem to, it is either because of a lack of insight or patience on our part, or else he is "nodding" in the sense of the term we apply to dope addicts rather than to Homer. But to what purpose should we dwell on these lapses of his or ours when there is so much that is irreplaceably rewarding in almost all of these pieces?

[1] Jean-Louis Baudry, in "Le Texte de Rimbaud," extends this view to a neo-Marxist, structuralist perspective: the later Rimbaud is deliberately undermining the language and myth of the bourgeois order. There is nothing really new in this, every critic of Rimbaud has more or less taken this for granted (indeed, what modern poet does not do this, in a sense?). Baudry's much-praised study, riddled with the contemporary pretentious jargon, in the end brings us nothing.

The revolution in syntax which the *Illuminations* is commonly deemed to represent is less thorough than Mallarmé's (*Igitur*, "Un Coup de Dés," etc.), but so perhaps is everyone else's. And Rimbaud had so little time. For years Mallarmé's creative contribution was largely ignored so that almost everyone, particularly the young, assumed that Rimbaud was the pivotal point of everything modern. But now that Mallarmé has finally come into his own, more objective justice can also be done to Rimbaud. He did superbly well what could be expected of a genius not yet out of his teens, or hardly so. In the end, on his own grounds, he is unique: in the pages to follow we will endeavor to appreciate him not comparatively— insofar as that is possible—but for his own incomparable self's sake.

I have nothing to add to the question of the dating of the *Illuminations*. The current view, that most were written before the *Saison en enfer* and a few after, seems acceptable. Hence, *faute de mieux*, I put the *Saison en enfer* at the end of this book. Not because I think it was a swan-song, or rather the *only* swan-song—most good poems implicitly, various of Rimbaud's explicitly, are that—but because I cannot find any compelling reason to do otherwise.

The word *Illuminations*, it is now generally accepted, refers both to visions ("epiphanies") and the English word for "painted plates" (implying a childishly intense and pure play of poetic colors). Rimbaud used the word *illuminé* early, in "Les Étrennes des orphelins," referring to the joyously lit fireplace when the orphans' mother had been there. That may seem a trivial usage, but it is distinctly relevant to the spirit of these very intimate poems.

Après le déluge

Rimbaud's total discontent with his circumstances at times extended to the cosmos. As much as the Mallarmé of "Hérodiade," or the Leconte de Lisle of "Dies Irae," he dreamed of apocalypse, a fresh start, rebirth.[1] In "Qu'est-ce pour nous, mon cœur" the *dies irae* came about through invasions and earthquakes. "Après le déluge" is a flood-version of that idea, much more fluid, refreshing, poetic, like the baptismal bath in the ocean of "Le Bateau ivre." The flood has undertones of actual birth (amniotic fluid), but I doubt that that was part of a deliberate artistic procedure. Nor, unlike Wallace Fowlie, do I see a consistent progression through "Enfance" and "Jeunesse," as if Rimbaud had an architecture of human growth in mind. No, each poem was written separately; that is a quite sufficient feat. And if they were shuffled into some sort of order, as in the

---

[1] Baudelaire, too, at times was discouraged with a world in which, for example, "action is not the sister of dream" ("Le Reniement de saint Pierre").

case of Baudelaire, the process did not get very far or become very convincing.

This poem is as familiar and concrete as a day thoroughly washed by sun. Or a glorious morning will do, preferably after sickness (as Baudelaire noted). Then the child "comes out" into the street, clean and triumphant as if from a dark womb. Miraculous phenomena emerge directly from a newly beautiful earth. A music arises therewith, and all sorts of things "happen" with immediacy, harmoniously, all participating in all. Some funny, disjointed things happen too. Eventually the dream "cools" (or "sours") as he says in "Départ." It does not last. Some note of disappointment with the cosmos, and more specifically the unsympathetic parent he had, creeps in through the image of the troubling *Sorcière*, a sort of Earth-Mother who will not reveal the secrets that might make joy more permanent, or repeat it.

> Aussitôt que l'idée du Déluge se fut rassise,

It is an *idea* of a Flood, just as in "Conte" the whole story is recognized as a fantasy that can disappear as rapidly as it came. Its magic *totality* is bought at the price of its *nothingness*, as Shakespeare's "gorgeous palaces . . . shall dissolve / And leave not a rack behind" in *The Tempest*. But, in any case, the flood-phase of the vision has now stopped ("rassise"), and the lovely aftermath, the birth of new phenomena can begin.

> Un lièvre s'arrêta dans les sainfoins et les clochettes mouvantes et dit sa prière à l'arc-en-ciel à travers la toile de l'araignée.

A hare is a timid and tentative creature, rather like Petit-Poucet, a little fellow coming out into the awesome light. At the newborn phase (as at earlier embryonic levels), we and the animals are very alike. That gives the poet a certain responsibility: he is the animal's spokesman (and even the earth's as Hugo, Guillén, and other poets have avowed): "Il est chargé . . . des *animaux* même" as the second "Lettre du voyant" puts it.

Though Rimbaud does not indicate it here, the moving bell-flowers—cf. "cloche de feu rose" in "Phrases"—are undoubtedly akin to those "fleurs de rêve [qui] tintent" in "Enfance I" (as Hackett noted); indeed, they are of childish appeal and decoratively frame the hare with almost Valentine-lace, as does the spider-web. The "sainfoins," furze or gorse, are healthy-sounding. The rainbow has the washed look of fresh watercolors. The prayer is sincere gratitude for survival, for the musical all: that signal from the divine is reflected in the "sceau de Dieu" below.

Unlike Yves Bonnefoy, I see no "mièvrerie" or "mauvaise foi" in these images.

> Oh! les pierres précieuses qui se cachaient,—les fleurs qui regardaient déjà.

The jewels are hidden underground but felt to be *there* just around the corner (like the jewels of Hérodiade's "enfance,"[2] about to dazzle her and us), adding expectation to an already delightful scene, like Christmas Eve. Jean-Pierre Richard speaks of their *pudeur*: they are shy as the hare and play at hide and seek. At the end of the poem they will again be "hiding themselves."

The flowers are coming out, anthropomorphically "looking," akin as the animals are to people at this level (in "Aube," one tells him its name). Flowers "look" because they look like eyes: Richard Wilbur speaks of nature's queen being "the flowers' cynosure" ("Ceremony").

> Dans la grande rue sale les étals se dressèrent, et l'on tira les barques vers la mer étagée là-haut comme sur les gravures.

The main street is dirty, as it is—Verlaine's "bruit des cabarets . . . fange des trottoirs"—and children love it as it is, littered, bustling, astir, with butchers' stalls going up, as here ("les étals se dressèrent," note "sale . . . étals"). The liveliness of workingmen recalls "Les Poètes de sept ans," "Bonne pensée du matin," etc.; here, with an added element of excitement the men are pulling boats toward the sea, as in "Le Bateau ivre." This ocean is, like the Flood itself, seen in fantasy, bigger than life, hyperbolic. So its image is *raised* as in primitive perspective or modern neo-primitive art like Cézanne's or the related Elstir-paintings described by Proust. That makes it more exhilarating (threatening-delightful), gives *more* of it to the eye (like the tilt in Cézanne's vases), thumbs its nose at flat academic perspective. It is a welling-up of instinctual life (id) from below: feminine, maternal (*mer-mère*).[3]

Valéry's Mediterranean Sea, deeply female (*chienne*), rose similarly: "Entre les pins palpite" and was seen as a *toit* ("Le Cimetière marin"), high as "étagée là-haut."

> Le sang coula, chez Barbe-Bleue,—aux abattoirs,—dans les cirques, où le sceau de Dieu blêmit les fenêtres. Le sang et le lait coulèrent.

---

[2] See *Toward the Poems of Mallarmé*, p. 80.

[3] In another context the sea will be a flood of tears, "faite d'une éternité de chaudes larmes" ("Enfance").

The blood flowing is also exciting—as Richard observes, it is like the vigorous bursting of life-juices from a ripe fruit. It is dangerous and deeply satisfying, smacking of brilliant life and of death, as Bluebeard does. (He also satisfies because he knows how to put women—like his mother?—in their place.) It mingles with milk (and the rain fall, still present). Both are life essences offering communion with the Source.[4] Blood and milk are both visibly present in the blood-suffused milky skin of the mother's breast, and the suckling child (cf. the little seeking mouth in "Les Déserts de l'amour") partakes, in a way, of both essences:

> Ivre du sang
>
> Qui coule, bleu, sous ta peau blanche
>   Aux tons rosés.
>
> ("Les Reparties de Nina")

The infant sometimes nips hard. It wants everything, and sometimes the world—in the guise of an unsparing mother or of a sacrificial god—gives all. This is what that transparent blissful rainbow, "the seal of God," seems to stand for: total gift. The still rainy windows are paled by it: physically by contrast with its intensity; spiritually, they are the glass through which we see only darkly compared to that transparent Light.

> Les castors bâtirent. Les "mazagrans" fumèrent dans les estaminets.

Beavers are more cousin-animals, pleasantly astir. Coffee shops are heart-warming too.

> Dans la grande maison de vitres encore ruisselante les enfants en deuil regardèrent les merveilleuses images.

The windows in the great house (which seems to be all windows) are still dripping, making a cozy feel for the indoor scene where enchanting pictures still emerge as from birth-waters. Who are the children "en deuil"? Rimbaud always was, for lost happiness. French children are often kept in their place, subjected to rigid adult rituals like the stiff Sunday Bible sessions in "Les Poètes de sept ans." But perhaps it is only a previous grief, rather than duty, that is meant to be felt here. Both help make images marvelous.

[4] As they are in the cheeks of Blanchefleur for Chrétien de Troyes's Perceval; or in Mallarmé's Hérodiade who dreamed of milk and had rose-like blood-suffused cheeks. See *Toward the Poems of Mallarmé*, pp. 53-55. Cf. Baudelaire's "Je respirais l'odeur de ton sang" ("Le Balcon").

> Une porte claqua,—et sur la place du hameau, l'enfant tourna ses bras, compris des girouettes et des coqs des clochers de partout, sous l'éclatante giboulée.

A door slamming is like the possible escape of "Les Poètes de sept ans," the "door which opened on evening" (perhaps the mention of the house, which can threaten to stifle, caused this image). Here the child is released onto the hamlet-square. All is his, and he takes symbolic possession of his kingly realm by broad gesture, turning his arms around, setting life in motion magically as in "Aube" "en agitant les bras." His subjects are the weathervanes and weathercocks—elevated, out of the adult area—(like the platform of "Villes, I" or the bridges of "Les Ponts"); they "understand" him, are him. The rain glistens on.

> Madame * * * établit un piano dans les Alpes. La messe et les premières communions se célébrèrent aux cent mille autels de la cathédrale.

The imagery becomes more dramatic, dynamic, expressionistic, closer to Van Gogh than to Pissarro or Monet. In a sense that is a step down: the best stylization is as close to the real world as possible, a new, more intimate and essential view of it. The expressionistic always smacks somewhat of caricature, manipulation, short-circuitry, the sensational. But this is a very relative matter.[5]

Here, the restless rhythms of a disjointed, fragmented cosmos begin to shake us. Things happen in all directions. It is certainly lively, like good jazz, already very twentieth-century. Nothing stagnant or conventional. Only by now, our ears are deafened and the manner has become automatic. We have seen or heard it all.

With Rimbaud it was really new.

The piano in the Alps is a satisfying, lightning-like marriage of remote entities, "surprising" (as Apollinaire would have it) as the encounter of an umbrella and a sewing machine. Maybe Flaubert's idea of a "piano in front of some natural setting" (*Madame Bovary*) inspired this, as has been suggested. But Rimbaud's image is more jolting and refreshing. Later, in

---

[5] The original Creation itself (reality) is already in a sense "stylization." (Cf. Pascal's idea that nature itself may be an early custom.) If we see it wholly adequately (as Spinoza would say) it is already "expressive"—it reveals an ecstatic plan, harmony. The canny artist can point this up with minimum "underlining"—the tiniest hint of an extra tilt here, a curvier curve there, etc.

I admire most of Van Gogh, but prefer his quieter views, like the *Kitchen Gardens at Arles*. And, in the end, the glory of the Creation is even more manifest in Pissarro's *L'Entrée du village*.

"Soir historique," the "clavecin des prés" (a cricket?) faintly seems to recall this image (along with the surreal "on joue aux cartes au fond de l'étang").

The theatrical cathedral becomes a swarming city, just as in "Villes, I" the city will become a theatre with pulleys and changing *décor. Tout est dans tout.*

> Les caravanes partirent. Et le Splendide-Hôtel fut bâti dans le chaos de glaces et de nuit du pôle.

Here again are the same principles: whee! caravans leaving from or going to exotic places (like Delius' never-never Samarkand). Keep it moving. The luxury hotel in the desolate cold places is another marriage, almost of heaven and hell. Cold is thus made cozy.

> Depuis lors, la Lune entendit les chacals piaulant par les déserts de thym,—et les églogues en sabots grognant dans le verger. Puis, dans la futaie violette, bourgeonnante, Eucharis me dit que c'était le printemps.

More exoticism, à la "le douanier" Rousseau. This time it is mixed with references to bucolic poems, including probably Virgil and a character from Fénelon's pastoral *Télémaque*: Eucharis. The "eclogues in wooden shoes grunting in the orchard" remind us obliquely of Rimbaud's sly, earthy peasant, glimpsed on his mysterious journey in "La Rivière de Cassis." We have seen the "violet grove" in "Bal des pendus," where we noted the poet's affection for this spiritual (and funereal) color combined with its radically opposite earth and forest. The shadowy grove, as Richard says, is the place of birth, a feminine essence in tense fusion with the "male" high-frequency light of *violette* (as in "Voyelles). The combination represents life at a vibrant peak poised as if to make a lyric spring into buds.

> Sourds, étang,—Écume, roule sur le pont et par-dessus les bois;—draps noirs et orgues,—éclairs et tonnerre,—montez et roulez;—Eaux et tristesses, montez et relevez les Déluges.

By now it is all beginning to pall. So he calls for a new round of apocalypse to refresh life again. Humbly, almost humorously, he invites the familiar little pond—we have seen it often in Rimbaud—to well up and do its flood-bit. The black flags and organs seem to echo death-like military movements (or pirates? see "Les Premières communions" where night is a "pirate"). In "Métropolitain" there are also "drapeaux noirs" in a dramatic moment of struggle for life-renewal. The fantasy recalls the invasion of "Qu'est-ce pour nous, mon cœur." The organs are awesome, churchly, appropriate to death, *dies irae*, etc. So are the thunder and lightning. The "tristesses" get into the act because they are the emotional black "waters" which must rise and drown life in sorrow before it can be reborn (cf. the first line with the "idea" of a flood).

As Py notes, the liquid r gives the tone to this passage and much of the poem.

> Car depuis qu'ils se sont dissipés,—oh les pierres précieuses s'enfouissant, et les fleurs ouvertes!—c'est un ennui! et la Reine, la Sorcière qui allume sa braise dans le pot de terre, ne voudra jamais nous raconter ce qu'elle sait, et que nous ignorons.

Since the floods stopped, he sighs—remembering the lovely coquettish jewels and the newly-open flowers that came with them—all is a bore. He blames this disaster on the mysterious "Reine, la Sorcière" who lights her embers in an earthen pot and will not tell what she knows. She is a familiar Earth-Mother figure. The link with his own mother is clear from a number of passages, for example in "Les Étrennes des orphelins":

> Elle a donc oublié, le soir, seule et penchée,
> D'exciter une flamme à la cendre arrachée.

In the *Saison en enfer* there is "la boue m'apparaissait soudainement rouge et noire, comme la glace quand la lampe circule dans la chambre voisine, comme un trésor dans la forêt!" ("Mauvais sang"). We find the same family-setting in "Les Déserts de l'Amour": "La lampe de la famille rougissait l'une après l'autre les chambres voisines. Alors, la femme disparut." The "trésor" and the *Sorcière* are again linked in the *Saison en enfer* when he calls the Muses, "la Beauté . . . la justice . . . O sorcières . . . c'est à vous que mon trésor a été confié."[6] Thus, the treasure (as Mauron says, it is strongly associated with the mother's breast), like embers in an earthen pot (gold in woods, a lamp in the night),[7] is the vestigial memory of the "mother," Beauty, half-hidden in guilt and forbidden passage, bitter disappointment, loss, etc., a consummation buried in ignorance: "Ne sachant rien de ce qu'il faut savoir" (Letter to Demeny, April 17, 1871).

---

[6] See "Veillées," III: "Les lampes et les tapis de la veillée font le bruit des vagues, la nuit, le long de la coque et autour du steerage. La mer de la veillée. . . ."

[7] The remote mother of "Les Étrennes des orphelins" was similarly associated with red and black.

Enfance

Childhood is primarily a time of purity: joys and terrors. The simplicity of innocence precedes the complications and sophistications of social life; it goes back to the source of earthly life, *la mer pure* ("Est-elle almée?"), the "vagues sans vaisseaux" here below.

In each of the five sections of "Enfance" there is a graceful Icarian curve. All of the sections are divided into an uneven number of paragraphs, usually five, sometimes three or seven. In most of them—to some extent in all—the voice spontaneously rises, the action or emotion reaches its height at approximately mid-point in the section. And then begins the turn of disappointment, the growing menace, the descent toward the eventual lonely dejection: ennui (I); tears (II); hunger and thirst and someone to chase you away (III); threat of the world's end (IV); bitterness (V).

I

> Cette idole, yeux noirs et crin jaune, sans parents ni cour, plus noble que la fable, mexicaine et flamande; son domaine, azur et verdure insolents, court sur des plages nommées, par des vagues sans vaisseaux, de noms férocement grecs, slaves, celtiques.

We note first the verbless construction throughout this opening section: each scene is presented as a pure impressionistic notation, in keeping with the idea of "Illuminations," or flashes.

This initial passage is composed of pleasantly infantile babble: savory, salty sounds, smartly incantatory assonances and alliterations ("noble . . . fable"; "vagues . . . vaisseaux"). It presents images ambiguously childlike and primitive (ontogeny, philogeny). The idol with black eyes and crude yellow mane[1] is thus both doll and totem. The sex is unspecified, but other uses in Rimbaud point to the feminine. Mainly, I suspect, she is a doll such as one of Rimbaud's sisters might have had. Certainly this is an essence of childhood reminiscence: that inanimate yet-so-alive creature which we cannot help believing in, like a snowman.

She maintains the black eyes of Woman ("regard noir") in "Les Sœurs de charité" and of the primal Woman, Cybele: "Déesse aux grands yeux noirs vainqueurs" ("Soleil et chair"). In the latter poem, Woman is described as an idol:

---

[1] It recalls the tradition of that combination in the Romantic era, e.g., Nerval's "Fantaisie," Gautier's *Mademoiselle de Maupin*.

253

—Et l'Idole où tu mis tant de virginité,
Où tu divinisas notre argile, la Femme,

But she is nobler even than these "fabulous" creatures, "plus noble que la fable," more original.

But "cette idole" has aspects of a strange flesh-and-blood child, perhaps a newcomer in the neighborhood or glimpsed through a fence like Proust's first image of haughty and aloof Gilberte, or the more-sophisticated orange-lipped little girl in the dream forest of the next section. The *insolence* is felt to be partly hers, the idol's, like the "cold and superior" *enfance d'Hélène* in "Fairy." She is made up of contrary qualities, real and unreal: personally "noble" and impersonally a totem, exotic and yet solid ("Mexican" and "Flemish"; although these adjectives modify "fable" they can also apply ambiguously to the "idole"). The black eyes seem to echo the Mexican, the yellow hair the Flemish: south and north.

Sky ("azur") and earth ("verdure") are her vast and wild joint domain as they were that of "Le Bateau ivre." Their insolence is the indifference of superiority, nature's:

> Et le printemps et la verdure
> Ont tant humilié mon cœur
> Que j'ai puni sur une fleur
> L'insolence de la Nature
> (Baudelaire, "A Celle qui est trop gaie")

Her estate *runs* joyously along the beaches in utter freedom. This dynamism of release along the edge of water will be repeated when Rimbaud, "l'homme aux semelles de vent," runs along the *quais* in "Aube"; at such times he leaves the *Assis* far behind.

Doll or girl, if the idol is parentless, that reflects Rimbaud's estate as well as his sympathy. And it gives her a royalty, a fatherless "nobility" like his, an *ex nihilo* purity. To be without a "court" is to be like the pair of "Royauté": noble from a higher source, rulers by divine right of juvenile omnipotence, trailing Wordsworthian clouds of true glory. Thus her provenance is the wide world; she is from nowhere and everywhere, like Maeterlinck's mysterious Mélisande. And what better place to meet this absolute child-companion than on a beach, "une plage pour deux enfants fidèles" ("Phrases")!

The native beaches are named—as if by vessel-less waves (pure primitive water without vulgar encumbrance, as in "Villes II": "bras de mer, sans bateaux"), babbling the names as they lap at them—"with ferociously Greek, Slavic, Celtic names"! This is *apparently* precise but basically impressionistic, like the "Italiennes, Espagnoles" used to give a general exotic effect in "Les Poètes de sept ans" or the "Sicile, Allemagne" of "Entends comme brame"; these places are simultaneously mythic and real. The lands here have the salty, smart tone ("férocement") of the above-mentioned "insolence." The slapping dry hard sounds of c and t have much to do with this effect, which is deliberately unsentimental to emphasize the *primitive* quality of the idol or doll. Thus Rimbaud, who needed this harsh, salt-like ingredient, admired the "dureté" of the "forçat intraitable" in the *Saison en enfer* ("Mauvais sang"), the suntanned returned explorer —"les brigands, les amis de la mort, les arriérés de toute sorte" ("Adieu"). In "Parade" such types predominate and clearly fascinate as well as frighten.

The place words refer to the related entities—ancient cultures, Greek or Celtic, and the comparatively primitive regions of Eastern Europe. Rimbaud looks back to his Celtic origin for support and authenticity in *Une Saison en enfer* ("Mauvais sang"). He admired the wholeness of the Greeks (second "Lettre du voyant"), and was fascinated by the Slavic element (cf. "Fairy" and "Fête d'hiver").

> A la lisière de la forêt—les fleurs de rêve tintent, éclatent, éclairent,—la fille à lèvre d'orange, les genoux croisés dans le clair déluge qui sourd des prés, nudité qu'ombrent, traversent et habillent les arcs-en-ciel, la flore, la mer.

The dream-setting is clear and familiar. The nude girl-form emerges into vision from the woods like the golden kiss of "Tête de faune" or *la belle au bois dormant*. She is a human flower or fruit with fetching vibrancy of light and color, like Proust's Gilberte seen through her Monet-like estate. Orange lips are naturally enticing as oranges (Proust's Marcel compared Albertine's lips to orangeade; Mallarmé speaking of oranges in "La Dernière Mode" refers to the "delicious taste we find in bright colors").[2]

The "clair déluge," already seen in "Michel et Christine," is literally a flood of light, refreshing or reviving nature, as in "Après le déluge." The rainbows here also recall that first *Illumination*: land and sky are united in its promise. There is almost a strobe-effect in the striations of light and shadow moving across the landscape; it is vibrant, impressionistic, renewed by life and motion (but *static* motion: gentle, not going anywhere, only *bringing*).

Lovely remote entities come and marry the setting as if wafted by a breeze: the distant sea (as in "Mystique": "la rumeur tournante et bondis-

---

[2] In "Métropolitain" the mysterious She has "green lips."

sante des conques des mers"), the rainbow from the sky. The light wells up from the meadows as if from an *inner* source (cf. the light *in* the girl who opens the barn door in Claude Simon's *La Route des Flandres*). It is earth-light, palpable, buttery as a child's flesh; the damp meadows and flowers are part of the surge. The tinkly flowers are like the "clochettes" of "Après le déluge" (cf. the "buzzing flowers" in part II, "une cloche de feu rose" of "Phrases"). They are alive to all the senses, synesthetically as in "Le Bateau ivre" ("phosphores chanteurs"), and indeed have an undersea-music or "happening" effect of organic sound and light phenomena. They are musical, dynamic ("éclatent") and luminous; they metamorphose before our eyes and ears.

In "Fleurs" the sea and the flowers come together similarly, as they did in "Le Bateau ivre" ("La mer . . . Montait vers moi ses fleurs d'ombre"), and in "Age d'or" ("Ce n'est qu'onde, flore").

We note that the idol was seen as motionless (like a doll held in the hands of a staring child); so is the little girl seated cross-legged in the wood. In the third paragraph a dance will begin, something of a moving spectacle, as the child-vision becomes more active, slightly sophisticated. This parallels the progression from simple colors (black, yellow, azur, verdure) to less simple (orange) and more nuanced ones ("arcs-en-ciel") and, finally, the adulteration of "vert-de-gris."

As the scenes progress, the simple dynamic movement of "court" (first paragraph) becomes in the second paragraph the tripartite rhythm of "tintent, éclatent, éclairent" or "ombrent, traversent et habillent"—almost a waltz rhythm, a 3-point circularity leading to the dizzy "tournoient" in the final paragraph. The progress is one of hallucinatory stir like the "tourbillons" of "Being beauteous" and other such vertiginously mounting moods in Rimbaud. The vertical oscillation between "enfantes et géantes" (supported by the an/é contrast) is part of this frenzy which by its very excess ends, as usual with Rimbaud, in a fall.

> Dames qui tournoient sur les terrasses voisines de la mer; enfantes et géantes, superbes noires dans la mousse vert-de-gris, bijoux debout sur le sol gras des bosquets et des jardinets dégelés,—jeunes mères et grandes sœurs aux regards pleins de pèlerinages, sultanes, princesses de démarche et de costume tyranniques, petites étrangères et personnes doucement malheureuses.
>
> Quel ennui, l'heure du "cher corps" et "cher cœur."

The ladies who gyrate on the terraces by the sea are romantic and exotic, as the creatures Rimbaud dreamed of in "Les Poètes de sept ans": "Espagnoles, Italiennes." There are also shades of the "fêtes de nuit sur la mer pure" of "Est-elle almée"? This is the original sea as in the "vagues sans vaisseaux" above. The terraces and flowers emerge from it again in "Fleurs" (see our extended comment on the image there). In "Mystique" there is a parallel *tournoiement* of dresses, with flowers and distant sea-echoes. "Girl-children and giantesses," both extremes please (cf. Baudelaire's pair in "La Géante" and "le vert paradis des amours enfantines," "Moesta et errabunda"). Blacks are beautiful to Rimbaud, as in the *Saison en enfer* or "les noirs inconnus" of "Qu'est-ce pour nous, mon cœur." The "verdigris" moss is green jewelry (cf. the grass of "Mystique," also metallic: "les herbages d'acier et d'émeraude" and the Sartrean anti-viscosity crystallizations of "Fleurs"). Moss is like the meadow grass, only more porous—it absorbs the underground water and brings it to the surface; it is a magic-fertile carpet. The corruption of vert-de-gris is fecund, like the damp gardens of dark winter-death preceding spring's rebirth. The thawed little gardens echo the damp plot of ground behind Rimbaud's house in "Les Poètes de sept ans," the suburban gardens bathed in a warm February south wind of "Ouvriers." T. S. Eliot describes this fecund, mysterious seasonal overlap as "Midwinter spring" ("Little Gidding").

"Jeunes mères" and "grandes sœurs" both blend opposites: Rimbaud applied this special note of tenderness to himself in "Délires I": "manières de jeune mère, de sœur aimée." Their looks are full of pilgrimages—fascinating far-away looks. Sultanas are exotic. Tyrannical costumes of the princesses are like the *insolence* of the idol's domain, a haughty or superb quality that adds sadistic spice to femininity. The "sweetly unhappy" females are at first romantically attractive, but their softness leads to a misogynous note as does the "pitié douce" and "monceau d'entrailles" of "Les Sœurs de charité." Rimbaud seems to mock Baudelaire's women in his "cher corps" and "cher cœur": "Car à quoi bon chercher . . . Ailleurs qu'en ton cher corps et qu'en ton cœur si doux?" ("Le Balcon"). Verlaine's sentimentality is ribbed in an allusion to his own "cher corps endormi" in "Délires I."

At the end of "Ouvriers," an adventure with a girl, he refuses to drag on any longer "une chère image."

In "Métropolitain," "cœurs" rhymes with "atroces fleurs" as well as "sœurs," all sentimentally disgusting at this point.

II

C'est elle, la petite morte, derrière les rosiers.—La jeune maman trépassée descend le perron.—La calèche du cousin crie sur le sable.—Le petit frère (il est aux Indes!) là, devant le couchant, sur le pré d'œillets.—Les vieux qu'on a enterrés tout droits dans le rempart aux giroflées.

Children do not dissociate well. For them, time is not so much chronological, or sequential, but rather an eternal present, simultaneous as in a dream or deep experience generally (the *totum simul* of mystics). If a child is told that someone familiar is dead, he has trouble understanding this total absence which to him is still presence: the *image* of the person persists (in memory, or imagination). So he imagines the absence as a removal to another spot, shadowy because of the pain and trouble associated with the death-announcement, mysterious, too, because the event is darkly puzzling and threatening: "behind the rosebushes" is a likely place and may add reassurance since there was a local legend about children being born there.

It is the same with the young mother. She is remembered, as Rimbaud writes, as eternally doing something characteristic, though he knows she too is dead. Perhaps Rimbaud's longing for a younger, more loving version of his own mother is "buried" here. Other puzzling events occur in a related way. In life, someone is always coming (the "cousin"), someone departing, or gone (the "little brother" is "in the Indies"). Life, the *Sorcière* of "Après le déluge," does not tell us why—things just happen to upset our routine, trouble us, fascinate us, and sometimes charm us. Though absent, the brother's image persists too, in a place and manner characteristic of him: "before the sundown, on the meadow of pinks." Those old men buried standing up in the ramparts covered with gilliflowers seem to be based on a local legend (soldiers from a past war may have been buried there and in a peculiar fashion, according to one of Rimbaud's familiars). But mainly it is just the odd sort of thing that awes and grips children's imagination. This image of dead men postured straight up is akin to the drowned men who go down backwards in "Le Bateau ivre."

> L'essaim des feuilles d'or entoure la maison du général. Ils sont dans le midi.—On suit la route rouge pour arriver à l'auberge vide. Le château est à vendre; les persiennes sont détachées.—Le curé aura emporté la clef de l'église.—Autour du parc, les loges des gardes sont inhabitées. Les palissades sont si hautes qu'on ne voit que les cimes bruissantes. D'ailleurs il n'y a rien à voir là-dedans.

The child, moving outward from his unsatisfactory home, investigates a possible refuge of happiness. A general's house is a possibility: a general is a promising and obvious father-figure[3] (in "Alchimie du verbe" Rimbaud calls the sun "Général"; he is the "fils du Soleil" in "Vagabonds"). But the general is absent, like Godot. And the church is locked.

[3] Compare Proust's old General, admired by the young hero, in *Jean Santeuil*.

The swarm of golden leaves around the house is like a halo. They (the family) are off in the south, another typical bit of puzzling and disconcerting information, the sort of unaccountable disappointment or *dislocation* in which life abounds.

The red road leads to another possible refuge, one we have seen in "Comédie de la soif" (and Baudelaire's "L'Irréparable"). The castle is another possible ideality, as in "Le Bonheur": it is not to be entered either (it is for sale) and somewhat dilapidated. (There is a premonition here of Meaulnes's domain and in a way Kafka's castle too.)

The keyless church is like the empty one the jaded couple come to in *L'Avventura.*

The guards' huts are also uninhabited, emphasizing the theme of no-comfort (in the next section the child is even chased away).

The fence is so high that one sees only the rustling tops of the trees. That is frustrating but exciting: exquisite presence-absence. Trembling leaves—nature's sympathetic sigh and caress—always console Rimbaud's deep sorrow, notably in "Ophélie" and "Mémoire."

Nothing to see inside, this is the final dejection we have witnessed so often at the close of a lyric curve in Rimbaud ("Le Bateau ivre," "Larme").

> Les prés remontent aux hameaux sans coqs, sans enclumes. L'écluse est levée. O les calvaires et les moulins du désert, les îles et les meules!

We have seen a similar, numbly suspended (as if by magic curse, or spell) landscape before, in "Les Corbeaux," "La Rivière de Cassis." The dam-gate is raised: so there is a rush of water, as in *Le Grand Meaulnes*, toward a promise, a humble break of the emotional pall. In section IV the sluices' "rumeur" accompanies the steps of the pilgrim-like searcher.

The horizontal way, like that of *Pilgrim's Progress*, goes past staccato vertical events: crosses, mills in deserted places, isles, haystacks. We saw these last, the haystacks, in rather frightening projections of darkness in "Entends comme brame." Here, rather, they are lyrically hailed. Moreover, the succession of "events" seems to lead on to meaning. And the islands and haystacks swell wholesomely.

> Des fleurs magiques bourdonnaient. Les talus le berçaient. Des bêtes d'une élégance fabuleuse circulaient. Les nuées s'amassaient sur la haute mer faite d'une éternité de chaudes larmes.

We have seen the flowers tinkling, now they buzz. Rimbaud's familiar "talus" now appear. They always represent gentle thresholds to promise, just out of sight. Here, they also cradle "him" like the typical womb-shapes of land in Cézanne. The fabulous and elegant animals are also consoling; elegant no doubt because prissyfooted like cats (Valery Larbaud's vagrant child in *Enfantines*—"L'Heure avec la figure"—dreamed of a blue-eyed animal in a forest).

The high sea corresponds to the tearful emotion welling in him to fill his basic emptiness; it is a recurrent image of emotional fullness. It recalls the sea "étagée là-haut" in "Après le déluge." And it is in itself a refreshing flood, tears washing away sorrow. The heavy clouds massing on them are no doubt the weight of sadness gathering still in his soul, veiling the dream of eternal happiness *là-haut*. There are some memories of his mother; in "Mauvais sang" she aroused the image of the sea overcast by smoke: "une mer de flamme et de fumée au ciel."

III

> Au bois il y a un oiseau, son chant vous arrête et vous fait rougir.

The bird through song gives its all, and by its total authenticity makes Rimbaud blush for his shortcomings (the seasons and castles had had a similar effect: "Quelle âme est sans défauts?"). Or, physically, the blush that results from this sudden penetration of violent beauty amounts to the same phenomenon: it so Real, I so full of bad faith. Mallarmé in "Petit Air II" will have the same experience: the bird "one hears only once in one's life" must have died, he felt, for this perfect gift of self. Richard Wilbur's birds "explode with joy" ("Wedding of the Puppets").

In "Fairy," "L'ardeur de l'été fut confiée à des oiseaux muets." These birds are only potentially givers of the all—the whole summer warmth—they contain. Like the golden kiss of "Tête de faune," the birds here and there sum up the woods and the day.

> Il y a une horloge qui ne sonne pas.

The clock, as we saw in "Les Étrennes des orphelins," is a fatherly entity: giver of order, like *raison* ("A une raison"). A stopped or silent clock (as in Pierre Reverdy's "Réalité immobile" from *La Lucarne ovale*) betokens a still point in a turning world, an end-of-cycle crisis, a numb moment of waiting, out of time (there is one in the *Saison en enfer*: "l'horloge de la vie s'est arrêtée tout à l'heure"; and in *Igitur*). It can be beautiful still, an ecstasy, or else panic fear; or both, in "awe." All three are present here.

Hackett sees the stopped clock as a symbol of the maternal heartbeat silenced at birth; this image may well underlie, and overlap with, the other. The patriarchal character of the clock is attested by numerous examples in French and German folklore,[4] in Nerval's *Sylvie* and *Aurélia* (*IV*), etc. The matriarchal image is classically Freudian.

The "Il y a" anaphora betokens the steepness of the *phenomena*, happenings as if without cause.

> Il y a une fondrière avec un nid de bêtes blanches.

This mudhole with its white creatures reminds me of the puddle in which T. S. Eliot saw a crab and poked at it with a stick ("Little Gidding"). In "Ouvriers" there is a pond with isolated fish. All these little areas are microcosms, psychic mini-theaters for important though puzzling symbolic events: for example, one sees one's own shrunken creatural self there. At any rate we all remember this adventurous, oddly sacrificial peering into holes and puddles for signs or meanings in the little life there.

> Il y a une cathédrale qui descend et un lac qui monte.

The sinking cathedral reminds us of *La Cathédrale d'Ys* and may be a revenge against his mother's religion, even as the rising water is associated (as in part I) with the emotion—usually grief—of the son-mother relationship. See the lake and the mother-figure of "Phrases."

> Il y a une petite voiture abandonnée dans le taillis, ou qui descend le sentier en courant, enrubannée.

The little carriage is nest-cozy and precious like the train-compartment in "Rêvé pour l'hiver" and, like it, might take him on a delightful escape to another, better world.

It is an *abandoned* carriage, arrested movement (cf. the *arrête* of the bird), like an empty *château* (e.g., the general's), vibrant with inner life, wonder. If it breaks the spell of wonder, it bursts right through a normal level of comprehensible activity and gives itself to the equally puzzling phenomena of *extreme* speed, ribbons streaming, beyond our reach and ken—but admirable, graceful, and lovable. Its being in a "taillis" (or on a "sentier") guarantees its grace—it is part of nature's own mystery, one with the seasons and the woods. The young nature of the woods—"taillis," new growth—offers a certain promise.

> Il y a une troupe de petits comédiens en costumes, aperçus sur la route à travers la lisière du bois.

[4] See Hoffman-Krayer, *Handwörterbuch des deutschen Aberglaubens* (Berlin, 1927), under "Uhr."

The little actors are also graced by the woods—on their edge, like the little orange-lipped girl (this is a privileged place to be, vibrantly outside and in, partaking of both nature and art). On a distant road, they elude our grasp and tantalize us, like a circus parade before children. We wanted to go too but were too small as yet. What prestige! (Rimbaud's father had this chic in "Mémoire.")

> Il y a enfin, quand l'on a faim et soif, quelqu'un qui vous chasse.

The end of the curve is a typically Rimbaldian dejection. Who is the "quelqu'un"? There are always some old neighbor-ladies or crabby householders, unfriendly to children or wayfarers. Like the *Sorcière*, this figure may well reflect the surliness of his own mother. Or of life. (That "enfin" seems to echo the "Sans qu'on dise: enfin" of "L'Éternité.")

I V

> Je suis le saint, en prière sur la terrasse,—comme les bêtes pacifiques paissent jusqu'à la mer de Palestine.

Here, the child makes a qualitative leap in growth, advances to the stage where he gingerly tries out various life-roles. It is very like Snoopy saying: "Here is the world-famous hockey player, or here is the World War I ace." But, soon, before this Petit-Poucet has gone far along one of these tentative ways, the mood darkens; there are dire forebodings of where it may lead. . . .

I believe many children know the attraction of sainthood. Their celibate and submissive condition makes it an easier step than for adults, and its rewards are obvious to them: utter smugness! So little Rimbaud dreams of beatitude. Serenity's natural objective correlative is a pasture (of heaven). Thus in "Voyelles" the "vibrements divins" were in the "Paix des pâtis semés d'animaux" (obviously the "paix/paissent" echo works on him in both texts). The terrace is akin in serenity, only man-made. There is another one in "Vies" (which, as its title indicates, extends the role-exploring mood): "O les énormes avenues du pays saint, les terrasses du temple!" Flaubert's *Hérodias* will open with such a perspective of lands extending to the Dead Sea.

> Je suis le savant au fauteuil sombre. Les branches et la pluie se jettent à la croisée de la bibliothèque.

A close corollary to sainthood is the scholar's ascetic life, with rewards for solitude in delicious laziness. Like the trees beyond the palisade of the *château*, the window is another such threshold of exquisite potentialities—branches and rain are nature's feminine caress. "Il pleut doucement sur la ville" is a poignant fragment of Rimbaud which Verlaine used as an epigraph for "Il pleure dans mon cœur" (cf. "Barbare").

> Je suis le piéton de la grand'route par les bois nains; la rumeur des écluses couvre mes pas. Je vois longtemps la mélancolique lessive d'or du couchant.

In our first essay on Rimbaud (1960), we spoke of the persistent central image in him as being that of the *piéton*: driven out from his beginnings, going curiously toward the unknown. Nor does he move fast: he takes a world of depth with him in every step (depth of nostalgia, and of qualms).

The dwarf woods add a puzzling and somewhat theatrical element: nature seems to adapt itself to the child's height (cf. the "little actors" in the "woods," above). Accordingly, on both counts it seems less serious, hopefully manageable.

The dam-gates were up in section II, allowing the promising rush. Here the waters rush on *too* promisingly: the child feels swept along. Menace creeps in with loneliness. Thus the wistful note of seeing for a long while the melancholy "gold wash" of sundown. That "lessive" is an aptly curdled effect like Baudelaire's "sang qui se fige" ("Harmonie du soir").

> Je serais bien l'enfant abandonné sur la jetée partie à la haute mer, le petit valet suivant l'allée dont le front touche le ciel.

The "abandoned child" needs no more explaining—and we note the self-pity of "petit" ("valet"). The pier going out to open sea is an excellent metaphor for a hesitant quest into the unknown (or future). In this context it is *not* promising, for a pier abuts nowhere (James Joyce called it "a disappointed bridge").

"Petit valet," a little farmboy, is what Rimbaud was in a sense, or could identify with, on his mother's farm at Roche where he spent some time. It might hark back to a local folklore version of Perceval who was called a *valet*, "varlet." Anyway, "valet" seems called up poetically by "allée"; he *is* his going.[5]

> Les sentiers sont âpres. Les monticules se couvrent de genêts. L'air est immobile. Que les oiseaux et les sources sont loin! Ce ne peut être que la fin du monde, en avançant.

[5] Similarly, in *La Condition Humaine*, Malraux's Ferral ambiguously declares, "Je suis mes routes." Rimbaud uses the same effect in "À la musique."

Now the going is frankly harsh as the mood gets heavier. The still air is at least partly a *menacing* pall, as in "Les Corbeaux" or section II of this *Illumination*. Even the birds and wellsprings—some comfort, some *points de repère* of life or stir—are far-off. In "Larme," the birds and flocks were left behind willingly. Here, however, the end of the world—in space and time—threatens whoever insists on going on alone too far: "par une route de dangers ma faiblesse me menait aux confins du monde . . ." ("Délires II"). (Rimbaud always returned home just in time. . . .)

V

> Qu'on me loue enfin ce tombeau, blanchi à la chaux avec les lignes du ciment en relief—très loin sous terre.

The child seeks refuge, finally, in a habitable tomb. At the end of "Les Sœurs de charité," it is death itself that the desperate and unwanted groper seeks. Here it is a snug underground womb or nest where the "enfant/Gêneur," the "si sotte bête" ("Honte") will be out of everyone's way. The ugly duckling does not really want to be a swan, just a self-sufficient egg. Is the light that breaks through botheration?—or a new life?

This is a practical tomb-habitation, neatly whitewashed. The geometric lines of cement are a reassuring sign of order, control (like the metal spheres farther on)—counterbalancing the other side, the *infinite* of repose which is the main object.

> Je m'accoude à la table, la lampe éclaire très vivement ces journaux que je suis idiot de relire, ces livres sans intérêt.—

The child here is like the one pictured at the beginning of Baudelaire's "Le Voyage," under a living room lamp savoring *estampes*. But the disappointment of the later parts of the "Voyage" are here too (and the final death-wish of the end is always *sous-entendu*).

Rimbaud desires to be away from it all. And yet, curiously, as in so many of his poems ("Veillées," "Mauvais sang") he is back safe at home. He always, in fact, came back. This is a familiar domestic scene: ordinary bourgeois boredom as on the Sundays of "Les Poètes de sept ans."

> A une distance énorme au-dessus de mon salon souterrain, les maisons s'implantent, les brumes s'assemblent. La boue est rouge ou noire. Ville monstrueuse, nuit sans fin!

At the midpoint, as usual, of his Icarian dream-flight, trouble sets in. The bother comes as a glimpse of the city that has followed him down to his retreat to haunt him. At first he states that it is "enormously" far away, above. Inoffensive houses are described. That is whistling in the dark. The vision soon clouds with "fogs" akin to the earlier overcast sea. But the image of red and black mud which haunts him equally in the *Saison en enfer* ("Mauvais sang") is an essence of cold, darkly threatening city. He sums up that idea: "Monstrous city, endless night!" In "Les Déserts de l'amour" the vision is the same: "Je sortis dans la ville sans fin. O fatigue! Noyé dans la nuit sourde et dans la fuite du bonheur."

The red and black, we have often seen, is a struggle of life and death forces (sometimes combined in a vehemence, purple rage, etc.). It is like the flame in the night of Andersen's "Little Match Girl" or the embers in the dark forest of "Après le déluge."

> Moins haut, sont des égouts. Aux côtés, rien que l'épaisseur du globe. Peut-être les gouffres d'azur, des puits de feu. C'est peut-être sur ces plans que se rencontrent lunes et comètes, mers et fables.

He sets up a sort of compromise between his deep retreat and the monster-city: sewers, midway between the two. It is a way of dealing with the problem: "OK, there's a lousy city, but at this level . . . , etc., etc." The sewer image seems to emerge naturally from the obsessive image of mud. Around them is an even more acceptable image, a fantasy à la Jules Verne of controlled danger as in science fiction. Americanized boyish man's tinkering can tame even those infinites that terrified Pascal. Actually, Rimbaud (and the tinkerers) *are* terrified. But it is controlled terror: exhilaration. So the gulfs of azur can plunge down, the wells of fire surge up, moons can roll along and comets swoosh by; it is all foreseen and numbered. The gentler, more feminine infinites of "seas and fables" are part of the reassurance he mixes with his fear.

> Aux heures d'amertume je m'imagine des boules de saphir, de métal. Je suis maître du silence. Pourquoi une apparence de soupirail blêmirait-elle au coin de la voûte?

The sapphire and metal balls are buoys of manly strength and resistance. Hence the proud boast of the would-be-dominator of mud, softness, and endless smothering silence: "Je suis maître du silence." (In "Les Premières Communions" there is the same night-silence-mother: "la nuit, Vierge-Mère impalpable, qui baigne / Tous les jeunes émois de ses silences gris.")

The air-hole, I believe, indicates the evasive child is not so sure of his strength after all. He needs contact with something up there, at human level. There is a breach in his self-sufficiency. The sturdy cement-lined retreat is not all that solid: a *pallid* opening occurs, i.e., something all-too-human, namby-pamby even, in his would-be-intransigent sight. The origin of the image, I suspect, is a crack of daylight, putting an end to an orgiastically happy and free night-vision, a *bateau-ivresque* voyage.

Hackett sees this as the other side of the air-hole ("soupirail") in "Les Effarés," as if now he is *inside* that warm baker's womb-room like a made-wholesome loaf. It is an interesting possibility. But the whole-feeling is now past. This is a time of "bitterness," the end of a Rimbaldian curve. He is back at mediocre earth-level, like the child squatting before the puddle in his own neighborhood, after the fantastic voyage of "Le Bateau ivre."[6]

Conte

The tone of "Conte" is unusually Baudelairian: it is particularly the Baudelaire of "Une mort héroïque" and "Spleen LXXVI."

There are reminiscences in both of Caligula and Nero, of princely Roman cruelty and sophisticated perversion generally.

In "Une mort héroïque":

> Le Prince n'était ni meilleur ni pire qu'un autre; mais une excessive sensibilité le rendait, en beaucoup de cas, plus cruel et plus despote que tous ses pareils. Amoureux passionné des beaux-arts, excellent connaisseur d'ailleurs, il était vraiment insatiable de voluptés. Assez indifférent relativement aux hommes et à la morale, véritable artiste lui-même, il ne connaissait d'ennemi dangereux que l'Ennui, et les efforts bizarres qu'il faisait pour fuir ou pour vaincre ce tyran du monde lui auraient certainement attiré, de la part d'un historien sévère, l'épithète de "monstre," s'il avait été permis, dans ses domaines, d'écrire quoi que ce fût qui ne tendît pas uniquement au plaisir ou à l'étonnement, qui est une des formes les plus délicates du plaisir. Le grand malheur de ce Prince fut qu'il n'eût jamais un théâtre assez vaste pour son génie. . . .[1]

The boredom and huge potential of this figure, the banality of his life despite the (inner) royalty, all this corresponds to aspects of Rimbaud's personality or mood: long waiting periods of pall, spiritual numbness in which even the thought—or imagined spectacle—of cruelty becomes banal, boring.[2]

---

[6] In "Après le déluge," "le sceau de Dieu blêmit les fenêtres" implied a divine visitation, but that hint is present here only by its absence.

---

[1] This *génie* may have some specific bearing on Rimbaud's prose poem.

[2] Compare Adolph Eichmann, according to Hannah Arendt.

In "Une mort héroïque," the monarch's genius can only blossom fully in the "right" time and place, or "theatre." Rimbaud's Prince believes that equally. The difference is that Baudelaire's figure finds an active way of reaching the extraordinary; true, he is moved by the great talent of his clown, Fancioulle, but it is he who brings about the remarkable love-death moment on the stage. Rimbaud's Prince, on the contrary, is overcome by a figure more powerful in every way than he, a kind of God or Father-figure of genius, as in the *Illumination* entitled "Génie." And, far more subtle than Baudelaire, Rimbaud discovers that the "Génie" was the Prince—or was part of him. Actually, even this is found in Baudelaire: "le personnage de Giglio Favio, le comédien atteint de dualisme Chronique . . . il se déclare l'ennemi du prince assyrien . . . et quand il est prince assyrien, il déverse le plus profond et le plus royal mépris sur son rival . . . Favia" (*De l'essence du rire*).

I suspect that Baudelaire's language helped Rimbaud, or supported him in his paradoxical insight. The passage about this reciprocal identity in "Conte" reads partly as follows: "Un Génie apparut, d'une beauté ineffable, inavouable même. . . . d'un bonheur indicible, insupportable même! Le Prince et le Génie s'anéantirent probablement dans la santé essentielle. Comment n'auraient-ils pas pu en mourir?"

The spirit of genius, for Rimbaud, is like that of Goethe's devil: "Der Geist der stets verneint"—the spirit that always denies. Certainly his Prince—and the whole Poe and Baudelaire prose tone imitated here—is ironic in his milder periods, fully negating in his annihilations and in his deeper moments. The reader will have noted the series of in- s clearly indicative of negation: "ineffable . . . inavouable . . . indicible . . . insupportable" (also the negations of "anéantirent" and "n'auraient-ils pas pu"). These in- s reflect the in- and its reverse form ni- (as in "nier" or "ironie," etc.) of the *Génie* and the *Prince*.[3]

The piece, then, describes a dull waiting period during which, as in Baudelaire's "Au Lecteur," boredom generates a frenzy of hate and destruction. Then comes the privileged moment when from nowhere the negation turns into exquisite spirit, genius, health (in the sense that Wallace Stevens says: "this health is holy"), beauty. It is a marriage of self with self, as all true moments of bliss are: e.g., Proust's wedding of a present self with a past one in "involuntary memory." A miracle.

But it is all put in understated, almost ironic terms. This is deliberate prose to *handle* a dangerously poetic topic, as Baudelaire's prose poems

[3] Genet shows a similar development of wild negation as adventurous spirit, sheer genius, according to Sartre's analysis and picture. Sartre, who is so hard on Baudelaire because of his *choices* in difficult situations, is curiously indulgent toward Genet.

often are. It has a remarkable special tension and high synthesis à la Kafka (ordinary real plus extraordinary). Even the title, "Conte," is an understatement, like Mallarmé's "Prose (pour des Esseintes)," recounting a moment of deepest vision.

> Un Prince était vexé de ne s'être employé jamais qu'à la perfection des générosités vulgaires. Il prévoyait d'étonnantes révolutions de l'amour, et soupçonnait ses femmes de pouvoir mieux que cette complaisance agrémentée de ciel et de luxe. Il voulait voir la vérité, l'heure du désir et de la satisfaction essentiels. Que ce fût ou non une aberration de piété, il voulut. Il possédait au moins un assez large pouvoir humain.

We have already explained this psychological configuration. Note the "désir et . . . satisfaction essentiels" reflected in the "santé essentielle" below, at the climax. "Que ce fût ou non une aberration de piété, il voulut" indicates the Nietzschean or Kierkegaardean drive "beyond morality," plus some hint of lingering fear, clinging to the props of traditional piety as a standard of (self-) judgment. The "large pouvoir" is Rimbaud's bragging—but not lacking in substance! The "assez" is, again, cautious.

> Toutes les femmes qui l'avaient connu furent assassinées. Quel saccage du jardin de la beauté! Sous le sabre, elles le bénirent. Il n'en commanda point de nouvelles.—Les femmes réapparurent.

This is quite straightforward. The whole spectacle is, as in "Après le déluge," recognized by the author (with Romantic irony) to be imaginary: a nothing-everything of fantasy. There is no strength in it, only power, to use a distinction of Coleridge's. Thus in "Barbare," after a striking image of flowers and seas, we read: "elles n'existent pas."

> Il tua tous ceux qui le suivaient, après la chasse ou les libations.—Tous le suivaient.

Même jeu.

> Il s'amusa à égorger les bêtes de luxe. Il fit flamber les palais. Il se ruait sur les gens et les taillait en pièces.—La foule, les toits d'or, les belles bêtes existaient encore.

He continues in the same vein. Women, men, new animals and palaces, the castles he could love more easily than people as in "O saisons, ô châteaux." So here he is cutting deeply into his own psyche, lacerating himself too, masochistically, in the process of sadistic destruction.

> Peut-on s'extasier dans la destruction, se rajeunir par la cruauté! Le peuple ne murmura pas. Personne n'offrit le concours de ses vues.

And all is in vain. Nothing really happens in this self-involved fantasy. When you are alone, there is no resistance, no stimulating life (as Sartre keeps insisting in his theoretical works on the imagination). He encounters neither solid negation from outside ("Le peuple ne murmura pas"), nor affirmation (no "concours"). This is the bottom: despair.

> Un soir il galopait fièrement. Un Génie apparut, d'une beauté ineffable, inavouable même. De sa physionomie et de son maintien ressortait la promesse d'un amour multiple et complexe! d'un bonheur indicible, insupportable même! Le Prince et le Génie s'anéantirent probablement dans la santé essentielle. Comment n'auraient-ils pas pu en mourir? Ensemble donc ils moururent.

Despite the despair, like Baudelaire's Don Juan or a desperate, damned Romantic hero, he goes on "proudly." Underneath, we can guess atrocious suffering of solitude, hubris, the awful sin of pride. But at the very bottom of Hell, in Dante's account, the way already leads up to hope (the "promesse" here) of total salvation: "santé essentielle." So they (he and his Father, or the genius-spirit and the son-spirit; the actual, or entelechy, and the potential) "die" together, as in Christ's confrontation with his Father on the agonizing and blissful cross. But Rimbaud refuses, out of *pudeur*, fear, and mainly out of youthful ignorance or tentativeness (caused largely by his mother's and the Establishment's contamination of these truths), to see it or put it in these terms. He maintains his ironic "superiority" and control—a horrible mistake like the Baudelairean dandy's determination to "ne pas être dupe."

> Mais ce Prince décéda, dans son palais, à un âge ordinaire. Le Prince était le Génie. Le Génie était le Prince. La musique savante manque à notre désir.

So life goes on banally, femininely (in horizontal, river-like movement[4])

---

[4] The famous quotation at the end of *Faust II*: "Das Ewig-Weibliche zieht uns hinan" is usually translated "the Eternal Feminine draws us upward." But *hinan*

despite the deep crisis. This could be wisdom—life *does* go on—but Rimbaud had not yet learned Goethe's middle-aged serenity. Rather in his case it is a confession of disappointment, *plus ça change*, as at the end of "Le Bateau ivre." But it is also ambiguous. Thus the statement "Le Prince était le Génie. Le Génie était le Prince" is at once a deep discovery of the oneness of truth (vision) and of Personality (with something of the total disinterestedness of pure friendship as in Montaigne's "Parce que c'estoit luy; parce que c'estoit moy" or his own image of "L'ami" in "Veillées," I).[5] And, simultaneously, the vision is turning sour as all visions do eventually: all nothings which are everything become nothing once again. I feel that the negative aspect of the reversible formula prevails at the end, because Rimbaud's poems tend to curve this Icarian way, and the tone of the last line is clearly dejected.

But what is the "musique savante [qui] manque à notre désir"? Something to give one a duration, a privileged and merited endurance, no doubt. Perhaps art could do this, as Proust thought. And in a work which is curiously haunted by that Proustian emotion, *La Nausée*, Sartre will come up with a useful phrase: "souffrir en mesure." Rimbaud too needs a classic dimension, a *rhythmic form*—"musique savante"—to immortalize his longings and satisfactions as art. "L'art c'est le désir perpétué" as Jules Laforgue will say in a *Moralité Légendaire* ("Pan et la Syrinx").

Parade

"Parade" is extremely obscure; no one, to my mind, has come anywhere near a satisfactory interpretation. I do not much care for riddles, and the proportion of sheer puzzle in relation to poetic substance is clearly excessive in this instance. Still, the page has its rewards, and not only exegetic ones.

"Parade" is essentially Rimbaud's impression of the world of mature modern men: "Quels hommes mûrs!" In "L'Impossible" he describes them as "des gens hargneux et joyeux, de faux élus, puisqu'il nous faut de l'audace ou de l'humilité pour les aborder. Ce sont les seuls élus. Ce ne sont pas des bénisseurs." His vision is extreme, fantastic, grotesque: "il [Rimbaud] avait des jours où tous les hommes agissant lui paraissaient les jouets de délires grotesques" ("Délires I"). That is largely because on the one hand he is extremely attracted to them (he yearns for virile attention;

---

can mean "along," according to my dictionary. This seems to me to be the profounder interpretation. And why not both?

[5] Montaigne was referring in this phrase to his friendship with La Boétie. Rimbaud is known to have memorized portions of the *Essais*.

as we have seen, without doubt his greatest lack is of a father or Father . . .); on the other hand, he is repelled by them. As the inevitable obverse of his attraction, he sees them also as "la foule barbare" ("Scènes"), and confesses: "j'ai tremblé à l'aspect des gardiens de colosses et officiers de constructions" ("Villes II"). Moreover, men are cruel to outsiders, "ugly ducklings" like Rimbaud; they try to scare them into line, even as they defend their own vulnerable sensitivities by this rough and gruff technique. Rimbaud's experience during the Commune ("Le Cœur volé") obviously did not help in this regard.[1]

Rimbaud's vision is more than personal; it overlaps with the whole fabric of the male-dominated modern city in a Western democracy like France. It is full of militant and missionary types, and the many *rôles* he discusses in various texts ("Enfance," "Vies," "Jeunesse," etc.): priests, soldiers, all the *métiers* and professions he scorns and rejects in the *Saison en enfer* ("Mauvais sang," "L'Éclair").

> Des drôles très solides. Plusieurs ont exploité vos mondes.

These are mature doers, as in "au service des plus monstrueuses *exploitations* industrielles ou militaires" ("Démocratie"; my italics; note this title); compare "Mouvement": "Ce sont les conquérants du monde," and "la barbarie moderne" of "Villes II."

> Sans besoins, et peu pressés de mettre en œuvre leurs brillantes facultés et leur expérience de vos consciences. Quels hommes mûrs!

"Sans besoins, et peu pressés" is their "coolness," irritating to Rimbaud's emotionality (young Proust admired "the hand that doesn't tremble when it writes" in his virile friend Henri). The rest describes something like Sartre's *docteur Rogé* in *La Nausée*; Sartre was equally enraged and fascinated by this old *salaud* of a doctor who had "seen it all" and who pinned you down with his knowing look.

---

[1] Proust similarly, in *Jean Santeuil*, described his terror of male passers-by as he tentatively approached manhood. Yet he is clearly attracted too (for example to the old General he passionately admired). The combination of extreme attraction and extreme repulsion creates a grotesque, baroque vitality. One version of that fascinating combination in Proust is Charlus, bigger than life—he is as horrid as he is attractive to the adolescent. (See the series of father-figures described in *The Writer's Way in France*, p. 259.) There is a similar "henormous" character in Vanbrugh's play *The Relapse*. Flaubert's *Garçon* and the whole concept of the *hénaurme* is pertinent here, as well as Jarry's *Ubu Roi*. Likewise much of Beckett.

The "expérience de vos consciences" seems to go with other hints of a religious procession of the sort Verlaine describes in his *Confessions*: "de jeunes gens de la ville en robes monacales de diverses couleurs . . . qui m'effrayaient passablement . . . je les appelais 'les fantômes.' "

Being a man is a problem: note, for example, Rimbaud's alienated italicization of the word *homme* in "un jeune, un tout jeune *homme*" ("Les Déserts de l'amour"); or his similar emphasis in "Jeunesse": "*Homme* de constitution ordinaire. . . ."

> Des yeux hébétés à la façon de la nuit d'été, rouges et noirs, tricolores, d'acier piqué d'étoiles d'or; des facies déformés, plombés, blêmis, incendiés; des enrouements folâtres!

Here, like Sartre (who imagines the doctor eaten by cancer), Rimbaud gets some revenge with the "yeux hébétés"; at bottom they are *geworfen*, parts of nature ("nuit d'été"). "Rouges et noirs" is his familiar formula, life and death together; undoubtedly it is only his fantasy—or are they dark and bloodshot?—which sees their eyes in terms of these basic forces, or of the "tricolores" which makes them mere militaristic puppets. The "steel flecked with golden stars" reminds me of Faulkner's description of the eyes of the cowboy sitting on the rail in "Spotted Horses": metallic virility (or his Popeye's tin look). The ravaged aspects of the faces are characteristic of a line-up of males anywhere. As is their "enrouement," hoarseness, sure sign of mature maleness (aftermath of the descent of emotion into the *bas-ventre*). The "fôlatres" is Rimbaud's fascinated double reaction: "It's wild!" Like Montesquieu's Frenchmen vis-à-vis the Persians he might be saying: "Comment peut-on être un homme mûr!"

> La démarche cruelle des oripeaux!—Il y a quelques jeunes,— comment regarderaient-ils Chérubin?—pourvus de voix effray- antes et de quelques ressources dangereuses. On les envoie prendre du dos en ville, affublés d'un *luxe* dégoûtant.

The "tinsel" is the tawdry finery of their role-trappings, military, priestly, or whatever. And "cruel" because it is aggressive, the essence of such male doing, proudly insulting to the beholder as badges or insignia can be. These are the "fils de famille" Rimbaud execrates in the *Saison en enfer* ("Mauvais sang"). The young are already dangerous with frightening voices. Beaumarchais's charming and tender Chérubin seems poles away, so Rimbaud asks, "How would they look upon him?" Clearly, he identi- fies more with *that* adolescent. Their strutting and luxury—bourgeois, military, etc.—is offensive at this point. Rimbaud is *hors de lui* as he strolls about the city ("en ville") in much the same spirit as Roquentin promenades among the Sunday-dressed bourgeoisie of Bouville (*La Nausée*).

> O le plus violent Paradis de la grimace enragée!

"Paradis" here comes from the sound of "Parade." Priests seem especially involved here, perhaps in a religious procession—but I suspect a broader vision, including all men with *missions*. The "enraged grimace" is his extreme alienation-attraction once again. For he admires their grim set purpose even if he fears its violence. Thus in "Enfance," the names of primitive places were "férocement grecs . . . celtiques," etc., befitting hardy ancestors of the savage sort he encountered in "Le Bateau ivre" (see "sauvage," last line here), once he had let go the haulers' ropes.

> Pas de comparaison avec vos Fakirs et les autres bouffonneries scéniques.

This is Rimbaud's way of dealing with these fearsome males: he makes them into a comic spectacle, like fakirs to a Westerner.

> Dans des costumes improvisés avec le goût du mauvais rêve ils jouent des complaintes, des tragédies de malandrins et de demi-dieux spirituels comme l'histoire ou les religions ne l'ont jamais été.

He continues to make them into mere actors, ham ones at that, with bad taste, playing at being demi-gods (here Rimbaud betrays envy . . .) with fancier "tragic" doings than those of religion and history.

> Chinois, Hottentots, bohémiens, niais, hyènes, Molochs, vieilles démences, démons sinistres, il mêlent les tours populaires, maternels, avec les poses et les tendresses bestiales. Ils interpréteraient des pièces nouvelles et des chansons "bonnes filles." Maîtres jongleurs, ils transforment le lieu et les personnes et usent de la comédie magnétique. Les yeux flambent, le sang chante, les os s'élargissent, les larmes et des filets rouges ruissellent.

After reducing them to a ridiculous list of grotesque exotics or play-actors, he sees them as part of the stream of evolution, coming down out of the night of time, "vieilles démences," with their old violences and evils, "démons sinistres."[2] Then he indicates that they have a disconcerting capacity to combine opposite qualities (cf. "Génie") but for low purposes: thus they know how to be nice, gentle, solicitous ("populaires"), even "maternal," as well as bestial. But even the brutality has its "tender" aspect as nature has its "pose" side (as Pascal would say, it is a "first custom"). So Rimbaud does justice to the complexity of all men.

Nor does he make things easy for himself. These men are flexible, adaptable, open to the new—"pièces nouvelles"—and have their own gentility: they are capable of singing "songs for good girls." Thus Rimbaud ambiguously mocks and admires the suppleness of modern scientists and philosophers, in "Mauvais sang": "On a tout repris . . . les remèdes de bonnes femmes et les chansons populaires arrangées." In fact these modern types are "master jugglers" and can use all the magic devices Rimbaud can, or artists can generally: "ils transforment le lieu . . . magnétique." Obviously, Rimbaud is not immune to this charisma (James Joyce's Shaun, Saul Bellow's extroverts, reveal the same amusingly protean and fascinating complexities). He describes intense emotive effects on "eyes," etc., his own not excluded.

In this section, Rimbaud seems to be haunted by father-figures in a dream or obscure vision, the male equivalents of the phenomena described in terms of an awesome mother-figure in "Being beauteous." Here: "Les yeux flambent, le sang chante, les os s'élargissent, les larmes et des filets rouges ruissellent." There: "des blessures écarlates et noires [cf. the "rouges et noirs" above] éclatent dans les chairs superbes . . . nos os sont revêtus d'un nouveau corps amoureux." In the "tears" I find a note of the deprived boy's sorrow. Tears[3] are an essence of a frustrated male-male relationship.[4]

> Leur raillerie ou leur terreur dure une minute, ou des mois entiers.

This is the haunting quality of mature males, the authoritative adult world at the end of "Le Bateau ivre."

> J'ai seul la clef de cette parade sauvage.

[2] Cf. the "chinois" of "L'Homme juste." For many Frenchmen as well as for Rimbaud the word *chinois* conveyed the essence of everything exotic, pleasantly different (for almost every Frenchman, it goes without saying, Montesquieu's "Comment peut-on être Persan?" can be generalized into "Comment peut-on ne pas être Français?"). See the expressions "casse-tête chinois," "chinois" (tricky), etc.

[3] See *The Writer's Way in France*, chapter on the Hunt.

[4] The described phenomena are inner ones, hence mainly applicable to the subject, Rimbaud, though it is possible to see them as projected into the transformed *personnes* (or even the men themselves).

274

The proud boasting (as in the series of "J'ai . . ." of "Le Bateau ivre") is offset by the timid obscurantism. In "Vies" he claims he has found "la clef de l'amour," and that is equally unconvincing.

Antique

> Gracieux fils de Pan! Autour de ton front couronné de fleurettes et de baies tes yeux, des boules précieuses, remuent. Tachées de lies brunes, tes joues se creusent. Tes crocs luisent. Ta poitrine ressemble à une cithare, des tintements circulent dans tes bras blonds. Ton cœur bat dans ce ventre où dort le double sexe. Promène-toi, la nuit, en mouvant doucement cette cuisse, cette seconde cuisse et cette jambe de gauche.

There is not much to go on here. The text presents a fairly coherent expression of something graciously Greek and partly animal (maybe a centaur), but I am not sure it is worth trying to identify it. In "Villes, I" "les centauresses séraphiques évoluent parmi les avalanches," and the suggestion there of slinky indolent or insolent motion seems to echo this creature's movement.

In "Soleil et chair" Rimbaud sang:

> Je regrette les temps de l'*antique* [my italics] jeunesse,
> Des satyres lascifs, des faunes animaux

and hymned the live fluids

> L'eau du fleuve, le sang rose des arbres verts
> Dans les veines de Pan mettaient un univers.

Here we have a "son" of that natural pagan *antique* era and that all-embracing Pan; likewise the "tintements [qui] circulent dans tes bras" seem to come from that same primal sap-source. The "tinkle" (cf. the dream-flowers of "Enfance"), like the associated music of the *cithare* of the breast goes back probably to the Pythagorean music of the spheres (see "Ma Bohème"), or Greek *harmony* in an ambiguous sense (see the second "Lettre du Voyant": "la poésie grecque, Vie harmonieuse").

The puzzling creature is obviously close to his creator. One thinks of the superbly naked and brown-skinned ephebe of "Les Sœurs de charité," and this creature's cheeks are "Tachées de lies brunes." The closely related figure of "Tête de faune" had a similar wine-dreg appearance: "Brunie et sanglante ainsi qu'un vin vieux, / Sa lèvre. . . ." In the shadowy park background behind all this may be Verlaine's old and brown "vieux faune

275

de terre cuite" (*Fêtes galantes*: "Le Faune"). The "white teeth" of "Tête de faune" are vaguely reflected in the shining "crocs" here.

But all this does not tell us what the thing really is, when Rimbaud saw him, etc. P. Arnoult guesses at a statue of a centaur in the Louvre. This is possible and would explain the hint of three legs (two thighs and a left leg) implying four. Plus the "bras." Maurice de Guérin's *Centaure* is another possibility. For example, he is comparably withdrawn: "dans les ténèbres d'un séjour reculé . . . au plus épais de l'ombre"; he is associated with a musical instrument: "Apollon . . . ayant mis sa lyre sur cette pierre, y laissa cette mélodie. . . ."

The heart is seen as beating in the "stomach," which is anatomically surprising, though not far off the norm. This emphasizes the animality and leads quickly to the "double sex." Apparently there is a feeling of hermaphroditism about the creature ("dort" implies it is not aroused, I suppose): "hors . . . de tout sexe" ("Solde"). Rimbaud wants it to move around. That means he is attracted to it, empathizes with it, and enjoys the idea of seeing it in motion. Animal grace, the movement of horses and such, *is* a pleasant thing to behold and feel into: all that muscled flesh harmoniously, rhythmically, naturally, almost insolently, consenting to function.

Why at night? It seems almost as if Rimbaud is afraid that such beauty is vulnerable in daytime (cf. "Est-elle almée?" and the "luxe nocturne" of "Vagabonds"). The creature comes shyly out of the night of time (Pan is dead) and perhaps is at home, or safer, in shadows, in mystery.

Being beauteous

The title may be construed either nominally as meaning "*a* Being who is beauteous" or verbally as in a phrase such as "being beauteous is costly." It comes to much the same thing, although I slightly prefer the first reading because of the expression "un Être de Beauté" in the initial sentence. What, then, is the Being? Essentially a mood that arises and "hits" the poet like the spirit of "Génie," only with the feminine (and maternal) emphasis, rather than the male (and fatherly) emphasis of "Génie."

The giddy rising of the mood is like the Christmas whirlwind of delight in "Les Étrennes des orphelins," the delirious "vertiges" he will boast of fixing in "Délires II." In the second "Lettre du Voyant" we read: "j'assiste à l'éclosion de ma pensée [poétique] . . . la symphonie fait son remuement dans les profondeurs, ou vient d'un bond sur la scène." And there are many other such from-the-depths ecstasies, whether creatively inspirational or passive, in "Matinée d'ivresse," "Royauté," "Phrases," etc.

The Being is clearly feminine, maternal: "notre mère de beauté." She is part of a long list of such awe-inspiring creatures, often called "Elle." With her "haute taille"—cf. the "géantes [qui] tournoient" in "Enfance"— she is like the giant apparition at the crossroads in the garden of Nerval's *Aurélia*, summing up the eternally returning lineage of Nerval's women, beginning with his own mother or the archetypal mystic version of her, the Goddess (cf. Robert Graves' *The White Goddess*).[1]

The essence of a strict mother, like Rimbaud's, is someone who is usually cold and absent and then, suddenly, there is a fantastic sweetness.[2] Hence her beauty is pitted against a snow-scene in an extreme daemonic contrast like the poignant embers versus the chilly night-forest of the *Sorcière* in "Après le déluge" (cf. "Matinée d'ivresse": "anges de flame et de glace"). Anna Karenina's universal appeal—her red lips warm against the northern city's flurries—is of this exquisite order. Thus in "Les Déserts de l'amour" the mother-figure "d'une noblesse maternelle . . . la Femme que j'ai vue dans la Ville" disappears into "la nuit sourde et . . . la fuite du bonheur. C'était comme une nuit d'hiver, avec une neige pour étouffer le monde décidément . . . Elle n'est pas revenue et ne reviendra jamais." In "Métropolitain" there is "Le matin où avec Elle, vous vous débattîtes parmi les éclats de neige . . . —ta force." (Cf. "par des nuits d'hiver . . . une voix étreignait mon cœur gêlé . . . te voilà, c'est la force," "Mauvais sang.") This is the feminine voice of life ("force") that comes despite the cold. In "Barbare" the voice comes to him with overwhelming beauty from a chilly absence, a distance: "O Douceurs, ô monde, ô musique! . . . et la voix féminine arrivée au fond des volcans et des grottes arctiques." In a real sense (as in Mallarmé's "Don du poème," "O . . . berceuse . . . ta voix rappelant viole et clavecin") the pure feminine voice *is* music for Rimbaud.

> Devant une neige un Être de Beauté de haute taille.

The "neige" is the infinite and cold purity from which miracles of beauty are born, like Venus from the sea. The image is found in "Ophélie" ("belle comme la neige") and "Comédie de la soif": "Dites-moi la neige . . . Dites-moi la mer" (the two are fused together in "Le Bateau ivre"). In "Fairy" there is "ses yeux et sa danse supérieures encore aux éclats précieux, aux influences froides."

In "Phrases" She appears briefly, bigger than life (in a sense, in "Métropolitain," where he struggles against her and for her, She *is* his life): "Quelle sorcière va se dresser sur le couchant blanc?"

[1] Compare Baudelaire's "C'est Elle! noire et pourtant lumineuse" in "Un Fantôme," and also his "Géante" and the *Elle* in the preface of the *Paradis Artificiels*.

[2] In *Portnoy's Complaint* by Philip Roth the mother is alternately a witch with a knife and a creature of fantastic sweetness standing before a summer window.

> Des sifflements de mort et des cercles de musique sourde font monter, s'élargir et trembler comme un spectre ce corps adoré; des blessures écarlates et noires éclatent dans les chairs superbes.

She emerges spirally from coils of the psyche (like Redon's organic visions), alternating Eros and Thanatos; the "circles of music" are the positive coils, the "sifflements de mort" are like serpent-coils of negation.[3] The vision rises and trembles, vibrant with wondrous feeling. The scarlet and black "blessures" are another coupling of life and death forces (as in the numerous such pairs, beginning with "Les Étrennes des orphelins"; "l'Homme saigné noir" of "L'Étoile a pleuré rose"; the "sang noir" of "Les Mains de Jeanne-Marie"). The major equivalent is the red embers and black night of "Après le déluge"; an exact parallel to those bleeding-delight ember-wounds is found in Hopkins' "Windhover": "blue-bleak embers, ah my dear, / Fall, gall themselves, and gash gold-vermilion." Baudelaire wrote "le rouge et le noir représentent la vie, une vie surnaturelle et excessive, ce cadre noir rend le regard plus profond et plus singulier" (*Le Peintre de la vie moderne*).

As J.-P. Richard notes, the "éclate" here is a bursting forth of excessive life-blood, like an overripe fruit (Mallarmé's pomegranate) and is parallel to the flowers ("éclatent") and even the "éclatantes" flies of "Voyelles." This is the process of metamorphosis, when a state of being reaches its limit and "bursts" into another state.

> Les couleurs propres de la vie se foncent, dansent, et se dégagent autour de la Vision, sur le chantier.

A dance of life-beauty. "Chantier," as in "Bonne pensée du matin," has an overtone of "song" combined with the notion of creativity (workyard). The *dégagement* is Rimbaud's usual break to freedom as in "L'Éternité" or "Génie."

> Et les frissons s'élèvent et grondent, et la saveur forcenée de ces effets se chargeant avec les sifflements mortels et les rauques musiques que le monde, loin derrière nous, lance sur notre mère de beauté,—elle recule, elle se dresse. Oh! nos os sont revêtus d'un nouveau corps amoureux.

The shivers are the ambivalent delight in cold, the essence of his mother. Perhaps she is glimpsed in her furs in winter (as Baudelaire recalled).[4]

---

[3] Mallarmé's Igitur hears "sifflements" of derisive dead ancestors in the staircase-coil of his past-intestines.

[4] In a study of Constantin Guys, Baudelaire speaks of remembrances of furs, as a prominent part of the *mundus muliebris* in every poet's childhood.

Thus in "Fairy": "Pour l'enfance d'Hélène frissonèrent les fourrures et les ombres . . . éclats . . . influences froides." The shiver of *ombelles* was associated with "Elle," his mother, in "Mémoire" (cf. "Voyelles": "frissons d'ombelles").

The rest of the sentence is clear. The new liquid delight of the bones (with "filial tears and bloody wounds") we have seen in "Parade": "Les yeux flambent . . . les os s'élargissent, les larmes et des filets rouges ruissellent." In the *Saison en enfer* he will say "L'amour est à réinventer." In "A une raison" "le nouvel amour" comes with "la nouvelle harmonie."

> O la face cendrée, l'écusson de crin, les bras de cristal!

This is mysterious. The ashen face is ghastly fear at this hint of maternal incest and death-wish as in Keats' "La Belle Dame Sans Merci" or those associated moments when he saw his mother's horrid death-face.[5] The closest note in Rimbaund is the "lèvres vertes" of "Elle," in the death-struggle of the cold night of "Métropolitain."

The "écusson de crin" is perhaps her hairy pudenda, recalling "Remembrances du vieillard idiot": "ma mère, avec sa cuisse . . . me donna ces chaleurs que l'on tait"; or the sister with "sa lèvre / D'en bas." Compare the "corset velu" of "Voyelles" and the "satin touffu" of the *Stupra*.

"Crystal arms" are the lightness of her springtime beauty as in the "air léger" of the next sentence; cf. "Villes, I," "chalets de cristal . . . qui se meuvent sur . . . des poulies invisibles," the ultimate refinement of mechanics, bones of the Being, appearing transparent as sheer air.

> Le canon sur lequel je dois m'abattre à travers la mêlée des arbres et de l'air léger!

This last is like the sacrificial hurling of self into a level confrontation with mother-nature in a light mood of trees and air, as in "Bannières de mai" (except that the nature was male as well as female there). Note the ar effect in "arbres-air" (and the liquid r also in "léger"); compare "L'air léger et charmant" in "Proses évangéliques," no. 2.

The "mêlée" here reminds me of a battle of trees in Robert Graves' account of the White Goddess, or of Tchelitchew's organic painting (*Hide and Seek*) in the New York Museum of Modern Art, where embryos grow from branches, and veins of children and trees are confused (cf. the "vignes et veines enchevêtrées" of "Bannières de mai"). To overcome incest-fear is a moment of truth as in war: to hurl oneself against a cannon, in love-death. Thus in "Mauvais sang" Rimbaud imagines "le

---

[5] See Aileen Ward's *John Keats, The Making of a Poet*, p. 340.

canon!" as overcoming his last resistance to a moment of grace, parallel to the exquisite vision following "Général, bombarde-nous" in "Alchimie du verbe." The victory is a vision which is as *good* as having the mother: *Being beauteous.*

The turbulent crisis of his emotions is readily expressed in images of war, or related baroque scenes of disaster, fire, storm. Thus in "Mauvais sang," the maternal suggestions in "la lampe circule dans la chambre voisine, comme un trésor dans la forêt" leads to "une mer [cf. mère] de flammes et de fumée au ciel; et à gauche, à droite [cf. the many other theatrical settings] toutes les richesses flambant comme un milliard de tonnerres . . . orgie . . . femmes." This is both the whirlwind (above) and the fiery sunset battle (as in "Mystique," q.v.).[6]

Flaubert, in an early story, "Ivre et mort," describes a similar hallucinatory vision:

> Le monde avait fini avec ses douleurs et ses amertumes, tout tournait devant eux en images fugitives et errantes, sans suite, comme une ronde de fées vêtues de toutes les couleurs, et qui passaient en tourbillonant. . . .
>
> Des clartés inconnues, des lueurs, des jours apparaissaient tout à coup sur les murailles, s'élargissaient sur la suie de la cheminée, montaient en réseaux et en gerbes de feu. . . .

Vies

In "Enfance," part IV, we witnessed the child's first glimmerings of possible roles, as the lifelong quest for Identity—that ever-receding mirage of a final love-death consummation of self with self—gets well under way in the young Rimbaud remembered there. "Vies" examines further some possible paths glimpsed there and adds some new possibilities: the saint, the walker, the savant. In "Alchimie du verbe," Rimbaud writes: "A chaque être, plusieurs *autres* vies me semblaient dues." Here are some of his.

I

> O les énormes avenues du pays saint, les terrasses du temple! Qu'a-t-on fait du brahmane qui m'expliqua les Proverbes? D'alors, de là-bas, je vois encore même les vieilles!

---

[6] Hérodiade's crisis leads to similarly apocalyptic and frighteningly beautiful effects (cf. also Mallarmé's "Victorieusement fui"; "Tison de gloire, sang par écume").

This seems to extend the sentence in "Enfance," IV, which begins: "Je suis le saint. . . ." The attraction here is the horizontal calm, the serenity of such a saintly prospect, reflected concretely in the huge avenues—utterly restful as on that quiet summer day in "Bruxelles" on the boulevard du Régent—and in the terraces of the solid temple. The flat a's (and discreet mute e's) in "avenues . . . terrasses . . . brahmane" (and "là-bas," below) have much to do with this appeal.[1] Mainly, of course, he is thinking of that idealized Orient we have seen in various poems and will see often again, "Asie" (again with that a: thus Ravel's "Asie" in *Shéhérazade* is sweepingly *largo*, as is Baudelaire's "langoureuse Asie" in "La Chevelure"). Israel is part of Asia and so is India: both could be the *pays saint*. The "brahmane" puts emphasis on India (and Suzanne Bernard sees the "Proverbes" as being the *Vedas*; perhaps Rimbaud got his figure from Voltaire's well-known *Histoire d'un bon bramin*), but we need not be too specific here: one scene melts into another for Rimbaud's mercurial fantasy, which is an ideal and yet very tangibly real place of spiritual repose.

The "vieilles" add earthy reality, as in Baudelaire's "Tableaux parisiens" or Rimbaud's biblical sketches with their scattered gritty urban scenes.

> Je me souviens des heures d'argent et de soleil vers les fleuves, la main de la campagne sur mon épaule, et de nos caresses debout dans les plaines poivrées,—Un envol de pigeons écarlates tonne autour de ma pensée.

Here the fantasy becomes country-lyrical. The "hours of silver and sun toward the rivers" remind one of the "rivière / Accrochant follement aux herbes des haillons / D'argent" of "Le Dormeur du val." The personification of country as lover (*compagne-campagne*) is like "Sensation" and, later, "Aube"; it may be vaguely influenced by Vigny's "La Maison du berger."

The "peppery plains" are like the crow-flecked fields of "Les Corbeaux" and "La Rivière de Cassis" (cf. Van Gogh's field landscapes); later, in "Démocratie" we may get a passing mysterious glimpse of them in the "pays poivrés." Birds are very likely in his mind here, since pigeons thunder and slap up and whirl around in the next sentence. Their somber and sober quality is savored, as in the "campagne aigre . . . sobre" of part II. The pigeons are "scarlet" because that, as we have seen, is the color of life; maybe also a sunset red. They are the swarming life of Vision, like the "million d'oiseaux d'or." Doves swooped up more gently with, and like, the rays of the dawn of "Le Bateau ivre."

---

[1] See *Toward the Poems of Mallarmé*, pp. 265-66.

It is a curious fact, noted by Bouillane de Lacoste, that "red" pigeons ("red turbets") figure on a list of English words Rimbaud jotted down.

> —Exilé ici, j'ai eu une scène où jouer les chefs-d'œuvre drama-
> tiques de toutes les littératures. Je vous indiquerais les richesses
> inouïes. J'observe l'histoire des trésors que vous trouvâtes. Je
> vois la suite!

As in "Les Poètes de sept ans," or "Parade," the dispossessed and "exiled" (see part II) child possesses all in his creative compensation: his little inner stages or scenes. The bragging about psychic riches is very characteristic: see later "Solde," "Nuit de l'enfer," "Nocturne vulgaire." The "history of treasures" that others found and the "suite" are like the genetic vision of art Rimbaud describes in the "Lettre du voyant."

> Ma sagesse est aussi dédaignée que le chaos. Qu'est mon néant,
> auprès de la stupeur qui vous attend?

He knows his vision is inaccessible to others. He sees it as the "nothing" from which everything is born, which is a momentarily "saintly" idea, lose all to gain all (or almost . . .). But then he is boyish and vindictive: when they *do* catch on, their "stupeur"—like the gaping hole of open mouths[2]— will be greater than his nothingness.

II

> Je suis un inventeur bien autrement méritant que tous ceux
> qui m'ont précédé; un musicien même, qui ai trouvé quelque
> chose comme la clef de l'amour.

This is simply more bragging about a role he will excel at ("inventeur"). Music and love indeed are the essential "keys" to art like Rimbaud's. The "music" is the metaphor of pure creation as in the second "Lettre du voyant" (cf. the "maison musicale" of "Phrases").

> A présent, gentilhomme d'une campagne aigre au ciel sobre,
> j'essaye de m'émouvoir au souvenir de l'enfance mendiante, de
> l'apprentissage ou de l'arrivée en sabots, des polémiques, des
> cinq ou six veuvages, et quelques noces où ma forte tête
> m'empêcha de monter au diapason des camarades.

[2] Compare Mallarmé's "Toast funèbre": "Vaste gouffre apporté dans l'amas de la brume / par l'irascible vent des mots qu'il n'a pas dits . . . ."

This seems to be a real look around at Roche,[3] his mother's farm where he was "exiled," perhaps after the trial or just as any child is caught in the family house in summer, as in the "Chanson de la plus haute tour" where the same word *veuvage* was prominent. He reminds one curiously of that earlier country gentleman in *his* tower, Montaigne. (Is that -agne in "campagne" and aig- in "aigre" an echo? He likes the former and repeats it together with the Montaigne-word *skepticism*.)

From here on Rimbaud seems to be a part of the *historique* of his inventory (cf. "histoire" above) by stirring up the recollections (cf. "mon imagination et mes souvenirs," "Adieu") that will go into his art ("j'essaye de m'émouvoir"). The "enfance mendiante" recalls, in addition to the "piéton" of "Enfance," his earlier flights (e.g., to Paris), memorialized again in "L'Impossible" of the *Saison en enfer*: "cette vie de mon enfance, la grande route par tous les temps, sobre [see the "sobre" here] surnaturellement, plus désintéressé que le meilleur des mendiants. . . ."

The "apprentissage" and arrival in "sabots" is like a scene from "Ouvriers": some memory of coming to a village or city, working, the ruggedly ingrained realistic poetry of living.

The "cinq ou six veuvages" refers no doubt to some or all of his losses: father, mother (in a sense), then his dead sister, Vitalie, Izambard, perhaps the girl of "Roman," Verlaine, etc. The "Chanson de la plus haute tour" tells of similar abandonment: "Mille veuvages / De la si pauvre âme."

The "noces" are vague, perhaps some poets in Paris, e.g., "les amis" of "Comédie de la soif." Here he may be regretting his well-known sulking in their company as in the painting by Fantin-Latour: *Le Coin de table*.

> Je ne regrette pas ma vieille part de gaîté divine: l'air sobre de cette aigre campagne alimente fort activement mon atroce scepticisme.

The divine gaiety is maybe the "noces" or perhaps some past pleasures amidst others, or just a more active and meaningful era as he looks back from this stagnant exile. He sees himself as becoming more and more sulking, "sceptical" and arid.

> Mais comme ce scepticisme ne peut désormais être mis en œuvre, et que d'ailleurs je suis dévoué à un trouble nouveau,—j'attends de devenir un très méchant fou.

---

[3] Roche as it appeared to me in the spring of 1970 is a beautiful place; but maybe in the heat of summer and in the hopelessness of Rimbaud's condition it appeared quite different.

He can not even make use of the scepticism—does this mean that he is abandoning literature as in the *Saison en enfer*? Then comes a reference to a new problem in his life, which is preventing his development. So he sees only nasty madness ahead. That too is a role. It is unclear what the problem is, and it is of no consequence to art: indeed this part is disappointing from that viewpoint.

III

> Dans un grenier où je fus enfermé à douze ans j'ai connu le monde, j'ai illustré la comédie humaine. Dans un cellier j'ai appris l'histoire.

This "grenier" is like the attic of "Les Poètes de sept ans" where he wrote or read novels of adventure. The cellar recalls the tombeau of "Enfance," part V. Both are places of exile, tomb-like isolation where art and adventure seem to incubate.

> A quelque fête de nuit dans une cité du Nord, j'ai rencontré toutes les femmes des anciens peintres.

"Est-elle almée?" tells of such a nocturnal festival, a masked ball, which is a more frivolous, visual, and fantastic—in sum, theatrical—version of the previously mentioned "Comédie humaine." Among influences from old painters one thinks naturally of Hélène Fourment, Rubens' wife. (He was of a *cité du Nord*, in Flanders.)

> Dans un vieux passage à Paris on m'a enseigné les sciences classiques.

This recalls the "bibliothèque" of the savant in "Enfance" but combines it with a prestigious and old place in fertile Paris: the mysterious "vieux passage" seems to lead to the past (*passé*) and dead glories.

> Dans une magnifique demeure cernée par l'Orient entier j'ai accompli mon immense œuvre et passé mon illustre retraite.

Here his dream-wish of glorious accomplishment in solitude has as its fantasy-backdrop its customary total site of magic, of juvenile omnipotence, Rimbaud's "entire" Orient: "Je retournais à l'Orient et à la sagesse première et éternelle" ("L'Impossible").

> J'ai brassé mon sang.

This recalls the monstrous "work" he promises to do on himself in the second "Lettre du voyant": "Ineffable torture où il a besoin de toute la foi."

> Mon devoir m'est remis. Il ne faut même plus songer à cela.
> Je suis réellement d'outre-tombe, et pas de commissions.

This resembles the ambiguous end of the *Saison en enfer* (which is not too surprising in the sense that "Every poem [is] an epitaph," T. S. Eliot). Rimbaud was almost always bidding farewell to his *old self*, that is why he is so original. His duty is handed back and exchanged for a new one. "Solde" will tell us more of such wholesale liquidations. This giving up and going into a grave, "back to scratch" (cf. the room-tomb of "Enfance") is the same experience described in "Nuit de l'enfer" where he announces "nous sommes hors du monde." He opts out; this is the meaning of "pas de commissions," as in "Solde" where he uses the exact same expression in the same sense, only negatively: "Les vendeurs ne sont pas à bout de solde! Les voyageurs n'ont pas à rendre leurs commission de si tôt" (Bernard, p. 293).

Départ

> Assez vu. La vision s'est rencontrée à tous les airs. Assez eu.
> Rumeurs des villes, le soir, et au soleil, et toujours.
> Assez connu. Les arrêts de la vie.—O Rumeurs et Visions!
> Départ dans l'affection et le bruit neufs!

We might say, with Rimbaud: "On ne part pas" ("Mauvais sang"); or we might add, in his spirit, "On ne s'arrête pas" (Goethe's "Verweile doch du bist so schön"), since "il y a des auberges qui pour toujours n'ouvrent déjà plus" ("Métropolitain"). But there are days when one leaves and stays at once. These are the glorious moments of threshold, the moments of boats trembling in the port, charged with the electricity of potential departure such as we will see in "Adieu"—"Un grand vaisseau . . . agite ses pavillons multicolores sous les brises du matin"—and have seen in Baudelaire's "L'Invitation au voyage."[1] That is what—despite the seemingly clear distinction between something left behind and something new—the poetry is about, or is, in this little piece.

The title has the transparent sound of ar, echoed in the "airs" (cf. the "mêlée des arbres et de l'air" in "Being beauteous" and "L'air léger et

---

[1]
> Vois sur ces canaux
> Dormir ces vaisseaux
> Dont l'humeur est vagabonde . . .

charmant" of "Proses évangéliques," and, especially, Baudelaire's "Parfum exotique" which has a dozen such effects). It is like the airy space over railroad tracks as one is about to go away! The station was obviously one of Rimbaud's favorite places of vibrant potential delight, of staying-and-going, as in that "charmante station du chemin de fer, / Au cœur d'un mont" in "Bruxelles." The *Génie* represents both the "charme" of fleeting places and the superhuman delight of "stations."

Rimbaud says goodbye to all that, he has *seen* enough of what he is leaving, perhaps the town behind him and the visions he has had in it heretofore. It is like saying goodbye to his poetry at the end of *Une Saison en enfer*. But does he? Well, yes and no. All authentic poetry hedges in this sense. "Nier A c'est affirmer A derrière une grille" (Valéry). That vision, those "airs," die hard. . . . The rumors are what he has *had* ("eu"). These faint stirrings of distant cities in the evening or in the sun—they are the essence of that poetic hovering as in "Il [le Génie] a fait la maison ouverte . . . à la rumeur de l'été" or Verlaine's:

> Mon Dieu, mon Dieu la vie est là
> Simple et tranquille.
> Cette paisible rumeur-là
> Vient de la ville.
>
> ("Le ciel est, par-dessus le toit")

"Rumeur," like art, is reality refined, made suggestive, through filtering distance: both here and there. "La ville, avec sa fumée et ses bruits de métiers, nous suivait très loin dans les chemin: O l'autre monde . . ." ("Ouvriers").

The "soir" is like that "soirée frissonnante" in which a boat hovers off shore ("Promontoire"). He pretends to dismiss the "arrêts," those repeated wayside inns. . . . But we are totally undeceived by that poignant cry: "O Rumeurs et Visions!" It is an ambivalence screwed to the breaking point.[2]

The "new affection" reminds one of the "nouvel amour" of "A une raison" and the "re-invented love" of "Délires I," or the "affection" of the pied-piper "Génie." The "new noise" is like the latter's piping ("ses souffles"); but is it, by definition, anything more than new *Rumors*? For this hail to departure is made on a sort of shore, is fixed on a page. *On part et on ne part pas* (just as, in "Nuit de l'enfer," he says: "Il n'y a personne ici et il y a quelqu'un"). The word "Départ" contains the excruciating word *art*. Still, there are times when the dream of breaking

---

[2] It resembles Quentin Compson's scream to the obsessive South: "I *don't* hate you!"

away from it all, including "all the books," seems the sole meaningful impulse: "Fuir! là-bas, fuir! Je sens que des oiseaux sont ivres . . ." (Mallarmé's "Brise marine"). Rimbaud is this too for us, particularly in this poem: a fresh start in life.

Royauté

> Un beau matin, chez un peuple fort doux, un homme et une femme superbes criaient sur la place publique: "Mes amis, je veux qu'elle soit reine!" "Je veux être reine!" Elle riait et tremblait. Il parlait aux amis de révélation, d'épreuve terminée. Ils se pâmaient l'un contre l'autre.
>
> En effet, ils furent rois toute une matinée où les tentures carminées se relevèrent sur les maisons, et toute l'après-midi, où ils s'avancèrent du côté des jardins de palmes.

Little need be said of this clear gem. We have all seen that flushing adolescent couple come running down a meadow together, being It. And they are.[1]

The atmosphere of the place with its "gentle people" has the Middle Eastern (Palestinian—cf. the Samarie of the "Proses évangéliques" or "Métropolitain"—or vaguely Oriental) calm of the beginning of "Vies." As in that poem, this too is a projected life-role; Baudelaire's prose poem "Les Projets" is probably remembered here: "Comme elle serait belle dans un costume de cour, compliqué et fastueux."

The festival of self lasts a day: it rises with morning light and proceeds through an afternoon toward a quiet evening. In this it is parallel to similar progressions in various of the poems in verse or prose.

There is a suggestion of glory in palms—"ô palmes! diamant!" ("Angoisse")—and even of a Christ-like entry into a Levantine city. Compare "L'air léger et charmant de la Galilée: les habitants le reçurent avec une joie curieuse" ("Proses évangéliques").

A une raison

In "L'Homme juste," Rimbaud had mocked Christ's *raison sereine.* Subsequently he had discovered a "right reason" of his own: "Enfin ô

---

[1] "This royal seasonal festival may justifiably be called the greatest and most central rite of archaic times. . . . From it are derived various specialized ceremonies . . . the marriage ceremony is recognizably descended from this sacred marriage, particularly as evidenced by the Eastern European customs of crowning the bride and groom as 'King and Queen for a Day' " (John W. Perry, *Lord of the Four Quarters,* pp. 22-23).

bonheur, ô raison" ("Délires II"). That is the story of the thorough revolutionary: Nietzsche, who begins by throwing off Judeo-Christian duty, ends with total obedience to the cosmos. Rimbaud's mother's *devoir* (in "Les Poètes de sept ans") was unacceptable, but the *devoir* of "L'Éternité," even more implacable, was his. This is something unfinal, of course, but each poem is a would-be or provisional finality (in an unending asymptotic or Sisyphean quest).

The human—as Aristotle said, "He spontaneously desires infinitely."—is never satisfied, but men even less than women (Rimbaud less than his mother). She has a fertile hollow in her, a fleshly womb. He, deprived of this, has a psychic hollow (Pascal's *le vide*, Baudelaire's *gouffre*, Proust's *néant*). He must fill this void with male creativity. But, in a sense, he is doomed never to fill this void, not in human life. Like the man who has denied God in the Christian scheme, he is fated to rise and fall and rise and fall. Or, less sectarianly, man is never content to be just man, less than IT (in a multiple sense: not woman, not his male model, not God).[1] Malraux's *condition humaine* and Sartre's *passion inutile* are in line here. But Rimbaud knew days of provisional triumph when *en-soi* and *pour-soi* seemed to coalesce (fire and rose are one, as Dante and T. S. Eliot saw it; or, as Breton put it, night and day cease to be seen as contraries). "L'Éternité" was such a moment. "Génie" will be another. "A une raison" is in the same spirit, although closer to "Génie" (more masculine) than to "L'Éternité."[2]

The Fatherly God-like *Génie* is an acceptable (original) *raison*: "raison merveilleuse et imprévue." He represents pure *amor fati*: "machine aimée des qualités fatales." This, in a sense, "metallic" necessity ("c'est trop beau! mais c'est nécessaire," "Est-elle aimée?") is essentially virile, with obvious affinities to the military: "L'ordre, éternal veilleur" ("L'Homme juste"). We have noted, in our Introduction (p. 25), the connection here with "Général . . . bombarde-nous" in "Alchimie du verbe." "A une raison" is full of such effects.

"Raison" has an echo of rai-, light-ray (which was the "arm" of the Général in the passage cited above, cf. the similar piercing "rayon" of "Bannières de mai") and *résonne*, the synesthetic equivalent of light, significant sound. Thus the -son of "raison" is echoed by "tous les sons" in the first line (as in "Génie": "l'Adoration . . . sonne, sa promesse sonne").[3]

---

[1] In a sense, man invests his feminine-self (anima) in the woman-figure, then mates with himself through her; this union approaches the suprasexual divine, Breton's "androgyne primordial."

[2] The *Génie* will include an *éternité* but revised in mood.

[3] See *L'Œuvre de Mallarmé*, p. 28.

As in "Mémoire," each musical sound, each ray of light, is an angelic sun-son ("fils du Soleil," "Vagabonds").[4]

> Un coup de ton doigt sur le tambour décharge tous les sons et commence la nouvelle harmonie.

This is akin to all sorts of cosmogonies. The first "coup" releasing all the others is very like the beginning of Mallarmé's "Un Coup de dés" as well as Vico's initial Thunderclap (the notion was taken up by Joyce in *Finnegans Wake*). This is a new creation, "repeating" in the Kierkegaardean sense the old. The "drum" gives it a military and/or primitive quality.

> Un pas de toi c'est la levée des nouveaux hommes et leur en marche.

The image is clear and warlike: one step of this giant releases thousands of ours; compare "Génie": "Son pas! les migrations plus énormes que les anciennes invasions." It evokes "Qu'est-ce pour nous, mon cœur" ("Noirs inconnus, si nous allions!") and the dark allies of the *Saison en enfer*: "la marche des peuples" ("Matin").

> Ta tête se détourne: le nouvel amour! Ta tête se retourne:—le nouvel amour!

The multiple faces of love, of spiritual vitality, are similarly seen in "Génie": "O . . . ses têtes."

The swiveling of the head, moreover, is a wooden masculine gesture of affection, reminding one of the abrupt "right face" of military homage, and it may just possibly recall the long-ago game of "peekaboo" with his father or just his miraculous consent to appear, after a prolonged absence: "Cela commença sous les rires des enfants, cela finira par eux . . . notre très pur amour" ("Matinée d'ivresse"). That combination of hardness and beauty is male, like the "machine aimée des qualités fatales" of "Génie." Men love by *relenting*: "l'épouvante de sa concession" ("Génie"). This is the fascination of the grim cowboy's eyes suddenly turning "pleasant" in Faulkner's "Spotted Horses."

Rolland de Renéville has suggested a connection between the idea of *numen* (divinity) and its etymon *nuo* (I nod). This seems far-fetched.

---

[4] The *fil-fils* (thread-son) ambiguity, exploited in "Mémoire," is matched in Mallarmé's "Une dentelle s'abolit": "Filial on aurait pu naître." Norman Brown in *Love's Body*, p. 74, discusses this idea-cluster.

> "Change nos lots, crible les fléaux, à commencer par le temps,"
> te chantent ces enfants. "Élève n'importe où la substance de nos
> fortunes et de nos vœux," on t'en prie.

As with "Génie," Rimbaud's faith and trust in this spirit is childishly
infinite. All evils (plagues) can be crushed by Him or It, even the evil
of "time" ("Le Temps [qui] mange la vie," according to Baudelaire). The
"children" are the same as in "Matinée d'ivresse" and "Enfance": they are
pure in heart and will inherit Rimbaud's earth.

> Arrivée de toujours, qui t'en iras partout.

The "arrival" (of the miracle) always or everywhere "goes away," like
the presence-absence of his own daemonic father. As in "Départ," he
wants to follow. The movement is the lightning-flash which is the essence
of (vertical, male, intense, creative) Spirit or Reason: "raison—ça passe
vite!" ("L'Impossible"). The flash comes only to go: "le temps de se
dissoudre" as Mallarmé noted in a fragment of *Les Noces d'Hérodiade*
referring to the instant vision of St. John. Or "foudre . . . le temps . . .
d'évaporer" in the "Coup de dés." "Au revoir ici, n'importe où" ("Démo-
cratie") is a comparable formula of permanent revolution.

Matinée d'ivresse

A hymn to earthly salvation, a moment of ecstatic vision—Rimbaud's
good, beautiful, true—"Matinée d'ivresse" may have been inspired by
drug-induced euphoria but that is only incidentally pertinent. As Baude-
laire noted at the close of his "Du vin et du haschisch," all you need is
"enthusiasm and will" in order to be intoxicated. So the *poison* may be a
drug, but it could be just the "tortures" (see below) which Baudelaire
also described as leading to explosive creative joys (in "Le Confiteor de
l'artiste"). A *matinée* is a prolongation of Rimbaud's favorite moment
of the day, dawn, cf. "Aube."

> O *mon* Bien! O *mon* Beau! Fanfare atroce où je ne trébuche
> point! Chevalet féerique!

The poem begins with the expression—in terms of the philosophically
classical "good" and "beautiful"—of an absolutely authentic moment of
individuality, when "It" is between self and self, or self and creator-cosmos.
Stirner's *Der Einziger und sein Eigentum* is one example among many of
this nineteenth-century phenomenon *par excellence*.

The "Fanfare atroce" is like the "Clairon plein des strideurs étranges" at the end of "Voyelles": an awe-inspiring, powerful and joyous climax. Again, Baudelaire's "Confiteor" is pertinent: "L'étude du beau est un duel où l'artiste crie de frayeur avant d'être vaincu."

The "chevalet féerique" merely extends this notion. *"Le Beau est toujours bizarre"* (Baudelaire, *Exposition universelle de 1855*).

> Hourra pour l'œuvre inouïe et pour le corps merveilleux, pour la première fois! Cela commença sous les rires des enfants, cela finira par eux.

The "unheard-of work" is the art on the page before us, emerging from this pure experience. The "marvelous body" is both this "homunculus" (*Faust*) or sylph (Mallarmé's "Surgi de la croupe et du bond"), the new creation, a product of male parthenogenesis, a *whole* creature, and also the integration of self in true creativity. This is the pagan Greek ideal—as opposed to Christian dichotomy of soul and body—recaptured by Nietzsche and Rimbaud, of total self-acceptance, acceptance of all that is: "mage ou ange, dispensé de toute morale" ("Adieu").

Rimbaud, ignorant of Nietzsche and of the true Mallarmé, could only assume he was the "first" to achieve this uncompromising wholeness. But like the German Romantic ideal of "das dritte Reich," the return of a Golden Age, expressed in his "Voyant" letters, this is in a sense a *rediscovered* wholeness; the early people had it and children have it, too.

But Rimbaud now integrates more than this: he (spirally) includes his adult sophistication or complexity, the "œuvre inouïe." The explosion of joy in a child's laugh (repeated below) was a pure *beginning*. Perhaps the end he envisages under these auspices will be another pure simplicity, beyond the "work," or perhaps *in* the work, it is hard to say.

> Ce poison va rester dans toutes nos veines même quand, la fanfare tournant, nous serons rendus à l'ancienne inharmonie.

The "poison" has been construed as drugs (see below), but I see it rather as an ambivalent (with negative accent, provocatively, stubbornly, or sulkily clinging to the honest half-awful truth others fear and shun) expression of the pure daemonic experience, just as Baudelaire referred to his beloved Jeanne, or his love for her, as "poison." ("Le Flacon"; see Mallarmé's "même un poison . . . à respirer si nous en périssons," "Le Tombeau de Charles Baudelaire.")

Rimbaud says that even if the experience sours (as in "le rêve fraîchit," of "Veillées," I) and the total harmony of truth and beauty crumbles, he will still believe in this experience, the "method." This clinging to *some* meaning in man, despite the absurd odds, reminds one of Dostoevski (Ivan Karamazov), Kafka, Camus.

> O maintenant, nous si digne de ces tortures! rassemblons fervemment cette promesse surhumaine faite à notre corps et à notre âme créés: cette promesse, cette démence! L'élégance, la science, la violence!

All this is obviously part of a "whole" experience: opposites of knowledge and violence come together like Blake's heaven and hell, "lion and lamb," etc.

> On nous a promis d'enterrer dans l'ombre l'arbre du bien et du mal, de déporter les honnêtetés tyranniques, afin que nous amenions notre très pur amour.

Likewise the categories of good and evil no longer prevail, as Nietzsche would have it (*Beyond Good and Evil*). The "tyrannical honesties" are those of the namby-pamby society, the family, the Church.

> Cela commença par quelques dégoûts et cela finit,—ne pouvant nous saisir sur-le-champ de cette éternité,—cela finit par une débandade de parfums.

The "dégoûts" correspond to the "encrapule" of the "Voyant" letters: it might be drunkenness or general debauchery,[1] even drugs, but mainly it is just the negative phase, the "tortures," which are half of the dialectic that culminates in a synthetic wholeness, according to the Hegelian pattern.

That "scattering of perfumes," volatilization (cf. "Le Flacon"), like a fireworks-explosion, in Joyce (the Gerty MacDowell episode) and Mallarmé ("séparer enfin ses froides pierreries," "Hérodiade"), is an *almost* adequate objective correlative of the experience of total joy. But he did not quite make eternity—just as in "Aube" he only felt the goddess's body *un peu*.

> Rire des enfants, discrétion des esclaves, austérité des vierges, horreur des figures et des objets d'ici, sacrés soyez-vous par le souvenir de cette veille. Cela commençait par toute la rustrerie, voici que cela finit par des anges de flamme et de glace.

---

[1] This might be a more specific reference to homosexual experience, cf. the "noirs parfums" of "Le Bateau ivre" and our comment there. But there are no good grounds for pinning down the experience in this way, other than anecdotal ones.

The last shall be the first, as in the Gospels; these are the underdogs, the humble and deprived: children ("a little child shall lead them"), slaves ("the meek"), virgins (like the suffering creature of "Les Premières Communions"). These are the spiritually promising, as were Faulkner's "children, Indians, and idiots." Humble in origin ("rustrerie"), they will emerge as angels. The "fire and ice" is another union of opposites that sums up a series of such extreme ambivalent delights, beginning in "Les Étrennes des orphelins" and culminating in the snow-and-sparks (or music) of "Being beauteous." Baudelaire describes very similar effects in "Les Paradis artificiels."

> Petite veille d'ivresse, sainte! quand ce ne serait que pour le masque dont tu nous as gratifié.

The mask is probably the work of art (as Yeats spoke of the man and his "masks," in the sense of his works or creative personality), something less than eternity but a fair facsimile.

The drunkenness reminds me of Baudelaire's "Enivrez-vous": "Il faut être toujours ivre."

> Nous t'affirmons, méthode!

The "méthode" is like the one of the *Voyant* letters: primarily the suffering.

> Nous n'oublions pas que tu as glorifié hier chacun de nos âges.

The "âges" refers to the child, with his pure laugh, rediscovered in the self. And by extension, in such integrating moments, all one's successive levels are resuscitated; cf. "Age d'or."

> Nous avons foi au poison. Nous savons donner notre vie tout entière tous les jours.

This is quite clear.

> Voici le temps des *Assassins*.

The "Assassins" are linked to hashish by some critics, because of the common etymology. They will recur in *Une Saison en enfer*. I see them as merely metaphors of the daemonic new artistic self, ruthlessly destructive of the sentimental, or "calumniating" (as Nietzsche would say) old ways.

293

Cf. the "Noirs inconnus" of "Qu'est-ce pour nous," the blacks of the *Saison en enfer*.

Phrases

Antoine Adam thinks this series of "phrases" is grouped in two poems, the first one ending after the third section. I see no such grouping, but rather only separate "phrases."[1] Adam also sees allusions to Verlaine everywhere, such as the "bois noir" (*La Bonne Chanson*) and the "deux enfants" ("Soyons deux enfants," *Ariettes oubliées*). I doubt it; poetry can hardly afford to be about anything so specific. And this is clearly poetry. It is at times also patently baffling, irritatingly obscure.

> Quand le monde sera réduit en un seul bois noir pour nos quatre yeux étonnés,—en une plage pour deux enfants fidèles,—en une maison musicale pour notre claire sympathie,—je vous trouverai.
>
> Qu'il n'y ait ici-bas qu'un vieillard seul, calme et beau, entouré d'un "luxe inouï,"—et je suis à vos genoux.
>
> Que j'aie réalisé tous vos souvenirs,—que je sois celle qui sait vous garrotter,—je vous étoufferai.

The voice is of a *celle*, in the lineage of all the numerous *Elles*, especially that of "Angoisse":

> Se peut-il qu'Elle me fasse pardonner les ambitions continuellement écrasées,—qu'une fin aisée répare les âges d'indigence [see the *luxe* of the old man] . . .
>
> Mais la Vampire qui nous rend gentils commande que nous nous amusions avec ce qu'elle nous laisse . . .
>
> Rouler aux blessures, par l'air lassant et la mer [cf. the *plage*].

In short, the She of both poems is life as a feminine (and *femme fatale*) principle like Mallarmé's "Mère qui créas . . . De grandes fleurs avec la balsamique Mort" ("Les Fleurs," which Rimbaud is known to have pastiched). She shows up again and again. In "Enfance" she was the orange-lipped little girl (like the initial apparition of Proust's Gilberte) at the edge of a wood; here, she is *in* the wood (cf. "Tête de faune," and "Ophélie," a sort of *belle au bois*). The eyes are dramatically pitted against

---

[1] There is a slight community of tone between the first and second "phrase"—and something rhetorical, interlocutory—but this does not extend to the third (i.e., although it addresses someone, so does the last of all). Not enough to base any thing solid on.

the dark of the woods, bringing out the paradoxical, pure relationship—reflexive and outgoing—of Rimbaud with his self, his *anima*, as well as with the girl who embodies it separately.

In "Délires I," Rimbaud has Verlaine say: "Je nous voyais comme deux bons enfants, libres de se promener dans le Paradis de tristesse." The sentimentality of this image rules it out as a parallel here.

He finds Her again on a beach, as in the just-quoted end of "Angoisse."[2] A beach is an obvious place for children to meet and play together. In "Enfance" the child-idol is on such a beach, running along "des plages nommées." At the end of *Une Saison en enfer*, in "Matin," Rimbaud further describes a Dufy-like strand. The shore, like the *talus*, is a place of promise, a threshold of the beyond.

The musical house reminds me, and possibly reminded Rimbaud, of the Verlaine poem, among his most intimate, where the piano stands near a window in a quiet love-filled interior (V of *Romances sans paroles*).[3]

The old man is the entelechy of Rimbaud himself: he has beauty, riches, and maturity, as in the "fin aisée" of "Angoisse." He dreamed of him in "Vies" (the "brahmane," the "gentilhomme") and "Enfance": "Le savant au fauteuil sombre" in his "bibliothèque." A handsome father-figure, he is a quieter version of the *Génie*. The Woman, Life, favors such successful old men in his fantasy, is "at their knees."

The "luxe inouïe" in quotes sounds like a purposeful cliché, à la Flaubert or Nabokov. If there is only *one* old man, that is the exclusive true glory of the sort Rimbaud sought: unique.

In the end, She gets even the most glorious of men: "Even if I have realized all your memories [i.e., all your childish aims], I'll stifle you." "Even if I know how to throttle you" is puzzling, but reinforces the cruelty, the irony of the gentle "She" who kills the one she "knows how" to handle, mother-like, as in "Angoisse": "la Vampire qui nous rend gentils [et nous] commande."

---

[2] This recalls the end of the film *Les Quatre Cents coups*, when the boy-child, deserted by his mother, walks into Mother-ocean and death. But in "Phrases" that is just the hinted feminine backdrop of the scene. In Mallarmé's "Livre," the boy hero similarly stands on a beach in "le grand air" with the appropriately feminine waves before him.

[3] It may slightly recall the specifically musical "household" (of Madame de Fleurville) where Rimbaud found Verlaine, but that was not poetic to Rimbaud: rather, the piano from that household found its way into some truly musical Verlaine poems. It resembles the sunlit, leafy room, dreamed of by Meaulnes in the sheepfold, with the girl (an overwhelmingly fetching young mother-figure) playing the piano. Or Coleridge's "damsel with a dulcimer," or Mallarmé's "berceuse" in "Don du Poème."

> Quand nous sommes très forts,—qui recule? très gais,—qui tombe de ridicule? Quand nous sommes très méchants,—que ferait-on de nous.
>
> Parez-vous, dansez, riez. Je ne pourrai jamais envoyer l'Amour par la fenêtre.

This is obscure, but seems to be an expression of la-de-da indifference to the world.[4] Whatever we do, nothing matters to others.

So if we are strong—who draws back, afraid?

So if we are very gay (and mock at the others)—who (among them) falls down from (our) ridicule?

So if we are very nasty—what could they do with us? (i.e., what would seriously affect us? Nothing, he implies.)

So, never mind *them*. Doll up, dance, laugh (as the children of "Matinée d'ivresse" did). The "pure love" of that play is echoed in the "Amour" he refuses to throw out the window here. In the *Saison en enfer*, his abandonment of the West is summed up in the primitive "dance, dance, dance. . . ." But the tone here is closer to Verlaine's *Fêtes galantes*: frivolously adolescent.

> —Ma camarade, mendiante, enfant monstre! comme ça t'est égal, ces malheureuses et ces manœuvres, et mes embarras. Attache-toi à nous avec ta voix impossible, ta voix! unique flatteur de ce vil désespoir.

Here is the Life-girl again, this time recalling the sweet little orphan girl-friend described by De Quincey in his *Confessions of an English Opium Eater* and Baudelaire in his reworking of him in *Les Paradis artificiels*, or the Henrika of "Ouvriers." The reference to "manœuvres" here reinforces that connection. Externally projected or not, she is the *anima* of Rimbaud, his dulcet but rough and real ("mendiante . . . monstre") poetic voice, like the one that comes to him in "Barbare": "O Douceurs! . . . la voix féminine arrivée au fond des volcans et des grottes arctiques." In "Age d'or," the voice was of a similar "sister." The "ça t'est égal, ces malheureuses et ces manœuvres, et mes embarras" seems to mean that for poetry the condition of the workers, men and women—Rimbaud's social concern—is beside the point.

> Une matinée couverte, en Juillet. Un goût de cendres vole dans l'air;—une odeur de bois suant dans l'âtre,—les fleurs rouies,—le saccage des promenades,—la bruine des canaux par les champs—pourquoi pas déjà les joujoux et l'encens?

---

[4] This passage is curiously close to a gypsy song found by Françoise d'Eaubonne (in Py, p. 121).

This is full of ambivalent—sooty, foggy—poetry in the Baudelairean "Crépuscule" and "Spleen" manner. The dull morning in July is like the pall over the countryside in "Enfance" or "Les Corbeaux" or the double, penetrating wind from the south in "Ouvriers": "Le temps était couvert, et ce vent du Sud excitait toutes les vilaines odeurs. . . ." The taste of ashes in the air is like the peppery crows in "Les Corbeaux," burnt seasoning (see the ink taste in the air in the last "phrase"). The odor of wood sweating in the fireplace is comparable. Steeped (i.e., flaccid) flowers ("arbrisseaux brûlés," in "Les Premières Communions"). The ravaged fields of the promenades ("jardins ravagés," "Ouvriers"). The mist over the canals through the fields. Shades of "Mémoire" and "Jeunesse," riverside promenades. In the *Saison en enfer* he says: "J'aimai . . . les vergers brûlés, les boutiques fanées, les boissons tiédies." As in wine and cheese, there is a mild savory death in fading passing time, the "grace of faded things."

Finally he revolts at this too-nostalgic memory. Hence the savage turning against "toys" and the "incense" of the Church which made him spiritually a child (cf. the "nana" babble of "L'Homme juste") and threatened to keep him one forever.

> J'ai tendu des cordes de clocher à clocher; des guirlandes de fenêtre à fenêtre; des chaînes d'or d'étoile à étoile, et je danse.

Contrasted to the memory of constraint at the end of the last phrase, this is a new freedom, the staking-out of a new, original, inner-outer space. Compare Apollinaire's "Liens." Comment is unnecessary: it is as clear as "Royauté" and as justly celebrated.

> Le haut étang fume continuellement. Quelle sorcière va se dresser sur le couchant blanc? Quelles violettes frondaisons vont descendre?

This is a sort of disappointed wedding ("L'azur et l'onde communient," "Bannières de mai") of father-sky and mother-water as in "Mémoire." The "high pond" echoes the one in "Ouvriers": "une flache laissée par l'inondation [cf. "Après le déluge"] du mois précédent à un sentier assez haut." Like the "mer étagée là-haut" of "Après le déluge" or the "haute mer faite d'une éternité de chaudes larmes" of "Enfance," this height of water bespeaks a high emotional charge. It is again associated with his mother, not only because of the *mer-mère* echo but because his memory of her, as in "Mémoire" (and "Jeunesse," "le long des rivières"), was confused with that of her sister-water. Thus, as in "Mémoire," her form rises up—there it was "Madame se tient trop debout"—bigger than life, too big for the stifled boy, and hard to shake off. As in "Being beauteous" she rises awesomely: there it was in front of snow—here it is before a "white" sundown. The sorceress of "Après le déluge" is clearly parallel: the smoking water here has obvious affinities with the embers in the sort of witches' cauldron there.

As in "Mémoire," the father principle is up high: it descends (like the sun there) to meet the earth and water: only here it is "violettes frondaisons." As we noted in "Voyelles" and "Comédie de la soif," violet (or ultra-violet) is from the upper range of the spectrum, hence a male principle in Rimbaud.

> Pendant que les fonds publics s'écoulent en fêtes de fraternité, il sonne une cloche de feu rose dans les nuages.

Like the fifth "phrase" and in strong contrast to the disappointment of the one above, this is a happy moment of union. What happens below is reflected above in the sky where a "pink firebell" rings joyously (with flowery cloud effect and synesthesia as in the tinkling bell-shaped flowers of "Enfance"). On earth or rather just above it the resultant effect is along the synthesizing mid-line, the horizontal plane of fraternity, communion of all men. And the public funds *flow*, like the promiscuous milk and blood in "Après le déluge."

> Avivant un agréable goût d'encre de Chine, une poudre noire pleut doucement sur ma veillée.—Je baisse les feux du lustre, je me jette sur le lit, et, tourné du côté de l'ombre, je vous vois, mes filles! mes reines!

The black dust is as agreeable as the peppery crows of "Les Corbeaux" and "La Rivière de Cassis." More closely, it recalls the "fleurs d'encre crachant des pollens en virgule" of "Les Assis"; or the "points noirs" he presses his eyes to see (or "pour des visions") in "Les Poètes de sept ans." Here he is about to have visions. But who are "mes filles, mes reines"? They may be like those nocturnal spectres of "Vies": "A quelque fête de nuit dans une Cité du Nord, j'ai rencontré toutes les femmes des anciens peintres"; or the "blêmes figures lunaires, feuilles, seins" he sees in "Nocturne vulgaire"; or the liquid light-shadows, "esprits des eaux," he sees in the "alcôves" of "Jeune Ménage." Then there are all the exotic women he dreamed of in "Les Poètes de sept ans." In the same lineage as these figures, the "filles" et "reines" pose no real problem.

Ouvriers

One of the roles dreamed of by the child in "Enfance" could easily have been that of a worker, knowing as we do the prestige the latter had for Rimbaud (see particularly "Les Poètes de sept ans" and "Bonne pensée du matin"). In this fantasy, Rimbaud imagines himself to be a rather harried and indigent itinerant *ouvrier* accompanied by his wife, looking no doubt for a job. The situation calls for some pity and bespeaks self-pity. Here is unrewarded merit, unrealized potential and a sacrificial humility corresponding to Rimbaud's own case, particularly as a child, and so the scene modulates to some "misérables incidents de mon enfance."

The whole tone is one of savored poverty which Rimbaud shared with the *peuple* children in "Les Poètes de sept ans" and which colored the rugged and "soupy" poetry of "Les Pauvres à l'église." The intimate ambivalent tone is reflected in many aspects of the landscape: the vibrancy between winter and spring, cold and warmth, outer indigence and inner riches (as in "Royauté"), between city and countryside in the haunting *banlieue*.

The "there" of the civilized city and the "here" of these earthy paths in the country combine in other ways through smell and sound: "La ville, avec sa fumée et ses bruits de métiers, nous suivait très loin dans les chemins" (see our comment on the "bruits" of "Départ"). Past and present are movingly joined in memory, as well as in the costumes from another century. The couple is suspended between two ages, youth and maturity, in unsure adolescence, not quite serious or fixed, on the road between this place and that.

Although the girl Henrika is called his wife (he may have had a wandering companion according to Delahaye), at the dejected end Rimbaud says: ". . . nous ne serons jamais que des orphelins fiancés." So even the married state is unsure, suspended between two possibilities.

There is a subtle tension between the northern color of this girl's Dutch or Flemish name and the hints of a southern influence; together they create a Van Gogh tone, a lowland lyric solidity.

The close is very ambiguous. One interpretation is that Rimbaud no longer wants to be suspended, but wants his psyche to be univalent, hard and determined as his arm is, or as a true mature worker is. For that, he would have to give up all play-acting art and imagination (as at the end of the *Saison en enfer*), hence no more "chère image." The second possibility is that he must give up (the) woman, for similar reasons; again, as at the end of *Une Saison en enfer* he says goodbye to women generally, as he leaves for a tough solitary life in the East. The two meanings overlap, and the ambiguity is probably intended. The *Saison en enfer* ends on just such an unsure note.

> O cette chaude matinée de février. Le Sud inopportun vint relever nos souvenirs d'indigents absurdes, notre jeune misère.

We have already commented on this. The "O" shows clearly how poignant this ambivalent poetry of cold February and warm wind from the South is for Rimbaud. It is very like T. S. Eliot's "Midwinter spring" or "April is the cruellest month, breeding / Lilacs out of the dead land" or Laforgue's "L'hiver qui vient."

> Henrika avait une jupe de coton à carreau blanc et brun, qui a dû être portée au siècle dernier, un bonnet à rubans, et un foulard de soie. C'était bien plus triste qu'un deuil. Nous faisions un tour dans la banlieue. Le temps était couvert, et ce vent du Sud excitait toutes les vilaines odeurs des jardins ravagés et prés desséchés.

Henrika's outmoded costume from another century reminds one of the clothes Meaulnes donned at the *fête étrange* in a quite comparably vibrant (winter-spring, rich-poor, old-young) atmosphere. "Sadder than mourning" conveys a stricken beauty. The poetry of the "overcast" surroundings is amply commented under the fourth section of "Phrases."

> Cela ne devait pas fatiguer ma femme au même point que moi. Dans une flache laissée par l'inondation du mois précédent à un sentier assez haut, elle me fit remarquer de très petits poissons.

This too has been largely elucidated under the sixth part of "Phrases." The flood, no doubt, like that of "Après le déluge," represents a baptism, a renewal of contact with the total life force: one is at home in the common deluge, or cosmic "Ocean," as in the "Poème de la Mer" of "Le Bateau ivre." But when it recedes, eventually, it leaves the isolated puddle, like the one at the end of "Le Bateau ivre." And then one is a sad small fish in that little pond of the lost isolated individuality. Eliot's ragged-clawed creature in "The Love Song of J. Alfred Prufrock" (or on the mountain path of "Little Gidding," where he pokes at it with a stick) echoes this. Compare the "nid de bêtes blanches" Rimbaud fascinatedly discovers in "Enfance."

> La ville, avec sa fumée et ses bruits de métiers, nous suivait très loin dans les chemins. O l'autre monde, l'habitation bénie par le ciel et les ombrages! Le sud me rappelait les misérables incidents de mon enfance, mes désespoirs d'été, l'horrible quantité de force et de science que le sort a toujours éloignée de moi. Non! nous ne passerons pas l'été dans cet avare pays où nous ne serons jamais que des orphelins fiancés. Je veux que ce bras durci ne traîne plus *une chère image*.

We have partly understood the urban "bruits" (of looms). The city represents a possible entelechy, but not yet for him. So he dreams of a full world, the ideal city, like the vision of "splendides villes" at the end of *Une Saison en enfer*. The sky and the shadows of foliage raise and caress, *bless* this authentic place, in a double (male and female) way. It smacks of heaven, ultimately.

Then, by contrast, intrudes the stirring of miserable memories, as in "Chanson de la plus haute tour," those desperate stagnant summers; or, as in "Mémoire," the childish numbness and powerlessness, the defeat by that inner family-disaster. Cf. "Des petits enfants étouffent des malédictions le long des rivières" ("Jeunesse").

He blames these circumstances and revolts (unconvincingly as did Nietzsche in his sick restlessness) against the present place, the "stingy country." (Stingy as his mother was in affection and was said to be economically; cf. "avare comme la mer" in the *Saison en enfer*.)

He wants to shake off this cowardliness and, alone—without soft art, or soft woman, or both—as at the end of the *Saison en enfer*, make a fresh start, prove he is an utterly tough independent male, like his soldier-father who left woman and all behind!

How very young and vulnerable and unwise he was![1]

Les Ponts

Along with "Villes," I and II, and "Métropolitain," "Les Ponts" sketches something like an ideal city. We noted earlier that the château of "O saisons, ô châteaux" was an ideal architecture of the soul, and these city-scenes represent an extension of that vision. Moreover, this city is a place

---

[1] In a study of Rimbaud, Robert Montal quotes a friend of Rimbaud to the effect that he was never seen in female company. This is surely an exaggeration. The little worker girl in "Les Poètes de sept ans" was without any question a real creature. Too many other poems, such as "Roman," indicate at least a passing amorous acquaintance with the opposite sex. Delahaye could not have made up out of whole cloth the episode of the girl companion.

of magic convergence, of increasing complexity to the point of utter ful-
fillment—like a rich cake of reality, as in Proust's Combray, an earthly
paradise. It takes up through distillation the excluded nature, and involves
it in a momentary higher synthesis, like a poem.

The effect is of a city-scape painting, with some of the haunting
geometric quality of a Piranesi drawing, or even the colonnaded surrealism
of Chirico (Py thinks of Monet and Sisley). Memories of Baudelaire's
cities—"Rêve parisien," as well as the drug-induced hallucinations of
Les Paradis artificiels—may linger here. There is a schizoid, dream-like
precision in this free-floating vision.

A bridge is a heady experience: under it is a breathtaking dose of noth-
ing. The victory over the void is akin to flying, an access of Spirit,
Aufhebung.

> Des ciels gris de cristal.

"Ciels" indicates artificial skies, in a painting or drawing ("dessin" in the
next sentence) like the ones in Baudelaire's "L'Invitation au voyage": "ces
ciels brouillés" (see the commentary of Judd Hubert in *L'Esthétique des
Fleurs du Mal*, p. 69). Rimbaud uses "ciels" in a comparable way in
"Guerre": "certains ciels ont affiné mon optique." The grayness of the sky
will be reflected in the gray water below; together they vertically frame
the tableau, as usual in Rimbaud.

The "cristal" creates an effect of transparency similar to the "chalets
de cristal" in "Villes," I and the "boulevards de cristal" of "Métropolitain."

> Un bizarre dessin de ponts, ceux-ci droits, ceux-là bombés,
> d'autres descendant ou obliquant en angles sur les premiers,
> et ces figures se renouvelant dans les autres circuits éclairés du
> canal, mais tous tellement longs et légers que les rives, chargées
> de dômes, s'abaissent et s'amoindrissent. Quelques-uns de ces
> ponts sont encore chargés de masures. D'autres soutiennent des
> mâts, des signaux, de frêles parapets. Des accords mineurs se
> croisent et filent, des cordes montent des berges. On distingue
> une veste rouge, peut-être d'autres costumes et des instruments
> de musique. Sont-ce des airs populaires, des bouts de concerts
> seigneuriaux, des restants d'hymnes publics?

The bridges, places of magic suspension between worlds (cf. "Ouvriers"),
grow as the banal banks diminish in size and in importance. They are
fantastically long, as English bridges were according to Germain Nouveau
in a letter dating from his time abroad with Rimbaud. They even usurp

the habitations (as the ancient London Bridge or the "Old Bridge" of Florence did). These "masures" are thus sublimated to magic, a new life. Or they take on other curious, neat, and smart details à la Klee. They can cross over into the realm of music, as did the house of "Phrases" or the singing phosphorus of "Le Bateau ivre." "Accords" and "cordes" are clear echoes, musical—melodic and harmonic—relation-lines paralleling physical ties; cf. Apollinaire's "Liens." Thus in "Mystique" "les bruits . . . filent leur courbe" and in "Soir historique" there are "fils d'harmonie."

Costumes, as in "Ouvriers," get into the act (cf. "Parade"): the "veste rouge" is like a visual flash on a player in an orchestra; then the other costumes, vaguely glimpsed, arise by association or proliferation. Music returns in the visual form of instruments. But it is heard music again in the next line, in a sort of Rousseauistic public festival, an idyllic concert such as the "musique des anciens" offered to "féeriques aristocraties" in "Métropolitain."

> L'eau est grise et bleue, large comme un bras de mer.

That wide arm of the sea is like the Whole coming in and blessing the part, the place. The gray (drunk?) water reflects the gray sky—obviously serene or static and harmonious with summer, as in the "ciel gris de chaleur" of "Mémoire."[1]

> Un rayon blanc, tombant du haut du ciel, anéantit cette comédie.

All that harmonious scene is too full; Rimbaud almost always ends on a note of breakdown. Like lightning punishing hubris, a ray from above descends. But here the vision (as in the *Saison en enfer*) is called a "comédie"; Rimbaud seems to be turning in revolt against his own creation before our very eyes. The avenging ray is his own, at least in part. We can easily suspect that he welcomes it, as a relief from his earlier *inauthentic* self, just as St. Paul speaks of his own conversion—the descending fire on the road to Damascus—as having killed the frivolous child in him. Thus Rimbaud will call down the beam that dissolves the ephemeral gnat ("Alchimie du verbe"). "Si un rayon me blesse / Je succomberai . . . moi je ne veux rire à rien" ("Bannières de mai") comments on a similar desire for reality.

---

[1] In his *Salon de 1845* Baudelaire describes a Delacroix painting: "Ce tableau est si harmonieux . . . qu'il en est gris—gris comme l'atmosphère de l'été, quand le soleil étend comme un crépuscule de poussière tremblante sur chaque objet."

Ville

Unlike the cities in "Les Ponts" or "Métropolitain," this is not at all an ideal *ville*, but rather a fantasied "modern" metropolis which owes much to late nineteenth-century London, almost Dickensian in atmosphere, seen by a fascinated visitor from the Continent. Verlaine and Rimbaud lived together in London from September to December 1872, and Rimbaud returned there several times later (with Verlaine and in 1874 with the poet Germain Nouveau). Through various poems and letters we know that Verlaine thought London to be a dirty and immoral place, and that Rimbaud agreed.

> Je suis un éphémère et point trop mécontent citoyen d'une métropole crue moderne parce que tout goût connu a été éludé dans les ameublements et l'extérieur des maisons aussi bien que dans le plan de la ville.

Rimbaud has an obviously jaundiced view of modern taste, cf. "la barbarie moderne" ("Villes," II). To friends he said "Je gobe assez Londres et ces mœurs-ci . . . c'est peut-être sain d'être parmi des barbares, un temps" (in Py, p. 128). Visitors to London still can know what he means: Paris, by contrast, maintains more of the old unitary principle of monarchy (and deity) in architecture and the "plan de la ville." But he is bemused, obviously, as a passing observer ("éphémère").

> Ici vous ne signaleriez les traces d'aucun monument de superstition.

London has *some* monuments of superstition, but fewer cathedrals, at least, than Paris. But Rimbaud's city goes farther in pagan modernity.

> La morale et la langue sont réduites à leur plus simple expression, enfin!

This may owe a bit to British laconic expression but mostly it is an extrapolation of modern tendencies Rimbaud with some irony could see developing (as did Baudelaire in his *Journaux intimes*).

> Ces millions de gens qui n'ont pas besoin de se connaître amènent si pareillement l'éducation, le métier et la vieillesse, que ce cours de vie doit être plusieurs fois moins long que ce qu'une statistique folle trouve pour les peuples du continent.

The democratic flattening to sameness makes life go faster for all and perhaps even for the whole society, which may speed to annihilation.

> Aussi comme, de ma fenêtre, je vois des spectres nouveaux roulant à travers l'épaisse et éternelle fumée de charbon,—notre ombre des bois, notre nuit d'été!—des Érinnyes nouvelles, devant mon cottage qui est ma patrie et tout mon cœur puisque tout ici ressemble à ceci,—la Mort sans pleurs, notre active fille et servante, un Amour désespéré, et un joli Crime piaulant dans la boue de la rue.

The "comme" is puzzling but otherwise the sentence makes sufficient (poetic) sense.[1]

From his observer's window Rimbaud sees the players in life's eternal dramas, as in "Bruxelles." In the (London) coal-smoke they take on a mythic unreal quality, as did Eliot's London Bridge in *The Waste Land*. He can see behind the contemporary figures, as Joyce could in *Ulysses*, their classic counterparts, and together they constitute a Joycean perspective of eternal return, reprises in new guises—*sartor resartus*—of the old gestures. Py rightfully compares this mood to that of Ulysses contemplating the shades of his past in "Cimmérie, patrie de l'ombre et des tourbillons" ("Délires II").

In place of the old Dionysian or Eleusinian groves, "woods" and "summer night," there is the modern darkness of the coal-smoke, whence emerge the new Erinyes, an up-to-the-minute Death (like a British servant girl, efficiently "active," "tearless," implying perhaps a Cockney directness and brutality), a desperate Love (some violent, nakedly modern passion of the sort one reads about in the papers), and lastly the "pretty Crime whining in the mud of the street," a contemporary ruthless character like Lacenaire, as seen in Carné's *Les Enfants du Paradis*. Rimbaud is fascinated and disgusted, cynical and heartsick as we all are—particularly T. S. Eliot—when we yearn for a milder or courtlier bygone world.[2]

The cottage is all his land and heart "since everything here resembles this," i.e., one window on the world sums it up, in this repetitive democratic order, and in this Viconian perspective.

Ornières

> A droite l'aube d'été éveille les feuilles et les vapeurs et les bruits de ce coin du parc, et les talus de gauche tiennent dans leur ombre violette les mille rapides ornières de la route humide. Défilé de féeries. En effet: des chars chargés d'animaux de bois

[1] Py suggests the reading "comme . . . je vois des spectres [je vois] la mort. . . ." This is dubious.

[2] Thomas Hanson in an unpublished study sees an Orestes (fantasied mother-killer) in the reference to Erinyes.

doré, de mâts et de toiles bariolées, au grand galop de vingt
chevaux de cirque tachetés, et les enfants et les hommes sur
leurs bêtes les plus étonnantes;—vingt véhicules, bossés, pavoisés
et fleuris comme des carrosses anciens ou de contes, pleins d'en-
fants attifés pour une pastorale suburbaine.—Même des cer-
cueils sous leur dais de nuit dressant les panaches d'ébène,
filant au trot des grandes juments bleues et noires.

Rimbaud easily sees a theatre in nature, as setting for visions such as this
circus parade. In "Mémoire" he creates a sort of picture or proscenium
frame of sky, river, hill and bridge-span. In "Mystique" there is a similar
right and left, an *en haut* and a *dessous*. Here the right side of the picture
is a dawn stir of light and leaves,[1] sounds (Rimbaud's favorite moment and
emotion), and the left is another savored effect: roads to freedom, damp
with fertile freshness, violet shadows with their ethereal lyricism yet
earthly solidity, "talus" which are both wombs of new life and sills of pure
promise, thresholds to the glorious All like a stage apron (as in "Mys-
tique").

The ruts themselves are a guarantee of communion with the happy
earth; eyeing them one is grooved into and ultimately a part of Her (we
dig Her, to use the good recent expression; She is groovy). But, in one of
Rimbaud's characteristic male-female combinations, the ruts also go off
somewhere, rapidly, dynamically, as the plow-furrows do in "Marine."

We note that the dark shadows, the feminine "left" area of the tableau,
are the "humid" womb-source of the latent events (fecundated, as it were,
by the male light).

There is a progressive focusing of the magic reality emerging from this
source: first, a general effect of *féerie*, then, following the "en effet," a
more precise imagery which is like "on closer look what do we see, ah!"
etc.

The vibrancy in the taut high-frequency violet (see under "Voyelles")
is the whirring-alive of the wonderful events.[2]

The only main verb is in the first sentence; after that, all is apposition,
sheer phenomena.

The rest is very like the *fête étrange* of *Le Grand Meaulnes*: delightful
fresh creatures, untainted by adult bourgeois fakery: horsemen, children,
animals, gay carriages. No women: the feminine source will become a

---

[1] Note "été . . . éveille" for é sounds presenting brightness as in "Aube": "Au réveil
il était midi." Note further that in this series of rapid *impressions*, there is only
one finite verb.

[2] The tension of ultra-violet frequency is in the series of bright i's and é's: "vio-
lettes . . . mille rapides . . . humide . . . Défilé de féeries." Observe also the repe-
tition of breezy f's in the last group.

smothering death at the end. Meanwhile, it is a *suburban* pastoral festival, vibrant like the *banlieue* in "Ouvriers" or "Villes," I, or the elegant *faubourg* of "Villes," II—unsure in mood as the city-country, past-present, youth-age, winter-summer of the *fête étrange*. Similarly through the woods of "Enfance" there came a troupe of mysterious *comédiens*.

As in "Marine" the wave-like (humid) ruts give birth to some sea images: masts and sail-cloths.

The animals of gilded wood are purest toy-fantasy; "chars chargés" is childish incantatory babble.

The pejorative "attifés" (implying a mockery of his mother's idea of Sunday) and a hint in the "pastorale suburbaine" indicate that the prettiness of the picture is turning before our eyes into sentimentality, then funereality, like a womb- or nest-like rococo coach in "Nocturne vulgaire": "Ce carosse dont l'époque est assez indiquée par les glaces convexes, les panneaux bombés et les sophas contournés. Corbillard de mon sommeil, isolé, maison de berger de ma niaiserie." As in the present poem, the scene changes rapidly into a death-ridden night.

The last phrase proves it is all a dream vision, mixing in a funeral as did "Après le déluge," with its "enfants en deuil." With the abruptness of reversal of Baudelaire's "Chambre double," this switch occurs in Rimbaud before we know it: the turnabout of mood from charm to nightmare is very like the one in "Nocturne vulgaire" or "Le Bateau ivre."[3] It seems that these rutted roads, like the paths of "Enfance," lead too far. . . .

"Blue and black" are solemn night-colors, thus paired; horses are powerfully charged, "cathected," as in Plato's *Phaedrus*, Picasso's *Guernica*, Pierre Gascar's stories, with forces from below. Perhaps the charge includes the hateful combination of blue-black—"azur . . . noir," "bleu qui ment"— we saw, with Rimbaud, in his mother's eyes.

Villes, I

We are again, as in "Les Ponts," on ideal territory, this time more varied, colorful, sprawling, baroque: dream-cities like multi-ringed circuses with operatic sideshows. Their dramatic gorges and heights make them somewhat Byronically Swiss, but there are Oriental, English, and French or Belgian touches as well.

Rimbaud has drawn on all times and places in his attempt to cram reality simultaneously into his ideal cities. Nature and urban sights, myths—"Toutes les légendes"—and new gadgets, heights and depths,

[3] The "grandes juments" are, literally, mares of night (before, they were just "horses"); this furthers the tone of growing feminine, or maternal-smothering, death.

violent motion and suspended moments of rest, all are lumped together kaleidoscopically in an orgy of vision. It is as if Rimbaud had set out to prove his boast: "toutes les possibilités harmoniques et architecturales s'émouvront autour de ton siège" ("Jeunesse"). Later, he regretted it: ". . . je me vantais de posséder tous les paysages possibles" ("Délires, II"). The solid single block of prose containing the description of the heteroclite metropolises adds to the feeling of density, agglomeration. After it comes a one-sentence paragraph: a palinode.

> Ce sont des villes! C'est un peuple pour qui se sont montés ces Alleghanys et ces Libans de rêve! Des chalets de cristal et de bois qui se meuvent sur des rails et des poulies invisibles.

"Ce sont des villes!" is an exultant boast: compared to my cities, the others are nothing. The "people" are similarly vaunted. The "Alleghanys" and "Libans" both refer to mountain-chains: the image is of primeval formations rising from the earth just as these dream-visions rise. This is mainly childish fantasy on place-names, as in Proust. Shades of the "Rocky Mountain cat" in "Honte," the "Greek, Slavic, Celtic" of "Enfance." "Alleghanys" smack of American freedom, "Libans" of Rimbaud's ideal Orient.

The chalets which move on rails (horizontally) and pulleys (vertically) are magically light ("cristal") and pure as air, as gleefully evanescent and frivolous as theater scenery, the "huttes d'opéra-comique" of "Fête d'hiver" (whose cascade also refreshingly puts in an appearance here, below). Some have seen an influence of Swiss mountain cog-railways. The vertical axis will be particularly exploited, as Richard noted; the scene shifts up and down dramatically as if moved by the above-mentioned pulleys.

> Les vieux cratères ceints de colosses et de palmiers de cuivre rugissent mélodieusement dans les feux.

There is an evocation of Vesuvius here: romantic fire from the depths and classic bric-à-brac (colossal statues) in a palm-fringed south, similar to "les feux à la pluie du vent de diamants jetée par le cœur terrestre éternellement carbonisé pour nous.—O monde!" ("Barbare"). The "copper" may be a result of volcanic ash. We note the oxymoron of "rugissent mélodieusement," typical of the dynamic contradictions running through the piece.

> Des fêtes amoureuses sonnent sur les canaux pendus derrière les chalets. La chasse des carillons crie dans les gorges.

In "Est-elle almée?" we had amorous festivals reminiscent of Musset's "Nuit vénitienne." One thinks too of painted Flemish boating parties.

Canals were a backdrop for Baudelaire's love-idyll in "L'Invitation au voyage." Rimbaud recalled walking sadly along the "canaux" in his frustrated childhood in "Phrases." (There are many canals in the region of Roche.) Their suspended height here expresses glee, a "high" emotional charge as in the elevated sea (below).

The "chasse des carillons" (in the gorges of this vaguely Swiss, or Alpine, décor), is a "pack," like all the other budding groups—corporations, fleets—which tend toward the total collective harmony of Rimbaud's ideal future.

> Des corporations de chanteurs géants accourent dans des vête-
> ments et des oriflammes éclatants comme la lumière des cimes.
> Sur les plates-formes au milieu des gouffres les Rolands sonnent
> leur bravoure.

This is the operatic effect—the "opéra fabuleux" of "Délires, II"—a chorus, with violent coloration as in "Parade." Accordingly, Roland seems like a Wagnerian *Heldentenor*. But he is plural, part of a phantasmagoria, which is prolonged in a number of classic or mythic figures. They will all be pastiched, grotesquely transformed as Rimbaud brings down the old legends, or metamorphoses them into something wildly new and his own.

Baudelaire earlier had spoken of "la prodigieuse musique qui roule sur les sommets" (Pléiade, p. 1543).

> Sur les passerelles de l'abîme et les toits des auberges l'ardeur
> du ciel pavoise les mâts.

The inn (as in "Comédie de la soif") is a haven of refuge for the deprived child's heart. Its roof is thus a place apart—like the weathercocks of "Après le déluge"—for an infantile scene of freedom. Hence the glorious atmosphere as in the ecstatic "Adieu" of the *Saison en enfer*, with its departing boats, its Dufy streamers. The "passerelles" are an essence of buoyancy, suspension (as in "Les Ponts"), victory over gravity and earth-mother threats. Wallace Fowlie sees a medieval hill-city here, with drawbridges reflected by "cities on the ocean with inns and masts in the sunset."

> L'écoulement des apothéoses rejoint les champs des hauteurs où
> les centauresses séraphiques évoluent parmi les avalanches.

All that crumbling stir of clouds and light or snow on upper fields, with exotic creatures mixed in, is good fun. The "écroulement des apothéoses . . . avalanches" is Hugolian: "Des avalanches d'or s'écroulaient dans l'azur" (*La Légende des siècles*: "Le Sacre de la femme"), echoed in

Mallarmé's "Les Fleurs" (pastiched by Rimbaud in "Ce qu'on dit au poète") : "Des avalanches d'or du vieil azur." The crumbling is of the old gods, "apothéoses." The "centauresses séraphiques" are another catachresis of the ancient world; they are like the slinky creature of "Antique." "Seraphic" adds a Christian touch to pagan creatures in a further saucy juxtaposition. The "évoluent" may refer again to the modification of old myths, or merely "maneuvers." Incidentally, the mountain-setting is appropriate to centaurs—they classically lived in the mountains of Thessaly.

> Au-dessus du niveau des plus hautes crêtes, une mer troublée par la naissance éternelle de Vénus, chargée de flottes orphéoniques et de la rumeur des perles et des conques précieuses,— la mer s'assombrit parfois avec des éclats mortels.

For the very high sea, see "Après le déluge" and "Phrases": it is a *high* charge of instinctual—feminine in a large sense—life, as in "Les Sœurs de charité" where the same sunken treasure ("diamants") rolls in the flood of feeling like potential delight in a restless adolescent's nocturnal bed (cf. the buried jewels of "Après le déluge"). The *orphéon*, male choral society (with a hint of Orphée developed below), is perhaps the eternal homage men pay to their maternal source, Venus ("Divine mère," "Aphrodité marine"—"Soleil et chair"). This is a whole *fleet* of such choristers, men drifting on the mother-sea of life and love, praising Her. Music clearly plays for Rimbaud something like the role it did for the Greek Orpheus: it enchants nature and all of life, transforms it, calls forth a new order (the "groups of belfries singing the ideas of the people" below). The rumor and stir of shells is heard again in "Mystique"; it is the oniric underground, or undersea music of the senses. Partly, the darkness is the atmosphere of latent birth, common in Rimbaud, but it is also a sense of doom. Venus is eternally born only at a high price.[1] This tableau of the desire to rise again and again is a counterpart to Brueghel's "Landscape with the Fall of Icarus."

> Sur les versants des moissons de fleurs grandes comme nos armes et nos coupes, mugissent.

These dream-flowers are sonorous, like the ones which tinkle in "Enfance," and are threatening mouths ("coupes") resembling the sickroom *ventouses* of "Le Bateau ivre," hence they bellow like the hysterical herds of that long poem, emerging no doubt from fever-delirium. Flowers, like vortices in

---

[1] In "Being beauteous," her sister *mère* had "blessures écarlates et noires [qui] éclatent. . . ."

water, are beckonings downward, throated like gladioli or lilies—cf. the sickroom "lys . . . Clysopompes" ("Lys," *Album zutique*) or "Lys . . . clystères" of "Ce qu'on dit au poète"—and can hence be a threat. The male aspect of them—pistils—is equally prominent in the gigantic "armes."

> Des cortèges de Mabs en robes rousses, opalines, montent des ravines.

The Shakespearean Fairy Queen of fantasy, from *Romeo and Juliet*, off-sets the threat from below by coming up in a cheerful, frivolous, buoyant apparition.

> Là-haut, les pieds dans la cascade et les ronces, les cerfs tettent Diane.

The stag is another offsetting—male—apparition. He is high up. His antlers point up (see our study of this image in *The Writer's Way in France*, pp. 250-56). Joyce wrote in some defiant young verse:

> I stand, the self-doomed, unafraid,
>
>   . . .
>
> Firm as the mountain-ridges where
> I flash my antlers on the air.
> ("The Holy Office")

If Rimbaud is descended from a woman, nevertheless she is here the highest and coldest, Diana, the moon-goddess, chaste huntress of stags. This may be a reminiscence of Gautier's "Ténèbres":

> Ils tettent librement la féconde mamelle;
> Et tout l'or du Pactole entre leurs doigts ruisselle.

But the heather ("ronces") makes me mindful of Scott's

> The stag at eve had drunk his fill,
> Where danced the moon on Monan's rill . . .
> ("The Lady of the Lake")

The general note of communion or promiscuity running through the poem is maintained in the image of Diana's giving suck to the stags: "L'azur et l'onde communient" ("Bannières de mai"). It certainly brings her down to earth.

> Les Bacchantes des banlieues sanglotent et la lune brûle et
> hurle.

The "Bacchantes des banlieues" are a pleasant old-new irony in the mode
of T. S. Eliot's Sweeney, Joyce's Bloom; compare the Sabines of "Bottom."
Clearly women, recalling the maenads in the myth of Orpheus (see the
"orphéon" earlier), are angry at this reluctant male (cf. Diana's disciple
Hippolytus and the fugitive male of "Bottom") and threaten to tear him
apart. The moon burns and howls as if in anger or lust, for it is the orb
not only of Diana but of witch-mother Hecate, and the regulator of
fecundity (echo of *sang* in "sanglotent"?).

> Vénus entre dans les cavernes des forgerons et des ermites.

Venus reobserved; as in classic myth, where she is wedded to Hephaestus,
she goes to see the smith. Rimbaud in "Soleil et chair" and "Le Forgeron"
favored such a union, as he did later in "Bonne pensée du matin":

> pour ces Ouvriers charmants
>
> . . .
>
> Vénus! laisse un peu les Amants, . . .

Hermits live in caves too and dramatically deserve such attentions;
Rimbaud thinks of them again in the *Saison en enfer*.
 A woman's voice penetrates into the caves of "Barbare." Is there a
vestige of Tannhaüser's Venusberg here?

> Des groupes de beffrois chantent les idées des peuples.

Compare the "fêtes de fraternité" of "Phrases," and the social poetry of
"Le Forgeron," etc.

> Des châteaux bâtis en os sort la musique inconnue.

This echoes "les rauques musiques . . . nos os sont revêtus d'un nouveau
corps amoureux" ("Being beauteous") and "le sang chante, les os s'élargis-
sent" ("Parade"). The inner architecture of vision which is the *château*
(see "O saisons, ô châteaux") is apparently linked with the inner human
physical structure, or architecture, of bones, the skeleton; but it is alive,
with flowing and enlarging love, marrowy. The combination of "possi-
bilités harmoniques et architecturales" ("Jeunesse") leads to something
like the "maison musicale pour notre claire sympathie" ("Phrases"), the
notion of a structured city where men will live in harmony in the future.

> Toutes les légendes évoluent et les élans se ruent dans les bourgs.

Stir in time ("légendes") and space (city-streets). It is like the myths of old Ireland, or Greece, prolonged in the Dublin streets of Joyce. The "élans" (elk) go back to the "cerfs" above; ambiguously, they can be *élans*: impulses, part of the general commotion.

> Le paradis des orages s'effondre.

A storm is the essence of paradisiac change; see under "Michel et Christine" for numerous examples in Rimbaud. Like the renewing flood of "Après le déluge," it recedes.

A "crumbling" is a hint of an Icarian down-curve as we near the end, a predictable pattern in Rimbaud.

> Les sauvages dansent sans cesse la fête de la nuit.

A foretaste of the savage (and in a sense Rousseau-like) dance that stubbornly beats down the cancerously proliferating mind in the *Saison en enfer* ("Mauvais sang"). The same theme of new toughness, action, operates in both texts.

> Et une heure je suis descendu dans le mouvement d'un boulevard de Bagdad où des compagnies ont chanté la joie du travail nouveau, sous une brise épaisse, circulant sans pouvoir éluder les fabuleux fantômes des monts où l'on a dû se retrouver.

The Bagdad boulevard is the dream, as in "Vies" ("avenues du pays saint"), of a calm new perspective of maturity and harmony in an ideal Orient poles removed from our contaminated Western bustle.

The "compagnies" are like the earlier "flottes orphéoniques"—male choruses—and the "corporations" which we linked with the mature singing males of "Parade." His dream of adult masculine doing as in "Ouvriers" (the "bras durci" there echoes the "bons bras" here, below, as well as passages of the *Saison*) is still accompanied by the old "fabulous phantoms" of the magic "heights" of revery, the mountains themselves; he cannot "elude" them. But the fact that these mountains which rose up at the beginning of the vision are now ghosts indicates a fall of inspiration. The rendezvous between Rimbaud and his "other" in this vision has ended in only a possible and past encounter: "l'on a dû se retrouver." He is not sure it really occurred and in any case it is over; the verb ("ont chanté") is in the past tense. A "thick breeze" seems to dim the scene as if in the evening, like the sighing breeze of "Mémoire."

The "se retrouver" implies a rendezvous with inspiration as in "Phrases": "maison musicale . . . je vous trouverai," or in "Génie" or "Conte." But the interjection of a particular "I" and a particular hour, "une heure," breaks the visionary mood, as does the past tense.

> Quels bons bras, quelle belle heure me rendront cette région d'où viennent mes sommeils et mes moindres mouvements?

A pathetic appeal to an absent father-figure—the nearby "travail" emphasizes this virile aspect of the "bras"—whose strong arms, as in "Génie," in a "beautiful hour" can show, and perhaps give, him this ideal of male effectiveness together with lyric delight. Baudelaire once cried: ". . . je sortirai . . . D'un monde où l'action n'est pas la sœur du rêve" ("Le Reniement de Saint-Pierre").[2] Rimbaud will, in "Génie," ask again for these superbly privileged (and original) moments which combine opposites in a higher synthesis: power from the Source, the power that gives movement as well as true rest.

Vagabonds

It is generally recognized that Rimbaud is describing, in this *Illumination*, his relationship to Verlaine. That has a certain anecdotal interest; the poetry comes only in a few remarkable snatches.

> Pitoyable frère! Que d'atroces veillées je lui dus! "Je ne me saisissais pas fervemment de cette entreprise. Je m'étais joué de son infirmité. Par ma faute nous retournerions en exil, en esclavage." Il me supposait un guignon et une innocence très bizarres, et il ajoutait des raisons inquiétantes.

Rimbaud's basic attitude towards Verlaine, as a weaker and more effeminate soul—"the vierge folle" of *Une Saison en enfer*—is borne out by these beginning lines. Their homosexual *ménage* was typically—as in Genet—unbearable at times, with sleepless Bohemian nights spent in mutual torment. He imitates Verlaine's nagging querulous voice, in indirect quotes: Rimbaud was not really interested in their joint enterprise, etc. Verlaine did regard his young friend as unreliable, demonic, and the recorded accusation rings true to life and what we know of the pair; as does the innocent and bad-luck hex ("guignon") Verlaine saw in Rim-

---

[2] Mallarmé took Baudelaire to task for this, in a letter to Cazalis; but the dilemma and impulse returned to haunt Mallarmé in his later work.

baud. The "raisons inquiétantes" he alleges might refer to Rimbaud's precarious sanity.

> Je répondais en ricanant à ce satanique docteur, et finissais par gagner la fenêtre. Je créais, par delà la campagne traversée par des bandes de musique rare, les fantômes du futur luxe nocturne.

Rimbaud's scornful reply is to escape youthfully—in vision or physically—by the window and light out across nocturnal country, with lyric zones ("bandes")—"bandes atmosphériques" ("Veillées," II)—as in "Mystique": "la bande en haut du tableau est formée de la rumeur tournante et bondissante des conques des mers et des nuits humaines." These nocturnal phantoms and luxuries are like the spectres and the music of ancestors he sees and hears in "Métropolitain": "crânes lumineux . . . les autres fantasmagories—la campagne . . . la musique des anciens." They are also related to the visions of "Entends comme brame" and the night feast with whirling apparitions in "Est-elle almée?"

Verlaine confirmed that the "satanic doctor" was himself, in a letter to Charles de Sivry (Pléiade, p. 782).

> Après cette distraction vaguement hygiénique, je m'étendais sur une paillasse. Et, presque chaque nuit, aussitôt endormi, le pauvre frère se levait, la bouche pourrie, les yeux arrachés,—tel qu'il se rêvait!—et me tirait dans la salle en hurlant son songe de chagrin idiot.

He returns from his "hygienic" excursion. But Verlaine keeps up his fitful tirade: on-running, "horizontal" like a woman's.

"Hurlant son songe" repeats a formula of Mallarmé's "Toast funèbre" ("Hurle ce songe"), but that is probably accidental.

> J'avais en effet, en toute sincérité d'esprit, pris l'engagement de le rendre à son état primitif de fils du Soleil,—et nous errions, nourris du vin des cavernes et du biscuit de la route, moi pressé de trouver le lieu et la formule.

By contrast Rimbaud's spirit is vertical, free, a sun-son's; we recall "Vin, fils sacré du Soleil" (Baudelaire, "Le Vin des chiffoniers"). No need to invoke Incas, etc.[1]—it is an obvious enough idea. The "Sun . . . General" is a clear father-figure in "Alchimie du verbe" and in "Bannières de mai":

---

[1] Phèdre, in Racine's version and in the original Greek of Euripides, was the daughter of the Sun.

"C'est rire aux parents, qu'au soleil." To his sister, on his deathbed, he said enviously: "Toi tu marcheras dans le soleil."

Finally, this is a scene, or one of a series of scenes, portraying their wanderings (hence the *vagabonds* of the title, which they notoriously were). They drink the wine of caverns. This may refer to fountains in caves, cf. "J'ai une soif à craindre la gangrène: les rivières ardennaises et belges, les cavernes, voilà ce que je regrette" (letter to Delahaye of June 1872). But it may refer to "les bouges où nous nous enivrions" ("Délires I"). They eat biscuits on the road, the typically tough fare of a wayfarer like the hardtack of voyagers. Rimbaud sees himself as the eternal seeker —a Wandering Jew as in "Comédie de la soif"—of the right place (like the restless Nietzsche) and the right expression, the *logos* that would say it all.

Villes, II

This is still the city which we saw emerging in "Les Ponts," and the earlier "Villes," as an ideal architecture: light, airy, above-it-all as a Klee painting (with some Piranesi effects, some baroque, operatic or theatrical features, and hints of a multi-ringed spectacle). There are certain clear reminiscences of London, which with it foreignness, its pragmatic and democratic sprawl, obsessed Rimbaud as an embryonic vision of the homogenized and technocratic future. But this city is more luxurious and aristocratic; it is a dream of a place almost without people—like Baudelaire's "Rêve parisien"; its magnificence is somewhat cold (snowy), indifferent or beyond his reach or understanding. What people there are seem rich and hurrying, or fearful, or vague. It is possible that Rimbaud was influenced in his vision by the drawings of John Martin, a contemporary English artist whose grotesque fantasies had much in common with those of Grandville (Rimbaud mentions the latter in "Ce qu'on dit au poète à propos de fleurs").

> L'acropole officielle outre les conceptions de la barbarie moderne les plus colossales.

The "acropolis," it has been recognized, may be the Crystal Palace built for the London Exposition of 1851. Dostoevski, in *Notes from Underground*, had made it his symbol of a manipulatory or Faustian modernity, against which nature, the irrational forces, would some day surge up in revolt. Rimbaud seems to be more suspended in his reaction: nothing is yet promised or foreseen. But the "barbarie" certainly indicates a tone of partial repulsion, as does the "outre." Nonetheless he is caught and held by the ambitions, highly fascinated by the "hénaurme," as Flaubert would say.

> Impossible d'exprimer le jour mat produit par ce ciel immuable-
> ment gris, l'éclat impérial des bâtisses, et la neige éternelle du
> sol.

The effect of colossal *flatness* and breadth is rendered by the word "mat,"
by the "gray," stable stretch of sky, the width implied in "bâtisses." The
flat a in "mat . . . éclat . . . impérial . . . bâtisses" enhances this effect.

The association of snow, eternity, and city repeats a scene from "Les
Déserts de l'amour": "la ville sans fin . . . avec une neige pour étouffer le
monde, décidément." A city is foreign to the provincial boy, a place of fear
and alienation, a future eternally without the home-comfort he really
wanted.

> On a reproduit dans un goût d'énormité singulier toutes les
> merveilles classiques de l'architecture.

He describes a typical heteroclite modern urbanity in quest of the varie-
gated swank of the past. We have seen it in many a big city on various
continents.

> J'assiste à des expositions de peinture dans des locaux vingt fois
> plus vastes qu'Hampton-Court. Quelle peinture!

There is no problem here, but no particular illumination either. So he
saw paintings in vast places. And was either impressed or depressed ex-
cessively, according to the exclamation mark. Maybe both. In "Alchimie
du verbe": "[je] trouvais dérisoires les célébrités de la peinture et de la
poésie moderne."

> Un Nabuchodonosor norwégien a fait construire les escaliers
> des ministères; les subalternes que j'ai pu voir sont déjà plus
> fiers que des [Br . . . , an unreadable word], et j'ai tremblé à
> l'aspect des gardiens de colosses et officiers de constructions.

A Babylonian hint (recalling the "roi de Babylone" of "Bonne pensée
du matin") that is extended through the fancy description of many-
leveled architecture. The "guards" of the places and "officers" supervising
construction echo the monstrously virile figures of "Parade." Rimbaud
fears and admires mature males with jobs or missions in both texts.

> Par le groupement des bâtiments en squares, cours et terrasses
> fermées, on a évincé les cochers.

The closed-in areas indicate a fear of snobbish exclusion, bearing out the
note of Rousseauistic alienation we detected earlier. Underwood has ob-

served that elegant houses in London were often arranged in private squares from which traffic was excluded (in Py, p. 143).

> Les parcs représentent la nature primitive travaillée par un art superbe.

This combination seems obvious enough in any city; it is a curiously direct observation.

> Le haut quartier a des parties inexplicables: un bras de mer, sans bateaux, roule sa nappe de grésil bleu entre des quais chargés de candélabres géants.

The invading sea-arm, is, as in "Les Ponts," a communion with the beyond. It is a high part of the city, raised up like the picture sea of "Après le déluge": Rimbaud was evidently moved by the powerful sublimation of that mass. Looking at the ocean, one is often surprised at seeing it *rise up* into the distance. Up and down join in a colossal wedding.

The candelabras along the water are probably vestiges of streetlights along the Embankment, or harbor lights. The term "candelabra" indicates a confusion between interior and exterior which is the reverse counterpart of "Les lampes et les tapis de la veillée font le bruit des vagues" ("Veillée," III). And we find similar confusions in "Les Déserts de l'amour" and "Le Bateau ivre." The indication "sans bateaux" echoes "des vagues sans vaisseaux" in "Enfance." This gives a feeling of frightening openness (as in the breaking away to boatless sea in "Le Bateau ivre") combined with comforting reminiscences in the lights, which he scorned in "Le Bateau ivre": "l'œil niais des falots," at least for a while. . . .

Cf. the "girandoles" of "Fête d'hiver."

> Un pont court conduit à une poterne immédiatement sous le dôme de la Sainte-Chapelle.

The significance of this detail escapes me. But it is a pleasant detail, architecturally. The Sainte-Chapelle reference, after Hampton Court, indicates that Rimbaud is playing with cities and with us, making an impressionistic amalgamation.

> Ce dôme est une armature d'acier artistique de quinze mille pieds de diamètre environ.

Crystal palace again, or something similar. The poetic *apport* is minimal.

> Sur quelques points des passerelles de cuivre, des plates-formes, des escaliers qui contournent les halles et les piliers, j'ai cru pouvoir juger la profondeur de la ville! C'est le prodige dont je n'ai pu me rendre compte: quels sont les niveaux des autres quartiers sur ou sous l'acropole? Pour l'étranger de notre temps la reconnaissance est impossible.

(Leonardo's sketch of a city was on levels like this.) Rimbaud is moved by the *depth* he sees from upper levels. The city reflects his inner verticality. Hence the puzzled fascination, the attempt to *fathom* it. But he is thwarted as at the end of "Mémoire"; the depth is too problematic. He is an eternal "stranger" in this world, which he cannot "reconnoitre."

> Le quartier commerçant est un circus d'un seul style, avec galeries à arcades.

This reminds me of the Place Vendôme, or the Place Ducale in Charleville. Underwood thinks of Piccadilly Circus (in Py, p. 144).

> On ne voit pas de boutiques, mais la neige de la chaussée est écrasée; quelques nababs aussi rares que les promeneurs d'un matin de dimanche à Londres, se dirigent vers une diligence de diamants.

Obscure memory of a city on an empty day, perhaps Sunday (cf. "Bruxelles") with rich people heading for luxurious carriages, all this is an apt image of his abandonment: the treasure is for others.

> Quelques divans de velours rouge: on sert des boissons polaires dont le prix varie de huit cents à huit mille roupies.

These velvet divans could be in rich restaurants in Paris; but the "roupies" open it again to a never-never city.

> A l'idée de chercher des théâtres sur ce circus, je me réponds que les boutiques doivent contenir des drames assez sombres. Je pense qu'il y a une police. Mais la loi doit être tellement étrange, que je renonce à me faire une idée des aventuriers d'ici.

This repeats the dramas of everyday life he described in "Ville." Vigny, in "Stello," described such a drama in a London shop. But here we sense sooty London crime as in "Ville." The related idea of police comes up. However, apparently due to his state of abandonment, alienation, Rimbaud finds it hard to think of any such *attention* from authority. So he speaks of a "strange" law and cannot work up the idea of resistance to it. He was not a criminal type and could not bring himself to get that attention, unlike the *forçat* he will admire in the *Saison en enfer*. True, there were provocations and escapades; but not enough and not now and not *really* —in this last he foreshadows our current student agitators.

> Le faubourg, aussi élégant qu'une belle rue de Paris, est favorisé d'un air de lumière.

In this final paragraph the mood lifts to a light airy elegance, *genre rue du faubourg Saint-Honoré*.

> L'élément démocratique compte quelques cents âmes.

The "democratic element," i.e., the number of relatively poor people, is minimal; like Rimbaud, they are marginal to the magnificent and over-bearing city built by virile and efficient men for the rich and powerful.

> Là encore les maisons ne se suivent pas; le faubourg se perd bizarrement dans la campagne, le "Comté" qui remplit l'oc-cident éternel des forêts et des plantations prodigieuses où les gentilshommes sauvages chassent leurs chroniques sous la lumière qu'on a créée.

The houses of this area, like the other constructions, do not lead any-where; they too exclude him by not presenting a discernible path to follow. So his mind wanders on into vague suburban outskirts. The thought of his own poor or worker status, as in "Ouvriers," makes Rimbaud think of his country-city vibrancy: he is marginal to advanced city life, half-sunk still in his Rousseau-like provinciality and other backwardness or his incapacity to "make it" in urban terms. Thus the "County,"[1] the rural background, emerges into view. Those country gentlemen are like the one he imagined himself to be in "Vies," a possible *role* for him if he is excluded from city life. But the "created light" and the "chroniques" in-dicate that city terms track such men into their pastoral havens: they "hunt for the news columns" as well as for game.[2] Their infinite sweep of forest and distant plantations is impressive but really too vague and vast for a resting place. Beyond all this, city and bucolic setting, is the un-settled and unsettling mystery of it all.

---

[1] "Comté" seems to be used in the sense of English "County" (Underwood).
[2] Some critics think "chroniques" refers to ancient chronicles, the "lumière" their painted illuminations.

Veillées

The title recalls the lost masterpiece, "Le Veilleur," and "L'ordre, éternel veilleur" ("L'Homme juste"), as well as various fragments such as the "âme sentinelle" of "L'Éternité"; the final section of "Phrases": "Je baisse les feux du lustre, je me jette sur le lit, et, tourné du côté de l'ombre, je vous vois, mes filles! mes reines!"; "Petite veille d'ivresse, sainte!" ("Matinée d'ivresse"); or "C'est la veille. Recevons tous les influx de vigueur et de tendresse réelle" ("Adieu"). In "Les Sœurs de charité" we see the sleepless young man turning in his bed. Scenes of "Le Bateau ivre" occur in an insomniac domestic setting which are echoed in the *veillée* of part III here.

Staying up at night and seeing visions, as Poe and Mallarmé did (either seated before a fireplace, like Rimbaud in "Nocturne vulgaire," or just lying in bed) is common enough. There is no more *voyance* here, *pace* Antoine Adam *et al.*, than elsewhere, and who cares really whether Rimbaud was using his drug-stimulated method or not? Indeed that over-used word *voyance* becomes pointless when applied to this clearly and even simply poetic piece, particularly part I.

"Veillées" imply being awake: wide awake, intensely alert to beauty; or something like a knight's vigil, waiting for a privileged moment of election. That "It" is the *Ce* of the series of "C'est."

I

> C'est le repos éclairé, ni fièvre, ni langueur, sur le lit ou sur
> le pré.

The privileged moment he seeks is expressed by the union of opposites in "repos éclairé," a Joycean stasis, a still intensity. This is a highly charged or electric of awareness, an "epiphany." "On the bed" bears out our impression of a nocturnal waiting in the usual place, but "on the meadow" shows that his title is flexible. "Ni fièvre ni langueur": he is balanced beatifically, avoiding extremes of restlessness and apathy. As in "L'Éternité," he has attained a sort of *ataraxia*: "pas d'espérance."

> C'est l'ami ni ardent ni faible. L'ami.

"Le Prince était le Génie" of "Conte" seemed to echo Montaigne's formula for pure friendship: "Parce que c'était lui, parce que c'était moi" (we noted that Rimbaud memorized portions of the *Essais*). That "c'était" is close to this "C'est": both express the ineffability of purity. The clearly separated phrases, surrounded by much clean space, seem to emerge reluctantly as a *pis aller* for silence, almost with an audible equivalent for a shrug: "Comment dire?" A friend is a friend is a friend. Easier to say what he is not: he is not too this or too that; neither "ardent" nor "weak," but just right. A friend. Or rather *the* friend. Note the sheer arrest, through isolated substantives surrounded by a halo of silence as in Mallarmé's frequently verbless utterances.

C'est l'aimée ni tourmentante ni tourmentée. L'aimée.

Mallarmé said to his mistress Méry: "Dame [soyez] sans trop d'ardeur." Here Rimbaud shows a comparably sincere, if wise, love of the opposite sex.

L'air et le monde point cherchés. La vie.

Here there is not even a "c'est." Beyond people is the static All in pure air itself. The world, as in "Génie" or "Barbare" ("O monde!"), is roundly perfect at such rare moments, given freely to one who is totally resigned, *désintéressé*. Then life is precious and entire.

—Était-ce donc ceci?

But the "ce"—the It—is fading, alas, as the curve starts downward like the shape of an inverted smile.

—Et le rêve fraîchit.

"Fraîchit" means mainly "turns sour." Or "gets cold," in the same sense of disappointment. "Le rêve" refers to the waking vision, the "epiphany."

Py believes that *fraîchit* implies a refreshing, a whipping-up of the vision; and he sees a connection between the fact that it is a marine term and the imagery of the sea in part III.

II

L'éclairage revient à l'arbre de bâtisse. Des deux extrémités de la salle, décors quelconques, des élévations harmoniques se joignent.

This vision is particularly nocturnal, shadow-colored. It is a dream ("Rêve intense"), with something of the night-setting, including prominently the framework of a room, mingled in.

A "bâtisse" is a frame building. The idea of "tree," an organic hierarchy of limbs, seems associated with the visible structure of such a building—cf.

the "armature d'acier" of "Villes II"—and, more intimately, with an inner
organization of the sleeper's body (and perhaps some outer equivalent in
the juncture of human limbs). There are many versions of these analogies
in modern, especially surrealistic, art (cf. the body as a boat and plank in
"Le Bateau ivre"). Rimbaud is fascinated with such a structure in
"Scènes," where he is influenced by the partitions of the seating in an
opera house: "L'opéra-comique se divise sur notre scène à l'arête d'inter-
section de dix cloisons dressées de la galerie aux feux." In "Nocturne vul-
gaire" an echo of the opera house is found in the "brèches opéradiques dans
les cloisons," another nocturnal vision of such an architecture (along with
toits, etc.).

The "harmonic elevations" are a sort of joining together, on a superior
plane (like the inn-roofs and the raised operatic platform of "Villes, I," or
the weathercock of "Après le déluge," the suspended convergence of cables
in "Ponts"), of diverse parts of the psyche (cf. the "succession psycholo-
gique" below) at an intersection, a unifying spire of the spirit to which
various strands of the self lead (cf. the circumflex in "arête," of "Scènes").
The "éclairage" is the psychic illumination (*Illuminations*) which ac-
companies and suffuses the celebration of integration. It has an objective
correlative in the passing or gliding luminosity of walls ("La muraille en
face du veilleur") at night in a dark room—in our time usually by the
headlights of wayfaring cars (as in Delmore Schwartz's "In the Naked
Bed"), in Rimbaud's rather by an early dawn glow, or an itinerant lantern,
perhaps on a carriage, or the maternal light down the hall described in
part III and in "Les Déserts de l'amour"; cf. the "esprits des eaux [qui] /
Entrent vaguer aux sphères de l'alcove" ("Jeune Ménage").

> La muraille en face du veilleur est une succession psychologique
> de coupes de frises, de bandes atmosphériques et d'accidences
> géologiques.—

This theatrical "happening" effect—reality decomposed into strips like
planes of sea, land, sky in a landscape (or his cityscapes of the "Ville"
series)—is very like the one in "Mystique":

> Et tandis que la bande en haut du tableau est formée de la
> rumeur tournante et bondissante des conques des mers et des
> nuits humaines,
> La douceur fleurie des étoiles et du ciel et du reste descend
> en face du talus ... et fait l'abîme ...

It also recalls "Villes, I": "Au-dessus du niveau des plus hautes crêtes, une mer . . . chargée de flottes orphéoniques et de la rumeur des perles et des conques précieuses. . . . Sur les versants des moissons de fleurs. . . ."

The "accidences géologiques" are such "bands," with a harder texture as in "Barbare" or "Soir historique" ("l'Allemagne s'échafaude vers des lunes; les déserts tartares," etc.).

> —Rêve intense et rapide de groupes sentimentaux avec des êtres de tous les caractères parmi toutes les apparences.

The people he sees are very diverse, including the "sentimental groups" of the jumbled human comedy, as in "Bruxelles," and perhaps the more grotesque ones of "Parade." One thinks particularly of the *dramatis personae* of "Mémoire" or the "jeunes mères et grandes sœurs" of "Enfance." The effect is kaleidoscopic, as in "Nocturne vulgaire."

III

> Les lampes et les tapis de la veillée font le bruit des vagues, la nuit, le long de la coque et autour du steerage.

This is the scene, as in "Le Bateau ivre" ("l'œil niais des falots"), of the maternal lamp down the hall, perhaps kept lit for a sick or fear-ridden child, a beacon of security as he undertook his fever-tossed nocturnal sea-voyage. There is a similar image in "Les Déserts de l'amour": "La lampe de la famille rougissait l'une après l'autre les chambres voisines." In "Après le déluge," embers glowed near a mother-like Sorceress; in "Les Étrennes des orphelins" "—Le rêve maternel, c'est le tiède tapis."

> La mer de la veillée, telle que les seins d'Amélie.

The sea of the initial image persists, its undulations now being likened to breast-shapes as in "L'étoile a pleuré rose . . . La mer a perlé rousse à tes mammes" or the "sein des grandes mers" of "Soleil et chair." Amélie is no one discernible; such mysterious feminine names: Hortense, Henrika, Louise Vanaen de Voringhem, etc., are scattered sparsely throughout the *Illuminations*, tantalizingly . . . Amélie is a very feminine name, and m is the most breast-related of letters, but this brings us scarcely farther.

> Les tapisseries, jusqu'à mi-hauteur, des taillis de dentelle, teinte d'émeraude, où se jettent les tourterelles de la veillée.

These "tapisseries" reflect no doubt real wall-hangings (or wallpaper). However modest, they are always a source of deep mystery to children.

Mallarmé was haunted by bird-flights (and *ramage*) emerging from embroidered tapestries in the "Ouverture ancienne d'Hérodiade." In "Barbare," "les formes, les sueurs, les chevelures et les yeux, flottant" spring from such an arabesquing wall-source. Mallarmé's maternal figures (e.g., *nourrice*) in the tapestry were "sibylline" with "buried eyes." In *Les Paradis artificiels* ("Théâtre de Séraphin"), Baudelaire described the vision of a friend: a cage-like room surrounded by trellises filled with birds and golden light. The vision in the sheepfold of *Le Grand Meaulnes* is comparable. All this is archetypal womb-tree fantasy à la Tchelitchew. The emerald tint here recalls a related vision, the wall of gold-shot greenery in "Tête de faune": "feuillée, écrin vert taché d'or . . . exquise broderie."

> La plaque du foyer noir, de réels soleils des grèves: ah! puits des magies; seule vue d'aurore, cette fois.

As in Mallarmé's famous *théâtre-âtre* ("Crayonné au Théâtre"), the *foyer* is a minuscule stage for the stirrer of ashes, or perhaps it is just standing across the room from the reclining poet, cloaked in shadowy mystery ("noir"), waiting to be illumined like a stage *rampe*. It is thus a "well of magic" since it goes up and down, in depth. In "Les Étrennes des orphelins," the hearth, like the above-mentioned carpet, was the locus (or *focus*, the Latin root of *foyer*) of the absent mother:

> Elle a donc oublié, le soir, seule et penchée
> D'exciter une flamme à la cendre arrachée.

In the joyous days when she was *there*:

> Un grand feu pétillait, clair, dans la cheminée,
> Toute la vieille chambre était illuminée [cf. *Illuminations*];
> Et les reflets vermeils, sortis du grand foyer,
> Sur les meubles vernis aimaient à tournoyer . . .

But now:

> Il n'est point de parents, de foyer. . . .

And still they dream that:

> Au foyer plein d'éclairs chante gaîment le feu. . . .

All this makes us strongly feel that in this *Illumination* there is a memory of hope of happy love for the mother, the home; a "dawn" of expectation of that felicity. The *veillée* was a waiting-up, among other possibilities, for that moment of It, the supreme apparition, as in Mallarmé's "Sonnet" ("pour votre chère morte") where the mother certainly participates in the fireplace-image, as Mauron and Cellier observe.

The black *foyer*, paradoxically, is a source, like night itself, of a blissful dawn, Rimbaud's favorite moment. Hence it is like a shoreline ("grève"), a horizon from which a sun will rise. In "Adieu" (*Une Saison en enfer*), "c'est la veille [cf. veillée] . . . Et à l'aurore . . . nous entrerons aux splendides villes," as he imagines a hopeful morning beach, "des plages sans fin . . . sous les brises du matin." The strand is the place of his imminent departure as well as that of the sun—and he is *fils du Soleil*.

A black puddle ("flache / Noire et froide"), in "Le Bateau ivre," was the theatre for the white flight of a sail.

Perhaps Verlaine's "Soleils / Couchants sur les grèves" ("Soleils couchants") is faintly remembered here. A sketch for the *Saison en enfer* reads: ". . . sur la grève le clair de lune" (Bernard, p. 334).

Mystique

This is a summer poem of "splendor in the grass" and the comforting warmth and nearness of the sky even at night.

> Sur la pente du talus les anges tournent leurs robes de laine dans les herbages d'acier et d'émeraude.

The "talus" which "cradled him" in "Enfance"—it is a gentle friendly haven for a child—is also, conversely, the threshold to the beyond. It has a near theatre in its grass (and later a far theatre over the ramp-like crest, the horizon). In "Mémoire" the light in the grass was also called "anges": "l'ébat des anges;—Non . . . le courant d'or en marche [the light reflected in the river], / meut ses bras, noirs, et lourds, et frais surtout, d'herbe." In "Le Dormeur du val" there was the same descent of light mingled with the river-reflection in the grass:

> C'est un trou de verdure où chante une rivière
> Accrochant follement aux herbes des haillons
> D'argent; où le soleil, de la montagne fière,
> Luit: c'est un petit val qui mousse de rayons.

And farther down: "dans l'herbe . . . son lit vert où la lumière pleut." In "Beth-Saïda" the light is again an angel: "ce reflet, pareil à un ange blanc," which is multiplied, in "Mémoire," into "mille anges blancs qui se séparent sur la route." The "laine" like the "haillons" is surprisingly concrete. Recalling the fragment of sky which shines through the leaves of "Roman" they stand out eidetically—a higher saturation of color will produce this odd effect.

Rimbaud, in his "laine dans les herbages," like Mallarmé, might have been influenced by the sonority of Verlaine's name: *vert* and *laine*. In "Tombeau" (*de Verlaine*) Mallarmé wrote: "Verlaine? Il est caché parmi l'herbe, Verlaine" and fused with this grassy image the "nubiles plis" of clouds. Here is a passage from our *Toward the Poems of Mallarmé* (p. 175): "The resonance of *laine*—adding subtle touches of fluffy white clouds emerging with spring—reminds one of the frequent use of the word *moutonner* in Verlaine, and the related image of sheep. For example, in *Sagesse*, which Mallarmé admired exceedingly (we suspect for the properly lyric poems in it like this one) there is the wonderful 'L'échelonnement des haies' which goes on:

> Moutonne à l'infini, mer
> Claire dans le brouillard clair
> Qui sent bon les jeunes baies.
>
> Des arbres et des moulins
> Sont légers sur le vert tendre
> Où vient s'ébattre et s'étendre
> L'agilité des poulains.
>
> Dans ce vague d'un Dimanche
> Voici se jouer aussi
> De grandes brebis aussi
> Douces que leur laine blanche . . .

Mallarmé was certainly in a Verlainian mood when he penned:

> Simple, tendre, aux prés se mêlant
> Ce que tout buisson a de laine
> Quand a passé le troupeau blanc
> Semble l'âme de Madeleine."

Here, in Rimbaud, the "laine" and the "herbages" create just such a mood. The "laine" may be a hint of sheep grazing in a meadow rising by association from daubs of light or white flowers (the "ombelles" of "Mémoire," etc.).

The "acier," I believe, has to do with the reverse side of *sharp* blades of grass when blown by the wind: a flat metallic look.[1] The "émeraude" is a more obvious effect of grass's greenness jeweled by light as in the

---

[1] Dhôtel's impression of railway tracks here seems beside the point.

"taillis de dentelle, teinte d'émeraude" of "Veillées," III, which we compared to the wall of greenery in "Tête de faune." This hardness, crystallization, of the organic is a common effect in Rimbaud: a higher synthesis in art.

> Des prés de flammes bondissent jusqu'au sommet du mamelon. A gauche le terreau de l'arête est piétiné par tous les homicides et toutes les batailles, et tous les bruits désastreux filent leur courbe. Derrière l'arête de droite la ligne des orients, des progrès.

The child's imagination is stirred more fearfully by the theatre at the crest and beyond it: all the awesome unknown of adult doing, such as wars, violence of all sorts—"les homicides et toutes les batailles." The stir is associated with flame-like waves of vegetation rising on the crest. On the left—West—is an area associated with disaster, sundown as in Mallarmé's apocalyptic "soir . . . crime, bûcher," of "Ouverture ancienne d'Hérodiade" or "tison de gloire, sang par écume" of "Victorieusement fui." On the right—East ("orients")—is a dawn area of buoyant promise, "progress."

The synesthesia of noises which "run a contour" (a surveying term) is duplicated in the "Des accords . . . filent" of "Les Ponts" (also in the flute melody which traces the line of a nymph's back in Mallarmé's "Faune").

> Et tandis que la bande en haut du tableau est formée de la rumeur tournante et bondissante des conques des mers et des nuits humaines,

These theatrical strips of sensation, like planes of a field-sky-water landscape placed in exciting depth perspective, were already seen in "Villes, I": "Au-dessus du niveau des plus hautes crêtes, une mer troublée par la naissance éternelle de Vénus, chargée de flottes orphéoniques et de la rumeur des perles et des conques précieuses, . . . Sur les versants des moissons de fleurs. . . ." In "Veillées," II, too, there is "une succession psychologique de coupes de frises, de bandes atmosphériques et d'accidences géologiques."

In "Les Sœurs de charité" we heard that stirring rumor of the inner sea on a love-tossed bed, the "nuits humaines" here: "Pareil aux jeunes mers, pleurs de nuits estivales, / Qui se retournent sur des lits de diamants."

> La douceur fleurie des étoiles et du ciel et du reste descend en face du talus, comme un panier,—contre notre face, et fait l'abîme fleurant et bleu là-dessous.

How unusual—yet absolutely typical—is this quietly happy love, in Rimbaud! Nature is gentle and close to the child. When we are full of emotion, the stars seem very near. The sky seems to come right down; that luminescence of the horizon—"l'abîme fleurant et bleu là-dessous"—on summer nights seems to bring out its quality of nearness and descend like a comforting bread basket lowered by a mother near a child's face. The stars are like snowy flowers ("fleurie") or snowflakes, or breadcrumbs, manna, hence the "panier" (recalling the bread-benediction in "Les Effarés"). Yeats expressed the nearness this way: "hid his face amid a crowd of stars." The relaxed and sincerely lyric mood is emphasized by the repetition "fleurie . . . fleurant." Cf. Hugo's "Nuits de juin" (*Les Rayons et les ombres*).

Aube

Aube is almost everybody's favorite *Illumination*. It is certainly one of the most accessible, and it is pure Rimbaud. Even the sound of his name (*baud*) echoes the sound of the title. The rubbery b's with the buoyancy of dawn are found in a telling sequence at the beginning and the end of the poem.

The title is without an article (like "Départ") : a sheer phenomenon.

Dawn, it is evident, is Rimbaud's elect moment. For example, in a famous letter to Delahaye he wrote: "A trois heures du matin, la bougie pâlit; tous les oiseaux crient à la fois dans les arbres: c'est fini. Plus de travail. Il me fallait regarder les arbres, le ciel, saisis par cette heure indicible, première du matin. Je voyais les dortoirs du lycée, absolument sourds. . . ." It is the moment of rebirth, with the ecstatic possibility of a self, a world made miraculously whole this time around.

In "Les Déserts de l'amour" he is "ému jusqu'à la mort par le murmure du lait du matin" (one thinks of Mallarmé's "Don du Poème" with its mysteriously commingled hunger for milky morning sky and musical nursing mother . . .).

> J'ai embrassé l'aube d'été.

The confident "J'ai" is like those in "Le Bateau ivre": he is taking possession directly. The child is king of this domain as in "Royauté"; Nature is his queen (as in "Sensation": "heureux comme avec une femme," or "j'ai assis la Beauté sur mes genoux," *Une Saison en enfer*). This *passé composé* looks forward to the burst of action of "J'ai marché" below; meanwhile the passive background is rendered by a series of imperfects. Later, the more fixed forms of the *passé defini* will be interspersed with the *passé composé*. They provide a naïve *Märchen* childlike paratactic narration: "et les pierreries regardèrent, et les ailes se levèrent . . . une fleur . . . me dit son nom."

Note the buoyant b's of "embrassé . . . aube . . . bougeait . . . ombres."

The light é sounds of "été" will be echoed in "réveil . . . était" at the end. These are rising acute accents.

> Rien ne bougeait encore au front des palais. L'eau était morte. Les camps d'ombres ne quittaient pas la route du bois. J'ai marché, réveillant les haleines vives et tièdes, et les pierreries regardèrent, et les ailes se levèrent sans bruit.

At first a lifeless pall is offered for contrast: still places, dead waters. This silent zone could be a memory of dawn in the city as in the letter just cited: "Je voyais les dortoirs du lycée, absolument sourds." In "L'Orgie parisienne" we saw the "palais morts" of a deserted city. These had "la lumière [qui] arrive intense et folle" in the morning, the pure light being a response to that rich decadence of the palaces. In "Bonne pensée du matin" the morning light, joy of the workers, was similarly contrasted with the stale preciosity of "lambris." Perhaps there is memory of Baudelaire's "Rêve parisien" here (see under "les quais de marbre" below).

"L'eau était morte" refers to the characteristic mat surface of water on a chilly morning. In "Mémoire," after the light has gone in the evening, we see a similar effect: "la nappe, sans reflets, sans source, grise . . . l'eau couleur de cendre."

The shadows are comparably subdued, but there is the beginning of life in their roundness, cf. the b of "ombre" and the p of "camps." One feels the *solid* weight of the shadow, like camps in the woods (Gide saw "des ombres plus franches" when he began to feel alive again, in *L'Immoraliste*). And the road through the woods is a lyrical, promising effect in itself; entertaining figures came along it in "Enfance." As in "Après le déluge" (the gesture to the roofs and the weathercock), the child (the King) actively directs nature, awakening the lively and warm breaths; later this is his "entreprise." As in "Après le déluge," stones look out as underground life stirs. Birds, too, rise gently. All is friendly.

> La première entreprise fut, dans le sentier déjà empli de frais et blêmes éclats, une fleur qui me dit son nom.

The child's relation to nature, again, is an active undertaking. He directs the orchestra of events. A flower responds like a player in the orchestra, yielding its intimate essence, in its name, like a new little friend. It is humanized in a sort of primitive animism typical of a child's world:

everything reflects him anthropomorphically. The woodsy stir gradually increases, as in the beginning of Ravel's *Daphnis et Chloé*. Note the cool discreet vowel sounds of "frais" and "blêmes."

> Je ris au wasserfall blond qui s'échevela à travers les sapins: à la cime argentée je reconnus la déesse.

As Auden says: "I know I love someone when he makes me laugh." Mallarmé's lover wants to "rire sa victoire" in "M'introduire. . . ."

The German (*Märchen?*) word *wasserfall* is cool and fresh like "strom" in "Mouvement." The water is "blond" with the dawn light. The double ss is graphically *échevelée* or *frissonnant*, cf. "tresses" in Baudelaire's "La Chevelure." At the silver crest of the waterfall (cf. the "haillons / D'argent" of the river in "Le Dormeur du val") is the goddess of dawn; he recognizes her, "knew her all along" innately. In "Bonne Pensée du matin" he associates the joyous moment with Venus (whom he asks to bring brandy to the workers). Cf. the Cybèle-Vénus-Aphrodité of "Soleil et chair."

> Alors je levai un à un les voiles. Dans l'allée, en agitant les bras. Par la plaine, où je l'ai dénoncée au coq. A la grand'ville elle fuyait parmi les clochers et les dômes, et courant comme un mendiant sur les quais de marbre, je la chassais.

The morning mists arising from the forest floor are "veils," removed one by one as in a dance; cf. Astarté in "Soleil et chair." Their softness is echoed in a series of l's. Again the child takes charge as in "Après le déluge," waving his arms like a *chef d'orchestre*, simply to show off, to push his weight around. In "Après le déluge" the weathercocks were his fiefs. Here the cock of the plain is his subject. The child "denounces" the dawn to the cock, i.e., he is the actor, *bout en train* and harbinger of it. Further, he is at this point the headstrong master of the dawn like a swaggering male dominating a woman (later he will be awed and humbled). He is on to Her tricks. He sees Her gliding around the buildings of the city. No matter that he rushes from the countryside to the city in his vision, he is in command of this poetic world. He has memories aplenty of Paris awaking. He had been destitute in Paris, "la cité énorme . . . Ah! les haillons pourris, le pain trempé de pluie, l'ivresse, les mille amours qui m'ont crucifié!" ("Adieu"). In the city ("Métropolitain") She came to him in the morning: "Le matin où avec Elle, vous vous débattîtes parmi les éclats de neige. . . ." We saw her again, "Dans les villes . . . une glace quand la lampe circule dans la chambre voisine, comme

331

un trésor dans la forêt . . . Mais l'orgie et la camaraderie des femmes m'étaient interdites" ("Mauvais sang"). In "Après le déluge" and "Being beauteous" we have seen how all the images come together and form a supreme figure, as here, of Woman as natural strength and happiness, natural life or (at the extreme point when female and male merge) life itself. In "Les Déserts de l'amour" it was

> . . . la Femme que j'ai vue dans la Ville. . . . J'étais en haillons.
> . . . La lampe de la famille rougissait l'une après l'autre les chambres voisines. Alors le femme disparut. Je versais plus de larmes que Dieu n'en a pu jamais demander.
> Je sortis dans la ville sans fin.

In "Aube" Rimbaud still sees himself as hungry for Her, chasing Her along the marble quais—he fears She will vanish soon. In that "chassais" there may linger a feeling of the eternal quest, the "hunt," as in "La Chasse spirituelle" (see our Introduction, p. 16). Taking possession of the long sweep of light along the river-fronts of Paris, seen from a bridge, we all know this search; thus the breathtaking domain of another (probable) Her, the idol in "Enfance," "court sur des plages"; in "Promontoire" there are "d'immenses vues de la défense des côtes" shimmering under the light of "L'aube d'or" which is very like the dawn here. In a similar dynamism of hunger for light, the deserted mother-figure "runs" after the departing sun in "Mémoire."

The "quais de marbre" are echoed in the "terrasses de marbre" fronting the sea in the next piece, "Fleurs." Both imply a sensational juxtaposition of finite culture and infinite nature, as in the topos of the tower by the sea.

> En haut de la route, près d'un bois de lauriers, je l'ai entourée avec ses voiles amassés, et j'ai senti un peu son immense corps. L'aube et l'enfant tombèrent au bas du bois.

The crest of the road (as in "Enfance," IV) is a privileged place, another threshold like a *talus*. Here too the essence of desire will be found just beyond. He feels he does find it for a rare moment. Together with her mist-veils, he "surrounds" her, much as he "embraced" her in the opening line. He conquers or feels her immense body only a "little"—but that is tremendous enough. They fall together, no doubt sexually, as in T. S. Eliot's "Burbank": "they were together, and he fell." I do not see the full defeat most commentators read in here. Those buoyant b's help to preclude that.[1]

---

[1] In "Les Déserts de l'amour" the effect of "tomber" in relation to the woman is quite different: that one occurs at night.

Au réveil il était midi.

There seems to be a blackout and considerable lapse of time in sleep, marked by the hiatus of the empty page.

The bright staccato sound and shape of the little last sentence is sharp like noon itself (cf. Valéry, "Midi le juste").

Fleurs

In "Ce qu'on dit au poète à propos de fleurs," Rimbaud proposes to Banville some new desentimentalized species: "des fleurs qui soient des chaises" and

> Des fleurs presque pierres,—fameuses!—
> Qui vers leurs durs ovaires blonds
> Aient des amygdales gemmeuses!

Although this is mainly spitefully playful virtuosity, Rimbaud's attack on the literary softness of Banville and *tutti quanti* is really an attempt to offset feared effeminacy. The hard—rock-like and gem-like—posies go with other willfully tough attitudes such as the attraction to the hardened criminal in the *Saison en enfer*. Rimbaud's "boules de saphir, de métal," in "Enfance" are a corollary dream of artistic immunity.

More than a willed attempt, each of these images also represents the successful momentary result of an inner struggle. An androgynous higher synthesis arises parthenogenetically from a male-female confrontation in the self. Born of soft flowers and hard jewels (or rocks) combining features of both, the resulting syntheses may be called *crystallizations*, which is what poetic images essentially are.

Crystals are not only ambiguous in the soft-hard sense (like glazed fruit), they are also suspended in a corollary way between the inanimate and the animate. Indeed modern philosophers like Hans Kayser regard crystals as representing the crucial point at which the organic rose out of the inorganic.[1] Authentically new poetic images share in this alive-dead vibrancy too. So Rimbaud's prose poem is partly a study of how such images arise.

In "Enfance" something comparable happens: "mousse vert-de-gris, bijoux debout sur le sol gras des bosquets et des jardinets dégelés"; the

---

[1] Hardness and softness are related to inanimate and animate in complex, paradoxical or reversible polarities; together the four poles form what we call a polypolar relationship (see *L'Œuvre de Mallarmé* or *The Writer's Way in France*). Rimbaud's new flowers are both harder and softer than their archetypes, just as any crystallized form, or new life, is.

boy actually saw crystalline fungoid forms rising from a damp maternal nature fecundated by a male force of light (or inspiration). (A similar transfiguring light metamorphoses the originally moist meadow of "Mystique" into "[herbages] d'acier et d'émeraude.") Light, in "Barbare" and "L'Éternité," turns sea-surface into satin (as had happened previously in Baudelaire's "La Chevelure").

> D'un gradin d'or,—parmi les cordons de soie, les gazes grises, les velours verts et les disques de cristal qui noircissent comme du bronze au soleil,—je vois la digitale s'ouvrir sur un tapis de filigranes d'argent, d'yeux et de chevelures.

The "gradin d'or" is another such crystallization on a grander scale: a whole sunlit meadow slope where Rimbaud sits, watching the metamorphosis of nature into imagination, is transformed magically into a mid-creature between hard and soft, natural and artificial, closely related to the "fleurs-chaises" (*gradin*: seating) of "Ce qu'on dit au poète." Sunlit sky was similarly transformed into steps in "L'Orgie parisienne": "des pleurs d'or astral tombaient des bleus degrés [from *gradus*]."

The word "gradin" indicates a characteristic theatrical setting in nature, as in "Mystique," "Scènes," etc. This is carried out in the "cordons de soie, les gazes grises, les velours verts et les disques de cristal." The "cordons" are like the ones which are draped in front of curtains; the "gazes" and "velours" are part of the décor or costumes, or even finery worn by the public; the "cristal" could refer to a chandelier. What are the natural phenomena from which this imaginary theater is synthesized? The "cordons" may be metamorphosed from vines or tendrils, "gazes grises" from insect wings or transparent petals of irises, "velours verts" from lush green leaves, "disques de cristal" from flat droplets of dew lying on foliage (thus Leconte de Lisle speaks of "les gouttes de cristal de la rosée"); the blackening could be dark reflections in them. This is admittedly unsure, but Richard's notion of a maternal darkness preceding a birth is even less sure. Moreover, unlike Richard and many another commentator, I do not always find this picture-puzzle very gratifying. Alas, it reminds me at times too much of a Soviet color film called *Stone Flower*. Or, worse, some clever department-store window displays.

The "digitale" represents a male-female fusion in its combination of opening cup and "finger" (*digit-*), borne out by the virile sound and shape of the i versus the broad a. The "tapis" is the underlying meadow with flowers for eyes—as in "Aube"—and vines, tendrils, etc., for hair. The silver is probably dew or snail paths. This carpet curiously recalls "les chevelures et les yeux, flottant" in "Barbare." These fragments of human form, particularly feminine, give personal life to nature though in a scattered sublimated way, rather as the golden kiss animated the foliage in "Tête de faune," cf. the orange-lipped girl bred from the forest in "Enfance." Children easily imagine animate forms emerging from or entering tapestries and rugs: "Les tapisseries . . . où se jettent les tour-terelles de la veillée" ("Veillées," III). Thus, like Rimbaud, Mallarmé in an air of fine symbolist, or surreal, mystery saw the eyes (and the silver) in his "Ouverture ancienne d'Hérodiade": "tapisserie . . . avec les yeux ensevelis . . . parmi l'argent noir."

Py sees these human fragments as suggestive of an audience before whom the spectacle arises. This is quite possible.

> Des pièces d'or jaune semées sur l'agate, des piliers d'acajou supportant un dôme d'émeraudes, des bouquets de satin blanc et de fines verges de rubis entourent la rose d'eau.

"Pièces d'or"—buttercups?—recall "Plus pure qu'un louis, jaune et chaude paupière / le souci d'eau" ("Mémoire"). They too arose angeli-cally, androgynously, from a taut male-female tension. And could see. "Agate" might be stones or pebbles, the mahogany pillars and emerald dome evoke tree-trunks and rounded foliage-bush; white satin bouquets could easily be lilies or the like. The "verges de rubis" are organic "rods," perhaps pistils. Suzanne Bernard notes that Rimbaud copied a phrase from Bernardin de Saint-Pierre into a notebook where flower stamens were compared to "solives d'or en équilibre sur des colonnes plus belles que l'ivoire poli"; in corollas were "des voûtes de rubis et de topaze."

The "rose d'eau" may well be the original protagonistic "digitale" now seen in a different light, something like a water-lily; it seems to have been invented parallel to the "souci d'eau" just mentioned (from "Mémoire") and out of a similar mood and need. Just as the idol, an independent royal creature, arose from the unsullied seas of "Enfance," this pure child of the imagination, whether the "souci d'eau" or the "rose d'eau," arises from the source: "Ce n'est qu'onde, flore / Et c'est ta famille" ("Age d'or"). The pristine "souci d'eau" was the emblem of a "foi conjugale" which was sadly lacking in the real marriage of Rimbaud's parents. The "rose d'eau" is similar; a rose is offered, not in traditional fashion, to a lady, but only to the cosmos.

Leconte de Lisle offered his rose in a comparable spirit:

> Ruisselante encore du flot paternel,
> quand de la mer bleue Aphrodite éclose
> étincela nue aux clartés du ciel,
> la terre jalouse enfanta la rose;
>
> ("La Rose")

Another Parnassian, Catulle Mendès, located his more directly in the water, in "La Fleur qui va sur l'eau": "la seule rose de toute la mer."

> Tels qu'un dieu aux énormes yeux bleus et aux formes de neige, la mer et le ciel attirent aux terrasses de marbre la foule des jeunes et fortes roses.

As in the "rayon violet de Ses Yeux" ("Voyelles") or the "regard" of the all-seeing "Génie," in these eyes are the power of the total cosmos which is both the source of the flowers and their magnet: the beauty of flowers is one with the love-light of divine eyes which created and behold them.

The god's eyes are the twin blue horizon-circles of sky and sea; such water-eyes are found in "Mémoire" and "Le Bateau ivre." The snow-forms are, in tune with the whole piece, crystallized versions of parallel whitenesses of clouds and foam. The marble terraces carry this crystallization a step farther in another parallel entity, the terraces which like the earlier "agate" are an earth-source or background made hard. These three whitenesses thus link sky, sea, and land in an orgy of white joy like the one at the onset of "Mémoire."

Out of this blue and white bliss in the divine eyes are born and beheld the roses. They are natural flowers but redeemed by the total setting, in an air of *obedience* like Nietzsche's. They are young and strong (hard) as his supermen. Their prolific vitality bespeaks that abundant flourishing of all life we see in "Génie."

Those marble terraces are well situated by the shore, as in some familiar Picasso Mediterranean canvases: a place of land-sea, here-beyond vibrancy and luxury. They are redolent of privilege and isolation. In "Enfance" exotic ladies in healthy abundance swirled about exclusively on them: "Dames qui tournoient sur les terrasses voisines de la mer." The Grand Hotel of "Promontoire" features such a sea-view, with its "terrasses à présent pleines d'éclairages, de boissons et de brises riches." In "Aube" we have compared the "quais de marbre," in this connection, with the traditional topos of the tower by the sea: solitary construction and natural infinity joined.

Matucci notes the progressive shift from the horizontal site at the beginning through pillars and rods in mid-paragraph to a startling total vertical. We would add to this vertical an equally sweeping new horizontal perspective, as in "Génie."

Nocturne vulgaire

The title indicates fairly well what is happening in this poem: a rather ordinary night vision (not as melodious as "nocturne" implies), quite familiar to all of us, I suspect. The kaleidoscopic dislocations and shifting scenes in the room (as in Proust's first pages of *A la Recherche*) are the stuff dreams are made of. We get hints, here and there, of fragments of other accounts of Rimbaud's haunted nights.

> Un souffle ouvre des brèches opéradiques dans les cloisons,— brouille le pivotement des toits rongés,—disperse les limites des foyers,—éclipse les croisées.—

The "souffle" is a breath of dynamic vision. "Opéradiques" (a port-manteau word including "operatic" and a neologism for "operational") seems to indicate a sensation of theatricality plus something like the organic structure we saw in "Veillées," with its familiar steep partitions of seating sections, the "cloisons" as in "Scènes": "L'opéra-comique se divise sur notre scène à l'arête d'intersection de dix cloisons dressées de la galerie aux feux."

In "Les Déserts de l'amour" there is a dream-shift into a menacing maternal world much like the one which is initially dissipated and re-forms here: "la cloison devint vaguement l'ombre des arbres, et je me suis abîmé sous la tristesse amoureuse de la nuit." That "abîmé" is like the suffocation in silk below. Cf. also Baudelaire's "La nuit s'épaississait ainsi qu'une cloison" ("Le Balcon"). In "Nocturne vulgaire," the "brèche" opens up the stifling solidity for a provisional breather.

The pivoting of the roofs is the sort of thing that happens in a fever, with shades of Hallowe'eny witchery, eerily weaving moonlit planes. The roofs are "rongés" in the sense of being invaded by other entities involved in the dislocations. The "foyers," one of which was a "théâtre-âtre" in "Veillées," are part of the theatrical scene-shifting, opening on magic, infinite and frightening vistas. The same with the "croisées" (Keats' "magic casements"); their familiar perspective gives way to wild ones now.

> Le long de la vigne, m'étant appuyé du pied à une gargouille, —je suis descendu dans ce carrosse dont l'époque est assez indiquée par les glaces convexes, les panneaux bombés et les sophas contournés. Corbillard de mon sommeil, isolé, maison de berger de ma niaiserie, le véhicule vire sur le gazon de la grande route effacée: et dans un défaut en haut de la glace de droite tournoient les blêmes figures lunaires, feuilles, seins;—Un vert et un bleu très foncés envahissent l'image. Dételage aux environs d'une tache de gravier.

The dreamer imagines, in a likely sequence, that he too is shifting, outside; as in "Les Poètes de sept ans" he imagines the places just outside his home, in the garden where he had childish visions before the similar "vines." Here the romantic detail of a gargoyle (from some church or cathedral, no doubt) is added. He uses it to make his romantic escape with some of the Germanic ("Leonore") atmosphere of "Entends comme brame" and "Métropolitain." The dream-carriage recalls the magically self-propelled one of "Enfance" (although there is a hint of horses in the "dételage"). It is momentarily *funereal* and *isolated* like the solitary dream in the death-colored night. But the central fantasy-image comes into familiar focus in vivid colors, reminiscent of "Le Bateau ivre" ("azurs verts").

Perhaps, indeed, because it is so childishly familiar, even stereotyped—cf. "carrosses anciens . . . pastorale suburbaine" of "Ornières"—Rimbaud sees it as part of the sentimental "niaiserie," whence also the "vulgaire" of the title.[1] We spoke of it as a snug womb-substitute (like the "nest" of the railway carriage in "Rêvé pour l'hiver"), hence those numerous belly effects of "convexes" and "bombés" and "contournés" (note the round b's and o's).[2] The *époque* is *assez indiquée*; again, this is a self-deprecatory note of sentimentality befitting the rococo pastoral eighteenth-century carriage (cf. the "bergers" of "Bonne pensée du matin" echoing the "maison de berger" here, with a passing reference to Vigny's poem of that name).

The deforming flaw in the carriage-window—cf. the "bouillons" of "Mémoire"—is a microcosm of the whole shifting scene. Idle children often note such flaws and the distorted processions of images that come through their moving optic, which are a welcome escape from the adult world in which they are being hauled around object-like. In Tolstoy's *Childhood* there is a vivid account of such a surreal child's-eye-view journey. The procession parallels a similar one in "Enfance" of "moulins . . . îles . . . meules." Or the "lieux fuyants" of "Génie," the fleeting scenes as if seen from a train-window, in "Larme."

That invasive color-effect is absolutely typical of such dreams. In "Ornières" the similarly pretty carriage also turned into a funereal nightmare with comparable splashes of color in the blue and black of the horses. The sudden humble place indication—a spot of gravel—is reassuring in this fearful, unfamiliar setting; "me," thinks the child; I am such a sterile locus of no importance but affectionately alive anyway and identifiable.

---

[1] "Vulgaire" presents a consonance with the "niaiserie," the theme of silky suffocation, etc. The letters v and u are feminine and the element *vulg* disgustingly so; see *Toward the Poems of Mallarmé* under the "divulgue" of "Tombeau de Baudelaire," also Appendix c, under v and g.

[2] For the element *con*, see *Toward the Poems of Mallarmé*, Appendix b.

—Ici va-t-on siffler pour l'orage, et les Sodomes—et les So-
lymes,—et les bêtes féroces et les armées,

The scene becomes menacing. Apocalyptic visions of atrocious beasts and
migrating troops are elsewhere associated by Rimbaud with landscape-
sweeping storms, notably in "Michel et Christine" and "Qu'est-ce pour
nous, mon cœur?" The biblical Sodome (and Solyme, the biblical name
for Jerusalem repeated in "Mauvais sang") indicates—as in Proust—a relic
of religious awe, fear of the sin, perhaps homosexual, which will bring
down thunder and brimstone upon him. The mature males of armies (as
in "Parade") and the beasts are clear father-principles (superego), agents
of God's wrath. The "siffler" is a reminiscence of a typical male way of
hailing (the dogs?) which could have caused Rimbaud malaise in all
sorts of fearful contexts such as the border guards with their "dogues" in
"Les Douaniers." The whistle gets bound up here with the menacing
sound of storms, etc.; cf. "sifflements de mort" in "Being beauteous." A
coup de sifflet signals Fancioulle's destruction in Baudelaire's "Une Mort
héroïque."

—(Postillons et bêtes de songe reprendront-ils sous les plus
suffocantes futaies, pour m'enfoncer jusqu'aux yeux dans la
source de soie)
—Et nous envoyer, fouettés à travers les eaux clapotantes et
les boissons répandues, rouler sur l'aboi des dogues . . .

Then comes a typical moment of suffocation—poets in particular have
notable trouble breathing at times (the backwash of the creative *souffle*
which opened the poem)—perhaps brought on by twisted bed clothes,
associated with a maternal element of silk, softly feminine and source of
the self (*soie-soi*; "source de soie"), harking back to the "sophas con-
tournés" of the round womb-carriage. In "Barbare" the equivalent element
is the "soie des mers," cf. Baudelaire's injunction to his "Mère des souve-
nirs" (Jeanne Duval) in "La Chevelure": "soyez la houle . . . ," or the
watered silk (*moire*) which was her ocean-and-light essence in the same
poem. Rimbaud's feminine "Éternité" was exhaled from similar "Braises
de satin." This emotion is here felt to be *suffocatingly* maternal, "niai-
serie," numbly childish and passive. The "futaie," as Richard says, is the
source of life. In its shadows, amidst the burgeoning, one may discern the
image of the organic inner tree, as in "Being beauteous." And the hairy
opening to the womb has some bearing here, cf. the "Satin touffu" of the
Stupra.

In "Les Déserts de l'amour" the protagonist lays the "maternal" woman in a "corbeille de coussins," but the dangerous proceedings are soon drowned in darkness as they are here.

The "postillons" are crude males (as in "Parade"; cf. Kessel's *Belle de jour*). They stand just outside the comforting interior like the monsters of "Rêvé pour l'hiver"; and, along with the ferocious beasts, they can drive him fearfully back—as the adult male prison ships did in "Le Bateau ivre"—to the protection of the carriage-silk. Those "dogues" (he fears them and their authoritarian masters in "Les Douaniers") represent, like Cerberus, sentinels of a male hell and, beyond, the authentic and awesome power of God, the hound of heaven of "Le Bonheur" (cf. Joyce's "dog-god" in *Ulysses*).

The "à travers les eaux clapotantes . . . rouler" will be repeated in "Angoisse": "Rouler aux blessures, par l'air lassant et la mer." It is like the end of Truffaut's *Les Quatre Cents Coups*: the abandoned child, fearful of the adult male world he is ill prepared for, rejected or suffocated by the female, faces the cosmos alone and "wades out" into solitary grief and despair, perhaps under the influence of alcohol: "les boissons répandues" echo the "taches de vin" of "Le Bateau ivre."

—Un souffle disperse les limites du foyer.

Nothing new. The repetition rounds off the vision with resignation, but there is relief in it too; the nightmare was only a dream. And there is buoyancy in the *souffle* still.

Marine

Les chars d'argent et de cuivre—
Les proues d'acier et d'argent—
Battent l'écume,—
Soulèvent les souches des ronces.
Les courants de la lande,
Et les ornières immenses du reflux,
Filent circulairement vers l'est,
Vers les piliers de la forêt,—
Vers les fûts de la jetée,
Dont l'angle est heurté par des tourbillons de lumière.

Rimbaud is said, on the basis of this poem and of "Mouvement," to be the originator of free verse. The two pieces remained unpublished until 1886, by which time other active claimants, such as Gustave Kahn, had arisen. Prose poetry, notably Aloysius Bertrand's *Gaspard de la Nuit* and Baudelaire's *Petits poèmes en prose*, had preceded Rimbaud's efforts, but

Rimbaud deserves some formal credit here, though I am not sure he would care or that, in a way, it is important. Genius like Rimbaud's is always innovating with its left hand, so to speak; that is to say, incidentally to its truer and deeper purposes of total expression of self, of truth. But in a way, too, it *is* important; there is no point in belittling literary history.

Rimbaud's land-sea exchange began in "Le Bateau ivre." Leconte de Lisle had presented a version of the mixed image in his "Épiphanie," where sails and butterflies get pleasantly confused. (Valéry will follow suit with pigeons in "Le Cimetière marin.")

This is more concrete, intimate. Rimbaud savors the land; he *feels* it as dynamically static, or vibrant, hence water-like even as it remains land-like. The prospect "takes off," opens up to infinite escape, like Mallarmé's "brise marine" in a landlocked bourgeois garden.[1]

An air-shimmer in midsummer heat can help do this; Van Gogh was comparably swept along into whirlpools of celebration by meridional French light.

The copper and silver "chariots" are, like the "char de fortune" of "Bannières de mai," basically sun-chariots; the sun may be playing on actual vehicles in this image, perhaps plows (*charrues*) which are digging up the "souches des ronces" and making the "ornières." In "Ornières" we observed that Rimbaud "dug" the earth, in the current hip phrase, "grooved" into it. It is his male communion with the Magna Mater, making his mark, his "wake" precisely as Joyce sees it (*Finnegans Wake*). The vast sweep of the Rimbaud-eye's view fuses with the whole landscape, takes possession of it like the broad swinging gesture of the child's arms in "Après le déluge." Transposing it thus in daring imagery, he makes it all his. The forest trunks as pilings of a jetty are apt, unforced imagery. Compare the "long pier en bois d'un bout à l'autre d'un champ rocailleux" ("Scènes").

The light coming down here in an intervention from on high is benign, not destructive as in "Les Ponts"—it is part of the sweep of possession by an allied child-spirit.

The linear dynamism of "filent" (the male wake) and the femininely graceful curve of "circulairement" seem to combine—a familiar kinesis-stasis pattern of Rimbaud's—in the spiral of the final "tourbillons."[2]

Fête d'hiver

Rimbaud hated cold but needed it, like some other true poets: "l'hiver, saison de l'art serein" wrote Mallarmé. René Char noted later that "the

---

[1] We note the watery transparent *ar* element as in "Départ," q.v.

[2] In "Mystique," "filent leur courbe" is a parallel movement.

poet performs well only under torture." "Sur les routes, par les nuits d'hiver, sans gîte, sans habits, sans pain, une voix étreignait mon cœur gelé . . . " ("Mauvais sang"). Winter is the enemy: "la fuite du bonheur. C'était comme une nuit d'hiver . . . " ("Les Déserts de l'amour").

But the "Being beauteous" appears against a background of snow. And the "douceurs" of the feminine voice come to him through "rafales de givre" in "Barbare." "Je redoute l'hiver parce que c'est la saison du comfort!" he cries in the name of an uncompromising ambivalence—winter must really sting him to the core to set him alive, create a "festival."

The chilly Russian overtones ("Rondes Sibériennes," later; cf. the "steppes" of "Fairy") prolong the frosty atmosphere against which background reassuringly appears the cosy lit circle of a stage, a comic opera interlude—nestled against all outdoors[1]—like that theatre of Baudelaire's:

> —J'ai vu parfois, au fond d'un théâtre banal
> Qu'enflammait l'orchestre sonore.
> Une fée allumer dans un ciel infernal
> Une miraculeuse aurore;
>
> ("L'Irréparable")

Gérard de Nerval's vision of Jenny Colon partook of a similar nestling need.

This winter festival, arranged against the cold rather than the dark, is otherwise analogous to the swirling and theatrically-costumed night-feast of "Est-elle almée?"—the "almée" was a fairy-spirit who threatened to disappear with the dawn.

> La cascade sonne derrière les huttes d'opéra-comique.

We have seen the "cascade," in "Villes, I" poised at a similarly dramatic elevation in the scenery. But here there is also the intimacy of the "Wasserfall" in "Aube," and a promise of refreshingly rushing water, as in the opened dam-gate of "Enfance." The *opéra-comique* provides the light touch of humor, of neo-classic control, not-too-seriousness; these figures are only dolls, like the childhood "idol" of "Enfance." Whence the "Boucher," below, to underline the eighteenth-century pastoral frivolity à la Watteau or Fragonard, or Favart (the Opéra-Comique in Paris is the Salle Favart), author of librettos admired and sometimes imitated by Rimbaud. Elsewhere—in "Nocturne vulgaire"—this prettiness evoked the scornful comment of "niaiserie"; and the term *Bergers*, for example in "Bonne pensée du matin," was likewise mocking. But on the other hand, Rimbaud ex-

---

[1] Cf. the train-interior of "Rêvé pour l'hiver."

pressed fervent admiration for Verlaine's *Fêtes galantes* ("adorable"); he was, after all, French.

> Des girandoles prolongent, dans les vergers et les allées voisins du Méandre,—les verts et les rouges du couchant.

The "girandoles" are an artificial echo of the sunset, cf. the decadent décor of "faux cieux" versus the morning light of "Bonne pensée du matin." The pastoral seventeenth- and eighteenth-century style of Fénelon's *Télémaque* brought a *verger* like the present one—neo-classic in tone—into "Après le déluge," along with the term *églogues* ("verger" seems to arise by association with "Berger"). Hence, along with the orchard here there appears the neo-classic reminiscence of the Méandre. But the green and red of the sunset are real and fiery (these colors were, incidentally, the essence of Delacroix for Baudelaire) and are merely "prolonged" artificially, prettily, by the girandolas.

Cf. the "candélabres" of "Villes, II."

In "Phrases" the sunset was the backdrop for a disturbing giantess. She, the Mother-figure, may be still present—an exiled, husbandless Andromaque—in the scene of the Méandre: "Une misérable femme de drame, quelque part dans le monde, soupire après des abandons improbables . . . le long des rivières" ("Jeunesse"). We saw the same scene in "Mémoire." And in "Phrases" there was a numb, defeated walk along canals.

> Nymphes d'Horace coiffées au Premier Empire,—Rondes Sibériennes, Chinoises de Boucher.

The rest is masquerade, with the neo-classic touches of Horace and French Premier Empire, notoriously imitative of the Greek (shades of Alain-Fournier's *fête étrange*, in which the masqueraders appeared in costumes from the same era).

The "Rondes Sibériennes" have been explained above, as has the mention of Boucher. The "Chinoises" are among the subjects Boucher painted (Py). They are, as we have seen, an essence of exotic strangeness for the French, including Rimbaud—*chinoiseries* are, as much as pastoral, a part of frivolous *décor*, beginning in the classical era. But for Rimbaud the Orient is also something more: the promise of a magically whole world.

Angoisse

Angoisse is, of course, *Angst*; ontological psychic pain as unbearable as Heidegger's.

Baudelaire referred to his muse and "vampire" as "C'est Elle! noire et pourtant lumineuse." Here too there is a central "Elle . . . Vampire," but not concretized, as for Baudelaire, in a contemporary; rather, She is a vestige of the awe-inspiring Mother beyond his mother (Graves' White Goddess who makes your hair stand on end).[1] The source of life, She is his "Amour, force." In "Métropolitain" he fights with "Elle," and the explosion of feeling surrounding this tussle is his fissioning strength which comes from his very adversary: "ta force." In "Les Fleurs," Mallarmé says she is the "Mère qui créas . . . De grandes fleurs avec la balsamique Mort" (Rimbaud pastiched "Les Fleurs" in "Ce qu'on dit au poète à propos de fleurs").

> Se peut-il qu'Elle me fasse pardonner les ambitions continuellement écrasées,—qu'une fin aisée répare les âges d'indigence,—qu'un jour de succès nous endorme sur la honte de notre inhabileté fatale?

He inquires of himself if his life will support his aims. It is a sort of prayer as well as self-analysis. The "fin aisée" is like the imagined entelechy of self as a serene *vieillard* in "Vies" or "Enfance." In "Honte" he pellucidly saw his weaknesses and hated himself with the "shame" described here, which is related to the clumsiness and "bad blood" he ascribes to his ancestors in "Mauvais sang." That heredity *is* a poor life-force to count on, he feels. But now as in "Elle est retrouvée" (note the *Elle*), he gets a flood of reassurance from Her, Eternity.

> (O palmes! diamant!—Amour, force!—plus haut que toutes joies et gloires!—de toutes façons, partout,—démon, dieu,— Jeunesse de cet être-ci: moi!)

The "palmes" are like the ones in "Royauté," signifying, and being, majestic feminine tree-shapes, the glory of life-strength (cf. Valéry's hymn to a mothering palm). The diamonds are dazzling strength from earth, from Magna Mater's bowels as in "Barbare." They are sons of earth, like the grass-borne angels of "Mémoire." Here "démon" and "dieu" are male entities (as in "Génie") from above, the sharp and lucid light which mysteriously draws its power from underground jewels. It is a true mystery, this paradox of masculine in feminine. Rimbaud does not go into it here, but in "L'Éternité" the marriage was blessed; "la mer allée / Avec le soleil."

---

[1] In *The White Goddess*, Robert Graves associates her with trees; compare the end of "Being beauteous."

> Que des accidents de féerie scientifique et des mouvements
> de fraternité sociale soient chéris comme restitution progressive
> de la franchise première? . . .

This is a question (another clause to the "Se peut-il"). Rimbaud was not
sure that nineteenth-century positivism and science were on his side. At
times he felt confident. He hoped, like most of us, that a better world
might emerge from the "féerie scientifique." The "mouvements" here echo
the poem "Mouvement" in their rigid dynamic progress toward reunion,
a creative democratic future (cf. "Villes, II"). Would it be *das dritte
Reich*, or rather, the Golden Age? "Franchise première"? The question
will be put again later (see "Mouvement," "Solde," etc.). In "Le Forgeron"
and "Soleil et chair" he believed in that Nietzschean cyclic return. Here,
the question mark stands for his later tentativeness. . . .

> Mais la Vampire qui nous rend gentils commande que nous
> nous amusions avec ce qu'elle nous laisse, ou qu'autrement
> nous soyons plus drôles.

His Life (Mother) says with universal and particularly French implaca-
bility: "Shape up totally or be a total outcast" ("drôle"). We learn from
the notes to "Les Poètes de sept ans" (Bernard) that his mother liked to
call him "petit drôle," or "misfit." "Ce qu'elle nous laisse" is probably the
male legacy after women get through dominating the core of existence.
As Suzanne Briet wrote in *Madame Rimbaud*, "her final triumph over
her son was complete."

The Vampire is reflected again in: "cette goule reine de millions d'âmes
et de corps morts et qui seront jugés!" ("Adieu"). It is Life seen as a
swarming *indifferent* city (cf. Joyce's Molly and Eternal Woman as
"amoral indifferent *Weib*"). It can swallow us up, murder us, "suffocate"
us ("Nocturne vulgaire"), judge us, as women do, by the very power of
their being *hors jeu*.

The struggle with Her in the big city is recorded in "Métropolitain":

> Le matin où avec Elle, vous vous débattîtes parmi les éclats de
> neige, ces lèvres vertes, les glaces, les drapeaux noirs et les
> rayons bleus, et les parfums pourpres du soleil des pôles,—ta
> force.

"Being beauteous" presents a comparable mortal snow-fight.

> Rouler aux blessures, par l'air lassant et la mer; aux sup-
> plices, par le silence des eaux et de l'air meurtriers; aux tortures
> qui rient, dans leur silence atrocement houleux.

The "blessures" were also Hers in "Being beauteous": life's sudden wounds and its outbursts, ours or Hers. The "tiring air" is the true locus of striving (inwardly, our panting breath), and our struggles with Her: "Je me suis séché à l'air du crime" (Preface of the *Saison en enfer*). In the moment of *Angst*, on a solitary religious beach between here and beyond (cf. "Adieu"), he sees the cruelty of it all like the abandoned young boy at the end of *Les Quatre Cents Coups*. That sea-air (*mer-mère*; cf. "Le Bateau ivre") can cleanse and support, or drown: "meurtriers." The *silence* is deadly indifference, as in Mallarmé's "A la nue accablante tu": the silent wisp of foam is like the "poor forked creature" (*King Lear*) lost in a struggle with all. Mallarmé in "Le Livre" describes a figure close to his little boy Anatole who stood alone on a similar metaphysical beach: little "mariner," with big eyes, he died—"Seul sur la plage . . . comme pour se commenter le grand air."

The "houleux" is like the ironic "rire" of the ocean in Baudelaire's "L'Homme et la mer." That meaningless "laugh" of noise makes any attempted meaning ridiculous, "Dans un tumulte au silence pareil" (Valéry, "Le Cimetière marin").

Métropolitain

This is a more resigned and passively Rimbaldian impression of an urban landscape than the ones we witnessed earlier. These are fleeting impressions as if seen from a train, the London Metropolitan Railway which is echoed in the title. Some of the touches of the other modern sketches—e.g., the crystal boulevards—are as if vestigial here, but the mood is less futuristically technical and architectonic. Rather, the present city merges in gentle, fluid vibrancy with the adolescent's childhood past and with some of its troubling ambiguities: country-city (suburbs), pleasure-pain (their ambivalently inviting and exclusive gardens), patrician-popular (the poor on the new boulevards versus the fleeting "fairy-like aristocracies"), youth-age (childish whims, frustrations of the closed inn versus adult battles and studies), here-there (reality and fantasy, France-*étranger*), and so on.

At the end he sums up this wandering quest for meaning—the splendors and bitterness, the new and the old—by the representative struggle between himself and his life-strength that he once had waged in a remembered crisis. No one seems to have won, but the struggle goes on; he has some resources left: "ta force."

> Du détroit d'indigo aux mers d'Ossian, sur le sable rose et orange qu'a lavé le ciel vineux, viennent de monter et de se

croiser des boulevards de cristal habités incontinent par de jeunes familles pauvres qui s'alimentent chez les fruitiers. Rien de riche.—La ville!

The initial effect is of land waters opening out onto coldly majestic northern seas, "mers d'Ossian."[1] The indigo strait, the orange and pink beach, and the winey sky are invitingly and exotically colored, like similar venturous sea-passages in "Le Bateau ivre"; for example, the *figements violets* of dawn, the *taches de vins*. The "cristal" may be an effect of rain or ice, as Underwood surmises.

But it is as if such bold or cold openness were now too challenging. The crystal boulevards which are open at least to the future (actually they are, as always, an element of reassuring human control) only momentarily maintain the daring mood; the poor and the fruit-vendors quickly warm the scene with their presence. That is disappointing in terms of total adventure or innovation: the poor are always with us, and we are less "with it," in sober reality. It is just a city.

Du désert de bitume fuient droit en déroute avec les nappes de brumes échelonnées en bandes affreuses au ciel qui se recourbe, se recule et descend, formé de la plus sinistre fumée noire que puisse faire l'Océan en deuil, les casques, les roues, les barques, les croupes.—La bataille!

The disenchanted mood colors the waste of macadam paving. A turbulent atmosphere, like the storm of "Michel et Christine" but less lyrical, sweeps across the horizontal landscape ("Satan, Ferdinand [qui] court avec les graines sauvages," "Nuit de l'enfer"), speaking of apocalypse and migration ("Qu'est-ce pour nous, mon cœur?"). The invasive temper of frightening or awesome adult-male doing—battle, black smoke (as if from the gunboats or prison-ships of "Le Bateau ivre")—is, no doubt, mingled with emotional distress from another source, the rising and dark sea of bitterness surrounding his relationship with his mother; that "Océan en deuil" recalls closely the floods of tears from "Enfance" and "Les Déserts de l'amour." The rising of dark smoke and fog—"le diable . . . au clocher" of "Nuit de l'enfer," "le vice . . . qui monte au ciel" ("Mauvais sang")—is very apt for this familiar emotional experience: who has not seen, in nightmare or day-vision, in the sky where promise should be, freedom and future, a sort of dragon (cloud-shape or forest peaks) arc up from the depths ("recule et descend") and threaten all in a towering struggle of light and dark forces? In Mallarmé's "A la nue accablante tu" the "ba-

---

[1] Ossian ("barde d'Armor") is alluded to in "L'Homme juste."

saltic" smothering storm-clouds reflect, and meet, the oceanic torment below.

In "Mystique" and "Veillées" we saw such "bands" of inner theatre, planes of feeling, especially associated with sundown (light-dark battle), apocalypse. An incantatory rhythm helps control the mood: "casques" and "barques" are like interlocking assonances alternating with echoing "roues" and "croupes." The succession of phenomena is like that of "Enfance" ("Moulins . . . îles . . . meules") or, even more, the railway and evening sky phantasmagoria (stations, pillars, lakes) in "Larme."

> Lève la tête: ce pont de bois, arqué; les derniers potagers de
> Samarie; ces masques enluminés sous la lanterne fouettée par
> la nuit froide; l'ondine niaise à la robe bruyante, au bas de la
> rivière; ces crânes lumineux dans les plans de pois—et les autres
> fantasmagories—la campagne.

Rimbaud the persistent promenader and voyager tells us to "raise our heads" with him and see the phenomena as they come at him: the arched wooden bridge is a possibility of another better world. Its humble wood leans, however, to the past rather than to a technical future: to the biblical world of his "Proses évangéliques" (distantly related to his magic Orient), for example, "A Samarie, plusieurs ont manifesté leur foi en lui." Certainly, at such times, he can see himself as the misunderstood itinerant figure of Christ—cf. the allusion to St. Paul on the road to Damascus, below—just as he was the Christ-like worker in "Ouvriers," approaching the vibrant here-there, ancient-modern *banlieue* with its humble kitchen gardens.[2] Next we see fantastic night-shapes as in "Nocturne vulgaire"; then a mythological shape, the undine in the river, appears to this Faustian (*Faust II*), this "Wandering Jew." (In "Comédie de la soif" the decorative mythical figure was similarly pretty-pretty and *niaise*, unsatisfactory to his eternal thirst.) The luminous skulls in the rows of peas are like the "chers Anciens" of "Entends comme brame," where the peas also figure in a mysterious moonlit landscape.

> Des routes bordées de grilles et de murs, contenant à peine
> leurs bosquets, et les atroces fleurs qu'on appellerait cœurs et
> sœurs, Damas damnant de longueur,—possessions de féeriques
> aristocraties ultra-Rhénanes, Japonaises, Guaranies, propres en-
> core à recevoir la musique des anciens—et il y a des auberges
> qui pour toujours n'ouvrent déjà plus—il y a des princesses, et,
> si tu n'es pas trop accablé, l'étude des astres—le ciel.

[2] In "Morts de Quatre-vingt-douze," the worker-soldiers are seen as "million de Christs." The worker as a Christ figure is a theme not limited to Rimbaud; Sartre clearly feels that way about him, as do numerous socialist writers.

Inviting roadsides, as in "Bruxelles," are not for him. A Hamletic bitterness against woman and comfort (as in "Enfance": "cher cœur," or "je redoute l'hiver parce que c'est la saison du comfort," "Adieu") dictates the outburst against sentimental "sister and heart" flowers. The "Damas damnant de langueur" (with its allusion to St. Paul on the road to Damascus) is his eternal road of waiting for the ray of illumination to stab him as in "Bannières de mai," "Si un rayon me blesse / Je succomberai sur la mousse." The eternal dissatisfaction is the endless "languid" length by which he is damned. Thus the inns (similar to the empty ones in "Enfance") are eternally unopened to the "Wandering Jew" of "Comédie de la soif."

Those lovely things—Faust's "Verweile doch du bist so schön"—belong to others, to the eternal possessors of this world, the "aristocrats," fairy people behind their palace-gates or beyond romantic[3] foreign borders like the distant princesses, below. They are in touch with the source (*vide* Kafka's emperor in *The Chinese Wall*) and with the original music. Rimbaud dreams of a fulfilled life as in "Enfance" or "Vies"; he studies that source as an inspired savant, the origin in the starry sky. The repeated "Il y a" formula is like the one of "Enfance": sheer phenomena of a better, purer world.

> Le matin où avec Elle, vous vous débattîtes parmi les éclats de neige, ces lèvres vertes, les glaces, les drapeaux noirs et les rayons bleus, et les parfums pourpres du soleil des pôles,—ta force.

The source is also the Her of his life-force.[4] And he relives the struggle with that *à même* essence of his being as if he wanted to dredge up strength for all his desires, all that he has not, from that source; compare "Le Bateau ivre": "Est-ce en ces nuits sans fonds que tu dors et t'exiles / . . . ô future Vigueur?" "She" is like the "Elle" of the dawn-goddess, happiness whom he chased like a love-hungry beggar in "Aube"—the beggar crucified by "a thousand loves" in "Adieu."

In the cold night of the city, like Delius (in *Paris, Song of a Great City*), in a sort of fever of hallucinated beauty, he saw the essential feminine soul, or *anima*, at the core of things.[5] The chilled "green lips"

---

[3] Germany is romantic for Rimbaud as it was for the French literary tradition generally (particularly in the nineteenth century), thus the spectral images of "Entends comme brame" are partly German; in "Mauvais sang" he dreams he was "[un] reître . . . sous les nuits d'Allemagne."

[4] There may be a comma before "avec"; he may have been accompanied by "Elle" in his struggle, but I prefer the other meaning.

[5] "C'est elle . . . 'Elle' il essayait de se demander ce que c'était, car c'est une

are far removed indeed—as far as the North Pole—from the warmly alive "fille à lèvre d'orange" in "Enfance." The former, in a modulation from the "face cendrée" of "Being beauteous," are like the "starv'd lips" of the death figure, *la belle dame sans merci*. Keats was to relive the image of his mother's horrid-ecstatic white face on her deathbed over and over again, death itself as the extreme of life or beauty.

The black flags were involved in the apocalyptic renewal of "Après le déluge," as the "rayons bleus" were in the trumpet call of eternity-sky in "Voyelles."[6] The polar sun was a similar extreme of sensation in "Le Bateau ivre" ("figements violets"); in "Barbare," "arctic flowers" offer comparable effects; in "Après le déluge" a Splendid Hotel is built amid the polar "chaos de glaces." See also "Dévotion."

Barbare

At the center of this "barbaric"[1]—savagely pure—vision is the infinite sweetness of a feminine voice heard at the bottom of a pit[2]—*de profundis* —where it comes like an Ariadne thread, a sublime umbilical cord leading to the total Mother, attaching Rimbaud to life. We hear it elsewhere: "Sur les routes, par des nuits d'hiver sans gîte, sans habits, sans pain, une voix étreignait mon cœur gelé" ("Mauvais sang"). The "sisters" in "Age d'or" were a source of this vital and crucial feminine appeal, which rings again in the music of the "Being beauteous."

---

ressemblance de l'amour et de la mort . . . de nous faire interroger plus avant, dans la peur que sa réalité se dérobe, le mystère de la personnalité" (Proust, *A la recherche*, vol. I, p. 308).

[6] His mother's blue eyes may be remembered here, transmuted to an infinite as in "Génie" or "Bruxelles."

---

[1] In "Mauvais sang," Rimbaud says his clothing is as "barbarous" as that of his Gallic ancestors. The word is thus used quite differently there (pejoratively), but there is a certain parallel in the historical perspective. Baudelaire in his "Peintre de la vie moderne" had written: "Ce qui peut rester de *barbare* et d'ingénu apparaît comme une preuve nouvelle d'obéissance à l'impression, comme une flatterie à la vérité . . . une *barbarie* inévitable, synthétique, enfantine qui reste souvent visible dans un art parfait (mexicaine, égyptienne ou ninivite). . . ." Compare "Enfance": "cette idole . . . plus noble que la fable, mexicaine . . . ."

In "Comédie de la soif" the poet desires to "mourir aux fleuves barbares."

[2] Richard Wilbur wrote, in "A Song":

> As at the bottom of a seething well
> A phosphorous girl is singing,
> Up whispering galleries trellised notes
> Climb and cling.
>
> It is a summer-song an old man wrote
> Out of the winter's wringing . . .

The voice comes as a climax to a series of visions fluttering about the idea of Woman—"the flesh that always says yes," in Joyce's phrase. She is a glorious resignation and yielding to the world as it is, passive delight in *being* which submerges some vestigial imagery of male doing or "heroism."

> Bien après les jours et les saisons, et les êtres et les pays,

A long period of wandering precedes the visions and the *douceurs*; as in Baudelaire's "Le Voyage," the world-weary tone is that of one who has seen it all in both time and space, the "Juifs errants" of "Comédie de la soif" seeking the final "Inn." The summing-up of time in "saisons" recalls briefly the sweeping embrace of "O Saisons, ô châteaux."

> Le pavillon en viande saignante sur la soie des mers et des fleurs arctiques; (elles n'existent pas.)

The pavilion is obscure, but one thinks first of Baudelaire's "pavillon de ténèbres tendues" referring to Jeanne's hair in "La Chevelure." Here the image is even more intimately feminine—although Baudelaire's "Les promesses d'un visage" already illustrated its daring possibilities. It is probably the raw interior of the mouth of the womb (Claude-Edmonde Magny, without my knowing it, had come to the same conclusion in a brilliant study). Undoubtedly we are on shaky exegetic ground here, but I fail to see, unlike Antoine Adam, why Rimbaud should be sent into such ecstasies by the Danish flag. One is emboldened by the fact that Rimbaud so often merged feminine parts with other natural entities, e.g., in "Soleil et chair" and "L'Étoile a pleuré rose." In the latter *blason*, the female sex is related, as here, to bleeding: "L'Homme [a] saigné noir à ton flanc souverain." In "Les Sœurs de charité," biological woman is an "excès de sang épanché tous les mois." "Voyelles" associates "sang craché, rire des lèvres belles" (cf. "sa lèvre / D'en bas," "Remembrances du vieillard idiot"). Blood ("petits caillots de marne rousse"), milk, tears ("larmier"), nest, sucking-cup all converge intimately in the central image of the last of the *Stupra*: a vagina, called a promised land, "Chanaan féminin."

In "Barbare" the suavity of the image (which will be related to a grotto and volcano below, cf. the erotic Venusberg cave of Wagner and the "Vénus . . . cavernes" of "Villes, I") is brought out by the smooth "soie des mers," with its easy overtone *mère* as in "Le Bateau ivre": "je me suis baigné dans le Poème / De la Mer." One thinks, again, of the silk in Jeanne's tresses (*moire*: watered silk) where Baudelaire swam, "glissant dans l'or et dans la moire," cf. Rimbaud's comparable combination in "braises de satin" ("L'Éternité"). In the second of the obscene poems entitled *Stupra*, female pubic hair is called "satin": "dans la raie / Charmante fleurit le long satin touffu." In "Mémoire," the white bodies of women (probably his mother and his sisters) were orgiastically likened to silken oriflammes in a medieval field of battle: "L'assaut au soleil des blancheurs des corps de femmes; / la soie, en foule et de lys pur, des oriflammes / sous les murs dont quelque pucelle eut la défense." Surely those silken white lilies are a feminine essence of receptivity. The salty white tears from this same passage will show up as part of the "douceurs" below ("larmes blanches, bouillantes"), and the white flowers are probably echoed in the "fleurs arctiques" (the "lys" or "ombelle" of "Mémoire," the chilly "frisson d'ombelle" of "Voyelles").

If "they do not exist," it is partly because, as in "Conte," this is sheer fantasy, but also because Rimbaud initially finds the old contact too powerful, too beautiful ("c'est trop beau," "Bruxelles") to bear. It is too original—"barbaric" (the title) in the sense of archetypal, in the realm of *die Mütter*, as Goethe called the womb of things.

> Remis des vieilles fanfares d'héroïsme—qui nous attaquent encore le cœur et la tête—loin des anciens assassins—

He tries to shake off the vision and says he is far from ("cured of") the old allies, the "assassins" of "Matinée d'ivresse" with whom in fact (as companions in hashish) or fancy he took off on his wild inner adventures. But those were male images, male doings. The female is deadlier, truly "barbaric," as Margaret Mead claims.

> Oh! Le pavillon en viande saignante sur la soie des mers et des fleurs arctiques; (elles n'existent pas.)
> Douceurs!

This image, the raw female, will not be shaken. There is no defense against the surging sweetness, from *below*, from the source.

> Les brasiers, pleuvant aux rafales de givre,—Douceurs!—les feux à la pluie du vent de diamants jetée par le cœur terrestre éternellement carbonisé pour nous.—O monde!—

The "brasiers" were related to maternal Woman in "Après le déluge," the "Sorcière" with her "pot de braise," and in "Les Étrennes des orphelins" the essence of the memory of the mother was the *foyer*. In "L'Éternité" the "braises de satin" were the image of silky-soft woman-water and sharp father-sun commingled. A clear overtone, indeed anagram, of *braises* is *baisers.* Thus Mallarmé in "Toute l'âme résumée" plays on this: "clair baiser de feu." No more parents in "Les Étrennes des orphelins" meant "point de foyer, de clefs prises / Partant point de baisers, point de douces surprises!"

Here, the gust of delight is like a kiss of the original mother-world. This is intensely Rimbaldian poetry, the pure description of the diamonds of joy in that lashing by wind and rain, the "paradis des orages" of "Villes, I" or of "Michel et Christine." Or "Enfance" where "Les branches et la pluie se jettent à la croisée" of the womb-like study, in sheer caress. Diamonds come from the world's bowels, from coal ("carbonisé"), as did jewels from the mud in Jeanne Duval or from her "tar" hair in "La Chevelure." This is the prime phenomenon of *crystallization* by virtue of which all our lives arose from the slime, or from amniotic fluid.

> (Loin des vieilles retraites et des vieilles flammes, qu'on entend, qu'on sent,)

Again, he tries to leave it behind—it is too much. This is exactly parallel to the mood in "Alchimie du verbe," where Rimbaud is saying goodbye to beauty, which dies very hard. Or the end of the *Saison en enfer*, when woman too is left behind.

In "Mauvais sang" "l'orgie et la camaraderie des femmes" were linked to "une mer de flammes" and the clearly maternal image of "la lampe circule dans la chambre voisine, comme un trésor dans la forêt" (see "Après le déluge"). The "vieilles retraites" are undoubtedly linked with the recurrent image of the quiet womb-like source, the "Inn" of "Comédie de la soif," etc., and the underground room of "Enfance."

> Les brasiers et les écumes. La musique, virement des gouffres et choc des glaçons aux astres.

The sweetness of the elements fire and water is presented in their various sublime or whipped-up forms ("brasiers," "foam," icy radiance of stars). That whipping-up, the rising whirlwind of joy—"virement des gouffres," from those depths—has been described in earlier chapters ("Les Étrennes," "Being beauteous," etc.). Compare the "cieux de braise" of "Le Bateau ivre." Odilon Redon captures the metaphysical feel of this archetype in his *Mysterious Juggler.* The *tourbillon* is a key image of the "Coup de Dés."

> O Douceurs, ô monde, ô musique! Et là, les formes, les sueurs, les chevelures et les yeux, flottant. Et les larmes blanches, bouillantes,—ô douceurs!—et la voix féminine arrivée au fond des volcans et des grottes arctiques.

The *tourbillon*, "epiphany" of gorgeous phenomena, is visibly feminine, as in "Being beauteous" or "Fleurs" where the same tapestry-effect of floating hair and eyes caught our attention (cf. Mallarmé's "Ouverture ancienne d'Hérodiade" where these images fluttered about the maternal nurse). "Sweats" recall the "sueurs froides de la lune" in "Comédie de la soif," droplets like tears, from an intimate source (*sueurs* has an overtone of *sœurs*). The tears themselves we compared earlier to the boiling white and sweetly consoling childhood ones in "Mémoire"—"ô douceurs!" But the feminine voice is the musical essence of such sweetness and light as it was for Mallarmé in "Don du poème": "O la berceuse, avec . . . ta voix rappelant viole et clavecin." Compare: "ta voix! unique flatteur de ce vil désespoir" ("Phrases") or "Quelqu'une des voix / Toujours angélique" of "Age d'or" and "votre danse et votre voix" ("Jeunesse").

In "Villes, I," the cavern visited by Venus is in a passage full of such feminine essences; "une mer troublée par la naissance éternelle de Vénus . . . fleurs grandes . . . coupes . . . Mabs . . . ravines . . . Diane . . . Bacchantes . . . sanglotent [cf. sang] et la lune brûle et hurle [cf. menstrual cycle] . . . Vénus entre dans les cavernes des forgerons et des ermites."

The voice comes in the cold arctic grotto as it did in the beggarly past: "Sur des routes, par des nuits d'hiver, sans gîte, sans habits, sans pain, une voix étreignait mon cœur gelé," reminding him of his life: "la force" ("Mauvais sang"). In "Being beauteous" this primal music arose "devant une neige."

Le pavillon . . .

The repetition brings a cyclic—or spiral, *tourbillon*—quality to the whole: it is musically organized, as was Baudelaire's "La Chevelure," or "Le Balcon" (in pantoum form), of which the "Renaîtras-tu?" could serve as an epigraph here. That is what the voice, the sweetness really mean: rebirth to authentic, original life.

Solde

Like Nietzsche, Rimbaud is offering here something ambivalent, beyond good and evil—"dispensé de toute morale" ("Adieu")—daemonic, extremely high and low, beautiful and ugly. The whole idea is as amorally dynamic as was fascism (according to Rauschning's authoritative definition). That is the main point of this *Illumination*, as of "Matinée d'ivresse." The tone is satanically exalted; but it is also vehemently ironic; for example the title: "On Sale," which we may render as "Nah, here, take this!" The drift is "Since you won't appreciate at their full value the things I bravely show you, I will offer them to you in a degraded form, at a cheap price; maybe you will take them that way, you mediocrities."

This virulent irony directed at the unworthy reader is borne out by a series of grammatical negations: the overall effect is one of brutal understatement, mucker-pose, litotes. Here are gorgeous riches offered under a cheap-price sign which is a reflection of our, the readers', cheapness.

There is, then, more than a hint of Rimbaud's going out of "the business" of writing, in a tone prophetic (or confirmatory) of the close, "Adieu," of the *Saison en enfer*. And he is showing us what we are losing.

> A vendre ce que les Juifs n'ont pas vendu, ce que noblesse ni crime n'ont goûté, ce qu'ignorent l'amour maudit et la probité infernale des masses; ce que le temps ni la science n'ont pas à reconnaître;

Beyond all known extremes is this ambivalent beauty: even the Jews, famed as merchants, have not offered *this* rare entity; even highest nobility or lowest crime has not reached the level of this "far-out" essence, which is both higher and lower; even "cursed love," such as that of the great lovers, Tristan and Yseut, Paolo and Francesca, is less extreme; likewise for the "infernal probity of the masses," another great emotion obviously admired by Rimbaud (cf. "Le Forgeron"); "the [our] time and science" are not up to recognizing this pure essence.

> Les Voix reconstituées; l'éveil fraternel de toutes les énergies chorales et orchestrales et leurs applications instantanées; l'occasion, unique, de dégager nos sens!

The Voices—or the "orchestral" symphony of the famous *voyant* letters—are like those of "Villes, I," "corporations de chanteurs géants . . . orphéoniques . . . Des groupes de beffrois chantent les idées des peuples . . . des compagnies ont chanté la joie du travail nouveau."

The opportunity to free our senses—"dégager nos sens!"—is echoed in "Génie": "le dégagement rêvé." The "Génie" is the pied-piper spirit who will open up a more exhilarating world.

> A vendre les Corps sans prix, hors de toute race, de tout monde, de tout sexe, de toute descendance! Les richesses jaillissant à chaque démarche! Solde de diamants sans contrôle!

The exaltation of the body takes up the Greek-pagan tone we saw running from "Soleil et chair" through "Les Sœurs de charité" ("le corps de

vingt ans . . . amour, appel d'action") and on to "Génie" ("son corps!").
It is beyond all known limitations of sex (as was the ambiguous creature
of "Antique"), or of race (we note the appeal to the Blacks in the *Saison
en enfer* and "Qu'est-ce pour nous, mon cœur?" and approving reference
to various exotic peoples in "Enfance," "Les Poètes de sept ans," etc.);
beyond all *descendance* implies the Manichean bias of non-usage of this
superior body for vile procreation; beyond "any world" is a total ineffa-
bility, as in "Conte." Those riches are put in images of jewels as was the
delight of "Barbare," with its rain of diamonds.

> A vendre l'anarchie pour les masses; la satisfaction irrépres-
> sible pour les amateurs supérieurs; la mort atroce pour les
> fidèles et les amants!

Anarchy is part of this wild joy; "irrepressible satisfaction" too, of the
sort he dreamed of in "Angoisse": "qu'une fin aisée répare les âges d'indi-
gence—qu'un jour de succès nous endorme sur la honte de notre inhabilité
fatale." But only for "superior," disinterested admirers of such satisfaction;
lovers—those sentimental *bergers*, as he calls them in "Bonne pensée du
matin"—and the Church faithful are excluded from these paradises;
rather, an atrocious death is for them, in Rimbaud's nasty terms which
sound disturbingly like the Nazis' at this point.

> A vendre les habitations et les migrations, sports, féeries et
> comforts parfaits, et le bruit, le mouvement et l'avenir qu'ils
> font!

Here, Rimbaud, as in "Mouvement," with much the same vocabulary,
rather disappointingly includes in his vision of salvation (things he is
"selling" *sub specie æternitatis*) a whole panorama of the modern world:
its houses, its restless mobility, its sports; magic doings (*féeries* is clearly
echoed by the "féerie scientifique" of "Angoisse") and "perfect comforts"
brought by a technical society, its movement and future—all this is un-
fortunately prolonged by the crass pragmatism of the post-poetic period of
Rimbaud. Camus was right to see that excess may easily end in extreme
banality in Lautréamont as well as in Rimbaud (in *L'Homme révolté*).

> A vendre les applications de calcul et les sauts d'harmonie
> inouïs. Les trouvailles et les termes non soupçonnés, possession
> immédiate,

Rimbaud seems to vaunt his deep vision for its affinity with modern
mathematics, philosophy, science, music, etc. Undoubtedly Rimbaud did

have moments of profound penetration into syntactical secrets—in "Vies" he calls himself an "inventeur autrement méritant que tous ceux qui m'ont précédé"[1]—as evolved in Mallarmé and Valéry and modern thought and art generally (cf. the comparable philosophico-aesthetic exaltation of Thomas Mann in *Dr. Faustus*, Hesse in his *Magister Ludi*).

"Immediate possession" keeps up the mucker-pose irony of "solde."

> Élan insensé et infini aux splendeurs invisibles, aux délices insensibles,—et ses secrets affolants pour chaque vice—et sa gaîté effrayante pour la foule.

This extreme "élan" can be expressed only in negative terms like the "ineffable" of "Conte." A series of in- prefixes here, as in "Conte," gives the incisive tone. The "maddening secrets" it brings to "each vice" is no doubt the huge stimulus this intoxicating essence gives to every expression —including the mass expression of gaiety in the crowd, joined in a divinely orgiastic outpouring as in the various other passages concerning the fraternal future society dreamed of by Rimbaud; the "Voix reconstituées" above.

> A vendre les Corps, les voix, l'immense opulence inquestionable, ce qu'on ne vendra jamais. Les vendeurs ne sont pas à bout de solde! Les voyageurs n'ont pas à rendre leur commission de si tôt!

A summing-up: the already-mentioned body, voices, riches ("diamonds" earlier); everything that no one will ever sell, "except myself here" being understood. No one will "ever" reach the height and depth of Rimbaud's renunciation and sacrifice of inner riches. This is what he means when he says the sellers are not finished, the traveling salesmen have still some selling-errands to perform; they, the future artists, have a long way to go. And since he has already indicated they will *never* attain this point, these last sentences are ironic understatements, instances of litotes.

Fairy

The English title is one of three in all of Rimbaud, the others being "Bottom" and "Being beauteous." This one, like "Bottom," seems Shakespearean. A reference to Mab, the fairy queen (*Romeo and Juliet*) in "Villes, I," encourages this feeling. Rimbaud, as much as Verlaine, ob-

---

[1] See also "J'ai tous les talents! . . . Je ferai de l'or comme des remèdes" ("Nuit de l'enfer").

viously appreciated the Shakespearean gossamer-delicate evocation of fairies, those elusive creatures representing the human in intimate union with mysterious nature: this is the tone, for example, of "Jeune ménage." The girl, Hélène (with something of the original Greek beauty), is appreciated by Rimbaud in this shimmering light; as much as the lovers of *Midsummer Night's Dream*, she is felt to be at one with the birds and woods, like the orange-lipped little girl at the forest edge in "Enfance" (with similar strobe-light effects in both).[1]

The hints of Russia bear this out: Russians, especially to Frenchmen, seem close to the earth (some entertainment, novel, play or musical drama with a Russian décor may well have worked on Rimbaud to this end[2]).

> Pour Hélène se conjurèrent les sèves ornamentales dans les ombres vierges et les clartés impassibles dans le silence astral. L'ardeur de l'été fut confiée à des oiseaux muets et l'indolence requise à une barque de deuils sans prix par des anses d'amours morts et de parfums affaissés.

This girl's life is charmed; magic effects in nature arise for her as if called up by someone (or Someone) who is putting on a show for her pleasure ("plaisir du décor") and adornment (thus, below, an effect is said to be "required" for the overall atmosphere). The show is in the four acts of the seasonal round: first the "saps" of spring in the "virgin shadows"; then summer ardor; an autumnal quality permeates the woodcutter's air; followed by the shivering furs and shadows and "influences froides" of winter.

The "ornamental saps" redolent of spring remind one of those in "Soleil et chair"; rising in the vegetable veins of Pan, they exude the universal love. The "virgin shadows" in which they are conjured up are like the "camps d'ombres" in the morning-forest of "Aube": a pristine spring womb-source whence the girl's appearance is likewise born. The "impassive brightness [conjured up] in the astral silence" refers to starry light, pure, impassive and superior ("un astre en vérité") like "Hérodiade" (Rimbaud could have read the "Scène" of "Hérodiade" in the second *Parnasse contemporain*); the hints of coldness below are well in line with this suggestion.

The quiet birds who sum up the sleepy yet intense warmth of summer are potential cousins of the bird who made him blush in "Enfance." In

[1] Compare Richard Wilbur's "striped blouse in a clearing by Bazille . . . the flowers' cynosure" ("Courtesy").

[2] Gustave Doré's cartoon history of Russia was published in 1854, based on the travels of the Marquis de Custine.

"Larme" the "Ormeaux sans voix" refer to such Keatsian "unheard music [which] is sweeter." The pervasive atmosphere of high summer drowsiness recalls Mallarmé's "Faune" (at this date yet unpublished); the "indolence" is "required," as we said earlier, for the performance being mounted with her as *star*. It is achieved by the passage of a slow funereal boat as in *Lohengrin* or "The Lady of Shalott," with overtones of his own "Ophélie"; its deathly aspect is ineffable, "priceless"; children are similarly surrounded by such a mixture of "deuil" and magic atmosphere in "Après le déluge." The inlet represents a sort of running aground of emotion we have seen in connection with the boat of "Le Bateau ivre": "bateau perdu sous les cheveux des anses." There, also, were dangerous perfumes: "Echouages hideux au fond des golfes bruns / Où les serpents géants . . . / Choient . . . avec de noirs parfums." In "Solde" "la mort . . . pour les amants" expressed Rimbaud's hatred of normal lovers whom he had such difficulty joining, and there are many such outbursts in him (e.g., "Les Sœurs de charité," various pages of the *Saison en enfer*). Here the nature of the dead love is not specified, but one senses that for this privileged charmed girl—as Mallarmé did for his "Hérodiade" (i.e., for himself too), Valéry for his Jeune Parque—Rimbaud fears the end of innocence. Summer is a time of ripeness, of maturity, and Rimbaud is not ready for that.

> —Après le moment de l'air des bûcheronnes à la rumeur du torrent sous la ruine des bois, de la sonnerie des bestiaux à l'écho des vals, et des cris des steppes.—

A buoyant moment as if from an operetta brings in a snatch of distant song; lady-woodcutters, like fairies, are a part of nature, and from their song (which seems to be addressed to the "torrent") we pass to a "rumor" of water running through these old woods, which is the feeling of holy promise in the forest the child wanders through in "Enfance," hearing the release of the *écluses* with the same "rumor": "par les bois nains; la rumeur des écluses couvre mes pas." To this is joined other magical effects, from bells on flocks to the echo of valleys and cries on the vast plains or "steppes," which add a definitely Russian note, cf. "déserts tartares" of "Soir historique," "Rondes Sibériennes" of "Fête d'hiver." The next paragraph prolongs this atmosphere.

> Pour l'enfance d'Hélène frissonnèrent les fourrures et les ombres—et le sein des pauvres, et les légendes du ciel.

This childhood was surrounded by deep Russian winter tones of shivering furs and shadows; the strobe-effects are assigned to a cold landscape here as opposed to that of the girl in "Enfance." The poor, with quivering breasts, are also Dostoevskian or generally Russian, and the legends of heaven are in line with their superstitions, or those of a childhood, Hélène's, which is the core here. An aristocratic childhood is implied as of Anna Karenina or the sleigh-borne girls in T. S. Eliot's *Waste Land*.

> Et ses yeux et sa danse supérieurs encore aux éclats précieux,
> aux influences froides, au plaisir du décor et de l'heure uniques.

At the heart of this apparition, visible in her eyes, is a "Being beauteous," a rising whirlwind musical essence of womanhood. Those "éclats" and the "danse" and the "influences froides" all occur in "Being beauteous": "devant une neige un Être de Beauté . . . des blessures écarlates et noires éclatent . . . les couleurs propres de la vie se foncent, dansent . . . . " Here, the essence in the eyes and the dance is said to be superior to the "éclats" and the "influences froides" (which, being influences, are by definition exterior) and to the general *décor* which Rimbaud and nature have arranged around this star. But an influence is something exterior which "pours into" the being, as in "L'étoile a pleuré rose" (the etymon of influence is a pouring down from the stars) where the star's essence *becomes* the resplendent woman.

In sum: in "Being beauteous," the Being and the atmosphere were fused whereas, arbitrarily, they are kept somewhat apart here; but one senses that the *décor* and the girl are eventually one. She is a privileged girl, and her dance of childhood innocence occurs in a unique hour, in magic circumstances. She is also Rimbaud, as we can judge from "Jeunesse": "mais à présent . . . votre danse et votre voix."

Guerre

Rimbaud dreams of becoming a Grown Man, as in "Enfance" or "Vies," but he is psychologically handicapped and knows it deep down, suffers from an inferiority complex on the ordinary human plane. So his fantasied man's role will be inevitably excessive, compensatory—and, we reflect, hollow underneath, like the swaggerings of Montherlant or Hemingway or a Nazi program of conquest, or that one imagined by the young Camus in his *Myth of Sisyphus*: "The Conqueror." The War he imagines is "logical" and "simple" as a "musical phrase"—too pure, in fact, and smacking of a schizophrenic's rigidity.[1] In "A une raison," the same

[1] Not that I agree with Fretet (*L'Aliénation poétique*) that Rimbaud was pathologically schizoid; I agree rather with Kretschmer (*The Psychology of Genius*) that schizophrenia is closely analogous to—or is a pathological version of—the

steely musical and rhythmic logic of the male *raison* had, as we said in discussing that poem, a left-or-right dictatorial quality, like the "soleil . . . Général" of "Alchimie du verbe" or "Bannières de mai."

The childhood memories are Rimbaud's usual looking-back for keys to the future. He is fairly honest in describing that past and the present: he was then the passive recipient of artistic impressions (though they were favorable in a way to his evolution), and he is now being "chased" around in the world where he "undergoes" some vague successes, ironically described as "civil"—obviously not the firm ones he dreams of but ones applauded by queer children (childish types like Verlaine or his earlier self) and by those with aberrant, excessive, or "enormous" affections; as at the end of the *Saison en enfer*, his artistic doings are not mature enough for his present perspective. But, ambiguously, this applause, these tentative doings, are promising as were the young Goethe's in *Wilhelm Meister*.

> Enfant, certains ciels ont affiné mon optique: tous les caractères nuancèrent ma physionomie. Les Phénomènes s'émurent. —A présent, l'inflexion éternelle des moments et l'infini des mathématiques me chassent par ce monde où je subis tous les succès civils, respecté de l'enfance étrange et des affections énormes.—Je songe à une Guerre, de droit ou de force, de logique bien imprévue.
>
> C'est aussi simple qu'une phrase musicale.

In "Mauvais sang" Rimbaud recalls: "Encore tout enfant, j'admirais le forçat intraitable . . . je voyais avec *son idée* le ciel bleu et le travail fleuri de la campagne." The construction (memory of childish visions) is parallel here. The "skies" which "refined" his "sight" refer to his poetic sensibility, now rejected; there are many nuancé depictions of skies in Rimbaud, in "Le Bateau ivre," "Larme," "Michel et Christine," "Les Ponts." The technical term "optique" is a characteristic de-poeticization, like the "hydrolat" of skies in "Mes petites amoureuses" and similar "chemical" effects of the heavens in "Mouvement."

The "characters" are human equivalents of the skies: there are various descriptions of human types in "Parade," "Vies," and various parts of the *Saison en enfer*. Rimbaud implies here that such chameleonic development of his *physionomie*—following this or that type as in "Vies"—is not to the point of the firm logical path he seeks in War.

The various phenomena which were moved in the "pathetic fallacy"

---

highest genius. But in isolated utterances such as this, Rimbaud approaches the sick state of his talent, as he does in the paranoia of "Je ferai de l'or, des remèdes" ("Nuit de l'enfer").

of his art (the sighing poplars of "Mémoire," the stirred willows of "Ophélie") are, again, too emotional for his present fixed purpose.

The "eternal inflection" of moments expresses the pressure of circumstances as opposed to his desired control over them. The "infinite of mathematics" stands, no doubt, for a sort of Lucretian cosmos of events he does not influence—on the contrary he is "chased" around and "undergoes" his successes (obviously not the "civil" ones—that is ironic—but the respect), which seem to be the result of mathematical combinations that he does not dominate.[2] Undoubtedly he would agree with Valéry who claimed that he would rather fail than achieve success that he did not consciously control. Or with Mallarmé's Igitur: "vous mathématiciens expirâtes; moi projeté absolu."

The "force" and "droit" are directly echoed in the program of adolescence—the aim to mature, using the resources of a young body and mind against all stifling odds—of "Jeunesse": "la force et le droit réfléchissent la danse et la voix à present seulement appréciées." Dance is physical like *force*, voice mental, like *droit*.

The idea of a perfect music runs throughout Rimbaud. It plays the same ideal role as does his magic Orient or pagan antiquity, which is at times expressed in musical terms: "la musique des anciens" ("Métropolitain"), the "petite phrase" of Proust, or Sartre's perfect jazz-line in *La Nausée* are comparably essential.

Jeunesse

"Enfance" was an evocation of childhood, clearly enough. "Jeunesse" is a stock-taking at the age of adolescence, with some glances back at the child, as is Rimbaud's wont. Thus there are flashes of the mood of "Mémoire" or of "Les Poètes de sept ans."

I: Dimanche

> Les calculs de côté, l'inévitable descente du ciel, et la visite des souvenirs et la séance des rhythmes occupent la demeure, la tête et le monde de l'esprit.

Sunday, as in "Les Poètes de sept ans," is a crisis-day[1] as it still is for many: how "make it" emotionally to start another week?

---

[2] The phenomenon of being swept along by cosmic laws and their apprehension in science and art is duplicated in similar terms in "Mouvement": "Eux, chassés dans l'extase harmonique,/ Et l'héroïsme de la découverte."

---

[1] Cf. Sartre's comments on the pathos of Sunday in *La Nausée*. Or the fact that suicides are apt to occur on this day ("Blue Sunday").

The "calculs" no doubt refer to the "étude" (below)—his creative method (as in the "Lettres du Voyant") which is put aside. In this piece his method is being surpassed by something more total—either a fuller creativity or a more human way, as in the *Saison en enfer* (at this point, as indeed at points of the *Saison*, it is hard to say just what is emerging). But the "étude"—the "optimisme studieux" (part III) of youth—is apparently being eclipsed as we watch.

The "calculs" are directly invoked again in part II: "à présent . . . toi, tes calculs, toi, tes impatiences."

The "inévitable descente du ciel" is a nonchalant way of describing the arrival of daydreams.[2] The "souvenirs"—clearly of his childhood, soon to reappear—are echoed by the "mémoire" of part IV and of the poem "Mémoire" which is close in mood to the next passage: remembrances of the obsessive family-drama that thwarted his inner life, reverberating still in the stagnation and pathos of his Sunday misery.

The combination of memory and creativity is invoked in "Adieu": "Je dois enterrer mon imagination et mes souvenirs."

> —Un cheval détale sur le turf suburbain, et le long des cultures et des boisements, percé par la peste carbonique.

That horse, like the "envols de pigeons" of "Phrases," is everything he is not: a free creature who "takes off" ("détale") as insouciantly as did his father-sun in "Mémoire." In "Le Forgeron" the free-spirited worker of the future was as if mounted on a horse:

> Chasseur des grands effets, chasseur des grandes causes,
> [Il] montera sur tout, comme sur un grand cheval!

The horse, since Plato's *Phaedrus* at least, has long symbolized power (in Plato's case spiritual or erotic power). This particular horse is felt to be wild, on the loose, in nature, like a stallion glimpsed running in an open field. The inner rhyme of "cheval" and "détale" is firm, rhythmic as hoofbeats.

"Sur le turf suburbain" is a curious series of *ur* sounds; Rimbaud enjoyed such consoling (soothing to his inner wounds) incantation for its own sake, cf. "Les roses des roseaux longtemps dévorés" of "Mémoire";

---

[2] Jacques Rivière has compared this to various interventions of sky, e.g., "un golfe de jour pendant du toit" ("Les Poètes de sept ans"). It just possibly may refer (ambiguously?) to an after-church "descent" or disenchantment as in "les mystiques élans se cassent quelquefois" ("Les Premières Communions"). In "Génie" "il ne redescendra pas d'un ciel" refers to a Jesus-like return to earth.

bright u and liquid r (as in *pur*) are an alluring combination: "azur et verdure" ("Enfance").

The "carbonic plague" obviously echoes "bubonic plague" with memories of coal, as in "Villes, I"—"éternelle fumée de charbon"—perhaps associated with English scenery (turf and cultivated fields and woods) in the D. H. Lawrence manner, i.e., a blight of coal-pits (cf. "aux bois puant l'usine," "Les Mains de Jeanne-Marie"). The passage, at any rate, impressionistically describes the stagnant country scene he was stuck in as an adolescent, the local farm fields and woods of Roche, just as in "Les Premières communions" the burned countryside—"arbrisseaux brûlés—or the "Prairie à l'oubli livrée" of "Chanson de la plus haute tour" or in "Mémoire" the "roseaux . . . dévorés" symbolized his numb discontent. In "Vies" we saw him as a "gentilhomme d'une campagne aigre," foundered in his memories of an "enfance mendiante" as here.

> Une misérable femme de drame, quelque part dans le monde, soupire après des abandons improbables. Les desperadoes languissent après l'orage, l'ivresse et les blessures. De petits enfants étouffent des malédictions le long des rivières.—

This scene strongly evokes "Mémoire": the deserted woman (the drama is hers and Rimbaud's both, cf. "Ophélie"); the desperadoes, like the runaway horse, echo the irresponsible *Lui* who takes off over the mountain—or, later, the hardened criminals admired by the boy in the *Saison en enfer*. The storm is always, for Rimbaud, a climate of refreshing change, as in "Michel et Christine," with its wild band of warriors, hard and independent as the desperadoes, who "yearn for" these dramas even as the woman "sighs for" them. The wounded child who, unlike them, is held back, stifles his curses along a river which is very akin to the one of the family outing in "Mémoire" (or the canal of "Phrases"); he will recall that stagnancy again in "Dévotion," with its stinking and buzzing summer grass, the "fever of mothers and children," or "les rages et les ennuis" ("Génie"). The river for Rimbaud would be the eventual channel of escape—the promise of the famous anchored boat in the Meuse—but, as at the end of "Le Bateau ivre," it is still held by the familiar local banks, going momentarily nowhere, closed in like the tiny puddle.

> Reprenons l'étude au bruit de l'œuvre dévorante qui se rassemble et remonte dans les masses.

He goes back to his methodical work—"ce fut d'abord une étude" ("Alchimie du verbe")—as the future creatively revolutionary vision—"dévorante" as in "Guerre"—which will overwhelm him is rising noisily in him, in his inner "masses" and/or the outer masses who will be his putative allies, the workers of "Le Forgeron," the "assassins" of "Matinée d'ivresse," the "marche des peuples" of "Matin." This fermenting or whirling rise is the central effect of "Being beauteous" and "Barbare" and other poems or passages of enthusiasm.

II: Sonnet

> *Homme* de constitution ordinaire, la chair n'était-elle pas un fruit pendu dans le verger, ô journées enfantes! le corps un trésor à prodiguer; ô aimer, le péril ou la force de Psyché? La terre avait des versants fertiles en princes et en artistes, et la descendance et la race nous poussaient aux crimes et aux deuils: le monde votre fortune et votre péril. Mais à présent, ce labeur comblé, toi, tes calculs, toi, tes impatiences, ne sont plus que votre danse et votre voix, non fixées et point forcées, quoique d'un double événement d'invention et de succès une raison, en l'humanité fraternelle et discrète par l'univers sans images;—la force et le droit réfléchissent la danse et la voix à présent seulement appréciées.

The title is obscure; it may refer to the rising lyric tone of this section and its allusion to love, "ô aimer . . . "—the sonnet is a characteristic form of adolescent self-consolation born of frustration; "Vos sonnets La font rire" ("Roman").

He calls himself *Homme* de constitution ordinaire," which is tantamount to saying nothing unusual about his physical self; however, the italicizing indicates, like the parallel usage in "Les Déserts de l'amour" ("Ces écritures sont d'un jeune, tout jeune *homme*") a certain doubt about his own manhood. The "Quels hommes mûrs!" of "Parade," a heavy irony directed at outwardly mature men, bears out this feeling of malaise.

In the continuing inventory, he looks at his adolescent resources as in "Les Sœurs de charité" ("le corps brun") and finds anew a young body as well as spirit. In "Les Sœurs de charité" the youth was seeking everywhere, offering himself to a cause, in vain. In "Mauvais sang" he will ask "A qui me louer?" and he goes on: "J'offre à n'importe quelle divine image des élans vers la perfection." When he was a child, that same physical and moral strength was intact. He savored the fresh body of the little girl next door in "Les Poètes de sept ans" and now remembers something like that—or Baudelaire's "plaisirs libertins" of childhood in "Moesta et Errabunda"—but sees the prodigal spending of that treasure (cf. the diamonds of "Les Sœurs de charité") as a peril to his soul, *Psyché,* and to his future vocation; the "expense of spirit in a waste of shame / Is lust in action," as Shakespeare put it in one of *his* sonnets (no. 129).

The earth with its slopes fertile in princes and artists is a vestige of "Enfance": the child wandered forth and saw all sorts of magic possibilities, of ways of life, like the troupe of *comédiens* in the woods, followed by flashes of future roles as savant, etc. As in Bergman's *The Magician*, the woods seemed to spawn them. Those slopes, then, are like the *talus* ("les talus le berçaient," "Enfance") or the slopes leading to the numb villages of that same poem: they are earth-fold wombs of imagination (in "Villes, I," the "versants" produced huge and fantastic flowers). Thus on the "terrasses voisines de la mer" of "Enfance" were born to him "princesses." The "comédiens" were artists arising in the same way. Cf. "Mystique."

The world or the earth, he feels, gave birth to these types in the past—princes and artists—and, through the race (the ancestors, as in "Mauvais sang" or "Comédie de la soif") induced him to an ambitious setting-forth, like Petit-Poucet or the *valet* of "Enfance," to danger, *crimes et deuils*. Thus for the questing youth the world is a *fortune* or *péril*. . . . But now, he feels, this work of setting-forth is over for him; he has tried his flights and various ways (as in the method of the "Lettres du voyant" or perhaps as in "Ouvriers") and now this activity ("calculs . . . impatiences"; striving or dashing off somewhere to Paris or London "moi pressé de trouver le lieu et la formule," "Vagabonds") gives way to mere unassigned strength: "votre danse et votre voix, non fixées et point forcés" (not pushed dutifully into action or role-playing).

Despite this availability, the strength of voice and dance (mental or spiritual power or grace) is the "Reason" (in the sense of "A une raison") of a new double event of invention and success—combined creativity and solidly effective achievement—the informing *raison* of a new human movement, "fraternal and discreet humanity throughout an imageless universe," i.e., a pure activity of new social organization, as projected in the *Saison en enfer*, with art left behind ("sans images"), a view later espoused by Otto Rank (*Art and Artist*) as it had been by various anarchists and other utopians.

"La force et le droit réfléchissent la danse et la voix à présent seulement appréciées" means that this new order—cf. the "force et droit" of "Guerre" —carries to fruition his strength of mind and body which now is for the first time appreciated (by himself and potentially all others), is truly fertile.

III: Vingt ans

Les voix instructives exilées . . .

His élan is provisionally broken; all our adolescent dreams tend to fall flat in this bitter way. At "twenty years," or at this approximate point (he occasionally exaggerated his age as in his letter to Banville) Rimbaud felt old and disenchanted.

These voices are like the voice (and dance) of the preceding passage: his inner élan or inspiration (perhaps from ancestral heroes; cf. "Comédie de la soif" for voices from the past).

> L'ingénuité physique amèrement rassise . . .

The bodily strength too has disappointingly dropped.

> Adagio.

The musical indication *Adagio* is a comment on the new slow-down of his resources. Or else: "take it easy," addressed to his impatient ("impatiences," above) self.

> Ah! l'égoïsme infini de l'adolescence, l'optimisme studieux: que le monde était plein de fleurs cet été! Les airs et les formes mourant . . .

A true description of adolescent "egoism" and "studious optimism": those studies, they think, will lead to total victory. And the world full of flowers that summer is, to me, the essence of the lyric reassurance the world often provides the sensitive adolescent, telling him he is It, as in "Royauté." The "airs" are the light transparent promise all about as in "Départ": one is open to the universe, or vice versa. The "formes" are the surrounding seductive phenomena (cf. "les Phénomènes [qui] s'émurent," in "Guerre") that pay court or appeal to this king. But they are dying as we watch.

> Un chœur, pour calmer l'impuissance et l'absence! Un chœur de verres de mélodies nocturnes . . . En effet les nerfs vont vite chasser.

He calls for a "chorus" to soothe his loss. That might be the fraternal chorus of mankind (as in "Phrases," and "Solde") which we hear throughout his work standing for his spiritual strength—"la voix," above—as in the "bruit de l'œuvre dévorante" of part I. But the "chœurs de verres de mélodies nocturnes" turns it into a sort of dirge played on water-glasses, a private little soothing performance.[3] For his nerves are empty and quickly go "hunting" for the lost strength, as in "Aube":

---

[3] Similarly, in "Comédie de la soif" water-glasses betoken sentimental evasion: "fleurs d'eau pour verres." Note the variant "verres, de."

"courant comme un mendiant . . . je la chassais." Compare the "future Vigueur" for which the tired-out voyager yearns in "Le Bateau ivre."

I V

> Tu en es encore à la tentation d'Antoine. L'ébat du zèle écourté, les tics d'orgueil puéril, l'affaissement et l'effroi.

He compares himself aptly to St. Anthony for fantastic visions and sudden drops of élan; the "sporting" of abruptly-stopped zeal, the tics of puerile pride, the flop, and the fright.

> Mais tu te mettras à ce travail: toutes les possibilités harmoniques et architecturales s'émouvront autour de ton siège. Des êtres parfaits, imprévus, s'offriront à tes expériences. Dans tes environs affluera rêveusement la curiosité d'anciennes foules et de luxes oisifs. Ta mémoire et tes sens ne seront que la nourriture de ton impulsion créatrice. Quant au monde, quand tu sortiras, que sera-t-il devenu? En tout cas, rien des apparences actuelles.

But he promises himself that he will get to the supreme work—"l'œuvre dévorante"—which he felt rising in him at the end of part I: the program is much the same as in the "Lettres du voyant" with some added growth. Here arises anew the juvenile pipe-dream of perfect beings working with him: people who are in touch with the magic Greece or Orient (like the superior and exotic "féeriques aristocraties" of "Métropolitain" who still hear the "musique des anciens"). As in the "voyant" letters he sees himself as a mere instrument for that cosmic voice: "le bois se fait violon," "Je est un autre." Thus his faculties, including the *mémoire* (of his childhood) that surged at the beginning (part I), will serve his creative impulse. He imagines himself, as in "Enfance" and "Vies," as being cloistered for this great work and wonders what will have happened to the world by the time he gets out. At the end, we have the impression that it will have changed considerably, implying that he will be holed up for a long time. And, vaguely, we get the feeling that somehow, magically, Rimbaud will have effected that change. Such is solipsism, of the narcissistic sort we savored in "Conte."

Promontoire

Somewhere between the ideal architecture of the individual *château* and the equally ideal structure of the public *ville* lies the Grand Hotel.

There is one ("Splendide-Hôtel") in "Après le déluge," excitingly located at the North Pole. This one is more gently situated but with beguiling touches of distant exotic lands and a privileged foundation, a promontory. A promontory is an impressive place, proudly humping up and condensing reality—making it "simultaneous"[1]—by heaping it up in terraces. Land and sea (as well as night and day, old and new) meet there in a vibrant atmosphere. It juts out like the "Péninsule" of "Le Bateau ivre" and proudly asserts itself.

> L'aube d'or et la soirée frissonnante trouvent notre brick en large en face de cette villa et de ses dépendances, qui forment un promontoire aussi étendu que l'Épire et le Péloponnèse, ou que la grande île du Japon, ou que l'Arabie!

This moment is compoundedly vibrant: between night and day and, ambiguously, either in the morning or the evening, and in a suspended position, where the sea confronts the land, on a boat, before the promontory. The "golden morning" points to Rimbaud's well-known partiality to that promising time of day. The shivering evening is partly its chill but, more importantly, as in Baudelaire's "Crépuscule du soir," "l'air est plein du frisson des choses qui s'enfuient." "En large," I agree with the experts, is probably used in the sense of *au large*, with an overtone of *en largeur* indicating sweep (Renée Hubert). The exotic names give the place stir and color and generally refer to well-known juttings of land on the map.

> Des fanums qu'éclaire la rentrée des théories, d'immenses vues de la défense des côtes modernes; des dunes illustrées de chaudes fleurs et de bacchanales; de grands canaux de Carthage et des Embankments d'une Venise louche; de molles éruptions d'Etnas et des crevasses de fleurs et d'eaux des glaciers; des lavoirs entourés de peupliers d'Allemagne; des talus de parcs singuliers penchant des têtes d'Arbre du Japon; et les façades circulaires des "Royal" ou des "Grand" de Scarbro' ou de Brooklyn; et leurs railways flanquent, creusent, surplombent les dispositions dans cet Hôtel, choisies dans l'histoire des plus élégantes et des plus colossales constructions de l'Italie, de l'Amérique et de l'Asie,

The immense stretch of view along a coast under an *aube d'été* recalls the chase of dawn along the *quais* of "Aube." Old "temples" and antique "processions" combine or contrast with modern military constructions;

[1] In his *Confessions*, Rousseau enjoys the spectacle of a mountain with different seasons at successive levels.

the dunes with hot flowers and bacchanales recreate the sustained feminine atmosphere of "Villes, I": "Sur les versants des moissons des fleurs grandes . . . Les Bacchantes des banlieues sanglotent."

Underwood informs us that this whole scene is copied from Scarborough in England (see below): the "fanum" duplicates an old Roman ruin there and the "rentrée des théories" corresponds to returning fishing boats. But it has not been established that Rimbaud saw the place.

The "canals of Carthage and embankments of a suspicious Venice" combine English and Italian and ancient touches in a futuristic mixture recalling "Ponts" and "Villes, II," etc. The "louche," in addition to the immemorial decadence of that magic city, probably connects with the general *bacchanale* mood preceding and following in the references to "soft eruptions of Etna"[2] and "crevasses of flowers," another feminine essence. From here on we have little comment, the futuristic and heteroclite impression is simply prolonged with materials from here and there, fragments of remembered pictures or scenes of hotels and places from Scarborough to Brooklyn, with gardens including his beloved *talus*, poplars from a romantic Germany (as in "Métropolitain"); amidst all that the dynamic thrust and excitement of railways—which refreshingly open up distances (escapes as in "Michel et Christine" or simply movement as in "Villes, I": "chalets . . . qui se meuvent sur des rails").

> dont les fenêtres et les terrasses à présent pleines d'éclairages, de boissons et de brises riches, sont ouvertes à l'esprit des voyageurs et des nobles—qui permettent, aux heures du jour, à toutes les tarentelles des côtes,—et même aux ritournelles des vallées illustres de l'art, de décorer merveilleusement les façades du Palais-Promontoire.

Here the mood becomes lyric, like a Proustian hotel on a beach. It is as if he moved over to the other side of the metaphorical wall separating him from the rich in "Villes, I": "quelques nababs . . . se dirigent vers une diligence de diamants. Quelques divans de velours rouge. On sert des boissons." The windows and terraces—"terrasses voisines de la mer" ("Enfance")—are open to the spirit of the voyagers and of the noble people, i.e., it is a cosmopolitan place, available to ideas from other places and from an inventive idle upper class like the "féerique aristocratie" which could appreciate ancient music, in "Métropolitain." From here on, it is generally recognized, the syntax is obscure, but one gathers something like this: travelers and nobles (with their openness) allow, in

---

[2] Compare the volcanic activity of "Barbare," also Mallarmé's "Après-midi d'un faune." Both have erotic overtones.

the daylight hours, the native folk dances (tarentellas) of the region (the coasts), and even the "ritournelles," well-known songs from the realm of art, to decorate the façades of the Hotel. In "Villes, I," we have similarly combined natural and artificial touches: "les parcs représentent la nature primitive travaillée par un art superbe."

Scènes

Here, as in "Bruxelles" or in "Vies," III, Rimbaud has a vision of an eternal human comedy, ancient and new—the juxtaposition of the two realms makes for bitterly amusing effects, as in T. S. Eliot's "Sweeney Agonistes."

In "Bruxelles" he had written:

> Boulevard sans mouvement ni commerce,
> Muet, tout drame et toute comédie,
> Réunion des scènes infinie,
> Je te connais et t'admire en silence.

In "Scènes" there are the same *boulevards* and the same *comédie—ancienne* and yet contemporary as the *foule barbare* which "evolves" there. That *foule*, the Boeotians below—the "pauvres et faibles" of "Soir historique"—are simply the others, all the weak souls who lack the proud vision of Rimbaud.

> L'ancienne Comédie poursuit ses accords et divise ses Idylles:

At first there is the summing-up statement, followed by a colonic construction which gives examples. The old (-new) "Comédie" carries on its "accords"—harmony reverberating between old and new, between this and that: analogies—and also "divides" its "Idylles," or different episodes: offers the variety of life.

> Des boulevards de tréteaux.

This sounds familiar: a modern boulevard with temporary stands for some ceremony, inauguration, or whatnot. In "Soir historique" they recur in a more open setting, with the same *comédie*: "La comédie goutte sur les tréteaux de gazon." In "Scènes" the effect is a combined one of prosaic street and poetic theater. Rimbaud's art, like Kafka's, depends on just such a combination. "Parade" was an allied effect of spectacle in a city, *Comédie humaine*; cf. the "foule barbare" below.

> Un long pier en bois d'un bout à l'autre d'un champ ro-
> cailleux où la foule barbare évolue sous les arbres dépouillés.

The pier is akin to the file of "tréteaux" and also recalls the pier—fusing
sea and land—in "Marine." The "champ" is a vibrant effect of a stretch of
ground in a city like Paris—e.g., Champ de Mars—which impression is
reinforced by the "stripped trees," struggling nature in an artificial set-
ting, like Baudelaire's decadent Paris with dusty trees ("Le Cygne," the
two "Crépuscules"). The "barbaric crowd" recalls the feared adult males
of "Parade"; cf. the awe-inspiring adult city of "Villes, II": "les concep-
tions de la barbarie moderne les plus colossales . . . j'ai tremblé à l'aspect
des gardiens de colosses."

> Dans des corridors de gaze noire, suivant le pas des prome-
> neurs aux lanternes et aux feuilles.

These corridors recall the night home-scenes from "Veillées" and "Le
Bateau ivre," mixed with some funereal street-scene. It is really dream-like,
nightmarish, as in "Nocturne vulgaire" where we have the same hallu-
cinating night and leaves and mysterious people: "Corbillard de mon
sommeil . . . blêmes figures lunaires, feuilles, seins." One guesses at the
lantern effects which naturally accompany a carriage in the dark. Here
the "figures" are "promeneurs," and this clearly prolongs the street-scene.
But the maternal nocturnal suffocation is similar, and very much in this
respect like the atmosphere of "Les Déserts de l'amour" where city,
strange endless night, and mother all combine in a pathetic thwarted
quest for a way out, past stifling home and feared male figures, to liberty
and life and happy love. But here I get also a Watteau tone of swirling
figures in a sort of *Fête galante* as Verlaine caught the mood in the col-
lection of his most admired by Rimbaud. This is borne out below.

> Des oiseaux des mystères s'abattent sur un ponton de maçon-
> nerie mû par l'archipel couvert des embarcations des specta-
> teurs.

The word *oiseaux* was followed by *comédiens* in the original manuscript,
then crossed out. They, landing on a sort of boat, recall thus the clamorous
birds of "Le Bateau ivre"—"ballottant sur mes bords . . . oiseaux clabau-
deurs"—and indicate, as has been noted, a sense of medieval passion for
mystères, at least in part, prolonging and nuancing the central theme of
scènes or theater. That pontoon of masonry is akin to the "Palais-
Promontoire" of the preceding *Illumination*, a land-sea combination, a

building and strip of land jutting into water which is, again, reminiscent of the boat-Peninsula of "Le Bateau ivre" (*ponton*: old prison-boat, as in "Le Bateau ivre"). As in "Marine," the spectators are in boats which seem land-bound. This curiously anticipates some landscapes of Proust's Elstir. But it is not at all clear how the bridge (or prison-boat) can be "moved" by the archipelago formed by the line of spectator craft. All of this is pretty obscure and elusive, a fantasmagoria *exprès*.

> Des scènes lyriques accompagnées de flûte et de tambour s'inclinent dans des réduits ménagés sous les plafonds, autour des salons de clubs modernes ou des salles de l'Orient ancien.

Here the old-new vibrancy, as in "Promontoire" (temples and railways), produces a T. S. Eliot effect already mentioned ("Sweeney Among the Nightingales," etc.). I get the impression of underground clubs in modern Soho, but with Watteau touches and a magic Rimbaud-Oriental background perspective. How the "nooks" are. arranged "under" the ceilings is a particularly puzzling point, but maybe he is just suggesting levels, as in "Villes, I."

> La féerie manœuvre au sommet d'un amphithéâtre couronné par les taillis,—ou s'agite et module pour les Béotiens, dans l'ombre des futaies mouvantes sur l'arête des cultures.

This is a combined theater and nature effect, as in "Villes, II": "au milieu des gouffres les Rolands sonnent leur bravoure." I suppose the Boeotians— the legendary stupid people of Greece—prolong the "foule barbare," "spectateurs." The "arête des cultures" indicates a platform-like crest amid fields ("cultures") recalling the one on which the theatrical scenes-in-nature ("les herbages," etc.) occurred in "Mystique": "le terreau de l'arête est piétiné par tous les homicides . . . Derrière l'arête de droite la ligne des orients, des progrès." This goes easily with the "taillis et futaies," "groves" which are (as for the pagans, including the Boeotians) natural cult-theaters. The "arête" below echoes this, only it belongs to an indoor theater, the *opéra comique*. There the *arête* is the peak where the partitions between the seating-sections join. This recalls part II of "Vieillées" ("Des deux extremités de la salle, décor gigantesque, des élévations harmoniques se joignent").

> L'opéra-comique se divise sur notre scène à l'arête d'intersection de dix cloisons dressées de la galerie aux feux.

The separation of the spectators into scenes (note the repetition of *divise*) emphasizes anew the idea of *comédie humaine*.

Soir historique

This is like a rehearsal for the *Saison en enfer*; a Faustian (or Flaubertian, in the *Saint-Antoine* or *Bouvard et Pécuchet* manner) tour of the past, his own cultural roots and visionary artistic career up to this point. Rimbaud is ready to leave it all in an apocalyptic moment, a sort of *dies irae* which he calls for at the end. He is the "touriste naïf," and his vision is a "vision esclave": its "magie" is "bourgeoise," etc. The tone is liquidatory like that of "Solde."

The "Soir" of the title is "any evening the tourist chooses to have a vision in" ("En quelque soir . . . que se trouve le touriste naïf"); on each and every one—hence "historique," the vain repetition encountered in the tour of all history (cf. "histoire: à bas!" in "Qu'est-ce pour nous, mon cœur?")—of these evenings the following banal visions, the "vision esclave" and "magie bourgeoise" occur. Thus "Les hallucinations sont innombrables," he says in a comparably clearing-out mood in "Nuit de l'enfer."[1]

The evening is the end of the day, the appropriate time for a summing-up; the imagery reflects this ("le couchant," below); dusk precedes the night that will end it all. Indeed, at the close the tone rises exasperatedly to a *true* sundown vision: the *sérieux* apocalypse that will put a stop to this procession of nonsense.

> En quelque soir, par exemple, que se trouve le touriste naïf,
> retiré de nos horreurs économiques, la main d'un maître anime
> le clavecin des prés; on joue aux cartes au fond de l'étang,
> miroir évocateur des reines et des mignonnes; on a les saintes,
> les voiles, et les fils d'harmonie, et les chromatismes légendaires,
> sur le couchant.

The "tourist" is himself, making the round of the visions he has had; thus we find scenes from other works: the "clavecin des prés" recalls the "piano dans les Alpes" of "Après le déluge"; the "cartes au fond de l'étang" echoes the "salon au fond d'un lac" of "Alchimie du verbe."

He is "retiré de nos horreurs économiques," i.e., away from the "barbarie moderne" ("Villes, II") of "le monde, les marchands" ("L'Impossible"); Rimbaud's fascinated horror of the contemporary ordinary world—much like Sartre's—was expressed in "Parade," "Paris se repeuple," and many another text. But here the term is seen as glib.

---

[1] But in "Nuit de l'enfer," Rimbaud regrets this contempt for history: "C'est bien ce que j'ai toujours eu: plus de foi en l'histoire, l'oubli des principes."

The "maître" is an ironic equivalent of the one in "A une raison"—"un coup de ton doigt"—or "Génie," the spirit which starts the inner music of vision going.

The "hand of a master" is a mocking allusion to a sentimental man's propensity to see shape or artistry in nature—something like "pathetic fallacy," or the naïveté of a Bernardin de Saint-Pierre, who detected the hand of a benign Provider in the form of fruits. But Rimbaud, whose earlier poems were filled with these anthropomorphic illusions ("Ophélie," "Tête de faune," etc.), is really mocking himself (Fongaro and others detect a slap at Verlaine here).

The "miroir évocateur des reines et des mignonnes" is no doubt the pond, which reflects some of the fantasmagoric figures of history: queens and *mignonnes*, darlings of kings—apparently, feminine equivalents of the well-known *mignons* of the seventeenth century (the pond also figures the mirrors that these women used). This line-up is prolonged in the "saintes," and the "voiles" which can refer ambiguously to brides, women in mourning, or sails of historical war-boats (cf. the "Monitors" and "voiliers" of "Le Bateau ivre"); the "fils d'harmonie"[2] and "chromatismes légendaires" extend their apparition through subtly interwoven forms of auditory and visual effects akin to the apocalyptic sunset battle-scenes in "Mystique," where "les bruits désastreux filent leur courbe." The promise of catastrophe in the evening skies will recur in "Mouvement." That theatre of vision can be compared to another, in "Phrases," where the pond and the sunset are paired as here: "le haut étang fume continuellement. Quelle sorcière va se dresser sur le couchant blanc?"

> Il frissonne au passage des chasses et des hordes. La comédie goutte sur les tréteaux de gazon. Et l'embarras des pauvres et des faibles sur ces plans stupides!

It is the tourist again. The "chasses" and "hordes" recall the *dies irae* of invasions of "Qu'est-ce pour nous, mon cœur?" and "Michel et Christine," as well as the *Saison en enfer*. The "comédie" is the human comedy of all history, including these violent forms: "un opéra bouffe / Où chaque histrion foule un sol ensanglanté" (Baudelaire, "Le Couvercle"). The "goutte" seems to imply blood: but violence is nothing under eternity or perhaps in the mere fantasy of these visions. "Sur ces plans stupides" can

---

[2] As in "fils du travail" of "Mémoire" there is an ambiguity between "thread" and "son." *Fils* may imply cords of a string-instrument or the "filial" sounds thereof (cf. Mallarmé's "[d'une] mandore . . . filial on aurait pu naître" in "Une dentelle s'abolit").

refer to either of these interpretations, i.e., the "poor and weak" are embarrassed here as opposed to the Nietzschean Rimbaud, or else they take mere visions seriously, in art and religion. At the end of "Qu'est-ce pour nous, mon cœur?" Rimbaud cried "Ce n'est rien" and "j'y suis toujours," thus triumphing both over the horrid visions and those who fear them. In "Conte," Rimbaud conjured up horrors similarly and with a wave of his hand dissipated them.

> A sa vision esclave, l'Allemagne s'échafaude vers des lunes; les déserts tartares s'éclairent; les révoltes anciennes grouillent dans le centre du Céleste Empire; par les escaliers et les fauteuils de rocs, un petit monde blême et plat, Afrique et Occidents, va s'édifier. Puis un ballet de mers et de nuits connues, une chimie sans valeur, et des mélodies impossibles.

More "enslaved" vision; a further inventory of his outworn fancyings: "l'Allemagne s'échafaude vers des lunes" is only the moonlit Germany of "Entends comme brame" as well as the "fairy" region beyond the Rhine in "Barbare." The "tartar deserts" recall the "steppes" of "Fairy," as well as the far places whence the hordes of "Michel et Christine" rode forth, cf. "Qu'est-ce pour nous, mon cœur?"[3] The "céleste empire" is even farther east,[3] a region whence stir and renewal may come (the East being the classic scene of religious renewals).

The "stairs and chairs of rocks" is a Goethe-like *Walpurgis*-mountain vision (or Ossianic, or late eighteenth- and early nineteenth-century Romantic landscape generally, e.g., Wordsworth's "rocks and trees"). On such a ledgy Romantic hill-theatre, as in the "arête" of "Mystique," scenes are played. If this world is "blême et plat," that is because Rimbaud sees it as a fraud. Over the hills, as in "Mystique," is a rumor of distant ocean associated with night and tossings: "rumeur tournante et bondissante des conques des mers et des nuits humaines," cf. "jeunes mers, pleurs de nuits estivales, / Qui se retournent" ("Les Sœurs de charité"). All this is now "chimie sans valeurs" (cf. "Alchimie du verbe") and the interior music (as in "Métropolitain" or "Les Ponts") started by the master-hand is now mere "impossible melodies"; they lead nowhere.

> La même magie bourgeoise à tous les points où la malle nous déposera! Le plus élémentaire physicien sent qu'il n'est plus possible de se soumettre à cette atmosphère personnelle, brume de remords physiques, dont la constatation est déjà une affliction.

[3] Cf. Kafka's "Chinese Wall" for a similar theme of events that seem at a remote (Chinese) source whence we hear only the faint echoes.

Wherever the "malle"—this vehicle refers to the sustained metaphors of the tourist of historical time or Rimbaud's vision of it—puts him down, there is the same "magie bourgeoise," more routine visions; this is the disenchantment of Baudelaire's "Le Voyage" or the end of "Le Bateau ivre": "toute lune est atroce et tout soleil amer." He puts it in hygienic terms: these visions are the result of mere physical indisposition; the "brume de remords physiques" echoes closely the vapeurs of "Honte": "cette cervelle, / Ce paquet blanc, vert et gras, / A vapeur jamais nouvelle." Even to think of these "vapeurs" is an "affliction." This "personal" romantic imagining is outmoded; he wants objective truth, action.

> Non! Le moment de l'étuve, des mers enlevées, des embrasements souterrains, de la planète emportée, et des exterminations conséquentes, certitudes si peu malignement indiquées dans la Bible et par les Nornes et qu'il sera donné à l'être sérieux de surveiller.—Cependant ce ne sera point un effet de légende!

These upheavals were described in "Qu'est-ce pour nous, mon cœur?": the "étuve" recalls the "braise"; the "mers enlevées" recalls the "Océan frappé"; the "embrasements souterrains" echoes the "volcans" (also, more happily, in "Barbare"); the "planète emportée" corresponds to "la vieille terre" and the "exterminations" to the "nappes de sang." All this was predicted in the Bible ("si peu malignement"; cf. the Nietzschean pose earlier) in the form of St. John's *Judgment* and the Flood (described in "Mouvement"). The "Nornes" may well be, as Lacoste has observed, a vestige of Leconte de Lisle's "Légende de Nornes," also predicting the end of the world. The final sentence "it won't be an effect of legend" could then refer to this poem: Rimbaud's vision will be caused by material facts, not legendary predictions. Thus, in "Fairy," the superstitious Russian poor are evoked with their "légendes" as the "poor and weak" are evoked here. But a more direct link is with the "chromatismes légendaires," the dismissed vision of sundown invoked above, in the first paragraph.

The "être sérieux" is contrasted to the "touriste naïf"; the former is Rimbaud now having overcome his visionary naïveté.

Bottom

The title is from Shakespeare's *Midsummer Night's Dream*. Shakespeare's "Bottom the weaver" was metamorphosed into a donkey beloved by the fairy queen Titania (the original title of Rimbaud's poem was "Métamorphoses"). This is very apt for the situation Rimbaud retails here: a humble being, son of the people, and/or donkey receives amorous attention (whether in fact or fancy: I suspect, on no good grounds, some concrete episode behind this) from an aristocratic lady. This was foretold in the dream of "Les Déserts de l'amour": "J'étais en haillons, moi, et elle, mondaine qui se donnait." The parallel of the class-disproportion with the universal Oedipal situation is fairly obvious.

> La réalité étant trop épineuse pour mon grand caractère,—je me trouvai néanmoins chez Madame, en gros oiseau gris bleu s'essorant vers les moulures du plafond et traînant l'aile dans les ombres de la soirée.

Reality is too thorny for his great character in the sense that he is so abstract and ideal, Hamlet-like, and cannot act; he is as self-ironic as Amiel's *Journal* on this point. Nevertheless, he manages this once to get to Madame's place.

Rimbaud, a creature of extremes, daemonic poet par excellence, is characteristically both above and below the norm. Like Baudelaire's Albatross, who may be remembered here, he either soars up majestically or flops about piteously "dragging his wings in the evening's shadow"; nothing much in between. Soul-brother to the notoriously socially clumsy Rousseau, he apparently committed gaffe after gaffe through an evening. The "big bird" is apt for his peasant's ungainly size; the "blue-gray" may refer to an actual Bohemian-dandy costume. But the effect of the whole scene is indeed one of metamorphosis. Rimbaud is transformed into a beast (bird or bear); animals like himself are traditionally both divine and inferior (cf. Mallarmé's faun, both demi-god and goat representing two aspects of himself). This is magic, the terrain of art; the normal measure of sanity is abandoned in the vertigo ot welling love and despair (or as Mallarmé puts it in the art-section of the "Coup de Dés": "hilarité et horreur"). Everything communes as "tout se fit ombre et aquarium ardent." The reality coalesces kaleidoscopically, and the *colors* carry the uncontrolled love, as splashes of delight. It is the swirling adolescent fairy world of *A Midsummer Night's Dream* illustrated by Chagall (that donkey head is one of the latter's hallmarks).

> Je fus, au pied du baldaquin supportant ses bijoux adorés et ses chefs-d'œuvre physiques, un gros ours aux gencives violettes et au poil chenu de chagrin, les yeux aux cristaux et aux argents des consoles.

An actual scene of Rimbaud getting as far as the canopy of a bed; but then, again, metamorphosis takes over instead of act; and again, lyric colors and light ironic laughter emerge from the blockage and the bitter despair. The most lyric of all colors is violet,[1] and here it is amusingly associated with the bear's gums.[2] The heavy end of the spectrum of universal rhythms (Bottom) is represented by the heaviness of the bear and its dark "chagrin"; the light end is (with the violet) in the crystal and silver reflections on the sideboard, etc., to which he *diverts* his attention (like Mallarmé's faun whose bubbly flute "diverts" his "trouble" after an amorous fiasco). The "consoles" are "consoling" in this punning sense.

The self-concerned pathos of animals repeats in similar terms in "Matin": "des bêtes poussent des sanglots de chagrin."

> Tout se fit ombre et aquarium ardent. Au matin,—aube de juin batailleuse,—je courus aux champs, âne, claironnant et brandissant mon grief, jusqu'à ce que les Sabines de la banlieue vinrent se jeter à mon poitrail.

The aquarium may well be an effect of mirrors, cf. the "poisson . . . hautes glaces" of Circeto in "Dévotion" (is he now also a "little fish" as in "Ouvriers"?). At this point the vertigo and the magic reach a peak. As in "Aube," at a climax there is a blank. What occurs? Again as in "Aube," it is ambiguous; the child there "fell" together with the dawn, which could mean a sexual climax or a defeat (like the Oedipal fall of "Les Déserts de l'amour"). I suspected the more buoyant result there. But here, with an actual woman, even if there was a victorious act of sorts, the result is grief. The "matin—aube de juin batailleuse" is not the happiness or relaxed sleep in nature of "Aube" but a controversial ("batailleuse") dawn, followed by a misery. The dawn is a battle in the sense that Rimbaud is undergoing a deep emotional struggle, mirrored in the conflict of night-cool versus day-heat in the midsummer month (which may reflect Shakespeare's time-setting; Mallarmé's will be the same in the "Faune" with a remarkably similar "matin frais s'il lutte" against the rising, searing sun). He runs away, precisely, to the comforting fields.

Those Sabines of the "banlieue" may be real events, girls who came to be nice to him. They recall the "bacchantes des banlieues" of "Villes, II." He obviously enjoys the jarring ironic juxtaposition of classic and modern (as in "Promontoire"). I would guess, however, that they are merely imaginary girls like the one he promenaded with in nature in "Les Reparties de Nina." But who can say?

---

[1] But it is so extreme—the ends meet—it is also the color of mourning; see our comment on "Voyelles."

[2] In "Jeune ménage," the gums of elves are glimpsed. Gums are a flash of intimacy; purple ones are an intimate exoticism, perhaps reminiscent of a surprising toy.

The Sabines, finally, put an end to his "aube de juin batailleuse" in the way they do in David's gigantic painting in the Louvre: "Les Sabines arrêtant le combat entre les Romains et les Sabins." Or else he read of the same event.

H

I believe Étiemble was on the right track in identifying "H" as a not very obscure parable of masturbation.[1] Arnoult concurs. This is not poetry, of course, but a sort of veiled confession, hence barely literary. When such episodes are ensconced in rich and rangy texts as in the case of Proust (particularly *A la recherche*) and Gide (*Les Cahiers d'André Walter*), that is another pair of shoes. But this is as unbalanced and mistaken, in a way, as *Portnoy's Complaint*.

Rimbaud penned other brutal bits in the *Stupra*, particularly the "Remembrances du vieillard idiot" which speaks of the "puberté tardive et le malheur / Du gland tenace trop souvent consulté" and ends "Tirons-nous la queue."

The title refers evidently to Hortense and initiates the atmosphere of puzzle. A well-known French scholar—I doubt that he would appreciate being identified here ("trouvez l'érudit!")—assures me that "Hortense" has long been the familiar term for the act in the French army. "She" substitutes for the absent female, as Proust remarks in the Combray section of his novel. There may be a slight suggestion in the element *tense*.

> Toutes les monstruosités violent les gestes atroces d'Hortense. Sa solitude est la mécanique érotique, sa lassitude, la dynamique amoureuse. Sous la surveillance d'une enfance elle a été, à des époques nombreuses, l'ardente hygiène des races. Sa porte est ouverte à la misère. Là, la moralité des êtres actuels se décorpore en sa passion ou en son action—O terrible frisson des amours novices sur le sol sanglant et par l'hydrogène clarteux! trouvez Hortense.

The "monstruosités" that "violate" the atrocious gestures of Hortense are no doubt the gestures of self-punishing brutality that Rimbaud administered to himself at various phases of the act. The phrase "atrocious gestures" registers his horror of his sex in its erection, convulsive climax, and jerky detumescence. The "solitude" of the deed is self-explanatory; to say it *is* the "mechanics of eroticism" seems to be shorthand (or an

---

[1] Bonnefoy compares it with "Matinée d'ivresse": it is another hymn to hashish. Others see pederasty (Adam), a bout with a prostitute (Rolland de Renéville), etc.

obscure way) for saying it is the *condition* for that; similarly, the "tired-ness" or relaxation accompanies the release, the "dynamique amoureuse." Under childish surveillance—i.e., practiced by children—it provided ardently hygienic outlet for the various races, that is to say, it made the prohibition of mature sexual performance possible before adulthood by offering substitute release. Étiemble further points out that in India it is even taught to children by their parents for this reason or as a preparation for developed experience. But, as Proust and Gide knew, its excess can lead to—open the door to—"misery." *Là*—in its realm—the morality of contemporary beings is decomposed; a clear and self-evident statement. (Its "passion" is perhaps the phase of desire, its "action" the act proper; but it is not clear why he spells this out here.)

The last sentence refers to the horror of the convulsive "shiver" of these "novice loves." The "bloody soil" implies metaphorically (I think) a battleground of self against self, cf. the "aube de juin batailleuse" for another problematic erotic encounter ("Bottom").

The last phrase, starting with the dash, is an exclamation: "O terrible shiver of novice loves on the bloody ground and by the clear hydrogen." The latter may refer to the strange fluid of the act. Then Rimbaud adds "find Hortense" and, ambiguously, "by the clear hydrogen" may refer to the light by which we are to investigate the mystery. But I am afraid there is not much of one.

Mouvement

This is one of the two free-verse poems which are included in the *Illuminations*, the other being "Marine." It records Rimbaud's experience on a boat, perhaps on one of his trips to or from London with Verlaine. Unlike the vessel of "Le Bateau ivre," which explored the private dream-life, the psychic depths of the cosmos, this one moves rather in a horizontal, social-historical direction. It represents the Faustian dynamism of modern technical times, rushing toward a monstrous but fascinating future.

At this juncture, Rimbaud is in the mood of the *Saison en enfer* and "Soir historique." He rejects his visionary past as being too passive, leading nowhere but to crisis, and he seeks an active way toward life—and yet he is held in flashes of remembered beauty. Like Baudelaire, he detests and fears the growing crassness of "la barbarie moderne" ("Villes, II"), but there may be an exciting adventure here leading to power and even glory. So there is a double ambivalence; he is torn as on a cross—or quartered—between the positive and negative poles of both (passive) art and (active) life. The whole uncomfortable posture can be summed up, schematically, in our philosophical term "tetrapolarity."[1]

> Le mouvement de lacet sur la berge des chutes du fleuve,
> Le gouffre à l'étambot,
> La célérité de la rampe,
> L'énorme passade du courant
> Mènent par les lumières inouïes
> Et la nouveauté chimique
> Les voyageurs entourés des trombes du val
> Et du strom.

The title is symbolic of the horizontal, kinetic tendency in the entire piece. This is reflected in the "mouvement" of the first line and a series of terms which betoken passage and speed through space and time. *Mutatis mutandis*, the word "movement" here takes on some of the cosmic generality of the word "wake" in Joyce's title *Finnegans Wake*.

First, there is the passing like a meandering thread or shoe-lace of the succession of waterfalls, perhaps locks. Then the rushing "gulf" at the rear of the boat where the couple of travelers, probably Rimbaud and Verlaine, are watching it all fascinatedly.

The "ramp" of water slopes down rapidly, part of the haste of technical modernism. They go, in an "enormous" passage[2] of the current: Rimbaud is boyishly awe-struck by the motion of big material bulks pushed by motors and active men's ingenuity. As in "Parade," his previous passivity and inwardness make him very sensitive to such doings of mature males wrestling with an equally vital and strenuous nature.

All this leads the travelers by way of "unheard-of lights," probably streaks of strange luminescence in the evening sky—cf. the "lumière diluvienne" at the end of the strophe—which portend awesome changes, new horizons. The "chemical novelty," new promising substances— "chimique" is repeated below—seem mirrored there, as in "Mes petites amoureuses": "Un hydrolat lacrymal lave / Les cieux . . . " Then in the third strophe we have "accidents atmosphériques les plus surprenants."

Around the travelers are more exciting rushings and swirlings of water, as in "Le Bateau ivre" where we saw those "waterspouts." The foreign word "strom" has the unfamiliar freshness of *Wasserfall* in "Aube," with the sibilance exploited by Goethe in "Tiefe Stille heerscht am Wasser." It refers probably to the open sea as opposed to the inland *val*.

---

[1] See *The Writer's Way in France*, Appendix c.

[2] *passade*: a "passing affair"; perhaps the huge passing caress of the boat by the water.

> Ce sont les conquérants du monde
> Cherchant la fortune chimique personnelle;
> Le sport et le comfort voyagent avec eux;
> Ils emmènent l'éducation
> Des races, des classes et des bêtes, sur ce vaisseau
> Repos et vertige
> A la lumière diluvienne,
> Aux terribles soirs d'étude.

These farers-forward are the conquerors of the world in the way that Rimbaud personally will soon actively seek by voyaging to distant places. The "personal chemical fortune" signifies their Romantic individualism ("personnelle"), and the gimmicky technical nature of their quest, with some ironical dubiety in the tone; "chimique" has overtones of *alchimie* (the ancestor of chemistry, cf. "Alchimie du verbe"), hence magic; probably also *chimérique*. The "cherchant" guarantees, in the idiom of Rimbaud, his metaphorical *sub specie aeternitatis* tone echoing the "Wandering Jew" of "Comédie de la soif," where the Quester sighs, "Si j'ai jamais quelque or" (foretelling the image of the hardened gold-seeker in the *Saison en enfer*). This cosmic mood persists in the vision of the boat as a microcosm of the planet which humanity rides through the universe, i.e., a sort of *Naarenschiff* ("Ship of Fools") but also, as we shall soon see, a version of Noah's ark ("arche," below). As in "Solde"— "sports, féeries et comforts parfaits, et le bruit, le mouvement [*nota bene*] et l'avenir qu'ils font!"—the vision of headlong modern humanity, and of all the things these conquerors "take along" (like the camera he will order from Ethiopia), includes "sport and comfort,"[3] etc. This is the common feeling we have on a big boat or plane or a Jules Verne balloon where people dine and enjoy all the creature comforts, play games and the like while rushing through space and time; here the idea is blown up to include the education of races, classes, and beasts (of whom Rimbaud said he had charge in his "Lettres du Voyant"); they too are part of the Noah's ark image that is gradually being evolved along with the flood ("diluvienne").

The "repos and vertige" are the combination of the stillness of the travelers and the speed of the vehicle. Rimbaud much appreciated this kinetic-static fusion, the "charme des lieux fuyants et le délice surhumain des stations" of "Génie."

The "lumière diluvienne" reminds us of the refreshing change brought by the "déluge" in "Après le déluge" as well as the expensive renewal

---

[3] "Comfort" is spelt this way in "Solde" and "Adieu"; Rimbaud seems to have been influenced in this respect by Baudelaire in "Les Paradis artificiels."

wrought by Noah's. The conquerors take all reality to this new light—"à la lumière diluvienne"—and to the terrible evenings—"aux terribles soirs d'étude," i.e., they carry the education of races, etc., to the all-changing flood which is future science and to the harsh study which is the price of Enlightenment. Just so, in "Jeunesse" his "étude" accompanied a rising flood within, the "œuvre dévorante."

> Car de la causerie parmi les appareils, le sang, les fleurs,
>   le feu, les bijoux,
> Des comptes agités à ce bord fuyard,
> —On voit, roulant comme une digue au delà de la
>   route hydraulique motrice,
> Monstrueux, s'éclairant sans fin,—leur stock d'études;
> Eux chassés dans l'extase harmonique,
> Et l'héroïsme de la découverte.

The atmosphere of mobile and casually enjoyed luxury, like a lounge in a space-ship, recalls the dynamically modern hotel with its railways under, over, and beside, and its "terrasses pleines d'éclairages, de boissons et de brises riches" in "Promontoire," or the similar one in "Villes, II" with its "chalets de cristal et de bois [qui] se meuvent sur des rails et des poulies invisibles."

The "sang" is surprising: it points up, no doubt, the bloody price, in wars of conquest ("conquérants"), of such progress; cf. "la comédie goutte sur le gazon" in "Solde."

"From this chatting amid flowers," etc., and "from the accounts agitated on this fleeting deck" (the expenses of all this luxury and technique, cf. "nos horreurs économiques" in "Soir historique"), one sees the fantastic stock of studies that go into the modern mind. This "stock d'études" is, as above ("la lumière diluvienne"), assimilated to skies "s'éclairant sans fin." Rimbaud's view of the civilized mind is likened, concretely, to a wall like an arriving flood's, a "dike" but one that is "roulant," possibly conjured up by cumulus clouds in a light-filled evening sky (see the "accidents atmosphériques" below), but possibly in a surge of deeper water "beyond the moving hydraulic route," the river ("fleuve," first line) through which they are passing on the way to open sea, where there are taller waves. This precise progression occurred in "Le Bateau ivre."

They, the passengers, are "chased," harried along, by their demon of Quest, expressed much as in "Solde" ("les sauts d'harmonie inouïs. Les trouvailles . . . ") by "l'extase harmonique" and the "heroism of discovery."

> Aux accidents atmosphériques les plus surprenants,
> Un couple de jeunesse, s'isole sur l'arche,
> —Est-ce ancienne sauvagerie qu'on pardonne?—
> Et chante et se poste.

The evening sky is full of strange effects as in "Le Bateau ivre": "les cieux délirants . . . ouverts au vogueur," etc.

The young couple isolates itself on the "ark," and "sings and posts itself" (like sentinels; cf. "l'âme sentinelle" of "L'Éternité"), waiting, like Noahs, for the new flood, the deluge of the fresh era of Enlightenment described earlier.[4]

In a parenthesis, this Nietzschean expectation is seen as a potential sin; it implies, like the Flood, that only a few will make it.[5] It is thus called "ancient savagery," this un-Christian urge which may go back to the youth of culture (Hebrew? pagan?) as it suits the youthful amoral spirit of the couple and of the contemporary neo-pagan mind generally. Rimbaud explores this ancient aspect of himself in "Mauvais sang." He looks to savages for allies in "Qu'est-ce pour nous, mon cœur?," "Matinée d'ivresse," and "Mauvais sang": "j'entre au vrai royaume des enfants de Cham." They are Noah's descendants (Ham was his son) on the dark—Cain-like daemonic—side which Rimbaud finds so promising.

Dévotion

Perhaps the most obscure of the *Illuminations*, "Dévotion" is also among the least satisfying.[1]

The title, and the whole, mocks at Rimbaud's mother's religion rather as the "Ballad of Joking Jesus" mocked at Joyce's mother's (less bitterly; it was Buck Mulligan who sang that). A series of ironic "devotions"—litanies—is proposed, saluting each time some saintly person ("à . . . ") in the name of, or for, needy persons ("pour . . . ").

> A ma sœur Louise Vanaen de Voringhem:—Sa cornette bleue tournée à la mer du Nord.—Pour les naufragés.

[4] Py sees only Rimbaud and his *génie* (as in "Conte").

[5] Cf. "Vous me choisissez parmi les naufragés, ceux qui restent sont-ils pas mes amis? / Sauvez-les!" ("Mauvais sang").

---

[1] Some commentators, most recently Margaret Davies in *Revue de littérature comparée*, no. 170 ("Melville et Rimbaud"), see a whale in the *-ceto* of "Circeto" combined with "poisson" and "ambre" (*ambergris*) and build a whole mystic quest thereon. I do not see this. The connection of fish with prostitute likely has a humbler undertone.

The good sister is likely imaginary, but the resemblance to known persons may not be coincidental. Her name invokes a certain alliterative and Nordic quality (cutting v's), a Flemish or Netherlandish tone. Hence she—her nun's headdress—is visualized as turned to the North Sea, like a *stella maris* Virgin Mary figure, as in "Le Bateau ivre": "pieds qui calmeraient la mer." This in turn evokes the shipwrecked who are being prayed for, again as in "Le Bateau ivre" ("des noyés pensifs"). The vignette is fetching.

> A ma sœur Léonie Aubois d'Ashby. Baou—l'herbe d'été bourdonnante et puante.—Pour la fièvre des mères et des enfants.

This sister's name produces an aristocratic English effect. Hence the "Baou" transliterates, faithfully, the English word "Bow" (the command "Make a bow"), which is apt for a devotion. The name and the "Baou" form another alliterative sequence which is curiously like the one at the end of "Aube": "L'aube et l'enfant tombèrent au bas du bois." Perhaps the "Au-bois" of the sister's surname is responsible for the thought of nature and the child here, but his ironic mood turns the scene sour. His mother's religion makes him think of the suffocation of summer grass buzzing and stinking as in "Chanson de la plus haute" tour or the archetypal scene of "Mémoire" (with its "pourritures" and "roses . . . devorées") and the same in "Jeunesse": "De petits enfants étouffent des malédictions le long des rivières." The stagnation of a provincial church has some comparable bearing on the "arbrisseaux brûlés" and the "campagne en rut" of "Les Premières Communions."

In "Phrases" there is a strange consonance with our present passage: "Une matinée couverte en Juillet. Un goût de cendres vole dans l'air;—une odeur de bois suant dans l'âtre,—les fleurs rouies,—le saccage des promenades,—la bruine des canaux par les champs—pourquoi pas déjà les joujoux et l'encens?" This contains the "cendres" (of Ashby), the "bois" (of Aubois), the scene of corrupt summer nature and the child ("joujoux," cf. *enfants*), as well as the mockery of religion.

> A Lulu,—démon—qui a conservé un goût pour les oratoires du temps des Amies et de son éducation incomplète. Pour les hommes! A madame * * * .

This is thought by Suzanne Bernard to refer to lesbians (*Les Amies* was a naughty collection by Verlaine), hence the "Lulu—démon" and the "éducation incomplète" followed by the bitingly ironic "Pour les hommes."

Perhaps Rimbaud remembers here the charge he leveled against the Church, in "Les Premières Communions," of ruining a woman's normal emotions through "le baiser putride de Jésus." Diderot's *La Religieuse* had explored this terrain.

No one seems to know who "madame" is. There is one, similarly truncated, in "Bottom," but it sheds no light.

> A l'adolescent que je fus. A ce saint vieillard, ermitage ou mission.

This recalls the adolescent he delineates in "Jeunesse"; he offers a religious salute to him unironically, for a change, as he does to a holy old hermit who is much like the old man he had seen as his life's goal in "Vies" (cf. the "anachorète" of the *Saison en enfer*).

> A l'esprit des pauvres. Et à un très haut clergé.

This recalls the poem "Les Pauvres à l'église."

> Aussi bien à tout culte en telle place de culte mémoriale et parmi tels événements qu'il faille se rendre, suivant les aspirations du moment ou bien notre propre vice sérieux.

This devotional passage is dedicated to *any* cult, in the spirit of this passage of "Mauvais sang": "j'offre à n'importe quelle divine image des élans vers la perfection." This will be in "any place that memorializes a cult amid any events wherever we have to go, according to the inspiration of the moment (i.e., the cult can be of any inspiration) or else according to our serious vice" (i.e., the cult can be of a Nietzschean order, a "serious vice" like the *élan* which perhaps needed pardoning at the end of "Mouvement," the assassins of "Matinée d'ivresse"; a demonic cult).

> Ce soir à Circeto des hautes glaces, grasse comme le poisson, et enluminée comme les dix mois de la nuit rouge,—(son cœur ambre et spunk),—pour ma seule prière muette comme ces régions de nuit et précédant des bravoures plus violentes que ce chaos polaire.

The salute seems to go ironically to a fat prostitute (shades of Circé?); the high mirrors are found in bordellos. She is fat as a fish (the mirrors, as in "Bottom," create an aquarium atmosphere). This word "glaces" is chosen, instead of *miroirs*, for its cold overtones befitting the "chaos polaire,"[2] the "cold feet" endemic to this situation (Mallarmé used *glace* in much the same way in "Hérodiade"). Thus in "Mauvais sang" we have: "rouge et noire, comme une glace quand la lampe circule dans la chambre voisine, comme un trésor dans la forêt"; cf. the "nuit rouge" here. This indicates that the reddish "ambre" (and the spark implied in spunk) may be involved in an Oedipal reminiscence. This is especially likely since the quoted passage in "Mauvais sang" is followed closely by "mais l'orgie et la camaraderie des femmes m'étaient interdites."

According to Py, Circeto may be compounded of Circé and Ceto (in Hesiod a divinity daughter of Earth and Sea, etymologically related to the whale). She is all "lit up" by much paint like a "red night lasting ten months," an allusion to polar nights, probably, see the "polaire" below. Her heart is "amber and spunk"; the amber, from the northern regions, is part of the polar garishness, brightness against long cold and dark; this is apt for the fascinating horror of a prostitute's chamber. I do not understand "spunk" except perhaps as a "spark" against the dark, or her earthly "courage."

This is offered in behalf of his "mute prayer," his spark of desolate feeling. His prayer is silent as the "night regions" in this "polar chaos" adventure. An emotional disaster as in "Bottom" is involved, probably because of similarly unresolved Oedipal problems. There he ran off to the fields, "brandishing his grief." Here a violent bravado is threatened—such as frustrated men often perform after their unsuccessful acts in bordellos—some typical Rimbaud outburst of emotion, aggressive and pathetic like the various misdeeds and provocations he was known to have committed in Paris.

> A tout prix et avec tous les airs, même dans des voyages métaphysiques.—Mais plus *alors*.

This last salute is like the ones in "Départ" or "A une raison" (which duplicates the "to . . . " formula): in "Départ," "la vision s'est rencontrée à tous les airs" refers to the universal presence of the beautiful vision. Rimbaud offers his greeting to that ubiquitous spirit here. "A tout prix" is similarly open. It is an amusingly ambiguous statement: "No matter what the cost," i.e., "I offer my homage to all costs," all infinite élans, including "metaphysical voyages" (cf. "Le Bateau ivre"). Those infinites, as in "L'Éternité," are his ways to salvation—and, as in that poem, which says "Sans qu'on dise enfin" (the maternally stifling opposite of the eternity, i.e., it is a formula often used by a reprimanding martinet mother

---

[2] In "Après le déluge" there was "le chaos de glaces et de nuit du pôle," but the situation there was far less ambiguous.

as in "Enfin veux-tu?" and is literally "finally"), here in a possibly similar spirit he rules out a typically bourgeois-maternal *alors*—"no more *alors*."

Démocratie

"Le drapeau va au paysage immonde, et notre patois étouffe le tambour.

"Aux centres nous alimenterons la plus cynique prostitution. Nous massacrerons les révoltes logiques.

"Aux pays poivrés et détrempés!—au service des plus monstrueuses exploitations industrielles ou militaires.

"Au revoir ici, n'importe où. Conscrits du bon vouloir, nous aurons la philosophie féroce; ignorants pour la science, roués pour le confort; la crevaison pour le monde qui va. C'est la vraie marche. En avant, route!"

The ambivalence of the later Rimbaud—the Rimbaud of the *Illuminations*—vis-à-vis the idea of progress becomes, in this piece, an especially harsh and savage irony, damning what it praises. It almost seems as if the effect is taken from the sound *crasse* in the word "Démocratie" (hence perhaps the "paysage immonde"). The atmosphere is also that of "Parade": the sordid male strutting of brute force, which Rimbaud fears and, after the *Saison en enfer*—"une réalité rugueuse à étreindre"—will espouse, homeopathically.

The "patois" here (Rimbaud hated the "paysan matois," "Rivière de Cassis"—which rhymes with it) is like the "enrouements folâtres" there ("Parade"). It stifles the "tambour" which, as in "A une raison," is the swelling rhythm of creative life, healthy revolt, "révoltes logiques," which they will "massacre" (cf. the "raison" of "A une raison" and "Guerre . . . de logique bien imprévu," "Guerre"). That is atrocious, murdering the old ideals of Rimbaud—but is not that what he is about to do, as he prepares to enter the "vrai royaume de Cham" ("Mauvais sang")? Camus, after wrestling with and repudiating this late Rimbaud, in *L'Homme révolté*, confronts anew the atrocity of this attitude in *Le Rénégat*.

The "cynical prostitution" recalls what the Versaillais did to Paris, in "L'Orgie parisienne." Now Rimbaud would like to try it. Or at least a horrid part of him that he has to express, however indirectly (between the quotation marks which begin and end the piece).

The "pays poivrés" are like the good "plaines poivrées" of "Vies," speckled with crows, spicy with potential life. In "Les Corbeaux" and "La Rivière de Cassis" the black birds made him think of heathen revolt, an "armée étrange." But here the country stretches have become "détrempés," as in "Mémoire" the fields became "pourriture." What has happened then is an industrial and military disease in a vision like D. H. Lawrence's; the *poivre* seems to modulate from crows to dirty coalpits, the "peste carbonique" of "Jeunesse," littering, blighting, and blackening the landscape as in the English locus of "Ville": "spectres nouveaux, roulant à travers l'épaisse et éternelle fumée de charbon."

The "Au revoir ici, n'importe où" is an ironic formula of general departure toward an ignorant future, no matter where or at what cost. In "A une raison" a similar formula bespoke, rather, insouciance, availability: "Arrivée de toujours, qui t'en iras partout." What a falling off!

These "conscripts" are uncomfortably close to the barbaric types that Rimbaud, in his wilder moments, claims as allies, most prominently in the *Saison en enfer*.

Their concepts are well-intentioned; but their "bon vouloir" is, as is well known, what paves the road to hell. Their ferocious philosophy, their ignorance of science, and their blasé attitude toward comfort make them capable of the worst. The "comfort" and "éducation" of "Mouvement" have come to a dynamic horror. The "en marche" of "A une raison" has become a "true march," a hideous and prophetic image of nascent fascism, emerging from the modern republics.

Génie

In "Bruxelles," Rimbaud exclaims:

> Je sais que c'est Toi qui, dans ces lieux,
> Mêles ton bleu presque de Sahara!

This is the supreme visitation. The *Génie*—we may read either "genius" or "the genius"—is something as simple and obvious as "the divine spirit of poetry": "une personnalité multiple et une, mystérieuse et rien que pure. Quelque chose comme le Génie, écho de soi, sans commencement ni chute, simultané, en le délire de son intuition supérieure . . . " (Mallarmé, "De même"). Or "un être vaste, immense, compliqué, mais eurhythmique . . . un animal plein de génie" (Baudelaire, *Fusées*, XXII).

The idea of holy frenzy comes down from the daemon of Socrates through Cicero, the neo-Platonic poets of the Renaissance, and the Romantics, but in Rimbaud's case it has a special flavor which—in addition to his other sophisticated complexities—comes from the absence of, and his hunger to adore, his father; and this remoteness engenders, in the Judeo-Christian way, a Father. There can be no mistaking the concrete filial tone which permeates this lyric masterpiece. In our Introduction (p. 20), we have indicated some of the determining points of this golden thread of inspiration which runs throughout Rimbaud's creative expression: there is the *Génie* from whom the needy adolescent of "Les Sœurs de charité" would have received affectionate attention in ancient Persia where he consented to appear (that far-away region in time and place expressed his inherent remoteness); then, the similar *génie* in "Conte"; the sun-god of "Bannières de mai" (Rimbaud is "fils du Soleil" in "Vagabonds"); the departing sun, clearly identified with his father in "Mémoire"; the "soleil, dieu de feu ... Général" of "Alchimie du verbe."[1] Numerous other allusions have received commentary in the separate studies of this book. It is perhaps not too much to say that "Génie" is a summary of Rimbaud's previous poetry—that is why it comes properly last in the *Illuminations*—so many of the well-known images find their appropriate locus here, are shuffled felicitously into an ambitious structure.

> Il est l'affection et le présent puisqu'il a fait la maison ouverte à l'hiver écumeux et à la rumeur de l'été, lui qui a purifié les boissons et les aliments, lui qui est le charme des lieux fuyants et le délice surhumain des stations. Il est l'affection et l'avenir, la force et l'amour que nous, debout dans les rages et les ennuis, nous voyons passer dans le ciel de tempête et les drapeaux d'extase.

Genius breaks open the confining home and lets in the fresh air of the world; the soul escapes through the breach in the bedroom walls to flights of poetry as in "Le Bateau ivre."[2] One is at last free, at Home in the cosmos where each creature depends only on the original creation: nature. The seasons are utterly consoling in this sense of flattering our absolute dignity, reflecting that endless expansion of self. At such moments, the "foamy winter," the snow,[3] is the objective correlative of the blinding light of Eros which fills us—with overtones of milk, manna, soma, the "mille anges blancs" of "Mémoire" (and the whole first strophe)—"toutes les blancheurs" as Mallarmé, after Gautier, quelled.[4] The rumor of summer is another rhythm of that bliss—we have felt it in "Départ": "Rumeurs des villes, le soir, et au soleil et toujours."

[1] We pointed out, for example, how zealously he strove, through his schoolwork and his poetry, to capture the attention of Izambard.

[2] The winter penetrates into the sleeping boy's room there in various modalities: "Moi, l'autre hiver"; "neiges éblouies."

[3] The snow is part of a sadly consolingly maternal nature in "Les Étrennes des orphelins": "la nouvelle Année . . . Laissant trainer les plis de sa robe neigeuse, / Sourit avec des pleurs, et chante en grelottant. . . ."

[4] See *Toward the Poems of Mallarmé*, Appendix A.

In these moments, the elements, the water we drink, the food we eat are blessed, "purified." The hydra-thirst of "Comédie de la soif" is quenched, the hunger of "Fêtes de la faim" is satisfied. The ideal synthesis of movement and rest, so often sought and sometimes found in the poetry of Rimbaud, comes off in a prime formula: "fleeting places," seen at times from a train, at times on foot, and the "superhuman delight" of stopping-places, "les arrêts" of "Départ," perhaps a station as in "Bruxelles," generally the artistic "stasis" of Joyce—these two joys, for a Kierkegaardian Instant, are one.

We note the superiority of the "délice surhumain des stations" over the mere "charm" of "fleeting places." Rimbaud—despite the emphasis of many critics, including J.-P. Richard and Sartre, on his dynamism—is more essentially a poet of stasis, and would certainly agree with Joyce on its primacy: his highest moments of happiness like Nietzsche's are in resignation to what is: "Je vis que les êtres ont une fatalité de bonheur: l'action n'est pas la vie, mais une façon de gâcher quelque force" ("Alchimie du verbe"). The later post-literary Rimbaud would move radically to the opposite pole. But his art is at its best a fusion of movement and rest in a higher synthesis, with the crucial preference or imbalance of artistic Faith—"the still point of the turning world" (T. S. Eliot)—inherently implied in the word "synthesis" itself.[5]

"Affection" expresses, as in "Les Sœurs de charité" ("Adoré") Rimbaud's sense of election by the Father-Genius: "the future" is what our life *élan* at the full inevitably generates: promise! "La force" which Rimbaud, like Kafka in his *Journal*, discovered at the bottom of his being even in deepest despair (as in the winter struggle of "Métropolitain" or the comparable one of "Angoisse") is definitely here, together with its psychic equivalent, "love" ("Amour, force," he wrote in an exultant moment of "Angoisse"). The numb child of "Mémoire" and the remembered

---

[5] We have discussed the theoretical basis for this preference in *L'Œuvre de Mallarmé: Un Coup de Dés*, Appendix I; also in *The Writer's Way in France*, Appendix III.

Sartre's conception of Rimbaud's explosive dynamism (in his *Genet*) is simplistic and superficial. The really interesting dynamism of Rimbaud is his inner energy, the spiritual fire, the total "fissioning" power (in which he is comparable to artists like Proust, Mallarmé, Joyce). Sartre regards these figures as "feminine" (so was Jesus, in this sense, and we have not soon finished with *Him*). But actually, Rimbaud sought as much as these others an "essentialist" unity through universal analogy, metaphor, etc. (as well as its dialectical opposite, mobility). The very example Sartre gives of his explosive virility ("L'aube exaltée ainsi qu'un peuple de colombes") is a clear analogy, a simile. Rimbaud's poetry is rife with these links: he is, in this sense, a symbolist, unifying the world. And at times he sees himself as "une femme à genoux" ("Le Bateau ivre").

version of him in "Jeunesse" ("des enfants étouffent des malédictions") is now resurrected for contrast with the glorious change of a storm—we have seen it in "Villes," "Michel et Christine," "Larme." There follows the symbol of the above-it-all spirit, departing for freedom in harmony with all the imagined fraternal Others: the flag, waving in the storm of "ecstasy," like the banners of the boat about to leave behind the shore of the provincial home-past in "Adieu."[6]

> Il est l'amour, mesure parfaite et réinventée, raison merveilleuse et imprévue, et l'éternité: machine aimée des qualités fatales. Nous avons tous eu l'épouvante de sa concession et de la nôtre: ô jouissance de notre santé, élan de nos facultés, affection égoïste et passion pour lui, lui qui nous aime pour sa vie infinie . . .

The "mesure parfaite et réinventée" is the "ordre éternel" of "L'Homme juste" or the golden mean of realism of "Veillées": "le repos éclairé"; the "raison merveilleuse et imprévue" is the newly enlightened knowledge of and obedience to—in the Nietzschean sense—what is, the laws of creation, as in "A une raison." The "eternity" is that integral truth which he had communed with—*âme sentinelle*—in the state of high consciousness of "L'Éternité." The "machine aimée des qualités fatales" is of that same implacably authentic order: it can be summed up in the Nietzschean phrase: *amor fati*. The "[religious] terror of his concession" is that "not-before-ripeness" relenting which is the essence of fatherly love: when he is good and ready. The young male imitates him: "et la nôtre." Then, when the conditions are strictly fulfilled—when we do not give in prematurely—then and only then do we enjoy to the full our health, the élan of our faculties, and that paradoxical union of extreme opposites where egotism and passion for another—for him—are one. The converse paradox is in him: He loves *us* for himself, his own infinite life. (We have read much of this in the great mystics, from St. Augustine through Dante to San Juan de la Cruz. But . . .).

> Et nous nous le rappelons et il voyage . . . Et si l'Adoration s'en va, sonne, sa promesse sonne: "Arrière ces superstitions, ces anciens corps, ces ménages et ces âges. C'est cette époque-ci qui a sombré!"

Here there is a strong reminiscence—"we remember him"—of the ever-departing personal father, as in "Mémoire," with that same shining "lui"

---

[6] In "Après le déluge," flags participate in the orgy of rebirth.

associated with the male sun: "Lui . . . s'éloigne par delà la montagne." Essentially, Rimbaud's father was a being who "traveled," was not there. He left behind the provincial city and its (his mother's) church: the superstitious "adoration" which "goes away" into a background now, and "rings" its futile bells as the new cult of his "promise rings" a fresh appeal; cf. "fêtes de fraternité, il sonne une cloche de feu rose dans les nuages" ("Phrases"). "Back with these superstitions, these old bodies, these [stifling] homes and these [past] eras. It is this [whole] era which has sunk!" This is breaking the table of values, as Nietzsche would say; spiritual revolt: "la naissance du travail nouveau, la sagesse nouvelle, la fuite des tyrans et des démons, la fin de la superstition . . . Le chant des cieux, la marche des peuples . . . " ("Matin").

> Il ne s'en ira pas, il ne redescendra pas d'un ciel, il n'accom-
> plira pas la rédemption des colères de femmes et des gaîtés des
> hommes et de tout ce péché: car c'est fait, lui étant, et étant
> aimé.

He will not go away,[7] unlike our prophets of the past, or come down from the sky, unlike Jesus[8]—that would be too narrowly specific, naïvely miraculous; he will not redeem women's anger and the converse joy of men (who exploit them; this was detailed in "Les Premières Communions") and all that sin (of the present unfair code); for it is already done, just by his being, and being loved.

The last part of this paragraph is inconsistent with the first part, which distinguishes the Rimbaldian version of Genius from bygone religious forms; the second part, rather, specifies things that he once thought ought to be remedied but do not really need to be once we have understood the spirit. Rimbaud now accepts, in his *amor fati*, what is, rather than militantly opposing it: "L'air et le monde point cherchés. La vie" ("Veillées").

> O ses souffles, ses têtes, ses courses; la terrible célérité de la
> perfection des formes et de l'action.

The "souffles" are inspiration, the stirring refreshing breeze of change, the "brises du matin" of "Adieu," the *souffle* of spirit—*âme, anima*—which opens up breaches of vision in the house of "Nocturne vulgaire."

---

[7] The father goes away but that is supreme indifference; in a sense, that is his presence. He is not limited by traditional dogma.

[8] In "Jeunesse" a similar formula, "L'inévitable descente du ciel," refers either to the arrival of daydreams or to a disappointing come-down after Sunday religious soaring: "Les mystiques élans se cassent quelquefois . . ." ("Les Premières Communions").

"Ses têtes" are like the varied modalities or expressions of the creative spirit in "A une raison": "Sa tête se détourne le nouvel amour; sa tête se retourne le nouvel amour." "Ses courses" are the dynamic aspect of change, like the "terrible swiftness" which is a *vis a tergo* sweeping us along in its overwhelming power and impulse as it brings the new action of spiritual rebirth and the static aspects of it, perfected forms.

> O fécondité de l'esprit et immensité de l'univers!

No comment is needed here.

> Son corps! Le dégagement rêvé, le brisement de la grâce croisée de violence nouvelle!
> Sa vue, sa vue! tous les agenouillages anciens et les peines *relevées* à sa suite.

"His body"; genius is incarnate, is acute presence, *Dasein* (as well as radical absence). The "dégagement" is the same as in "L'Éternité": "tu te dégages et voles . . . . " Grace like this breaks us—as St. Paul said ("When the law came I died")—breaking the tables, in its "new violence" which is "crossed with"—intimately bound up with—the grace.

"Sa vue." This is ambiguous: his active look, ahead or upon us (this can include what we see of it, as in "Ses Yeux" of "Voyelles" or the "bleu" of divine sky-eyes in "Bruxelles") or else his appearance. No doubt both. It is enough to raise up old kneelings in a double sense: the formerly superstitious will no longer bow down to false images; the physically or morally bowed-down—this goes with "peines"—will be raised up as in the biblical "pick up your bed and walk" or Rimbaud's ironic version of it in "Beth-Saïda" (*Proses évangéliques*): "Le Paralytique se leva, qui était resté couché sur le flanc, et ce fut d'un pas singulièrement assuré qu'ils le virent franchir la galerie" as he left Christ behind.

> Son jour! l'abolition de toutes souffrances sonores et mou-
> vantes dans la musique plus intense.

"Son jour" (this will be repeated at the very end): it is the light of this supreme "Illumination" as it is of the total genius of nature: "les boutons d'or et les marguerites demandant grâce au jour" ("Beth-Saïda"). All previous noise (the *rumeurs des villes* of striving and suffering men in "Départ" and "Ouvriers"), the bustle of the world will be drowned out in this intense harmony—the chorus of "Métropolitain," the music of "Being beauteous" and "Barbare," the "maison musicale" of "Phrases."

> Son pas! les migrations plus énormes que les anciennes invasions.

"His step": a giant step is taken by this revolt, this awareness: "un pas de toi c'est la levée des nouveaux hommes et leur en marche" ("A une raison"). This was the clear aim of the seer of the famous *Voyant* letters: "il sera multiplicateur de progrès." Horizontally, the equivalent is framed in terms of vast sweeping migrations, as in "Michel et Christine," and "Qu'est-ce pour nous, mon cœur?"

> O lui et nous! l'orgueil plus bienveillant que les charités perdues.

"O lui et nous": a pure father-son relationship. The father is implacably authentic, existential as the old Jehovah: "I am what I am" (JHVH). His unswerving selfhood is pure "pride" but paradoxically—like the egotism which is affection, above—it is pure generosity, "bienveillant," unlike the sentimental, partial, former *charités*.[9]

> O monde! et le chant clair des malheurs nouveaux!

This world-spirit is round and whole as the letter O (or the o in "monde"). The "clear song" is like the piercing cock-call in "Le Bonheur" ("O saisons . . . "), cf. *chantecler*; a bugle-like call to greatness as in the "O suprême clairon . . . Mondes" of "Voyelles," a call to a non-denial (unlike Peter's) of the Source, cost what it may—*amor fati*—in "malheurs nouveaux."

> Il nous a connus tous et nous a tous aimés. Sachons, cette nuit d'hiver, de cap en cap, du pôle tumultueux au château, de la foule à la plage, de regards en regards, forces et sentiments las, le héler et le voir, et le renvoyer, et sous les marées et au haut des déserts de neige, suivre ses vues, ses souffles, son corps, son jour.

The all-embracing father. Let us be up to him ("Sachons . . . "), Rimbaud appeals. Facing the worst—the "nuit d'hiver" was the nadir of despair in "Les Déserts de l'amour," the *de profundis* setting-out point of "Le Bateau ivre"—embracing, like him, all: cape to cape, from the farthest remote pole ("Après le déluge") to the local chateau ("O saisons . . . "), from the bustling crowd in the midst of affairs to the beach ("Enfance")

---

[9] Thus Proust, near the beginning of *A la recherche*, sees in a coldly efficient nurse "le visage de la vraie bonté."

which is the threshold of the beyond, from look to look of all individuals (the fraternal social poems), leaving behind old "strengths and feelings," let us hail and see him, and send him off to new victories, and everywhere in nature—under the tides ("Le Bateau ivre"), on heights of snowy wastes ("Being beauteous," "Fairy"), follow his looks, his breaths, his body, his light. These last four key words occur previously in the text; we explained them as they arose.

IV

UNE SAISON

EN ENFER

Introductory Synopsis

THIS IS by far Rimbaud's longest single work. Complex, and often un-controlled, as it is, nevertheless there is a perceivable line of development: it tells a hectic "story" about Rimbaud's inner evolution—a crisis and a proposed solution—at a crucial moment of his young life. For these rea-sons, it seems useful to present, at first, a synopsis, followed by detailed comment on significant passages.

Une Saison en enfer is Rimbaud's most stubborn attempt at sustained creation, at producing one work which would climax and sum up his fledgling career. Simultaneously, like any other artistic expression, it is an effort to earn release from the tension between mind and body—and between the various other dangerously divergent parts of the creatively "schizoid" personality—to integrate, in this sense, and to atone for the characteristic creative lag. But, even more, in this instance it was the means of shaking off an insatiable drive to spiritual power which was threatening his very existence. Its deepest purpose—best evidenced in the part called "Nuit de l'enfer"—is thus a homeopathic cure, a purging of his artistic being by its own radical expression.[1]

Being a coming-to-grips with self in a crisis, through the medium of the written word, it is a spiritual autobiography of a concentrated sort, written in a highly-charged, occasionally poetic, prose. Like many such confessions, thoroughly turned in upon self—Rousseau's *Confessions*, Dostoevsky's *Notes from Underground*—it is largely ambivalent, drawing power from its failures, pride from its humiliation and self-mockeries, abandoning art to raise it momentarily even higher,[2] thirsting for God to better blaspheme (and vice versa), and so vertiginously on. To plunge into the whirling drift of Rimbaud's peripeties is to know the giddy experience of truth: *hypocrite lecteur*, it is the story of us all.

We ought to admit from the outset that, aside from the limitations inherent to the genre, *Une Saison en enfer* leaves a great deal to be desired artistically. Partly it is a patchwork affair, put together in obvious haste; there are some needless obscurities, gratuitous repetitions; the whole suffers from a lack of organization or composition. True to the youth of its author, there is even an adolescently rhetorical, sensational quality to

[1] There was, of course, no guarantee that such a cure would succeed permanently: being so radical, it could conceivably destroy the patient—this has happened to several writers—or again it might earn temporary repose followed by a relapse. But, with luck, the effort, by its extremeness, precipitates a convulsive crisis of the whole organism which may then definitively change course in a way useful to its survival. This was what happened to Rimbaud.

[2] Some later practitioners of this subtle maneuver will be called "terrorists" by Paulhan.

certain passages like "J'ai avalé une fameuse gorgée de poison" or those scenes in which he summons up a nineteenth-century street-theater demon.[3] But mainly its shortcomings have to do with the quality of its obsessiveness: for all our fascinated involvement, eventually one tires of the umpteenth reversal of direction and go-around again of that slender Kabbalistic serpent chasing its own tail, just as we may tire of a compulsive thinness in Dostoevsky or Kafka. It will be instructive to compare *Une Saison en enfer*, in this respect, with a quite similar attempt on the part of Mallarmé, *Igitur*.

The work (tentatively called *Livre païen*, then *Livre nègre*) begins with an untitled preface, a reminiscence of his former aliveness: "Jadis, si je me souviens bien, ma vie était un festin où s'ouvraient tous les cœurs, où tous les vins coulaient." Soon we learn—and it is a keynote of the entire confession—that he has become almost mortally exhausted, "sur le point de faire le dernier *couac*." Obviously, he still has the strength for this final expression, but, like so much modern literature, it is written in a kind of second or third wind, "on the nerves," venturing dangerously into the frontier zones of the spirit, where a man may hope to surpass himself with a supreme sacrificial effort. Not having the capacity, the desire, or the sheer necessity to radically change his overall course as yet, he will therefore press forward to precipitate a crisis and let nature take over via the utter exhaustion of his life-strangling mental faculties.

Now, the once-worshipped Muses of Beauty (responsible for the poems) and of Justice (the political fling) are invoked only to be disavowed as dead ends: "O sorcières, ô misère, ô haine, c'est à vous que mon trésor a été confié!" In an earlier poem, "Les Sœurs de charité" he had paid homage to these two, "la Muse verte et la Justice ardente . . . deux Sœurs . . . " and added a third, "O Mort mystérieuse, ô sœur de charité." This third muse, in slightly tempered form, is the one he now seeks as the only remaining avenue back to life: "la charité est cette clef." By charity here

---

[3] In his struggle for power over the literary Fathers, the adolescent arms himself with a sneer; his aim to replace rhetoric by popular speech, *jargon potache*, macaronic Latin, "queer" words (like Rimbaud's repeated *baver*, scientific terminology, big words), and so on works with the process of pseudo-primitive *déculture* to renew art dialectically, as we have noted. Thus the addition of the adolescent tone, with its particular form of bitterness, scatology, misogyny, tentativeness, is as valuable to art as the discovery of childhood. At best this tone is subsumed into ambitious later works which meet the Fathers head on: thus there are survivals of the *Stephen Hero* manner in *Ulysses*, in purposeful perspective and balanced proportion. But with Lautréamont, Jarry, even Laforgue and Corbière somewhat, the inchoate tone retains the limelight, and, often jelled into a pose, a new kind of rhetoric, becomes one of the relatively *minor* manners of modern literature. Rimbaud is a bit reduced by its presence in *Une Saison en enfer*.

he means not quite death but something near to it: total renunciation of his former self, or his art, which he nows sees as artifice, mere fakery. Charity is pure abnegation, gift of self without compensation. We shall see that although it is never accepted by Rimbaud in its Christian garb— he envisions this only to dismiss it—it takes on momentarily a bare pagan shape of love of God and, even, fleetingly, of love of his fellow-men. But these forms are soon rejected as involving specific commitment, however little—"je veux la liberté dans le salut"—and at the end charity means nothing more than the renunciation of art, his past striving, in favor of a rebirth to undefined life. At times Rimbaud sees death as the true "sister of charity." In the present chapter, the devil who reduced him to his sunken state whispers "Gagne la mort"; later he wonders "la charité serait-elle sœur de la mort?" But, like all the literary *tricheurs* (Magny), he manages to survive and "détacher ces quelques hideux feuillets de mon carnet de damné." By now, the manner of this preface has a familiar literary ring—but what has not?

Part II, "Mauvais sang," traces his ancestry to the pre-Christian Gallic barbarians, in an attempt to escape cloaking his charity with any later Western guise. Rimbaud has not yet the strength or the humility to embrace any part of the normal life against which his whole being has been hitherto clenched: his new ideal of charity is utterly naked. Hence he identifies himself with the lazy irresponsibility of those imagined distant ancestors: "surtout mensonge et paresse . . . J'ai horreur de tous les métiers." He will soon seek contemporary equivalents of these barbarians in pagan Africa. Meanwhile, in a rapid tracing, he sees successive generations of his forefathers[4] as belonging to "the inferior race," the people as opposed to the lords and their allies in the official Church: "Seigneurs—représentants du Christ." This lower caste is now rising up in modern times to supplant their rulers and the Church through progress, science, *l'Esprit*, constituting a new kind of "horizontal" religion; "l'Évangile a passé." Rimbaud is somewhat horrified at the idea, at the people and its Homais-like science, but he is also horrified at himself and, lacking alternatives, will turn repeatedly to this hope of redemption

---

[4] During this struggle of late adolescence to pin the angel of unfulfilled manhood, given the absence of his father and the general thorny problems of this area, there is a momentary attempt here to "go over his parents' heads" and find more remote ancestry on whose discovered strength one might base one's self-assurance. Thus Rimbaud here goes back to his peasant—at least biologically sound!—forebears, just as in "Comédie de la soif" he evokes the following: "Nous sommes tes Grands-Parents / Les Grands!" Mallarmé's ancestors had likewise egged him on to achievement in *Igitur* (cf. Vigny: "ils descendront de moi"). Fournier's Grand Meaulnes was particularly attracted to children and grandparents, with a significantly vague parental zone of affection. (Cf. Baudelaire's *vieux* and *vieilles*.)

through the dogged march of mind, somewhat in the spirit of Renan. As a member of the inferior race, "[il] attend Dieu avec gourmandise," but it is this new-old glory in a God without any Western institutional form.

Rimbaud now toys with a program of leaving Europe to live among dark savages, but soon drops the idea: "On ne part pas," and he continues to search for a concrete direction which he can accept: "A qui me louer?" He considers also becoming a military man, like his father—"Dans quel rang marcher?"—but without any identifiable moral cause: "La vie dure, l'abrutissement simple." He really does not know what he is seeking: "j'offre à n'importe quelle divine image des élans vers la perfection." Not finding any in his mind, he is profoundly discouraged and mocks at his very search: "O mon abnégation, ô ma charité merveilleuse! Ici-bas, pourtant." Which is to say that he has ended up amid the harsh reality of his continuing problem; "After such knowledge what forgiveness?" (T. S. Eliot).

There follows a peculiar hymn, "Encore tout enfant, j'admirais le forçat intraitable sur qui se referme toujours le bagne. . . . Il avait plus de force qu'un saint . . . lui, lui seul! pour témoin de sa gloire et de sa raison." This dangerous and beautiful vision of purity, perversely wrought, like the château, from utter isolation and sulking guilt is subtly associated with the irresponsible father who is "intraitable," absolutely unyielding of his presence, hence the recurrence of the key themes of "lui, lui" and "raison." Rimbaud's intransigence is patterned on this image. He wandered on so utterly alone, "Sur les routes, par des nuits d'hiver, sans gîte, sans habits, sans pain," so different from his fellow-men—whether exhausted in spirit or retreated into another world—that "ceux que j'ai rencontrés ne m'ont peut-être pas vu."

In self-pity, he now describes his orphan moments of misery and delight, "un trésor dans la forêt"[5]—the sudden gleam of flame in "The Little Match Girl"—and how even women were alien to him. The best, once again, is to leave Europe, to foresake thoughts, words, culture, to dance, dance, dance, and forget.

Having won to innocence by his abnegation and precisely *because* he has rejected the West and its Church, now, in a Dostoevskian reversal, he can envision momentarily—part mockingly—an acceptance of Christianity

---

[5] The completer phrase, "la lampe qui circule dans la chambre voisine, comme un trésor dans la forêt," evokes an incestuous orgy reminiscent of the one in "Les Déserts de l'amour": "une mer de flammes et de fumée au ciel; et à gauche, à droite, toutes les richesses flambaient comme un milliard de tonnerres." Cf. Mallarmé's "Etna . . . tonne . . . ou s'épuise la flamme. Je tiens la reine! O sûr châtiment . . ." In the Rimbaud passage there is an equal threat of punishment, and so "Mais l'orgie et la camaraderie des femmes m'étaient interdites."

from missionaries who will find him in Africa! Being totally devoid of any responsibility to it, having thrown it off sacrificially, he can imagine that the Church will transport him like a child to a pure paradise, without any of the sad dutiful trappings which Rimbaud associated with the institution he knew in Charleville. Still, the very hint of this makes him yell, "Vite! est-il d'autres vies?" in place of this untrustworthy cult, and, finding no answer, he returns to the dream of his pure conversion: "je loue Dieu."

In the next section, he makes very sure that it is God and not the Christian God or Church: "Je ne me crois pas embarqué pour une noce avec Jésus-Christ pour beau-père. . . . J'ai dit: Dieu. Je veux la liberté dans le salut. . . ." This cautionary remark is followed by the statement that, having dreamed of pure love, having inwardly achieved his innocence, he is absolved of any given action or form: "Plus besoin de dévouement ni d'amour divin. Je ne regrette pas le siècle des cœurs sensibles [the age of official religion]. Chacun a sa raison, mépris et charité; je retiens ma place au sommet de cette angélique échelle de bon sens," which is somewhat a reaffirmation of the natural religion of the Enlightenment, somewhat a Kierkegaardian belief that his tie to God is absolutely solitary.[6] But this victory, like Kierkegaard's flaming Instant which threatens to consume the moth, is very close to nothingness, and he faces this fleetingly: "Comme je deviens vieille fille, à manquer du courage d'aimer la mort." But, rejecting this total solution, he imagines a possibility of innocence on earth: "Si Dieu m'accordait le calme céleste, aérien, ta prière,—comme les anciens saints.—Les saints, des forts! les anachorètes, des artistes comme il n'en faut plus!" But this—sainthood, art—is obviously *tricherie*, a mere *form* of life, role-playing, an artifice, as he had already decided: "Farce continuelle? Mon innocence me ferait pleurer. La vie est la farce à mener par tous." So there is no perfect solution, no total honesty *ici-bas*, and yet he is stuck here, a latter-day Hamlet. The ephemeral dream of innocence enjoyed is now expiated by its inner concomitant, a vision of atrocious struggle in a spiritual hell. In the last portion of "Mauvais sang," it begins as a battle scene with a tiny thought that this might be a concrete way to salvation (another of his repetitions), but soon it becomes the sincerer vision of the struggle with the angel in the major part which follows.

In "Nuit de l'enfer," Rimbaud hits the bottom of the gravest crisis in his prolonged agon. The *Saison en enfer* was written over a period of months, and in between the various fragments he recuperated some

[6] The Enlightenment paved the way equally to the existential view and the social bias; Sartre has both.

strength. At this point, however, he is quite exhausted and thus is ready to try that one horrible extra step to force his system to take over from his mind, which by now had become a cancerous growth threatening the very life of the organism. In the sense that Rimbaud did render his art, at least, indigestible to himself, he was successful. (On his deathbed he told his sister "C'était mal.") But insofar as he was not yet sufficiently changed inwardly to accept roughly normal existence (love of others, family, work)—and this was undoubtedly too much to expect from one crisis—his success was only partial. These limited results begin to burgeon in the later fragments, especially "Adieu," which must have followed closely, in conception, "Nuit de l'enfer."

In the present part, we have the usual rises and dips, twistings in and out, but with a difference: this is for keeps. He is suffering atrociously from his self-torment and his exhaustion, but forcing himself to write on, beating his sides to empty himself: "les entrailles me brûlent. . . . Un homme qui veut se mutiler est bien damné." But he calls for more: "Va démon." In a further effort to damn his own soul he mocks at his recent dream of conversion, "Les nobles ambitions!" He longs to commit a crime to this same suicidal end: "Un crime, vite, que je tombe au néant. . . . " And like Eliot's Thomas à Beckett he sees *this too is pride*—"Orgueil"— this too is his failure to be humbled by a higher Power, Whom he continues to bait. Receiving no final condemnation, he pushes on with this pride, digging at the pocket of his deepest thirst, evoking the poetic glory of his childhood. But this flash of evanescent beauty is soon invaded and smothered by his sense of doom: "Le diable est au clocher." For a poignant instant he has delusions of "others" who come to help him, but no, "jamais personne ne pense à autrui." No, he is alone and damned and damned for being undamned: his pride pops up anew to tell him he is the greatest visionary of all time, but his obverse fear then tells him to bury it all quick: "Je suis mille fois le plus riche, soyons avare comme la mer." We may reflect that as yet he is caught between violent extremes: total generosity or total tightness, which he easily assimilated from his emotionally and financially stingy mother.

At this point his text presents close parallels to Mallarmé's *Igitur* (which preceded the *Saison en enfer* by a few years, but remained unpublished until after Mallarmé's death). In general tenor, both have their place in that lineage of spiritual combats which we now identify as the existential experience of the "absurd." The image of the clock-heart stopped in a flash of spiritual suicide occurs in each, and the inner attempt to kill the individuality (like Kirilov or Empedocles outwardly) to become a quasi-divine impersonal being ends in very similar statements of paradoxical victory: "Il n'y a personne ici et il y a quelqu'un," says Rimbaud;

Igitur gingerly proclaimed "Il y a et il n'y a pas de hasard." Both having achieved the experience of the absurd, they find their victory to be quite Pyrrhic, absurdly self-destructive: having all they have nothing, if having nothing they have all. And both soon realize the predicament, for the struggle, the writhings and writing, goes on. The outstanding difference between *Igitur* and *Une Saison en enfer* is that Mallarmé's fragments represent a more serious, stubborn, protracted effort to stay with the central problem, without incarnating it into a finished work. *Igitur* was, in this sense, a fertile failure, preparing the naked armature upon which, after a lifetime of patient accumulation of means, Mallarmé would build his *œuvre*. Rimbaud—despite his persistent use of the word *patience*—was less patient, sought and forced an immediate success of sorts, the finished text which is his peak achievement in terms of scope and finality, at a very early age.

The chapter goes on much the same, with a new exultation of pride brought by the triumph of the absurd: "Je ferai de l'or, des remèdes," which megalomaniac flight is not far, at this point, from true madness. But Rimbaud realizes himself that this lucidity is *too* complete and prefers to descend to real life once more at the cost of whatever suffering, which he calls for and gets in an obviously strong dose: "Mon Dieu, pitié, cachez-moi, je me tiens trop mal" (his pride is the "mal"). And the fire of this pagan hell blazes higher.

"Délires I" ("La Vierge folle") is the least worthy of the parts, being of primarily anecdotal interest. It tells of Rimbaud's attempts to convert Verlaine to his primitive state of "fils du Soleil," of Verlaine's sentimental softness, of Rimbaud's ultimate rejection of him.

"Délires II" ("Alchimie du verbe") is, on the other hand, the richest, formally, of the parts, largely because it includes some of Rimbaud's finest poems in verse (with many variants) but also because it must have been conceived in a moment of truce in the struggle, a grace between horrors, while the poet lapsed into a reminiscence. First he tells of how he made himself a *voyant* by his "dérèglement systématique" and his rejection of stale, self-consciously literary writing. There follows a particularly fine passage: "J'aimais les peintures idiotes, dessus de portes, décors, toiles de saltimbanques, enseignes, enluminures populaires; la littérature démodée, latin d'église, livres érotiques sans orthographe, romans de nos aïeules, contes de fées, petits livres de l'enfance, opéras vieux, refrains niais, rythmes naïfs."

This is justly celebrated, for it is one of the milestones in the modern poetic *déculture* leading to surrealism, Dada, Jacob, Picasso, Pop Art, what-have-you. All of which is very worthwhile but is usually gained at a stiff price, the renunciation of the highest—late Romantic or Symbolist—

ambitions. (Not necessarily: a Joyce picks up some of the gains and assimilates them to a Symbolist effort.) As for the *dérèglement*, every valid poet—and thinker too: e.g., Descartes—must go through some form of this radical return to the sources, the roots of spontaneity and original-ity. The revolt, when authenticated, made good, is called "creative free-dom"; when not (as is always partly the case with genius) it seems akin to madness.[7] But, although necessary, the convulsive revolt is not sufficient. If persisted in for its own sake it becomes automatic, "gimmicky." At a certain point it must give way to consolidation, synthesis, and a steady-plugging sense of *métier*, free to start all over again when up to it. *Dérèglement* alone is certainly no substitute for a lifetime of researches on the resources of the French language, as we gather immediately from "Voyelles" which, despite Rimbaud's claim to have invented a new poetic language, reveals a groping, botched attempt compared to Mallarmé's meditations concerning the shapes and sounds of letters. Moreover, Rim-baud's youthful boast rings rather hollow when we realize that—although he brought significant gains in syntax, particularly in the open forms of the *Illuminations*—he accomplished relatively little in the way of organiz-ing his (or our) total vision.

Rimbaud did supremely well what he could be expected to do, and, despite his youthful haste and the short period he had to work in, he managed to rewrite considerably, as his corrected manuscripts show, the result being a group of masterpieces which on their own grounds need no defense; it is only when unreasonable claims are made for him by somewhat hysterical partisans that reservations have to be brought in.

In this part we find the revealing passage to which we have previously alluded: "Général, bombarde-nous. . . . " This is followed by a poignant phrase, also cited, which is pure Rimbaud: "oh! le moucheron enivré à la pissotière de l'auberge, amoureux de la bourrache, et que dissout un rayon!" The multifaceted paradox of such beauty is that it touches us in the tiniest last bit of soul for an ephemeral instant—yet with a sense of all and forever—and raises to delight the humblest of creatures and its

---

[7] Valid art depends on a sense of reality as strong as the adventurous spirit. The former is guarantee of communication, for the real is in one of its essential phases the shared, the universal. Granted that a cultured public can be expected to have experienced practically everything the poet has experienced and can therefore re-spond providing he finds the proper "key" (Proust) to unlock or dig up the buried treasure, still there is a point beyond which the writer disappears into the private, the accidental: detailed description of fortuitous arrangements in space, local allu-sions, specialized vocabularies, dialect. Chance inner associations are even more gratuitous: at a certain point of *dérèglement* anything goes, everything recalls everything else. Rimbaud occasionally gives in to this automatism and monotony: the surrealists will go much farther.

scatological *milieu*. The young Joyce's epiphanies of dirty, hopeless Dublin are often very near in spirit to this essential Rimbaud, which he vastly admired.

We also come upon, in this section, the "Enfin, ô bonheur, ô raison [keynotes of the father-theme] j'écartai du ciel l'azur, qui est du noir, et je vécus, étincelle d'or de la lumière *nature*." And the part almost ends on this note of *bonheur*, the piercing voice of the absent Father. But at the very last there is the cryptic: "Cela s'est passé. Je sais aujourd'hui saluer la beauté." Did this mean he had reached a new mastery of his craft or did it imply the mockery he now made, in the *Saison*, of this perfidious muse? But it undoubtedly is meant to be ambiguous, for, at the moment of recording his past glories, Rimbaud was both caught up in a renewal of his old sense of poetic power and yet aware that the crucial point was nigh when he must give it all up for good.

Accordingly, in the next chapter, "L'Impossible," he unambiguously renounces art and his childhood thirst for beauty as "sottise"; at the same time he rejects the life of the Bohemians he once emulated: "ces bonshommes qui ne perdraient pas l'occasion d'une caresse, parasites de la propreté et de la santé de nos femmes, aujourd'hui qu'elles sont si peu d'accord avec nous." For, in fact, Rimbaud's escapes had always ended under the protection of some woman. Now, by contrast, he turns to an opposite, male, model of hardness—the father ingredient which his mother unpardonably deprived him of and which would have prodded him into a release of his emotions along liveable lines: "des gens hargneux et joyeux, de faux élus, puisqu'il nous faut de l'audace ou de l'humilité pour les aborder. Ce sont les seuls élus. Ce ne sont pas des bénisseurs!" (He is equally repelled by his fear and attracted by his need.) Theirs is the path of plugging, "horizontal" achievement against the steady resistance of life which he himself might follow, the hard road of the "réalité rugueuse à étreindre" at the end of which, in a radically divergent direction from that of his (vertically transcendent) art, he might obscurely hope to attain manhood. But in his present state of exhaustion and confusion, he will explore this direction, for the next page or so, in the double mood of his persistent ambivalence,[8] "Bon! voici que mon esprit veut absolument se charger de tous les développements cruels qu'a subis l'esprit depuis la

[8] It is this ambivalence which has him trapped until life, through purging defeat, takes him over univalently: clearly, he cannot choose the path of normal work forthrightly while his need is to take only the harshness of it, failing to see the pleasures of it. He can only choose some excessive form of it which he thinks will lead to pure joy, as long as he does not act it out but tries to think it out. For since his thought is an excessive growth, *anything* he thinks will have this exaggerated form. What he needs to do most is to dampen his mental life: "l'esprit . . . il faudrait le faire taire."

fin de l'Orient. . . . Il en veut, mon esprit! . . . L'esprit est autorité, il veut que je sois en Occident. Il faudrait le faire taire pour conclure comme je voulais." He means by this, first, that he must face the fact that he is in and of the West: since he is solving his problems by thinking them out he must mentally "swallow" the history of the West, think it through to locate himself; second, he rebels against this burden and wants to silence his Western mind, "le faire taire" by facing it down. This is so difficult that he now tries to justify himself for wanting to escape from the Western mind to the East: "Pourtant je ne songeais guère au plaisir d'échapper aux souffrances modernes." But the Western way is "un supplice réel," too horrible to be ever accepted by Rimbaud, for it is arid and insincere: " . . . l'homme *se joue*, se prouve les évidences, se gonfle du plaisir de répéter ces preuves, et ne vit que comme cela." Its insincerity and dishonesty mean that the deep life of nature will simply shuck it all—the bourgeoisie, their practical science, the Church—some day: "La nature pourrait s'ennuyer, peut-être! M. Prud'homme est né avec le Christ."

In the next paragraph he postulates the answers the Western Church and philosophers would give him. The first would say, "You are seeking for Eden, perfection." And Rimbaud momentarily agrees (though suspecting a trick). The second say, "East, West, the problems are basically the same." And Rimbaud thinks that, while taking the *sub specie æternitatis* view, this too is a ruse to trap him in Western schemes and defeat his individual revolt. So he rejects both "eternities," the churchly and the metaphysical, as being short-circuit escapes in his old vertical pattern. "Pas de partis de salut violents. Exerce-toi!" And he returns to his exploration of science, obviously hoping to push it to its own infinite goal, as a radically new path for him. But he is too tired: "Mon esprit dort." Still, in a flash, he sees the infinite end as "O pureté, pureté! C'est cette minute d'éveil qui m'a donné la vision de la pureté!—Par l'esprit on va à Dieu!" But then there is the tiredness again: "Déchirante infortune!"

In "L'Eclair" a new start in this direction is made: "Le travail humain! c'est l'explosion qui éclaire mon abîme de temps en temps." For several paragraphs he struggles with this potentiality, first with a partly mocking but partly hopeful invocation of the steady progress: " 'Rien n'est vanité; à la science, et en avant!' crie l'Ecclésiaste moderne, c'est-à-dire *Tout le monde.* . . . Ah! vite, vite un peu; là-bas, par delà la nuit, ces récompenses futures, éternelles . . . les échapperons-nous?" But he is afraid that he knows in advance the limits of this path: "je le vois bien. C'est trop simple . . . on se passera de moi [i.e., I'll be tempted to quit, drop out of step]. J'ai mon devoir, j'en serai fier à la façon de plusieurs, en le mettant de côté. [I'll be tempted to side-step, content with my awareness and foreknowledge.]" And he sees it all, anyway, leading to the old farce of religion, art, and the artifice of all Western institutions: "les apparances du monde, saltimbanque, mendiant, artiste, bandit,—prêtre!" This last possibility particularly revolts him, for it evokes the love of death: "Sur mon lit d'hôpital l'odeur de l'encens m'est revenue si puissante; gardien des aromates sacrés, confesseur, martyr . . . " He rejects this saintly death image, "Je reconnais là ma sale éducation d'enfance." He queries, why not just live like the "others"; certainly that would be gratuitous and sincere for *me*: "Aller mes vingt ans, si les autres vont vingt ans . . . " But this career is too light for his intense need: "Le travail paraît trop léger à mon orgueil: . . . [ce] serait un supplice trop court. Au dernier moment, j'attaquerais à droite, à gauche . . . " So, finally, he has investigated this direction and rejected it and nothing is left: "Alors,—oh!—chère pauvre âme, l'éternité serait-elle pas perdue pour nous!"

In "Matin" Rimbaud is, then, all the way down again, having exhausted the possibilities: "Vous qui prétendez que des bêtes poussent des sanglots de chagrin, que des malades désespèrent, que des morts rêvent mal, tâchez de raconter ma chute et mon sommeil. . . . *Je ne sais plus parler.*" But at least his season in hell is almost over. Each morning he arises to life hoping against despair: "Quand irons-nous, par delà les grèves et les monts, saluer la naissance du travail nouveau, la sagesse nouvelle, la fuite des tyrans et des démons, la fin de la superstition, adorer—les premiers!— Noël sur la terre? . . . esclaves, ne maudissons pas la vie." This is, unknown to him, the note of his future existence, the Adamic striving (poetically, now, rather like the long marches and appropriate *versets* of Perse) along the road of life as most men know it once their youthful fling is over, but here with an added dose of expiatory harshness. Still, as the cliché has it, where there is life there is hope: even Kafka could confide to his diary that within the deepest despair known to those condemned or graced to live, there is buried the gleam of another start.

In "Adieu" this start toward happiness is made with the uncompromising Rimbaldian intensity: "nous sommes engagés à la découverte de la clarté divine. . . . " He envisions the city, Paris, which he thinks will be the scene of his striving, and shudders at the memory of the miseries he suffered there. This reminds him too of the poetic visions which were born from city mud, and there is a lingering adieu to beauty:

> Quelquefois je vois au ciel des plages sans fin couvertes de blanches nations en joie. Un grand vaisseau d'or, au-dessus de moi, agite ses pavillons multicolores sous les brises du matin. J'ai créé toutes les fêtes, tous les triomphes, tous les drames . . . Eh bien! je dois enterrer mon imagination et mes souvenirs! Une belle gloire d'artiste et de conteur emportée! . . . Je suis

rendu au sol, avec un devoir à chercher, et la réalité rugueuse à étreindre! Paysan!

Such poetry dies hard and threatens to carry Rimbaud with it; he wonders whether this renunciation is not a disguised step toward the grave: "la charité serait-elle sœur de la mort pour moi?" But even if it is, he has done his best, "Enfin, je demanderai pardon pour m'être nourri de mensonge. Et allons." One last cry of distress: "Mais pas une main amie! et où puiser le secours?"

In the last paragraphs, he feels the hour of decision has finally arrived, difficult as it is: "Car je puis dire que la victoire m'est acquise." And the direction of his resolve is made quite clear: "Il faut être absolument moderne." He glances back over the combat. "Dure nuit! le sang séché fume sur ma face, et je n'ai rien derrière moi, que cet horrible arbrisseau." The exhausted nerves of his system are left like the skeleton of a burning bush after the consuming season in hell. (The same image of bushes burnt out after a hot summer—the *Saison*, incidentally, was finished after such a summer—is found in "Les Premières Communions": "près des blés lourds . . . ces arbrisseaux brûlés. . . .") There is grim resignation in his reflection: "Le combat spirituel est aussi brutal que la bataille d'hommes: [about the same time G. M. Hopkins spoke of the dangerous precipices of the mind] mais la vision de la justice est le plaisir de Dieu seul," which is to say that peace and justice are not for men, only Adam's sweat and struggle.[9] But then arises a glimmering vision of a rainbowlike promise: "Cependant, c'est la veille. Recevons tous les influx de vigueur et de tendresse réelle. Et, à l'aurore, armés d'une ardente patience, nous entrerons aux splendides villes." This is the earthly paradise, the remote goal—despite the boyish impetuousness of his anticipation—of what he knows will be the long, hard road of his future, which road he thinks he must go alone: "Que parlais-je de main amie! . . . j'ai vu l'enfer des femmes là-bas;—et il me sera loisible de *posséder la vérité dans une âme et un corps.*"

At the very end of his agon, therefore, his victory is incomplete: he is not yet ready to understand the implications of his change. No man can remain entirely sufficient to himself for very long on this way, though he begins and ends it alone. Even the artist that Rimbaud might have become in this direction would have somehow anchored himself more stably in existence through companions, perhaps a family. This was Rimbaud's expressed desire in his letters from Abyssinia. One can only regret that he did not get his wish. The artistic vocation really comes into its own when,

[9] There is a good deal of Old Testament toughness to Rimbaud's spiritual vision; cf. Pascal, Kierkegaard.

in later years, the learned patient striving[10] is worked in with the old daemonic aspirations to weave together the generous canvas of the mature *métier*: through it the flowers of expression insinuate, curlicue, and pose as enticingly as ever—only more luxuriantly, in the image of life.

Jadis, je me souviens bien . . .

1, "Jadis": Rimbaud speaks here of the privileged moments or "epiphanies" of childhood in language which recalls "Après le déluge."

4, "Un soir": This period of innocent delights came to an end in a crisis of adolescence, clearly like the present one. Beauty itself seemed a dead end, attached as it was to the dangerous imperialism of spiritual and mental excess. He burned what he had adored, "cursed" it.

6, "Je me suis": Justice, the wildly ambitious social revolutionary cause, was a corollary visionary excess. He "armed himself" against it in the same sense that, in the next paragraph, he strangled his joys. I do not agree with Suzanne Bernard, and others, that the justice he turned against here was the traditional "establishment" brand of it (as in "Qu'est-ce pour nous, mon cœur?": "à bas . . . justice"). That is inconsistent with the series of rejections of what he formerly believed in.

7, "Je": Parallel to "Les Sœurs de charité"—the two "witches," are the same as a pair of "Sisters" there—which illustrates the recurrent nature of such crises.

12, "J'ai appelé": A striking image of cosmic revolt: even as he lucidly accepts evil as a part of things he hates it, rather as Ivan Karamazov did ("Even if . . . "). The lucidity itself is an attempt to deal with the pain by facing it: the calling on "executioners," "plagues," etc., is of this same homeopathic order, only more active. Misfortune becomes his god in the same ambivalent way that it becomes that of the twisted figure in Camus' *Rénégat*. Rimbaud speaks elsewhere in the *Saison* of his experience of sleeping in city mud. The "air of crime" he steeped himself in is less certain,

---

[10] Since Rimbaud embraced his vocation while so very young—though rooted in the earliest, it is the last and highest form of love, implying the most difficult balancing feat of all—various other aspects of his personality which had remained latent and unsatisfied burst out, following his setback, as drudging labor, mercenary bourgeois spirit (inherited from his mother), and the technical and scientific attitude (inherited from his father and his own adolescence, period of special growth of this masculine, narrowly dynamic drive). He grubbed after outer success, wanted to become an engineer, expressed belief in the crassest progress. These things had been sporadically evident, often pointlessly, in his writing, but now they monopolized his horizon as he tried to right his balance.

though we know of some quasi-criminal acts he performed against fellow-poets in Paris. That he skirted madness is obvious, beginning at least with his *voyance* experiments in his sixteenth year.

17, "Et le printemps": Which "spring"? Probably, as has been surmised, the one following his wild winter in Paris, etc., with Verlaine in 1871-72. Spring, it is well known, is the likeliest time for breakdowns of this sort.

18, "Or": Rimbaud was not brought close to death by the light wound inflicted upon his wrist by Verlaine's shot; rather, he came back to Roche in a state of cumulative despair and was no doubt close to suicide. He thought of seeking the "key" to spiritual rebirth in the former psychic health and joy of his childhood. "Charity" is the key, in the sense of abandonment of the egoism of individualistic Pride, which betokens, as in the Gospels ("if you do not become as one of them"), a return to the innocence of childhood (Camus, in his preface to a late edition of *L'Envers et l'endroit*, spoke of a similar need). But it seems impossible—one seldom has the strength for spiritual death and rebirth—so he cries that he must have been dreaming when he got that idea.

23, "Tu resteras": The devil whom he imagines as having brought him to this state of utter oblivion ("poppies") of his past power now tells him he lacks the strength for that rebirth—he is nothing but a lowly animal—and counsels him to betake himself to true death, with all his appetites, egotism, and capital sins—he will never make it to redemption here.

27, "J'en ai": "I took too much" may refer either to the poppies of oblivion or to death. He asks Satan to be less severe in his reproving look, his insistence on death, that cowardly and damning way out—"les quelques petites lâchetés en retard"—which Rimbaud wants to put off while he knocks off for the devil (who likes amoral writing of this sort) some pages from his damned-man's notebook.

Mauvais Sang

1, "J'ai": The first sentence is clear and factual. The second shows a Baudelairian scepticism about progress. The third is ironic in the Montaigne manner of "quoy? ils ne portent point de haut-de-chausses" ("Des Cannibales"), i.e., a mockery of what men esteem an advantage over primitives.

5, "Les Gaulois": Idolatry, in the sense of his former worship of Beauty and Justice, as above. The "magnifique, la luxure" is a bitter irony at the expense of his own sexual experiences, no doubt, cf. "H" in the *Illuminations*.

10, "J'ai": He rejects all role-playing. The insult "tous paysans, ignobles" goes with other indications of his feelings about peasants (his neighbors at Roche), e.g., the "paysan matois" of "La Rivière de Cassis," the "Paysan!" of "Adieu." The hand is the essence of *métier*, and he wants no part of this Western way involving "domesticity" which "leads too far," i.e., takes you over and destroys integrity ("Moi, je suis intact"). Even beggars are role-players, "honest" in the sense of supportive of a general bourgeois order. Criminals too, he thinks, as disgusting as "castrated men" who are subject to the order, made powerless by it.

17, "Mais": He has used his wits, his perfidious tongue to survive in that order as a parasite, a wandering one. Observing all the types of the European human, apparently free, he is bound to it all (exactly as Sartre sees the bourgeois writer). He has known all the bourgeois sons, who come from backgrounds like his, and, knowing them, feels part of them, compromised.

24, "Si": He finds nothing to support nobility in his racial past, no courage for true (cosmic) revolt, only petty revolts for material pillage; his ancestors were ignoble as wolves parasitically preying on corpses that other creatures killed.

31, "Je me": A survey of the Christian past, crusades, pilgrimages; a glance at the era when the cult of Mary mingled with pagan vestiges. A vignette of a leper, typical of those times, seated—a vagabond (see below) —by a road. A mercenary soldier in Germany. A witches' sabbath rite in the woods (from Michelet's "La Sorcière," perhaps).

42, "Je ne": He feels stuck in that tradition, sees himself back in it in imagination, always alone as he is now, alienated from power in the Church- or Christianity-dominated state, because of his refusal to believe in the Church; *non serviam*, as Joyce would put it.

47, "Qu'étais": No use trying to see himself in a previous century, all he finds is his present self. Now there are no more vagabonds (unlike the leper), no more of those vague idealistic wars of the distant past. The inferior *peuple* has taken over: modern science, nationalism (this "reason" is not the beautiful "raison" of "A une raison").

51, "Oh": The modern religion, science, has done everything over; as viaticum we have now, *in extremis*, medicine and philosophy, goodwives' remedies and popular songs (instead of hymns, no doubt). The games of princes—wars for glory, masques, etc.—they, the moderns, have ruled those out (Rimbaud implies a Homais-like comedown here). Instead, we have only those sciences with ugly names.

57, "La": He mocks at progress. Indeed, why emphasize linear movement? (Nietzsche agreed.)

59, "C'est": It *is* an epoch of numbers, leading to Spirit, in the Hegelian pattern. Cf. "l'infini des mathématiques" in "Guerre." Rimbaud is ambivalent here and farther on. He feels an old pagan religious surge at the thought of this new pagan ideal. But that implies a vast paradox of radically new and radically old which mutes him.

62, "Le sang": This vast prospect continues: if Spirit is near, as he thought, where is the Christian rise of spirit he (being inevitably in his tradition) should feel? Where is Christ's help? (This is contradictory but in a way it makes sense, for under the Christian, as he said earlier, is the pagan and the two should rise together.) But, alas, the Gospels are finished (so both sink, apparently). Hence, the last time the word "Évangile" is used it lacks an exclamation mark.

66, "J'attends": He waits for God somehow anyway (before Didi and Gogo); he is eternally of an inferior species (a) because of his absurd hope or (b) because he feels no supportive spirit. It is not clear which, probably both.

68, "Me voici": Since his Western tradition leads nowhere for him, he dreams of leaving Europe. The cities lighting up are part of the romantic drama, redolent of what he is leaving, as in "Matin." He dreams of the simple life, like all of us who are fed up with our Faustian scramble.

75, "Je reviendrai": This carries him to a fallible idea of cashing in on his new purity, by coming back, like any hero from the renewing dark venture (cf. Malraux's Ferral from Asia), to dominate his homeland. That "Sauvé" is pathetically inconsistent, all-too-human (and ironic too). But he feels no real strength for even this human effort, all he is is damned; he hates his homeland without the power to do anything about it. Better just sleep, drunk, on that beach, without leaving (as he will go on to say).

82, "On ne": One does not leave; specifically he cannot now, lacking the strength and, generically, a man of his poetic ilk is apt to find it meaningless (later he will say action is only a way of "wasting some energy"); cf. des Esseintes or Baudelaire's "Le Voyage." The vice is unidentified, but one senses a general force of gravity, sexual probably.

86, "La dernière": He denounces the preceding thought; he must feel no more concern about an arbitrary morality which calls whatever he does "vice" (above), no more timidity about surmounting that weakness (which is only temporary always). Enough said. Don't carry around, or wear on your sleeve, these disgusts and these betrayals of spirit; surpass or forget them. Let's go (or come on): strike out stubbornly, horizontally, plug on, cost what it may in boredom or anger, *live*, get going, don't be "hung up." . . .

92, "A qui": He looks for a cause. Any cause. With bitter irony he proposes a beast-idol, a religious image to defend against some attack, hearts to break (a conquest of women), a lie—myth—to uphold, a bloody war to fight.

96, "Plutôt": No sentimental campaign for justice (see the earlier "je me suis armé contre la justice"). Just struggle and then die (like Vigny's stoic wolf or Camus's "Conqueror"), go sit in the coffin quietly and stifle. This will avoid old age, and dangers such as terror, which is un-French. In this unflattering reference to his countrymen, Rimbaud is making fun of his own shallowness, his escapism.

100, "Ah": This is more sincere: he yearns for a sacrificial cause.

102, "O mon": But he quickly repents of this earnestness, this "charity" or self-denial. He knows himself to be incapable of it, too earth-bound (actually he is not, merely dispirited at the moment). He mocks at his *de profundis* mood, calls himself "silly."

105, "Encore": A reminiscence of a childishly amoral admiration of the daemonic male, with overtones of his missing and irresponsible father.

112, "Sur": By contrast, out of his present flaccid mood, he remembers equally empty past episodes, with only an ultimate voice of "feminine" raw life-force to reassure him that he was alive, existent: "te voilà"; cf. the end of "Qu'est-ce pour nous, mon cœur?" Otherwise, he was so null that he felt invisible.

120, "Dans": A poetic remembrance of home-thoughts amidst wandering misery; compare our comments on the end of "Après le déluge" and footnote 25 of our Introduction. The Oedipal crisis stirred up herewith makes him whistle in the dark, wish himself "Good luck." The emotional stir has apt objective correlatives in the "mer" (*mère*) involved with stormy flames (no calm marriage of light and sea here, contrary to "L'Éternité"); dark smoke representing anguish from his depths rises up menacingly to contaminate and menace any bright "male" notions: it is an apocalypse; all burns miserably. That it is indeed an Oedipal crisis is confirmed by the next line.

126, "Mais": So heterosexuality is ruled out by this unresolved inner drama. He is utterly companionless; and alienated, moreover, from society, self-pityingly so. But he removes himself wilfully, sulkingly from society, will not accept even their pity or pardon; he is *hors jeu* (like Meursault), or out of *that* game; his *jeu* is directly cosmic, Nietzschean, amoral.

137, "Oui": He is a "beast, a negro" insofar as he is outside the laws of the West. He sees all the role-players as being, underneath, equally dae-monic or amoral but "false negroes" because they deny it with typical bourgeois bad faith. Even the sick and old are such "respectable" fakes (infected with Sartre's "esprit de sérieux"). They ought to be boiled alive. So let's leave for a pagan Africa, leave this continent where pure madmen like himself (or Meursault) are hostages of those sane wretches. For him the true kingdom is of the innocently childlike, the descendants of Ham.

149, "Connais-je": A moment of doubt: does he really want the natural, does he know nature enough to say he can take it? Does he know himself well enough to assure that? He tries to still his doubt by telling himself to shut up; since his words are expressions of the West, to silence them is to approach the natural. The silenced words are the "dead" which he buries in his unconscious, his "ventre." Becoming unconscious thus, he will not fear even a possibility that the whites will come and find him in Africa and make him null again (but his thinking of this is proof his qualms remain).

154, "Faim": The hunger and thirst are the sacrificial cost of the primi-tive life he yearns for; he calls out for all this.

155, "Les blancs": The qualm returns. The Rimbaud who feared the prison-ships at the end of "Le Bateau ivre," and was constantly haunted by the dread of being called for military service, imagines that adult males will triumph over him, subdue him with cannon. He will have to submit to all the Western code which he hates.

157, "J'ai": He imagines receiving the final *coup* of Baptism, conversion in his heart (with a pun on the *grâce: le coup de la grâce*). This was un-expected. One senses the irony ready to burst forth at every turn, yet he will now pursue the idea of salvation with apparent earnestness.

159, "Je n'ai": He feels momentarily saved in Christian moral terms: he has done no harm, he will need no repentance. He will not be judged, with a soul dead to good, by severe light of conscience, like funeral tapers. That is the fate of the bourgeois boys, that deadness of soul covered like a premature coffin with tears of remorse. He rejects sin, debauchery, vice. As a reward the hours will not always sound pure pain. He feels himself rising (like the chastened Stephen of *Portrait of the Artist*) to innocence, to play like a child in paradise.

169, "Vite": Fear of what this entails, in acceptance of society, makes him yell suddenly for other lives, ways. Bourgeois riches, as in the Gospels, kill peace of soul. Riches are public, not deeply private. Only divine love (he is back to his new grace-hope) gives true knowledge. Nature, in this sense, is good. So goodbye selfish illusions, ideals, errors (we are back on the track of Charity).

174, "Le chant": The previous image of militant missionaries is now seen as a grace-bringing boat. The two loves of Christians—fellow-man ("terrestre") and God ("dévouement")—are invoked. But he feels qualms about being elect, concern for the others who will not be saved (this is a true dilemma of grace).

180, "Sauvez": This may be a moment of true Charity.

185, "La raison": There is a note here of true religious grace. He speaks of God, not Christ (see below).

189, "Je ne": But he is slipping: he wants freedom, hence no subjection to beatings, unlike the masochists, weak spirits he denounced in "Les Premières Communions" and "Soir historique." Hence, no marriage with the world in which Christ would serve as father-in-law. No institution-Church (cf. Dostoevsky, Gide, *et al.*).

192, "Je ne suis": Here, insensibly, the insistence on freedom carries him out of his new religious grace—frivolous—to unidentified, wide-open grace. He does not miss the sentimental religious past. He is his own Church; every man is complete, with "reason"—i.e., total awareness—charity and its shadow, scorn. He keeps his place at the top of the angelic ladder of "good sense," the modern freethinking spirit which is cosmically rooted (angelic) in God but untrammeled by any institutions; perhaps there is some echo of Descartes in that *bon sens*, which refers back in any case to his just-completed analysis.

199, "Quant": Further veering from the religious interlude. No bourgeois code for him. No domesticity, no work, no action (that favorite locus of ordinary man). He is too dissipated and weak, on the dark side, too superior, high-flying, volatile on the bright side, for that.

204, "Comme": Back to despair; he ought to love and seek death.

206, "Si": Again, hope of peace from God. And an ambivalent evocation of saints, spiritually strong people, hermits, artists—these last being "such as we don't need anymore"; insensibly, the revolt against all role-playing, including his own art, returns.

209, "Farce": All is fake. Even his dreamed-of innocence would be so fake that it makes him weep. Life is a farce to be played out by everyone. Cf. Shakespeare: "All is but toys"; "a tale told by an idiot" (*Macbeth*).

211, "Assez": The punishment is something like Adam's curse: plug on! Specifically, in the curative pattern of Rimbaud's veering from transcendence or pride, it is an injunction to live "horizontally," just go on. Because of his unredeemed pride, it has a harsher tone than that of most of our Adamic paths and already resembles his rough anabases in Africa. He imagines the harsh advance of an army, hopes he will be killed and so end his misery. "Shoot me or else I'll surrender [to utter despair, I suppose]" indicates he is still striving, by extreme self-punishment, to rise to salvation.

219, "Ah": Ironic; even this one gets used to so it is all not very serious—just more farce (he has a mild return of strength). And he mocks this way too, for it is still a French one, the road to honor. He seems to shudder at his military farce.

Nuit de l'enfer

The title was, at first, "Fausse Conversion," referring to Rimbaud's near return to faith, on his hospital bed in Brussels, after the drama with Verlaine. He plays with this holy fire in the previous section, "Mauvais sang," as we saw. Now, at some time during the summer of the writing, he plays again with it and gets burnt. His vaunted paganism notwithstanding, he has the God-impulse inextricably rooted in him, the pure kind which goes with an equally pure sense of hell. It need not be Christian—he distinguished God from Christ in the previous section—but why quibble on this point?

1, "J'ai": The "poison" is something which opened up hell with heaven, little matter whether it was alcohol, a drug, sex, or just plain awareness-in-depth. At all events, now he is far down inside himself. And, like Proust when he began his delayed suffering for his grandmother's death, he eggs the pain on out of a sense of deserving it absolutely. No doubt, the counsel he blesses is the one which told him to take the "poison." (Unlike the character in the Sartrian hell of *Huis Clos* who says, "One never suffers enough." Rimbaud is getting a solid dose.)

8, "J'avais": He recalls the vision of grace and tries to describe it, not very persuaded that one can, or that he can, in this state. But at this level extremes tend to meet, and (as Baudelaire knew) hell gets strangely poignant glimpses of heaven. But his strength is not unlimited here, and he ends with a limp irony (". . . que sais-je?"), followed by a bitter one.

14, "Et": "Et c'est encore la vie!" registers his very human surprise that one goes on after such heights and falls—in a way, this going-on is (femininely) frivolous, almost disappointing to male concerns. One is not so serious (here he rejoins Sartre). But he thinks his damnation may go beyond life, through eternity, which is serious—he fears this and wants, obviously, to fear it. Then he reassures himself that he is in hell since he wants to mutilate himself (cf. "Honte") and since he *believes* he is ("je pense donc je suis"). This sense of damnation he owes to his tradition, which now he turns against; he tries to escape through his claim to being pagan. Again, there is the ennui of life's going on, now with a double sense of continuing nightmare and frivolity. But the latter may stop later, he may attain new depths of hell ("délices" is ironic). He may also escape it by a crime which will make him suffer so much as to homeopathically blot out the hell, by falling very low just on a-religious, human-psychic terms.

23, "Tais-toi": His desire to curatively fall is offset by thought and speech (exactly as in *Igitur*), so he tells himself to shut up. The thought, he says, comes from Satan who counsels him not to take pain seriously— the shame and reproach tell him he cannot make it—but to escape, as before (in the Preface), in a cowardly way, by babbling on as he did formerly in his art. He incorrigibly is tempted to do so now (even by writing the *Saison*, another "error" perhaps in the purest sense which he courts), with more "magic," "fake perfumes," "childish music" (we have discussed the perfumes in our Introduction to the *Derniers Vers*).

27, "Et dire": A burst of Pride tells him he is above all this and then the Pride—hubris—takes an awful fall. But at the low point there is the old thirst, the *sitio*—just as at the bottom of Dante's Hell there started the upward climb to Paradise. Rimbaud is dangerously oscillating between extremes in his "trip." A poetic vision of childhood—grass, rain, lake over pebbles, moonlit midnight bell-tower (as in Reverdy)—is immediately contaminated by devil-horror. The appeal to Mary is only partly ironic. The "horror of my stupidity" is his disgust at the whole absurd human condition which is doomed to these opposites, this failure to conclude.

35, "Là-bas": He thinks Others may help him, perhaps phantoms from the past (like Hamlet's father, equally remote; or the ancestors of *Igitur* or the old folk who might pardon in *Le Grand Meaulnes*)—such as were invoked in "Comédie de la soif," "Entends comme brame," "Métropolitain." They cannot hear him since he has a pillow over his mouth—he cannot communicate with pure figures, his human condition makes him mute. Besides, no one ever helps anyone (true, in a sense; but too true to be liveable). So he plays independent—and feels more hell burning ("roussi") because of his solitary hopeless pride.

40, "Les": The preceding were only visions such as he has always had (and no belief in history, like Valéry, nor social principles: only direct phenomenological experience). He feels their power again and brags that his visions could eclipse all those of other poets and visionaries, but mainly he regards all that as an error of his past. But despite the renunciation, Rimbaud's *awareness* that he was the richest and is deliberately being stingy—keeping the visions for himself, or just keeping quiet—this is dangerous pride indeed.

The sea is stingy because indifferent, does not give a hoot about us even as we drown; there is a possible overtone of his avaricious *mère* (and of *avare-avarie*).

45, "Ah": This tense cancellation of opposites seems to lead to a dead point, a stasis, momentarily: the world-clock stops. From this mid-point he sees the high and low of life, heaven and hell, as in the doctrine of (Christian) theology which he says is "serious," veracious in this matter. Finally, there is a mingling of the opposites in ecstasy and nightmare and, again, in the kinesis-stasis of sleep and flames. That nest of flames is rather like the final synthetic vision of Dante, fire and rose as one (only this one is less beatific).

49, "Que": His phenomenological "attention," he recalls, yields mysterious forces in nature; Satan, Ferdinand (a local name for the devil), runs with wild grain. Jesus seems to walk, in a childish vision, on the heather, without bending it. As in a picture, unidentified, Jesus appears, walking on the water in a dramatic and colorful image.

55, "Je vais": More bragging: both impressive and pathetic.

58, "Écoutez": An example of his power: as in mystic tradition, he has discovered the core-paradox (as many of us have anew; and it *is* powerful). Some specific boasts which barely skirt paranoia. And are funny, like Camus' Caligula's apparition as Venus ("dance of houris"). He knows it is funny.

64, "Fiez": He feels superior. He asks others to believe in him; obviously the Jesus-image spills into himself ("no prayers"). But there is irony . . . that "marvelous heart" is not very Christian; he's mocking it.

70, "Et": Ironically, he thinks of himself as well as the others (he is not so selfless . . .). This burst of self-important vision causes him to say that the world was well lost for it. He has been lucky, it has cost him relatively little in suffering (compared to Jesus?). Maybe he should have suffered more—he regrets that his life was only "sweet follies."

73, "Bah": Aware of the grotesque in the preceding, he eggs himself on like a self-tormenting child making faces in a mirror (cf. Joyce yelling "hooray for the damned idiot" at his adolescent mirror-image).

He feels out of life; this twisting self-involvement carries one far from the center of men; there is no sound, no "feel" for reality. By contrast, he invokes reminiscences of vivid earlier impressions: chateau, willow-grove, exotic dream of Saxony. Evenings, mornings, etc. But now he is only tired.

78, "Je": A queer idea of multiple *ad hoc* hells. This shows that his hell is not yet the *final* one.

81, "Je meurs": He asks for that finishing touch from Satan.

85, "Ah": Now, instead, he wants to rise to life (the normal man takes over in him for a moment). He wants to see plainly, sanely or soberly, what he even now (as other men in usual life would do) sees as aberrations. The "poison" is, as we said, either a drug or other stimulant, artificial paradises, bestowing a cursed "kiss," or just awareness; this too he now rejects as error, deformation. He blames his weakness on the world's cruelty. He asks God for help, to hide him from this pitiless aberrant self-examination of the *Saison*. But he is hidden already (as we all are; we really cannot see ourselves); and yet . . .

90, "C'est": More pain. He has not burned out.

Délires I: Vierge Folle L'époux infernal

This, it is well recognized, is a speaking portrait of Verlaine, a weak sister as Rimbaud sees him, wailing to Jesus over his stormy relations with the daemonic (or demonic) Rimbaud. It presents few difficulties and, outside of a few famous lines and some anecdotal qualities, little of interest.

1, "Écoutons": Rimbaud suggests we hear the confession of his hell-companion.

2, "O": Verlaine confesses to Jesus his impurity (sins with Rimbaud and before).

5, "Pardon": The later tears will be of remorse, upon his full conversion (below).

7, "Plus": "L'autre" is R.; V., confessed, is invulnerable.

9, "A présent": The "amies" implies that Verlaine turns to women for comfort in his weak-sister state. But women—his wife Mathilde and her mother—were not friendly. "Tout pourtant m'est permis" is Verlaine's weakness and bad faith, as Rimbaud sees it.

15, "Enfin": This "répéter" is hardly flattering to Verlaine.

17, "Je suis": Verlaine sees Rimbaud as a Demon Lover, like the devil who caused the Foolish Virgins to miss their marriage with the Divine Lover. Verlaine is such a Foolish Virgin, as in the subtitle. "On ne me tuera pas!" means that, despite the demon Rimbaud, he, Verlaine, will be saved.

25, "Je": "Veuve" implies bereft of his Divine Lover, Jesus, with some probable allusion to his wife's leaving him.
"La vraie vie est absente" is religious escapism, an invocation of a better world as an excuse for inadequacies in this one. "Nous ne sommes pas au monde" has the same bearing. This line is often quoted out of context as an example of Rimbaud's dissatisfaction with life.

34, "Il dit": Rimbaud speaks his misogyny, his need for a new, superior form of love-relation. But this is canceled by his recognition of women he could be happy with (alas, they are already ruined by brutal men).

68, "Je voyais": Rimbaud's desire to "escape reality" is of a different order from Verlaine's, not religious but revolutionary: i.e., "change life." But Verlaine denies he has found ways to do this.
Rimbaud's "charity"—his generosity of spirit—has bewitched Verlaine, enslaved him. No other soul but Verlaine's could stand it (his charity), could stand being protected and loved by Rimbaud. Verlaine cannot imagine Rimbaud with a different soul; one only knows who one's own Angel is (i.e., Rimbaud), not someone else's Angel (a soul different from Rimbaud's). Verlaine feels he inhabits Rimbaud's soul (love) unworthily —all others had been emptied from it, as from a palace, in order that Rimbaud should not find in him anyone so unworthy as Verlaine.

117, "Ah": "Il veut vivre somnambule" means that Rimbaud, refusing to work and live like others, will be trying to live a dream.

139, "Tu vois": Rimbaud has Verlaine compare himself to a mistreated bourgeoise. A dirty trick—but Rimbaud himself is seen as being tender as a woman at times: "ses manières de jeune mère, de sœur aimée." This is ruthlessly honest as the passage in "Le Bateau ivre": "ainsi qu'une femme à genoux . . . ." Verlaine confirmed the "douceur" of Rimbaud in his "Hommes d'aujourd'hui" (cf. Suzanne Bernard, p. 468). But it is "mortal," sometimes, as Rimbaud thinks Verlaine sees it—surely a less gentle and tame variety than Verlaine's.

152, "Un jour": An ironic view of Verlaine's adoration, mocking both Verlaine and himself. Verlaine rightly saw Rimbaud as wishing to rival God: "O je serai celui-là qui sera Dieu" ("Dédicace"). In "Nuit de l'enfer," Rimbaud mocked at this same ambition.

155, "Drôle": A disabused and amused final comment on that queer relationship, now disavowed, not without some saving grace of humanity and humor.

Délires II: Alchimie du verbe

This is the most rewarding chapter of the *Saison*, not only for the valuable variants of the poems cited there but, altogether, as Rimbaud reminisces about his *folie*, art, and social vision, his genius returns momentarily—in a grace between horrors—and inspires some of his finest prose.

1, "A moi": "A moi" is "It is my turn," "Let's speak of me now" (after leaving Verlaine in the previous chapter).

2, "Depuis": This is justly celebrated: it leads to much in modern art, by a dialectical or spiral renewal through *déculture*, contact with popular culture or familiar scattered imagery of ordinary reality.

16, "J'inventai": Rimbaud brags about his advanced poetics but, as we noted in our comment on "Voyelles," they were not thought through. Brilliant beginnings in this direction for a boy, to be sure. The "accessible à tous les sens" implies exploitation of the visual and aural aspects of language and the tactile and olfactory qualities of imagery, one supposes. This was not unprecedented, of course (e.g., Baudelaire went far in this direction, as did Hugo, etc.).

"Keeping the translation" implies the hermetic difficulties of such a poetics.

Rimbaud had announced this program in his "Lettres du Voyant." It began to be put in practice with the later-manner poems he quotes here.

First he studied the verbal possibilities, or tried them out in poems such as the ones quoted. The "silences, des nuits . . . inexprimable . . . vertiges" were indeed part of the phenomenological advances we find in him and in coeval poets. As examples he quotes "Larme" and "Bonne pensée de matin."

We skip the poems, having noted the important variants (for our purposes) in connection with the preceding versions.

24, "La vieillerie": There is indeed a strong traditional vein in Rimbaud's poetry.

25, "Je m'habituai": Baudelaire, in *Les Paradis artificiels*, had remarked on the amazing and even "terrifying" depths which wallpaper or a sign could take on for the drugged mind (referring to "un titre de vaudeville dressait des épouvantes devant moi"). But Rimbaud does not seem to be speaking of a drugged condition here.

31, "Puis": The "hallucination des mots" probably refers to the wild associations arising from words (overtones, letter-shapes)—every good poet, every child, knows and plays with these phenomena.

33, "Je finis": This debauch of vision led to mental fever, naturally enough. Rimbaud dreamed of "dropping out" of life, as we all have, envying the simplicity of animals, etc. His caterpillar reminds me of a drawing by Blake (portraying larval innocence). Or the "modest buds" of Hölderlin's *Schicksalslied*. Mallarmé similarly probes into the limits between worlds (death and life) at the moment of birth, in "Surgi de la croupe et du bond."

38, "Mon": He became sour against the world, blaming it for his disorder, and said goodbye to it in verse, e.g., the cited "Chanson de la plus haute tour" which looks to a future better time, while the poet goes into a sort of sulking exile in his "tower."

35, "J'aimai": His exiled mood carries him to out-of-the-way places and appreciations. The "burned orchards" and "faded shops" are fine modern subtle moods. Those closed eyes remind one of the deprived child of "Les Poètes de sept ans," closing and pressing his eyes "pour [avoir] des visions." As in "Bannières de mai," he hopes to be related at least to the cosmos, the sun-god, taken in hand by that Father-spirit. In "Mauvais sang," the cry "j'offre à n'importe quelle divine image des élans vers la perfection" was out of a similar *délaissement* and need.

39, "Général": We noted in connection with "Bannières de mai," "Mémoire," and "Génie" the link of the sun-god with the (military) father-image. Compare also: "Le Poète . . . ses rayons d'amour flagelleront les Femmes ("L'Orgie parisienne"). The "ruined ramparts" imply some irony about God's presence in the modern world; the image was influenced by the ramparts of a ruined fort which used to exist in old Charleville; Rimbaud's awe at the haunting dead soldiers reputed to be buried there was expressed in "Enfance." The blocks of dried earth as missiles is apt for a harsh dry beating down of the sun. But the image modulates to reflections in store-windows, inside salons (as in "Bottom" and the "flagelleront les Femmes" above). It is called upon to beat down the dust of the city in its vast implacable downpour; to rust the gargoyles; to fill boudoirs (like the salons) with the dazzle of "burning ruby-dust."

45, "Oh": What an exquisitely earthy-ethereal pure Rimbaldian image! The tiny gnat, like the least object in the impartial light of a Vermeer, humbly bound to the urinal, is drunk with light and dirty substance; he is intense as an epiphany, ephemeral and eternal, struck as Rimbaud yearned to be by that supreme attention of Light. This touches us in the most intimate corners of our soul. All, the least part of us, is saved.

Compare: "Le grand soleil met un rubis" ("Les Mains de Jeanne-Marie").

The poems next quoted, "Fête de la faim" ("Faim," here) and "Le loup criait" prolong the theme of yearning.

47, "Enfin": This is the supreme moment: *bonheur*—that of "L'Éternité" quoted following, or the next after that "O saisons, ô châteaux" (sometimes called "Le Bonheur"); the *raison* juxtaposed synonymously is the fiercely fatherly one of "A une raison" (later the *bonheur* is a piercing divinely male "fatalité . . . remords"). Here, the pure fatherly light replaces in the sky the blackly hateful blue or azure ("bleu regard—qui ment," "Les Poètes de sept ans"). He is, as in "Mémoire," an Angel of light, a sun-son, a spark of nature in this sense.

Joyous at this identification, he hymns in a wild paean this light, married, however, in a moment of cosmic reconciliation (as hoped-for in "Mémoire"), with the feminine sea, "L'Éternité."

51, "Je devins": His vision enlarges to include fabulously "operatic" scenes (cf. "Nocturne vulgaire," "Villes, I"). The note of *bonheur* as *amor fati* is sounded. This Nietzschean total acceptance—female in appearance but really a higher synthesis of male-female attained in the creative domain mainly by sacrificial males—leads to a statement of rejection of (ordinary) action; this is, contrary to Richard, Sartre, and others, the central Rimbaud. The stance implies also an above-it-all amorality.

55, "A chaque": The cosmic vision reaches out to develop from each individual various of the potential other lives which are buried there ("Chaque homme porte la condition humaine toute entière," Montaigne), including lives from the "lower" orders, as well as the higher: dogs, angels. The "pig" could well have been Verlaine in one of his avatars. This vision is based on the facts of evolution, made simultaneous and developed upward to mystic higher orders as well.

60, "Aucun": He now sees all the foregoing as dangerous madness.

63, "Ma santé": He was carried to the edge of reality, with a fine pagan-hell metaphor taken from the *Aeneid*: Cimmérie is the remote part of the underworld. The "tourbillons" are the negative side of the joyous "vertige" he claimed he "fixed" in poems earlier (see our comments on this intimate archetype of the psyche, under "Les Étrennes des orphelins," "Being beauteous," "Barbare").

69, "Je dus": As in the free open sea-moments of "Le Bateau ivre" he feels saved by being bathed in the total cosmic ocean à la Nietzsche, baptismally. The sign of the cross which arises therefrom (like the prayer of dove-flights in "Le Bateau ivre") is immediately rejected as being caused by the sentimental hope, the false promise of the Old Testament sign of the rainbow, as in "Après le déluge" (cf. "Mouvement"). Now he accepts only *amor fati*; he had been "damned" by this God-promise in his Christian training, as he has said in previous chapters. But he has passed beyond this. *Bonheur* is absurdist "fatality"; the human condition condemned him to it, along with its negative side of "remorse" (as in the scene of Peter's treason to Christ; the cockcall follows below). Total "immense" life includes the realization that happiness, or the true God, is the bite (remorse, from *re-morsus*) or "agenbite of inwit," the sting of conscience—implacable as the tooth of the hound of heaven, "dog-God" or "hangman God" (Joyce), who kills us for rebirth to total truth. This life is bigger than his old myths of strength (social power, revolution) and beauty (art).

76, "Le Bonheur": The death-life totality of true *Bonheur* is recalled to him in a morning of rebirth by a distant cockcall; he is "warned" as Peter was not to escape authenticity. The image of Christ comes in here naturally, as it did for the anti-Christian Nietzsche in his *Ecce Homo*. The "darkest cities" are the places of utter alienation from nature and cosmos; we have seen this locus of vision, *de profundis*, in many a Rimbaud text: "Les Déserts de l'amour," "Métropolitain."

This happiness is now sung in Rimbaud's purest poem, using the same terms: "O saisons, ô châteaux."

428

79, "Cela": A vibrant paradox closes this radiant chapter, fittingly: for his progression to truth and happiness is nothing if not dialectical—a dialectic of past-present, in glowing epiphanous reminiscence, along with vibrances of pleasure-pain (*amor fati*), heaven-earth. "Cela s'est passé" can mean either "it happened" or "it's finished." Both are true: "it happened," thus affirmed, implies "it is happening still," which it obviously is, only now it has evolved spirally, into something fresh and more embracing. The same ambiguity haunts "Je sais aujourd'hui saluer la beauté." Is it a new sweeping vision, as of his enlarged happiness, a beauty not to be recorded in art, now rejected? Or is it the old beauty which, obviously, is dying hard and which he greets as with a handkerchief-wave from the deck of that ship which is about to leave from the shores of the present in "Matin"? I feel it is both.

L'Impossible

Rimbaud, having looked back at his ancestry and having offered a provisional panorama of the modern scene, in "Mauvais sang," having reminisced about his visionary flings in "Délires, II," now takes a closer look at the Western mind or spirit as he prepares to leave it: he finds it "impossible" and justifies his "disdains."

1, "Ah": First, a glance back at his wandering boyhood—the flights from home—with its poetic pride, now rejected (only now does he see its stupidity). It was still a part of the impossible West. That wide-open road through all sorts of weather, that supernatural drunkenness of life itself, without artificial stimulus ("sobre"), that freedom and almost religious gratuitousness, beyond that of even the best of beggars—all that can sound very attractive to less adventurous, jaded, role-bound men who read it. But Rimbaud was seeking further freedoms.

6, "J'ai": The invoked beggars were not independent enough: they, unlike Rimbaud, would accept caresses from clean and healthy bourgeois women on whom they depend for handouts, or in other ways. Rimbaud wants nothing to do with them, for in his view, as he said in "Délires, I," they have been ruined by Western men, turned into something which is not in *accord* with "us," meaning men like Rimbaud. That note was sounded earlier in "Les Premières Communions" and in the "Lettres du Voyant."

10, "J'ai": Rimbaud, the purist, sees *damnés* everywhere, as often as Sartre sees *salauds*, both including themselves. We lack charity, he says: the truly disinterested, Olympian spirit, generosity of soul. Oh, we are polite enough, in the usual French manner. But how would the authentically elect regard us? (He does not specify who these might be.) We have *fake* elect, harsh and joyous people—the successful men that it takes courage and humility to approach (cf. "Parade")—and they are our only elect; apparently there are no true elect, which would explain why he does not specify who they are. These fake "élus" are not "blessers"—no real charity there. This contrasts totally with the all-giving spirit of "Génie."

26, "M'étant": In a flash of insight—his pure *raison*—he sees that his troubles come from not having understood early that we are in the messy, or marshy, West. Not that he thinks nature—light, forms, movement—is out of whack here; so it must be something else. So his mind wants to trace what happened since the end of his ideal Orient, to see where Western soul went off the track. He mocks at this tremendous ambition.

Scholars still debate whether Rimbaud could have gotten a detailed knowledge of Oriental mysticism—ancient Hindu, as in the Vedas, etc.—from the Charleville library. It seems to be doubtful. But the really rather simple notions he had of this lore could have been gleaned from all sorts of local French vulgarizing sources: Leconte de Lisle, Cazalis, Louis Ménard. This was common coinage in the later nineteenth century. I do not see any important problem here.

34, "Mes": His flash is over. He cannot get out of his Western mind enough to see its evolution. He would have to silence it, be reborn in a different tradition.

37, "J'envoyais": He had dismissed Western religious ways (sainthood), art, invention, conquest; he had gone back in spirit to that integral Orient of his vision. Alas, it was only, apparently, a fantasy bred by crude laziness. So there is no way *back*. Rimbaud must press forward.

42, "Pourtant": Rimbaud's lucidity was not an attempt to escape modern suffering. Hence his *amor fati* (see "Délires, II") is not Oriental—Muslim—fatalism, which is a lazy escapist kind (the "paresse" just mentioned; cf. Suzanne Bernard, p. 474). Still the spirit of Christianity and its Western partner, modern science (or the positivistic bourgeois mind generally: M. Prudhomme), is disgusting: it plays with itself (or deceives itself) in rejecting the old mysticism, seeking narrow Cartesian proofs for everything in its less-than-total blinkered way. Nature might get fed up with this imposed construct, throw it off. This is prophetic of our polluted, destructively and explosively manipulated era.

52, "N'est-ce": The "fog" seems to refer back to the "Western marshes" above: lack of lucidity. Rimbaud is "fils du Soleil" (still, on occasion, as in

"Entends comme brame," the *brouillard* is poetic and so were the vegetables; in "Honte," however, he complained about *vapeur*). The rest is unproblematic.

58, "Les gens": He agrees with the Western religious men who might say it is Eden he was dreaming of: lost innocence. The last sentence is ambiguous: either the purity of old races, such as his Orient, is insufficient for his new vision, or Eden itself, included, is not up to his need. So he rejects the churchly solace.

63, "Les": He rejects too the Western philosophic solace which says "make your own Orient, through free thought, in the West," i.e., be one of us and stay. Like Heidegger, Rimbaud is beyond philosophy. Those philosophers are bogged too in Western marshes.

68, "Mon": Rimbaud is put on guard by these two transcendental ways, religion and philosophy. He has suffered from excessive transcendence, spiritual greed or pride, and he fears "violent choices of salvation." "Exerce-toi" is part of his new emphasis on horizontal striving—of his own radical sort: "la réalité rugueuse à étreindre" ("Adieu")—which combined with his vertical spirit, one assumes, will give the whole rounded new world he seeks, the "new Jerusalem." Modern science goes in this direction—as we have seen ("nous allons à l'*Esprit*"; "Mauvais sang")—but evidently not fast enough for him (Rimbaud does not realize that in this direction he will find pride and excessive vision as well: the dimensions of the human spirit meet in their extreme extension).

71, "Mais": But the march of Spirit is delayed; his spirit is dormant now.

72, "S'il": Otherwise he would soon be there, arrived at truth. The vision of weeping angels and of God—forgiveness, innocence regained—confirms our remark about the ends of the dimensions meeting. He accuses his sins of holding back that spirit, sins that occurred as far back as he can remember. The cry of "purity" sounds sincere; but it is hardly Claudelian conversion.

As so often after flights of this sort, Rimbaud's spirit flags.

L'Éclair

The flash of the title is the explosion of work which lights up (cf. *the Illuminations*) his abyss of despair from time to time. Rimbaud speaks of "travail humain" as if work generally had the creative *éclat* of his own effective moments. In a way it does, but there is obviously some difference of degree. Rimbaud tended to idealize the Worker, as we have seen often enough, and to make him over in his own image: he was to be an ally in a harmonious new world, hymned particularly in "Matin": "travail nouveau, la sagesse nouvelle, la fuite des tyrans et des démons, la fin de la superstition . . ."

1, "Le": The modern "Teacher" (Ecclesiastes) or prophet offers a formula which is the reverse of "All is vanity"; he believes, with a naive positivistic optimism, that science and progress will obliterate evil. He is, like Homais, representative: he is everybody. But evil persists: the corpses of the wicked and lazy fall on the hearts of the conquerors, hit them in their conscience. This dilemma makes Rimbaud anxious and hurried ("vite, vite un peu"), as if by acceleration we could get way out there somewhere to the moment of reconciliation he envisioned at the end of "L'Impossible." That "far out there" is the new note of horizontal striving which is the curative essence of the *Saison*; it sounds most clearly in the next section, "Matin." The "les échappons-nous?," referring to the "récompenses éternelles," is a curious way of saying, "Will we miss out on them?" (miss the boat leaving in "Adieu") by dawdling or insufficient zeal. It is, simply, expressive of need, anxiety.

9, "Qu'y": Discouragement and reversal; he *knows* work (and it is implied that it did not get us anywhere crucial). And science is too slow in its advance. He hopes more from prayer—it goes fast—and from flashes of vision (again the "éclair" of the title, with a synesthetic overtone of thunder in the "gronde"). Work and science are too simple, and besides it is too hot to work; the others will have to go on without him. Rimbaud has his own duty, he will be proud of it like some other eccentric types, and he will stand aside.

14, "Ma vie": But he feels too tired, too worn out, for true duty. So he proposes self-mockingly a cowardly program of self-amusement, dreaming of futile fantasies, complaining and resentfully lashing out at the illusions others believe in; he will be a "charlatan, beggar, artist, bandit—priest!" Insensibly, the humble outsider role has turned in its sacrificial gratuitousness—recalling Dostoevsky's prostitutes—into a supreme dignity. This is another essence of the *Saison*, this sort of violent reversal. The priest is both mocked and elevated simultaneously, or almost so in a crucial ambiguity or paradox. The sincerity of the evocation of his near-conversion on the hospital bed in Bruxelles is evident—and yet . . .

22, "Je": That supreme moment was just the result of a dirty bourgeois-Christian upbringing. So forget it; and then? Just go on another twenty years or so to death, as others will do. The twenty years was almost prophetic but that is coincidence (actually he made only seventeen more). I suppose he felt, as people tended to do then, that a man had reached his upward peak at forty or so; and it is roughly true (Robert Graves thinks forty-six is the climacteric year; Dante chose thirty-five; Rimbaud is somewhere in between).

25, "Non": But that resignation, acceptance of a dull road toward death, revolts him now. Still, he will not accept work as the form of his particular striving. His pride needs some more daemonic revolt or "betrayal" of the world and its ordinary fatality—he needs more torture, an agony, to betray it well, to protest against the human condition. He knows that if he enlisted in the common form of striving he would burst out of the ranks eventually and would lash out frenziedly in all directions.

29, "Alors": But then, on his own, victim of his pride and isolation, might he not lose eternity? Might he not, it is implied, fall into the same hell he had already fallen into in this *Saison*? The "nous" seems to arise from the dialogue between mind and soul; it is self-address. The soul appears here as a weak sister in his mocking self-depreciation; it has something of Verlaine's sentimentality, judging from the term "chère pauvre âme" which was used for the Foolish Virgin in "Délires, I" (Suzanne Bernard, p. 475).

Matin

Rimbaud has by now seen his central drama from all angles, and repetitively. Yet again he looks back to the privileged moments of his childhood in an attempt to understand what went wrong, what brought about his "faiblesse actuelle." Of course, it was the very power of that privilege, become Pride, that led to his hell. Suspecting this absurdity, that reason and speech can do nothing about such basic human dilemmas, he gives up utterance for a despairing moment. Then hope arises again from the depths like a Christmas star. He will start forth again on a dogged march, hoping to thus live down that pride, tame it at least, somehow combine the old (vertical) and the new (horizontal) impulses into a "sagesse nouvelle."

1, "N'eus": "Trop de chance" indicates an at least obscure realization of the excess of that youthful lyric pride. Yet he queries "Why?" He asks an explanation of men who have looked tragedy in the face, seen it rooted in pathetic animal existence (reminiscent of "Bottom") rising in the despair of the sick, prolonged even in the uneasy sleep of the dead (a vision of a sort of lost afterlife, hell). As for himself, he has no more answer than the beggar who can only stupidly repeat formulas of prayer.

10, "Pourtant": But some hope springs up; at least he is out of the woods of his confessional struggle in this recorded Hell, a Hell which, as he has understood in his previous accounts of his Western tradition, arose with the new high consciousness of Christ.

13, "Du même": The hope is still rather languid, merely nascent. But the very lyric note gradually rising in the long phrases expresses some promise. The doggedness, the implied repetition of *même . . . même*, express a world-weariness, mingled with that hope; but also, insensibly, that insistence is turning into the new program of stubborn striving, resignation to his version of the Adamic way. In the following sentence, the star, which failed to stir his faculties, kindles a buoyant clarity. Much of the spirit of "Génie," a *vita nuova* with an unidentified star for Beatrice, surges forth and up, despite the resignation to the wearying distance of the way and despite the question mark, the asking: When will we go?— perhaps even: When will we start out?—beyond the shores and the mountains to salute the marvelous new world. Some reminiscence of the Christian guiding star of Christmas eve is surely there (as it was for Dante).

Although resignation to man's Adamic lot might betoken a potential maturity, some note of caution is needed here. As we know, Rimbaud's future path across shores, mountains, deserts was in a way like his previous transcendent efforts: the insistence was excessive. Although, as we noted in our Introduction, Rimbaud made some promising progress toward growing-up just before he died (or at least expressed hopes for it), we strongly suspect that Rimbaud would have found himself again in this would-be new direction. Whatever maturity he mastered might have combined with his daemon to produce rich and ripe later works—but alas this was not to be. But it *could* have happened and this part of his *Saison* *could* have been prophetic, a germ of artistic or utopian things to come. Rimbaud followed another course, money-seeking and health-seeking adventure and struggle, and so now we tend to read this passage as prophetic of his mundane wanderings. But what he himself had in mind is less certain.

21, "Le chant": The new vision is put now in terms of whole nations, masses of people, as in "Génie." Low as we may be—we human "slaves"— and bound as we are to an earthy path, still let us not give up hope but strive on under the star; not curse the darkness but seek light.

Adieu

This is Rimbaud's goodbye to "all that"—his former visions, artistic or social—as he is about to depart for the "splendid cities," the new vision, "la vérité," largely undefined but of which we have gotten some idea in previous sections, if only negatively. Vaguely, one senses—again depending on previous utterances—that it is a goodbye to the West; here we are further, unduly, influenced by the actual facts of his subsequent wanderings. Certainly, it is a farewell to Hell as he seeks a "divine clarity."

He is going on to greater things. Despite the sacrifice of his literary expression, the ambiguous talk of "charity," there is nothing of Christian humility here. Whatever he comes up with, one is to feel, it will not be ordinary or mild.

1, "L'automne": The autumn following the summer during which Rimbaud wrote his *Saison en enfer* is approaching as he pens these final pages. But he is beyond concern for the seasonal decline: it is "divine light" he seeks, far from men who "die," or whose spirits sink, with the physical sun.

5, "L'automne": The "boat" is his imagination, as in "Le Bateau ivre"—related to the vessel which is the symbol of departure, below—and it now turns back to all he is glad to leave: the miserable city which sums up Western culture (shades of foggy London, Paris) and where he almost died of starvation. It is a "goule," devouring *femme fatale* figure of city-life with undertones of Death itself, which sucks in the surroundings, like the "putain Paris" of "L'Orgie parisienne" (the dangerous "Elle" of "Métropolitain" is somewhat related, the "Elle"-vampire of "Angoisse" is closer). The dark whirlpool wheel of Vigny's Paris may be remembered here. All the dead bodies—alienated from nature—and souls of this pestilential culture will be judged by some God in Rimbaud's image; cf. "I had not known death had undone so many" of T. S. Eliot's foggy London, in *The Waste Land* (after Dante).

The "sky splashed with fire and mud" is a baroque painterly touch, reminiscent of Baudelaire's "A Paris" (*or et boue*). It goes back to the imagery of the earliest Rimbaud poem we have, "Les Étrennes des orphelins," this archetypal pairing of blood-fire-life and fecal mud-cinder-death. Bread soaked with water is strangely poetic in its misery, with echoes of Christ's hyssop-sponge on the cross, hence the ambivalent "crucifié"—this is the "thousand loves" of drunkenness and the perverse lyricism of city-misery that crucified in the sense of consummation in delight and near-death. He could have died in the city, and he execrates the misery. Yet . . .

16, "Et": He fears winter because it is the time of bourgeois nestling indoors; this is, like the foregoing passage, an ambivalent attraction which he wants to leave behind. The anglicized "comfort" (cf. "Mouvement"), with a possible allusion to London, seems to echo Baudelaire's "tout le comfort exige une température rigoureuse"—speaking of the joys of winter in *Les Paradis artificiels* (Matucci).

18, "Quelquefois": This makes us feel most keenly, in addition to the anticipatory joy of imminent setting-forth by day, all that we are to lose as he buries his talent, his inventive "imagination," and his "memories." One thinks of Nero's "qualis artifex pereo."

28, "Moi": This defines as closely as anything the new way: the Adamic, horizontal path of striving at human level, the level of the surface of the planet—not above, in an Olympian amoral realm, not below in hell—the "sol," horizontal, stretching out of sight so that only steady plugging effort will get us there, no sudden flashes will do. Over the horizon, as we saw in the previous section, there is a future something, a duty to be *sought*, yet undefined or undefinable. This is the rough road of reality as most men—waiting for Godot or something—know it, but with an added bite, given Rimbaud. The "Paysan!" is double: he wants to pitch in at the peasant level, the soil-level, but he despised the "paysan matois" as we saw, hence there is a typical return of self-mockery as he reaches a provisional peak.

So he wonders if he is not wrong, once again. This sacrifice of his art is a sort of "charity"—though not, as we said, a true Christian humility—but its departure leaves him so empty now that he fears he is nearing death. In "Les Sœurs de charité," death was the final "sœur de charité"; now he is terrified of that sister.

He is talked and reasoned out; all he can do is ask for pardon if, with limited human means, he was mistaken in his decision to leave it all. So onward.

But a qualm: he's going it alone. The "friendly hand" is one everyone needs. (Reverdy's "D'un autre Ciel" ends "Personne n'est venu me prendre par la main.")

36, "Oui": He plucks up the courage to face the departure, acknowledging the difficulty of the crisis. He feels the worst is behind him, the season in hell almost over—the devilish sounds taper off. His lingering regrets at not having played certain roles disappear: even the purest of Western types in his eyes—independent spirits such as brigands, beggars (the saint and the priest mentioned earlier are perhaps implied in the "friends of death, retarded characters of all sorts")—all these are damned with the rest, and he thinks of vengeance against them. This is charity? One remembers Dante. . . . There is a young lifetime of bitterness behind that phrase.

44, "Il faut": A famous phrase; "modern" has a particular ring in Rimbaud's mouth, and it has nothing to do with modern art—that is behind him. He means his whole utterly independent new path, best defined negatively as not the traditional Christian one: "Point de cantiques." Just keep going in the direction one has started in. Nothing behind him (of his struggle, his past) but that horrible bush—the burning bush of his spiritual combat is extinguished, like those "arbrisseaux brûlés" in late summer (the time of this pronouncement) in "Les Premières Communions." Anyone who has had such a vision knows that that bush is an apt objective correlative for the exhausted nervous and cerebral system. One need not rule out the "tree of good and evil" which he referred to in "Matinée d'ivresse"; it is really the same thing, as the Valéry of "Ébauche d'un serpent" knew.

Spiritual combat is brutal; only God knows the peace implied in a vision of justice, not us men.

50, "Cependent": It is the eve of departure. Like the "âme sentinelle" of the vigil of "L'Éternité," he is filled with vigor and affection as a reward for his long waiting. The fresh ardor is added to the patience of the vigil to give the "ardente patience" which is the combination of horizontal and vertical spirit in his special would-be-rounded maturity, adequate to the full world, reality ("réelle"). The "splendid cities" are this brave new world of promise—a "new Jerusalem"—not the old ghoulish city he knew too well.

54, "Que": He feels his oats, thinks he can go it alone. A last gibe at couples is appropriate to this dangerous solitary pride—that is hell, dependence on women; this is a desperate attempt to wean himself from his mother (and her surrogates) as his father did, be a man, in the classic and vulnerable way so many men have tried. He will be truly independent, self-sufficient: Plato's ideal of the whole man, the healthy mind in the healthy body, becomes this Rimbaldian ideal: truth in a soul and a body— or one soul and one body. This unity can be opposed, too (as Richard thought), to the earlier dispersion of his artistic imagination. In any case, and this is more to the point, a man trying to get hold of himself seeks a base in a unitary identity or independence.

Few—a saint here or there—have made it for long alone along this proud path. Rimbaud certainly tried for a while. Later he spoke of marriage in letters to his mother. Was her ultimate triumph over him complete, as Suzanne Briet claims? Surely she made some gains: he sounded and acted like her more and more as he grubbed after money and a position. But no one wins a final triumph in this life. Nor did Rimbaud. But what an exemplary struggle!

BIBLIOGRAPHY

OF PRINCIPAL WORKS

CONSULTED

Note: Standard cultural references are not included. An extensive bibliography on Rimbaud is available in Étiemble, *Le Mythe de Rimbaud*.

I. *Rimbaud's Works*

Rimbaud, Jean-Arthur. *Œuvres*, ed. Suzanne Bernard. Paris, 1960.
—— *Œuvres complètes*. Paris, 1960.

II. *Books on Rimbaud*

Arnoult, Pierre. *Rimbaud*. Paris, 1955.
Bonnefoy, Yves. *Rimbaud par lui-même*. Paris, 1961.
Bouillane de Lacoste, H. de. *Rimbaud et le problème des Illuminations*. Paris, 1949.
Briet, Suzanne. *Madame Rimbaud*. Paris, 1968.
Carré, Jean-Marie. *La Vie aventureuse de Jean-Arthur Rimbaud*. Paris, 1949.
Daniel-Rops, Henry. *Rimbaud, le drame spirituel*. Paris, 1936.
Delahaye, Ernest. *Souvenirs familiers à propos de Rimbaud, Verlaine, Germain Nouveau*. Paris, 1925.
Dhôtel, André. *Rimbaud et la révolte moderne*. Paris, 1952.
Eaubonne, Française d'. *Verlaine et Rimbaud ou la fausse évasion*. Paris, 1960.
Étiemble, R. *Le Mythe de Rimbaud*, V. 1: *Genèse du mythe*. Paris, 1952. V. 2: *Structure du mythe*. Paris, 1954.
—— and Gauclère, Y. *Rimbaud*. Paris, 1950.
Fowlie, Wallace. *Rimbaud*. Chicago, 1965.
Frohock, W. M. *Rimbaud's Poetic Practice*. Cambridge, Mass., 1963.
Gengoux, Jacques. *La Symbolique de Rimbaud*. Paris, 1947.
Hackett, C. A. *Le Lyrisme de Rimbaud*. Paris, 1938.
—— *Rimbaud l'Enfant*. Paris, 1948.
—— *Rimbaud*. New York, 1957.

439

Houston, John Porter. *The Design of Rimbaud's Poetry*. New Haven, 1963.

Izambard, Georges. *Rimbaud tel que je l'ai connu*. Paris, 1946.

Magny, Claude-Edmonde. *Arthur Rimbaud*. Paris, 1949.

Matarasso, Henri and Petitfils, Pierre. *Vie d'Arthur Rimbaud*. Paris, 1962.

Mondor, Henri. *Rimbaud ou le génie impatient*. Paris, 1955.

Montal, Robert. *L'Adolescent Rimbaud*. Lyons, 1954.

Noulet, Émilie. *Le Premier Visage de Rimbaud*. Brussels, 1953.

Py, Albert. *Arthur Rimbaud: Illuminations*. Geneva, 1967.

Rivière, Jacques. *Rimbaud*. Paris, 1930.

Rolland de Renéville, R. *Rimbaud le voyant*. Paris, 1947.

Ruff, Marcel. *Rimbaud*. Paris, 1968.

Starkie, Enid. *Arthur Rimbaud*. New York, 1961.

III. *Articles on Rimbaud*
(including chapters of books)

Adam, Antoine. "L'Énigme des Illuminations," *Revue des Sciences Humaines*, Oct.-Dec., 1950, pp. 227-45.

Baudry, Jean-Louis. "Le Texte de Rimbaud," *Tel Quel*, no. 35 (Autumn 1968), pp. 46-63, and no. 36 (Winter 1969), pp. 33-53.

Claudel, Paul. "Rimbaud," in *Positions et Propositions*, Paris, 1928, vol. I, chapter 3.

Cohn, Robert G. "Rimbaud," in *The Writer's Way in France*, Philadelphia, 1960, pp. 267-326.

Davies, Margaret. "Melville et Rimbaud," *Revue de Littérature Comparée*, 43rd year, no. 4 (Oct.-Dec., 1969), pp. 479-88.

Faurisson, R. "A-t-on lu Rimbaud?" *Bizarre*, nos. 21-22, 1961, entire issue.

Fretet, Jean. "Arthur Rimbaud," in *L'Aliénation poétique*, Paris, 1946, chapter II.

Hubert, Renée Riese. "The Use of Reversals in Rimbaud's *Illuminations*," *L'Esprit créateur*, vol. IX, no. 1 (Spring, 1969), pp. 9-18.

Lapp, John. "Mémoire: Art et Hallucination chez Rimbaud," *Cahiers de l'Association Internationale des Études Françaises*, vol. 23 (May, 1971), pp. 163-75.

Mallarmé, Stéphane. "Arthur Rimbaud," in *Œuvres complètes*, Paris, 1945, pp. 512-19.

Richard, J.-P. "Rimbaud ou la poésie du devenir," in *Poésie et profondeur*, Paris, 1955, pp. 189-250.

Smith, Madeleine. "La Chasse spirituelle," *PMLA*, LXIV, no. 3 (June, 1949), pp. 325-39.

Underwood, V. P. "Rimbaud et l'Angleterre," *Revue de Littérature Comparée*, January-March 1955, pp. 5-35.

Verlaine, Paul. "Arthur Rimbaud," in *Les Poètes maudits*, Paris, 1920, pp. 20-40.

Weinberg, Bernard. "Le Bateau ivre or the Limits of Symbolism," *PMLA*, LXII, no. 10, (March 1959), pp. 165-93. Reprinted in *The Limits of Symbolism*, Chicago, 1966.

IV. *Other Books Used in This Study*

Brown, Norman. *Love's Body*. New York, 1966.

Cassirer, Ernst. *An Essay on Man*. New York, 1953.

Cohn, Robert G. *L'Œuvre de Mallarmé: Un Coup de Dés*, Paris, 1951.

───── *Toward the Poems of Mallarmé*, Berkeley, 1965.

Graves, Robert. *The White Goddess*. New York, 1948.

Hubert, Judd. *L'Esthétique des "Fleurs du Mal."* Geneva, 1953.

Jung, C. G. *Psyche and Symbol*. New York, 1958.

Kayser, Hans. *Der hörende Mensch*. Berlin, 1932.

Kretschmer, Eugene. *The Psychology of Men of Genius*. London, 1931.

Laplanche, Jean. *Hölderlin et la question du père*. Paris, 1961.

Neumann, Erich. *The Origins and History of Consciousness*. New York, 1954.

Painter, George. *Proust, the Early Years*. Boston, 1959.

Perry, John W. *Lord of the Four Quarters*. New York, 1966.

Prévost, Jean. *Baudelaire*. Paris, 1953.

Sartre, Jean-Paul. *Baudelaire*. Paris, 1947.

INDEX

Library of Congress Cataloging in Publication Data

Cohn, Robert Greer.
    The Poetry of Rimbaud.

    Bibliography: p.
    1. Rimbaud, Jean Nicolas Arthur, 1854-1891.
I. Title.
PQ2387.R5Z589   841'.8   72-5377
ISBN 0-691-06244-7